Lourenço da Silva Mendonça and the Black Atlantic Abolitionist Movement in the Seventeenth Century

This groundbreaking study tells the story of the highly organised, international legal court case for the abolition of slavery spearheaded by Prince Lourenço da Silva Mendonça in the seventeenth century. The case, presented before the Vatican, called for the freedom of all enslaved people and other oppressed groups. This included New Christians (Jews converted to Christianity) and Indigenous Americans in the Atlantic World, and Black Christians from confraternities in Angola, Brazil, Portugal and Spain. Abolition debate is generally believed to have been dominated by white Europeans in the eighteenth century. By centring African agency, José Lingna Nafafé offers a new perspective on the abolition movement, showing, for the first time, how the legal debate was begun not by Europeans, but by Africans. In the first book of its kind, Lingna Nafafé underscores the exceptionally complex nature of the African liberation struggle, and demystifies the common knowledge and accepted wisdom surrounding African slavery.

José Lingna Nafafé is a senior lecturer in Portuguese and Lusophone Studies at the University of Bristol.

Cambridge Studies on the African Diaspora

General Editor:

Michael A. Gomez, New York University

Using the African Diaspora as its core defining and launching point for examining the historians and experiences of African-descended communities around the globe, this series unites books around the concept of migration of peoples and their cultures, politics, ideas and other systems from or within Africa to other nations or regions, focusing particularly on transnational, transregional and transcultural exchanges.

Titles in the Series

Crystal Nicole Eddins, *Rituals, Runaways, and the Haitian Revolution: Collective Action in the African Diaspora*

Merle L. Bowen, *For Land and Liberty: Black Struggles in Rural Brazil*

Michael A. Gomez, *Reversing Sail: A History of the African Diaspora, Second Edition*

Jorge L. Giovannetti-Torres, *Black British Migrants in Cuba: Race, Labor, and Empire in the Twentieth-Century Caribbean, 1898–1948*

Daniel B. Domingues da Silva, *The Atlantic Slave Trade from West Central Africa, 1780–1867*

Rashauna Johnson, *Slavery's Metropolis: Unfree Labor in New Orleans during the Age of Revolutions*

Lourenço da Silva Mendonça and the Black Atlantic Abolitionist Movement in the Seventeenth Century

JOSÉ LINGNA NAFAFÉ
University of Bristol

Shaftesbury Road, Cambridge CB2 8EA, United Kingdom

One Liberty Plaza, 20th Floor, New York, NY 10006, USA

477 Williamstown Road, Port Melbourne, VIC 3207, Australia

314–321, 3rd Floor, Plot 3, Splendor Forum, Jasola District Centre, New Delhi – 110025, India

103 Penang Road, #05–06/07, Visioncrest Commercial, Singapore 238467

Cambridge University Press is part of Cambridge University Press & Assessment, a department of the University of Cambridge.

We share the University's mission to contribute to society through the pursuit of education, learning and research at the highest international levels of excellence.

www.cambridge.org
Information on this title: www.cambridge.org/9781009573726

DOI: 10.1017/9781108974196

© José Lingna Nafafé 2022

This publication is in copyright. Subject to statutory exception and to the provisions of relevant collective licensing agreements, no reproduction of any part may take place without the written permission of Cambridge University Press & Assessment.

First published 2022
First paperback edition 2025

A catalogue record for this publication is available from the British Library

ISBN 978-1-108-83823-8 Hardback
ISBN 978-1-009-57372-6 Paperback

Cambridge University Press & Assessment has no responsibility for the persistence or accuracy of URLs for external or third-party internet websites referred to in this publication and does not guarantee that any content on such websites is, or will remain, accurate or appropriate.

Contents

List of Figures	*page* viii
List of Tables	xi
Acknowledgements	xii

Introduction   1
- 0.1 The Portuguese Empire Operation in Angola: Kings, Governors, Councils and Local Rulers   11
- 0.2 Studies and Sources for Mendonça's Work and Historical Context   23
- 0.3 Methodology and Use of Sources   48
- 0.4 Chapter Breakdown   51

1. The Municipal Council of Luanda and the Politics of the Portuguese Governors in Angola   57
   - 1.1 The Structure of the Luanda City Council   76
   - 1.2 Correia de Sousa, the Treachery and Seizing of Kazanze People, a Vassal of Kongo   81
   - 1.3 Protests against Correia de Sousa's Actions and the Illegal Sending of Kazanze People to Brazil   93
   - 1.4 Correia de Sousa's Unjust War against Bumbi, Another Vassal of Kongo   100
   - 1.5 Antonio Bezerra Fajardo's Investigation into Portuguese Crime in Angola and Kongo   104
   - 1.6 Correia de Sousa's Unrest in the City of Luanda   114
   - 1.7 The Feud between Correia de Sousa and Álvares   116
   - 1.8 Kongolese Captives Return from Brazil (1623–1627)   129
   - 1.9 Concluding Remarks   135

2. Ndongo's Political and Cultural Environment: Alliance, Internal Struggle, Puppeteering and Decline   138
   2.1 Ndongo's Political, Social and Cultural Structures   147
   2.2 The Term 'Slave' in Ndongo Society   153
   2.3 King Philipe Hari I of Pungo-Andongo (1626–1664)   159
   2.4 Election of Philipe Hari I as Puppet King of Portugal   163
   2.5 The Introduction of *Baculamento* as a Tax System by Governor Fernão de Sousa   169
   2.6 Ngola João Hari II, King of Pungo-Andongo (1624–1671)   176
   2.7 Francisco de Távora 'Cajanda': Portuguese governor of Luanda (1669–1676)   178
   2.8 João Hari II's Claim of Independence from Portugal and the Destruction of Pungo-Andongo   181
   2.9 Concluding Remarks   192
3. The Journey of Mendonça: The Princes of Pungo-Andongo in Brazil   193
   3.1 The House of Ndongo: João Hari II and Diogo, the First Generation of Alliance Breakers   200
   3.2 The House of Pungo-Andongo's Role and Former Loyalty to Portugal   207
   3.3 The Sending of the Ndongo Royals to Portugal and Brazil as Prisoners of War and Sá's Plans for Angola   209
   3.4 The Royals' Experiences and Network in Brazil   212
   3.5 The Royals' Experiences, the Sugar Plantation and Antonil's Whistleblowing Work on the Treatment of the Enslaved Africans in Bahia   222
   3.6 The Quilombo dos Palmares and its Alliance with the Indigenous People   239
   3.7 The Quilombo dos Palmares, Cristovão de Burgos and the Royals of Ndongo   256
   3.8 The Quilombo dos Palmares and Father António Vieira   260
   3.9 Concluding Remarks   270
4. Mendonça's Journey to Portugal and Spain, and the Network of the Hebrew Nation and Indigenous Americans   275
   4.1 The Ndongo Royals: From Brazil to Portugal and their Distribution to Different Monasteries   280
   4.2 Lourenço da Silva Mendonça in Vilar de Frades, Braga, c.1673–1677   296
   4.3 Mendonça and the Confraternity of Our Lady of Rosary of Black Men in Portugal   300

	4.4 Mendonça's Network with New Christians in Portugal and the Indigenous Peruvians in Toledo, 1674–1681	312
	4.5 Concluding Remarks	320
5.	Mendonça's Discourse in the Vatican: Liberation as a Wider Atlantic Question	323
	5.1 African Voices of Protest Before Mendonça's Discourse in the Vatican	331
	5.2 Mendonça's Criminal Court Case Presentation in 1684	345
	5.3 Reactions to Mendonça's Court Case	353
	5.4 Mendonça on Natural, Human, Divine and Civil Laws in His Closing Statement in 1668	367
	5.5 Mendonça's Argument in His Court Case in 1684 and in His Closing Statement in 1686	371
	5.6 Concluding Remarks	382
6.	Mendonça's Quest for Abolition and the Tussle between the Portuguese Overseas Council and the House of Ndongo	384
	6.1 The Portuguese Overseas Council and the House of Ndongo	386
	6.2 The Portuguese Crown and Mendonça's Impact at the Vatican	392
	6.3 Mendonça's Tussle with the Portuguese Overseas Council	402
	6.4 Concluding Remarks	408
	Conclusion	414
Bibliography		431
Index		461

Figures

1 APF, SOCG. vol. 495a, fl. 58. Photograph taken by the author. *page* 5
2 Lourenço da Silva Mendonça's family tree, part 1. By the author, based on manuscripts. 17
3 Lourenço da Silva Mendonça's family tree, part 2. By the author, based on manuscripts. 18
4 Mendonça's presentation of the 'complaints' and 'appeals' of the various confraternities he represented to the Vatican court. SOCG, vol. 495a, folio, 393. 45
5 Intersection of power between the Crown, the Portuguese Overseas Council and the Municipal Council of Luanda. By the author. 79
6 Map dated 1623 of the seige of Kazanze. Biblioteca da Ajuda, Lisbon, Portugal, [BAL], cartografia, MS. [Topografia (...) Provincia da Quissama, Angola, CA 1622, ARM, met. X 51-IX-20, fl. 2.]. Photograph by the author. 88
7 Map of Luanda, Angola, in the seventeenth century. Biblioteca da Ajuda, Lisbon, Portugal. [BAL], cartografia, MS. A descrição da barra do reino de Angola, 51-IX-21 (fl. 2.), Armário Met.X. Photograph by the author. 117
8 Map of Kongo, Angola and Benguela. Jacques Nicolas Bellin, 1747, Biblioteca Digital Luso-Brasileira (http://bdlb.bn.gov.br/acervo/handle/20.500.12156.3/14333). 146
9 Ndongo's (Angola's) political structure, in the fourteenth to the seventeenth centuries. By the author, based on manuscripts and available literature. 150

List of Figures

10 Ndongo's (Angola's) social structure in the fourteenth to the seventeenth centuries. By the author based on manuscripts and available literature. 152
11 Seh Dong-Hong-Beh, a female soldier from Dahomey. Forbes, 1851. 191
12 Salvador Correia de Sá e Benavides (1648–1651). Museu de História Militar, Luanda, Angola. Photograph by the author. 203
13 Branding symbols used to mark the forehead or the side of the face or arm, so that people knew who a slave belonged to. Livro de Banguê, Arquivo Santa Casa, Salvador. Photograph by the author. 228
14 View of St. Salvador. Artist unknown, Museu de Arte da Bahia (MAB), Salvador. Indigenous people are depicted in the foreground, roasting the limbs of their enemies before eating their flesh. Photograph by the author. 235
15 Map indicating *engenhos* in seventeenth-century Bahia. *Atlas Universal*, João Teixeira Albernaz (1640). 236
16 Map of Palmares, in the south of the Captaincy of Pernambuco, by Barleus (1647). There are no contemporary paintings of Palmares and Barleus's work is perhaps the only one available that shows Palmares. Public domain. 242
17 Graph illustrating the arrival of the four groups of royals in Portugal. By the author, based on manuscripts. 281
18 Francisco Gonçalvez Ferráz's letter, Arquivo Público de Salvador, Bahia. In the letter he talks about six slaves, then corrects himself by saying he had received six princes. Photograph by the author. 290
19 Igreja e Mosteiro de Vilar de Frades/Mosteiro de São Salvador, where Lourenço da Silva Mendonça studied for three to four years. Public domain. 297
20 Pope Gregory XII, without papal hat. Vilar de Frades Chapel, Braga, Portugal. Photograph by the author. 298
21 Pope Gregory XII, with papal hat. Vilar de Frades Chapel, Braga, Portugal. Photograph by the author. 299
22 *Chafariz d'el Rey em Lisboa*. Artist unknown, 1570–1580. Interracial depiction of the city of Lisbon. Public domain. 304
23 Cover of the Confraternity's *compromisso* (constitution) of Our Lady of Rosary of Black Men. Biblioteca Nacional de Portugal. Photograph by the author. 305
24 Garcia II, king of Kongo/Nkanga a Lukeni, Albert Eckhout, 1641. Public domain. 340
25 Mendonça's criminal court case and documents classification A, B, C. By the author. 349

26 Activism of 'men', 'women' and 'youth' from confraternities in Brazil, Portugal and Spain. By the author.   352
27 Coat of arms of Propaganda Fide surrounded by the text *Morir Es Lo Mas Cierto*, drawn by Gaspar da Costa de Mesquita in his recommendation letter. Image created by the author.   374
28 Original coat of arms of Propaganda Fide surrounded by the text *Morir Es Lo Mas Cierto*. Image created by the author.   375
29 Signature and Propaganda Fide coat of arms with text *Morir Es Lo Mas Cierto* on the recommendation letter by Gaspar da Costa de Mesquita. Photograph by the author.   376
30 Last Judgement of Hunefer with scales of justice, Book of the Dead, *c.*1275 BCE, papyrus, Thebes, Egypt (British Museum). Public domain.   381

Tables

1. The system of Mendonça's court case documents, as filed in the Vatican. Photograph by the author *page* 45
2. Wealth of Gaspar Álvares, Portuguese trader and resident of Angola in the seventeenth century, based on his correspondence and will. By the author 119
3. Number of houses (*fogos*) in each of the parishes (*freguesias*) and how many people (*almaj*) lived in each parish in the city of Salvador in the mid-eighteenth century. By the author, based on manuscripts 217
4. Number of sugar-cane mills in Bahia from the sixteenth to the nineteenth centuries. By the author, based on Berenstein de Azevedo (2009) 219
5. The 129 farms in Canindê and Peauhy, Palmares. By the author, based on 'Documento n. 65' 249
6. Unconquered Tapuyas who were at war with New Parish of N. S. da Victoria, Palmares. By the author, based on 'Documento n. 65' 254
7. Conquered Indigenous people in Bahia, Brazil, in their respective villages and the missionary societies that set them up. By the author, based on based on 'Documento n. 65' 264
8. Distribution of the Ndongo royals to different monasteries. By the author, based on 'Carta de António da Costa de Sousa a Manuel Barreto de S. Paio' 295

Acknowledgements

I dedicate this book to my sister Dang Lingna Nafafé, who passed away in 2017.

The research for this monograph began in 2001. However, it gathered real impetus in July 2016 when I was awarded a Leverhulme Research Fellowship and the University of Bristol Research Fellowship, which allowed me to take research leave for eighteen months; these were followed by a European Research Council Advanced Grant (ERC) in August 2018. The Leverhulme Research Fellowship helped me put my long-term research strategy for this book back on track; I am grateful to the Leverhulme Trust for funding my time on the project 'Freedom and Lusophone African Diaspora in the 17th-Century Atlantic', which played a crucial part in the making of this book, allowing me to carry out research around the world. In 2016 and 2017, I undertook research in Angola, Brazil, Portugal, Spain, Italy and England in thirty-six archives, libraries and museums. I am grateful to the ERC for funding my time on the project 'Modern Marronage? The Pursuit and Practice of Freedom in the Contemporary World', which helped me develop the ideas in the book. I offer my thanks also to the Vice-Chancellor Fellowship from the University of Bristol for their support; and to the University of Bristol for financial support and the Faculty of Arts and the School of Modern Languages, which helped me make a research visit to Brazil. My special thanks go to the Faculty of Arts Research and Impact Support Fund and to Elle Chilton-Knight. I am profoundly grateful to my colleague and friend Dr Carlos da Silva Jr, who helped me find documents that revealed where Prince Lourenço da Silva Mendonça came from for giving me documents about the princes of Ndongo in 2015.

Acknowledgements

I would like to acknowledge my indebtedness to various individuals whose assistance has made it possible to complete this book: Professor Matthew Brown, for his encouragement, advice and scrutiny, for reading the entire manuscript twice and providing excellent feedback; Professor Toby Green, for his support in reading the book proposal and the entire manuscript and for his scholarly observations, useful additions and the invitation to present my findings in two joint workshops at the University of Oxford in 2021. I am grateful also to Professor Andreas Schönle, Professor Martin Hercombe, Dr Sally-Ann Kitts and Dr Caroline Williams, for reading parts of the manuscript and for their invaluable comments and advice. I would like to extend my gratitude to Ms Vanessa Christine Mariano, for her indispensable support in transcribing Portuguese texts and for technical support in drawing tables and figures for the book. My thanks also go to Professor Linda Heywood and Dr Saima Nasar, for reading several chapters of the book draft and for their feedback, and to Professor Carolin Overhoff Ferreira, for ideas for the book cover, for reading the first draft twice and editing the footnotes and for helping with the caption where the images and tables would go. I offer my thanks to Professor John Holmwood, for his invaluable feedback on the book proposal and to Professor Julia O'Connell Davidson for her invaluable advice, for editing the text and for her support, ideas and academic advice. I would also like to give thanks to: Professor Linda Heywood, for reading and making comments on the book; Professor John Thornton, for reading the draft and for his invaluable suggestions and for giving me archival material for the book; Professor Madge Dresser, for support; Professor Werner Ustorf, for academic advice and for giving me the initial impetus to carrying out research on Lourenço da Silva Mendonça; Professor Mariana Cândido, for reading the first draft and for excellent feedback; Dr Sandra Nerves Silva, for support, feedback and for sending me useful research archival materials and secondary sources; and Professor Giorgio de Marchis, Professor Mariana Cândido and Professor John Thornton for their wonderful endorsements.

I would also like to thank: my copy-editor on the first draft, Kay Celtel, for her excellent editing skills and outstanding professionalism; my good friend Dr Ramon Sarro, for recommending Kay to me; Jessica Zausmer, for taking on the initial copy-editing of the book; Warren Shaun Greig, for proofreading the first draft and helping to make it read better; David Perkins de Oliveira, for translating key words from Portuguese to English; Dr Gustavo Infante, for his invaluable support in transcribing manuscript text, translating Latin texts into Portuguese and checking and proofreading my transcription in Portuguese; Marc Lingna Nafafé, for his support and technical skill in drawing some of the figures in the book; Barnabé Costa Lingna Nafafé, for checking the legal terms used in the book; Walter Mariano, for technical design of the book cover; Hanan Almatan, for creating the bibliography; Dr Denise Vargiu, for her support in translating texts from Italian to English and for transcribing Italian texts; Paola Collenely and Dr Vera Castiglione, for transcribing and translating Italian texts into English; Connie Bloomfield, for her kind support in proofreading Chapter 5 and useful feedback; Dr Deogratius Joseph Mhella, for proofreading Chapter 1; Dr Botelho Isalino Jimbi and Dr Joseph Dalcantara, for clarifying Kimbundu terms; and Dr Maria Adelina Amorim, for transcribing some of the original manuscript texts.

It is a pleasure to thank all those who made it possible for me to present earlier versions of this research at conferences or seminars, interviews, festivals and on podcasts: Professor Toby Green, Professor Phillip Rothwell, Professor Fabiana Schleumer, Professor Jaime Rodrigues, Dr Carlos Junior, Dr Patrícia Godinho, Dr Gerhart Seriber, Dr Juliana Barreto Farias, Dr Carlos da Silva Junior, Professor Giorgio de Marchis, Dr Dorothée Boulanger, Dr Leslie Fesenmyer, Simon Bright, Janet Kirk, Dr Anna Moore and Dr Tomáš Kunca. I would particularly like to thank Peninah Achieng-Kindberg, for inviting me to present my research at the Afrika Eye Festival in Bristol; Dr Rosie Doyle, for her invitation to present my research at a University of Warwick seminar – and Dr Selina Nascimento, for her comments on my University of Warwick presentation; Dr Joana Palminha of RTP Africa, for the invitation to be interviewed on RTP Africa; Professor Mariana Cândido, and Gaspar Micolo, for inviting me to be interviewed in *Jornal de Angola*; Dr Joana Serrado, for her invitation to present my work on Lourenço da Silva Mendonça at her conference; Mário Agostinho, for lending me his camera to take pictures during my research in Rome; and Dr Ali Bennett, Rory Boyle, Moya Lothian-McLean, Jaja Muhammad and Renay Richardson, from Broccoli Productions, Podcast Production, Sony Music Entertainment, UK; Ana Naomi de Sousa, for the interview with *Al Jazeera* about the book's findings.

I am profoundly grateful to my colleagues in the Hispanic, Portuguese and Latin American Studies department, the School of Modern Languages, the Faculty of Arts and School of Sociology Politics & International Studies at the University of Bristol. I extend my thanks to: Professor David Brookshaw, Dr James Haweky, Madalena Pires, Dr Paco Romero Salvado, Dr Edward King, Dr Caragh Wells, Dr Jo Crow, Dr Christabelle Peters, Professor Andrew Ginger, Dr Bethan Fisk, Arismende da Silva Contreiras, Ana

Suárez Vidal, Itziar Martinez, Professor Robert Vilain, Dr Ruth Bush, Professor Siobhan Shilton, Dr Tristan Kay, Dr Bradley Stephens, Professor Catherine O'Rawe, Professor Charles Burdett, Professor Madge Dresser, Dr Joanna Burch-Brown, Professor Susan Harrow, Professor Charles Burdett, Hannah Blackman, Anne Payne, Nick Bartram, Dr Charlotte Goudge, Dr Erna Johannesdottir, Dr Jessica Moody, Dr Richard Stone, Professor Katharine Robson Brown, Professor Mark Norton, Professor Robert Bickers, Dr Samuel Okyere, Dr Pankhuri Agarval and Dr Angelo Martins Junior.

My special thanks to Dr Claire Williams, Professor Shelley Godslands, Dr Clive Harris, Professor John Holmwood, Professor Gurminder K. Bhambra, Malia Bouattia, Dr. Patricia Odber de Baubeta, Dr John Naryan, Professor Kai Andrews, Dr Eghosa Ekhator, Dr Conrad James, Genisete de Lucena Sarmento, Dr Barbara Castillo Buttinghausen, Katiuska Ferrer Portillo, Dr Marina Temudo, Karine Mariano, Genite Mariano, Dr Miriam Franchina, Dr Christianne Silva Vasconcellos for their invaluable support. My special thanks to Kate Newnham, Senior Curator, Visual Arts, Bristol Museum & Art Gallery, for her invaluable support.

I am grateful to colleagues I have met and friends I have made on my research travel around the world and especially to: Dr Giorgio Guzzetta's family in Vatican City, for their hospitality; Patrícia Paco, for organising a tour of Recife and a visit to the parishes and for helping me to visit the Black Brotherhood of the city of Recife; Dr Zé Kouyate, Dr Carlos da Silva Jr and Juliana, for their hospitality in Salvador; Dr Cândido Domingues, for advice on archives in Salvador; Dr Ana Maria Maia, for her support, her introduction to Brazilian arts, advice on museums in São Paulo and for allowing me to see her exhibition in São Paulo; Dr Iracema Dudley and Dr Ariel Rolim, for invaluable support and for hospitality in São Paulo and Campinas; Dr Aramis Luis, for hospitality in São Paulo; Dr Zé Kuoate, for hospitality in Rio de Janeiro; Dare Rose from the Museu da Bahia; Dr Juliana Barreto Farias, for recommending archives in Rio de Janeiro; Juliana de Oliveira Souza Caffé, for introducing me to the Hotel Cambridge in São Paulo; Carlos and Nené Ranger, for their hospitality in Lisbon and Pastor Apolinário da Silva, for his generous support and hospitality; Luís Bengui Gange, for providing me with contacts in Angola; Professor Abdizia Maria Alves Barros, for her hospitality; Jonas António Alves Barros, for his tour of Palmares and Alagoas including Muquem and for taking me to Palmares at night; Dr Moritz Hermann, for providing me with vital contacts in União de Palmares; Genisete de Lucena Sarmento, for the insights she gave me into the history of

Palmares and for sharing documents about Palmares with me; Rev Deacon Bakang Morris Malila, Rev Antonio Samalali and Rev Verdiano Ndafiuda, for their support in Rome; and Filipe Nafafé, for his hospitality.

I am also grateful for the assistance and the excellent support of the archive, library, museum and art gallery staff around the world, in Portugal, Angola, Brazil, the UK, Italy and Spain for their support and for permission to publish and reproduce documents. I send my thanks to Rosana Santos de Souza, Diana Santo Souza and Adriana Basto from the Arquivo da Santa Casa da Misericórdia da Bahia. My also thanks are due to Marlene Oliverira and Jacira Vitório from the Arquivo Público de Salvador for their support.

My thanks to Professor Evana Lima Stolze, for her support and for her guide to accessing the archives in Rio de Janeiro; Professor Pátricio Batsikama Mampuya Cipriano, for his feedback on Angolan culture; Professor Patrícia Teixeira Santos, for providing me with valuable contacts in União dos Palmares, Maceió; Roberto Ferreira Machado and Gildete Silveira dos Santo, for their wonderful support and hospitality in Cachoeira and for taking me to see the *engenho* de Victoria in Cachoeira, Bahia; Professor Flávio Gomes, for the invaluable discussion on Palmares in Rio de Janeiro; Dr Margarida Cerqueira, Biblioteca da Ajuda; Dr Alicia Campos Serrano, for her invitation to Madrid; Dr Margarita Rodríguez, for her guide to getting to the Archivo de Deciona in Toledo; Dr Moritz Herrmann, for providing me with contacts in Alagoas; Dr Ariane Carvalho, for sending me a copy of her Ph.D. thesis; Dr Roberta Stumpf; and Dr Aparecida de Jesus Ferreira, for her support.

I am also very grateful to the anonymous reviewers of this book, and to the excellent team at Cambridge University Press – particularly Professor Michael A. Gómez, series editor, Cambridge Studies on the African Diaspora; Cecelia A. Cancellaro and Deborah Gershenowitz, senior editors; Victoria Inci Phillips, editorial assistant; Rachel Blaifeder, editor; Ruth Boyes, senior content manager; Charles Phillips, copy-editor; and Felinda Sharmal, project management executive – for all their support and extremely helpful recommendations, professionalism and extraordinary commitment, skills and dedication. It has been a privilege and a pleasure to work with you all.

Introduction

In 1684, Lourenço da Silva de Mendonça from the kingdom of Kongo in the Indies[1] 'arrived in Rome to take up an important role for Black peoples'.[2] That role was to bring an ethical and criminal *kufunda*[3] (case) before the Vatican court, which accused the nations involved in Atlantic slavery, including the Vatican, Italy,[4] Spain and Portugal, of committing

---

[1] See Archivio della Propaganda Fide (Archives of Propaganda Fide, hereafter APF), Scritture Original Riferite Nelle Congregazioni Generali, Vatican, Rome, Italy (hereafter SOCG), SOCG, vol. 495a, folio (fl.) 393, 'Lourenzo deSilva de Mendonza delReyno diCongo nell'Inde venutó à Roma'. What was known as the kingdom of Kongo then was situated in West Central Africa in what is today part of northern Angola. The territory also makes up the western part of the modern Democratic Republic of Kongo as well as the southern part of Gabon. For detailed studies of the kingdom of Kongo, see John Thornton, 'The Origins and Early History of the Kingdom of Kongo, c. 1350–1550,' *The International Journal of African Historical Studies*, 34(1), 2001, pp. 89–120. See Marina de Melo e Souza, 'Congo in the Americas and Brazil', Oxford Encyclopedia, 2020: https://oxfordre.com/africanhistory/view/10.1093/acrefore/9780190277734.001.0001/acrefore-9780190277734-e-430. The spelling of 'Congo' with 'C' is kept when there is a direct quote in both Portuguese and Italian sources of the seventeenth or eighteenth centuries to maintain the sense of originality of these sources.

[2] See APF, SOCG, vol. 495a, fl. 392.

[3] *Kufunda, maka* or *maca* are Kimbundu words (Mbundu is one of the ethnic groups in the Angolan population), meaning a case to be heard in court or a case taken to court, a court case or talk; see António de Oliveira Cadornega, *História Geral das Guerras Angolanas 1680*, vol. I, Lisbon: Agência Geral das Colónias, 1972, p. 614 and p. 616. Kimbundu was Mendonça's mother tongue. He may also have spoken Portuguese, Spanish and Italian, considering his education, travels to and stay in Portugal, Spain and Italy. The Portuguese language would have been natural to him, because of his family connections to Portugal.

[4] Italy here refers to northern Italy, that is, Mantua, which was ruled by the duchess of Mantua and Montferrat of the Gonzagas family. Mantua was a protectorate of Spain in the seventeenth century. The Gonzagas family intermarried with Spanish nobility. Mantua's

crimes against humanity. It detailed the 'tyrannical sale of human beings ... the diabolic abuse of this kind of slavery ... which they committed against any Divine or Human law'.[5] Mendonça was a member of the Ndongo royal family, rulers of Pedras (Stones)[6] of Pungo-Andongo, situated in what is now modern Angola.[7] He carried with him the hopes of enslaved Africans and other oppressed groups in what was a remarkable moment that, I would argue, challenges the established interpretation of the history of abolition.[8]

Legal, moral, ethical and political debate on the abolition of slavery has traditionally been understood to have been initiated by Europeans in the eighteenth century – figures such as Thomas Buxton, Thomas Clarkson, Granville Sharp, David Livingstone and William Wilberforce.[9] To the

---

links with Spain in the seventeenth century connected to the Atlantic world. Mantua joined the kingdom of Italy in 1866. There is also, of course, plenty of literature on the involvement of Italian merchants from for example Florence and Genoa in the Atlantic slave trade. See Luís L. de Cadamosto, *Navegações de Luís de Cadamosto, Texto Italiano, e Traducao Portuguesa*, Lisbon: Instituto para a Alta Cultura (1507), 1944; Trevor P. Hall, *Before Middle Passage: Translated Portuguese Manuscripts of Atlantic Slave Trading from West Africa to Iberian Territories, 1513–26*, Farnham: Ashgate, 2015; and Sergio Tognetti, 'Trade in Black African Slaves in Fifteenth-Century Florence', in Tom F. Earle and Kate J. P. Lowe (eds.), *Black Africans in Renaissance Europe*, Cambridge: Cambridge University Press, 2005, pp. 213–224.

[5] See APF, SOCG, vol. 490, fl. 140r, 'che da tal tirannica vendita d' humano ... dall' abuso diabolico di tal schiavitú ... usano contro ogni legge Divina, et Humana'.

[6] See Cadornega, *História Geral*, vol. III, p. 156 and p. 167, where a note by José Matias Delgado states that Pungo-Andongo, prior to becoming the seat of King Philipe Hari I, was called Matadi Maupungo or Matadi ma Unpungu (Pedras Altas ou Pedras de Altura) [High Stones].

[7] Angola is in fact the Portuguese version of the precolonial name Ngola, which was the name of a king who reigned over that kingdom. See Cadornega, *História Geral*, vol. I, p. 167. The kings of Ndongo were subordinated to the kingdom of Kongo, and so Ndongo was technically one of its provinces. I will use the term Angola to refer to both people groups that inhabited the region, the Mbundu and the Ovimbundu. All the Portuguese governors sent to the region were called governors of Angola in the seventeenth century, even though the country obviously did not exist as the modern nation state we know today. See 'Carta de Doação a Paulo Dias de Novais' [Letter of Grant to Paulo Dias de Novais] Arquivo da Torre do Tombo (here after ATT), Chancelaria de D. Sebastião (Doações), livro [liv.] 26, fls. 295–299, 19 September 1571, pp. 36–51.

[8] I will not attempt to modernise spelling, punctuation or capitalisation in all quotations from primary sources from the sixteenth to seventeenth centuries in order to maintain a sense of the originality of the work I have used.

[9] Thomas F. Buxton, *The African Slave Trade and Its Remedy*, London: J. Murray, 1839; Thomas Clarkson, 'A Summary View of the Slave Trade and of the Probable Consequences of its Abolition', London: J. Philips, 1787; Thomas Clarkson, *An Essay on the Slavery and Commerce of the Human Species: Particularly the African, Translated from a Latin Dissertation, Which Was Honoured with the First Prize in the University of Cambridge, for*

extent that Africans are recognised as having played any role in ending slavery, especially in the seventeenth century, their efforts are typically confined to sporadic and impulsive cases of resistance, involving 'shipboard revolts', 'maroon communities', 'individual fugitive slaves' and 'household revolts'.[10] Studies of these cases have never gone beyond the obvious economic disruptions caused by enslaved people resorting to poisoning, murder and attacks on plantations and their masters' household properties. Even those former enslaved Africans who gained their

the Year 1785, London: Longman, Hurst, Rees and Orme, 1808; Thomas Clarkson, *The History of the Rise, Progress, and Accomplishment of the Abolition of the African Slave-trade by the British Parliament* (1808), New York: John S. Taylor, 1836; Prince Hoare, *Memoirs of Granville Sharp*, London: Henry Colbourn, 1828; Granville Sharp, *A Short Sketch of Temporary Regulations, (until Better Shall Be Proposed) for the Intended Settlement on the Grain Coast of Africa, Near Sierra Leona*, London: H. Baldwin Publication, 1786; Granville Sharp, *The Law of Retribution: Or, a Serious Warning to Great Britain and Her Colonies, Founded On Unquestionable Examples of God's Temporal Vengeance Against Tyrants, Slave-holders and Oppressors*, London, 1776. For discussion of Livingstone, see Tim Jeal, *Livingstone*, London: Heinemann. 1973; David Livingstone and James I. Macnair (ed.), *Livingstone's Travels*, London: J. M. Dent, 1954; George Seaver, *David Livingstone: His Life and Letters*, New York: Lutterworth Press, 1957. For a detailed discussion of Wilberforce, see Wayne Ackerson, *The African Institution (1807–1827) and the Antislavery Movement in Great Britain*, Lewiston, NY: E. Mellen Press, 2005; Peter Bayne, *Men Worthy to Lead; Being Lives of John Howard, William Wilberforce, Thomas Chalmers, Thomas Arnold, Samuel Budgett, John Foster*, London: Simpkin, Marshall, Hamilton, Kent & Co. Ltd, Reprinted by Bibliolife, 1890; and Kevin Belmonte, *Hero for Humanity: A Biography of William Wilberforce*, Colorado Springs, CO: Navpress Publishing Group, 2002. On other abolitionists see Leslie Bethell and Murilo de Carvalho (eds.), *Joaquim Nabuco, British Abolitionists, and the End of Slavery in Brazil: Correspondence, 1880–1905*, London: University of London Press, 2009; and Carolina Nabuco, *The Life of Joaquim Nabuco*, Stanford, CA: Stanford University Press, 1950; Padre Antônio Vieira, *Obras Escolhidas*, Lisbon: Sá da Costa, 1951–1954; Padre Antônio Vieira, *Sermões* (15 vols., Lisbon, 1679–1748), 2nd ed., Lisbon: Editorial Comunicação, 1982.

[10] See David Richardson, 'Shipboard Revolts, African Authority, and the Atlantic Slave Trade', *The William and Mary Quarterly*, 58(1), 2001, pp. 69–92; for discussion of maroon, see Flávio dos Santos Gomes, *Histórias de Quilombolas: Mocambos e Comunidades de Senzalas no Rio de Janeiro, Século XIX*, Rio de Janeiro: Arquivo Nacional, 1995; see also slaves' revolt in São Tomé, Gerhard Seibert, 'São Tomé's Great Slave Revolt of 1595: Background, Consequences and Misperceptions of One of the Largest Slave Uprisings in Atlantic History', *Portuguese Studies Review*, 201, 18(2), pp. 29–50; on fugitive slaves, see Ivana Lima Stolze and Laura Carmo (eds.), *História Social da Língua Nacional, Diápora Africana*, Rio de Janeiro: FAPERU, 2014, and for household revolts, Harold Livermore, 'Padre Oliveira's Outburst', *Portuguese Studies*, 17, 2001, pp. 22–41; and Antonio Andreoni (ou André João Antonil), *Cultura e Opulência do Brazil por suas Drogas, e Minas, com Varias Noticias Curiosas do modo de fazer o Assucar; Plantar, & Beneficiar o Tabaco; Tirar Ouro das Minas & Descubrir as da Prata; e dos grandes Emolumentos, que esta Conquista da America Meridional dá ao Reyno de Portugal com estes, et Outros Generos, et Contratos Reaes*, Lisbon: Conselho Nacional de Geografi, [1717] 1963.

freedom through sheer endeavour and subsequently argued in the strongest terms for the abolition of slavery in the late eighteenth and nineteenth centuries, such as Olaudah Equiano and Ottobah Cugoano, were seen as limited in scope, without international imapct and reliant on their European counterparts.[11] Curiously, to date, no historians of slavery of West Central Africa, Africanists or Atlanticists have researched the Black Atlantic abolition movement in the seventeenth century; and those who have attempted to engage with the debate often conclude that any action driven by Africans was a localised endeavour.[12] No historian has yet provided an in-depth study of the highly organised, international-scale, legal court case for liberation and

[11] Gunn recently argues that Cugoano's biblical rhetoric on abolition of the enslaved Africans is standard within the abolitionist tradition. See Jeffrey Gunn, 'Creating a Paradox: Quobna Ottobah Cugoano and the Slave Trade's Violation of the Principles of Christianity, Reason, and Property Ownership', *Journal of World History*, 21(4), 2010, pp. 629–656; see also Olaudah Equiano, *The Interesting Narrative of the Life of Olaudah Equiano, or Gustavus Vassa, the African, Written by Himself*, vol. I, London: Printed and folded for the Author, by T. Wilkine, 1789, online: https://www.bl.uk/collection-items/the-%20life-of-olaudah-equinao.

Ottobah Cugoano, *Thoughts and Sentiments on the Evil of Slavery* (1791), New York: Penguin, 1999. See also Randy J. Sparks, 'The Two Princes of Calabar: An Atlantic Odyssey from Slavery to Freedom', *The William and Mary Quarterly*, 59(3), 2002, pp. 555–584.

[12] See Richard Gray, 'The Papacy and the Atlantic Slave Trade: Lourenço da Silva, the Capuchins and the Decisions of the Holy Office', *Past and Present*, 115, 1987, pp. 52–68. Gray provides an erudite examination of Mendonça in the Vatican but does not see it as a legal case. Ferreira's recent analysis of individuals working for the abolition of the slave trade focuses on challenges to the institution of slavery in the nineteenth century in West Central Africa and does not address the international abolition that Mendonça fought for in the seventeenth century: see Roquinaldo Ferreira, *The Costs of Freedom: Central Africa in the Age of Abolition, 1820 ca.–1880 ca.*, Princeton, NJ: Princeton University Press (forthcoming). Research on cases of individuals challenging their own enslavement in the West Central Africa, see also José C. Curto, 'The Story of Nbena, 1817-20: Unlawful Enslavement and the Concept of "Original Freedom" in Angola', in Paul E. Lovejoy and David Trotman (eds.), *Trans-Atlantic Dimensions of Ethnicity in the African Diaspora*, New York: Continuum, 2003, pp. 43–64; José C. Curto, 'Un Butin Illégitime: Razzias d'esclaves et relations luso-africaines dans la région des fleuves Kwanza et Kwango en 1805', in *Déraison, Esclavage et Droit: Les fondements idéologiques et juridiques de la traite négrière et de l'esclavage*, ed. Isabel de Castro Henriques and Louis Sala-Molins, Paris: Unesco, 2002, pp. 315–327; Vanessa Oliveira, 'Donas, Escravas e Pretas Livres em Luanda (séc. XIX)', *Estudos Ibero-Americanos*, 44(3), 2018, pp. 447–456; Mariana P. Candido, 'The Transatlantic Slave Trade and the Vulnerability of Free Blacks in Benguela, Angola, 1780–1830', in Mark Meuwese and Jeffrey A. Fortin (eds.), *Atlantic Biographies: Individuals and Peoples in the Atlantic World*, Leiden: Brill, 2013, pp. 193–210, and Mariana P. Candido, 'O Limite Tênue entre a Liberdade e Escravidão em Benguela durante a Era do Comércio Transatlântico', *Afro-Ásia*, 47, 2013, pp. 239–268.

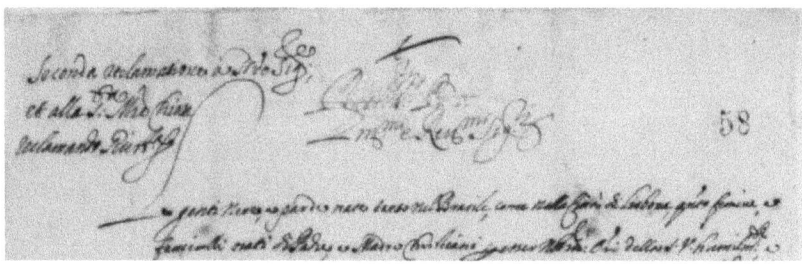

FIGURE I Mendonça's Second Legal Challenge 'Second Complaint' – [Seconda Reclamazione] APF, SOCG. vol. 495a, fl. 58. Photograph taken by the author.

abolition spearheaded by Lourenço da Silva Mendonça[13] (see Figure 1), or as Mendonça called it the 'complaint (*reclamazione*)[14] ... complaining about Justice (*reclamando Giustitia*)'.[15]

The letter (Figure 1) clearly indicates that Mendonça's first legal challenge was a court case, and that he presented the case again, as the 'second complaint' demanding justice ('Requesting Justice') to the Office of

---

[13] See the letter, SOCG, vol. 495a, fl. 54.   [14] APF, SOCG. vol. 495a, fl. 58.
[15] See the following documents: SOCG, vol. 495a; 'Indie Orientali, Sig. Card. Azzolino; Indie Orientali, Die 19 Jannuarij 1686, Signitures', 19 January 1686, folio 58, 'Seconda reclamazione à N'tro Sig.^{re}, et alla S:^{ma} Mad. Chiesa Reclamando Giuttitia', 'Beatist:^{mo} Pd:^{re} Em.^{mie} Rev.^{mi} Sig.^{ri}' – [Second complaint to Our Lord, and Saint Mother Church claiming Justice], [Most Blessed Fathers, Most Eminent and Most Reverend Lords]. Terms such as 'complaint' (*reclamazione* ... *Reclamando*), '*doghaàze*' and '*nicorhi*' (complaints and appeals) referred to a court case. Folios 54, 55, 56, 57, 58 60, 62 were kept in the file signed as C. 'Alla Sacra Congregato.^{ne} d. PropagandaFide Per la Gente Nere e Parde natè nel Brazile, Portugalle, e Spagna' ['to the Congregation of Propaganda Fide for the Black People and dual heritage born in Brazil, Portugal, and Spain'], was the name given to folio 59. However, folios 54, 55, 56 and 62 dealt with the method deployed for capturing Africans to enslave them, and folio 62 gave the solution to end the enslavement of the Africans. This was the solution adopted by the Vatican. Folio 62 was fundamental to ending slavery. The confraternities wrote folio 62 to express their frustrations with the Vatican, as they argued strongly for an end to slavery. Before this, the folio was kept in the file. Hence, it did not draw the attention of those dealing with the issues of slavery. I have given great attention to the documentation to highlight the importance of the folios as they are often misunderstood because they are inconsistently arranged in the file. It makes it easy for the reader to miss some of the folios. Folios 56r, 57, 58, 59, 60r and 60v are put in between 60 and 62. This might have prevented researchers such as Gray from piecing together their analyses. Thus, Gray missed out on the legal argument of the confraternities. Moreover, folio 56, which was a letter from Madrid detailing the conversation between Cardinal Milini, the Marquise of Astorga and the Prince of Gonzaga, dated 20 April 1684, was misplaced in the file. Likewise, folios 57r and 57v dated 1 May 1684, were another letter from the Vatican Nuncio in Lisbon, misplaced in the file. Folio 58 contains the appeal to the case, as seen in Figure 1.

Propaganda Fide, or 'General Congregation', which was charged with dealing with any issues arising overseas.[16] The document is undated, but it is clear that it was a continuation of his earlier legal challenge. It reads: 'S:^{ma} Mad. Chiesa Reclamando Giustitia' 'Beatist:^{mo} Pd:^{re} Em.^{mi} e Rev.^{mi} Sig.^{ri}' [Second appeal to Our Lord and to Saint Mother Church Requesting Justice], 'Beatist:^{mo} Pd:^{re} Em.^{mie} Rev.^{mi} Sig.^{ri}' [Most Blessed Fathers, Most Eminent and Most Reverend Lords].

In this book, I examine in detail how Mendonça and the historical actors with whom he was involved – such as Black Christians from confraternities in Angola, Brazil, Caribbean, Portugal and Spain – argued for the complete abolition of the Atlantic slave trade well before Wilberforce and his generation of abolitionists.[17] Providing an in-depth analysis of Mendonça's abolition movement, this book offers new perspectives on the abolition history of the seventeenth century and the associated debates that re-emerged in the eighteenth and nineteenth centuries.[18] It reveals, for the first time, how legal debates were headed not by Europeans, but by Africans.

Drawing on new data uncovered in a variety of archives around the world and never before used by historians of the Lusophone Atlantic, this book links Mendonça's activity to that of New Christians (Jews converted to Christianity, also known as the 'Hebrew Nation') and the Indigenous Americans (an Indigenous people who inhabited what is today known as Brazil before the Portuguese arrival).[19]

I argue that there is an important and previously overlooked connection between Africans seeking the abolition of slavery and the New Christians and Indigenous Americans in their common search for liberty and understanding of how the denial of religious freedom was connected

---

[16] For further discussion of the topic, see Oskar Garstein, *Rome and the Counter-Reformation in Scandinavia: Until the Establishment of the S. Congregatio de Propaganda Fide in 1622, Based on Source Material in the Kolsrud Collection*, vol. 1, Oslo: Universitetsforlaget, 1963; see also Pius Malekandathil, 'Cross, Sword and Conflicts: A Study of the Political Meanings of the Struggle between the Padroado Real and the Propaganda Fide', *Studies in History*, 27(2), 2011, pp. 251–267.

[17] See on the internationalisation of Confraternities' pledge to aboilish the Atlantic slavery, see APF, SOCG, Series America Meridionale, fl. 309, and see SOCG, vol. 495a, fl. 62.

[18] See Equiano, *The Interesting Narrative*, and Cugoano, *Thoughts and Sentiments*.

[19] On the Hebrew Nation, see Florbela Veiga Frade and Sandra Neves Silva, 'Medicina e Política em dois Físicos Judeus Portugueses de Hamburgo, Rodrigo de Castro e o Medicus Politicus (1614), e Manuel Bocarro Rosales e o Status Astrologicus (1644)', *Sefarad*, 71(1), 2011, pp. 51–94; and also Sandra Neves Silva, 'A "Obra ao Rubro" na Cultura Portuguesa de Seiscentos: o Cristão-Novo Manuel Bocarro Francês e seus Versos Alquímicos de 1624', *Cadernos de Estudos Sefarditas*, (8), 2008, pp. 217–244.

with the denial of enslaved Africans' humanity.[20] I also contend that by allying himself with these different constituencies in the Atlantic, Mendonça carried his abolitionist message of freedom far beyond Africa.[21] His claim for liberty was universal: it went beyond the predicament of enslaved Africans to include other oppressed groups in Africa, Brazil, the Caribbean, Portugal and Spain.[22]

To fully comprehend Mendonça's work, it is crucial that we understand from the outset that the enslavement of Africans was part of the Portuguese conquest of West Central Africa, where Mendonça was born.[23] Slavery went hand in hand with conquest in Portugal's encounter with Central or West Africa, and the enslavement of Angolans was inseparable from Portuguese military aggression in the region.[24] From the

---

[20] See Freire de Oliveira, *Elementos para a História do Município de Lisboa*, Lisbon, 1885, and John Ford Maxwell, *Slavery and the Catholic Church: Teaching Concerning the Moral Legitimacy of the Institution of Slavery*, London: Rose [for] the Anti-Slavery Society for the Protection of Human Rights, 1975, and A. C. de C. M. Saunders, *A Social History of Black Slaves and Freedmen in Portugal 1441–1555*, Cambridge: Cambridge University Press, 1982. See Gray, 'The Papacy', and the discussion of Brazil by Andreoni (Antonil), *Cultura e Opulência*.

[21] See 'Carta de Giacinto Rogio Monzon' [Letter by Giacinto Rogio Monzon], APF, Scritture Riferite nei Congressi, Series Africa, Angola, Congo, Senegal, Isole dell' Oceano Atlantico Dar, Vatican, Rome, Italy, 1645 al 1685, [S.C. Africa], vol. 1, fl. 487, Madrid, 23 September 1682. See also Stuart B. Schwartz, *Blacks and Indians: Common Cause and Confrontation in Colonial Brazil*, Yale University, no date.

[22] On the Caribbean's involvement see SOCG, vol. 495a, fl. 62.

[23] See 'Carta de António da Costa de Sousa a Manuel Barreto de S. Paio' [A Letter of António da Costa to Manuel Barreto de S. Paio], Arquivo Histórico Ultramarino de Belém (hereafter AHU), AHU_CU_001, cx. 11, d. 1326, Lisboa, fl. 678v, 24 August 1673. See also Beatrix Heintze and Katja Rieck 'The Extraordinary Journey of the Jaga Through the Centuries: Critical Approaches to Precolonial Angolan Historical Sources', *History in Africa*, 34, 2007, pp. 67–101 and Jan Vansina, 'Ambaca Society and the Slave Trade c. 1760–1845', *Journal of African History* 46(1), 2005, pp. 1–27.

[24] See Cadornega, *História Geral*, vols. I–III. My understanding of the conquest differs from a new wave of Brazilian-born scholars, who have been emphatic about using the term 'colonialism' and stressing territorial conquest, taxation and enslavement as part of the colonial expansion. See Mariana P. Candido, *An African Slaving Port and the Atlantic World: Benguela and Its Hinterland*, New York: Cambridge University Press, 2013; Flávia Maria de Carvalho, *Sobas e Homens do Rei. Relações de Poder e Escravidão em Angola (séculos XVII e XVIII)*, Maceió, Alagoas: Edufal, 2015; Crislayne Alfagali, *Ferreiros e fundidores da Ilamba: uma história social da fabricação do ferro e da Real Fábrica de Nova Oeiras* (Angola, segunda metade do século XVIII), Luanda: Fundação Agostinho Neto, 2018. I am using the term in the Anglo-Saxon and Luso-African way, as argued by Walter Rodney, that colonialism was a total domination and did not start before the end of the nineteenth century; see Walter Rodney, *How Europe Underdeveloped Africa*, London; Brooklyn, New York: Verso, 2018; and *History of the Upper Guinea Coast: 1545–1800*, Oxford: Clarendon Press, 1970. See also Amilcar Cabral, *Return to the Source: Selected*

beginning of Portuguese settlement there in the mid-sixteenth century, war was waged against the West Central African people.[25] This was the catalyst for the enslavement of ordinary civilians.[26]

If we are to grasp the rationale behind the capture of enslaved people[27] in the region and understand how they were obtained, it is crucial to recognise the role played by the Muncipal City Council of Luanda, which regulated the shipment of the enslaved Angolans sent to Brazil.[28] Indeed, it is impossible to understand the significance of Mendonça's court case without taking account of the involvement of the Muncipal City Council of Luanda in the slave trade. Central to the argument of this book, then, is the story of the destruction of Pungo-Andongo and the death of its last king, João (John) Hari II, who was Mendonça's uncle.[29] Exiled as prisoners of war, Ndongo's

---

Speeches of Amilcar Cabral, New York: Monthly Review Press, 1973; and *Unity and Struggle: Speeches and Writings of Amilcar Cabral*, New York: Monthly Review Press, 1979; and José Lingna Nafafé, *Colonial Encounters: Issues of Culture, Hybridity and Creolisation, Portuguese Mercantile Settlers in West Africa*, Frankfurt am Main: Peter Lang, 2007.

[25] I am employing the term West Central Africa (WCA), which has been used by historians of the region or Africanists, but of course this was not a designation at the time. WCA is a subregion that includes the African Coast between Cape Lopes and the Southern part of the African continent, comprising the Angolan, Kongolese and Loanguese ports. For detailed information see A. M. Caldeira, 'Formação de uma cidade afro-atlântica: Luanda no século XVII', *Revista Tempo, Espaço, Linguagem*, 5(3), 2014, pp. 12–39. The region was called Libia Inferior or Ethiopia Menor. See 'D. António Nigrita, Embaixador do Rei do Congo', AV – Fando Borghhe, Série I, vol. 721. (DIARIORUM CAEREMONIALIVM / IOANNIS PAVLl MVCANTII ROMANI i. V. D. / APOSTOLICARVM CJEREMONIARVM / MAGISTRI, 2 January 1608, MMA, p. 393 'Aethiopia inferior' (pp. 393–403).

[26] See Mário Martins de Freitas, *Reino Negro de Palmares* [1954], Rio de Janeiro: Biblioteca do Exército Editora, 2nd ed., 1988. See also Heintze and Rieck, 'The Extraordinary Journey of the Jaga'; Vansina, 'Ambaca Society'; and David Birmingham, *Trade and Conquest in Angola*, Oxford: Clarendon Press, 1966. All these authors have analysed at length how Portuguese conquest in Angola provided enslaved people.

[27] I use the term 'enslaved people' instead of 'slave' to indicate the process of enslaving the Africans and support the argument that there were no pre-existing slaves in Africa before the arrival of the Europeans. The term 'enslaved people' is already being used in Brazil by the Black Movement, as well as in philosophy and history by various authors in the Anglo-Saxon context.

[28] There may have been some enslaved Angolans who ended up in Brazil as contraband or who were smuggled illegally from the Portuguese point of view of tax payment. However, the Muncipal City Council of Luanda controlled and managed the trade.

[29] See Relaçam/ Do FELICE SVCCESSO, QUE / confeguiraõ as armas do Sereniffimo Princepe D. Pedro N. S. gouernadas por Francifco de Tauora, Gouernador, & Capitam General do Reyno de Angola contra a Rebeliaõ de Dom Ioaõ Rey das Pedras, & Dongo, no mez de Dezembro de 1671', Biblioteca Nacional de Lisboa, Reservado, 903, pp. 1–11; Cadornega, *História Geral*, vols. I and II; and Delgado's note in Cadornega, *História Geral*, vol. II, pp. 548–549.

royals, including Mendonça, his brothers, uncles, aunts and cousins, were sent first to Salvador in Bahia, then to Rio de Janeiro and other captaincies in what is nowadays Brazil, and finally to Portugal.[30] Crucially, to fully understand the involvement of *sobas* (Angolan local rulers) in the slave trade in Angola and perhaps elsewhere in Africa, I contend that it is necessary to take into account the introduction in 1626 by Fernão de Sousa, the Portuguese governor in Angola, of *baculamento*, a tax payment of enslaved people, in place of *encombros*, a tax payment in produce.[31] This is a piece of new data that has not been used by historians of West Central Africa, Africanists and Atlanticists. I argue that it had far-reaching consequences for the historiography of the region in the eighteenth and nineteenth centuries. Unaware of this legislation, West Central African historiography on 'taxation', 'wars', 'debt' and 'legal practices' has unwittingly been prevented from truly understanding the reasons for and methods of enslavement.[32] These historians of West Central Africa have remained ignorant of Sousa's introduction of the *baculamento*. Subsequent governors and their captains in the *presidio* (Portuguese outpost) in Angola used the *baculamento* for centuries to naturalise the Atlantic slave trade. And the *baculamento* has remained obscure until now; most West Central African historians have taken it as accepted wisdom that slavery was an African practice,[33] and the idea that Africans colluded in Atlantic slavery has never been challenged.[34] Generations of scholars have studied systems of 'taxation', 'wars', 'debt' and 'legal practices' without interrogating the the Portuguese institution of *baculamento*, which overrode local practices; instead, blame has been placed on the Angolan institutions. All Angolan *soba* allies of the Portuguese conquest were obliged to make a payment of 100 enslaved people annually to Portugal. This Portuguese taxation, which was named after the local *baculamento*

---

[30] See Delgado's note in Cadornega, *História Geral*, vol. II, pp. 546–547.
[31] *Encombros* were tributes paid by *sobas* to the Portuguese; tribute included produce, such as cows, timbers, palm oil and chickens. See 'Informação de Fernão de Sousa a El-Rei' (Information by Fernão de Sousa to the King), BAL, ms. 51-VIII-31, fls. 5–9 v, 7 December 1631. Sobas were noblemen responsible for the districts into which the kingdom of Ndongo was divided.
[32] See Charles R. Boxer (ed.), *South China in the Sixteenth Century: Being the Narratives of Galeote Pereira, Fr. Gaspar da Cruz, O.P. [and] Fr. Martín de Rada, O.E.S.A. (1550–1575)*, London: Routledge, 2010, p. 152. For the original work of Gaspar da Cruz, see Gaspar da Cruz (O.P.), *Tractado em que se Co[m]tam Muito por Este[n]so as Cousas da China, co[n] suas Particularidades, [e] assi do Reyno Dormuz*, Madrid: Em Casa de Andre de Burgos, 1569.
[33] See Eugénio Ferreira, *Feiras e Presídios: Esboço de Interpretaçào Materialista da Colonizaçào de Angola*, Lisbon: Edições 70, 1979.
[34] See Boxer (ed.), *South China in the Sixteenth Century*.

practice[35] – a tribute system – profoundly disrupted the Angolan sociopolitical and legal system and resulted in social upheaval. Communities and their rulers were turned against each other, a new local judicial procedure was imposed that served the interests of the Atlantic slave trade, putting judicial officers in local courts in Angola to adjudicate local cases in their own interest – what Kimbwandende K. B. Fu-Kiau called a turning point in African governance and leadership in West Central Africa.[36]

Following from this, I scrutinise the history of runaways to gain an understanding of how those who escaped enslavement in Angola, São Tomé and Brazil conceived their plight. Many enslaved peoples ran away in these regions because they rebelled against a system that dehumanised them, which Portugal had imposed upon them. While in Brazil, Mendonça may have had contact with communities there of such runaways, come to understand their suffering and connected his experience with theirs, especially those who joined *Quilombo dos Palmares*, one of the earliest, largest and most successful maroon communities in Brazil.[37]

---

[35] *Baculamento* is a Kimbundu term that means 'tribute'. For a detailed discussion of *baculamento* as a tribute, but not as a tax in human beings, see Aida Freudenthal and Selma Pantoja, *Livro dos Baculamentos que os Sobas Deste Reino de Angola Pagam a Sua Majestade 1630*, Luanda: Arquivo Nacional de Angola, D.L., 2013; Beatrix Heintze, 'The Angolan Vassal Tributes of the 17th Century', *Revista de Historia Economica e Social*, 6, 1980, pp. 57–78; Beatrix Heintze, 'Luso-African Feudalism in Angola? The Vassal Treaties of the Sixteenth to the Eighteenth Century', *Revista Portuguesa de História*, 18, 1980, pp. 111–131; Beatrix Heintze, *Angola nos Séculos XVI e XVII. Estudo Sobre Fontes, Métodos e História*, Luanda: Kilombelombe, 2007; and Beatrix Heintze, 'Angola nas Garras do Tráfico de Escravos: As Guerras Angolanas do Ndongo (1611-1630)', *Revista Internacional de Estudos Africanos*, 1, 1984, pp. 11–59; and Toby Green, 'Baculamento or Encomienda?: Legal Pluralisms and the Contestation of Power in Pan-Atlantic World of the Sixteenth and Seventeenth Centuries', *Journal of Global Slavery*, 2, 2017, pp. 310–336; Mariana P. Candido, 'Conquest, Occupation, Colonialism and Exclusion: Land Disputes in Angola', in *Property Rights, Land and Territory in the European Overseas Empires*, ed. José Vicente Serrão et al., Lisbon: CEHC-IUL, 2014, pp. 223–233; Mariana P. Candido, 'O Limite Tênue' entre a Liberdade e Escravidão em Benguela durante a Era do Comércio Transatlântico', *Afro-Ásia*, 47 (2013), pp. 239–268.

[36] See Overseas Council edit of 1698. For a detailed discussion of the evil of slavery brought by the Portuguese in Angola, see Vansina, 'Ambaca Society'. Even though the author's analysis is that of the eighteenth century, it is worth noting that the process of slavery in the region has been of *longue durée* (the process of history is a long-lasting one). A crucial author to understand the changes in the conceptions of law and crime is Kimbwandende K. B. Fu-Kiau, *African Cosmology of the Bantu-Kongo – Principles of Live and Living*. Poland Sp. zo.o.; Wroclaw: African Tree Press, 2001.

[37] For literature on Palmares, see Edison Carneiro, *O Quilombo dos Palmares* [1947] 2nd ed., São Paulo, Brasiliense, 1958; de Freitas, *Reino Negro de Palmares*. See also Glenn Alan Cheney, *Quilombo dos Palmares: Brazil's Lost Nation of Fugitive Slaves*, Hanover, CT: New London Librarium, 2014.

Looking at Mendonça's later life and journey to Portugal, I argue that his stay in Braga and Lisbon helped him to form an alliance with the family of the apostolic notary in Lisbon, Gaspar da Costa de Mesquita, and the New Christians in Portugal.[38] Then I examine his journey, undertaken with the support of the papal nuncio in Portugal, to Toledo – where he formed a network with Indigenous Americans at the Royal Court of Madrid.[39] I argue that to understand Mendonça's court case one must understand his family, who were coerced by the Portuguese into becoming involved in the slave trade. The weight of this history and the resulting psychological burden constituted one of the most compelling reasons for Mendonça's journey to the Vatican and his deep desire to see the Atlantic slave trade abolished. He wanted the Atlantic slave trade to be *tánuka*, a term in his language, Kimbundu, meaning 'to be torn, destroyed or shattered'.[40] Equally, he wanted all the other ill-treated constituencies such as the New Christians and the Indigenous Americans freed, due to 'Pan-Atlantic' solidary.[41]

This book thus explores for the first time how enslaved Africans were part of a wider Atlantic economic network in the seventeenth century, encompassing Africa, Brazil, the Caribbean, Portugal and Spain. It examines how they used transatlantic connections to join with other oppressed groups so as to fashion a league of confederation to achieve freedom. In the following pages and before engaging with this account in detail, I briefly introduce the historical context of Mendonça's court case by giving a first overview of the Portuguese Empire operation in Angola and Mendonça's family tree and life story. I go on to discuss the studies and sources that I have used to analyse Mendonça's work and historical context. I then explain the book's methodology. This is followed by a detailed breakdown of the book's chapters.

0.1 THE PORTUGUESE EMPIRE OPERATION IN ANGOLA: KINGS, GOVERNORS, COUNCILS AND LOCAL RULERS

The Municipal Council of Luanda was founded on 11 February 1575 by Paulo Dias de Novais, a nobleman who was appointed as a captain and the

---

[38] See 'Carta de Giacinto Rogio Monzon'. [39] See APF, SOCG, fl. 486.
[40] For a detailed dicussion on Kimbundu family language on West Central Africa, see Patrício Batsîkama, 'As Origens do Reino do Kôngo Segundo a Tradição Oral', *Sankofa, Revista de História da África e de Estudos da Diáspora Africana*, 3(5), 2010, p. 24, tánuka 'ser rasgado, destruir, usar ou pôr em pedaços'.
[41] See Toby Green, *The Rise of the Trans-Atlantic Slave Trade in Western Africa, 1300–1500*, Cambridge: Cambridge University Press, 2012.

first governor of Angola by the Portuguese Crown on 19 September 1571.⁴² The council was the governing authority that ran the affairs of the Portuguese enclave in Luanda. Executive power in the Municipal City Council of Luanda lay with its governors, members, a senior crown judge, scribes, judges and war council (which had the power to veto wars in the region). The head of the council was the governor, directly appointed by the Crown in Lisbon. Aside from the executive body, the council had other functionaries, such as the apostolic notary.

Conquered, and subjected to Portuguese rule, Angolan kings and *sobas* loyal to the king of Portugal were made subject to annual tax payment in human beings in 1626, thus turning people into a currency.⁴³ This was particularly the case for Angolan kings, because 'native' soldiers were recruited directly from the region where the Portuguese had established control and maintained fairs (markets).⁴⁴ The Municipal Council of Luanda was charged with dividing land already conquered from the Angolans between the Portuguese and African war captains, so-called *guerra preta*.⁴⁵ The council was also responsible for paying the salaries of the governors, the soldiers and secular priests, and regulating trade and

---

[42] See 'Carta de Doação a Paulo Dias de Novais'. See also Ilídio do Amaral, *O Consulado de Paulo Dias de Novais: Angola no Último Quartel do Século XVI e Primeiro do Século XVII*, Lisbon: Ministério da Ciência e da Tecnologia, Instituto de Investigação Científica Tropical, 2000, and Linda M. Heywood, *Njinga of Angola: Africa's Warrior Queen*, Boston, MA: Harvard University Press, 2017.

[43] All loyal *sobas* in both Angola and Kongo were conquered by the Portuguese and forced to give obedience to the Portuguese Crown in five areas: (1) pay annual tax in enslaved people to the Crown; (2) allow recruitment of solders for war to fight alongside the Portuguese contingent of soldiers stationed in Angola or Kongo against fellow Angolans or Kongolese; (3) open local and regional markets for the Portuguese to freely trade and impose their rule; (4) allow Portuguese priests to build churches and carry out Christian mission activities in the area; (5) allow land to be alienated for the Portuguese use. In return, *sobas* were granted protection from their Angolan enemies, and their children offered Portuguese education. See BAL, cód. 51-IX-20, fl. 241 v, MMA, pp. 1624–1630. For further discussion of *undar* or *under* in Angola, see Heintze, *Angola nos Séculos XVI e XVII*; Carvalho, *Sobas e Homens do Rei*; Green, 'Baculamento or Encomienda?' and for discussion of vassalship, see Candido, *An African Slaving Port*.

[44] See Birmingham, *Trade and Conquest*.

[45] *Guerra preta* was a term used to refer to Angolan soldiers who were recruited by force from the Portuguese-controlled or -conquered region of Angola. Portugal recruited in these areas as part of the agreements they had with *sobas*. *Sobas* allied to Portugal were obliged by force to allow, (1) their territory to be used for commerce by the Portuguese; (2) recruitment of soldiers; and (3) to make payment of tax in enslaved people. *Guerra preta* is used interchangeably with *quilamba*: the term *quilambas* or *kilambas* designated captains of *guerra preta*; In the Kimbundu language *quilamba* or *ilamba* means 'war captains'. See 'Carta de Constantino Cadena a Fernão de Sousa' [A letter of Constantino Cadena to Fernão de Sousa], AHU – Angola, cx. 2., 16 September 1626; MMA pp. 479–481 and

tax revenues.⁴⁶ On 19 November 1664, members of the Municipal Council of Luanda showed their power by lodging a complaint with the Crown that was adjudicated by the Portuguese Overseas Council, which dealt with all overseas affairs:

That the trade of the same Kingdom [Angola] consists only in the enslaved that is carried out in the lands of Soba's vassals of His Majesty, that is, from presidios such as Lobolo, Dembos, Benguella, and from those that are mostly conquered by that government ... that the most important thing that there is in that kingdom, which is in need of maintaining, is the Royal standard tax duty in slaves that they dispatch from the factory of Your Majesty. It is not that its profit is great, but also for being used for sustaining the Infantry, and to pay governors' salaries of five presidios of hinterland, of secular priests in Kongo, and of other clergy of that kingdom, and other salaries, and budgets.⁴⁷

This clearly demonstrates that the City Council's budget depended entirely on revenues from enslavement.⁴⁸ The slave trade in Angola was the lifeblood of the council and maintained the Portuguese project of conquest; without it, there was no Portuguese Empire. Hospitals in Angola were dependent on the slave trade for their existence, and so were education and missionary activities in the region.⁴⁹ The council

---

'Carta do governador de Angola a El-Rei de Portugal' [A letter of the governor of Angola to the king of Portugal] AHU – Angola, cx. 2., 9 de Março de 1643; MMA, pp. 28–38.

⁴⁶ See 'Relação de Antonio Bezerra Fajardo' [High Court of Appeal of, Antonio Bezerra Fajardo] BAL, Manuscrito [ms.] 51-VIII-25, fls. 29–32, 24 February 1624, pp. 205–214. See also 'Consulta ao Conselho Ultramarino', AHU, cód. 16, fl. 135v, MMA, 19 November 1664, pp. 509–510.

⁴⁷ See 'Consulta ao Conselho Ultramarino', AHU, Códice 16, folio, 135v., 19 November 1664, MMA, pp. 509–510, 'que o comercio do mesmo Reino cõsiste só no resgatte dos escrauos, que se faz nas terras dos souas vassallos de V. Magestade, assy dos prezidios, como do Lobolo, Dembos, Benguella, e nos mais sogeitos àquele gouerno ... que a cousa de maior importância que tem aquele Reino, e em que consiste a sua conseruação, hé o direito Real dos escrauos, que se despachão na feitoria de V. Magestade, não porque seu rendimento seja muito grande, mas porque com elle se sustenta a Infantaria, e paga o ordenado dos gouernadores de cinco presídios do certão, dos Cónegos de Congo, e do mais clero daquele Reino, e outras ordinárias, e despesas. E se faltarem aqueles direitos, todos estes Ministros, e officiaes padecerão grandíssima falta, e aquela praça correrá muito risco, faltandolhe a Infantaria, por falta de pagas'.

⁴⁸ See Manuel Seuerim de Faria, 'Sobre a Fundação de Seminários para a Guiné', [On the Foundation of the Seminars in Guinea], Academia Real de la Historia, Madrid, [ARHM], Salazar y Castro, ms. B-4, fls. 95–105 v; MMA, January 1622, pp. 666–690.

⁴⁹ On 29 January 1695, the hospital in Luanda, Angola, requested permission from the Portuguese Crown to sell 500 enslaved Angolans per year to meet the cost of its staff, which included 'sirurgiaõ, medico, e barbeiro' (a surgeon, a doctor and a barber), 'medicamentos" (medicines). See AHU., Angola, cx. 15, doc. 65. The hospital 'was granted its wish by the Crown' [S. Magestade fez mercê] on 13 February 1695. See the same document: Angola, cx. 15, doc. 65. A formal letter was again issued to Luanda hospital

interfered in local politics and elections, and particularly in the role of the local *ngola* (kings).⁵⁰

The Council of Luanda, which was composed mainly of Portuguese merchants and some retired soldiers who had fought wars in Angola, also exerted undue pressure on the *sobas'* governance of their provinces.⁵¹ They controlled the market and charged their *pombeiros* (local conquered traders, including enslaved people owned by the Portuguese) to carry trading into hinterland markets.⁵² The City Council's interests were often at odd with those of governors, the Portuguese Overseas Council and the Portuguese Crown.⁵³ Let us look now at the ruling royal family from which the City Council drew its influence and also at where Mendonça came from and his family tree.

Prince Lourenço da Silva Mendonça was probably born in the kingdom of Pedras of Pungo-Andongo, and certainly in Angola, but his date of birth and place of death remain unknown. He may have been twenty-two or twenty-three years old when he left Angola in 1671. He was a member of the Mbundu, one of the people groups in Angola.⁵⁴ Beyond this, not much is known for certain about his early life.

---

a month later on 5 March 1695. See AHU., Cód. 554, fl. 82: – Caixa 15, 5 March 1695. Almost a century earlier, in 1515, King Manuel issued an edict allowing every ship arriving in Lisbon from the West and West Central Africa to donate one enslaved person to the 'Hospital de Todos-os-Santos' [Hospital of All Saints in Lisbon] in order to meet its expenses. See ATT – Gavetas, II-2-62, 17 September 1515; MMA, pp. 118–119. Similarly, on 3 May 1504, King Manuel offered six enslaved Africans to help with subsistence and expenses *pera ajuda do sostimēto e despeesas* for the hospital in the Portuguese settlement of São Tomé. For detailed discussion of Portuguese expenditure in the Atlantic in the seventeenth century, see Faria, 'Sobre a Fundação de Seminários'. Faria's work is important for understanding the economic logic of the Atlantic slave trade and how the profit accrued from sale of the enslaved African people enabled the Portuguese to reach India and build its empire.

⁵⁰ See BAL., Cód. 51-IX-20, fl. 241 v, 1624–1630, MMA. See also 'Relação de Antonio Bezerra Fajardo' and 'Carta de João Correia de Sousa ao Marquês de Frecilha' (Letter of João Correia de Sousa to the Count of Frecilha), AHM – 9 – 1 – 6/B-4, fls. 130–133, MMA, 3 June 1622, p. 21.

⁵¹ See Heywood, *Njinga of Angola*; Heintze and Rieck, 'The Extraordinary Journey of the Jaga'; Vansina, 'Ambaca Society'; and Birmingham, *Trade and Conquest*.

⁵² See Birmingham, *Trade and Conquest*, p. 78.

⁵³ See Cadornega, *História Geral*, vol. II, p. 533.

⁵⁴ I use the term 'people group' in this book instead of 'tribe', a term introduced by the Portuguese that does not do justice to the people or African nations. Almada in the sixteenth century used the term 'nation' rather than tribe to refer to people he encountered on the West Coast of Africa. Each group had their own language, culture and political organisation, independent of others. See André Á Almada, 'TratadosBreue dosRejnos deguine docaboverde' [Treaty of the Kingdoms of Guiné and Cape Verde], BNL, 1594.

Pedras of Pungo-Andongo was the seat of the first Angolan allied to the king of Portugal, Philipe de Sousa, or Philipe Hari I (Ngola Aiidi), or Dom Henrique Rei do Pungo-Andongo, known in Angola also as Samba a Ndumba. He ruled for thirty-eight years.[55] Mendonça's father was Dom Ignaçio da Silva,[56] the son of King Philipe Hari I; his mother's name is unknown. He had three brothers: Simão, Ignacio and Ignacio (the two latter shared a name).[57]

Within Angola, I have traced the royal family of Pungo-Andongo back to the celebrated Queen Njinga (1624–1663). Ngola Aiidi (Philipe Hari I) was her half-brother on his father's side, as well as half-brother to King Ngola Mbandi; Cadornega's work confirms this.[58] His mother was the third wife (Mocama or Mukama) of King Ngola Kiluanje Kia Ndambi.[59] However, a letter I discovered in the Arquivo historico Ultramarino de Bélem, from the former governor of Angola, Salvador Correia de Sá e Benavides (1648–1651), states that Philipe Hari I was Queen Njinga's uncle; we know for certain that they were relatives.[60] Her brother, King Ngola Mbandi, died in mysterious circumstances, and writings from that time suggest that Queen Njinga killed him in order to take over the throne of Ndongo and rule the Mbundu people. However, after Philipe Hari I was elected king of Ndongo with the aid of the Portuguese on 12 October 1626, Njinga's rule was confined to Matamba, east of Ndongo. Philipe Hari I and Njinga ruled for thirty-eight and thirty-nine years, respectively.

---

[55] Ngola Aiidi or Philipe Hari I was a conquered *soba* prior to being elected as King of Ndongo by the Portuguese. See BAL, cód. 51-IX-20, fl. 241 v, MMA, pp. 1624–1630 and See D. Frei Francisco do Soveral, 'Relatório de D. Frei Francisco do Soveral na visita "Ad Sacra Limina"', 'Jnfra scriptam relationem de statu Cathedralis ecclesiae Sancti Saluatoris transmittit ad Sanctissimum D. N. Vrbanú Papam Octauum et Sacram Congregationem Concilli Tridentini Prater Pranciscus de Soveral, Episcopus. Anno Domini de 1631' (Friar Francisco de Soveral, Bishop, transmits the following written report on the state of the Cathedral church of São Salvador to the Most Holy Our Lord Urban Pope Eighth and to the Holy Congregation of the Council of Trent. Year of the Lord 1631.), ARSI – Goa, vol. 40, doc. IV, 1 April 1631, and see also MMA, pp. 121–125.

[56] See AHU_CU_001, cx. 11, d. 1326, fl. 678v, Lisboa, 24 August 1673. See also Cardonega, *História Geral*, vols. I, II and III.

[57] Both brothers have the same name.

[58] See Cadornega, *História Geral*, vol. I, p. 164. See 'Carta de Salvador Correia de Sá e Benavides' [A Letter by Salvador Correia de Sá e Benavides], AHU_CU_001, cx. 11, d. 1272, 21 August 1672. What we know for certain is that they were relatives.

[59] See Cadornega, *História Geral*, vol. I, p. 164. Mocama was a third wife. For detail study on lineages, see Vansina, 'Ambaca Society'.

[60] See 'Carta de Salvador Correia de Sá'.

Mendonça's family tree (see Figure 2 and Figure 3)[61] demonstrates that he was descended from the kings of Kongo who ruled over what is today known as West Central Africa and were the first royals to adopt Christianity in the region. Afonso I (1509–1543),[62] the king of Kongo, is said to have been related to Mendonça's great-grandfather, Ngola Kiluanji Kia Samba (1515–1556), king of Ndongo and Matamba.[63] It was not a far-fetched statement, therefore, when Mendonça made the claim in the Vatican that he was descended from the 'royal blood of the kings of Kongo and Angola'.[64]

Given Mendonça's origins in Kongo and Angola, Africans were demonstrably the prime campaigners for the abolition of African enslavement in the seventeenth century. In presenting his court case in the Vatican about the plight of enslaved Africans in Africa and in the Atlantic, and the oppression of Natives and New Christians in Portugal,[65] he put forward a universal message of freedom – all these groups included people whose humanity was being denied. This challenges the accepted view that 'the conduct of the slave-trade involved the active participation of the African chiefs'.[66] There were, indeed, many within Africa who refused to accept and actively opposed the Atlantic slave trade, and who abhorred its ideology and practice. Mendonça represented those constituencies from his own family – his grandfather, Philipe Hari I, and father, Ignaçio da Silva – who were coerced into the slave trade by the Portuguese regime in Angola.[67]

---

[61] The family tree is based on the following sources: 'Carta de António da Costa de Sousa a Manuel Barreto de S. Paio'; SOCG, vol. 490, folios, 140r-v, Cadornega, *História Geral*, vols. I and II, and secondary sources. It covers the period 1506–1673.

[62] Mvemba a Nzinga or Nzinga Mbemba was Afonso I's African name before he converted to Catholicism. Name changes were an important tool of the Portuguese in ensuring that African royals felt allegiance. See AHU, Guiné. 1a Secção, Caixa 3, doc. 95, 1694; and L. Silveira (ed.), *Peregrinação de André de Faro à Terra dos Gentios*, Lisbon: Na Officina Tipographia Portugal – Brasil, 1945.

[63] Guida M Jackson, *Women Who Ruled: A Biographical Encyclopedia*, Santa Barbara, CA: ABC-CLIO, 1990. See also SOCG. 490, folios, 140r.

[64] SOCG. 490, folios, 140r, 'Lorenzo deSilva, é Mendoza della RegioStirpe de' i Re diCongo, et Angola' [Lorenzo de Silva e Mendoza of the Royal Blood of the Kings of Kongo and Angola]. I have constructed his family tree using archival documents housed in 'Carta de António da Costa de Sousa a Manuel Barreto de S. Paio'; and SOCG vol. 490, folios, 140r-v. and Cadornega, *História Geral*, vols. I and II and secondary sources.

[65] I am using the term Natives and Indigenous interchangeably in the book because of my sources.

[66] See C. R. Boxer, *Portuguese Seaborne Empire*, London: Hutchinson, 1969, p. 31.

[67] See 'Carta de Antonio da Costa de Sousa a Manuel Barreto de S. Paio' [A Letter of Antonio da Costa de Sousa to Manuel Barreto de S. Paio], Angola, cx. 10, 24 August 1673, and 'Sobre os Principes Negros do Dongo Unidos no Navio Sao Verissimo'. The names Ngola Aiidi, Philipe I de Sousa and D. Henrique Rei do Pungo-Andongo all refer to the same person: Philipe Hari I.

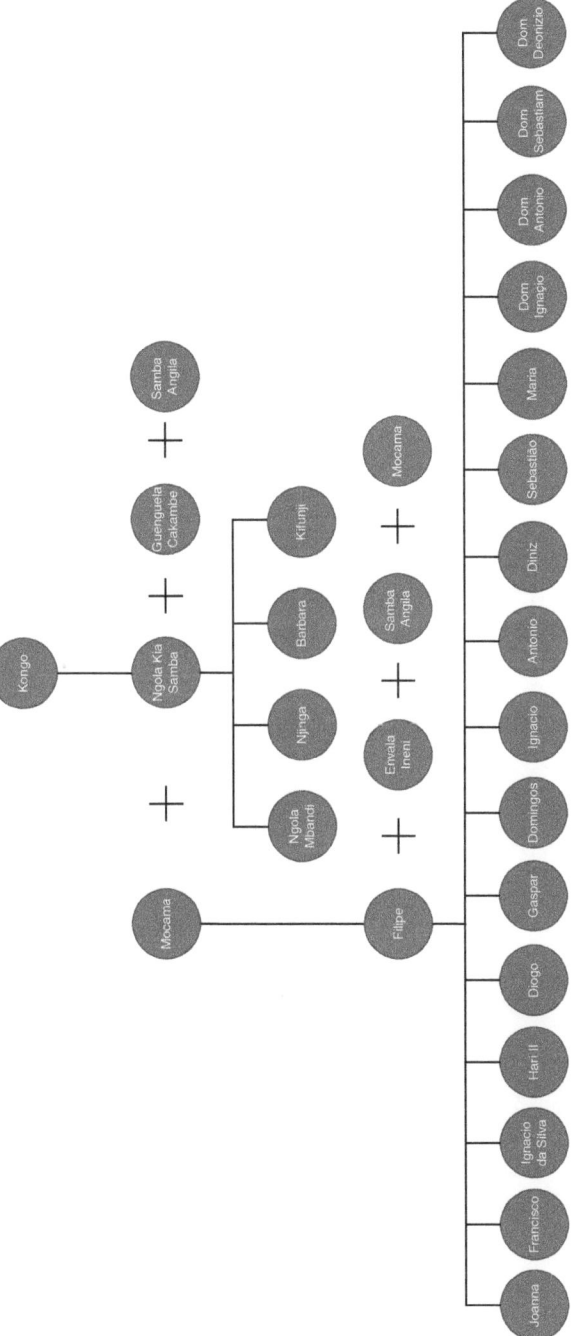

FIGURE 2 Lourenço da Silva Mendonça's family tree, part 1. By the author, based on manuscripts.

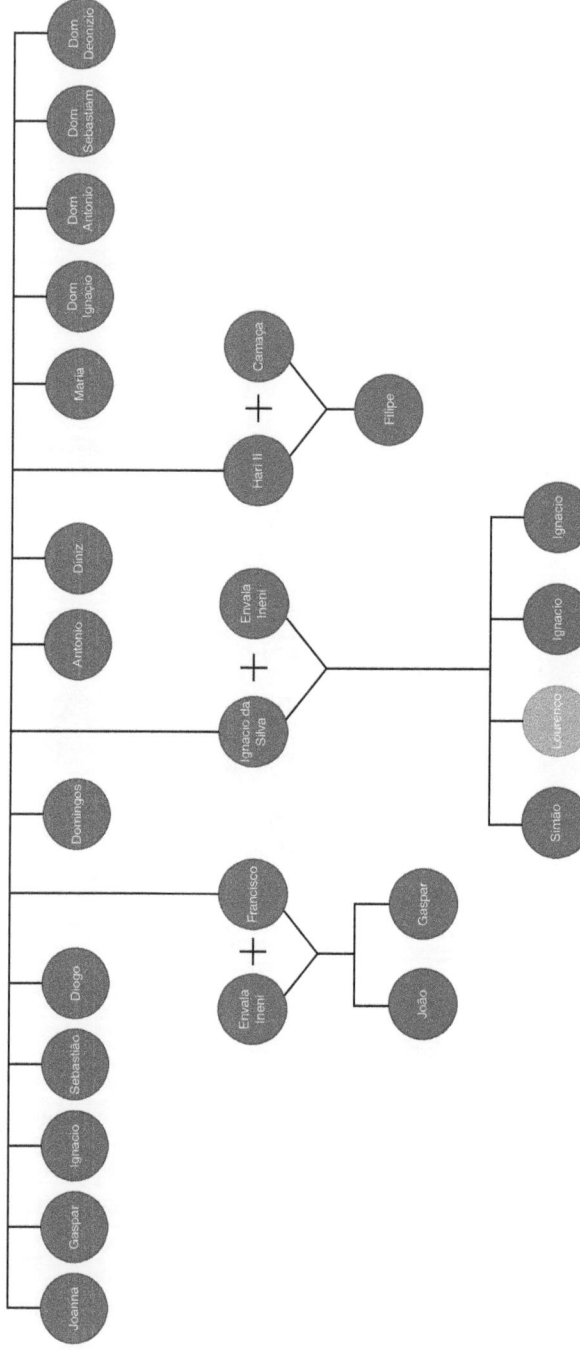

FIGURE 3 Lourenço da Silva Mendonça's family tree, part 2. By the author, based on manuscripts.

In my view, and in accordance with the documentary sources used in this book, it was unquestionably Ignacio da Silva's son Lourenço who went to Rome to present the case for abolition there on 6 March 1684; he took his father's surname to become Lourenço da Silva e Mendonça, or, in some documents, Lourenço da Silva de Mendonça.[68] It is possible that Lourenço may have been given the surname Mendonça by the governor of Bahia, Afonso Furtado de Castro do Rio de Mendonça, with whom the Angolan royals stayed for sixteenth months of their stay in Salvador.[69] The uncertainty about Lourenço's surname stems from the fact that only his first name appears in the original documents in the Portuguese archives.[70] In fact, only the first names of his brothers, uncles, aunts and cousins were recorded.[71] There is a second possibility in that he could have used the surname Mendonça at home, in Ndongo, as this was not unusual. Mendonça's uncle, a Portuguese captain, António Teixeira de Mendonça, who had lived with his aunt (Philipe Hari I's daughter) for more than 10 years, also had the same surname.[72] It would not be far-fetched to suggest that Mendonça was so named in his honour.[73] He may have also received the surname Mendonça, if António Teixeira de Mendonça was his godfather, at his baptism. Such was the case with Mendonça's grandfather, Ngola Aiidi, who was given the name Dom Philipe de Sousa when he was baptised in Luanda on 29 June 1627 in

---

[68] The doubts surrounding the identification of Lourenço da Silva Mendonça stem from his court case presentation in the Vatican, in which he stated that he descended from 'Kings of Kongo and Angola' without further explanation. Gray has assumed that he came from the Kongo. However, the archival evidence I have recently found in the Arquivo Histórico Ulramarino de Bélem, Portugal, shows that he came from Pungo-Andongo and not from the Kongo. His line of descent, however, goes back to the Kongo, as he claimed in the Vatican. In the Portuguese original letter from Madrid, his name appears as Lourenço da Silva Mendonça, without the preposition 'de'. See Gaspar da Costa de Mesquita, Archives of Propaganda Fide, Rome, Scritture Riferite nei Congressi, Series Africa, Angola, Congo, SC Africa, fl. 486, Lisbon, 15 February 1681. Mesquita was an apostolic notary in Lisbon and a New Christian.

[69] See 'Carta de António da Costa de Sousa a Manuel Barreto de S. Paio'; and 'Sobre os Principes Negros do Dongo Unidos no Navio Sao Verissimo' [Concerning the Black Princes from Dongo United on the Saint Verissimo Ship Fleet Captain], cód. 97, A.H.U, cód. 17, fls. 129–130, 1670–1686, Lisbon, 9 November 1673.

[70] See 'Carta de António da Costa de Sousa a Manuel Barreto de S. Paio'.

[71] See 'Carta de António da Costa de Sousa a Manuel Barreto de S. Paio'.

[72] António Teixeira de Mendonça was made captain major by Salvador Correia de Sá e Benevides on 8 April 1649. He was one of the heroes of the war in Angola, and served in many posts from 1623 onwards.

[73] Antonio de Teixeira Mendonça was his brother-in-law, see 'Carta de Salvador Correia de Sá'.

honour of Dom Philipe III of Portugal and Philipe II of Spain, and Sousa in honour of his godfather, Fernão de Sousa, the governor of Angola.[74]

As mentioned, towards the end of 1671, after the war of Pungo-Andongo,[75] Mendonça, his brothers, uncles, aunts and cousins were sent to Salvador, Bahia, by the governor of Luanda, Francisco de Távora 'Cajanda' (1669–1676); they lived there for eighteen months.[76] In 1673, Mendonça was then taken to Rio de Janeiro, where he lived for, possibly, six months.[77] After spending two years in Brazil, he was sent to Portugal in August 1673. In Portugal, he stayed at the Convent of Vilar de Frades, Braga, by order of the Portuguese Crown. His three brothers were sent to Braga, too, but to different monasteries: Basto, Moreira and Selzedas.[78] Mendonça probably studied law and theology in Braga for three or four years, from 1673 to 1676 or 1677, before returning to Lisbon, where he stayed for perhaps four years from 1677 to 1681.[79] The exact details of Mendonça's life over the next five years are unclear, though a few details are discernible from a recommendation letter that he carried with him from the apostolic notary in Lisbon, Gaspar da Costa de Mesquita. In 1682 he departed for Madrid.

It is intriguing that the family name Mendonça [Mendoza], according to Lope de Barrientos, was a Jewish surname.[80] The aristocratic Mendoza family 'originated from the town of Mendoza in the province of Álava in the Basque countries' in Spain. The Mendoza family in Spain wielded considerable power and influence when Álava joined the kingdom of Castile

---

[74] See Cadornega, *História Geral*, vol. III, p. 447. If this was the case, when Mendonça arrived in Brazil, he might have been twenty-two or twenty-three years of age. António Teixeira de Mendonça might have died at the end of Sá's governance in 1651 or during the governance of Rodrigo de Miranda Henriques (1652–1653); see Cadornega, *História Geral*, vol. II, pp. 577–578.

[75] For the war of Pungo-Andongo, see Relaçam/ Do FELICE SVCCESSO.

[76] Távora was questioned by the Overseas Council on his return to Portugal, see 'Consulta do Conselho Ultramarino Sobre os familiars do Rei do Dongo' [Overseas Council Minute on the Family of the King of Dongo], AHU, cód. 17, Consultas Mixtas, vol. 13, fl. 301, 18 July 1679; see also MMA, vol. 13, pp. 507–508 (Palmares is being mentioned, rather than Mocambo, p. 507). His surname Távora is used here in conjunction with his second and African surname 'Cajanda', which was given to him by the Mbundu people of Luanda, meaning 'someone who walks with the centre of gravity in the body'.

[77] He was sent to Rio de Janeiro in 1673, but the exact date is uncertain. Afonso Furtado de Castro de Mendonça's letter of 18 August 1673 does not specify the time of his journey.

[78] See 'Carta de António da Costa de Sousa a Manuel Barreto de S. Paio'.

[79] See 'Sobre os Principes Negros do Dongo Unidos no Navio São Verissimo'; and Monzon, S.C. Africa, vol. I, fl. 486.

[80] See the Geni Genealogy family tree: https://www.geni.com/projects/Mendoza-Ancestors-Research/243 (obtained on 12 September 2018). I am indebted to Professor Madge Dresser for providing me the link.

during the reign of Alfonso XI (1312–1350). The surname's history might not have any direct bearing on Mendonça's own name, nor on his alliance with Jewish descendants, the New Christians, in Portugal. Nonetheless, it is significant for my argument in this book as far as Mendonça's dialogue with and the support he gained from Gaspar da Costa de Mesquita, the apostolic notary in Lisbon, in the 1680s is concerned. The Mendonça name is suggestive, as there might be a link to the New Christians in Angola. There is, indeed, evidence that New Christians in the Kongo, Angola and Cacheu [in modern Guinea-Bissau] were marrying into the ruling class and forming alliances in order to gain political influence and protection in the sixteenth and seventeenth centuries.[81] Some of the New Christians helped the African kings with intelligence information on Luso-Hispanic operations in Africa. The Crown in Madrid was very unhappy with this situation and accused the Vatican of turning a blind eye to what was happening. This may sound trivial to Mendonça's family and personal history, but it is important to his case as it demonstrates the existence of a ready-forged network between the New Christians and the élite classes in West Central Africa, to whom Mendonça belonged.[82] A royal letter from Madrid, dated 28 August 1618, stated that:

> The complaints from the King of Kongo are fostered by some restless people from the Hebrew Nation[83] who, out of fear of the Inquisition Tribunal, left Portugal and now live in that part of the world. For that, they see themselves as having a place with the King. They helped him with writing letters and provided him with intelligences together with others from the same Hebrew Nation that reside in this Curia.[84]

The conviviality that existed between the New Christians and the Africans in West Central Africa and in West Africa moved beyond inter-group

---

[81] 'Carta Régia ao Cardeal de Borja' [Royal Letter to the Cardinal Borja], Archive of Spain Embassy in the Vatican Maço, 56, fl. 471, 28 August 1618; see also MMA, pp. 323–325. For a discussion of the New Christians' marriages with Africans in the seventeenth century, see Lingna Nafafé, *Colonial Encounters*.

[82] For further discussion about Jews and Africans living together in Africa, see Tudor Parfitt, *Black Jews in Africa and the Americas*, Cambridge, MA: Harvard University Press, 2013; Toby Green, 'Masters of Difference: Creolization and the Jewish Presence in Cabo Verde, 1497–1672', unpublished Ph.D. thesis, University of Birmingham, 2006; Green, *The Rise of the Trans-Atlantic Slave Trade* and Lingna Nafafé, *Colonial Encounters*.

[83] 'Hebrew Nation' here refers to Jews converted to Christianity; they are also called the New Christians.

[84] 'Carta Régia ao Cardeal de Borja', pp. 323–325, 'as queixas d'ElRey de Congo, saõ fomentadas de alguãs pessoas da naçaõ hebrea inquietas, que com temor do castigo do S.t° Officio, se ausentarão de Portugal, e uiuem naquellas partes, as quaes por estes me[i]os trattaõ de ter lugar com o Rey, e se ajudão da correspondência, e inteligencias de outros da mesma nasçaõ que residem nessa Curia'.

solidarity to infiltrate the highest-level institutions such as the Curia Vaticana. It would not be far-fetched to assume that Mendonça tapped into this existing network.

The letter of recommendation that Mendonça carried with him from Lisbon to the Vatican, dated 15 February 1681, raises questions over Mendonça's racial heritage. In the letter, Mendonça was described as a *homen pardo*. This translates in Italian as *morrate*, which in Spanish could have been translated as *moreno* – that is, a dual-heritage person;[85] Richard Gray translates it as 'mulatto'.[86] However, according to Hebe Mattos, the term *'pardo'* in the seventeenth century could mean both 'Black' and 'mulatto'.[87] In seventeenth-century Spanish America, the term *pardo* could mean someone who is born free,[88] and I favour this latter meaning, 'born free', when referring to Mendonça's identity. Mixed marriages in seventeenth-century Angola were not unusual, and King Philipe Hari I could well have married dual-heritage or Portuguese women. The Portuguese Crown decreed in the sixteenth century that any allied African king's daughter should marry within the Portuguese royal family, or, if there were no royal heir, marry into the Portuguese nobility. In the sixteenth century, the king of Caio (in modern Guinea-Bissau) travelled to Cape Verde with his nobility, and declared that his daughter, who was of marriageable age, was expected to marry Portuguese nobility. When he arrived in Cape Verde, he sent a message to the Portuguese Crown that a marriage to his daughter should be contracted.[89] Among the Peniche group (the brothers of Mendonça who were not sent to Brazil with him, but who instead were despatched directly to Portugal and on to Peniche town) was 'Francisco the Black', which

---

[85] See Mesquita, S.C. Africa vol. I, fl. 486.   [86] Gray, 'The Papacy', p. 53.
[87] See Hebe Mattos, '"Pretos" and "Pardos" between the Cross and the Sword: Racial Categories in Seventeenth Century Brazil', *European Review of Latin American and Caribbean Studies*, 80, 2006, pp. 43–55. Even in the sixteenth century, *pardo* means both 'Black' and 'Mulatto'. See ATT – Legitimações de D. Sebastião, liv. 26, fl. 136v., 11 September 1566; see also ATT – CC-II- 2 40-22, 25 April 1545.
[88] See Kathryn Joy McKnight and Leo J. Carofalo (eds.), *Afro-Latino Voices: Narratives from the Early Modern Ibero-Atlantic World, 1550–1812*, Indianapolis, IN/Cambridge: Hackett Publishing Company, Inc., 2009, p. 334; 'Moreno in colonial Spanish America, a person of African descent, possibly enslaved, but usually signifying a person who has freed herself or himself', p. 334; 'pardo/a, brown, mulatto; can also refer to a zambo. In mid-colonial Spanish America, a person of colour born or raised as a free person', p. 335.
[89] See 'Mensagem de Rei Caio para El'Rei' [Message of the King of Caio to El'Rei], Arquivo Vaticano (AV), Fondo Confalonieri, vol. 15, fls. 297–298v, 'treslaclo da carta que mandarão ao Bispo de Cabo Verde, estante em Lisboa', 10 June 1596. See also MMA, pp. 390–394.

indicates that Mendonça and his relatives may have been of dual heritage. Francisco was the servant ('free' servant or subordinated rank and not a chattel enslaved person)[90] of Ignacio, the illegitimate son of King Philipe Hari I.[91] The Portuguese decree could be viewed as contradicting the purity of blood doctrine that was sacrosanct at the time. However, more research is needed in order to come to a definitive conclusion here.

Ultimately, there may have been many Lourenço da Silva Mendonças in Angola, Kongo or Brazil. However, according to our documentary sources, few would have been princes and had a bloodline going back to the kings of Kongo and Angola, as Mendonça's did. Situating Mendonça in his political landscape in West Central Africa is pivotal to our understanding of his court case, since only in this way can we rethink the historiography of Atlantic slavery with regard to so-called African slavery.

0.2 STUDIES AND SOURCES FOR MENDONÇA'S WORK AND HISTORICAL CONTEXT

Richard Gray was the first historian to bring Mendonça's work in the Vatican into the public domain. In his pioneering article, 'The Papacy and the Atlantic Slave Trade: Lourenço da Silva, the Capuchins and the Decisions of the Holy Office', Gray argues that Mendonça's presentation in the Vatican was a petition in which he appealed to the Holy Office to deal with the suffering of enslaved Africans in the Atlantic.[92] In Gray's

---

[90] For further discussion of the meaning of the term, see B. J. Sokol, *Shakespeare and Tolerance*, Cambridge: Cambridge University Press, 2008, pp. 144–160. On how northern Europeans classify their southern European neighbours in terms of intellectual ability, see Giovanni Botero, *Relations, of the Most Famous Kingdoms and Commonweals, Through the World Discoursing of Their Situations, Religions, Languages, Manners, Customes, Strengths, Greatnesse, and Policies*, London: Printed by Iohn Hauiland, and are to be sold by Iohn Patridge at the signe of the Sunne in Pauls Church-yard, 1630.

[91] See 'Carta de António da Costa de Sousa a Manuel Barreto de S. Paio', 'negro Francisco se lhe dê hum vestido de parrilha' (Francisco the Black be given saragoça gown).

[92] Gray uses the term 'petition' in Mendonça's case to identify it as a request to seek a solution to alleviate the plight of the enslaved Africans; he takes no account of the legal argument embedded in the case. This is where I differ from him. According to Roman law there were different types of petition: 'private petitions to the Roman emperor' and 'subscriptions of legal sources'. The first were issued to make a case for clarifying the law on behalf of private individual petitioners who had questions about it. Generally, the 'petitioners had no interest in legal matters at all; they wanted honours, jobs, and financial concessions'. The 'subscriptions of legal sources' on the other hand 'contained formulations of principle ... they were a response not to intellectual difficulties, but to practical ones. Petitioners went to the imperial government to get action, not advice.' Normally, they were written by legal professionals or lawyers. The presentation Mendonça delivered

view, Mendonça did not argue for the universal condemnation of slavery, but rather for the liberation of enslaved African Christians and their offspring. Gray's findings centred on the Vatican archives and did not include data on Mendonça from Spain, Portugal and Brazil. He was well aware of this limitation and, in fact, kindly recommended that I carry out research in those countries' archives.[93]

In an attempt to widen the scope of Gray's research into the Black Atlantic, a Brazilian historian, Hebe Mattos, has published a comparative study on Mendonça and Dias entitled '"Pretos" and "Pardos" between the Cross and the Sword: Racial Categories in Seventeenth Century Brazil'.[94] Her main interest is to look at categories of *pretos* (Blacks) and *pardos* (mulattos or free people), and their emergence in Brazil. She argues that 'the two cases presented here appear to suggest a more central role for the early demographic impact of access to manumission in colonial society and the possibilities for social mobility among the free peoples of African descent'.[95] Mattos employs these categories to unpick the roles played by both Henrique Dias, governor of Crioulos and commander of the *Terço da Gente Preta*,[96] in Brazil in the mid-seventeenth century, and

---

contained a statement of principles. For this reason, it cannot have been a petition in the first sense: it was not simply a request to end the suffering of the enslaved Africans in the Atlantic, but was a legal claim, supported by legal argument. I am indebted here to William Turpin, 'Imperial Subscriptions and the Administration of Justice', *Journal of Roman Studies*, 81, 1991, pp. 101–118. Mendonça's court case was inclusive of five principles of law: human, natural, divine, civil and canon law. For a detailed study of petitions see J. L. White, *The Form and Structure of the Official Petition: A Study in Greek Epistolography*, Missoula, MT: Society for Biblical Literature, 1972; J. E. G. Whitehorne, 'Petitions to the Centurion: A Question of Locality?' *Bulletin of the American Society of Papyrologists* 41, 2004, pp. 155–170. See also John Finlay, 'The Petition in the Court of Session in Early Modern Scotland', *Parliaments, Estates & Representation*, 38(3), 2018, pp. 337–349.

[93] I met Gray at a conference on *Lusophonia* organised by Professor Newitt at King's College London in 2002. We had a long fruitful conversation about Mendonça's work. His recommendation to me at the time was that I needed to look for data on Mendonça in Portugal and Brazil, which he could not do, because he did not speak Portuguese at the time. He was adamant that there was data on Mendonça in those archives. However, little did he know that Mendonça came from modern Angola. After working on the archives in Brazil, Portugal, Spain and the Vatican, I returned to London in 2016, eager to share my findings with Professor Gray, only to be told by Professor Newitt that he had sadly passed away.

[94] Mattos, '"Pretos" and "Pardos"', pp. 43–55.

[95] Mattos, '"Pretos" and "Pardos"', p. 44.

[96] *Terço da Gente Preta* was 'a regiment of enslaved and freed enslaved people that played a decisive role in the battles against the Dutch' – see Mattos, '"Pretos" and "Pardos"', p. 45.

Lourenço da Silva Mendonça, a procurator general from the confraternities of Black Brotherhood. However, Mattos does not include Mendonça's network in Brazil in her study, nor explore his connection with Indigenous Brazilians. Most importantly, Mendonça's Vatican court case does not feature at all in her work. She acknowledges Gray's research but does not detect that Mendonça's intervention is a court case nor that his abolition message was for all Africans, across the Atlantic region – and not only in Brazil but in the entire Aermican continent; nor does she recognise his interconnection with Black confraternities in Portuguese America, Brazil and Spain. This was not through lack of interest, but simply because of a lack of data to support a more in-depth analysis of the debate about the abolition of slavery in the Atlantic in the seventeenth century. Gray and Mattos are the only two contemporary scholars to have focused on Mendonça.

When it comes to historical sources, in 1682 the Jesuit missionaries Francisco José de Jaca and Epifanio de Moirans, who knew and supported Mendonça's court case, completed their work *Servi Liberi Seu Naturalis Mancipiorum Libertatis Iusta Defensio* (Freed Slaves or the Just Defence of the Natural Freedom of the Emancipated).[97] Both also offered a critique of the capture of Africans in Africa who were then taken to the Americas as enslaved people. While renowned Spanish Jesuit Bartolomé De las Casas (1484–1566)[98] defended the Indigenous Americans against slavery, the lesser-known Jaca and Moirans also spoke out against the enslavement of Africans using the legal arguments of the time. Their work, however, did not come to the fore in the debate on the Atlantic slave trade until the beginning of the 1980s, when their defence was translated from Latin to Spanish by José Tomas López García as *Dos Defensores de los Esclavos Negros en el Siglo XVII* (Two Defenders of the Black Slaves in the Seventeenth Century). Neither Jaca nor Moirans went to Africa as missionaries, but they both worked as Jesuit priests in Venezuela and Cuba, where they met. Their defence is a major work on the injustice of African

---

[97] See Francisco José de Jaca and Epifanio de Moirans, Order of Friars Minor Capuchin (Ordo Fratrum Minorum Capuccinorum) [OFM Cap.], *Servi Liberi Seu Naturalis Mancipiorum Libertatis Iusta Defensio* (Freed Slaves or the Just Defence of the Natural Freedom of the Emancipated), Archivo General de Indias, Sevilla, Audiencia de Santo Domingo, Legajo 527, 1682, in José Tomas López García, *Dos Defensores de los Esclavos Negros en el Siglo XVII*, Maracaibo, Caracas: Biblioteca Corpozulia, 1982.

[98] See Bartolomé de Las Casas, *Brevisima Relacion de la Destruccion de Africa* (1556) (estudo preliminar, edição e notas de Isacio Perez Fernandez), Salamanca, San Estéban, 1989.

enslavement in the Americas, and on the abolition of slavery in the Atlantic, yet it is almost unknown. They analysed in great depth the same legal terms that were used by Mendonça in the Vatican, such as 'natural', 'human', 'divine', 'civil' and 'canon law (jus canonico)', challenging why Atlantic slavery was being practised against these laws.[99] They argued that the Atlantic slave trade was illegal, stating that 'when we begin with natural law, all men are born free'.[100] They contended that the responsibility for those enslaved Africans in the Americas lay with the pope, because 'the lords of blind slaves with their ambition to impress the Governor (the governors in the Indies are subject to the Catholic King and the kings are subject to the Pope)'.[101] This chain of responsibility made it necessary for the pope to punish the guilty parties committing such crimes, particularly the Portuguese governing authorities in Africa, Brazil and the Americas. And this obligation also implicated the pope in a crime against humanity: the Atlantic slave trade. Indeed, Jaca and Moirans stood in the witness box in the Vatican to testify on behalf of Mendonça's court case, arguing that each 'person is free by natural law'.[102]

In their thesis, Jaca and Moirans also asked uncomfortable questions as to why Christians bought enslaved Africans, who were captured using force, fraud, intimidation, kidnapping and theft. They argued that the transaction carried out and the value of the things exchanged for human beings were worthless in comparison to the human beings bought. For them, such exchanges should never have taken place. They asked:

Would Christians like this to be done on their lands and in their regions? Would they like to be made slaves and be bought? Would they like to be captured with violence and fraud and tied up and transported? How can they commit such lawless things and how could they harden their hearts to the evil, the force of sins against *natural, positive,* and *divine* laws?[103]

They used their knowledge of the Americas and their experience with enslaved Africans to strongly support Mendonça in the Vatican.

---

[99] See SOCG vol. 490, fls., 140r-v 'usano contra ogni legge Divina, et Hummana ... legge naturale' ['they practised slavery against every Divine and Human law ... Natural law'], see also folio 62 'jus canonico'.

[100] See Cap. Iur. Civ. Dig., 50, 17, 32, fl. 36, p. 12, 'iure enim naturali áb initio omnes homines liben nascebantur', Jaca and Moirans, OFM Cap., *Servi Liberi*, p. 200.

[101] Jaca and Moirans OFM Cap., *Servi Liberi*, p. 181, 'los señores de los esclavos ciegos de ambición impresionaron al Gobernador (los gobernadores en las Indias están sujetos al Rey católico y los reyes están sujetos al Papa)'.

[102] See Jaca and Moirans, OFM Cap., *Servi Liberi*.

[103] See Jaca and Moirans, OFM Cap., *Servi Liberi*, p. 209.

Furthermore, they openly criticised the Atlantic slave trade and demanded that the enslaved Africans' owners pay back what they owed the enslaved for their work and release them from bondage.[104] For them, as for Mendonça, *natural, human, divine* and *civil* laws were universal, and had been broken by the enslavement of Africans.

Dating from the same time, the three-volume history of the Angolan wars completed by Antonio de Oliveira Cadornega in 1681 is fundamental to understanding the socio-political and cultural circumstances surrounding Mendonça's court case, the context of the Portuguese conquest and the wars waged on the Ndongo kingdom.[105] Cardonega came to Angola with Governor Pedro Cesar de Menezes in 1639, serving in the military. He initially became a captain, but then followed a civil and subsequently political career, becoming ordinary judge in 1660 and municipal councillor of the City Council in Luanda in 1671. Not only does he give details on the wars, but he also offers ethnographic and geographic insights into the period.

Two and a half centuries later, in 1944, Father António Brásio, a Portuguese priest, missionary and historian, compiled his vast collection *Monumenta Missionaria Africana*, an account of the activities of Portuguese missionaries in Africa. The text covers the period from the arrival of the Portuguese in Africa in 1446 to 1700. While he included documents on Mendonça, he did not know of his role and does not mention Mendonça's work in the Vatican at all. He also wrote a book, entitled *Os Pretos em Portugal* (Blacks in Portugal), about the freedom of enslaved Africans in Portugal.[106] He examined historical documents on the existence of Black Brotherhoods in Lisbon and described how some members had gained their freedom within the law using the rights conferred on them in the sixteenth and seventeenth centuries. However, this work does not extend much beyond Portugal, since the only mention of another Black Brotherhood in the Atlantic sphere is the confraternity of Massangano in Angola.[107] Brásio uses his work on Black Brotherhoods in Portugal to argue that the treatment of enslaved people in Portugal was not as brutal as many people might have been led to believe. Writing in the twentieth century, he used the freedom of the enslaved Africans in sixteenth-century Portugal to deny that Portuguese society was racist, using it

---

[104] See Jaca and Moirans, OFM Cap., *Servi Liberi*.
[105] Cardonega, *História Geral*, I, II and III.
[106] António Brásio, *Os Pretos em Portugal*, Lisbon: Agência Geral das Colônia, 1944.
[107] See António Brásio, 'As Misericórdias de Angola', *Studia* 4, 1959, pp. 106–149.

as a defence against charges levelled at Portugal in the eighteenth and nineteenth centuries and at colonialism in general.[108] For Brásio, enslaved Africans in Portugal were treated humanely. He argues that the country had no equal in its civilising mission and race relations in any part of the world, and was – for that reason – superior to the United States of America.[109]

French historian Didier Lahon, who has continued the work begun by Brásio on Black Brotherhoods[110] in Portugal, is more aware of Mendonça but argues that his achievement with these confraternities was limited because of the social and political constraints of the time.[111] Brásio and Lahon stand for one of two key arguments used to sanitise slavery and colonialism: firstly, that they were part of a greater civilizing mission and secondly, that slavery was already in existence and widely practised by Africans in Africa. For Lahon, the presence of African confraternities in Portugal somehow diluted and contradicted Portugal's ideology as an enslaving society. However, the author does not recognise the African agency and fight for freedom through the Black Brotherhoods because he does not conceive of them as possible in this historical moment.

Like Lahon, Brazilian scholar Lucilene Reginaldo, who works on Brazilian and Angolan Black Brotherhoods and the circulation of Black men in the Atlantic world,[112] does not engage with Mendonça's work. However, her work is important in understanding confraternities of Black

---

[108] For more detailed discussion, see George J. Fonseca, 'A Historiografia Sobre os Escravos em Portugal', *Cultura*, 33, 2014, pp. 1–22.

[109] Gilberto Freyre's work could be in this light. See Jeffrey D. Needell, 'Identity, Race, Gender, and Modernity in the Origins of Gilberto Freyre's Oeuvre', *The American Historical Review*, 100(1), 1995, pp. 51–77.

[110] I will use the term Black Brotherhood and confraternity of Black Men (*homens pretos* in the original) interchangeably throughout the book. Confraternities were guilds within churches. They began as organizations for white members but were extended to include African Christian members of the Church. Later on, churches were built that had emerged from Black Brotherhoods and carried the title in the Church's name.

[111] See Didier Lahon, 'Da Redução da Alteridade à Consagração da Diferença: as Irmandades Negras em Portugal (Séculos XVI–XVIII)', *Projecto História*, São Paulo, 44, 2012, pp. 53–83.

[112] See Lucilene Reginaldo, 'André do Couto Godinho: Homem preto, formado em Coimbra, missionário no Congo em fins do século XVIII', *Revista História*, 173, 2015, pp. 141–174; and Lucilene Reginaldo '"Não tem Informação": Mulatos, Pardos e Pretos na Universidade de Coimbra (1700–1771)', *Estudos Ibero-Americanos*, 44/3, 2018, pp. 421–434. Reginaldo in her work on André do Couto Godinho shows the struggle of the African élites resistant to the Portuguese discriminatory educational process in the eighteenth century. However, Godinho's work was a struggle for personal freedom, whilst Mendonça's case demonstrated an effort to gain freedom for many.

Brotherhood in Brazil, particularly in Salvador, Bahia, where Mendonça received great support for his court case in the Vatican.[113] For Reginaldo, Black confraternities in Bahia were Africanised through practices they brought from Kongo and Angola.[114] They preserved their tradition with the memory of the king of Kongo. According to Reginaldo 'the King of Kongo represented the triumph of continued strategies to preserve links with Africa'.[115] She argues that the Angolans were the first to form brotherhoods in Bahia. They used them as a space in which to overcome their daily challenges and as a legal support for themselves.[116] For Reginaldo, confraternities were 'channel[s] of expression and integration of the Black people in the colonial period'.[117] She pointed out that Angolans made up the great majority of Bahian confraternity members and dominated the groups' leadership.

With regard to the question of slavery in Africa, in the nineteenth century Pedro de Carvalho, Portuguese secretary to the governor in Angola between 1862 and 1863, stated in his book *Das Origens da Escravidão Moderna em Portugal* (Origins of Modern Slavery in Portugal), that 'Africa is a land of slavery by definition. Black is a slave by birth.'[118] Contrary to the lone voice of Portuguese priest Father Oliveira, who in *Elementos Para a História do Município de Lisboa*[119] criticised Portugal as an enslaving society by seeing it as the only country responsible for Atlantic slavery, Carvalho argued that 'we [the Portuguese] did not invent Negroes' slavery; we have found it there, which was the foundation of those imperfect societies'.[120] Other Portuguese historians have also defended Portugal's involvement in the Atlantic slave trade by echoing sentiments expressed by both Carvalho and Brásio.[121] Among them is the nineteenth-century writer and patriarch

---

[113] See Lucilene Reginaldo, *Os Rosários dos Angolas – Irmandades de Africanos e Crioulos na Bahia Setecentista*, São Paulo: Alameda, 2011.
[114] Reginaldo, *Os Rosários dos Angolas*, p. 69.
[115] Reginaldo, *Os Rosários dos Angolas*, p. 226, 'o Rei do Congo representava o triunfo das estratégias contínuas para preservar as ligações com a África'.
[116] Reginaldo, *Os Rosários dos Angolas*, pp. 240–241.
[117] Reginaldo, *Os Rosários dos Angolas*, p. 345, 'canal de expressão e integração da população negra no período colonial'.
[118] António Pedro de Carvalho, *Das Origens da Escravidão Moderna em Portugal*, Lisbon: Tipografia Universal, 1877, p. 45, 'A África é por essência a terra da escravidão. O preto é escravo por Nascimento'.
[119] See Oliveira, *Elementos para a História do Município de Lisboa*.
[120] Carvalho, *Das Origens da Escravidão*, p. 45, 'não inventámos a escravidão dos Negros; encontrámo-la formando a base daquelas sociedades imperfeitas'.
[121] For full discussion of the Portuguese historiography, see Fonseca, 'A Historiografia Sobre os Escravos'.

of Lisbon, Father Francisco de S. Luís. In *Nota Sobre a Origem da Escravidão e Tráfico dos Negros* (Reflection on the Origin of the Slavery and the Traffic of Enslaved Black Africans) – an answer to French authors Christophe de Koch and Frédéric Schoell, who had accused Portugal of being responsible for the slave trade[122] – Luís contributed to the invention of the seductive and misleading narrative that Arabs and Africans were already trading in enslaved people in Africa before Portugal became involved in the Atlantic slave trade. This has become the dominant version of the history of slavery in the region and is intended above all to shift responsibility and guilt from Europeans to Africans.[123]

The historiography of West Central Africa initially focused on *ita*[124] – 'war' – as an enslavement method. Historians working with this focus have included John Thornton, David Birmingham, Beatrix Heintz, José C. Curto and Mariana P. Candido;[125] others such as James Walvin, Paul E. Lovejoy and Patrick Manning have focused on *ita* but for Africa as a whole rather than West Central Africa.[126] Away from the focus on 'war',[127] historians have paid particular attention to *xicacos* (tributes of vassalship) – or 'taxation'.[128] Both Beatrix Heintze and Mariana P. Candido have considered these two elements

---

[122] Christophe G. de Koch and Frédéric Schoell, *Histoire Abrégée des Traités de Paix entre les Puissances de l'Europe Depuis la paix de Westphalie*, vol. XI, Paris: Nabu Press, 1817–1818, p. 171.

[123] See Boxer (ed.), *South China in the Sixteenth Century*; see John Thornton, *Africa and Africans in the Making of the Atlantic World, 1400–1680*, New York: Cambridge University Press, 1992, and Boxer, *Portuguese Seaborne Empire*, p. 31.

[124] *Ita* or *kita* is a word for war and plural *kita* in Kimbundu language. See Cadornega, *História Geral*, I, p. 615.

[125] See Thornton, *Africa and Africans*, p. 99 and John Thornton, *The Kingdom of Kongo: Civil War and Transition, 1641–1718*, Madison, WI: University of Wisconsin Press, 1983; Birmingham, *Trade and Conquest*; Beatrix Heintze, 'Ngonga a Mwiza: um Sobado Angolano sob Domino Português no Século XVII', *Revista Internacional de Estudos Africanos*, 8–9, 1988, pp. 221–234; Heintze, *Angola nos Séculos XVI e XVII*; and Heintze, 'Angola nas Garras do Tráfico de Escravos'; José C. Curto, 'Experiences of Enslavement in West Central Africa', *Social History*, 41(82), 2008, pp. 381–415; Candido, 'Conquest, Occupation, Colonialism and Exclusion'; Candido, 'O Limite Tênue'.

[126] James Walvin, *Black Ivory: A History of British Slavery*, London: Harper Collins, 1992; Patrick Manning, *Slavery and African Life*, Cambridge: Cambridge University Press, 1990, pp. 60–148; Paul E. Lovejoy, *Transformations in Slavery: A History of Slavery in Africa*, Cambridge: Cambridge University Press, 2011, pp. 140–245.

[127] See also Ariane Carvalho, 'Guerras nos sertões de Angola: Sobas, Guerra Preta e Escravização (1749–1797)', unpublished PhD thesis, Universidade Federal do Rio de Janeiro, 2020.

[128] See Cadornega, *História Geral*, I, p. 621: *xicacos* are tributes of vassalship, vassalage. However, these are different from the Portuguese taxation system, which was obligatory. *Xicacos* were tributes in kind.

together and engaged with the significance of the fact that 'raiding' and 'taxation' were important as a source of income to cover the Portuguese administration's expenditure in seventeenth-century Angola. Subsequently, the focus on 'war', 'raiding' and 'taxation' has given way to an emphasis on 'debt'. Historians such as Joseph Miller, Jan Vansina, José Curto and Roquinaldo Ferreira[129] have used this as a focus in their analysis of the ways in which Africans were enslaved in West Central Africa in the eighteenth and nineteenth centuries. Alongside 'debt', historians have also examined 'judicial proceedings'[130] – the *tribunal de mucanos* (*mucanos* tribunal). A tribunal of *mucanos* means 'legal verbal proceedings in their disputes and demands' in the Angolan language Kimbundu.[131] *Mucanos* were local courts, indigenous to West Central Africa, used to deal with legal cases. The above-mentioned historians have used these local legal structures to argue that the enslavement of Angolans was part of the West Central Africans' culture, and that enslavement was used as a punishment for those found guilty of breaking the law. Ferreira argues that civil and criminal cases were used by *sobas* to enslave the guilty in the seventeenth and eighteenth centuries.[132] He challenges West Central African historiography that views enslaved Africans in the region as war captives and calls for its revision, deploying individual cases to reveal that enslavement was carried out through acts of kidnapping and betrayal. In a similar vein, Candido has demonstrated that in Benguela the Portuguese governing authorities were not only waging war as a method of capturing Angolans but also using debt and judicial practices to enslave them.[133] Similarly, Joseph Calder Miller in his work *Way of Death* has argued that the Portuguese used the judicial system to obtain enslaved Africans in the region by enforcing debt recovery as a method in the seventeenth and eighteenth centuries. For Miller, the enslavement of Angolans was carried out in regions far away from areas of Portuguese settlement.[134] Alongside historiography on *ita*, Curto has demonstrated the problem of social conflict that was

---

[129] See Roquinaldo Amaral Ferreira, *Cross-Cultural Exchange in the Atlantic World: Angola and Brazil During the Era of the Slave Trade*, Cambridge: Cambridge University Press, 2014; and Candido, *An African Slaving Port*. Judith Spicksley has argued that the Portuguese in Angola were somehow morally superior to the Angolans in their dealing in enslaved people. However, this interpretation is contradicted by Sousa's argument. See Judith Spicksley 'Contested Enslavement: The Portuguese in Angola and the Problem of Debt, c. 1600–1800', *Itinerario*, 39(2), 2015, pp. 247–275.
[130] See Ferreira, *Cross-Cultural Exchange*.   [131] Cadornega, *História Geral*, I, p. 618.
[132] See Ferreira, *Cross-Cultural Exchange*.
[133] See Candido, *African Slaving Port*, p. 195.
[134] Joseph Calder Miller, *Way of Death: Merchant Capitalism and the Angolan Slave Trade, 1730–1830*, Madison, WI: University of Wisconsin Press, 1997, p. 268.

created by the slave trade in which people were 'kidnapping' others in revenge for enslaving their family members, particularly the slave-traders in the region. This social conflict was actually driven by the need to pay debt.[135] Recently Daniel B. Domingues da Silva has endorsed the claim, made by both Candido and Ferreira, that the Portuguese-enslaved captives sent to Brazil from Angola came from the region controlled by the Portuguese, rather than from a distant territory, as Miller's work showed.[136]

Intriguingly, the idea of the legal system being used to capture and enslave Angolans, which has dominated the recent historiography of West Central Africa, is not new. It stemmed from the earlier seventeenth century, with the introduction of *baculamento* as a form of payment of taxes in enslaved people. Raiding in the region controlled by the Portuguese is not new, either. An example of this is Correia de Sousa capturing Kazanze and Bumbi people. No historian has identified the true importance of the introduction of *baculamento*, which became the basis of the ensuing system of enslavement in the eighteenth and nineteenth centuries. Mendonça's argument in the Vatican in 1684 pieced together these themes, which later became the subject of debate in the eighteenth and nineteenth centuries in the historiography of West Central Africa. These were already subjects discussed among the confraternities of Black people in Brazil, Portugal and Spain in the seventeenth century.[137] None of the historiography mentioned above made this connection.

Just as the historiography of West Central Africa has focused mainly on the eighteenth and nineteenth centuries, so the debate on the abolition of slavery in the region has concentrated on the same period – as if abolition were not a theme of the seventeenth century. What is more, the abolition of Atlantic slavery is understood to have been an almost exclusively European endeavour, in which the fundamental part played by Africans remains in the background. Within Western scholarship, the Africans' contributions to the debate on the abolition of the Atlantic slavery in particular and to world history in general have been, and continue to be, neglected. This led Michael Gomez, in his recent work *African Dominion: A New History of Empire in Early and Medieval*

---

[135] See Curto, 'Experiences of Enslavement'. See also José C. Curto, 'The Legal Portuguese Slave Trade from Benguela, Angola, 1730–1828: A Quantative Re-appraisal', *África*, 17 (1), 1993/1994, pp. 101–116.

[136] See Daniel B. Domingues da Silva, *The Atlantic Slave Trade from West Central Africa, 1780–1867*, New York: Cambridge University Press, 2017.

[137] See APF, SOCG, fls. 54 and 58; see SOCG vol. 490, fls., 140r-v.; and SOGC, vol. 495a, fl. 54.

West Africa,[138] to question why so little attention has been paid to their role in shaping history. He states that even when historians have worked in fields in which the impact of Africans was obvious, their contribution has been brushed aside: 'world history as well as the imperial annals require substantial preparation and endeavour, often an impressive, invaluable feat of erudition. It is therefore all the more disappointing that Africa continues to receive such short shrift.'[139] Toby Green endorsed this view in his work *A Fistful of Shells*, stating that 'the modern world emerged from a mixed cultural framework in which many different peoples from West Africa and West Central Africa played a significant part. Yet, knowledge of these studies remains thinly spread.'[140]

The sense of guilt among the continents involved in the slave trade – Asia, Europe and Africa – has often eclipsed the debate to the extent that the evidence-backed argument that Africans made a valuable contribution to abolition tends to provoke the response that both Africans and Europeans were active and willing participants in the slave trade. It has become almost anathema to make the point that the Africans were under significant pressure from their European allies to deal in enslaved people. The seventeenth-century Angolan form of offering service to their fellow human beings, known as *mobuka* (which can be translated from Kimbundu as 'at your service')[141] was grossly misinterpreted by European settlers and missionaries alike as a form of slavery.[142] For Angolans, *mobuka* did not categorise a person as a 'slave' in the European understanding of the word, and Africans never had interpreted the labour they offered each other in that way. Those offering *mobuka* were nonetheless branded by the Europeans as 'enslaved people' and sold

---

[138] See Michael A. Gomez, *African Dominion: A New History of Empire in Early and Medieval West Africa*, Princeton, NJ: Princeton University Press, 2018.

[139] Gomez, *African Dominion*, p. 13 and Michael A. Gomez, 'African Identity and Slavery in the Americas', *Radical History Review*, 75, 1999, pp. 111–120.

[140] See Toby Green, *A Fistful of Shells, West Africa from the Rise of the Slave Trade to the Age of Revolution*, Milton Keynes: Penguin Random House UK, 2019, p. 8. See also Green, *The Rise of the Trans-Atlantic Slave Trade*; Toby Green, 'Beyond an Imperial Atlantic: Trajectories of Africans from Upper Guinea and West-Central Africa in the Early Atlantic World', *Past and Present*, 230(1), 2016, pp. 91–122. See also Joseph E. Inikori, 'Africa and the Globalization Process: Western Africa, 1450–1850', *Journal of Global History*, 2(1), 2007, pp. 63–86.

[141] Pedro Dias, *A Arte da Língua de Angola, Oferecida à Virgem Senhora N. do Rosário, Mãe e Senhora dos Mesmos Pretos*, Lisbon: Na officina de Miguel Deslandes, impressor de Sua Magestade, 1697.

[142] See Luis de Molina, *De Justitia et Jure, Opera Omnia*, Bousquet, 1733.

into the Americas. The correlation between *mobuka* and slavery only emerged in the context of Atlantic slavery, and was, in the words of Suzanne Miers and Igor Koptyogg, an 'unusual historical creation'.[143] Mendonça included criticism of this cross-cultural misrepresentation in his court case. What was meant exactly by the word 'slave' or 'slavery' and the practice of slavery in Europe and how these concepts were transferred to Africa and applied there contributed to significant misunderstanding. Accordingly, the complexities of African practice, and how both cultures approached the reality of service being offered and the general penal system in West Central Africa, have been misread.[144] As Gray remarks, 'indeed those African peoples who were by the late-seventeenth century exposed to the Atlantic slave trade accepted within their own various degrees of servitude. Yet seldom, if ever, was the slavery in African societies rigidly perpetuated over the generations.'[145]

The case studies of the people of Ndongo and Kazanze examined in this book engage with studies by Africanists, West Central African historians and authors who work on the African diaspora such as Birmingham, Linda M. Heywood, Heintze and Thornton, among others, but, above all with new historical sources that go beyond those from Cardonega and Brásio and that I encountered in many different archives.[146] These datasets show that Africans were coerced into slave-trading, particularly

---

[143] See Suzanne Miers and Igor Kopytoff, 'African "Slavery" as an Institution of Marginality', in Suzanne Miers and Igor Kopytoff (eds.) *Slavery in Africa: Historical and Anthropological Perspectives*, Madison, WI: University of Wisconsin Press, 1979, pp. 1–26.

[144] On the penal system in Angola, see Cadornega, *História Geral*, vol. II, pp. 350–353. Mocano or *mucano*, in Kimbundu language, means tribunal or legal disputes. A dispute was resolved in private as well as in a public *terreiro*. Witnesses or *banges* in Kimbundu were called upon to give their testimonies about particular cases. Disputes were heard by the respective attornies (*procuradores*) and envoys (*inviados*). Cases were heard too in the presence of *sobas*, councillors, *macotas* and envoys. After all parties concerned in a dispute had been heard, the judge decided who was guilty and who was not guilty. Then the guilty party would be asked to restitute the loss to the plaintiff. The guilty party was not sent into slavery but might undertake 'mobuka'. The dispute generally ended in peace 'composto em paz'. For detailed discussion of Angolan tribunals in eighteenth-century Begula (Angola), see Candido, *An African Slaving Port*, pp. 214–215, 234.

[145] Gray, 'The Papacy', p. 59.

[146] See Birmingham, *Trade and Conquest*; Candido, *An African Slaving Port*; Heywood, *Njinga of Angola*; Heintze, 'The Angolan Vassal Tributes of the 17th Century'; Heintze, 'Luso-African Feudalism in Angola?'; Heintze, 'Ngonga a Mwiza'; Heintze, *Angola nos Séculos XVI e XVII*; Beatrix Heintze, 'Written Sources and African History: A Plea for the Primary Source. The Angola Manuscript Collection of Fernão de Sousa', *History in Africa*, 9, 1982 (1982), pp. 77–103; Thornton, *Africa and Africans*.

through the introduction of *baculamento* in Angola by the Portuguese governor, Fernão de Sousa, in the seventeenth century. Certainly, some of the African ruling class in different areas of Africa who were conquered were also coerced into the slave trade, including Mendonça's grandfather, Philipe Hari I, and even his own father, Ignaçio da Silva. While their involvement could easily be generalised as normative, a product of its time, there exists no data to substantiate such a claim. The practice of *baculamento* could be seen as evidence for African collusion with slavery,[147] but in order to repudiate this interpretation I set out to examine original archival sources rather than rely on the same old secondary sources.

If we are to understand the different legal practices of coloniser and colonised in the Atlantic with reference to Mendonça's court case, Lauren Benton's discussion of the dialogical nature of this exchange in *Law and Colonial Cultures: Legal Regimes in World History* is very useful. She writes about the intersection of legal regimes from the Western and non-Western worlds in the process of colonial formation in Africa, Asia and the Americas, and argues that local social history played a fundamental role in shaping Western legal theory in the contact zones, where there were 'conscious efforts to retain elements of existing institutions and limit legal change as a way of sustaining social order'.[148] Western legal jurisprudence was transformed as it entered into dialogue with local legal systems that were already operating in these regions before the Europeans came there. What emerged from this encounter is what she terms 'global legal regimes'.[149] However, Benton pays less attention to the familiar legal and international law applied by both Africans and Europeans in disputes about ending the Atlantic slave trade. In the seventeenth century, the Supreme Court of Christendom in the Vatican was used to arbitrate on abuses of Africans and Indigenous Americans in the Americas.[150] My

---

[147] See Richard Reddie, *Abolition! The Struggle to Abolish Slavery in the British Colonies*, Oxford: Lion Books, 2007.
[148] Lauren Benton, *Law and Colonial Cultures: Legal Regimes in World History, 1400–1900*, Cambridge: Cambridge University Press, 2002, p. 3.
[149] Benton, *Law and Colonial Cultures*, p. 3.
[150] On Portuguese settlers 'raiding', 'hunting' and 'kidnapping' Indigenous Americans and turning them into enslaved people in Maranhão, Brazil, in the seventeenth century, see Walter Hawthorne, *From Africa to Brazil, Culture, Identity, and Atlantic Slave Trade 1600–1830*, Cambridge: Cambridge University Press, 2011, pp. 34–37. See also Sebastião da Rocha Pitta, *Provincia da Bahia, História da America Portugueza, Collecção de Obras Relativas á História da Capitania Depois a Sua Geographia Mandadas Reimprimir ou Publicar pelo Barão Homem de Mello, Do Conselho de Sua*

argument in this book is that Mendonça used the Supreme Court, bypassing local courts, such as the Angolan, Kongolese, Brazilian, Portuguese and Spanish courts. Instead, he went to the Vatican to present his legal case against Atlantic slavery.[151]

What is more, his criminal court case went beyond the denunciation of the enslavement of Africans. Proposing the concept of the 'Black Atlantic abolition movement' is an attempt not only to make sense of the philosophy underlying Mendonça's case in the regional setting from which it developed but also to align it with other compatible themes in the Atlantic world of the Americas and Europe. The alignment of Africans with other Africans that began in West Central Africa, in which Kongolese and Angolans allied with each other, helped them to unite with wider constituencies of those whose freedom was being denied in the Atlantic, such as the New Christians.[152] However, Mendonça's exile to Brazil and Europe provided him with the impetus to act and solidarity with those who were on the receiving end of global Atlantic injustice: enslaved Africans in the Americas, Indigenous Americans and New Christians. Applying the concept of a Black Atlantic abolition movement is to engage with the Atlantic as a political and legal space, and to engage with the nexus of dialogue and interactions between its different constituencies, which have not so far been included together in the Atlantic debate. This is a more nuanced understanding than seeing it, as Paul Gilroy does, as a space of cultural meaning and 'historical production'.[153] I use the idea of a Black Atlantic abolition movement to move away from the notion of the 'Black diaspora of the Atlantic', which is understood to only include

---

Magestade o Imperador, Presidente da Mesma Provincia, Bahia: Imprensa Econômica, 1878.

[151] See APF, SOCG, vol. 490, fl. 140r; SOCG, 490, fl. 141r-v; SOCG, vol. 490, fl. 54; SOCG, vol. 495a, fl. 58; SOCG; SOCG, 495a, fl. 62vol. 495a, folio (fl.) 392; SOCG, vol. 495a, fl. 393, and C. Africa, 1, fl., 486.

[152] There are forms of connection in the Atlantic between Africans and the Indigenous Americans. However, these connections are not between these three different constituencies: Africans, Indigenous Americans and the New Christians. For further discussion of Atlantic connections between Africans and the Indigenous Americans, see Schwartz, *Blacks and Indians*.

[153] Paul Gilroy, *The Black Atlantic*, London: Verso, 1993, p. 15. For Gilroy, 'cultural historians could take the Atlantic as one single, complex unit of analysis in their discussions of the modern world and use it to produce an explicitly transnational and intercultural perspective'. See also Priscilla Naro, Roger Sansi-Roca and David Treece (eds.), *Culture of the Lusophone Black Atlantic*, London: Palgrave Macmillan, 2007, p. 4. Gilroy sees the Black Atlantic as an inclusive space beyond the rigid configurations of essentialism of culture and absolute identity.

Black Americans, British and West Indians. The concept of the 'Black diaspora of the Atlantic' does not embrace other oppressed constituencies, such as Indigenous Americans and the New Christians who circulated in the Atlantic and in the metropolitan centres of Europe (Portugal, Spain and the Netherlands), along with white descendants of enslaved people in the Americas.[154]

Accordingly, I understand the Black Atlantic abolition movement as a project of solidarity and a common search for freedom. The relationship that was formed between whites, Africans, New Christians and Indigenous Americans emerged from a shared desire for and working towards liberty that was articulated in Mendonça's court case as a discourse to defend this position.[155] I use 'discourse' to refer to his speech in the Vatican as a form of utterance, but also in its Foucauldian sense,[156] to indicate how language and practice (institution) regulate ways of speaking that in turn define, construct and produce objects of knowledge, because knowing what counts as regulated truth involves relations of power and knowledge.[157] Mendonça presented his court case as utterance, but also as discourse in his attempt to refute the merchants and governing authorities in Brazil, Africa and the Iberian Peninsula's version of discourse on Atlantic slavery.[158]

Mendonça's court case cannot be discussed outside the wider context of his royal background, West Central African history and how the Portuguese project of conquest shaped it. This brings us back to the

---

[154] See Mendonça's recommendation letters, S.C. Africa, vol. 1, fl. 486 and fl. 487, and SOCG 54. 'Black Diaspora of the Atlantic' offers a more complex reality than the one proposed by Gilroy. See Robin Cohen, *Global Diasporas: An Introduction*, London: Routledge, 2008, and Emmanuel Akyeampong, 'Africans in the Diaspora: The Diaspora in Africa', *African Affairs*, 13, 2000, pp. 183–215.

[155] See APF, SOCG, vol. 490, fl. 140r; SOCG, 490, fl. 141r-v; SOCG, vol. 490, fl. 54; SOCG, vol. 495a, fl. 58; SOCG; SOCG, 495a, fl. 62vol. 495a, folio (fl.) 392; SOCG, vol. 495a, fl. 393, and C. Africa, 1, fl., 486.

[156] For further discussion of discourse see the books by Michel Foucault, *The Archaeology of Knowledge*, New York: Pantheon, 1972; *The Birth of the Clinic*, London: Tavistock, 1973; *Discipline and Punish*, London: Allen Lane, 1977; and also Charles Barker, *Cultural Studies, Theory and Practice*, London: Sage, 2003.

[157] Discourse then, by its very nature, is a production of knowledge in an intelligible form that excludes other forms of seen reality as unintelligible. It gives credence to a particular way of talking about objects, regulates maps of meaning and how institutions (practices) are given meaning. Discourse therefore regulates not only what can be said at any given time, but who can speak, when and where. See Foucault, *The Archaeology of Knowledge*, and Barker, *Cultural Studies*.

[158] SOCG, vol. 495a, fls. 54 and 55; SOCG, vol. 495a, fl. 57, Vieira – 'O Problema de Escravatura', and Barreto, Monstrusidades do Tempo e da Fortuna, ms. 16, fl., 189 v.

problem of historical sources. Although there is some debate concerning the origin of the kingdom of Ndongo, I will not address it in detail here.[159] Suffice to say, records of the myths of origin of African kingdoms written down in the early period of the European encounter with West Central Africa in the fifteenth and sixteenth centuries do not convey their full meaning.[160] Myths of origin of African kingdoms and places lie at the intersection of political, cultural, religious and economic power, and they need to be understood from these multifaceted perspectives.[161] In an attempt to engage with the history of Ndongo from the seventeenth century, one is clearly dependent on accounts written by missionaries, administrators, soldiers, travellers and overseas envoys. Most of these were Portuguese, with a handful coming from Italy, Spain and the Netherlands.[162] All, however, had an overtly Christian civilising mission and a political agenda that aimed to exploit the African subjects of their writings and to condone the taxation of Africans and the existence of African slavery.[163] In other words, their writings were not apolitical – as can be perceived in the historical documents themselves; and, as post-colonial scholars and historians have pointed out, their own positionality was determined by a distinct identity framed within the context of time and space and within the social settings and power relations of the

---

[159] For a fuller debate on the origin of Kongo and Ndongo, see Batsîkama, 'As Origens do Reino do Kôngo'; Patrício Batsîkama, 'O Poder Político Entre os Mbûndu', *Sankofa*, 9(16), pp. 96–134; J. Cuvelier, *L'Ancien Royaume de Congo*, Bruxelles: Desclée, 1946; J. Cuvelier and L. Jadin, *L'Ancien Congo d'Après les Archives Romaines (1518–1540)*, Bruxelles: IRCB, 1954 and O. De Bouveignes, *Les Anciens Rois du Congo*, Namur: Grands Lacs, 1948 and J. M. Decker, *Les Clans Ambuund (Bambundu) d'Après Leur Littérature Orale*, Bruxelas: Institut Royal Colonial Belge, 1950.

[160] See, for example, myths relating to the Cape Verde Islands. These were believed to be uninhabited islands when Europeans arrived in West Africa and thereafter. For discussion of Cabo Verde, see M. Barros, *Litteratura dos Negros: Contos, Cantigas e Parabolas*, Lisbon: Typographia do Commercio, 1900; Hall, *Before Middle Passage*.

[161] For a detailed discussion, see Cécile Fromont, *The Art of Conversion: Christian Visual Culture in the Kingdom of Kongo*, Chapel Hill, NC: University of North Carolina Press, Chapel Hill, 2014, pp. 24–32. See also Koen Bostoen, Odjas Ndonda Tshiyayi and Gilles-Maurice de Schryver, 'On the Origin of the Royal Kongo Title Ngangula', *Africana Linguistica*, 2013, pp. 53–83 and Batsîkama, 'As Origens do Reino do Kôngo'.

[162] For a detailed discussion of sources for West Central Africa, see Vansina, 'Ambaca Society'; Heintze, *Angola nos Séculos XVI e XVII*; Batsîkama, 'As Origens do Reino do Kôngo' and Giovanni Antonio da Cavazzi Montecuccolo, *Istorica Descrizione de Tre Regni Congo Matamba e Angola*, book 5, Bologna: Giacomo Monti, 1687.

[163] 'Carta de Salvador Correia de Sá', 'Sobre o que escreve e Governador de Angola Fr. De tavora, acerca da v. q. alcansou delRey de Dongo, e forma qse deve ter có D. Philipe có e Irmaó do mesmo Rey ...'

period.[164] Heintze and Katja Rieck have warned us about the problems of dealing with written sources on Ndongo's history, in that, 'most texts ... often were written by eyewitnesses, or at least by contemporaries, but they were written to serve Portuguese assessments, decisions and actions'.[165] It is this positionality, 'the who, where, when and why of speaking, judgement and comprehension',[166] that constrained their thought.[167] This is not to suggest that sources written by Africans themselves would have been free from ideological overtones. However, sources collected and written by Europeans, whether Portuguese, Spanish, Dutch or Italian, are not to be considered as original, unbiased sources in themselves; nor are they to be used as the yardstick for the interpretation of oral African histories.[168] Most of these sources were oral in their circulation long before the Portuguese wrote them down, and it is imperative that African perspectives and voices are included in the writing and interpretation of African history.[169] European sources have long been considered authoritative, despite the political conditioning of their authors, while African voices, even those documented within European sources, have remained in the background. What I am advocating is that a cautious and

[164] See 'Relação da costa de Angola e Kongo pelo Ex-Governador Fernão de Sousa' [A Report on the Angola and Kongo Coast by former Governor Fernão de Sousa] BAL, ms. 51-VIII-31, fls. II-18v, 21 February 1632, also in MMA, vol. VIII, pp. 113–130, and Archivum Romanum Societatis Iesu [ARSI], 'História da Residência dos Padres da Companhia de Jesus em Angola, e Cousas Tocantes ao Reino, e Conquista Lusitana' [History of the Resistence of the Fathers from the Society of Jesus in Angola, and Other Questions Concerning the Kingdom and Lusitan Conquest], 106, fls. 29–39, 1 May 1594, see also MMA, vol. III, pp. 546–581. See also Edward Said, *Orientalism*, New York: Pantheon, 1978.

[165] Heintze and Rieck, 'The Extraordinary Journey of the Jaga', p. 68.

[166] Barker, *Cultural Studies*, p. 388.

[167] On issues of how these authors carry with them their background and political positioning, see Ingrid Silva de Oliveira, 'As "Histórias" de Angola e seus Autores nos Séculos XVII e XVIII: um Estudo de Caso dos Militares Antonio de Cadornega e Elias Alexandre Correa', Anais do XV Encontro Regional da História da ANPUH-RIO, 2012, pp. 1–11; and Catarina Madeira Santos, 'Um Governo "Polido" para Angola: Reconfigurar Dispositivos de Domínio (1750–1800)', unpublished PhD thesis, New University of Lisbon, 2005.

[168] John K. Thornton, 'Legitimacy and Political Power: Queen Njinga, 1624-1663', *The Journal of African History*, 32(1), 1991, pp. 25–40.

[169] See Cadornega, *História Geral*, vol. I, p. 25. See also Green, 'Beyond an Imperial Atlantic'; Barros, *Litteratura dos Negros*; Wyatt MacGaffey, 'African History, Anthropology and the Rationality of the Natives', *History in Africa*, 5, 1978, pp. 101–120; Barbara Cooper, 'Oral Sources and the Challenge of African History', in John Philips (ed.), *Writing African History*: Rochester, NY: University of Rochester Press, 2005, pp. 191–215; Phyllis Martin, 'Sources and Source–Criticism', *Journal of African History*, 29(3), 1988, pp. 537–540.

balanced reading of these sources must be conducted if we are to give voice to both Europeans and Africans of the time.[170] The historical sources of Mendonça's court case are probably the most outstanding examples of this. Let me explain where I found them and of what they consist.

When I began my research I thought, as Gray had always maintained, that the case Mendonça took to the Vatican was a petition to obtain the abolition of African slavery. However, the documents I discovered in Arquivo de Torre do Tombo (Archive of de Torre do Tombo), Arquivo Histórico Ultramarino (Overseas Historical Archive in Belem, Brazil), the Archivo del Palacio Real (Archive of the Palace in Madrid, Spain) and the Archivio della Propaganda Fide (Archive of Propaganda Fide, Vatican) forced me to abandon my assumptions. Mendonça's case was not a petition, but a fully fledged criminal court case: 'Lourenço de Silva, arrived in Rome several times to report the complaints, the appeals of the poor Blacks enslaved and the burdens they receive in those parts.'[171] His liberation discourse was not just directed at African slavery, but was a universal message of freedom for all those, including Indigenous Americans, Brazilians and the New Christians in the Americas, Spain and Portugal, who were not members of the 'Jewish race nor pagans, but only following the Catholic faith, akin to any Christian, as is known'[172] – on the receiving end of injustice in the Atlantic region.

By 1686, two years after the Vatican adjourned Mendonça's court case, confraternities of Black Brotherhoods from across Brazil and the Americas had organised themselves to send a memorandum of grievance to the Vatican, which was taken there by Paschoal Dias, a freed Angolan enslaved in Salvador (then the capital of Brazil).[173] The confraternities declared that 'their miserable condition' was being overlooked. They claimed the daily deaths of enslaved people were being ignored by the Supreme Court of Christendom, even though they were members of the Universal Church. And they sought to 'inform the Pope of the miserable state in which all the Black Christians of this city and all the other cities of this Kingdom of

---

[170] See Batsîkama, 'As Origens do Reino do Kôngo' and Patrício Batsîkama, *Dona Beatriz Nsimba Vita*, São Paulo, Ancestre, 2021.
[171] See APF, SOGC, vol. 495a, fl. 393, see also SOCG, vol. 495a, folio, 393, 'Lorenzo desilva de Mendoza delRegno diKongo nelle' Indie' and 'Lorenzo diSilva venutó à Roma più volte per por' tare le doglianze, e ricorsi de poveri schiavi Negri l'aggravij che ricevono in qtte parti'. See also Gray, 'The Papacy'.
[172] See his final appeal letter, APF, SOCG, vol. 490, folio, 140.
[173] See APF, SOCG, Series America Meridionale, fl. 309.

America are'.[174] The aim of the Salvador memorandum was to confirm in the strongest terms the brutality and ill treatment suffered by the enslaved African Christians in Brazil.[175] Six confraternities from the city of Salvador – Our Lady of Rosary of Desterro, Our Lady of Rosary of Black Men from São Pedro, Our Lady of Rosary of Conceição, two confraternities from São Benedicto and Our Lady of Rosary from the Main Cathedral[176] – led the complaint and demanded a review of the case in the light of their evidence. The memorandum from Brazil was approved by the bishop of Brazil, Dom João, and his judge's scribe, Francisco da Fonsequa [Fonseca].[177] Fonseca was the scribe of the 'Cathedral of the City of Salvador, Bahia and of the kingdom of Brazil in the Americas. He was in charge of the Public Office and other roles in the City. He was nominated by order of His Highness.'[178] He gave Paschoal Dias the authority to carry the evidence in memorandum to the Vatican on 2 July 1686.[179] The memorandum was a universal condemnation of slavery, made with the aim of abolishing slavery.[180] Mendonça and the confraternities of Black Brotherhood included a case in the Vatican from the Caribbean islands as they sought to find the best solution to ways in which they were being treated and to gain freedom for enslaved Africans in Brazil and elsewhere. They appealed for the indentured servants' law of the French Constitution to be applied in the New World to alleviate the death toll among enslaved

---

[174] See APF, SOCG, Series America Meridionale, fl. 309, 'dizendolhe omizaravel estado enque estam todos os osnegros cristam desta edetodas as mais cidades deste Reino da America'.

[175] See APF, SOCG, Series America Meridionale 1, fl. 309.

[176] Seee APF, SOCG, Series America Meridionale 1, fl. 309, affidavit [letter of attorney] of Francisco da Foncequa, Bahia, fl. 309, 'Com procurasam damenza dos negros danosa Senhora do Rozario da Confraria denosa Senhora do destero [1], Comprocurasam dorozario que esta enSam Pedro dopretos [2], Comprocurazam da Comfraria de nosa Senhora dorozario daigreja denosa Senhora daComseiCam [3], Com otra procuracam de duas Confrarias que estam em Sam benedito [4, 5], Com outra procurasam daComfraria denosa Senhora do rozario que estana se catredal.'

[177] See APF, SOCG, Series America Meridionale 1, fl. 309, 'todas estas Comfrarias fizeram do Senhor arcebispo Dom Joam oqual mandou pacar esta cirtidam dando as sobre ditasConfrarias poder e aturidade'.

[178] See APF, SOCG, Series America Meridionale 1, fl. 309, 'Francisco daFonsequa oscrivam doiuizo dosenhor arcebispo dasanta Se desta cidade da bahia doreino do brazilda Americas I publico nas couzas desta por provizam deSua Alteza'.

[179] See APF, SOCG, Series America Meridionale 1, fl. 309, 'oqual mandou pacar esta cirtidam dando as sobre ditasConfrarias poder e aturidade apascoal dias negro foro, para que venha aCuria Romana'.

[180] Gray has not allowed for such universal condemnation and the fight to abolish slavery. See Gray, 'The Papacy'.

people in the Atlantic. The French indentured servants' law known as *engagés* or *trente-six mois* (thirty-six months), was passed on by Act of Parliament in 1663, and this allowed poor French emigrant citizens to move to the French Caribbean and work for three years for a French slave-master. After this period of service, then they would be set free.[181] Based on this evidence, I will argue that Mendonça's criminal court case was a universal condemnation of the Atlantic slave trade. It provided a global voice against the Atlantic slave trade, which was an attack on humanity itself. Atlantic slavery was undermined the human values of natural, human, divine and civil laws, he argued. What distinguishes us from animals was reversed in the Americas: human beings were treated as animals, whilst animals were treated better than human beings.[182] Some slave-owners had, in fact, descended to a level in which it did not matter how humans were treated.[183]

Mendonça's court case began on 6 March 1684 and lasted for two years.[184] Mendonça travelled numerous times to the Vatican to make his case.[185] Louise Kallestrup states that, in Roman legal procedures, 'more complicated trials were held in close communication with the Holy Office'.[186] Mendonça demanded the intervention of the Holy Office so 'that Your Holiness will deign to give this subject back to the Holy Congregation of the Holy Office and to the one or Propaganda Fide'.[187]

---

[181] For Mendonça and Confraternities seeking the French Caribbean model, see SOCG, vol. 495a, fl. 62. French minister Jean-Baptiste Colbert introduced *engagés* or *trente-six mois* to French colonies in the Caribbean in 1663. Here I am indebted to Robert Taber '"To Strengthen the Colonies": French Labor Policy, Indentured Servants, and African Slaves in the Seventeenth Century Caribbean', *Library Research Grants*, 10, 2007, pp. 1–35. See also Alexandre Prouville de Tracy, 'Réglement de M. de Tracy, Lieutenant Général de l'Amérique, touchant les Blasphémateurs et la Police des Isles, 19 June 1664,' in Moreau de Saint-Méry, *Loix et Constitutions des colonies françoises de l'Amérique sous le vent*, vol. I, Paris, 1786.

[182] See Andreoni (Antonil), *Cultura e Opulência*.

[183] Andreoni (Antonil), *Cultura e Opulência*, p. 21.

[184] See APF, SOCG, vol. 495a, fl. 54, 'in the General Congregation of the 6th of March 1684 has been read a Memorial given by the Sanctity of Our Lord, in which were reported the cruelties practiced in the Indies against the Blacks', [Nella Cong:^{ne} g^{o}le de 6 Marzo 1684 fù letto um Mem.^{le} rimefso dalla San'tà di N'ro Sig.^{re} nel quale fi rappresentava le crudeltà che se pratticavano nell' Indie contro de Negri]. See also SOCG, vol. 495a, fl. 393, 'Alla Sacra Cong.^{ne} de Propaganda Fide ... Die 26 Martij 1686' [To the Sacred Congregation of the Propaganda Fide ... on 26 March 1686].

[185] See APF, SOCG, vol. 495a, fls. 392 and 393, 'Lorenzo di Silva venuto à Roma più volte' [Lorenzo de Silva, having arrived in Rome several times].

[186] Louise Nyholm Kallestrup, *Agents of Witchcraft in Early Modern Italy and Denmark*, Basingstoke and New York: Palgrave, 2015, p. 54.

[187] See APF, SOCG vol. 490, fl. 138 and 140, 1684, 'che la st.à v. Si degni rimemere questa materia alta sacra Congregatione delS. Officio, ò à quella di Propaganda Fide'.

Introduction 43

The Vatican's response was that the people involved in buying and selling enslaved Africans, particularly those found committing crimes against Christians, should be punished, and the Vatican put huge pressure on Spain and Portugal to stop such cruelty to enslaved Christians in Africa and in the Atlantic.[188] Both Carlos II of Spain and Pedro II of Portugal, whose reigns coincided with Mendonça's court case, wanted to abolish Atlantic slavery, but they were prevented from doing so by advisors including the Council of Indies and the Portuguese Overseas Council.[189] The Portuguese Crown responded to the Vatican's demand of 18 March 1684, made in response to Mendonça's court case,[190] by improving conditions of shipment for enslaved Africans being taken from Angola and Cape Verde to Brazil.[191] The Portuguese Crown also pledged to punish governors or merchants found to have committed crimes against the enslaved in Brazil and elsewhere.[192]

Mendonça began his *reclamazione*[193] (see Figure 1) or court case in the Vatican not with African involvement in slavery, but rather with a bold statement of his argument and evidence about how the capture of Africans was implemented, and the methods that were deployed to enslave them.[194] In doing so, he refuted the established thinking that Africans were willing participants in the Atlantic slave trade, and the idea that there were existing markets in Africa for enslaved Africans.[195] Mendonça

---

[188] See the letter from the Vatican nuncio sent to the Propaganda Fide, SOCG, vol. 495a, fl. 57, 1 May 1684.
[189] Charles R. Boxer, *The Church Militant and Iberian Expansion 1440–1770*, Baltimore, ML, and London: The John Hopkins University Press, 1978, p. 35.
[190] See Dom Pedro II's Transatlantic Slave Trade Law, AHU_CU_001, cx 13, d. 1554, Angola, 18 March 1684, and A. J. R. Russell-Wood, *Fidalgos and Philanthropists: The Santa Casa da Misericordia of Bahia, 1550–1755*, London: Macmillan, 1968, p. 385.
[191] See 'Lei sobre a arqueação dos navios', AHU, Arquivo de Cabo Verde, liv. 42, fls. 29v-32v, – cód. 544, fl. 50v, 28 March 1684.
[192] See APF, SOGC, vol. 495a, fl. 393.
[193] See SOCG vol. 495a, fl. 58, 'Seconda reclamazione à N'tro Sig.^{re}' – [Second complaint to Our Lord].
[194] See SOGC, vol. 495a, fl. 54, and an Italian text written by Cardinal Alexandrino 'Relazione del Viaggio, Fatto Dall Ilmo, e R.mo Fr. Michelle Bonnello, Cardinal Alexandrino Del Tit: di S. Ma. Sopra Minerva, Nipotte di Pio V, Legato Alli Serenis.mi Re, Di Franca, Spangna, e Portogallo, Colle Annotarioni delle Citta, Terre, e Luoghi, Descritto Da Mes.r Gio: Battista Ventu: Rino da Fabriano, l'anno 1571', Biblioteca da Ajuda, Lisboa [BAL] – 46-IX-3.
[195] See Boxer, *Portuguese Seaborne Empire*, p. 31, and Thornton, *Africa and Africans*, p. 6. See also Padre Baltasar Barreira, who was Novais' confessor and claimed that there were African slave markets, 'Informação Acerca dos Escravos de Angola' [Information about Slaves in Angola] (1582–1583), Biblioteca e Arquivo Distrital de Évora, Portugal, [hereafter BADE], BADE, cód. cxvi/1/33, fls. 168–168v, see also MMA III. For Barreira,

accused the Vatican, Italy, Portugal and Spain of crimes against humanity, claiming, 'they use them [enslaved people] against human law'.[196] The legal concept of a 'crime against humanity' may not have been current at the time of Mendonça's case, although it is implicit in both natural and human laws. However, the term is frequently used in the documents Mendonça presented in the Vatican, and Roman legal jurisprudence has influenced the European legal system since that time.[197] I believe that Mendonça's use of the term 'crime against humanity' anticipated its use in modern times. Atlantic slavery, as he saw it, was an attack on the human values of freedom, liberty and free will. For him, slavery was indeed a crime against humanity according to four principles of law known to human societies: *natural, human, divine* and *civil*.[198]

The documents for Mendonça's court case in the Vatican were later organised into three categories, based on the order in which they were presented and their importance, using the letters (A), (B) and (C) (see Figure 4 and Table 1), which indicates how the documents were preserved. (A) referred to Mendonça's presentation of the first case as an attorney (procurator). (B) relates to the defendants' responses, that is, the responses from the political governing authorities in Italy, Spain and Portugal, and the slave-masters in Spain, Portugal and Brazil. Documents labelled (C) record the plaintiff's cases and the voices of the Africans from different

---

Africans would mean people from regions we now call Angola, Kongo, Guinea, Sierra Leone, Ghana and Nigeria (Benin). After all, the category Africa, which included the political geography of demarcation, came later. As Valentin-Yves Mudimbe shows, the concept of 'Africa' did not really exist until the eighteenth century. The participation of some Africans in the Atlantic slave trade has often been generalised so as to include the whole continent. The reason for Africans' involvement has not been critically analysed in light of the allegiances they were obliged to declare – in particular, to the Portuguese. See Valentin-Yves Mudimbe, *The Invention of Africa: Gnosis, Philosophy and the Order of Knowledge*, Bloomington and Indianapolis, IN: Indiana Press University, 1988, and MMA III.

[196] *AllaSantita di N.ro Sig're, Innocenzo* ..., SOCG, 490, folio, 140r, 'usano contro ogni legge ... humana'.

[197] On the Roman legal system's influence on European jurisprudence, see Peter Stein, *Roman Law in European History*, Cambridge: Cambridge University Press, 1999; James Q. Whitman, *The Legacy of Roman Law in the German Romantic Era: Historical Vision and Legal Change*. Princeton, NJ: Princeton University Press, 1990; Greg Woolf, *Becoming Roman: The Origins of Provincial Civilization in Gaul*, Cambridge: Cambridge University Press, 1998; Greg Woolf, 'Monumental Writing and the Expansion of Roman Society in the Early Empire', *Journal of Roman Studies*, 86, 1996, pp. 22–39, and Reinhard Zimmermann, *The Law of Obligations: Roman Foundations of the Civilian Tradition*, Oxford: Oxford University Press, 1996.

[198] See *AllaSantita di N.ro Sig're, Innocenzo*.

Introduction 45

TABLE 1 *The system of Mendonça's court case documents, as filed in the Vatican. Photograph by the author*

A	B	C
Mendonça's evidence-based discourse	Governing authority response (Italy, Spain and Portugal) and decision to stop slavery	Enslaved Africans' complaints and activism (Africa, Spain, Portugal, and Brazil)

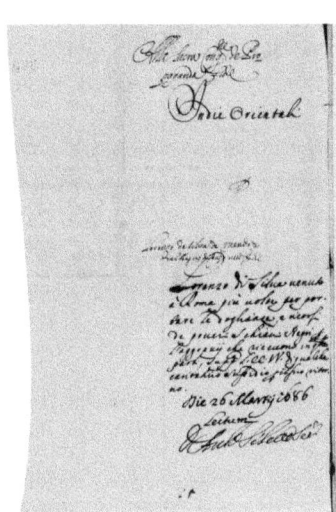

Folio 393

Alla Sacra Cong.ne de Propaganda Fide
Indie Orientali
C
Lorenzo desilva de Mendoza delReygno diCongo nelle' Indie Lorenzo diSilva venutó à Roma più volte per por' tare le doglónze, e nicorsi de poueri schiavi Negri l'aggraauij che rice vono en qtto parti, supp.ca l'ee. VV. Diqualehe canitahùo sufidio pilsuo ritorno

Die 26 Martij 1686

Lectum
Signature

Folio 393

To the Sacred Congregation of Propaganda Fide
Oriental Indies
C
Lorenzo de Silva de Mendoza from the Kingdom of Kongo in the (Indies) Lorenzo de Silva, having arrived in Rome several times to report the **complaints**, the **appeals** of the poor Black slaves and the burdens they receive in those parts, pleads the [Initials] for some charitable grant for his return [to the Indies].

26 of March 1686

Lectum
Signature

FIGURE 4 Mendonça's presentation of the 'complaints' and 'appeals' of the various confraternities he represented to the Vatican court. SOCG, vol. 495a, folio, 393.

organisations, confraternities, including constituencies of 'men', 'women' and 'young people' within the confraternities themselves, and other interest groups.[199] Cases (A) and (C) are similar in content, although (C) reinforces (A). (B) responds to (A). The contents of (B) – the Spanish, Portuguese and Roman governing authorities' responses – were met with huge protest from the Black Africans in Africa, Spain, Portugal and Brazil, and the pressure groups represented by (C). The 'men', 'women' and 'young people' of those Black confraternities sent their grievances to the pope, disapproving of what was said by the constituency of (B). Indeed, waves of protest were driven towards the Vatican: 'after receiving his replies, the Blacks have complained again to this Congregation raising the same grievances and pleading to provide to their miserable condition as in the paper C'.[200]

It is imperative to note that many court cases were brought by enslaved Africans against their masters and vice versa and by those subject to the Inquisition in the Atlantic in this period of the seventeenth century.[201] They were, however, presented as individual cases and, unlike Mendonça's case, were not taken to the Supreme Court of Christendom, the Propaganda Fide or 'General Congregation' at the Vatican, which was charged with dealing with any issues arising overseas, including missionary work in Africa, Asia and the Americas.[202] The constitution issued to the Black African confraternities in 1526[203] gave enslaved Africans the legal right to seek their freedom as Christians within churches of which they were members.[204] The constitution also allowed them to elect their attorneys. Accordingly, Mendonça was elected as an international lawyer in Portugal in the 1680s, and at the Royal Court of Madrid, Toledo, on 23 September 1682 and therefore allowed to practise 'throughout the whole of Christendom in any kingdom or dominion' and 'using the economic and political right which is conferred to him'.[205]

After Mendonça presented his case in court, the Vatican requested eyewitnesses. The confraternities selected, 'three priests who have been missionaries in those areas. Two of them were Spanish and one

---

[199] See APF, SOCG, vol. 495a, fl. 58, 'tanto huomini, come femine, e ragazzi'.
[200] See SOGC, vol. 495a, fl. 56.
[201] See Lucilene Reginaldo '"África em Portugal": Devoções, Irmandades e Escravidão no Reino de Portugal, Século XVIII', *Studia Historica, Historia Moderna*, 38(1), 2016, pp. 123–151, and Lahon, 'Da Redução da Alteridade'.
[202] For further discussion of the topic, see Garstein, *Rome and the Counter-Reformation in Scandinavia*; see also Pius Malekandathil, 'Cross, Sword and Conflicts'.
[203] See Lahon, 'Da Redução da Alteridade'.
[204] See Reginaldo, 'África em Portugal', pp. 123–151, and Russell-Wood, *Fidalgos*.
[205] For his election in Toledo, see 'Carta de Giacinto Rogio Monzon'.

Portuguese'.[206] They gave evidence similar to Mendonça's. Two of the eyewitnesses were the above-mentioned priests, Jaca and Moirans, who were both asked by the confraternities or Brotherhoods of Black Christians from Brazil, Portugal and Spain to stand as witnesses for Mendonça in the Vatican. The document relating to their testimony, classified in (C), declares, 'Mons. Secretary says that to provide against such illegal contracts it was proposed by the zeal of some Capuchin missionaries to declare wrong and to forbid, under punishment ... some propositions which were sent to the Saint Office, but it is not known which decision has been taken about them.'[207] Both men confirmed the atrocities suffered by enslaved Africans in the Atlantic.[208] Before standing in the witness box in the Vatican, Moirans had already completed a thesis on the defence of Africans from enslavement.[209] The inhumane treatment of enslaved people was widely known in Brazil, Portugal, Africa and Spain by the seventeenth century, but the merchants and the governing authorities in the Iberian Peninsula who had long dominated the trade had covered up its abuses. In fact, and as referenced, they promoted slavery throughout Europe as benign, and in the Atlantic as a triumph of Christian missionary activity.[210]

Mendonça's court case was also shaped by the Council of Trent, held between 1545 and 1563. Among the issues dealt with at the Council of Trent were the doctrinal challenges presented by the Protestant Reformation and the renewal of the Roman Catholic Church in the face of Protestant expansion. These challenges coincided with the age of European expansion to Africa, the Americas and Brazil.[211] The Council of Trent thus provides the background to the politico-religious landscape Mendonça encountered in the Vatican. The need to recruit new members for the Catholic Church meant that one of the outcomes of the Council of Trent was the requirement for Catholic kingdoms – Spain, Italy and, in particular, Portugal, with its monopoly of Africa – to invest the revenue

---

[206] See APF, SOCG, vol. 490, fl. 138, 'da tre sacerdoti, due Spagnoli, et un Portoghese'.
[207] See SOGC, vol. 495a, fl. 62.
[208] See the documents that they presented in the Vatican confirming the atrocities and methods used to capture Africans. See Propaganda Archives, series: Acta de anno 1685, no. 26, March 12, fls. 35–37.
[209] See Jaca and Moirans, OFM Cap., *Servi Liberi*.
[210] See Gomes Eanes de Zurara, *Crónica de Guiné, Introdução, Novas Anotações e Glossário de José de Bragança*, Lisbon: Livraria Civilização, 1972 and Esmorald. See also the Vatican Nunico's letter from Portugal, SOGC, vol. 495a, fls. 54–55.
[211] For further discussion, see John W. O'Malley, *Trent: What Happened at the Council*, Cambridge, MA: The Belknap Press of Harvard University Press, 2013.

garnered overseas on the expansion of Christianity, provide Christian education and formal education of Indigenous people, including Africans, the Indigenous Brazilians and the Natives in India.[212] At the Vatican, Mendonça was calling for the revitalisation of the inclusive principles that emerged from the Council of Trent. His appointment in Portugal as a lawyer for Blacks in Brazil, Portugal and Spain was made on the understanding that he supported the principles of Trent, and his appointment as an international lawyer in Toledo reinforced that understanding. His letter of recommendation from the papal nuncio in Portugal explicitly stated that Mendonça was given the affidavit in the spirit of the Council of Trent.[213]

0.3 METHODOLOGY AND USE OF SOURCES

The book deploys a microhistorical methodology, opening a window onto an exceptionally complex and important period of colonial interconnections in the seventeenth century through the personal life story of Mendonça and that of his royal family, namely his brothers, uncles, aunts and cousins. The book thus offers one of the earliest Black Atlantic microhistories and uncovers an extraordinary story of an abolition movement that included other oppressed constituencies such as New Christians and Indigenous Americans, shedding light on Africa, Europe and colonial America in a crucial period of world history. It deals with the objective strategy and operation, network and universal nature of

---

[212] See 'Carta do Rei D. Pedro II para o General de Alcobaça'.
[213] See Mesquita, S.C. Africa, vol. I, fl. 486. According to the Council of Trent, Indigenous people were to be trained to play a Christian role in their respective societies; they were also to be paid with the revenue gathered from their local regions. The confraternities of Black Christians in Africa, Brazil, Portugal and Spain grew out of this requirement. See Faria, 'Sobre a Fundação de Seminários'. Confraternities in Lisbon were paid 500 reis, directly from the state treasury, for any ship that returned from the Americas and India. Joaõ Gago, the Treasurer of the House of Guinea [Casa de Guyne] was ordered to Royal decree to pay 500 Reis to Black confraternities for every ship that returned from Mina [West Africa], 'Alvará à Confraria dos Pretos de Lisboa' [Permit to the Black Brotherhood in Lisbon], ATT, Chancelaria de D. João III, liv. 22, fl. 100, 18 April 1518, 'quynhemtos reis desmolla em cada caruella que vyer da Myna'. These confraternities joined together from Brazil, Portugal and Spain to make a universal declaration against injustice levelled at the enslaved people in the Atlantic. Mendonça's court case was aligned with his role as an international lawyer tasked with defending the oppressed groups, be they Indigenous Americans, the New Christians or white Christians who were treated as subhuman and lived lives not worthy of humanity as a result of the political and economic injustices found in the Atlantic.

Mendonça's criminal court case and abolition discourse that he presented to the highest court of the Christian world: the Vatican.

It is the prime purpose of this book to reveal the inclusive processes at work in Mendonça's case as a Black Atlantic abolition movement that embraced the African enslaved, New Christians and Indigenous Americans. His case forced me to ask some fundamental questions about slavery that have previously been given unsatisfactory and ideological answers and to which this book attempts to offer new and perhaps uncomfortable responses: Were the enslaved Africans in the Atlantic already enslaved? How were they obtained? Who was a slave? If slavery was a normative practice in Angola, why would the enslaved run away to gain their freedom? More daring responses to these questions require an understanding of the conceptual issues around slavery in West Central Africa as understood by the Africans themselves, and the clarification and revision of some of the stereotyped views held about African slavery.

Crucial to the book is the question of how far Mendonça provokes us to rethink our methodological approach to studying Atlantic slavery and the abolition movement. Moreover, the research asks how the debate that surrounds the work on Mendonça extends and challenges our understanding of the African diaspora in the Atlantic. To engage with the complexities of Mendonça's criminal court case and the troublesome issues that he raised in the Vatican, such as kidnapping, wars waged on Africans, treachery and robbery, with his legal defence based on *natural*, *human*, *divine* and *civil* laws, and with his universal freedom message for all, offers us a new understanding of Africa's and Africans' denunciation of slavery as a crime against humanity.

I have found it necessary to employ a loosely chronological and regional approach. However, the book also adopts a thematic approach, since I believe that the complex issues involved cannot be dealt with adequately through a chronological perspective alone.

This study builds on my prior research on Portuguese merchants, which has made it possible for me to question established interpretations of slavery in West Central Africa and to engage critically with the stances taken by the Vatican, and Italian and Luso-Hispanic merchants, and the methods they used to defend Atlantic slavery.[214] To engage with Mendonça's abolition discourse, I have relied for the most part on primry sources, as explained above. This is generally new material that has not so

---

[214] Lingna Nafafé, *Colonial Encounters*.

far been used by historians, and which I encountered in archival and library records, and in various languages: in Latin, Kimbundu (one of the Angolan languages), Portuguese, Italian and Spanish.

The book's findings are based on more than fifteen years of research, undertaken in fourteen cities and in thirty-seven archives.[215] I have uncovered new data in a variety of archives from three continents (Africa, America and Europe) and six countries (Angola, Brazil, Portugal, Spain, Italy and the USA) and each document encountered offered new insights and connections. The sources I found in Arquivo Histórico Ultramarino de Belém (AHUB), Torre do Tombo, Lisbon; Arquivo Nacional de Rio de Janeiro, Brazil; and both the Arquivo Municipal and Público de Salvador, Brazil, link Mendonça and his relatives directly to Quilombo de Palmares, something not previously known. Archival material encountered in the Torre do Tombo connects Mendonça to a wider Atlantic network of New Christians (Jews) in Portugal and Brazil. Other material found in the El Archivo General de Palacio de Madrid and the Archivo General de Simancas, Valladolid, Spain, links Mendonça with a Native American network. I traced trajectories from Ndongo to Salvador, Bahia; from Salvador to Rio de Janeiro; and from Rio de Janeiro to Portugal and then researched Mendonça's journey from Lisbon to the Royal Court of Madrid, Spain and from there to the Vatican. This led to my carrying out research in Archivo de Diociano de Toledo; Angola Museu de Antropologia; the Archives of Propaganda Fide; Bibliotheca Apostolica Vaticana;

[215] These different archives include museums, monasteries and libraries such as: the Arquivo de Antropologia de Angola, Luanda, Angola; Arquivo Histórico Ultramarino de Belém; Torre do Tombo; Palácio Nacional da Ajuda; Biblioteca Nacional de Lisboa, Lisbon; Museu de Peniche, Peniche; Mosteiro de Alcobaça, Alcobaça; both Arquivo Público de Braga and Biblioteca de Braga; Mosteiro de Vilar de Frades; Mosteiro de Tibans, Braga; Museu de Vilar Viçosa, Viçosa, Portugal; Arquivo Nacional do Rio de Janeiro; Biblioteca Nacional do Rio de Janeiro; Arquivo Público do Estado do Rio de Janeiro; Museu Nacional do Rio de Janeiro; Arquivo Geral da Cidade do Rio de Janeiro; Instituto Geográfico do Rio de Janeiro; Arquivo da Cúria do Rio de Janeiro, Rio de Janeiro; and both the Arquivo Municipal and Público de Salvador; Arquivo da Santa Casa de Misericórdia; Arquivo da Cúria da Universidade Católica; Instituto Geográfico e Histórico da Bahia; Museu de Arte da Bahia; Museu Carlos Costa Pinto, Salvador; Instituto Histórico e Geográfico de Alagoas, Maceió, Brazil; Arquivo Público de Pernambuco, Recife, Brazil, Quilombo dos Palmares [Parque Memorial], Maceió, Brazil; El Archivo General del Palacio de Madrid; Archivo General de Madrid; Museu del Prado, Madrid; Archivo General de Simancas, Valladolid; Archivo Diocesano de Toledo, Spain; the Archives of Propaganda Fide; Santa Maria Maggiore; Vatican Archive and Biblioteca Vaticana, Rome, Italy; and Brown University Library, Rhode Island, USA.

Introduction 51

Archivum Secretum Vaticanum; and the Historical Archives of Santa Maria Maggiore, Rome, Italy.[216]

Regarding published sources, I have used the aforementioned sixteen volumes of Father António Brásio's collection, *Monumenta Missionaria Africana*, in which he has brought together and carefully transcribed an extensive number of documents from different archives in France, Portugal, Italy, Spain and the Netherlands. The volumes cover the period of Portuguese expansion from the mid-fifteenth to the end of the seventeenth century. As observed earlier, the vast majority of the documents are not commented upon by him, but he sometimes makes explicit the names and people associated with a particular place and role. As Brásio's work was commissioned by the Vatican, it is dominated by records of missionary activity in Africa; but Brásio has also transcribed many documents of wider political and cultural interest.

In order to question the established ideas on slavery and its abolition in the seventeenth century, I thought it imperative to carry out research based on archival documents that are scattered around the world. The fact that Mendonça had to move across the Atlantic in order to try to change the African predicament suggested to me a way of developing a methodology that could do justice to his cause by following in his footsteps.

Let me now present the chapter breakdown to explain how I have structured the narrative that is the outcome of my research.

0.4 CHAPTER BREAKDOWN

Chapter 1 deals with the Municipal Council of Luanda and the politics of the Portuguese governors in Angola in the seventeenth and eighteenth centuries. The Municipal Council of Luanda became the site of political intrigue, jealousy, deceit and mutiny; it was a political landscape in which

---

[216] The research for the monograph was carried out in six countries: Angola, Brazil, Portugal, Spain, Italy and the USA. I have consulted archives in the following places: the Angolan archive, Salvador (Curia, Santa Casa, publico, Municipal and Instituto historical geográfico), Rio (arquivo nacional, Curia, Instituto geografico de Rio de Janeiro, Biblioteca nacional do Rio), Portugal (Torres do Tombo, bibioteca nacional de Lisboa, arquivo historical ultramarino, Palacio e Ajuda), Braga (Arquivo e biblioteca de Braga), Coimbra (biblioteca de Coimbra), Madrid, Rome. The research was carried out over three and half years, and in six languages: Portuguese, Spanish, Italian, Latin, Kimbundu, and English. I also visited places such as Palmares in Alagoas, Engenho of Victoria in Cachoeira, Bahia, Brazil, and the monasteries of Vilar de Frades, Tibans, Carnide, Gracas, Alcobaça, Peniche, Fotres of Sao Juliao de Barra.

the main drive was for economic gain, and the enslavement of Angolans was a key part of that package. The methods deployed to capture Angolans – through wars, pillage and treachery – formed the basis for Mendonça's Vatican court case.

Chapter 2 introduces the Ndongo and focuses on its relationship to Kongo in terms of political and social structures. It looks at the election of Philipe Hari I to the throne of Pungo-Andongo. It examines his rivalry and family ties with Queen Njinga, and how the Portuguese used his election to foster their trade relationships in Angola by introducing the *baculamento* tax system. The chapter then explores the role of João Hari II (Dom João de Sousa), also known as Ngola Aiidi,[217] the son who succeeded Philipe Hari I, and the ideology of Francisco de Távora 'Cajanda', the Portuguese governor of Luanda at the time.[218] It investigates the destruction of Pungo-Andongo and the sending of the kingdom's princes and princesses, Queen Njinga's nephews and nieces, to Brazil. The chapter is concerned with exploring the political environment of Angola and the wider region as the backdrop to Mendonça's debate on freedom and the integration of enslaved Africans in the Atlantic.

Chapter 3 investigates the journeys of the Ndongo royals as political exiles to Salvador and Rio de Janeiro in Brazil. It examines how their dismissal was aligned with the power struggles in Luanda. The House of Ndongo, that is Mendonça's family, was led at the time by members of a generation that confronted the Portuguese alliance their predecessors had endorsed. They broke away from this alliance at a critical period of Portuguese history, when the country was achieving independence from Spain (1640–1668). I argue that the first generation of rulers of the House of Ndongo (which began with Philipe Hari I and was preceded by the House of Matamba), who were graduates of the Jesuit College of Luanda,

---

[217] Dom João de Sousa. After his baptism, he was given the surname Sousa because governor Fernão de Sousa was his godfather. His African name was Ngola Aiidi. He took the throne of Pungo-Andongo after the death in 1664 of his father, Dom Philipe de Sousa, known as Philipe Hari I or by an Angolan name, Ngola Airi. He took the throne as Dom João Hari II when André Vidal de Negreiros was governor of Angola. For further information see, Cadornega, *História Geral*, vol. III, pp. 307 and 309; and p. 453.

[218] The kingdom of Ndongo or Maupungo, later called Pungo-Andongo, was created on 12 October 1626 by the Portuguese when Philipe I was elected as a king and baptised in Luanda on 29 June 1627. It lasted until 29 November 1671, when it was destroyed by the Portuguese. *Baculamento*, the tax system in enslaved Angolans began with the creation of the new kingdom, Pungo-Andongo, and then the system was applied to all sobas allies and became law in Angola for the subsequent centuries. See Cadornega, *História Geral*, vol. II, p. 156; vol. III, p. 453 and vol. III, pp. 308–310.

sought a return to the traditions of their forefathers. The chapter focuses on the royals' lives in Brazil, and on what they saw there of the general treatment of enslaved and of Indigenous Brazilians. It also explores how their stay there was shaped by the African slave communities in both Salvador and Rio, that is to say the Black Brotherhoods. The royals' stay in Brazil acquainted them with the predicament of enslaved Africans and helped them establish political ties with the Angolans in Salvador who later supported Mendonça at the Vatican. The chapter also looks at how these experiences shaped Mendonça's discourse in the Vatican, where he criticised the Portuguese trade model deployed in Africa to enslave Africans. It examines the case of runaway enslaved Africans mentioned in Chapter 2 and connects it with the runaway enslaved people of Quilombo dos Palmares in the state of Alagoas, Brazil, by exploring the ideology of the Quilombo dos Palmares community and the idea of liberation as a question of power. The chapter looks at new data on Palmares, and investigates how the community forged a political and economic alliance with Cristovão de Burgos de Contreiras, known simply as Cristovão de Burgos, a judge in the High Court of Salvador, and a man at the heart of the Portuguese governing class in Brazil. In contrast to the view of some members of the religious authority in Brazil, the Jesuits, de Burgos envisioned Palmares as a new colonial power emerging from the country. I argue that Palmares presented a different economy and, as such, provoked the governing authorities in Bahia to reconsider their strategy, which led them to send the royals away from Salvador to Rio de Janeiro. The governing authorities in Brazil feared that their royal status could help strengthen the enslaved fugitives' community, which would in turn endanger Portuguese economic interests. They believed that Palmares contained many Angolan enslaved who came from the royals' people group. This explains the authorities' fear that Palmares potentially represented a new colonial power in Brazil, and that the Palmarists not only had the support of the Natives for their cause of freedom and liberation, but also of some members of the Brazilian-born élite of the time who viewed them as economic partners. I also focus on how the Ndongo royals' presence in Salvador and Rio continued to be connected with the innovative power of Palmares. This chapter is a vital contribution to Brazilian historiography since Palmares has often been seen as an African state or African republic in Brazil that had little to do with those born in Brazil.

Chapter 4 looks at Mendonça's journey to Portugal and Spain, and the network he created with the Hebrew Nation (New Christians) and Indigenous Americans. It examines Mendonça's education in Braga,

Portugal, his appointment as an attorney of the Confraternity of Our Lady Star of the Negroes in Lisbon and Toledo, Madrid, and the alliances he formed with the New Christians in Lisbon, and in particular the Mesquita's family. Then it examines his alliance with Indigenous Americans in Toledo by means of his education in Vilar de Frades in Braga and the confraternity of Toledo, Madrid. It explores the period 1670–1681 in Lisbon as crucial to his networking with the apostolic notary in Lisbon, Gaspar da Costa de Mesquita, and his connection with the New Christian 'Hebrew Nation' question in Lisbon and in the Atlantic, which revolved around events in Odivela, Lisbon and the efforts of Vieira (a Portuguese Jesuit priest, philosopher and writer, who worked in Salvador, Maranhão, Brazil, in the seventeenth century) to free the New Christians from the Inquisition. The New Christians' search for freedom is then examined in relation to the denial of the enslaved Africans' freedom. The unity of the regional confederation in West Central Africa shaped Mendonça's engagement with the freedom of enslaved Africans in Angola, Brazil, Spain and Portugal. It also served as a springboard for his networking with the Indigenous Americans and the New Christians in the Atlantic, Portugal and Spain. I contend that my findings on the intersection between slavery and freedom are new, as is my discovery of the networks between the Portuguese 'Hebrew Nation', Indigenous Americans and Africans seeking their freedom in the Atlantic. I argue that engaging with this dialogue provides a better understanding of how those whose liberty had been denied sought to overcome this by allying with different constituencies in the Atlantic.

In Chapter 5, I explore Mendonça's court case in the Vatican and argue that liberation of enslaved Africans in Brazil, Portugal and Spain was part of a wider Atlantic question. I also maintain that, by allying himself with these different constituencies in the Atlantic, Mendonça's message and claim of freedom was universal and his urging of abolition transcended the African frontier to include the equally suffering New Christians and Indigenous Americans. The chapter reveals how Mendonça's evidence-based court case challenged the established seventeenth-century assertion that Africa was a slaving society that already took part in and willingly aided the European Atlantic slave trade. His evidence demonstrated how the Atlantic slave trade operated on the ground in Africa, and how violence was used as a strategy for maintaining slavery's existence. The accused were the Vatican, and the Italian, Portuguese and Spanish political governing authorities, and Mendonça brought together African accusers from different organisations, confraternities and interest groups, including constituencies of 'men', 'women' and 'young people'[219] within the confraternities themselves. I conclude the chapter with remarks on the significant reinterpretation of slavery and abolition that it offers, and on the new understandings it reveals of Mendonça's criminal court case in the Vatican as a Black Atlantic abolition movement.

Chapter 6 engages with the debate about the freedom of enslaved Africans as a tussle between Mendonça, his family and the Portuguese Overseas Council. This was a struggle initiated by his grandfather, Philipe Hari I, in 1658, and continued by his uncle, João Hari II, from the 1670s onwards. The chapter examines the Crown's slave legislation of 18 March 1684, seeing it as a direct response to Mendonça's court case in the Vatican. It looks at the sphere of the Portuguese Overseas Council's jurisdiction in relation to the internal affairs of the kingdom, that is, Portugal, and its attempt to overturn Mendonça's court case verdict in the Vatican via a discreet, anonymous letter. It examines how Mendonça marshalled his legal arguments to uphold the Vatican's verdict ensure it was influential on the Portuguese Overseas Council. It analyses three types of political struggle, centred on the Overseas Council, the Portuguese Crown and Mendonça's court case. The chapter argues that the court case was a tussle between Philipe Hari I and João Hari II of the House of Ndongo and the Portuguese Overseas Council, which vetoed a decision that Philipe Hari I would continue payment of *baculamento* – that is, make tax payments in enslaved people. João Hari II rebelled against the payment of tax in enslaved people and declared the independence of Pungo-Andongo from Portugal in 1671. This was a struggle that Mendonça continued to argue in the Vatican in 1684–1687. I contend that Mendonça, in taking his criminal court case to the Vatican, sought not only the abolition of African slavery and liberty for Indigenous Americans and New Christians, but also to shake off the burden of his own family's involvement in the slave trade. In the tussle between himself and the Portuguese Overseas Council, Mendonça succeeded where his family had failed. However, I argue, the positive response of the Portuguese Crown to Mendonça's court case failed to address the radical abolition that Mendonça and the Black confraternities demanded.

So far, the story of slavery has been told as a narrative in which the Africans were the victims of their own crime. That crime is said to have consisted in the enslavement of their own people by their governing bodies, embedded in their socio-political, economic, religious and legal

---

[219] See APF, SOCG, vol. 495a, fl. 58, 'tante huomini, come feminine, e ragazzi'.

system. The abolition of Atlantic slavery, on the other hand, has mainly been told as a narrative in which the morally superior Europeans came to rescue the Africans from this very system. Both narratives made it possible for the European colonising nations to explore Africa while exploiting African labour in a dehumanising and violent fashion, through an intervention whose only purpose was economic gain and political power, corrupting their own Christian morality by using it to validate this domination and the turning of human beings into currency. Mendonça's criminal court case makes it clear that these narratives are nothing more than treacherous tales aimed at justifying the unjustifiable. The case not only points up that a role in the abolition movement was taken by Africans with a sophisticated understanding of the connection between divine, natural, civil and human law but also that they showed political nous by uniting other oppressed constituencies with the Black Atlantic. Indeed, Mendonça's universal pledge for freedom made it clear that Atlantic slavery was introduced to Africa by Europeans. It was the Vatican as a seat of Christendom with its universal ethics and the European colonising nations that were implicated in this crime against humanity. To this day, we live with the consequences of the false criminalisation of Africans and their descendants, while the true perpetrators have not been held accountable. Mendonça's story makes this unquestionable.

I

The Municipal Council of Luanda and the Politics of the Portuguese Governors in Angola

On 6 March 1684, when Mendonça presented his evidence-based court case in the Vatican, he began with statements on how Africans were captured and enslaved.[1] As a member of the Royal Court of Pungo-Andongo, he would doubtless have recalled historical cases of ordinary people having been rounded up from their homes, fields and daily lives and having been enslaved in Angola; he would have experienced war; and he would have heard stories of people being seized in raids, kidnapped and taken to the Americas as enslaved people.[2] He would have heard from his grandfather, father, uncles, aunts and brothers – all allies of the Portuguese – about illegal wars conducted, treachery used and robbery carried out on Angolans captured, enslaved and shipped to Brazil on

---

[1] See APF, SOCG, fls. 54 and 58.
[2] See APF, SOCG, fl. 54. For a full discussion of the idea that there were no enslaved people out there in West Central Africa and all was being done by the Portuguese illegally and using force of arms to capture people and turn them into enslaved people, see High Court of Appeal 'Relação de Antonio Bezerra Fajardo'. For people captured in wars instigated by the Portuguese, see 'Descrição da Batalha de Ambuíla' [A Description of the Battle of Mbwila], BLN, Mercúrio Portuguez, 1666, Res. 110 (V), 20 October 1665, MMA, vol. XII, pp. 575–581; see also an account of the battle in 'Relação da Batalha de Ambuíla' (Report of Mbwila Battle), 29 October 1665, Museu Britânico [British Museum, BM], Additional n. 20.953, fls. 227–229, MMA, vol. XII, pp. 582–591. On the use of courts created in the outpost by the Portuguese to handle cases in their favour, see Frei Melchior da Conceicam, 'Alvaras, Cartas, Provizioes, Regimentos' and on the 'forced gift' or 'buttering-up gifts' forced on *sobas* to provide the Portuguese with enslaved people, see Carta do Governador Fernão de Sousa a El-Rei Angola-are [A Letter of Governor Fernão de Sousa to the King and Angolans], BAL – Ms. 51-VIII-30, fls. 242–242v, 27 March 1627; also, in MMA, vol. XII, pp. 506–507 and Frei Melchior da Conceicam, 'Alvaras, Cartas, Provizioes, Regimentos' just mentioned above.

behalf of Portugal.³ His report in the Vatican confirms cases of 'those who have been "abducted", "kidnapped", "hunted", "snatched", "taken from the fields with fraud" and "sold" to "merchants"'⁴ who would in turn 'sell them in Europe like animals'⁵ or in the Americas for that matter.

So to begin to understand Mendonça's criminal court case about the predicament of enslaved Africans in the Atlantic, it would be useful to start in West Central Africa, where he first experienced his people being seized and carried off into slavery in the Americas.⁶ It is essential that we locate his work in the political, legal and economic landscape of Kongo and Angola.⁷ It is also fundamental that we understand from the beginning that enslaving Africans was an integral part of the Portuguese conquest of West Central Africa.⁸ This is evident from the 1512 brief to the kings of Kongo, and later Angola, by Dom Manuel, King of Portugal.⁹ It is, therefore, impossible to draw a distinction between what we might perceive as a 'slavery period' in Africa at the beginning of the Portuguese encounter with West Africa or West Central Africa in general and the conquest.¹⁰ That is not to suggest that some Africans conquered by the Portuguese – whether kings or *sobas* in West Central Africa – did not unwittingly become involved in or were coerced into the trade we now call the 'slave trade', in which ordinary African men,

---

³ See the agreement made with Philipe Hari I to make a payment of 100 enslaved people per year, 'Carta de Fernão de Sousa a El-Rei' [A Letter by Fernão de Sousa to the King], BAL, Ms. 51-VHI-30, fl. 321–331 v, 22 August 1625.
⁴ See APF, SOCG, vol. 490, fls. 136 and 137; and APF, SOCG, vol. 495a, fl. 54 and actual fl. 56.
⁵ For Mendonça's evidence-based report, see APF, SOCG, vol. 495a, fl. 54 and actual fl. 56.
⁶ On people being taken to the Americas, see 'Carta de João Correia de Sousa ao Marquês de Frecilha', pp. 17–24. For a detailed description of Correia de Sousa's activities in capturing Kazanze people, see 'Padre Mateus Cardoso's High Court of Appeal'. On the illegality of captives in the region, see High Court of Appeal 'Relação de Antonio Bezerra Fajardo', and on Captain-Majors from outposts' in using plots to capture people in the conquered zones, see Carta do Governador Fernão de Sousa a El-Rei Angola-are [A Letter of Governor Fernão de Sousa to the King and Angolans], BAL – Ms. 51-VIII-30, fls. 242-242v, 27 March 1627; also, in MMA, vol. VII, pp. 506–507.
⁷ For further studies on Angolan politics, see Birmingham, *Trade and Conquest* and Batsîkama, 'O Poder Político'.
⁸ See Birmingham, *Trade and Conquest*; Candido, 'Conquest, Occupation, Colonialism and Exclusion'; and Heintze, 'Ngonga a Mwiza'.
⁹ See 'Regimento de D. Manuel a Simão da Silva (1512)', [Brief or Set of instructions from Manuel to a Simão da Silva], 1512, ATT – Leis, 2–25, MMA, vol. I, pp. 228–246.
¹⁰ For further detail studies on Angolan conquest, see J. Vansina, 'Long-Distance Trade-Routes in Central Africa', *The Journal of African History*, 3(3), 1962, pp. 375–390; Joseph C. Miller, *Kings and Kinsmen: Early Mbundu States in Angola*, Oxford: Clarendon Press, 1976; Heintze, 'Ngonga a Mwiza'; Ferreira, *Feiras e Presídios*; Vansina, 'Ambaca Society'; Ferreira, *Cross-Cultural Exchange*; and Batsîkama, 'O Poder Político'.

women, young people and children were captured and made slaves.¹¹ However, for our understanding of Mendonça's criminal court case and his presentation in the Vatican, we need to be fully aware of his experiences in Angola. That means that it is also imperative that we understand the role played by the Muncipal City Council of Luanda, which regulated all shipments of enslaved Angolans to Brazil.¹²

It was in the city councils, such as that of Luanda, that decisions were made about how Africans were to be captured and enslaved.¹³ The councils were the places in which decisions were made about conquest – the so-called 'just war' – and the wages of the soldiers fighting in those wars were paid.¹⁴ Those who disagreed with the politics of the council and its decisions were exiled to Brazil or São Tomé.¹⁵ Such was the fate of the Portuguese governor of Luanda, Correia de Sousa,¹⁶ as well as of Mendonça's family, which was considered a threat to the 'common good' of the council.¹⁷

---

¹¹ See the shocking description of how women and children were being 'snatched', 'taken away' by force and turned into enslaved people by the order of Portuguese captains, and captains-major from the outposts in Angola, in Frei Melchior da Conceicam, 'Alvaras, Cartas, Provizioes, Regimentos'.
¹² Some enslaved Angolans might have ended up in Brazil as contraband, smuggled illegally. However, the Muncipal City Council of Luanda controlled and managed the trade as one of its main attributions.
¹³ On 15 November 1664, the Municipal Council of Luanda asked the king of Portugal for a special dispensation to prevent people leaving Angola and returning to Portugal, and allowing them to stay and marry in Angola, because there were many widows and maidens in Angola whose husbands and parents had died during the war against the Dutch from 1641 to 1648, see Consultas Mixtas, liv. 4, fl. 135v, 15 November 1664.
¹⁴ The idea of a 'just war' was an ancient concept with a moral justification for waging war, often based on a theological interpretation. It was a prerogative and praxis reserved to the royal court. For Mbundu's court, it was the *macotas* who decided when a war was to take place; for the Portuguese in Angola, it was the Luanda City Council on behalf of the Crown. For further discussion of the concept of 'just war', see Augustine of Hippo, *The City of God Against the Pagans*, translated and edited by R. W. Dyson, New York: Cambridge University Press, 1998; F. Russell, *The 'Just War' in the Middle Ages*, Cambridge: Cambridge University Press, 1975; and J. Langan, 'The Elements of St. Augustine's "Just War" Theory', *The Journal of Religious Ethics*, 1984, 12(1), 19–38. On West Africa in the Early Modern period see also V. Fernandes, *Description de la Côte Occidentale d'Afriqe (Sénégal au Cap de Monte, Archipels) par Valentim Fernandes (1506–1510)*, Bissau: Centro de Estudo da Guiné Portuguesa, 1951.
¹⁵ Sousa sent some of the leaders of Kazanze people to São Tomé. Farras, while governor of the bishop in Luanda, sent a secular priest to São Tomé. On war cabinet in Luanda in the seventeenth century, see High Court of Appeal 'Relação de Antonio Bezerra Fajardo', and see also Birmingham, *Trade and Conquest*.
¹⁶ See Consultas Mixtas, n. 4, fl. 233, 1 September 1667.
¹⁷ See AHU-CU-001, Angola, Cod. 17, Consultas Mixtas, fl. 187, Oversea Council Inquiry about the relatives of the King of Dongo, 28 November 1675; and fl. 301.

Early historiography of West Central Africa tended to emphasise that the capture and enslavement of Angolans were a means of financing the Portuguese conquest of the region. Both Heintze and Candido have put considerable effort into demonstrating that raiding and taxation were important mechanisms of the Portuguese administration in maintaining their economic strength.[18] Whilst Ferreira explores the idea that markets/ *feiras* in eighteenth-century Angola were used as a means of obtaining enslaved Angolans, he indicates that their regulations were carried out by *sobas*. However, he concedes that the Portuguese authorities in Angola created these markets in an attempt to bridge local trading regulations.[19] Vansina has taken this debate further and examines a different perspective on the markets, arguing that the Portuguese intervened to introduce a new 'distance' market in the region in enslaved Angolans, using caravans. For Vansina that market was based on the slave trade.[20] Curto argues that African rulers in West Central Africa were involved in the Atlantic slave trade, including enslaving their creole élites.[21]

Thornton, Heywood and Curto have argued that the very foundation of Kongo was based on slave labour and that Afonso I [1509–1543] was complicit in the slave trade during his reign.[22] According to Thornton and Heywood, Afonso I's co-operation with Portugal in the slave trade is attested by his letters to Manuel I, king of Portugal (1495–1521).[23] Thornton states that the 'warfare in this time was nevertheless important, for Nimi aLukeni's (1380–1420) father was said to be a raider who had sought his fortune by reducing one or another local stronghold and demanding tribute'.[24] However, Thornton appears to have been reliant on the oral sources of Father Giovanni Antonio Cavazzi da Montecuccolo (1621–1678), an Italian Jesuit priest, sent to Angola by the Vatican, in his

---

[18] Heintze, 'Ngonga a Mwiza'; Heintze, *Angola nos Séculos XVI e XVII*; Candido, 'Conquest, Occupation, Colonialism and Exclusion'; Candido, 'O Limite Tênue'.

[19] See, Ferreira, *Feiras e Presídios*, pp. 19–22, 25–28, 31–48, and 39–44.

[20] See Vansina, 'Ambaca Society'.   [21] See Curto, 'Experiences of Enslavement'.

[22] See Thornton, *Africa and Africans*, p. 74.

[23] See 'Carta do Rei do Congo, A. D. Manuel' [A Letter of the King of Kongo to A. D. Manuel], ATT-CC-I-16-28, 5 October 1514, MMA, vol. I, pp. 294–323; for full discussion of D. Manuel, see also Thornton, 'The Kingdom of Kongo'; José Curto, *Enslaving Spirits: The Portuguese-Brazilian Alcohol Trade in Luanda and Its Hinterland c. 1550–1830*, Leiden, 2004; Linda M. Heywood, 'Slavery and Its Transformation in the Kingdom of Kongo: 1491–1800', *The Journal of African History*, 50(1), 2009, pp. 1–22; and Curto, 'Experiences of Enslavement'.

[24] See Thornton, 'The Kingdom of Kongo: The Development of an African Social Formation', *Cahiers d'Études Africaines*, 1982 (87–88), pp. 325–342 (p. 332). The House of Kilukeni/Lukeni kanda starts from 1390s to 1568.

assessment of pre-colonial Kongo, particularly with regard to Afonso I; a point he acknowledged in his work.[25] The difficulty with Cavazzi's oral sources lies in the fact that they were collected in the seventeenth century and translated from Kikongo (one of the Kongo languages) into Italian, his Native language; he would have been inclined to use terms such as 'slave' or *servus* (Latin for slave) in describing situations in which conquered Africans in Europe were obliged to offer slave labour to their conquerors.[26] This practice was found in the Luso-Iberian political project of reconquest of the Iberian peninsula (formerly known as the Reconquista) from the eighth to the fifteenth centuries that was based on *encomienda* system.[27] Robin Blackburn declares that 'the Spanish and Portuguese use of African slaves was heavily influenced by medieval, Mediterranean and Roman legacies'.[28] As we saw in the Introduction, servitude had no direct correlation with slavery in the Western understanding of the term.[29] Missionary sources such as those collected by Cavazzi cannot be viewed as reliable, given his Christian ideology, the fact that he was ignorant of local cultural practices and the language he used in rendering terms from Kikongo in Italian. Based on the evidence of what he said about Jaga being cannibals, his understanding of the local practices needs to be taken with some degree of caution.[30] The very 'Society of Jesus' that he was serving as a priest owned enslaved Africans in Kongo and Angola, and he never condemned the practice of Atlantic slavery: on the contrary, he endorsed it.[31] It cannot be taken for granted

---

[25] See Thornton, 'The Kingdom of Kongo'.
[26] For further discussion of how Venetian Christians treated their enslaved people, from antiquity to the early modern period (the sixteenth century), see Sokol, *Shakespeare and Tolerance*, pp. 152–155.
[27] See Robert Himmerich y Valencia, *The Encomenderos of New Spain*, Austin: University of Texas Press, 1991; Lesley Byrd Simpson, *The Encomienda in New Spain*, Berkeley, CA: University of California Press, 1950; R. Altamira, 'El Texto de las Leyes de Burgos de 1512', 4, 1938, *Revista de Historia de América*, pp. 5–79.
[28] See Robin Blackburn, *The American Crucible, Slavery, Emancipation and Human Rights*, London: Verso, 2011, p. 21.
[29] See Nell Irvin Painter, *The History of White People*, New York: W. W. Norton & Company, 2011, Cheikh Anta Diop, *The African Origin of Civilization, Myth of Reality*, ed. and trans. Mercer Cook, Chicago, IL: Lawrence Hill Books, 1974, and John G Jackson, *Introduction to African Civilizations*, New York: Citadel Press, 1970.
[30] See Giovanni Antonio Cavazzi Montecúccolo, *Descrição Histórica dos Trés Reinos do Congo, Matamba e Angola*, vols. I–II., trans. Graciano Maria de Leguzzano, Lisbon: Junta de Investigaçoes do Ultramar, 1965.
[31] There was an interesting discussion between Luis Brandão and Padre Alonso de Sandoval in 1611 about whether African war captives were caught justly. Brandão avoided telling Sandoval that the captives had not been captured in a just war and had been stolen instead.

that he had lived in Kongo and Angola because his collection of oral materials appears to be genuine and to have been collected at the time of political tension in Kongo.[32] Cavazzi's sources remain questionable as they may not reflect the political reality of the time. In other words, there are no other comparative sources available to us to confirm his claims.[33]

Heywood has developed Thornton's argument further and argued that 'slavery as an institution existed from the time that Kongo emerged as the dominant power in West Central Africa in the fourteenth century'.[34] Heywood was also reliant on Cavazzi's oral sources. She states that 'Cavazzi collected the earliest oral traditions on slavery from Kongo informants in the mid-seventeenth century, noted that the traditions claimed that the first slaves in the kingdom appeared at its founding by Kongo's first conqueror king, Lukeni lua Nimi.'[35] According to Heywood, the existence of slavery as an institution in Kongo is attested in 1502 by the Cantino Atlas.[36] For Heywood, Afonso I was directly involved in the slave trade and it was in his rule as a king that we gain an understanding of slavery in Kongo. She remarks: 'the several letters from King Afonso I (1509–43) to the Portuguese kings form the bedrock of any understanding of the social categories that existed in the kingdom and the place of slavery in it'.[37] Heywood went further to reconstruct the social structures of Kongo from Afonso I's letters, using terms such as *gente, naturaes, naturaes forros, espcriuos/esprauos* and *peça* (freeborn Kongolese, citizens, free citizens, captives/slaves and piece of merchandise).[38] She states: 'at this time Afonso operated an open slave

---

He went on to say that people do not ask the captives whether they were caught justly, because the captives would say that there were stolen – knowing that once they had done this, they would be liberated. Luis Brandão was a director of the College of Jesus Society in Luanda, Angola, whereas Sandoval (1576–1652) was a Spanish Jesuit priest and missionary in Colombia. See 'Carta do Padre Luis Brandão, S.J. ao Padre Alonso de Sandoval, SJ.' [A Letter of Father Luis Brandão, S.J. to Father Alonso de Sandoval, SJ], *De Instaurando Aethiopum salute*/Historia de Etiopia, pelo Padre Alonso de Sandoval, S.J., 21 August 1611, BNM – R.14.775, pp. 100–101, MMA, vol. VI, pp. 442–443.

[32] See Thornton, 'The Kingdom of Kongo'.
[33] For further debate on oral sources in Kongo, see Batsîkama, 'As Origens do Reino do Kôngo'.
[34] Heywood, 'Slavery and Its Transformation', p. 3.
[35] Heywood, 'Slavery and Its Transformation', p. 3.
[36] For the Cantino Atlas as cited by Heywood, see Armando Cortesão and Avelino Teixeira da Mota (eds.), *Portugalliae Monumenta Cartographica* (6 vols.), Lisbon: Imprensa Nacional-Casa da Moeda, 1960–1962, pp. 1, 12 (plates 4–5).
[37] See Heywood, 'Slavery and Its Transformation', p. 3.
[38] For detailed correspondence from Afonso to Manuel and to João III, as cited by Heywood, see Afonso to Manuel, 5 October 1514, MMA, 295; see also Afonso to João III,

market in the capital, for he notified King Manuel that the enslaved people who had been captured were 'in our compound (*terreyro*)'.[39] Terms used by Heywood need further analysis in the light of the *Regimento* (brief or set of instructions) of 1512 sent by Dom Manuel, king of Portugal, to Afonso I two years earlier.[40] This brief gives the reasons behind Afonso I's response to Manuel and João III. The brief has not been cited by both Thornton and Heywood. Manuel's *Regimento* of 1512 formed the background to Afonso I's letters; one cannot understand the rationale of the letters without analysing them in tandem with the *Regimento*.[41] Terms such *gente*, *naturaes*, *naturaes forros*, *espcriuos/esprauos* and *peça* used in Afonso I's letters were there to explain his Christian commitment and to inform Manuel of it; Manuel had been keen to see Kongo model its governance on Christian European states. Manuel also expected Afonso I to pay back the expenses incurred for the education of his children whom he had sent to Portugal previously. He stated:

and remind him [Afonso] of the great expense that we make with the sending of these ships, friars and clerics and things that we have sent him and those that have gone before you, and so the expense that is made here [in Lisbon] for the maintenance and teaching of his children, for that he must load said ships as fully as he can.[42]

These 'expenses' included personnel, Portuguese soldiers' wages and items stated in Manuel's 1512 *Regimento* that were shipped to Kongo for Afonso I, such as: *arma*s (firearms)[43] and *escudos darmas* (coats of arms),[44] *o seello das armas* (cell weapons),[45] *bamdeira das armas* (flags bearing coats of arms),[46] *gemtes e armadas* (soldiers),[47] *oficiaes*

---

[38] 18 October 1526, MMA, vol. I, p. 489; and João III to Afonso, end of 1529, MMA, vol. I, p. 526.
[39] See Heywood, 'Slavery and Its Transformation', p. 4.
[40] See 'Regimento de D. Manuel a Simão da Silva (1512)' [Brief or Set of instructions from Manuel to a Simão da Silva], 1512, ATT – Leis, 2–25, MMA, vol. I, pp. 228–246.
[41] See 'Regimento de D. Manuel a Simão da Silva (1512)'.
[42] See 'Regimento de D. Manuel a Simão da Silva (1512)', p. 240 'e lembramdolhe a gramde despesa que fazemos com a emviada destes nauios, Frades e clerigos e cousas que lhe emviamos e que já amtes de vós foram, e assy a despesa que se cá faz na mātença e ēsyno de seus filhos, por homde elle deue de car[r]egar os rrant nauios o mais abastadamēte que ele poder'.
[43] See 'Regimento de D. Manuel a Simão da Silva (1512)', pp. 232 and 233.
[44] See 'Regimento de D. Manuel a Simão da Silva (1512)', p. 233.
[45] See 'Regimento de D. Manuel a Simão da Silva (1512)', p. 235, 'o seello das armas que lhe emviamos' (cell weapons we have sent).
[46] See 'Regimento de D. Manuel a Simão da Silva (1512)', p. 235.
[47] See 'Regimento de D. Manuel a Simão da Silva (1512)', p. 232.

macanicos (mechanical officers or armed engineers),[48] *hū letrado* (a judge),[49] *frades e clerigos* (priests: friars and clerics)[50] and other material goods. In summary, Manuel declared: 'and aside from all the things that you took, there were freights, provisions, and a lot of payment that we made, for that reason it would not be good for the ships to return empty'.[51] These items were to help Afonso I set up his court along the lines of those kept by Christian monarchs in Europe, 'as from the beginning of your Christendom, we hope that in those parts there a lot will follow in the service of Our Lord and the addition to his holy Catholic Faith'.[52] Manuel remarked:

there is an acknowledgment of his [Afonso I's] conversion and the news of his Christian faith which we have passed on to the Holy Father as he is a great and powerful King. And it is in keeping with what Christian Kings and Princes do, so we must do. He must send his obedience to his Holiness, as all Catholic princes do, as the Vicar of Jesus Christ to his Church of Saint Peter in Rome, who is the head of all the Christian Faith.[53]

What was said during the embassy of Pedro, Afonso I of Kongo's cousin, who was sent to Portugal as an ambassador between him and Manuel, we may never know. However, what is clear from that diplomatic correspondence is that the Crown wanted enslaved people, minerals and a trade monopoly between Kongo and Portugal. From Manuel's brief there were many issues that were not included in the *Regimento*. They were left for the Crown's envoy to communicate to Afonso I directly 'for the King, you will tell him as we spoke here with Dom Pedro his cousin'[54] as soon as they arrive in Kongo, such as the intention that he be given firearms and their use 'for him to be well informed of the foundation [reason] we have and

---

[48] See 'Regimento de D. Manuel a Simão da Silva (1512)', p. 232.
[49] See 'Regimento de D. Manuel a Simão da Silva (1512)', p. 234.
[50] See 'Regimento de D. Manuel a Simão da Silva (1512)', p. 240.
[51] See 'Regimento de D. Manuel a Simão da Silva (1512)', p. 240, 'e de todas as cousas que leuastes, nos quaes e asy nos fretes e mantimentos e soldos nós gastamos muyto e que por yso nam serya rezam os nauyos se tornarē de vazio'.
[52] See 'Regimento de D. Manuel a Simão da Silva (1512)', p. 231, 'asy como as costumamos dar e emviar aos Reis e primcipes christaos'.
[53] See 'Regimento de D. Manuel a Simão da Silva (1512)', p. 242, 'ha noteficaçã que de sua cŌversam e cristyndade temos dada ao samto Padre e como hé Rey de grande poder. E que por guardar o que os Reis e príncipes christaaõs guardamos, elle deue madar sua obidiemcia a sua Samtidade, como todos os primcipes catholicos o fazemos, como a vigairo de Jhesu Christo na sua Igreja de sam Pedro de Roma, que hé cabeça de toda a religiam christâa.'
[54] See 'Regimento de D. Manuel a Simão da Silva (1512)', p. 242, 'A elRey direes como nos fallamos cá com dom Pedro seu primo.'

for giving him the firearms'.⁵⁵ It is clear from the *Regimento* that he was expected to use these gifts to establish his kingdom in the likeness of Portugal: the army and arsenal were to be used in accordance with Portuguese institutions and customs, including Christianity, the Church, defence, justice and governance.⁵⁶

Manuel made it clear that slave-capture and metals were the main purpose of his alliance with Kongo.⁵⁷ In other words, the goal of the Crown was to gather slaves: 'mainly, the ships [sent to Kongo] should return full of slaves and other merchandises'.⁵⁸ Manuel went further in his plea to Afonso I: 'tell him [Afonso I] if slaves are traded in his country then merchandise will be taken [from Portugal] to trade them'.⁵⁹ The Crown also promised further aid, if Afonso I cooperated; Portugal would help him when he needed it. Manuel remarked 'with great pleasure, you will always find help and favour from us'.⁶⁰ The aid he received from Portugal came about because of his commitment to Christianity 'just as we usually give and send them to the Christian Kings and Princes'.⁶¹ African kings who did not profess Christianity would not meet the criteria for aid 'as for the heathens and non-Christian kings and princes we do not send them gifts or greetings'.⁶² Afonso's war captives from part of his own kingdom (Ndongo) were to help him fulfil his obligation to Manuel. The description makes clear that the social division he made among the inhabitants of his kingdom was an attempt to protect his people from the vicious Portuguese slave trade. Afonso did not have enslaved people in his compound. He had to go and wage war

---

⁵⁵ See 'Regimento de D. Manuel a Simão da Silva (1512)', p. 233, 'pera elle ser bē ēformado do fundameto que teemos e dar as armas'.

⁵⁶ See 'Regimento de D. Manuel a Simão da Silva (1512)', p. 241, 'como antes vos dizeemos, a elRey de Manicomguo seruy nas cousas da paz e da gueerra e da gouernança da teerra, asy como elle vollo ordenar e mandar, poemdoas no costume de cá'.

⁵⁷ See 'Regimento de D. Manuel a Simão da Silva (1512)', pp. 228–246.

⁵⁸ See 'Regimento de D. Manuel a Simão da Silva (1512)', p. 240, 'e primcipalmente venham bē car[r]egados descrauos e das outras cousas'. On the Portuguese relations with Kongo and the Crown interest in trading in enslaved people, see Ferreira, *Feiras e Presídios*.

⁵⁹ See 'Regimento de D. Manuel a Simão da Silva (1512)', Manuel's letter to Afonso I, sent with Simão da Silva, MMA, vol. I, p. 240, 'dizēdolhe que se ē sua terra se resgatarem escrauos leuareys mercadoria pera se resgatarem'.

⁶⁰ See 'Regimento de D. Manuel a Simão da Silva (1512)', p. 232, 'senpre em nós achará ajuda e fauor, com muy boõa vomtade'.

⁶¹ See Manuel's letter to Afonso I, sent with Simão da Silva, MMA, vol. I, p. 231, 'asy como as costumamos dar e emviar aos Reis e primcipes christaos'.

⁶² See Manuel's letter to Afonso I, sent with Simão da Silva, MMA, vol. I, p. 231, 'porque a Reis e primcipes jmfyes e que nam sam christaaos nam emviamos ecomêdas nem saudações'.

against Matamba and Ndongo to get them for the Portuguese Crown. He was armed by the Crown, which expected him to act as Christian monarchs acted. It took Afonso two years to organise the trade in enslaved people for the Portuguese Crown.[63]

The word *terreyro* that Heywood interprets as a market is ambiguous. It can mean a 'square' but this does not necessarily imply 'market' as Heywood suggests. Curto argues that Afonso I opened a market in São Tome, when in fact it was a Portuguese market.[64] In fact, he sent his people there to ensure that people being stolen from his kingdom were not enslaved or made into war captives. Moirans points out that a just war did not take place in Africa.[65] Miller has argued that there were slaves' markets in the interior of Angola into which the Portuguese tapped.[66] For him, Queen Njinga of Matamba was involved in the slave trade, selling many Angolans into slavery in the Americas.[67] C. R. Boxer has endorsed the view that slavery was natural in Africa and that it cannot be compared to China where enslaved people were state property. Boxer compared the taking of Chinese *muitsai* or kidnapped children for use as enslaved people to that of Africans. The former, he said, were state property and not for sale, whereas there were no legal precedents for what was done to the Africans. Once again, historians of the Atlantic such as Boxer simply advance a problematic version of African culture that lacks critical engagement with the available writings. He identifies

---

[63] See the date of Afonso I's letter to Manuel I ['Carta do Rei do Congo, A. D. Manuel', ATT-CC-I-16-28, 5 October 1514]. 'Terreyro' could mean a sacred place, an abode of ancestors – a kind of homestead built for housing objects that belonged to the ancestors. In some cases, a 'terreyro' was a small square between houses; in others a sacred tree or trees were planted to represent the ancestors' abode. For Afonso I to do this might have meant that he consecrated his victory to the ancestors by placing the captives in the 'terreyro'. Thus, as understood above, 'square' cannot be understood as a place in which market transactions were conducted. Markets were normally built outside the houses or some miles away from where people livde. For a detailed description of an African market in the sixteenth century, see Fernandes, *Description de la Côte Occidentale d'Afriqe*, p. 120. See also Lingna Nafafé, *Colonial Encounters*, pp. 73–87. For a detailed description of sacred places, see Albano Mendes, Ramon Sarró and Ana Temudo, *O Museu Etnográfico Nacional da Guiné-Bissau: Imagens Para uma História – El Museu Etnográfico Nacional de Guiné-Bissau: Imágenes Para una Historia*, Lisbon: Instituto Camões, 2018.

[64] See Curto, 'Experiences of Enslavement'.

[65] See Jaca and Moirans, OFM Cap., *Servi Liberi*, p. 218.   [66] See Miller, *Way of Death*.

[67] Miller, *Kings and Kinsmen*; Joseph C. Miller, 'Capitalism and Slaving: The Financial and Commercial Organization of the Angolan Slave Trade, according to the Accounts of Antonio Coelho Guerreiro (1684–1692)', *The International Journal of African Historical Studies*, 17(1), 1984, pp. 1–56. Heywood echoes that view in her recent book, *Njinga of Angola*.

Atlantic slavery as an African problem rather than a European one, declaring:

> prisoners of war were, in fact, State slaves. There is, however, no need to dispute the accuracy of Caspar da Cruz's main contention viz. that Chinese domestic slaves were in a very different category from the Negro and other slaves who were bought and sold like cattle in the Portuguese colonies – and that consequently the Portuguese had no legal or moral right to purchase either *muitsai* or kidnapped children for use as slaves.[68]

In a similar vein, Augustin Holl, President of the Scientific Committee of UNESCO's General History of Africa, stated in an interview for the BBC with journalist Zeinab Badawi aired on 27 October 2020, that African coastal peoples were directly involved in the Atlantic slave trade as they were given guns to hunt people from the interior. He declared: 'One cannot expect the Europeans to mount expeditions in the hinterland of Africa to catch slaves or enslave people. It is coastal political groups that organise the expedition. Coastal people were armed with the latest technology – guns – and were able to capture their neighbours.'[69] However, Holl was not able to explain why this was when asked by Badawi. He said: 'it is really hard to say but we have to remove morality from this kind of issue. What is the common expression for that? It is called *realpolitik*, meaning there are no sentiments there. Coastal people used their power to seize people and sell them for profit.'[70] However, Holl is taking a leap here in his analysis. There is ample evidence in this book from European accounts that the coastal people were conquered by Europeans and had to pay them tax in enslaved people, otherwise they would have been taken into slavery themselves.[71] Walter Rodney argues that: 'in the Congo, the slave trade did not get under way without grave doubts and opposition from the king of the state of Kongo at the beginning of the sixteenth century'. There is clear evidence that Portugal intended to trade in slaves in Kongo.[72] In Rodney's analysis, 'the King of the Kongo had conceived of possibilities of mutually beneficial interchange between his people and the European state, but the latter forced

---

[68] See Boxer (ed.), *South China in the Sixteenth Century*, p. 152.
[69] See Augustin Holl's interview with the BBC: 'Slavery and Suffering: The History of Africa with Zeinab Badawi', episode 16: https://www.youtube.com/watch?v=ajI8lkYdmAk.
[70] See Holl, 'Slavery and Suffering'.
[71] For a detailed discussion of *baculamento*, see 'Informação de Fernão de Sousa a El-Rei' [Information by Fernão de Sousa to the king] and other forms of taxes including 'buttering-up gifts' or 'forced gifts', see Frei Melchior da Conceicam, 'Alvaras, Cartas, Provizioes, Regimentos'.
[72] Rodney, *How Europe Underdeveloped Africa*, p. 80.

him to specialize in export of human cargo'.⁷³ According to Rodney, Afonso I's expectation was not met. 'He asked for masons, priests, clerks, physicians; but instead, he was overwhelmed by slave ships sent from Portugal, and a vicious trade was opened up by playing off one part of the Kongo kingdom against another.'⁷⁴ None of these historians who have argued for the existence of slavery in West Central Africa were aware of Sousa's edict of 1626, which transformed the landscape of trade and currency in West Central Africa.⁷⁵

In my view, the changes in taxation introduced by governor Fernão de Sousa gave birth to slave-raiding. Unaware of it, neither Heintze and Candido viewed the 1626 changes as a legal intervention that arose as a natural result of the Portuguese conquest.⁷⁶ *Soba* allies were obliged to pay the tax in the form of human bodies – that is, enslaved people. Since this tax system was not a viable method, they resorted to raiding people to pay the tax imposed on them. Heintze and Candido were unable to unlock the distinction between taxation in produce and its substitute as a monolithic tax based on human beings. What is new in my interpretation is the understanding that the new tax system in enslaved people was deliberately imposed by the Portuguese and became part of the constitution of the Muncipal City Council of Luanda.⁷⁷ Based on new primary sources, I uncovered this law and realised that the taxation system based on it was designed to be permanent in West Central Africa. Fernão de Sousa was successful in naturalising this abhorrent law and it became an unquestioned norm in the region in the eighteenth and nineteenth centuries.

---

⁷³ Rodney, *How Europe Underdeveloped Africa*, p. 80.
⁷⁴ Rodney, *How Europe Underdeveloped Africa*, p. 80.
⁷⁵ For a full discussion of African involvement in the slave trade, Curto, 'Experiences of Enslavement' and Heywood and Thornton, *Central Africans*. Brásio stated that Garcia II, the king of Kongo, was involved in sending enslaved people as present to the Dutch. 'Carta de D. Garcia II Rei do Congo ao Padre Reitor do Colégio de Luanda' [A Letter of King Garcia II of Kongo to Father Rector of the Society in Luanda], AHU – Angola, cx. 2., MMA, vol. IX, p.18, 'no documento precedente a oferta espontânea de escravos aos holandeses, lamentando que fossem poucos!' [in the preceding document the spontaneous offer of slaves to the Dutch, regretting that there were few]. Despite the fact that it was Garcia II who gave details about the brutality of the enslavement of Angolans and Kongolese in the region and on the social and economic environment of the West Central Africa, by his time the exchange currency of the region was human beings.
⁷⁶ See 'Informação de Fernão de Sousa a El-Rei' [Information by Fernão de Sousa to the King], BAL, ms. 51-VIII-31, fls. 5–9 v, 7 December 1631.
⁷⁷ See See 'Consulta do Conselho Ultramarino', AHU., Cód. 554, fs. 90v.-91v., 7th March 1698, fol. 90v.

We must also bear in mind that the acquisition of enslaved Africans was not so straightforward a transaction as we have been led to believe. There were no markets in which natural-born or captured Africans could be bought as enslaved people in Angola in the seventeenth century; such markets were only found in Portugal, Brazil and the Americas.[78] Those who have argued for the existence of markets in Angola – such as Heintze, Miller, Ferreira and Boxer – have missed the point since they were ignorant of the 1626 changes.[79] Documentary sources available to us do not support their speculations.[80] From the accounts of both Antonio Bezerra Fajardo and Frei Melchior da Conceicam, there is no reason to equate *kitanda* (feiras or markets) with a market at which enslaved people were to be found for sale. Angolan institutions and practices cannot be held responsible for the ruthless methods (including kidnapping) used by the Portuguese to capture people in the region. Furthermore, Mendonça's claim in the Vatican refutes this interpretation.[81] Angolans saw *kitanda* as places for the exchange of goods but nevers as marketplaces for the sale of human beings. People in West Central Africa never conducted the sale of human beings as a business in an open space. People in Angola who had been unjustly 'convicted' of a crime they did not commit, 'snatched', 'kidnapped' or 'stolen' from their families could not be stocked and sold in a public space. The testimonies of former enslaved Africans such as Equiano,

---

[78] 'Natural-born' Africans were citizens (members of the clan or inhabitants of the territory controlled by a king) and were distinguished from non citizens (other Africans who were not part of the clan and might have been captured in wars). For the existence of slave markets in Portugal and Brazil in the sixteenth and later in the seventeenth, eighteenth and nineteenth centuries, see Cardinal Alexandrino 'Relazione del Viaggio, Fatto Dall Ilmo' and Robert Edgar Conrad, *Children of God's Fire: A Documentary History of Black Slaves in Brazil*, 3rd ed., University Park, PA: Pennsylvania State University Press, 1997. See also Pitta, *Provincia da Bahia*. On practices of slavery in Europe prior to the Europeans arrival in Africa, see Painter, *The History of White People*, and Blackburn, *The American Crucible*.

[79] The use of *kitanda* (feiras or markets) as places for exchange of produce was widespread in Angola, but they were not used as for the sale of human beings. Fajardo's enquiry in the region in the seventeenth century attested to this fact. See the High Court of Appeal 'Relação de Antonio Bezerra Fajardo'. On the existence of markets and their importance for *sobas*, see Heintze, *Angola nos Séculos XVI e XVII*; see also Vansina, 'Long-Distance Trade-Routes'; Miller, *Kings and Kinsmen*; Miller, 'Capitalism and Slaving'; Heintze, 'Ngonga a Mwiza'; Ferreira, *Feiras e Presídios*; Vansina, 'Ambaca Society'; and Boxer (ed.), *South China in the Sixteenth Century*.

[80] See High Court of Appeal, 'Relação de Antonio Bezerra Fajardo'; Frei Melchior da Conceicam, 'Alvaras, Cartas, Provizioes, Regimentos'.

[81] See APF, SOCG, fls. 54 and 58.

Guguano, Baquaqua and so on tell us a different story;[82] Mendonça's court case gives us a different, more accurate understanding of what the enslavement of Africans in the region was like.[83] Angolan markets such as those of 'S. José do Ecncoje, Dondo, Lembo, Lucamba and Ambaka's presídio, were created by the Portuguese'.[84] They were attached to local *presidios* (Portuguese outposts) and regulated by the authority in Luanda as well as their respective captains and captains-major. Early exchange of enslaved Africans was taking place in *presidios*. These forced negotiations between the Portuguese and their conquered allies' *sobas* were carried out in the outposts. Even the *sobas* did not consent to them.[85]

From the sixteenth century onwards, court cases in West Central Africa were being run under the Portuguese legal system in conquered areas.[86] From the sixteenth century, in the conquered zones in Angola, court cases were run by the Portuguese from their *presidios*.[87] People employed by captains-major in theses outposts were overriding court cases in favour of the captains who in turn were doing a service for the governor.[88] After the

---

[82] Equiano, *The Interesting Narrative*; see also Cugoano, *Thoughts and Sentiments*; Mahommah Gardo Baquaqua, *Biography of Mahommah G. Baquaqua, a Native of Zoogoo, in the Interior of Africa (a convert of Christianity), with a Description of that Part of the World, Including the Manners and Customs of the Inhabitants*, Chapel Hill, NC: University of North Carolina [1854] 2001, and see High Court of Appeal 'Relação de Antonio Bezerra Fajardo'.

[83] Since the historians do not understand the underlying mechanism of enslavement in West Central Africa, the central focus of their studies is on markets as places for the enslaved or at least places in which slavery transactions took place, rather than what they were: markets for exchange of local produce. The historians created the misleading idea of a society with slave markets, believed to be governed by *sobas* who were seen as willing to sell human beings as goods for a transnational market in the Americas. Thus, the brutal reality of a legalised taxation system – introduced in the seventeenth century and rife in the eighteenth- and nineteenth-century Angolan society, controlled by the armed Portuguese over conquered subjects – was overlooked. See Ferreira, *Feiras e Presídios*, pp. 19–22; 25–28; 31–48, and 39–44. See also Vansina, 'Ambaca Society'. For further analysis, see Miller, *Kings and Kinsmen*; and Ferreira, *Cross-Cultural Exchange*. For the political, commercial and market control of the region by the Portuguese, see Flávia Maria de Carvalho, 'O Reino do Ndongo no Contexto da Restauração: Mbundus, Portugueses e Holandeses na África Centro Ocidental', *Sankofa. Revista de História da África e de Estudos da Diáspora Africana*, 4(7), 2011, pp. 7–30.

[84] See Ferreira, *Feiras e Presídios*, p. 34. For full detail of these proceedings in the outpost *mocanos*, see Frei Melchior da Conceicam, 'Alvaras, Cartas, Provizioes, Regimentos'.

[85] For a detailed discussion of the Portuguese method of acquiring enslaved Angolans, see Frei Melchior da Conceicam, 'Alvaras, Cartas, Provizioes, Regimentos'.

[86] See 'Regimento de D. Manuel a Simão da Silva', pp. 233–234.

[87] See 'Consulta do Conselho Ultramarino', AHU., Cód. 554, fs. 90v.-91v., 7 March 1698, fol. 90v; and see also Frei Melchior da Conceicam, 'Alvaras, Cartas, Provizioes, Regimentos'.

[88] See Frei Melchior da Conceicam, 'Alvaras, Cartas, Provizioes, Regimentos'.

Dutch occupation of Angola (1641–1648), there was a major shift in terms of the Portuguese military organisation in Angola. From 1666, each *presidio* – such as Mbaka, Cambambe, Massangano or Muxima – was composed of: one captain, one captain-major and twenty-five soldiers.[89] They were manned with *pumbeiros* and *Quimbar* (a pejorative term used to describe 'a half-civilised Black person' that comes back to his village after living for sometimes in towns where the Portuguese were).[90]

The most significant element of the outposts was the incorporation of *mocano*[91] in them. For each *mocano* to carry out their deliberation in these outposts, the following members had to be present: governor, captain, tribunal priest, secretary, scribe and eyewitnesses.[92] The court's officials employed in these outposts were charged with the task of obtaining enslaved people from local *sobas* under the control of Portuguese outposts by false verdicts. These controlled *sobas* were obliged to accept 'forced gifts' or 'buttering-up gifts' such as *ocombas* (okombas) and *ynfucas* (infucas) from the captain and captain-major of the outposts.[93] *Ocombas* and *ynfucas* are Kimbundu words. How these terms were used in a 'disciplinary power'[94] on conquered *sobas* in Angola are described by Sousa himself, as stated by Brásio:

according to Fernão de Sousa, *ocombas* [okombas] consists of a pearl of wine, cloth, or another good that the captain of the *presidio* [Portuguese outpost] send to *sobas* of his district, or any other White person similarly send to the *soba*, with the

---

[89] For a detailed discussion of *presidios* and their reform, see Gastão Sousa Dias, 'A Defesa de Angola: a Estratégia Militar Portuguesa no Período da Grande Guerra, do Gapitão Gastão Sousa Dias', *Revista Militar*, 1932, pp. 598–620.

[90] See Brásio, *Monumenta Missionaria Africana*, vol. VII, p. 507, 'preto meio civilizado que volta das localidades de certa importância para o sertão'.

[91] *Mocano* or *mucano*, in the Kimbundu language, means tribunal or legal dispute. On the penal system in Angola, see Cadornega, *História Geral*, vol. II, pp. 350–353. The *mocano* in the outposts cannot be confused with the *mocano* locally run by the Portuguese. These *mocanos* run by the Portuguese in the seventeenth century were under direct control of the Portuguese and their appointed officials.

[92] See Frei Melchior da Conceicam, 'Alvaras, Cartas, Provizioes, Regimentos'.

[93] See Carta do Governador Fernão de Sousa a El-Rei Angola-are [a letter of Governor Fernão de Sousa to the King and Angolans], BAL – Ms. 51-VIII-30, fls. 242-242v, 27 March 1627; also, in MMA, vol. IX, pp. 506–507.

[94] Foucault used the term 'disciplinary power' to show how techniques were deployed in nineteenth century to punish dissident people who were not behaving according to the accepted rules. The intent here is to make these people behave via punishment, hence, to making them become 'docile bodies'. See Foucault, *Discipline and Punish*; Schwan, Anne and Shapiro, Stephen, *How to Read Foucault's Discipline and Punish*, London: Pluto Press, 2011; M. Sargiacomo, 'Michel Foucault, Discipline and Punish: The Birth of the Priso', *Journal of Management and Governance*, 13(3), 2009, pp. 269-280.

intention that the soba pay him back. They do it with the pretence of friendship and of a good relationship. According to the same Fernão de Sousa, another gift, *Ynfutas* [infutas] consists of selling the 'forced gift' or 'buttering up gift' to the sobas, with kind words and ways in which it does not appear to them that they will either pay or that they will not pay it later. They give them these goods either on request or by force, and then the time passes by, they then return to demand that these gifts be paid back, under the penalty of arresting their women, children, and vassals (children of *Morinda*) who are free, and to sell them as slaves[95].

Another Kimbundu term used in the period was *encombros* or *emcombos*, meaning a muted goat, which I will discuss later in this chapter. *Emcombos*, also known as *emponda* or *mponda*, was a traditional gift given to appease a person high in the hierarchy or establish a friendship with him/her. It was a form of a contract or testament that made an agreement binding and committed both parties to peaceful interaction. To make it legal and binding required the presence of high dignitaries such as ambassadors who were witnesses of the agreement and were responsible for taking the gift with them back to the king. In Cadornega we have a case in which an agreement was made between the Portuguese living in Luanda, who feared an imminent attack from the powerful army of *soba* Mani Mulaza, 'Mani Sundi' of Loango or Zaire in the seventeenth century. The Portuguese in Luanda did not have a powerful army to repel him; they decided that the best thing for them was to appease him before he sent his army against them. For this agreement to be made, Mani Mulaza sent his *macunges* or 'ambassadors' to seal the agreement. It was made binding by *emcombos*, accompanied by *motetes de Luco*, which were baskets made of palm trees (they might give four baskets of maize flour or *fuba*). This was not a payment in enslaved people as the Portuguese made it to be when they came to dominate politics and the economy of the time for the people they conquered in Angola[96].

Customary practices such as *ocombas* and *ynfucas* used for building communities in West Central Africa were used by the Portuguese for their

---

[95] Brásio, *Monumenta Missionaria Africana*, vol. VII, pp. 506–507, '[Ocomba] segundo Fernão de Sousa consiste em mandar o capitão do presídioaos sobas do seu distrito, ou qualquer outro branco ao soba com que corre, uma peroleira de vinho, ou pano, ou outra fazenda, com tenção de lha pagar o soba, com fingimento de amizade e boa correspondência. [Ynfucas] consiste, segundo o mesmo Fernão de Sousa, em vender aos sobas de fiado, por modos e palavras que lhes parece que ou não pagarão ou o farão tarde, pondo-lhes as fazendas por pedidos ou por força, e passado certo tempo exigindo que lhas paguem, sob pena de lhes prenderem as mulheres, filhos e vassalos (filhos da Morinda) que são forros, e de os venderem como escravos.'

[96] See Cadornega, *História Geral*, III, pp. 277–280.

own ends. They appropriated these terms, which sounded natural to the Mbundu people, but the way they applied them changed the Angolans' understanding of them. To the outside world these terms would appear to be used in accordance with Mbundu practices. However, they were taken out of context and used to serve a purpose for which they were not intended – to obtain slaves. The buying and selling of enslaved people was not an established practice; the Portuguese aligned their criminal acts with the Angolans' cultural practices.[97]

The approach to studying African history and the history of Africans' involvement in the Atlantic slave trade has been centred on two not entirely exclusive axes. On the one hand are those who sought an understanding of the African past from broad African institutional practices and argued for a mutual relationship based on give and take, i.e. that Africans were active players in Atlantic history. Thornton argues that Africans contributed to world history in the same way as their European counterparts.[98] On the other are those who argued that Africans' relations with Europeans were based on an unequal footing. For Lovejoy, as far as the Atlantic slave trade was concerned, Africans participated by using European systems to advance their economic and political ambition.[99] It is my position that the argument that Africans were positively involved in world history needs to be carefully made so as not to make Africans participants in a crime they did not commit or align them to a European system that wanted to annihilate them and which they were actually

---

[97] See Frei Melchior da Conceicam, 'Alvaras, Cartas, Provizioes, Regimentos'.
[98] For further discussion of European and African relations, see Thornton, *Africa and Africans*; John K. Thornton, *A Cultural History of the Atlantic World, 1250–1820*, Cambridge: Cambridge University Press, 2012; Jan Vansina, *How Societies Are Born: Governance in West Central Africa before 1600*, Charlottesville, VA: University of Virginia Press, 2004; Jan Vansina, *Kingdoms of the Savanna*, Madison, WI: University of Wisconsin Press, 1968; and Jan Vansina, *Paths in the Rainforests: Toward a History of Political Tradition in Equatorial Africa*, Madison, WI: University of Wisconsin Press, 1990; Philip J. Havik, *Silences and Soundbites: The Gendered Dynamics of Trade and Brokerage in the Pre-Colonial Guinea Bissau Region*, Münster: Lit Verlag, 2004; Philip D. Curtin, *Economic Change in Precolonial Africa: Senegambia in the Era of the Slave Trade*, Madison, WI: University of Wisconsin, vol. I. 1975; Philip D Curtin, Steven Feierman, Leonard Thompson and Jan Vansina, *African History: From Earliest Times to Independence*, Edinburgh: Longman Pearson Education, 1995; David Birmingham, *Empire in Africa: Angola and Its Neighbors – Research in International Studies*, Africa Series, Athens, OH: Ohio University Press, 2006; and Rodney, *How Europe Underdeveloped Africa*.
[99] See Lovejoy, *Transformations in Slavery*, and Paul E. Lovejoy and Nicholas Rogers, *Unfree Labour in the Development of the Atlantic World*, London: Frank Cass Publishers, 1995.

fighting against.[100] We also need to guard against the position that tends to see African encounters with Europeans as asymmetrical.[101] Documentary sources from the period do not support this claim fully.[102] The Atlantic exchange between Africa and the Americas took place in the initial phase in the fifteenth and sixteenth centuries on an equal footing. However, even in these early centuries of contact, relations were still influenced by other elements based on coercion and persuasion. In its first contact with the region of West Central Africa, Portugal sought a contractual agreement: this led to the vassalship of conquered African rulers under legal, economic and political systems already in existence in Europe.[103] Dom Manuel's brief to his counterpart Afonso I stated that: 'we will send him our judge that administer legal proceedings in his Kingdoms in accordance with our system and in the same way this applies to things relating to war that they be carrying out in our manner from here'.[104] The legal system in West Central Africa was thus transformed. In this brief Manuel made it clear to Afonso I that the 'slaves, likewise copper and ivory'[105] were the main trade objectives that Portugal wanted to consolidate in Kongo. This document undermines Curto's argument on the legality of slavery in West Central

---

[100] Painter, *The History of White People*.

[101] For discussion of the asymmetrical relationship between Europeans and Africans in the sixteenth and seventeenth centuries, see Lingna Nafafé, *Colonial Encounters* and José Lingna Nafafé, 'Europe in Africa and Africa in Europe: Rethinking Postcolonial Space, Cultural Encounters and Hybridity', *European Journal of Social Theory*, 16(1), 2013, pp. 51–68.

[102] For discussion of the encounter between Europeans and Africans, see Lingna Nafafé, *Colonial Encounters* and Rodney, *History of the Upper Guinea Coast* and Jerome Münzer, 'Itinerarium, De Inventione Africae Maritimae et Occidentalis Videclicet Genee Per Infantem Heinrichum Portugallie', fls. 280–88, 1494.

[103] For further debate on the application of the European system in Africa, see Blackburn, *The American Crucible*, pp. 20–24. Historians have focused on the economic dimension of the slave trade and not on its legal basis, which stems from the seventeenth century. Therefore, their key argument for the slave trade was to understand the need to obtain enslaved Africans for the Americas. This has led some historians to emphasise the importance of *kitanda – feiras* (as slave markets, which they are not), making it look as though slavery was a normal practice among the Angolans. On market see Umbundu terms such as a *quitanda – kitanda, itanda –* fair or market, Cadornega, *História Geral*, I, p. 620. See also Heintze, 'Ngonga a Mwiza'; Heintze, *Angola nos Séculos XVI e XVII*; Candido, 'Conquest, Occupation, Colonialism and Exclusion'; Mariana P. Candido, 'O Limite Tênue entre a Liberdade e Escravidão em Benguela durante a era do comércio transatlântico', *Afro-Ásia* 47, 2013, pp. 239–268.

[104] See 'Regimento de D. Manuel a Simão da Silva (1512)', pp. 233-234, 'nós lhe emviarmos huũa pesoa nosa que menestrase as cousas da justiça em seus, p. 234 – rranta noso costume e asy tambem êtemdese nas cousas da gueerra e a metese em uso ao modo de cá'.

[105] See 'Regimento de D. Manuel a Simão da Silva (1512)', pp. 233-234, pp. 239-240 'assim de escravos como de cobre e marfim'.

Africa.[106] Because of the violence to which West Central African people were subjected, the Portuguese Overseas Council in 1698 introduced a new measure under which the creation of courts (*mocanos*) were to be brought to centres of the Portuguese control to 'avoid such sensitive violence ... to the miserable Africans'.[107] However, the violence used to secure enslaved Africans was never halted. *Mocanos* in the City of Luanda and outposts were used simply to disguise the aim of the project, which was to enslave Angolans.[108]

Having set out the context and historiographical debates arising from it, the rest of this chapter moves on to look at a specific case involving Correia de Sousa, governor of Luanda City Council (*Senado da Camara da Cidade de Luanda*) because it demonstrates how economic interests were at play in Angola. Furthermore, it shows the questioning of the slave trade by Jesuit priests and the involvement in it by the Church and the Luso-Hispanic Crown, as well as the factual illegality of the slave trade even within Portuguese jurisdiction, given its alliances with the Angolan and Kongolese Christian kings. All this is vital for our understanding of Mendonça's argument that the slave trade was preposterous and that it was imperative that African enslavement in the Atlantic be abolished.

The first step is to look at the structure of the Municipal Council of Luanda, and to examine how treachery was used to capture and enslave the Kazanze and Bumbi people who lived in the region and who were vassals of Kongo. We will then explore the intervention made by the crown judge, Antonio Bezerra Fajrado, who was sent to Angola to look into injustices against Angolans and Kongolese. Correia de Sousa's abuses during his period of rule included causing unrest in Luanda, which we will also examine. We then engage with Correia de Sousa's dispute with Gaspar Álvares, a Portuguese Christian merchant who lived in Luanda

---

[106] See Curto, 'Experiences of Enslavement' and Curto, 'The Story of Nbena, 1817–20'.
[107] See 'Consulta do Conselho Ultramarino', AHU., Cód. 554, fs. 90v.-91v., 7 March 1698, fol. 90v, 'e por se lhe euitar estas violências taõ sençiueis ... nos mizeraueis negros'.
[108] By the eighteenth and nineteenth centuries the Angolan judicial system was operating in a *mindele* (docile) way, and was adulterated by the imported Portuguese legal practices. *Mindele* is a Mbundu term used to describe a Mbundu individual who adopted European customs or culture and behaved accordingly, considering him- or herself civilised. The term is used here to describe legal proceedings in Angola after the change introduced by Sousa in 1626. For the use of the term, see Cadornega, *História Geral*, I, p. 617. See also Frei Melchior da Conceicam, 'Alvaras, Cartas, Provizioes, Regimentos'. By the mid-seventeenth century, the Portuguese Crown had made changes to legal proceedings in Angola, under which Portuguese judicial officers were to be part of the local court's proceedings in Angola, AHU, cód. 17, Consultas Mixtas, 18 July 1679, fl., 301, and AHU, cód. 17, fls. 59–59v, 21 August 1672.

and was one the wealthiest traders in Angola. His story clearly shows the double standards of the Church's involvement in the slave trade. Finally, we take a critical look at the appeal by King Pedro II of Kongo (1622–1624) to return the Kazanze and Bumbi people from Brazil, where they had been taken illegally.

The chapter is based on rich and newly discovered archival sources about the cases, mainly the correspondence of Correia de Sousa, letters from Jesuit and Italian priests reporting to the Crown and the Vatican, correspondence from the administration of the Crown in Madrid and Fajardo's appeals. This data has not been used by Africanists, Atlanticists or historians of West Central Africa, most of whom have focused on the eighteenth and nineteenth centuries.[109]

1.1 THE STRUCTURE OF THE LUANDA CITY COUNCIL

The Municipal City Council of Luanda was composed of governors, a senior crown judge, scribes, judges and other functionaries employed by the council and the Vatican, such as ordinary judges, officers, councillors, an attorney, prison officers, a porter and apostolic notaries. The governors of Luanda, like those in Salvador and Rio de Janeiro, were mainly members of the aristocracy,[110] whose interests were quite different to those of the city residents and the Kongo and Angolan kings. There were two ordinary judges, three councillors and one procurator (attorney) or councillor attorney of the city. Ordinary judges were adjudicators, likely to support the Crown's interests over those of city dwellers and plantation owners. Councillors were administrators who functioned as tax officers, fixed the price of goods and deliberated over the public interest with regard to the needs of local business. The attorneys were executive legal representatives, who represented the interests of the city

---

[109] Heintze, 'Ngonga a Mwiza'; Heintze, *Angola nos Séculos XVI e XVII*; Birmingham, *Trade and Conquest*; Ferreira, *Cross-Cultural Exchange*; Curto, 'Experiences of Enslavement'; Curto, 'The Story of Nbena, 1817–20'; Vansina, 'Long-Distance Trade-Routes'; Miller, *Kings and Kinsmen*; Curtin et al., *African History: From Earliest Times*; Candido, 'Conquest, Occupation, Colonialism and Exclusion'; Candido, 'O Limite Tênue'; Linda M. Heywood and John Thornton, *Central Africans and Cultural Transformations in the American Diaspora*, Cambridge: Cambridge University Press; Lovejoy and Rogers, *Unfree Labour in the Development of the Atlantic World*; Lovejoy, *Transformations in Slavery*; Manning, *Slavery and African Life*; Gomes, *Histórias de Quilombolas*; and Ferreira, *Feiras e Presídios*.

[110] Arlindo Manuel Caldeira, 'Dimensão Sociopolítica do Município de Luanda Durante o Século XVII', *Cadernos de Estudos Africanos*, 30, 2015, p. 43.

council before the Royal Court of Lisbon. Municipal council officers were generally elected from the pool of city dwellers deemed reputable people, or 'good-men'.[111] They could be of any nationality – Luanda was significantly multinational, with Flemish, German, Spanish and New Christian inhabitants – and could also be members of the city council.[112] Aside from the council officers, there was a scribe or secretary who was a council functionary whose role included fixing the price of goods and maintaining control of the currency and trade regulations. The scribe was also charged with writing official documents. There was also a porter, who acted as a messenger and publicly announced the decisions of the Municipal City Council. A minister of prisons was responsible for the imprisonment of criminals and war captives.

In the City of Luanda, there were also several other roles in the Municipal Council. Among them was the apostolic notary. At first sight, the apostolic notary would appear to be an ecclesiastical position, but the notaries' political role in feeding back information to the Roman Curia cannot be ignored. There were apostolic notaries in most European countries and in other countries where Christianity was established, including Kongo.[113] In Angola, there were also Jesuit religious leaders who played an influential role in the politics of the Municipal Council of Luanda and who, on several occasions, acted as interim governors.[114] There was also a senior crown judge, whose role was to defend the interests of the Crown and the Crown's subjects in Luanda. By 1665, there were 326 European residents in Angola, 132 of whom were in the city and 124 of whom were in the conquest zone.[115] More than 1,000 Portuguese residents were living in Kongo in 1623.[116] The economic interests of these Portuguese residents often clashed with those of the Crown, particularly around the subject of taxes, which were often negotiated in the Crown's favour.

In 1665 the Municipal Council of Luanda, together with the Portuguese residents, put forward a motion responding to the Crown's intention to increase the annual tax. The Crown needed to pay a 'dowry'

---

[111] João Adolfo Hansen, 'Representações da Cidade de Salvador no Século XVII', *Sibila Sibila, Revista de poesia e crítica literária*, 2010, http://sibila.com.br/mapa-da-lingua/representacoes-da-cidade-de-salvador-no-seculo-xvii/3343.

[112] For further discussion see Caldeira, 'Dimensão Sociopolítica', pp. 33–37.

[113] See 'Relaçaõ para o Ill.mo Sñr Collector'. See also 'Relação do Padre Mateus Cardoso' [Padre Mateus Cardoso's High Court of Appeal], Archivum Romanum Societatis Iesu (ARSI), las., cód. 55, fls. 51–54v; MMA, vo. VII, pp. 176–193.

[114] Fryer Simão de Mascarenhas, governor and captain general (1623–1624).

[115] See Delgado's note in Cadornega, *História Geral*, vol. II, p. 533.

[116] See 'Relaçaõ para o Ill.mo Sñr Collector'.

of 4 million cruzados to the English, for losses accrued when they supported the Portuguese in the Dutch war in Brazil. Portuguese municipal councils in Angola and Brazil were ordered to contribute to this sum. The Municipal Council of Luanda rejected the Crown's demand for 22,500 cruzados per year in taxes. In response, the Crown instead proposed 360,000 cruzados divided into twenty-four instalments over sixteen years. Eventually, the council agreed to pay 15,000 cruzados annually over 24 years.[117] Meanwhile, residents of Pernambuco, Brazil, paid 400,000 cruzados at the rate of 25,000 per year for a period of sixteen years,[118] and Bahia residents paid 1,280,000 cruzados at the rate of 80,000 per year for a period of sixteen years.[119]

Outside the Angolan context, the Crown appears to have been the victim of its own decrees, which were often discarded by ruthless governors or municipal councils pursuing their own interests. Gilberto Freyre, the famous Brazilian sociologist, has reviewed the power and economic relations between the municipal councils and the Crown in the Atlantic. He argues that 'the king of Portugal was a ruler without government. The Municipal Council members, the words of these political families, soon limited the power of the Kings and later on imperialism itself.'[120] The political environment in Angola is telling. Issues between the Crown, governors and other members of the Municipal Council of Luanda (see Figure 5) dated back to the inception of the Council of Luanda in the sixteenth century, when the Portuguese Royal House of Aviz (1385–1580) was slow to grant the Portuguese general Paulo Dias de Novais a charter to become the first captain and governor of Luanda in 1571. When the charter was finally passed, Novais began to lay the foundations for what would become the Municipal Council of Luanda in 1575. This process took place against the backdrop of uneasy relationships with the kings of Kongo and Angola. It has been claimed

---

[117] See Cadornega, *História Geral*, vol. II, p. 533.
[118] See *Documentos Históricos do Arquivo Municipal de Salvador*, vol. V, 1928, pp. 431–433.
[119] See *Documentos Históricos do Arquivo Municipal de Salvador*. Atas da câmara (DHAMAC), vol. IV, 1949. 136–140. For a detailed discussion of the treaty between England and Portugal, see Edgar Prestage, *As Relações Diplomáticas de Portugal com a França, Inglaterra e Holanda de 1640 a 1668*, Coimbra: Imprensa da Universidade, 1928, pp. 148–149; and Borges de Castro et al., *Collecção dos Tratados, Convenções, Contratos e Actos Publicos: Celebrados Entre a Coroa de Portugal e as Mais Potencias Desde 1640 ate ao Presente*, Lisbon: Imprensa Nacional, 1856.
[120] Gilberto Freyre, *Casa Grande & Senzala, Formação da Família Brasileira Sob o Regime de Economia Patriarcal*, 4th ed., Rio de Janeiro: Livraria José Olympio, 1943, p. 108.

Municipal Council of Luanda & Politics of the Portuguese 79

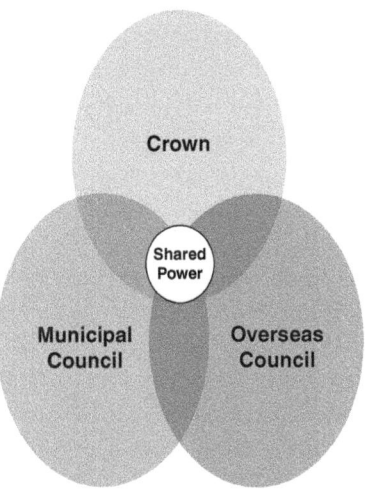

FIGURE 5 Intersection of power between the Crown, the Portuguese Overseas Council and the Municipal Council of Luanda. By the author.

that Novais was granted a stake in Luanda's settlement by the king of Kongo, although there is no evidence of this in archives in either Portugal or Angola.[121] Reference is, however, made to the good will of Kongo's authorities in allowing the Portuguese settlement even after the restoration of the House of Braganza (1640–1910) to the thrones of Brazil and Portugal. In the interim, between the ruling periods of the Aviz and the Braganza, the House of Habsburg (1581–1640) and the Hispanic-Portuguese Crown were distracted by the opposing lures of trade in Angola and in Brazil.[122]

---

[121] Brásio has stated that there was no evidence of this in either the Angolan and or the Portuguese archives, MAA, p. 468.
[122] The House of Habsburg in Portugal was also known as the Philippine Dynasty. It was the third Royal House of Portugal (1580–1640) and followed the second dynasty, the House of Aviz (1385–1580). Braganza was a Portuguese dynasty; it came to power after Portugal separated from Spain and ruled from 1640 to 1910. See Ignacio de Vilhena Barbosa, *As Cidades e Villas da Monarchia Portugueza que Teem Brasão d'Armas: Volume I*, Lisbon: Typographia do Panorama 1860; Edward McMurdo, *History of Portugal: Volume 3*, London: S. Low, Marston, Searle, & Rivington, 1889, and Leslie Bethell, *The Cambridge History of Latin America*, Cambridge: Cambridge University Press, 1984.

To maintain trade and to continue the exploration of Angola, especially with regard to the exploitation of the region's metal deposits (with silver being of particular importance), the Portuguese Crown needed to nurture a local labour force. However, the lucrative plantations of Brazil also required African labour. Angola and Brazil both held great potential for economic gain, and the Crown sought to maintain a fine balance between the two. In both regions, however, the governors' interests lay primarily in creating personal wealth, which was done most quickly through the Atlantic slave trade. The governors of Luanda often had businesses in Brazil because many of them came from there; they exploited Angola, enslaving its people and sending them to work on their sugar plantations in Brazil. These conflicting interests created great and unceasing tension between the governors, the Muncipal City Council of Luanda, the Crown and the *sobas* and African kings in the region. The business of slavery was central to everything that was done in Angola. Faria, a Portuguese economist of the seventeenth century, stated that the wealth accrued from Africa made it possible for the Crown in Portugal to conquer the Far East and Brazil. He declared:

> it is of note to those who have news of business of this Kingdom [Portugal] that the concentration and rights of the Coast of Guinea have been for many years the principal Revenue of the Crown of Portugal, and with it has become wealthy. And it gave it leverage to conquer the Orient and the New World. With it came the right of the import from Cape Verde, and Rivers of Guinea, Mina, São Tomé and Angola nearing 200,000 per annum.[123]

Let us now take a closer look at Governor Correia de Sousa's struggle with wealthy businessman Gaspar Álvares for control of the slave trade. Álvares had made his fortune from the slave trade in the region. The case in question deals with Correia de Sousa's interaction with the City Council and Álvares, and the breakdown of relations over their conflicting opinions on the methods to be used to secure enslaved Angolans in the region. Part of the problem with Álvares's business was that the Church and the Jesuit College of Luanda were not willing to challenge him for his involvement in the slave trade and the brutality that went with it; rather,

---

[123] For detailed information, see Faria, 'Sobre a Fundação de Seminários', pp. 697–698, 'notório hé a quem tem noticia das cousas deste Reyno, que a contratação e direitos da Costa de Guiné foraõ por muitos annos a principal Renda da Goroa de Portugal, e a com que elle se enriqueceo, e lhe deu cabedal pera poderem fazer as conquistas do Oriente e Nouo Mundo, porque importauaõ os direitos do Cabo Verde, e Rios de Guiné, Mina, S. Thomé e Angola, perto de duzentos contos'.

they wanted to appropriate his wealth for the Church. It is thus through the prism of this marriage of convenience between the Church and the economic sphere that Mendonça's court case is to be comprehended. Indeed, the official silence from the Church and the Vatican was one of the major concerns of Mendonça and the confraternities of Black Brotherhoods in Africa, Brazil, Portugal and Spain. I will also look at the challenge by the Kongolese authorities about the injustice of their subjects being taken into slavery, and the involvement of the Spanish Crown in Madrid (the Philippine administration that united the crowns of Spain and Portugal), which took a different view on enslaved Kongolese. They were interested in the slave trade rather than administrating justice for the Angolans and Kongolese taken to Brazil as enslaved people illegally. This lack of justice for the millions who had been enslaved in the Americas constituted the basis of Mendonça's cry for freedom.[124]

1.2 CORREIA DE SOUSA, THE TREACHERY AND SEIZING OF KAZANZE PEOPLE, A VASSAL OF KONGO

Correia de Sousa's account of slave-trading injustice related to the Kazanze people, Luanda's neighbours and vassals of the kingdom of Kongo, and the case of Bumbi (a trading town in Kongo). These are among many stories from the region characterised by what Mendonça described in his presentation in the Vatican as 'kidnapping' and 'treacherous' methods of capturing Africans. Correia de Sousa's account is supported by reports made by other governors of the period, including André Vidal de Negreiros (1661-1666) and Manuel Cerveira Pereira (1603-1607 and 1615-1617) who also deployed these methods during their tenures in Angola. The demand for African labour in Brazil's sugar plantations and for use in general agriculture and mining increased the incentive for war in Angola to supply Angolans for the slave market.[125] Carl Wadström, in his *Essay on Colonization, Particularly Applied to the Western Coast of Africa* (1794), stated that the Atlantic slave trade began with the Italians, who wanted to open a market in the New World. Once their attempt to recruit Indigenous Americans had failed, they turned

---

[124] See António Brásio, Capítulos da Embaixada do Rei do Kongo, 'Eminetissimi e Reuerendissimi Signori' [Most Emminent and Reverend Lord], APF – SRCG, vol. 247, fls. 165-165v, 9 May 1648, pp. 139-144. See especially his criticism of Kongo's involvement in slavery in footnote 14, MMA, vol. X, p. 142.

[125] See Carl Bernhard Wadström, *An Essay on Colonization, Particularly Applied to the Western Coast of Africa*. London: Darton and Harvey, 1794.

their attention to supplying enslaved Africans as labourers on the sugar plantations:

> ... without undervaluing the West Indian sugar colonies, we may venture to observe, that their importance, nay, according to the planters themselves, their very existence, depends on Africa. That continent supplies them with slaves, whom they call by the soft name of, 'Negro labourers,' and who alone confer a value on their property. Some affirm, with much probability, that they also owe to Africa the very object of their labours.[126]

Wadström's remarks show how slavery permeated Atlantic society, and why enslavement of Africans persisted for so long. They also suggest the reason for the silence in connection to liberation and demonstrates the flaw in current historiography on Atlantic slavery about Africans' willingness to participate in the slave trade.

Returning to the issue at hand, Correia de Sousa's case is significant in terms of our understanding of the mechanisms of slave capture and its legality, which is often neglected when debating issues relating to Atlantic slavery. It is also significant in delineating the guiding principle that steered the municipal councils and their governors, and their relationships with the African ruling classes in West Central Africa.

Prior to his arrival in Angola on 4 October 1621,[127] Correia de Sousa received a letter from the former governor of Angola, Manuel Cerveira Pereira (1603–1607 and 1615–1617). Pereira had also founded the city of São Philipe in Benguela, Angola, in 1617,[128] and he wrote the letter in question from there, urging Correia de Sousa to provide him with military personnel. Pereira stated that he had fifty-five people,[129] old and young, and that he himself was not in good health: he had an ulcerated arm and was also blind in his left eye. Nonetheless, he was ready to make battle with the enemy, who in his view recognised their miserable state. This letter became a turning point for Correia de Sousa's mission in Angola because it indicated what he needed to do.

On the day he received the letter, Correia de Sousa was aboard a ship to Luanda. He wrote a letter to the king of Spain regarding the news from Pereira, stating: '... all is in turmoil and in a confused state. If I could but

---

[126] Wadström, *An Essay on Colonization*, p. 4.
[127] Pereira's letter was filed in 'Correspondência de Manuel Cerveira Pereira e Do Governador de Angola' [Correspondence of Manuel Cerveira Pereira to the Governor of Angola], MMA, vol. VI, 4 October 1621, p. 584.
[128] See Cadornega, *História Geral*, vol. III, p. 465.
[129] See 'Correspondência de Manuel Cerveira Pereira e Do Governador de Angola'. In the letter of 7 November 1621, Pereira mentioned fifty people.

deal with the issues of the soldiers, where there is a lot to be done in so little time, and they are of very low morale. I will offer Angola to God, in all that is in me, I will serve Your Majesty with good will.'[130] However marginal it may sound, this statement led to the invasion of Kazanze; Correia de Sousa later betrayed the Kazanze people and waged war on them to appease the soldiers fighting in Angola and give them land, since their wages had not been paid.

While in Angola, Correia de Sousa met with Njinga, who was not queen at the time but was a *macunze* or ambassador of her brother King Mbandi.[131] Mbandi had sent Njinga to Luanda to negotiate a peace agreement between the Portuguese and the kingdom of Ndongo. Njinga made it clear to Correia de Sousa that his trade terms, which included a proposal to obtain enslaved people from Ndongo, were not acceptable.[132] She explained that while Correia de Sousa's predecessor, Luís Mendes de Vasconcelos (1617-1621), had had temporary success in Ndongo, forcing Mbandi out to the Kindonga islands on the River Coanza, it would be a mistake for Correia de Sousa to take this as a sign of vassalship and attempt to make Mbandi pay tax in enslaved people. Mbandi was not a conquered king and the Ndongo kingdom was still in Mbandi's hands. If Correia de Sousa wanted to enter into trade with Mbandi and Ndongo, it had to be on the basis of different merchandise, not enslaved Africans. The outcome of that meeting forced Correia de Sousa to rethink his approach to trading and obtaining enslaved people from the Ndongo and Matamba regions. He dispatched his own embassy to Ndongo to negotiate with Mbandi in the Kindonga islands. That delegation included 'Father Dionizio de Faria Barreto, a son of the land [Native of Angola], who spoke the language well, and with him, Manoel Dias, and after they arrived on the islands, they offered him peace and friendship on the part of the governor; from there they left via inland.'[133] The message that came back from that mission was a firm demand from Mbandi regarding the sovereignty of Ndongo. The

---

[130] On the same day, 4 October, Correia de Sousa arrived in Benguela. Following a probable meeting with Pereira there, he landed in Luanda on 12 October 1621, according to 'Resposta do Governador' in 'Correspondência de Manuel Cerveira Pereira e do Governador de Angola', MMA, vol. VI, 4 October 1621, p. 585: see also Cadornega, *História Geral*, vol. II, p.566.

[131] For further discussion of Queen Njinga's later rule, see Heywood, *Njinga of Angola*.

[132] Birmingham, *Trade and Conquest*, pp. 88–89.

[133] 'Relação de Fernão de Sousa a El-Rei' [Court of Appeal of Fernão de Sousa to the King], BAL, ms. 51-VIII-31, fls. 30–32 v, 2 March 1632, p. 156, 'P.e Dionizio de Faria Barreto, filho da terra, que sabia bem a lingoa, e cõ elle Manoel Dias. E chegados a ellas lhe offereçeraõ da parte do Gouernador paz e amizade, saindosse delias pera a terra firme'.

terms of the agreement between Mbandi and Correia de Sousa were unprecedented, and I agree with Joseph Miller that there was more to Njinga's diplomatic mission to Luanda than we are led to believe.[134] Though we do not have the documents in which the terms of their agreement were stipulated, it is clear that Mbandi's demands had to be met before any trade negotiation with Luanda could take place:

> [Mbandi] had accepted the proposal on the condition that to have a secure passage [for trade], first Jaguar Kazanze must be expelled, who is currently waging war on him, and that the [governor] must restore to [him] the *sobas* and *Quisicos* [subjects] that the governor Luis Mendes had taken away from him, for he could not be a king without *sobas*, nor a lord without subjects to serve him.[135]

Mbandi's position throws further light on our perception of slaves in the region: he put up resistance to trade with the Portuguese, to slavery and to foreign domination. In Mbandi's view, a monarch required chiefs to run his kingdom, with subjects to labour for the kingdom – and not to be used for slavery. Without king, chiefs and subjects, there could be no realm. Mendes may have driven Mbandi out of his palace at Kabasa to the islands, but Mbandi's flight was not a sign that he was ready to give up his role as king, forget his people or deny them their liberty. Mbandi's declaration was to show Correia de Sousa that, as king of the Mbundu people, his role was to defend and protect them. It demonstrated that his customs and manners ran counter to Correia de Sousa's and the Council of Luanda's understanding of the power relations between them.

Correia de Sousa submitted Mbandi's proposal to the Municipal Council of Luanda. The council decided unanimously in favour of Mbandi's demands: 'the governor has presented the proposal to the Council, Captains, and more people (as it is customary in that Kingdom). All have agreed that it will be good for the Kingdom to do what the King has asked for.'[136] The decision was based on what Anselmo termed the 'common good' of the residents represented by the council

---

[134] Miller, *Kings and Kinsmen*.
[135] 'Relação de Fernão de Sousa a El-Rei', p. 157: 'aceitou o Rey a offerta có declaração que pera se passer seguramente se auia primeyro desalojar da terra ao jaguar Casanze, inimigo comum, que actualmente lhe fazia rrant, e se lhe auiaõ de restituir os Souas e Quisicos que o gouernador Luis Mendes lhe ttinha tomado, porque naõ podia ser Rey sem vassalos, nem Senhor sem catiuos que o seruissem.'
[136] 'Relação de Fernão de Sousa a El-Rei', p. 157, 'proposta pello gouernador hà camera, capitaens e mais pessoas (como hé costume naquelle Reyno) se assentou por todos conuinha pera remédio do Reino conçederse ao Rey o que pedia'.

members.[137] Following the council ruling, Correia de Sousa came to the realisation that he was not going to succeed in exerting his will over Angola if he continued to seek approval for all his motions from the council, which prioritised its own interests. Instead, he turned to the army to be the enabler of his political will. Soldiers wielded great power in Angola thanks to their role in the region's conquest. Significantly, their salary had often presented a stumbling block for many governors in Angola, as they were paid from the booty that came from war, conquered lands and captured people, often in local currencies such as *patacas* and *libongos*.[138] Governors had generally been extremely accommodating of army demands, recognising the need to lubricate and continue the mechanism of conquest. The City Council simply did not have the economic resources to sustain the conquest without waging illegal wars on ordinary people, including those already considered allies of Portugal.

Given the resistance of King Mbandi and in order to fulfil his ambition and reward the soldiers, Correia de Sousa invaded Kazanze's territory on the pretext that there were enslaved Africans belonging to the Portuguese who had escaped and hidden there.

Correia de Sousa's invasion of Kazanze was, by all European and Christian precedents, illegal – a fact that later came back to haunt him. He made it clear that he was taking over from where his predecessor, Luís Mendes de Vasconcelos – whom Correia de Sousa claimed had stationed a contingent of twenty-five Portuguese soldiers and some Angolan *guerra preta*, the Angolan contingent forces who fought alongside the Portuguese, in Quilunda near Kazanze ' ... to oblige the enemies to surrender' – had left off.[139] Correia de Sousa explained his seizure of Kazanze land on the grounds that the Kazanze were murderers, for they stood accused of killing Portuguese men during the time of Governor Novais, almost fifty years earlier. He also claimed that they were harbouring runaway enslaved people from Luanda, and stealing Portuguese goods and livestock. He claimed, too, that the Kazanze had aided the release of two important enslaved political figures: 'Manigonge'[140] and 'Manicorinha', who from their titles we can deduce were allies of the kings of Kongo.[141] Correia de Sousa himself

---

[137] Hansen, 'Representações da Cidade de Salvador no Século XVII'.
[138] See 'Carta Régia ao Governador de Angola' [A Royal Letter to the Governor of Angola], AHU, cód. 275, fl. 354, 5 November 1664; MMA, vol. XII, pp. 506–507.
[139] 'Carta de João Correia de Sousa ao Marquês de Frecilha', p. 20.
[140] Manigonge or Manigango was once a vassal of Portugal, 'Carta de João Correia de Sousa ao Marquês de Frecilha', p. 20–21. See also Cadornega, *História Geral* vol. III, p. 56.
[141] 'Carta de João Correia de Sousa ao Marquês de Frecilha', p. 21

acknowledged in a letter on 3 June 1622 that Kazanze was a vassal of Kongo: 'Kazanze is a Lord who has under his jurisdiction 16 *sobas* each with his many people; all pay allegiance to this Kazanze, who is the Lord of all of them and they also said that these Kazanzes were always obedient to the Kings of Kongo and were subjects to the governance of the Dukes of Bamba.'[142]

Let us now look at how the siege of Kazanze led to treachery being employed in capturing Angolans and turning them into slaves. The attack was what Heywood and Thornton describe as a 'violent and duplicitous war against Kazanze'.[143] The war strategy was described in Correia de Sousa's letter to the Crown in Madrid, sent on 3 June 1622. It was intended that a detailed map or *lenço* of the landscape extending across Angola and into Kongo's territory would accompany the letter. The map was not included, but a copy of it later arrived in Lisbon, where it is now housed in the Palacio of Ajuda and has been cited only minimally by historians of Angola. In his letter to Madrid, Correia de Sousa stated:

I wished to send with this letter a scarf [map] that I have had made, that contains only this island and the city of Luanda, lands and the war with Kazanze, of which Your Majesty is Lord, from the River of Dande to Coanza, be in truth as it is all placed. And for the hastiness this map cannot go, it is being left, a consideration of which I say, when I go and I will deal with what I have been through in this so risky and unplanned war from the day I arrived until 11 May 1622, in which God be served giving the end full of his mercy as I will say, saying the truth I am used to.[144]

The problem Correia de Sousa had on arrival in Angola was the extremely low morale of the soldiers, which was made worse by their not having been paid. This was perhaps because – as the records show –the amount of tax collected in the period was low. Correia de Sousa knew of the problems facing the army, and knew also that to survive and fulfil his economic ambitions, he required their support. His discontented soldiers needed reimbursement in the form of land, and the territory of neighbouring

---

[142] 'Carta de João Correia de Sousa ao Marquês de Frecilha', p. 18
[143] Heywood and Thornton, *Central Africans and Cultural Transformations*, p. 136.
[144] See Letter of João Correia de Sousa to Marquês de Frecilha, 3 June 1622; MMA, vol. VII, p. 18, 'estimarej que possa ir com esta carta hú lenço que tenho mandado fazer, que conthem somente esta ilha e cidade de Loanda, terras, e enfinda de Casange e tudo o de que Sua Magestade hé senhor, do Rio Dande tee o Rio Coanza, bem na uerdade de como tudo está lançado. E se pola breuidade naõ puder ir este lenço deixese a consideração do que digo para quando vaa e tratarej do que que tem pasado nesra tam arrisquada como inportuna g[u]erra, dês do dia que aqui entrej tee onze de majo de 622, em que foi Deus seruido darlhe hú fim tam che[i]o de mercês suas como direj, tratando a verdade que costume.'

Kazanze presented the perfect solution. However, while Correia de Sousa ingratiated himself with his soldiers, he did not curry favour with the Crown in Madrid, which was well apprised of the chaos he was creating in Angola. Correia de Sousa's claim to 'give Angola to God' translated as an ambition to loot the lands, raid, kidnap and then send the people into slavery in Brazil, São Tomé and the Spanish West Indies.[145]

Correia de Sousa's war was unjust, and based on an economic rationale, and not on the Kazanze people's rejection of Christianity, which was the main condition for waging a 'just war' on them. One of his main reasons for invading Kazanze (see Figure 6) was that their lands were good,[146] consisting of a great deal of fertile soil[147] famed for its superior maize production:

> ... it produces grain, like a muted apple, and a thick apple, as they call it in the idiom of the Kimbundu language of these kingdoms, and our muted maize and coarse corn; the muted is another caste than ours from Portugal, because he gives humps cobs or coats very big and large in tall canes, and he has the most substantial sustenance that are produced in these parts.[148]

The considerable value of the Kazanze's lands, rather than the pretext he claimed – that the people of Kazanze were rebellious and a threat to Portuguese existence in the region – provided the driving motive for Correia de Sousa's war. Soon after the war, Correia de Sousa divided Kazanze land among his Portuguese soldiers: '... twelve leagues around Luanda were cleared and divided among veteran soldiers, so that they might till it, which will be of great benefit to the state'.[149] The Kazanze case, in which 1,211 people were rounded up and kidnapped, including children and women, is used here as an optic through which to comprehend the call for justice and application of law in the Atlantic, particularly with regard to the capture of enslaved people.

---

[145] 'Carta de João Correia de Sousa para o Marquês de Frecilha', pp. 7–24.
[146] See 'Relaçaõ para o Ill.mo Sñr Collector'.
[147] Cadornega, *História Geral*, vol. III, p.45.
[148] Cadornega, *História Geral*, vol. III, p.45, writes: 'chovendo a seu tempo, dá e produz bastimento, como he maça muida, e maça grossa, que se chama no idioma da lingoa ambunda destes reinos, e a nossa milho miudo e milho grosso; o miudo he de outra casta do que o nosso de Portugal, porque dá humas maçarocas ou caxas muito bastos e de grandura em canas altas, e he o mais substancial mantimento que têm estas partes criado nella.'
[149] Biblioteca Nacional de Lisboa [BNL], ms. 241 (F. G.), fls. 174, 189–189v. pp. 182–183, 'de modo que doze legoas ao redor de Loanda ficarão despejadas, e se repartirão aos soldados veteranos, para as cultiuarem, o que será com grande beneficio daquele Estado', and in *História Política de Angola* (1622–1623), MMA, vol. VII, p. 79.

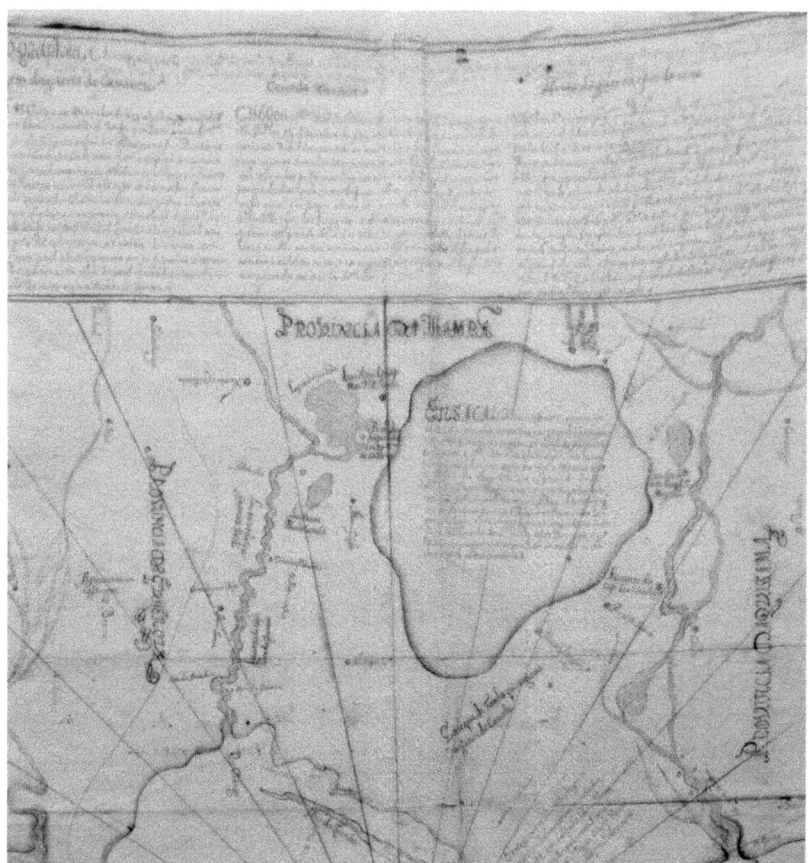

FIGURE 6 Map dated 1623 of the seige of Kazanze. Biblioteca da Ajuda, Lisbon, Portugal, [BAL], cartografia, MS. [Topografia (...) Provincia da Quissama, Angola, CA 1622, ARM, met. X 51-IX-20, fl. 2.]. Photograph by the author.

Correia de Sousa's justification for invading Kazanze was riddled with contradictions. Moreover, it demonstrated the power of the governors in Luanda and their lack of respect for the will of the Crown in Madrid. Correia de Sousa stated that the region he had invaded belonged to the Crown: it stretched from '... the city of Luanda and the enclave of Kazanze and of all that Your Majesty is Lord, from the River Dande to the River Coanza'.[150] If this claim is to be taken at face value, he had therefore invaded the lands of the king he was charged with serving, and

---

[150] See 'Carta de João Correia de Sousa ao Marquês de Frecilha', pp. 17–24.

hence breached the law that governed his tenure in Luanda. By declaring Kazanze a land belonging to the king of Spain, he also rendered it a Christian land, which should never have been subjected to war by the Portuguese. This makes sense of Mendonça's claim in the Vatican that enslaved Africans in Brazil and the Americas, such as those from Kazanze, were already Christians. We will return to this issue shortly. Suffice it to say here that most of the Africans shipped to Brazil as slaves were not slaves at all, but were likewise 'Christian' people captured under the same circumstances as the Kazanze.

By his own account of the attack on Kazanze, Correia de Sousa appears to have used African war tactics and Angolan mercenaries to starve the enemy and force them to surrender.[151] According to his report and as documented in a map from 1623,[152] he encircled Kazanze with five ditches, in which he stationed five captains and sergeants.[153] He ordered all the captains and their soldiers to cut down the trees with axes, sickles and cleavers to allow their 'arrows to reach the enemies'. According to the battle report, the Kazanze defended themselves, wounding between twenty-five and thirty Portuguese soldiers and Angolan mercenaries. Many Kazanze soldiers surrendered, and the Kazanze [chief] fled with five of his *sobas*; he was later captured and brought to Luanda. Correia de Sousa interrogated them there and, having extracted important information, ordered the beheading of the 'Kazanze' [chief] and two *sobas* for their role in 'robbing properties in Tombo'. 'They were brought to Luanda, where they were decapitated publicly for justice, with two

---

[151] See on the Papel people group of Guinea-Bissau war, José Lingna Nafafé, 'Mission and Political Power: Subversive Power Relations in Luso-West Africa (Guinea-Bissau) 1886–1914', in A. Seldtkeller (ed.), Series, *Missionsgeschichtliches Archiv. Studien der Berliner Gesellschaft für Missionsgeschichte*, volume 10, Franz Steiner Verlag: Berlin, 2005, pp.229–241.

[152] The map from 1623 describes the 'origin of the Kazanze war' and 'siege of Ensaca', (I have drawn the circles to indicate the siege positions), 'terms of the war' and the 'end of the siege'. The acquisition of the land through conquest accompanied the enslavement of the Angolans. Atlantic slavery was based on injustice and rarely on transaction. Biblioteca da Ajuda, Lisboa [BAL], cartografia, MS. [Topografia (...) Provincia da Quissama, Angola, CA 1622, ARM, met. X 51-IX-20, fl. 2.

[153] Soldiers were stationed in the following: (I) Captain Pero de Sousa (the military Chief of Staff), in Lake Quilunda; (II) Captains Roque de Sao Miguel; (III) Captain Lourenço Cardoso with a Sergeant Major along the River Coanza; (IV) Captain Luis Gomez Machado in command of the cavalry; (V) Pero de Gouea Leite along the banks of the River Bengo; (VI) Captain Gomes Roíz between Quilunda and another part; and (VII) Captain Antonio Brito was in charge of the soldiers carrying arrows. See 'Carta de João Correia de Sousa ao Marquês de Frecilha', p. 19 and see the map, Figure 1.

other *soba* allies. And finally, they arrested Grunhe, brother of Kazanze, to whom justice was administered in the same way.'[154]

Following the execution of their leaders, the Kazanze were called on by Correia de Sousa to carry out an election, which was customary practice in Angola following the death of a *soba*. The ceremony by which a new *soba* was elected was called *undar*. Correia de Sousa's successor, Fernão de Sousa, gave a dense description of *undar*:

> *Undar* is a ceremony in which they anoint *sobas* when they succeed in the lands after the death of the Lord of the Land, or when by means of justice, according to their laws and customs, a Lord has been thrown out of the land, and *macotas* who are Councillors then elect another Lord, who is usually the nephew of the dead, son of his Sister, who they regard as a legitimate Lord, and not the son, who they say could be a bastard. Even though elected by them, and even before they have chosen him, they inform the Governor of him, asking him to show good will, stating that they would like to elect him, which is the same thing as to be confirmed in the land. And in *undar* the new *soba*, lies on his chest on the ground before the Governor as a sign of vassalisation to his Majesty. A little flour is thrown over him, and he takes it with his hands, and rubs it on his breast and arms, and now he is declared the Lord of the land. Then he is sent to dress after being endowed with the power of the *soba*, according to the law.[155]

Correia de Sousa's demand for an election was in fact a deception. He called the *macotas* (elders or councillors) of Kazanze to Luanda to perform the ceremony there. They went in good faith, but on arrival found there was to be no election. Correia de Sousa declared: 'I have sent captain major Pero Coelho de Sousa that he brings me all *sobas*, *macotas* that are their advisors including *tendalas* and *maculuntos*, that are their ministers of war, because I wanted them to have an election that is accepted in their lands.'[156] He knew that they, including 'the four *gingos* that are the heirs and pretenders for the Kazanze's throne' would come to be elected as their lord of the land, 'and they all came willingly, and I did not inform the captain of my intention'.[157] He used treachery to detain them. When they

---

[154] BNL, ms. 241, 'trazido a Loanda, onde o degolarão por justiça publicamente, com outros dous sovaas seus aliados, e ultimamente prenderão também o Grunhe (?) jrmaõ de Caranze, o qual do mesmo modo foi justiçado', and in *História Política de Angola*, MMA, vol. VII, p. 79.

[155] BAL, cód. 51-IX-20, fl. 241 v, MMA, vol. VII, pp. 1624–1630.

[156] See 'Carta de João Correia de Sousa ao Marquês de Frecilha', p. 21, 'mandej ao capitão mor Pero de Sousa que me trouxesse todos hos souas macotas, que saõ os seus conselhejros, tendalas e maculuntos, ministros de suas g[u] erras, perque os queria undar, que hé confirmalos nas suas terras'.

[157] See 'Carta de João Correia de Sousa ao Marquês de Frecilha', p. 21, 'e quatro gingos, que saõ os erdejros e pretensores de Casange, que tanbem viessem para escolhrem hü para

arrived, he had them rounded up and put on a ship to Brazil to become the subjects of Governor Diogo de Mendonça of Salvador, Bahia. The *murinda* (ordinary subjects) were then called to Luanda under the pretext of the election. All the *murinda* (a total of 1,211) were forced to board five ships hired by Correia de Sousa and sent to Brazil. Many of them were children and elderly men and women. Almost half of them – a total of 583 – died onboard due to the appalling and inhumane conditions[158] and poor physical health. The ship was not fit for long-distance travel. In contrast, those between fifteen and twenty-five years of age and who were of able body had a much higher survival rate. Their death was beyond doubt caused by Correia de Sousa's treachery. At least their deaths were documented, but thousands upon thousands of such deaths have not been recorded.[159]

The case of the war in Kazanze and the exile of its inhabitants to Brazil as enslaved people by Correia de Sousa in 1622 is key in enabling us to understand the socio-political environment in which Portuguese slave-trading developed in Angola, and the wider practice of slave-trading unfurled in the Atlantic. It also highlighted the raiding, kidnap and treachery used to capture ordinary people. It was within this context that Mendonça contextualised and refined his anti-slavery statement. The idea of so-called African slavery – that is, the idea that Africans were complicit in slavery – has overshadowed cases such as Kazanze's, which is just one example among many. What has come to dominate Lusophone historiography is the element of transaction between Africans and the Europeans, but the siege of Kazanze and the enslavement of its people shows another side of the story that has often been overlooked.

Aside from Correia de Sousa's own account, the most valuable insight into the war waged on Kazanze comes from Catholic priests working in Angola and Kongo at the time. After the enslavement of the Kazanze, they launched an appeal at the High Court of Appeal, describing what Correia de Sousa had done. This appeal was recorded in several documents: Mateus Cardoso's case in the High Court of Appeal;[160] a collector's *relação* or High Court of Appeal case;[161] Mateus Cardoso's letter to

---

ficar senhor da terra; os quais vierão todos com boa vontade e sem o Capitão mor saber minha tensaõ'.
[158] Heywood and Thornton, *Central Africans and Cultural Transformations*, p. 137.
[159] See Dom Pedro II's Atlantic Slave Trade Law of 1684.
[160] See 'Relação do Padre Mateus Cardoso'.
[161] See both 'Relaçaõ para o Ill.mo Sñr Collector', and 'Relação do Padre Mateus Cardoso", pp. 176–193.

Father Nuno Mascarenhas, 20 October 1623;[162] Antonio Bezerra Fajardo's High Court of Appeal case, 24 February 1624;[163] and Collector Albergati's report to the pope, 23 September 1623.[164] These priests' descriptions of the Kazanze invasion and its motives contradict Correia de Sousa's account of events, and to a large extent reflected the Portuguese governors' attitudes, which were motivated by economic gain. All the High Court appeals argued strongly against the invasion as an unjust act and claimed that there was no justification for the exile of the Kazanze people and their *sobas* to Salvador, Bahia. The exception was the account of Albergati, which focused mainly on the brutality of the invasion on Kongo that followed the Kazanze attack. All the High Court Appeal writers claimed that Correia de Sousa had constructed the invasion to suit his own interests.

It appears from the sources available to us that, contrary to Correia de Sousa's claim, there was no war in Kazanze. De Sousa's account also included some doubtful assertions that the only people who had died in battle were Angolan *guerra preta* and other African contingent forces. It also suggested that only Portuguese soldiers were wounded.[165] The Portuguese and *guerra preta* may have encircled Kazanze as the map showed, but the details of the actual battle that took place were unclear, according to the priests' reports of the case in the High Court of Appeal held on 20 October 1623. Their reports were, as aforementioned, highly critical of Correia de Sousa's campaign in Kazanze. According to them, during the siege, the *sobas* went to the chief priest of the Jesuit College of Luanda, Father Jerónimo Vogado, wanting to reach a settlement with the Portuguese and repledge their allegiance to the Portuguese Crown. They went unarmed, seeking a peaceful resolution to the crisis and used Father Vogado as a mediator. The *sobas* confided in Vogado, whom they deemed a trustworthy mediator, and Correia de Sousa appeared to offer them safe passage to a meeting with him. So, according to these alternative accounts of events in Kazanze, the Kazanze *sobas* went willingly to Correia de Sousa and were not, as claimed by him, captured while trying to escape and then brought to him. Instead, Correira de Sousa clearly betrayed his agreement with Vogado, and slaughtered the *sobas*. As Cardoso reported:

---

[162] See 'Relação do Padre Mateus Cardoso', pp. 176–193.
[163] See High Court of Appeal 'Relação de Antonio Bezerra Fajardo'.
[164] 'Carta do Collector Albergati ao Papa, "Beatissimo Padre"', [Letter of the Collector Albergati to the Pope] Nunziatura di Portogllo, vol. 14, fls. 122–122v, 23 September 1623, MMA, vol. VII, pp. 148–149.
[165] See 'Carta de João Correia de Sousa ao Marquês de Frecilha', pp. 17–24.

... for them to stop the war, vassals of Kazanze decided to leave its protection, and to return to the old alliance with the king of Portugal. In order to obtain a treaty and to surrender, they went to Father, the Councillor of the Society of Jesus, to be their godfather before the Governor. As a result, three *sobas* came at night to the [Jesuit] College, saying that they would like to pledge their allegiance with all their vassals and with more *sobas*, and that other parts of Kazanze would pledge allegiance too, and they had come for the Governor that he would receive them. Immediately, the Councillor took this news to the Governor, who received it well. He gave order that they go to our settlement, which they did immediately, and with this example more *sobas* came out of the forest to our settlement, unprotected by their Head Kazanze, and they entered in the same way to our settlement on the goodwill of the Governor. Seeing that the enemy came without people [soldiers], immediately they were taken away, and brought to Luanda, where he had them decapitated.[166]

From the evidence of this text, there is a clear indication that the enslavement of the Kazanze was illegal, the war against them was neither 'just' nor legal and the killing of their leaders was motivated by economic interest. What becomes evident is that Correia de Sousa was interested only in enslaving the Kazanze people and securing their land for the unpaid soldiers. The individuals captured in Kazanze and taken to the Americas as enslaved people were ordinary civilians, not given the protection that would have been offered to soldiers, who would come under the category of *kijiko*.

1.3 PROTESTS AGAINST CORREIA DE SOUSA'S ACTIONS AND THE ILLEGAL SENDING OF KAZANZE PEOPLE TO BRAZIL

Correia de Sousa took the Kazanze people from the Jesuit compound and not, as he claimed in his own reports, from the *undar* ceremony. Correia de Sousa account was not supported by the evidence supplied in the High Court of Appeal on 20 October 1623, nor in Cardoso's High Court of Appeal hearing in the same year entitled, 'Father Nuno Mascarenhas' High Court of Appeal of what befell in Angola in the year 1623 about the imprisonment of the King Crown Judge, and Municipal Councillors, and the Priests of the Society of Jesus'.[167] The Jesuit High Court of Appeal hearing states that:

... the vassals of Kazanze were in our allegiance, in our settlement, then the Governor brought in a resolution of his own, which he took by himself. And he

---

[166] 'Relaçaõ para o Ill.mo Sñr Collector' and 'Relação do Padre Mateus Cardoso'.
[167] See 'Relação do Padre Mateus Cardoso', pp. 176–193.

hired five ships and filled them with those miserable people, who came to show their allegiance; he sent them to Brazil and, paying the cost of shipment and food packages to the ships' masters, left their land depopulated, without a sign of people.[168]

These were people who had come from their land of their own free will to the priests' settlement in Luanda. Among those sent to Brazil were distinguished *sobas* who had long served Portuguese interests in Luanda, and whose contribution to the Portuguese project in Angola was acknowledged by its priests and residents. For example, they had helped in the building of the fort in Luanda. They had served in the Portuguese army and fought for the Portuguese in Angola. One had been a fisherman for the Portuguese in Luanda alongside his role in the army.[169] In summary, they had dedicated their lives to and believed in the Portuguese project of the conquest of Angola.[170] In 1623, prior to the case in the High Court of Appeal written by Mateus Cardoso, Vogado's advice to Correia de Sousa was that he should not harm the Kazanze *sobas*. However, Correia de Sousa ignored this advice. Father Mateus Cardoso stated:

> ... it seems to all people that the resolution was unjust, bearing in mind these *sobas* came of their free will to pledge their allegiance; some of them came to speak to the Councillor and other Priests who tried to dissuade the Governor from his decisions, for it appears that it was just that the poor *sobas*' words were kept. In particular, it was not fair to ship them and make landless *soba* Quisso and the other two or three who had pledged their love for us, them having served in our army, helped to build our fort, and one them having fished for our soldiers.[171]

In Correia de Sousa's case, we face the fundamental issue of the legality of the Atlantic slave trade in Angola. The rights afforded to Angolans and

---

[168] 'Relaçaõ para o Ill.mo Sñr Collector', p. 529, 'estando os vassalos de Cassange á nossa obedienssia, em nosso Campo, sahio o Gouernador com huã resolusaõ, que consigo só tomou. E foi, mandar aprestar sinquo nauios e enchelos daquella mizerauel gente, que se ueo á obedienssia, e leualos ao estado do Brazil, pagando com alguns delles o frete, e matalotagem aos mestres dos nauios, dexando toda aquella terra despouoada, e sem rastro de pessoa'.

[169] 'Relaçaõ para o Ill.mo Sñr Collector', p. 509.

[170] See Peter Mark, *'Portuguese' Style and Luso-African Identity: Precolonial Senegambia, Sixteenth-19th Centuries*, Bloomington, IN: Indiana University Press, 2003.

[171] 'Relaçaõ para o Ill.mo Sñr Collector', p. 509, 'paresseo a todo o pouo esta rezolussaõ ser aleiuosa, supposto que aquelles Sobas se uieraõ de sua liure uontade á obedienssia; uieraõ alguãs pessoas ter com o P.e Rector e maes P.es que quizessê despersuadir desta determinassaõ ao Gouernador, poes paressia que era iusto guardar a palaura áquelles pobres Sobas, e sobretudo naõ era iusto embarquar, e desterrar ao Soba Quisso e a outros 2 ou 3, que tinhaõ por amor de nós perdido suas terras, e andaraõ no nosso exerçito peleiando, e aiudaraõ a fazer huã rranta, e hum delles pescaua o pexe para os soldados'.

Kongolese at the time were based on their identity as Christians. The priests' case in the High Court of Appeal stated that they were Christians and vassals of Portugal. Christian identity was used as an ontological point of departure from which to defend their human rights. Conceptually, being Christians, they were members of the universal Roman Catholic Church, had the same personal rights as all followers of God[172] and were entitled to the rights and protection of natural law.[173] A key pillar of natural law was the assumption that Christians were creatures of divine origin, enlightened and deserving of protection against violations and threats to their rights.[174] Despite this, the governors of Luanda implemented their own rules in Angola in order to capture people and enslave them, ignoring what the Portuguese Overseas Council called neglect of Africans' rights under natural law.[175]

Vogado's argument sought to disabuse Correia de Sousa of any notion that he was entitled to the Kazanze, and to make a distinction between the governor and the Kazanze, whom he was treating as enslaved. He based his argument precisely on the Kazanze people's Christian identity, which made them universal subjects of the wider Christian community – 'those *sobas* were not guilty, nor warranting of degradation, and were worthy of rewards'.[176] Vogado took his defence of the Kazanze, together with complaints from the residents of Luanda who opposed Correia de Sousa's actions, to the governor's residence. Their concerns were dismissed. Correia de Sousa's position was market-driven and, in the name of economic gain, the status and rights of the Kazanze were ignored. He responded to Vogado, saying that in 'sending all of these people away, he would be giving His Majesty more rewards for conquering Kazanze himself, and he did not want any vassal of Kazanze in Angola'.[177]

---

[172] See Richard Swinburne, *The Coherence of Theism*, Oxford: Clarendon Press, 1989, pp. 222–226.
[173] On natural law, see H. L. A. Hart, *The Concept of Law*, Oxford: Clarendon Press, 1961, and Anthony J. Lisska, *Aquinas's Theory of Natural Law: An Analytic Reconstruction*, Oxford: Clarendon Press, 1998.
[174] See Father Mateus Cardoso's argument in 'Relação do Padre Mateus Cardoso', pp. 176–193. I will deal with this in more detail in Chapter 6.
[175] 'Consulta do Conselho Ultramarino', AHU, cód. 15, fls. 32v-33v, 14 December 1652.
[176] 'Relaçaõ para o Ill.mo Sñr Collector', p. 509, 'aquelles Sobas naõ tinhaõ culpas para serem degradados, antes eraõ dignos de lhes fazer merssês'.
[177] 'Relaçaõ para o Ill.mo Sñr Collector', p. 509, 'por embarquar todos aquelles lhe auia de fazer Sua Magestade maes merssês, que por uensser o proprio Cassange, e que naõ queria que fiquasse vassalo algum de Cassange en Angola'.

Crucially, the war against the Kazanze demonstrates the injustices of slavery, and how the wars used in the period to justify the enslavement of Africans were based on a fraudulent claim.[178] Correia de Sousa alleged he was fighting a 'just war', but evidence suggests that this was not the case, and his actions in Kazanze were driven purely by economic motives. Moreover, there is very little evidence of the already preposterous argument of a 'just war' being fought by Kongo and Angola, to justify the capture of people who were then enslaved. The decision to enter into war with Angolans was made unilaterally by the governor and the Municipal Council of Luanda, without consultation with the Crown in Madrid, and the grounds necessary to declare a 'just war', as prescribed by the Crown, were starkly absent. Moirans, indeed, argues that there was never a 'just war' waged against Africans during the Atlantic slave trade. For a 'just war' to occur, according to him, there needed to be a 'just prince' capable of taking a decision as to whether there should be a war; however, in the case of Africa, wars were waged in regions that had no such prince.[179] Moreover, the substance of Madrid's orders to the governors of Angola was that war could only be declared if Angolans were preventing the preaching of the Gospel. There is no evidence from primary sources that this was the case; on the contrary, the governors of Angola gave reasons such as that the Angolans were making a trade blockade or were not opening the market for trade that the Philippine administration (the Madrid Crown) had sanctioned.[180] Vogado's advice to Correia de Sousa was rooted in theology, but Correia de Sousa responded that he did not need theology, that natural and divine laws were both a lived experience – that is, part of culture – and that there was no need for a priest to interpret his decision in terms of theology:[181]

> For the conscience, do not give me advice unless I have asked you; before you were born, Father, I had been governing. I know my conscience more than you do; there is no need for theology for a man to know what is required by his conscience, for an old person could be saved without knowing theology ... do not advise me, do not advise me, I know what I am doing.[182]

---

[178] On 'just war', see Jaca and Moirans, OFM Cap., *Servi Liberi*; and Michael W. Brough, et al. (eds.), *Rethinking the 'Just War' Tradition*, Albany, NY: SUNY Press, 2007; James M. Dubik, *'Just War' Reconsidered: Strategy, Ethics, and Theory*, Lexington, KY: University Press of Kentucky, 2016, and Thom Brooks, *'Just War' Theory*, Leiden; Boston: Brill, 2013.

[179] See Jaca and Moirans, OFM Cap., *Servi Liberi*.

[180] See 'Carta de Fernão de Sousa a El-Rei', 22 August 1625.

[181] 'Relaçaõ para o Ill.mo Sñr Collector', p. 510.

[182] 'Relaçaõ para o Ill.mo Sñr Collector', p. 510, 'na concienssia naõ me dé conselho, senaõ quando lhe pedir, que antes que Vossa Paternidade nasesse iá eu gouernaua, que eu sei

Here once again is the old conflict between faith and politics, between religion and economics. Vogado brought into the discussion a third person, a Native Angolan graduate theologian originally from Matamba, Father Dionizio de Faria Barreto, who was an ecclesiastical magistrate and vicar general of Luanda at the time. Father Barreto was extremely experienced in matters of Angolan diplomacy; he often acted as a bridge between the governors and the Angolan ruling class and was an expert in conflict resolution.[183] In spite of the expertise and counsel offered to him, Correia de Sousa maintained his position[184] and followed through with his decision to send the Kazanze people to Brazil. From then on, the relationship between the governor and the Society of Jesus soured, and Correia de Sousa began to persecute the Society.

From these reports, we learn what perhaps has not been made explicit in many debates about the wars waged on Angola and Kongo and about slavery in the region. There was a theological rationale for how Christian kingdoms and regions like Kongo, in which Christianity was established, were to be protected. As part of Christendom, Kongo was afforded protection against attacks by other Christian kingdoms, for there was mutual respect between all Christian monarchs. This interpretation was documented by priests in Luanda at the time and posed a challenge to the treatment of Christian Angolan slaves, which Mendonça later raised in the Vatican. The priests' report stated:

The Governor João Correia de Sousa, before the Judge of the High Court left Angola,[185] marched into a war, not only against heathens, but also against Christians who are vassals of the King of Kongo, Brothers in Arms to Your Majesty, that has a Seat and a Court of Bishops. And in that Kingdom come and go Portuguese who trade as in this land of our King and Lord; there, there are more than one thousand Portuguese, trading their goods, from which trade comes thousands of cruzados to the Royal Treasury. These were not good enough reasons for João de Sousa to wage war on a Christian Kingdom in the month of May 1622.[186]

---

maes de minha conciencia que Vossa Paternidade, nem hé neçessaria tanta Theologia para hum home saber o que lhe conuê a sua concienssia, porque huã velha sem saber Theologia se pode saluar ... naõ me dé conselho, naõ me dé conselho, que eu sei o que fasso'.

[183] 'Relaçaõ para o Ill.mo Sñr Collector', p. 510.
[184] 'Relaçaõ para o Ill.mo Sñr Collector', p. 510.
[185] See 'Relação de Antonio Bezerra Fajardo', p. 177.
[186] 'Relaçaõ para o Ill.mo Sñr Collector', pp. 512–513, 'O Gouernador Ioaõ Correa de Souza, antes de se partir de aquelle Reino o desembargador, mandou toquar caxas, e marchar á guerra, não para pouos gentios mas christaõs quaes saõ os vassalos de ElRei de Congo, Irmaõ en Armas de sua Magestade, que tem See e Bispo en sua Corte, e naquelle Reino entraõ e sahem os Portuguezes a resgatar como se foraõ ter[r]a de ElRei

In their report to the Crown, the Jesuits summed up the problems that befell the captives of Kazanze before they reached Brazil: 'so these poor people were shipped to Brazil, where they gave much to talk about. And there were no more to be found in all the five ships except old men and women and children; and they were asked what had happened to the people of war who had embarked from near Luanda.'[187] Correia de Sousa instructed the governor of Salvador, Diogo de Mendonça, to give the captives 'land where they are to be, together or separated, until His Majesty decrees what is to be done to them'.[188] De Mendonça was also warned to watch them closely as there was a chance that they would stage a rebellion or form a dissident group in Brazil. Let me state again that all of the Kazanze were subjects of the Crown and all were Christians. By their own laws and beliefs, the Portuguese should never have sent them to Brazil as captives. According to the priests' representations to the High Court of Appeal, Correia de Sousa had, in effect, violated the law set by the pope and the kings of Portugal and Spain.[189] In Salvador, Bahia, judges were brought to give their view on the legality of the situation. Their view was clear: the exile and enslavement of the Kazanze was illegal, the captives were to be returned to Angola, and His Majesty must order Correia de Sousa to pay for their return with his own money:

> The Governor and the Judge of the State of Brazil, seeing how these poor people came on board the ship, questioned their conscience, at which point they sought the advice of the Attorneys (Judges), who felt that Your Majesty ought to order that these poor people be sent back to settle again in their lands. Such a view has already been approved by Your Majesty, and a decree that the cost be paid out of João Correia de Sousa's property, so that he return these *sobas* and the poor to their lands, though this cannot be the case, for almost all of them have died from illness and lack of necessities.[190]

---

nosso Senhor, e andauaõ actualmente nelle passante de mil Portuguezes, resgatando con suas fazendas, de cuio resgate procedem muitos mil cruzados á Fazenda Real; naõ foraõ contudo bastantes estas razoens, para Ioaõ Correa de Souza dexai de meter guerra en o Reino Christaõ en o mes de Maio de 622.'

[187] 'Relaçaõ para o Ill.mo Sñr Collector', p. 510, 'e naõ aproueitaraõ as boas rezoens, e asim foi embarquada aquella apobre gente, para o Brazil, onde deu muito que falar, naõ se achar en todos aquelles 5 nauios, maes que uelhos, uelhas, e mininos, e preguntauaõ que fora feito da gente de guerra que metia em aperto a Loanda.'

[188] 'Carta de João Correia de Sousa ao Marquês de Frecilha', p. 21.

[189] See also 'Relação do Padre Mateus Cardoso', p. 177.

[190] 'Relaçaõ para o Ill.mo Sñr Collector', p. 510, 'o Gouernador e Rolaçaõ do estado do Brazil, uendo o como aquella pobre gente uinha embarquada, entraraõ en escrupulo de consienssia, e para isso tomaraõ paresseres dos Letrados, que iulgaraõ que Sua Magestade deuia de tornar a mandar aquella gente pouoar outra uez suas terras, o qual paresser tem aprouado Sua Magestade, e mandado que á custa da fazenda de Ioaõ

Correia de Sousa had taken a unilateral decision without consulting his governing authority, the City Council in Luanda, leaving some council members outraged by his actions and methods. Questions were asked in Brazil, too, about the morality of the slaves' capture. The case of Kazanze was seen as grossly inhumane, and generated concern about the process of enslavement and the mechanisms of slave-trading.

Correia de Sousa's claim that the Kazanze were harbouring runaway slaves – that is, those who had been captured and enslaved in the territory – echoed an accusation constantly made by previous governors of Angola. The problem of runaway slaves in Kongo and Angola was not new. A report written at the time of the governorships of Bento Banha Cardoso (1611–1615) and Luís Mendes de Vasconcelos (1617–1621), the direct predecessors of Correia de Sousa, stated that the problem of runaway slaves was dealt with through peaceful negotiation with the authorities of the lands in which runaways had sought sanctuary. War was not used as a resolution. The report declared that:

> ... there were years in which complaints were made by the Governors of Angola to a *soba*, lord of large lands, and vassals of the King of Kongo, saying that there were many common Portuguese slaves who were running away and hiding in the lands of that *soba*, and that he was receiving them and protecting them. Many times governors sent him requests that he return the runaway slaves, which he did indeed do in the time of the Governor Bento Banha Cardoso and during the time of Luis Mendez de Vasconcellos, who sent Captain Pero de Gouveia Leite there to the *soba*, who many times and on numerous occasions gave to the Portuguese more than 500 slaves he had found who had run away to his lands.[191]

Correia de Sousa claimed that the Kazanze were legally the spoils of war – that is to say, war captives. In other words, they were all runaway slaves: 'for all of these persons [Kazanze], for reason of war and justice, they are slaves, if they did not come, they [soldiers] would have been obliged to

---

Correa de Souza se tornem aquelles Sobas e pobre gente a suas terras, o que naõ será de effeito, porque quasi todos saõ mortos com trabalho da nauegassaõ e falta do necessário'.

[191] 'Relaçaõ para o Ill.mo Sñr Collector', p. 513, 'Auia annos que se quexauaõ os Gouernadores de Angola de hum Soba, senhor de grandes terras, e uassalo de ElRei de Kongo, dizendo que para aquelle Soba fugiaõ ordinariamente muitos escrauos dos Portuguezes, e que elle os recolhia, e emparaua. Foraõ lhe en uarios tempos os Gouernadores mandandolhe alguns requados que restituísse os escrauos fugidos, o que elle foi fazendo em tempo do Gouernador Bento Bainha Cardoso e en tempo de Luis Mendez de Vasconçellos, que lá mandou para esse effeito o capitão Pero de Guouea Leite, e o Soba, que por uarias uezes e en uarios tempos tem entregue aos Portuguezes passante de quinhentos escrauos, que achara fugidos nas suas terras.'

enter to their forest and for not being killed, they have chosen the remedy by giving themselves up without any party'.[192] However, the Crown in Madrid had not intended that people be removed from their lands to Brazil; on the contrary, its policy in West Central Africa encouraged increasing the population in the region to support trade and the production of goods. Despite this, Correia de Sousa continued his military offensive in Angola.

1.4 CORREIA DE SOUSA'S UNJUST WAR AGAINST BUMBI, ANOTHER VASSAL OF KONGO

In 1622 Correia de Sousa invaded Bumbi, another vassal of Kongo, having accused its *soba* leader, Duke Paulo Affonso Nabangogo, of hiding runaway slaves.[193] On 3 June that year, Correia de Sousa sent his soldiers to the land of Nabangogo and demanded that he return the runaways, using the pretext that the enslaved people in question had been stolen from their Portuguese owners in Luanda. Nabangogo's response was that there were no enslaved people there; if there had been, he would have returned them. This was a similar response to that given by Queen Njinga a few years later, when the same pretext was used against her kingdom. Nabangogo claimed that there were no enslaved people in Bumbi because they had returned to their original lands, and in so doing had regained their freedom and ceased to be enslaved.

Correia de Sousa's intervention in Bumbi ignited a fierce political confrontation that resulted in war with Kongo. His actions demonstrated another form of injustice in the region: war was used to capture Kongolese men, who were then labelled as enslaved. The governing authorities in Kongo questioned the legality of Correia de Sousa's war in Bumbi. Whilst the pressure of war was mounting, Father Barreto led efforts to find a peaceful solution to the crisis. He drew on his long experience as a mediator between governors and Angolan kings and *sobas*, and on his knowledge of Angolan customs and socio-political dynamics, and dispatched his own servants (helpers) from Luanda to Nabangogo to enquire

---

[192] 'Carta de João Correia de Sousa ao Marquês de Frecilha', p. 21, 'porque toda esta gente, em rezaõ de g[u] erra e justiça hé catiua, porque se naõ vieraõ senaõ obrigados de lhe terem já entrados os seus matos e polos naõ matarē, escolherão o remédio de se entregarem sem partido nenhũ'.

[193] See 'Carta de João Correia de Sousa ao Marquês de Frecilha', pp. 17–24. The title of duke was given to *soba* leaders by the Portuguese Crown in order to bring into Africa corresponding European terms for the local nobility.

about the alleged fugitive slaves.[194] Nabangogo told them to give him time to find the enslaved people, holding that the geography of the region made it difficult to determine their whereabouts. Correia de Sousa secretly sent his military chief of staff, or captain, Pero Coelho de Sousa, to Bumbi, where the duke of Bumbi, Paulo Affonso Nabangogo, and another *soba* leader, Marques de Pemba, Dom Cosme, could be found. The duke had two European priests as confessors, indicating that he was an ally of the Madrid Crown. Nevertheless, Sousa sent Jagas soldiers (one of the people groups of Angola) and *guerra preta* to fight Duke Nabangogo.[195]

Correia de Sousa demanded that Nabangogo return 2,030 alleged runaway enslaved and send him 50–100 further enslaved people as compensation.[196] Without giving Nabangogo adequate time to comply with his wishes, Correia de Sousa sent troops to Bumbi and many prisoners of war were taken, including Nabangogo, Cosme and other *sobas*. They were brought to Luanda, sold as enslaved people and then shipped to the Spanish Indies, Brazil and São Tome.[197] The enslavement and sale of Nabangogo and his people caused outrage amongst the religious authorities in Luanda, who began to question Correia de Sousa's motives.[198] Correia de Sousa's following campaign into Kongo territory sparked another outcry among priests, members of Kongo's élite and residents of Luanda.

Four major economic and political imperatives had prompted Correia de Sousa to wage war on the Bumbi. Firstly, he would stop at nothing to gain control of the region's natural resources, demanding that Pedro II, king of Kongo, hand over copper mines in Kongo and Pemba to the Portuguese. Secondly, he demanded Portuguese ownership of the island of Luanda, where *zimbu* (shells used as currency in Angola and Kongo) were found in abundance. Thirdly, he sought to open a passage between the rivers Dande and Bengo. Lastly, he demanded that Pedro II must accept his authority, and threatened to remove him from his throne if he did not comply. He said he would have Pedro II and his confessor, Brás

---

[194] Father Barreira had been a mediator between governors and kings in Angola, and between *sobas* and the governors. He had served as an interpreter, using his Native language Kimbundu to have *baculamento* deals settled between governors and *sobas*. See Freudenthal and Pantoja, *Livro dos Baculamentos*, p. 125.

[195] For a detailed discussion of Jagas and their military role in Angola and Kongo, see Anne Hilton, 'The Jaga Reconsidered', *The Journal of African History*, 22(2), 1981, pp.191–202.

[196] See 'Relaçaõ para o Ill.mo Sñr Collector'.

[197] See 'Relaçaõ para o Ill.mo Sñr Collector', p. 514.

[198] See 'Relaçaõ para o Ill.mo Sñr Collector', pp. 508–529; and 'Relação do Padre Mateus Cardoso', pp. 176–193.

Correia, arrested and brought to Luanda in chains,[199] claiming that 'in the name of the king of Portugal, he was given the authority to elect and confirm Kings of Kongo'.[200] Pedro II's response was pragmatic: he claimed that because of the unjust war waged on his kingdom, it was impossible to open the markets, because the law in Kongo and Angola held that in times of war no trade was to be conducted and all markets were to be closed.[201] This was a problem for the more than 1,000 Portuguese merchants who lived and traded in Kongo. Their safety was paramount for the Municipal Council in Luanda, which was highly concerned that, following the war in Bumbi, Kongo would retaliate by targeting those Portuguese merchants.[202] Gaspar Álvares, a wealthy businessman, wrote to the governor protesting that he had 150,000 cruzados-worth of enslaved people in Kongo, and that the war should not have gone ahead as it paralysed his business there.[203] Thus, there was an important economic argument against Correia de Sousa's war on Kongo.

During the war, several dukes of Bumbi were killed along with other noblemen, and many people were taken captive.[204] Back in Luanda, Correia de Sousa ordered the arrest of Gaspar Álvares, the senior crown judge and city councillors. He then sacked the other council members and replaced them with people loyal to himself. He ordered the house arrest of all priests, warning that if they left the Jesuit College of Luanda they would be arrested and sent out of Angola.[205] Correia de Sousa acted in this way in order to implement his method for capturing Angolans and Kongolese.

Fifty-five Portuguese residents in Kongo signed a petition demanding Correia de Sousa return the war captives. Indeed, the evidence of this petition reinforces my argument that Mendonça's presentation in the Vatican was not a petition, but a court case.[206] At the same time, the people of Kongo wanted to take matters into their own hands and accused Pedro II of giving Portuguese residents protection at the expense of the safety and well-being of his own people. The people of Kongo branded

---

[199] See 'Relaçaõ para o Ill.mo Sñr Collector', p. 515.
[200] See 'Relaçaõ para o Ill.mo Sñr Collector', p. 515.
[201] See 'Relação do Padre Mateus Cardoso', p. 177.
[202] See 'Relaçaõ para o Ill.mo Sñr Collector', p. 518.
[203] See 'Relaçaõ para o Ill.mo Sñr Collector', pp. 518–519.
[204] See 'Relaçaõ para o Ill.mo Sñr Collector', p. 519.
[205] See 'Relaçaõ para o Ill.mo Sñr Collector', p. 519.
[206] See 'Relaçaõ para o Ill.mo Sñr Collector', MMA, vol. VII, p. 522–523.

Pedro II a 'puppet Portuguese king'[207] for not allowing them to take their revenge on Correia de Sousa. Pedro II, however, was aware that Correia de Sousa's aggression was not merely directed towards Kongo, but also at people within the Portuguese administration, including members of the Municipal Council of Luanda, Portuguese residents and merchants, as well as the Jesuit priests.[208] To ensure the safety of the Portuguese residents in Kongo, Pedro II had them brought into his own compound. Only then did he launch a diplomatic attack on Correia de Sousa, sending formal letters to Madrid and the Vatican complaining that Correia de Sousa had illegally invaded Kongo, and stating that he must return the captives that he had stolen from Kongo and sold as enslaved people, and who were already bound for Brazil and São Tomé.

Officials, including some of those sacked from the Municipal Council of Luanda, wrote to Correia de Sousa. One letter was written by Payo d'Araújo, senior municipal judge,[209] and was sent on behalf of the king of Portugal and Spain, Philipe III (1621–1640). It highlighted that Luanda was dependent on Kongo for trade and that war against Kongo would strain trade relations because, as noted above, according to the law in Kongo and Angola no trade was to be conducted and all markets were to be closed in times of war.[210] This alone would have severe economic implications in the region. However, D'Araújo's letter went further, emphasising that enslaved peoples were the backbone of Luanda's economy and its conquest. If trade were prevented due to war, Luanda would suffer greatly.[211] While D'Araújo represented the dominant argument against the war shared by members of the Municipal Council, it is important to highlight that he was the captain of the *presidio* and the Fort of Our Lady of the Rosary of Kambambe from 1603–1604, and owned several *senzalas* (houses) of enslaved people in Luanda,[212] so war would also have adversely affected his own interests.

The relationship between the governor and the Municipal Council of Luanda had come to a standstill during the administration of governors before de Sousa. Furthermore, the relationships of governors Manuel

---

[207] Visconde Paiva Manso, *Historia do Congo*, Lisbon: Typ. da Academia, 1877, p. 176.
[208] For further details on Pedro II, see Manso, *Historia do Congo*, pp. 176–178.
[209] See Freudenthal and Pantoja, *Livro dos Baculamentos*, p. 64.
[210] 'Relação do Padre Mateus Cardoso', p. 177.
[211] See also 'Relação do Padre Mateus Cardoso', p. 177.
[212] For more detail on Paio D'Araújo D'Azevedo, see Freudenthal and Pantoja, *Livro dos Baculamentos*, p. 64. See also Cadornega, *História Geral das Guerras*, vol. I, pp. 146–147 and p. 151.

Pereira Forjaz (1607–1611), Bento Banha Cardoso (1611–1615), Manuel Cerveira Pereira (1603–1607, 1615–1617) and Luís Mendes de Vasconcelos (1617–1621) with the African rulers of the region had often come to a point of crisis that required the intervention of the Crown. The Crown had been informed of the abuses of power and the crimes committed against Angolans and Kongolese, and these reports had been the catalyst for sending Antonio Bezerra Fajardo to Angola in 1623 to conduct an official *devassa* (enquiry) into the political and military conflicts in the region. Let us examine Fajardo's judicial investigation of the crimes committed in the region and the unlawful capture of the Angolans and Kongolese who were then enslaved, as it resonates with the themes of Mendonça's court case in the Vatican.

1.5 ANTONIO BEZERRA FAJARDO'S INVESTIGATION INTO PORTUGUESE CRIME IN ANGOLA AND KONGO

Antonio Bezerra Fajardo was a fiscal crown court judge from Madrid who was sent, in 1623, to investigate the behaviour of Angola's governors – in particular, Luís Mendes de Vasconcelos (1617–1621), Correia de Sousa's predecessor as governor of Luanda. Fajardo was tasked with regulating the governors' power in Luanda, as well as their involvement in raiding, kidnapping and treachery in the region.[213] He was also vested with power to investigate how the governors, as representatives of the Crown, conducted their relationship with Kongolese and Angolan kings and *sobas*.[214] It is in this context that Fajardo's role, which sheds light on Mendonça's later court case in the Vatican, needs to be understood. In his case in the High Court of Appeal, Fajardo attempted to regulate the governors' abuse of power and promote a peaceful resolution between them and the Kongolese and Angolan authorities. Surprisingly, his investigation into the crimes committed against Angolans and Kongolese and the illegality of the slave trade in the region has not yet been explored by the historians of Kongo and Angola. Scholars such as Heywood and Thornton have mentioned Fajardo in passing while addressing issues relating to the sale of firearms to the 'heathens' in Kongo.[215] Yet Fajardo's investigation is significant for our understanding of the illegality of the Portuguese operation in Kongo and Angola – in particular, the trade in enslaved people

---

[213] See Freudenthal and Pantoja, *Livro dos Baculamentos*, p. 58.
[214] See 'Relação do Padre Mateus Cardoso'.
[215] Heywood and Thornton, *Central Africans*, p. 170.

practised by the city council, the governors and captains of the *presidio*, as well as their relationship with the *sobas*, who were coerced into trading in enslaved people through the use of force. In some instances, *sobas* were armed and obliged by the Portuguese authority to help secure captives in Angola. There were, as mentioned before, no 'just wars'. As Fajardo explained, the bulk of war captives in West Central Africa did not in fact fit the category: 'not even these slaves that are taken from these wars can be war captives, because they are taken from unjust wars, which they [the governors] wage on them against the decrees and brief from His Majesty'.[216]

In 1623, the Crown instructed that the white *pombeiros*, the Portuguese slave-traders who visited different regions to buy Angolans and Kongolese who had been caught in raids, kidnapped and enslaved, must stop attending Angolan markets because they were causing conflict between Angolan and Portuguese residents. In Angola, Birmingham claims that 'the earliest *pombeiros* were Europeans', but that 'the high mortality among them soon led the Portuguese to use mestiços and trusted enslaved Africans as *pombeiros*'.[217] The Crown further issued a decree to the Portuguese residents in Angola that all trading in enslaved people should be carried out by Black *pombeiros*, rather than white. Judicial proceedings demanded that the *pombeiros* should not live with the Angolans in their fields. Their presence among the Angolans was a cause for constant revolt against the Angolan *sobas*, who were often forced to flee their lands. The Crown wanted the *macotas* and the *sobas* to find a local solution to these conflicts, so it instructed that their advice be sought. Captains of the *presidio* were told not to ask the *sobas* to come to the *presidio* too often. *Sobas* who went to the *presidio* were forced by the captains to accept the demand to bring them enslaved people. Those *sobas* who were reluctant to comply were severely beaten and those who did not meet their agreed target were punished.[218] Judicial proceedings from Madrid declared that those *sobas* who had been left without land because of internal conflict must be given land to settle. *Sobas* were told

---

[216] See 'Relação de Antonio Bezerra Fajardo' [High Court of Appeals of Antonio Bezerra Fajardo]; 'Lembrança das Couzas que se hao de declarer a S. Magestade tocantes ao Reyno de Angola' [Remembering things that are to be declared to His Majesty relating to the Kingdom of Angola], 24 February 1624, BAL – Ms. 51-VIII-25, fls, 29–32, MMA, vol. VII, p. 208, 'nem estes escrauos que nestas guerras se tomaõ, podem ser catiuos, por serem tomados em guerras injustas, que se daõ contra as ordens e Regimento de Sua Magestade'.

[217] Birmingham, *Trade and Conquest*, p. 78.   [218] See Heywood, *Njinga of Angola*.

not to trade with white *pombeiros* who came to live on their lands. The kings of Angola were to be allowed to live in peace and harmony. Captains were not to invoke Philip III's name to acquire any benefits from the *sobas*.[219] All of this suggests that *sobas* were often being asked in the name of the Crown in Madrid to carry out the task of securing people as enslaved people for the Portuguese. In other words, *sobas* were the point of contact for captains of *presidios* seeking to obtain enslaved people through illegal means. This is a crucial point, not often taken into account when discussing the mechanisms of the slave trade in Angola.[220]

Fajardo's investigation into the crimes committed in the region is a major piece of work that deserves deeper analysis. It also highlights the conflicting interests of the Crown in Madrid and the Muncipal City Council of Luanda. If we are to understand Mendonça's claim in the Vatican of the illegality of the slave trade, Fajardo's enquiry into the Portuguese relationship with local authorities in Angola and Kongo is of great significance. Fajardo was instructed to investigate which *sobas* were allies of Portugal, and those whose allegiance was currently being solicited. He needed to ensure that they were treated in a dignified fashion and that the will of the *macotas* responsible for electing the kings of Angola and Kongo was respected according to their cultural practices. The primary task was to 'detect from the sobas the reason for their revolt... who was behind it... and whether any captains of the *presidios* (captaincies) had incited revolt by making promises to them so that they would act against the law and against the *macotas* who had elected them according to their laws'.[221] Portuguese interference in local politics is telling because their interest in slavery was harmful to the political status quo supported by the elders, the *macotas*. The local kings' power and authority was by proxy. The king was accountable to his council of elders, who could challenge his power but not veto it. These *macotas* not only exercised a strong social and religious role, they also played an influential political role in decision-making.

Through carrying out his enquiry in Luanda, Fajardo obtained firsthand information on the tense relations that were causing problems

---

[219] See 'Regimento do Governador de Angola' [A Brief to the Governor of Angola], AHU, cód. 169, fls. 18–25; Angola, cx. 9, MMA vol. 13, 10 April 1666, p. 18.

[220] See Curto, 'Experiences of Enslavement'.

[221] 'Regimento do Governador de Angola', p. 18, 'tomareis o mesmo conhecimento de todos os Sovas... e que cauza houve, quem lha deu para se levantarem e eximirse della... por offertas que fizesse a alguns Capitaês dos Prezidios, e por esta cauza sustentaõ nelles contra a justiça e vontade dos macotas que os devem eleger como entre elles se costuma'.

between the Native and European people living in Angola, on the infighting within the Municipal Council of Luanda and on how the *sobas* were being ill-treated by the Portuguese for failing to raid and kidnap their neighbours for sale as enslaved people. Fajardo advised that the Crown take action to prevent Portuguese injustice and cruelty in Angola and Kongo. In his High Court of Appeal report, Fajardo shed light on the complexity of the issues he had investigated. He summarised the issues in eighteen clauses, which became statutes and were written into the Constitution of the Muncipal City Council of Luanda: 'and a chapter of brief from His Majesty has been written in the City Council of Luanda Constitution by the Judge Antonio Bezerra Fajardo, that His Majesty had sent as a Judge to these kingdoms. He ordered it to be copied in the said Constitution, in which the chapter from His Majesty had decreed that nor offensive war be waged on them.'[222] The following is précis of each clause:[223]

1. Some governors were instigators of wars in Angola and there was a danger of 'losing Angola because of these wars'
2. There was 'a need for military experts in Luanda who make decisions regarding wars'
3. 'There was unjust treatment of Angolans and the enslavement of captives'.
4. The issues of 'just war' and the 'royal fifth'
5. The situation of '*sobas* fleeing, thus voting with their feet'
6. The 'Portuguese captains being relieved of their duties by governors'
7. The business of 'regulating the Council of Luanda so that it reflected the administrative structure found in Lisbon'
8. The 'need for regulated trade', which was interconnected with the regulation of the council
9. The need to ensure 'no killings of *sobas* by governors'

---

[222] 'Relação do Padre Mateus Cardoso', p. 177, 'e achando registado no liuro da Camara hũ capitolo do regimento de Sua Magestade, que o dezembargador Antonio Bezerra Faiardo, que Sua Magestade mandara áquelles reinos por syndícante, mandou tresladar no dito liuro, no qual capitolo Sua Magestade mandaua que se não desse guerra alguma offensiua'. Fajardo had also advised King Philipe IV of Spain to pass on this brief to Governor Fernão de Soua. See also BAL, ms. 5I-VIII-30, fls. 7-11 e 13-14, 19 March 1626.
[223] All quotations but one are to be found in 'Relação de Antonio Bezerra Fajardo', pp. 205–214.

10. The issue of 'providing respectable priests to aid captains of *presidios* in their dealings with Angolans akin to the systems found in Goa and India'²²⁴
11. 'No firearms were to be given to any *sobas* either for defensive or offensive purposes'
12. 'Sending annual certificates to the council treasury documenting all ships leaving Luanda for Brazil and India'
13. That 'no ships should trade in Lugano'
14. 'No interference with the appointment of scribes and municipal councillors'
15. '200 reis duty was to be paid for each slave leaving for Brazil'
16. 'Governors were not to take deposits in their subscriptions'
17. That 'no private property owned by residents was to be confiscated by governors'
18. That 'fiscal officers of His Majesty should give no special treatment to any individual, including governors'

What follows is my interpretation of what the most relevant of the clauses reveal:

[1] The accepted view was that the inter-group wars between Angolans and their distant neighbours for territorial control were the cause of many conflicts in Angola. However, further consideration of the evidence from Fajardo's own findings suggests that those wars were related to known political and economic struggles between the City Council and the governors. In this context, the internal politics of the Muncipal City Council of Luanda and the council's desire for enslaved people facilitated the constant waves of invasion and war experienced by the Kongolese and Angolan people.

[2] According to Fajardo, many of the wars that were judged to have derived from intra-Angolan and Kongolese conflict were myths, and the Portuguese interventions were most often unwarranted. The idea of a 'just war' was used as a pretext for the acquisition of Africans for slavery in Brazil. The so-called wars in the region were fomented by warlords, motivated by gain. Scrutiny of the justness of those 'wars' would uncover hardly any real war in Angola and Kongo at all. In Moirans's argument, there was no 'just war' waged on Africans because their kings were not involved in decision-making about the wars that aided the capture of the Africans.²²⁵

---

²²⁴ Heywood, *Njinga of Angola*.   ²²⁵ See Jaca and Moirans, OFM Cap., *Servi Liberi*.

[3] Fajardo was in agreement with Mendonça's court case about the ill-treatment of the Africans, including Angolans, and maintained that their enslavement was based on fraud.

[4] The use of 'just war' as a defence for the enslavement of Angolans is implausible, and there are several reasons to doubt the explanation. One of the reasons that Fajardo was sent to Angola and Kongo was that the revenue that should have flowed to Madrid from the booty of a 'just war' was simply not there. The Crown in Madrid was entitled to a royal fifth of the booty of any 'just war' in the region. However, since these wars were not just, there was no royal fifth, as we shall see in the case about the return of the Kazanze people from Brazil to Angola. The explanations for 'just war' were regularly used by Portuguese apologists to brush aside the brutality and the injustices of Atlantic slavery.[226]

[5–6] Fajardo moves on to deal with *encombros*, a tax that was replaced with *baculamento*, the complicity between the governors and their captains in capturing Angolans, and the situation of '*sobas* fleeing, thus voting with their feet' and the 'Portuguese captains being relieved of their duties by governors'. *Sobas* were forced to pay tax in enslaved people and, as a result, many fled their lands. Some, who had joined the Portuguese project of conquest and been involved in capturing their fellow countrymen could not return to their lands because they had created internal enemies. Captains of the *presidios* worked in tandem with their governors carrying out raids and treacherous attacks. Those captains who failed to meet the expectations of their governors were sacked from their posts. These two clauses show that there was not a ready-made market for enslaved people, and that enslaved people were secured by illegal means.

[7–8] The Crown in Madrid wanted to maintain vassalage and tribute payments from the *sobas* as part of a long-lasting business plan for the region. Conversely, the city council was interested in making a quick profit, and the slave trade – based on illegal wars fought against Angolans –was their priority.

[9–10] The need to ensure 'no killings of *sobas* by governors' and the issue of 'providing respectable priests to aid captains of *presidios* in their dealings with Angolans akin to the systems found in Goa and India' is significant in giving us a better understanding of Mendonça's court case. The killing of *sobas* by governors went in tandem with the enslavement of

---

[226] See Molina, *De Justitia et Jure*.

the Angolans. *Sobas* were coerced into raiding and kidnapping their own people as part of their vassalage. Those who did not comply with the rules were severely punished, often by death.[227] The call from Fajardo to bring a respectable priest into the *presidio* was clearly an attempt to control the brutality of the governors and their captains. The presence of a priest would at least guarantee some humanity in the treatment of *sobas*. It is important to note that the harsh treatment inflicted on *sobas* by the Portuguese officials was to ensure that *sobas* carried out their duties – that is, the providing of Angolans for slavery. To obtain the number of captives that were required each year, *sobas* had to resort to using different methods. They used raiding, kidnapping and treachery to acquire enslaved people, as the sporadic wars waged against Angolans and Kongolese were not sufficient to meet Portuguese demand, and because the use of firearms by *sobas* was prohibited at some point in the first quarter of the seventeenth century.

[11–12] The capture of Africans for slavery caused social issues in Central Africa and created a cycle of violence and unnecessary war that was used to feed the market in the Americas. Waging war became the norm for settling the scores of those who lost their family members through raiding and kidnapping. *Sobas* who were on the side of the Portuguese used warfare to maintain their safety and that of their family. Mendonça's court case in the Vatican was not delivered in a vacuum. He took on board the regional cases that arose where he and his family lived. Fajardo's recommendation was that trade in Angola and Kongo be carried out in a manner similar to other Portuguese contact zones, such as Brazil and India, where trade was regulated by 'sending annual certificates to the Council Treasury documenting all ships leaving Luanda for Brazil and India'.

[14] For Fajardo the role of the scribes and municipal councillors was to be protected. There was to be 'no interference with the appointment of scribes and municipal councillors'. They were the regulators of the economy in the region, they fixed the price of the goods and stabilised the currency. Politically, they were under pressure from the city council to represent its interests and suppress any negative reports. To control the scribes and municipal councillors was to control information in the region and to be able to misinform the Crown. Suffice it to say that the suppression of information from these regions was one of the fundamental

---

[227] See Heywood, *Njinga of Angola*.

reasons why Mendonça went to the Vatican, where he could reveal the truth about the crimes committed against Angolans and Kongolese, including members of his family.[228]

In reading Fajardo's findings, one may reasonably state that many so-called 'slaves' were not in truth 'slaves', because they had been captured illegally. According to his findings, there were hardly any enslaved people in Angola who had been caught legally, that is, captured in a 'just war' as defined by the Crown in Madrid. If there had been, and they had been captured in what was judged to be a 'just war', then, he posited, the Crown in Madrid was entitled to one-fifth of all the enslaved people captured. As it stood, cases where people had been captured legally were extremely rare. In 1452 Pope Nicholas V passed a decree, *Dum diversas*, to King Alfonso V, allowing the Crown of Portugal to conquer Saracens and pagans and to reduce them to perpetual slavery if they refused to accept the teachings of the Christian message. However, the Portuguese Crown did not interpret the fifteenth-century papal bulls that urged Christians to wage wars on infidels as an unfettered mandate to turn Africans into enslaved people. As explained, only if the Africans rejected the preaching of the Gospel could a so-called 'just war' be waged against them. Indeed, the concept of lawful slave capture emerged following the Portuguese Restoration. In the time of Tristão da Cunha's governorship of Angola and that of his successor, Francisco de Távora 'Cajanda', the royal fifth raised from the destruction of Pungo-Andongo was valued at one-fifth of 710,000 reis' worth of *presa* (war captives); another fifth went to the governor, another to the generals in the army and the other two-fifths went to the soldiers, making a grand total of 3,551,000 reis.[229] In other words, of the enslaved people extracted from Angola, the majority were taken illegally, because they were not war captives captured in a 'just war'. The royal fifth shows the emergence of the idea of 'lawful' slave capture in Angola, or at least shows that justifying slave capture as lawful was in the interests of the Crown, because they gained economically from it, while illegally captured enslaved people went unrecorded, with no benefit to the

---

[228] See 'Relação de Antonio Bezerra Fajardo' [High Court of Appeal].
[229] See Cadornega, *História Geral*, vol. III, pp. 547–550. On page 547, Delgado states: 'por curiosidade digo que o 5° das presas desta guerra foi de 710$200 reis os quais o Príncipe mandou vir para cá. Consta isto da carta régia de 26-7-1673 para o provedor da Fazenda de Angola, Domingos de Azevedo Coelho, o qual a fez cobrar' [out of curiosity I say that the fifth of the captives of this war (Pungo-AndDongo) was 710$200 reis, which the prince sent here. This appears in the royal letter of 26 July 1673 by the Angolan Commissioner of the Treasury, Domingos de Azevedo Coelho, who charged it.]

Crown. This fact was an important reason for Mendonça's outcry at the Vatican, where he called on Pope Innocent XI (1676–1689) to take action.

According to my understanding of Fajardo's appeal, any war conducted by the Portuguese against their African allies in the region must be minutely examined in terms of its justification and legality. Fajardo wanted new processes to be instigated whereby decisions regarding war would be made by a wider body of representatives from Luanda's various constituencies that should exclude Luanda's own governors, captains and residents.[230] He claimed that the latter's personal interests had always been served by waging war for the procurement of enslaved people, and that captains were often acting on the orders of governors, as was clear in the case of Correia de Sousa. Fajardo stated that:

> His Majesty should decree with grave consequences that there should never be wars against *sobas*, except defensive wars, and that when war is waged, let that decision be made with the council of the Bishop or his representative, and with the Director of the Society [of Jesus], Senior Crown Judge, Fiscal Officer of His Majesty, and the City Council of São Paulo [Luanda]; and let it be that captains and the representative of the people should not be part of such votes, for the captains and the city residents want nothing except that there are wars so that they can take slaves and benefit from them. Many people are dying in wars, as well as from hunger, and many others are eaten by Jagas who keep the people they kill. And if possible, first give to all a warning against such wars to stop; it is very necessary.[231]

Persistent warring and abuse of *sobas* were undoubtedly a valued means of control for the Portuguese governors and their captains in Angola and underlay the role of the Muncipal City Council of Luanda in the region. Indeed, the very existence of the City Council was based on securing the Angolans as enslaved people. Wars were primarily conducted with a single aim: to gather enslaved people. Most decisions taken by the war cabinet in Luanda had no legal basis for their implementation. In the light of this evidence, who were the enslaved that populated the Americas? The

---

[230] See 'Relação de Antonio Bezerra Fajardo'.

[231] 'Relação de Antonio Bezerra Fajardo', p. 208, 'Deue Sua Magestade mandar com granes penas que se naõ dem guerras aos souas senaõ defenciuas, e quando se ouueré de dar seya por conselho do Bispo ou de quem em seu lugar estiuer, e do Reytor da Companhia, e Ouujdor Geral, e feitor de Sua Magestade, e a Camara da Cidade de Saõ Paulo, e que naõ intreuenhaõ nos tais uottos os capitais nem a gente do Pouo, porque os capitais e moradores da Cidade naõ querem mais, senaõ que aja guerras pera dahy tirarem pessas, e se ualerem delias, e more muita gente como ditto hé, assy na guerra como á fome, e outra muita que come os Jagas, que se manto da gente aue mataõ, e sendo possiuel que primeiro se auize a Sua Magestade que se dem as tais guerras, será muy conueniente.'

answer to this question is that they were ordinary people who had been raided, captured and stolen. They did not fit any of the categories of people whom the Portuguese would define as slaves. They were not fighters, called *kijikos*, who had been captured in war. Nor were they debtors, those who had not paid their dues or owed someone money or had been caught stealing someone's property.

The notion of capturing people did have a place in the political, economic and legal environment of Angola and elsewhere in Africa at the time.[232] It was not without legal precedent, but was a practice bound by clearly understood reciprocal duties and responsibilities. The *kijikos* and debtors were under the legal protection of those who had taken them. Those who had *kijikos* and debtors in their service had a duty of care towards them. The captors were monitored by the watchful eye of Mbundu (the whole of society) to ensure that they fulfilled their responsibilities until such time as the *kijikos* and debtors had completed their term of service and were released.[233] It seems that the African concept of 'slaves' – that is, of debtors and *kijikos* – views the condition as temporary and bound by respect and responsibility, not a matter of ownership and servitude as in the Western version. *Kijikos* and debtors were never owned as such by their captors; indeed, Thornton states that the term *kijiko* is a description of a free person.[234] Those who argue for the existence of slavery in African society in seventeenth-century Angola have based their argument on anti-abolitionist literature of the nineteenth century rather than on sound evidence-based historical analysis.[235] From this evidence, therefore, we may conclude that so-called 'slaves' in Angola in this period were not in fact slaves and that the category 'slave' needs to be revisited. I will now turn to Correia de Sousa's role in the Muncipal City Council of

---

[232] See Walter Rodney, 'African Slavery and Other Forms of Social Oppression on the Upper Guinea Coast in the Context of the Atlantic Slave Trade', *Journal of African History*, 7, 1966, pp. 431–443; J. D. Fage, 'Slavery and the Slave Trade in the Context of West African History', *Journal of African History*, 10(3), 1970, pp. 394–404.

[233] A conversation in 2018 with an Angolan lawyer who is also a Mbundu person at King's College, London, revealed that the term *kijiko* does not refer to an enslaved individual in terms of the Atlantic slave trade. A *kijiko* (current pronunciation is *kashico*) is a trusted person charged with rendering service to, and often performing confidential duties for, his superior. He (*kashico*) acts as an ambassador in the service of his superior. His superior would never call him a *kashico*, although those outside the relationship might call him a *kashico*, because of the service he gives to his superior. This practice persists in modern-day Angola, and the relationship between a *kashico* and his superior is one of intimacy and closeness.

[234] See Thornton, *Africa and Africans*.

[235] See de Carvalho, *Das Origens*, and Fonseca, 'A Historiografia'.

Luanda and how he attempted to influence members of the war cabinet to support his method of capturing Angolans and how, in the absence of support, he resorted to sacking them.

1.6 CORREIA DE SOUSA'S UNREST IN THE CITY OF LUANDA

A major accusation made by the religious authorities in Luanda was that Correia de Sousa used his newly appointed scribe to pen his own version of events in letters to Madrid. He also censored all letters addressed to the Crown in Madrid, rewording them to suit his own interests.[236] Using his power as governor, Correia de Sousa refused to allow priests to leave Angola and sent soldiers to the port in Luanda to ensure that no priests or previous members of the Municipal Council left for Portugal without his consent.[237] He promised high office to many of his new council members in exchange for their loyalty.[238] He arrested wealthy residents, including one of the wealthiest merchants of the time, Gaspar Álvares, whom he saw as a threat to his mission. He suspected that Álvares would use his wealth to curry favour with the senior judge in Luanda and turn the judge against him.[239] Cardoso declared that:

> ... there was also an order that our brother Gaspar Álvares should be arrested. The soldiers surrounded his house, but he took shelter by an escape door and hid himself. And the next day at night he sneaked into our school, half dead and out of breath, saying, 'Priests, I have been wishing to enter the Society, for I see that God calls me because I am an old man and never had a shotgun in my house and there is no-one who complains about me with anger. And yet John Correa says that I am a traitor and a mutineer; this is from heaven, God calls me, I want to enter the Society soon.' And so he trimmed his beard and wore a cassock.[240]

Personal financial gain was always the motive for Correia de Sousa's actions. Eliminating his major rival Álvares, who was blocking

---

[236] See 'Relaçaõ para o Ill.mo Sñr Collector'.
[237] See 'Relaçaõ para o Ill.mo Sñr Collector'.
[238] See 'Relaçaõ para o Ill.mo Sñr Collector'.
[239] 'Relação do Padre Mateus Cardoso', p. 181.
[240] 'Relação do Padre Mateus Cardoso', p. 180, 'Tãobem estaua dada ordem que prendesse ao nosso irmão Gaspar Alu[a]res, e cercandolhe a caza os soldados, elle por hüa porta escusa se acolheo e escondeo. E ao dia seguinte de noite entrou ás escondidas no nosso collegio meyo morto e sem fôlego, dizendo: padres, eu andaua dilatando o entrar na Companhia, porem uejo que Deus me chama, porque eu sou homem velho e que nunqua tiue em caza espingarda né arma algúa, não auendo alguém que se queixe de mi [m] de reuoltozo, e contudo João Correa diz que eu sou tredor e amotinador; isto hé do ceo, Deus me chama, eu quero logo entrar na Companhia; e cortando a barba se vestio cõ huma roupeta.'

Correia de Sousa from capturing Angolans and Kongolese, made it easy for Correia de Sousa to implement his method of capturing the Angolans and controlling the slave trade. Father Cardoso wrote, 'and so all this is the Governor's wickedness, for he has planned to get rich by diabolical manners'.[241] Correia de Sousa had a notice pinned to the pillory declaring that traitors should give themselves up, among them Gaspar Álvares. I will in due course return to Álvares's case.

Correia de Sousa indeed claimed that he was changing the political and economic landscape of the Municipal Council of Luanda. To achieve this, he used his power to buy the support of many of the priests, although senior priests remained averse to his economic strategy. The two priests who were the leading supporters of his cause were Marçal de Figueiredo and Bento Ferrás, whom Cardoso branded 'unworthy clerics of that office' in his submission to the High Court of Appeals. He singled out Ferrás, in particular, as 'an idiot cleric, a cheat and a liar'. Ferrás was the confidant of another priest, Gasper Preto, whom Cardoso described as 'a messenger cleric who, with the collectors, is capable of anything, does what he wants in all matters and demands and cheats'.[242]

Farrás's allegiance was undoubtedly bought by Correia de Sousa on the basis of 'cash for sermons and trade'.[243] Farrás used the pulpit to voice his support for Correia de Sousa publicly. In his sermon entitled 'I had a dream', in which he declared that there was a plot to have Correia de Sousa arrested, it was clear that he was alluding to the former members of the Municipal Council of Luanda as well as influential Jesuit figures. Cardoso in his submission to the Court of Appeal states, '[Farrás] said in a sermon that he had a dream that they wanted to arrest the Governor; after this, he left for his business in the Spanish Indies without waiting for the Lord Bishop.'[244] Correia de Sousa had forbidden any priests and members of the Municipal Council to leave Angola, and had positioned soldiers in the port in Luanda to monitor those leaving. That Farrás was allowed to travel freely from Luanda to the Spanish Indies demonstrates his complicity with Correia de Sousa. Correia de Sousa also had the

---

[241] 'Relação do Padre Mateus Cardoso', p. 181, 'e assi tudo hé maldade do gouernador que traçou emriquecer cõ manhas diabólicas'.
[242] 'Relação do Padre Mateus Cardoso', p. 187, 'clérigo da legacia que cõ os colleitores podem muito, faz o que quer, em matéria de demandas e trapaças'.
[243] 'Relação do Padre Mateus Cardoso', p. 187.
[244] 'Relação do Padre Mateus Cardoso', p. 187, 'disse em huma pregação que sonhara que queriao prender o gouernador; este depois que fez seu negocio se foi pera as índias de Castella, sem esperar pollo Senhor Bispo'.

support of three other priests, Marçal de Figueiredo, Gaspar Preto (who was Angolan) and Diogo Nabo Paçanha. It was undoubtedly this kind of formal support for Correia de Sousa that led Mendonça to accuse the Church of participation in slavery in his court case.

In 1622, Correia de Sousa was arrested, after having fled to Cartagena, for not returning the enslaved Kazanze and Bumbi people to Angola, and for causing unrest in Angola, Kongo and the Municipal Council of Luanda. He returned to Portugal for imprisonment by the Madrid Crown: 'João Correia de Sousa, who left this government last year, and went to Cartagena in the New World, was there arrested by the order of His Majesty; and in Lisbon he escaped from the blame put on his government.'[245]

The Municipal Council of Luanda (see Figure 7)[246] was left in the hands of a military junta led by Captain Pero Coelho de Sousa, who in 1622 was 'one of those who sentenced the King's Senior Crown Judge to death, and was the one who came from the war with the soldiers to arrest him, and that he [Correia de Sousa] begged everyone to recognise him as his own person until the governor made it back, that at latest would be eight months.'[247]

1.7 THE FEUD BETWEEN CORREIA DE SOUSA AND ÁLVARES

I will now further develop the theme of the slave trade in Angola and Kongo and detail the intersection between the Church and slavery. The Church in Angola, and the Jesuits' Society, were silent with regard to criticising the slave trade. Their lack of criticism indicates that they were

---

[245] BNL, ms. 241, fls. 198v.-199 e, 'Joaõ Correa de Souza, que deixou este governo o anno passado, e se foi para Cartagena do novo Mundo, veyo de lá prezo por ordem de S. Magestade, e em Lisboa se livra das culpas do seu Gouerno.' See also pp. 212–213 and MMA, vol. VII, p. 298. Kara Schultz has recently explored the commercial links between the slave trades in Spanish and Portuguese America during the Iberian Union (1580–1640). This connection was more than a merely commercial link, but included elements of politics, as well. See Kara Schultz, 'Interwoven: Slaving in the Southern Atlantic under the Union of the Iberian Crowns, 1580-1640', *Journal of Global Slavery*, 2017, pp. 248–272.

[246] The map shows the trading of the time. For the most part, the trade with the Atlantic was in slaves. It is estimated that about 10,000–12,000 enslaved Angolans were shipped to the Americas every year in the seventeenth century.

[247] 'Relação do Padre Mateus Cardoso', p. 189, 'que foy hum dos que sentenciarão á morte o ouuidor dei rei, e que ueyo da guerra cõ os soldados pera o prender, e que pedia que todos o reconhecessem como a sua própria pessoa até elle gouernador tornar, que ao mais tardar serião oito mezes'.

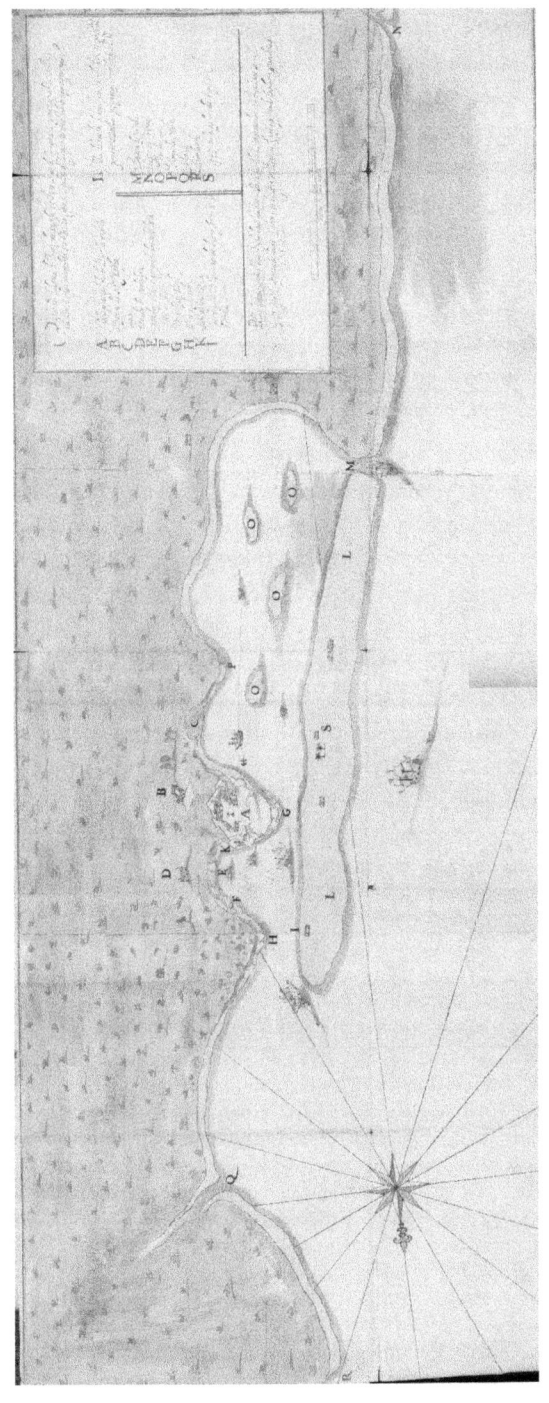

FIGURE 7 Map of Luanda, Angola, in the seventeenth century. Biblioteca da Ajuda, Lisbon, Portugal. [BAL], cartografia, MS. A descrição da barra do reino de Angola, 51-IX-21 (fl. 2.), Armário Met.X. Photograph by the author.

complicit with the merchants who were members both of the Muncipal City Council of Luanda and of the Church, and suggests that the Church benefited from the slave trade. In his writings, Cadornega describes the feud between Gaspar Álvares and Governor Correia de Sousa, outlining – as discussed above – that Álvares complained about Correia de Sousa before going to the Jesuits in Luanda to train as a novice. Cadornega was in agreement with Cardoso about the events that befell Álvares in Luanda:

> Gaspar Álvares [Devil Boy] was born in Lisbon and was an extremely wealthy merchant in Angola. Due to some issues with the Governor João Correia de Sousa, he went to the Jesuit College of Luanda and became a novice. He made a will on 13 February 1623 and granted this to the Jesuits for the founding of seminaries in the Kongo and in Luanda. Gaspar Álvares died in November 1623.[248]

Álvares had accumulated his wealth through slave-trading between Angola and Brazil and Argentina, and the sum he set aside in his will for the founding of seminaries was 20,000 cruzados, the worth of 400 enslaved people (see Table 2). Álvares wrote his will almost three months before he was to be executed on 2 May 1623 in the city of Luanda by order of Correia de Sousa. The execution did not take place, but Alvares nonetheless died that year, on 23 October 1623. The following year, on 20 April 1624, an attorney general from the Society of Jesus in the Court of Madrid, Antonio Colaço, 'sent a petition to the Crown asking for the Mission in Kongo to waive a customs tax of 400 slaves, equivalent to the 20,000 cruzados that Gaspar Álvares had outlined in his will, which the Society of Jesus had not received'.[249] Three governors were appointed to preside over the petition before it reached any

---

[248] Cadornega, *História Geral*, vol. III, p. 312, 'Gaspar Álvares [Menino Diabo] era natural de Lisboa e foi comerciante riquissimo emAngola. Por virtude de umas questões com o Governador João Correia de Sousa, recolheu-se ao Colégio dos Jesuítas de Luanda e veio a ser noviço. Fes testamento em 13 de Fevereiro em de 1623, e dêle consta uma importante verba testamentária a favour dos Jesuítas para a fundação de seminários no Congo e em Luanda. Gaspar Álvares faleceu em November de 1623.' The text does not explain why he is named 'Devil Boy', but it was probably on account of his business dealings. It was common practice for people to leave wealth to religious organisations in their wills in the seventeenth century, particularly in Salvador and Bahia, Brazil. And many wealthy slave plantation owners or *senhores de engenhos* left their wealth to the Santa Casa da Misericórdia of Bahia, Salvador, between the sixteenth and eighteenth centuries. See A Cópia do Livro 2. de Tombo 1652-85, Arquivo Santa Casa da Misericórdia de Bahia, Salvador, Brazil.

[249] 'Petição de Antonio Colaço, Religioso da Companhia de Jesus' [Petition by Antonio Colaço, Priest in the Society of Jesus], Fundação do Colégio do Congo, AHU, cód. 35-A, fls. 83v-85, 20 April 1624), 'Pede a V. Magestade seja seruido de ajudar a este sane to intento, com lhe perdoar os direitos de 400 peças que podem montar os dittos vinte mil + +. dos que o ditto Gaspar Alu[a]rez daa para a fundação do ditto Colégio, mandando os elle a índias de Castela', p. 229 (pp. 228–231).

TABLE 2 *Wealth of Gaspar Álvares, Portuguese trader and resident of Angola in the seventeenth century, based on his correspondence and will. By the author*

Items	People	Value description	Value
Build colleges: Luanda and Kongo		10,000 cruzados	10,000
		10,000 cruzados (2 cural of sheep and cattle)	10,000
		20,000 cruzados (estimated value of slaves held)	20,000
Seminary in Luanda	For 10 or more pupils, to include: clothing, food, maintenance and teaching. For children of the poor men of the kingdom	20,000 cruzados (worth 10,000 of Kongo cloths and another 10,000 of slaves' worth)	20,000 10,000 10,000
		500 cruzados from interest on slaves leaving for Bahia, Pernambuco for the seminary in rights plus 10,000 cruzados in Kongo cloths	500 10,000
His own lands near the Santa Casa da Misericordia de Lisbon; there, two houses to be built for rent for the Luanda Hospital		20,000 cruzados (estimated price of the two houses)	20,000
	To Paschoal Antunes 60 sheep, plus 20,000 cruzados, plus a slave named Antonio, and one named Lucrecia, and other people		20,000 10,000?
	To children of João Álvares, who is a neighbour in Abrantes 600,000 reis in credits	600,000 reis	600,000

(continued)

TABLE 2 *(continued)*

Items	People	Value description	Value
To Santa Casa da Misericordia House de Lisbon		600,000 reis	600,000
To what he owed to Santa Casa da Misericordia de Lisbon as the President of the Board		360,000 reis	360,000
Debt collected and given to Captain Henrique Dias da Estrada of the Santa Casa da Misericordia House de Lisbon		200,000 reis	200,000
More debt to be collected from Cartagena as witnessed in the books kept in the drawers, and more money sent via Brazil, Rio de Prata, assigned documents, accounts in the book in which many properties owed to me are written		Value not known	
Francisco Charamela lent to the Governors a debt which should be collected	To be given to the priests of The Society of Jesus	1,000 cruzados	1,000
Other properties not mentioned		Values go to the Society of Jesus for the building of college in Kongo or in another kingdom or seminary. If nothing is done	40,000

(continued)

Municipal Council of Luanda & Politics of the Portuguese   121

TABLE 2 *(continued)*

Items	People	Value description	Value
		towards that, then 40,000 goes to the Orphanage House	
To Confraria de Nossa Senhora da Conceição in Lisbon		For retable, 100,000 reis	100,000
To Casa Professa de Santo Antonio		4 slaves to send from Lisbon beautiful retable	??
To Manuel da Silva		For retable 80,000	80,000
Has built a chapel and there built 3 houses: a factory with a floor and 3 houses that follow for everyday prayer	Used by the São José's priests / Used by Paschoal Antunes and his children	130,000 reis / Rent value more than 200,00 reis / More 150,000	130,000 / 200,000 / 150,000
	To Luís Gonçalves Bravo	4 slaves	??
To the priests of São José to build a church		4,000 cruzados of city cloths / To be also given more money from his houses rent from now to July 1624 (March 1623–July 1624	4,000 / ????
	To the poor both men and women	2,000 cruzados	2,000
	For the sister of João Baptista to enter the monastery of Abadeça	4,000 cruzados	4,000
Any property found after this will, it should go to orphan houses, and the poor people, and a quarter of what is left should go to orphan houses	Poor people and orphans	?	?
To build a hospital in Alcantra	To Capucho Freiry, Francisco Antonio de santo Estevão	20,000 cruzados	20,000

(continued)

TABLE 2 *(continued)*

Items	People	Value description	Value
If the plan fell through, the money must go to wed orphans, and with poor			
	Any known relatives of his in Lisbon	To them 100,000 reis each	100,000
	For those orphans that I have asked to be wedded from my property are daughters of Gaspar Carneiro	200,000 reis of cloth each (200,000 x ???)	200,000??
20000 masses to be carried in Lisbon	For people, he may have done wrong to	Value not known. In Bahia, it varies from priest to priest	???
Money that comes from Rio de Prata for brotherhoods	To Father Duarte Vaz	200 patacas	200
Houses of stone that he has made from their senzala	A young woman of dual heritage that is in the house of Paschoal Antunes, he is setting free, called Catherina; he should marry her whom he has left with a young black girl	200,000 reis of cloths, a slave that she brought up by the name of Maria Ambuela with her sons	200,000

Sum total = 3,321,393 Cruzados
Gaspar Álvares' worth was 3,321,393 Cruzados in Angola, which equated to 664, 279 persons of enslaved Angolans and Kongolese taken to the Americas.

tribunal; two of them, Dom D. da Silva and Dom D. de Castro, approved the petition, and the third, D. Simão Soares, declined to sign it.[250]

[250] 'Petição de Antonio Colaço, Religioso da Companhia de Jesus', 'e o doutor Simaõ Soarez foj na resolução, posto que naõ assinou'.

The events that led to Correia de Sousa ordering Álvares's execution, and the subsequent wrangle over Álvares's inheritance, began in 1623 when Kongo noblemen wrote a letter of petition to the senior crown judge, André de Moráes Sarmiento, considered 'a man of justice and virtue', demanding that Correia de Sousa be stopped in his actions against Kongo.[251] The senior crown judge called a meeting with the municipal councillors and sergeants Antonio Bruto, Martim Correa and Lourenço de Figueiredo,[252] who accepted a brief containing the eighteen clauses written by Fajardo and approved by the Council of Luanda and the Crown.[253] As foremory mentioned, the brief sought radical political and commercial reform in Angola. In particular, the council sought to stop the governor having the final say over whether war would be waged or not. They asked that the judge, Captain Major Payo de Araujo, be present when they negotiated with Correia de Sousa.[254] In the first meeting, Correia de Sousa rejected the council's proposal not to wage wars against Angolans and the Kongolese. At a second meeting with Correia de Sousa, Dionizio de Faria Barreto, an African priest and judge, read out the brief to Correia de Sousa. This infuriated Correia de Sousa, who turned against the senior crown judge and the municipal councillors. He summoned the army, led by Pero Coelho de Sousa,[255] to Luanda under the pretext that he was to be imminently arrested by the city's Municipal Council.[256] When the army arrived, he divided the men into two groups and sent them to arrest members of the Municipal Council: the first group arrested the senior crown judge; the second group went to the house of Antonio Bruto, who escaped into the night on horseback.[257] Luanda was put under curfew that night, while soldiers opened fire and the residents were left in disarray.[258] Cardoso recounted that the city was in shock: 'all were in fear and confusion knowing the cause; it was that the soldiers surrounded the senior crown judge's house, who arrested him, and took him before the Governor, who received him with harsh words, called him a traitor, and declared that his head be removed; he ordered him to be chained and put in prison'.[259]

[251] See 'Relação do Padre Mateus Cardoso', p. 177.
[252] See 'Relação do Padre Mateus Cardoso', p. 176.
[253] See 'Relação do Padre Mateus Cardoso', p. 176.
[254] See 'Relação do Padre Mateus Cardoso', p. 176.
[255] See 'Relação do Padre Mateus Cardoso', p. 189. Pero de Sousa was one the people who executed the crown senior judge.
[256] See 'Relação do Padre Mateus Cardoso', p. 179.
[257] See 'Relação do Padre Mateus Cardoso', p. 179.
[258] See 'Relação do Padre Mateus Cardoso', p. 180.
[259] 'Relação do Padre Mateus Cardoso', p. 180.

Correia de Sousa ordered d'Araujo's execution for 2 May 1623, just a day before he himself was to be extradited to Portugal for imprisonment: 'and before he left on board the ship, on 2 May, he ordered the Judge Payo d'Araujo to be beheaded, the municipal councillors, Antonio Bruto, Martim Correa and Lourenço de Figueiredo and our Brother Gaspar Álvares novice, all placed in the pillory'.[260] The Crown in Madrid, having received unceasing complaints from Pedro II, the king of Kongo, about Correia de Sousa's invasion tactics in Kongo and Kazanze, had finally ordered his arrest and extradition to Portugal. The Luandan officials seized by Correia de Sousa were not executed and, if the Vogado report is accurate, Gaspar Álvares died in Luanda four months later, on 24 October 1623. There is, however, disagreement between Vogado and Cadornega surrounding Álvares's death: Cadornega stated that 'Gaspar Álvares died in November 1623' in the prison of Limoeiro.[261] It had been Álvares's desire to invest some of his wealth in the education of Native Angolans and Kongolese. Following his death in 1623, new teachers of Latin, philosophy, humanities, arts and rhetoric arrived in Luanda. Funded by Álvares's will, they taught the children of the *sobas* and noblemen of Angola and Kongo (see Table 2).[262] The will was strongly contested in court by his living relatives in Lisbon, especially by Antonio de Bairros Pereira and other heirs, for four years after his death. The case was heard by the Tribunal of Consciousness and Orders on 17 November 1627.[263]

However, the biggest legal challenge to Álvares's will came from the Crown itself on 16 October 1624, during the Luanda governorship of Correia de Sousa's successor, Fernão de Sousa (1624–1630). The Crown

---

[260] 'Relação do Padre Mateus Cardoso', p. 180, 'e antes de se embarcar, aos 2 de Mayo, mandou degolar em estatua ao juis Payo dAraujo, aos u [e] readores Antonio Bruto, Martim Correa e Lourenço de Figueiredo e ao nosso Irmão Gaspar Alu[a]res nouisso, todos postos no pelourinho'.

[261] Cadornega, *História Geral*, vol. III, p. 317, 'Gaspar Álvares faleceu em November de 1623'.

[262] See *História Política de Angola* (1622–1623), MMA, vol. VII, p. 79, 'El Rey de Angolla se tem outra uez reduzido á nossa amizade, e correm já as feiras. Chegarão este anno os Mestres pera darem Cadeiras de Latim, Casos de Consciência, e outras boas artes aos naturaes da terra, pera os quaes applicou bastantes rendas Gaspar Alueres, antigo cidadão de Loanda, e com o mesmo zello da honrra de Deos, e do bem das almas daquella dezemparada christandade de Congo e Angola, quer instituir huma Rezidencia da Companhia em Congo, e hu Seminário em Loanda, pera nelle se criarem os filhos dos Sovaas e de outros Ethiopes nobres nos costumes da Jgreja, e Letras Sagradas, per o grande effeito que estes taes faraó na conuersaõ de seus naturaes.'

[263] See 'Mesa da Consciência e Ordens' [Tribunal of Consciousness and Orders], ATT, liv. 30, fl. 79v., 17 November 1627, MMA, vol. VII, p. 279.

contested the will on two fronts: political and legal. Politically, the Crown claimed that it had to respond to the needs of its subjects 'with the desire that justice is done to all, as it is my obligation, and to avoid the outcry from the heirs of the deceased'.[264] The Crown had been informed about mismanagement by some of the officials in Angola and Kongo, the Church's complaints about Correia de Sousa in particular and Fajardo's complaints in general. It could be argued that Fajardo's claim to the High Court of Appeals had probably reached Madrid. The Crown pointed a finger at the Treasurers of the Deceased and Absent,[265] which was the office in Luanda charged with dealing with the property of the deceased, claiming that money was not being passed on to the relatives. The Treasurers had allegedly been appropriating the money, 'using it as if their own, to which great loss has been incurred from the heirs of the deceased, who have been in the city requesting their payments'.[266] The Treasurers of the Deceased and Absent should have passed any money to the Bureau of Consciousness and Orders; instead, they failed to declare it.

The Crown appointed Judge Diogo Nabo Peçanha to carry out an enquiry into the case and to ensure that all the money was returned to Álvares' family. In the absence of Peçanha, Correia de Sousa was then to appoint a bailiff of trust, who would keep hold of the money and who be responsible for sending it to Portugal and Spain. Meanwhile, the Crown in Madrid accused King Pedro II of Kongo's two confessors, André Cordeiro and Brás Correia, of corruption, after having been informed of their abuse of power in appointing 'treasurers, scribes and presidents of the Board of the Deceased'.[267] The Crown threatened to repatriate these priests if they failed to cooperate with the enquiry commissioned by the Crown.

The complication with Álvares's will was not only that he had become a novice and left his wealth to the Society of Jesus in Luanda but also that

---

[264] 'A Contestção do Testamento de Alvarés' [The Crown's Contestation of Alváres' Will], BAL, cód. 51-VIII-30, fls. 2t–2iv., 23–23v. c 25–25v., 16 October 1624, MMA, vol. VII, p. 266, 'cō intento de que a todos se faça iustiça, como tenho de obrigação, e euitar os clamores dos herdeiros do dito deffuncto'.

[265] For detailed information on this, see 'Sobre os Bens dos Defuntos e Ausentes de Angola' [Wills About the Deceased and Absents from Angola], ATT, ms. 871 (Livraria), fl. 52, MMA, vol. III, 18 March 1587, pp. 153–154, and 'Alvará Sobre o Dinheiro dos Defuntos e Ausentes de Angola' [Royal Decree About Money of the Deceased and Absent from Angola], ATT —Ms. 871 (Livraria), fl. 52, 26 June 1588, MMA, vol. III, pp. 368–370.

[266] 'A Contestção do Testamento de Alvarés', p. 266, 'uzando delle, como de cousa sua própria, de que resulta notauel perda aos herdeiros dos deffunctos, que nesta cidade andaó requerendo seus pagamentos'.

[267] 'A Contestção do Testamento de Alvarés', p. 267, 'que com seu poder elegem thesoureiros, escnuaes e prouedores dos deffunotos'.

his will had not been properly witnessed. There had been no witnesses present at its signing, aside from the priests from the Church who were implicated in its signing by Vogado, the director of the Jesuit College in Luanda. Álvares left a colossal sum of money to the Society of Jesus, in the region of 400,000 cruzados, equal to the value of 8,000 enslaved people and more than the cost of twenty colleges on the scale of the Jesuit College in Salvador, Bahia (see Table 2). It was clearly an amount that was envied by the Crown itself.

The Crown accused Jesuit leaders of corruption and embezzlement, claiming that the Treasurers of the Deceased and Absent were given backhanded pay-outs to ensure that the will was authenticated. It was asserted that 'the Religious [priests] corrupted the officers with bungs: each was paid 3,000 Cruzados and another 1,000 cruzados went to a person who appeared for the absentees. The officers had forgotten what they owed to my service and the obligation of their office; they have abandoned the treasury for their own interests.'[268] Madrid urged the Jesuits in Luanda not to obstruct justice through religious censorship or to omit any information regarding the case; rather they should comply with the rules of the enquiry and return the money to the appointed judge. 'If they attempt to obstruct justice with any censure, that person or persons, be they religious [priests] or otherwise, will have disobeyed my decrees and will immediately be sent back to this kingdom [Portugal–Spain].'[269]

Four months later, on 10 February 1625, governor Fernão de Sousa was able to defuse the conflict between the Crown and the Society of Jesus in Luanda by proposing that it was in the interest of both the Crown and the Álvares family that the money be kept in the possession of the Jesuits, rather than in the hands of the Treasurers, until a solution was found. He assured the Crown that 'the inventory of Gaspar Álvares's wealth will be implemented, and it will not get lost for being in the hands of the priests of the Society of Jesus, it being much safer in their hands than in the hands of

---

[268] 'A Contestção do Testamento de Alvarés', p. 267, 'os dittos Religiozos corronpendo os ditos officiaés cõ peitas, e dandolhe[s] tres mil cruzados a cada bum, e outros mil cruzados á pessoa que requeria pellos auzentes, esquecendosse os ditos officiaés do que deuiaõ a meu seruiço, e á obrigação de seus officios, lhe[s] largarão toda a fazenda pello dito interesse'.

[269] 'A Contestção do Testamento de Alvarés', p. 278, 'e sendo caso que os ditos Religiozos perturbem fazer iustiça cõ algũas sensuras, a tal pessoa ou pessoas, posto que eclesiásticas sejaõ, que o intentarem, e naõ obedecerem a meus mandados, os embarcareis logo pêra este Reino'.

the Treasurers'.[270] He went further, suggesting that the Treasurers of the Deceased and Absent must be overseen by the newly appointed senior crown judge, who should have the role of Chief Commissioner of the Deceased. Whilst in post, he should appoint the Treasurers of the Deceased, who must trust him, and who ought to be moneyed people who would give him '*residência*' or an 'official judicial review' after he completed his term in office. For Fernão de Sousa, this would prevent the mismanagement of the Treasury and hold the officers charged with the job to account. Giving him an 'Official Judicial Review' – that is, auditing him – would also prevent him from running away to Brazil or to other regions such as the Spanish Indies, because 'he must return to the kingdom, and he would not dare to do wrong, and if he does it, he will be punished, and his Majesty will not make use of his services again'.[271] Sousa did not want a repeat of the Gaspar Ferras's case, in which Ferras – the president of the Treasurers of the Deceased in Luanda – having been accused of corruption in the handling of Gaspar Álvares's will, had fled to Pernambuco after learning that the Crown had issued a warrant for his arrest. As Fernão de Sousa recorded:

... with this will comes the inventory [will] and more papers that belong to the Treasury of which Gaspar Alu[a]rez made in the Jesuits College in this City; with them I sent Simaõ de Niza to prison, who was the Treasurer of the Deceased and Manoel Paez who served as a Scribe. Not Gaspar Ferras, who was the President of the Deceased, for when a letter was issued, and an order given by His Majesty to arrest and send him there, he had already gone to Brazil. In that it was precarious to arrest him in Pernambuco, I have written to Governor Mathias de Albuquerque that when arrested it would be favourable that he is sent to the Bureau of Consciousness.[272]

---

[270] 'Carta de Fernão de Sousa a El-Rey', BAL, ms. 51-VIII-30, fls. 320–320v, MMA, vol. VII, 10 February 1625, p. 322, 'o jnuentario da fazenda de Gaspar Alu[a]res se fará, e naõ se té perdido em estar esta fazenda em mãos dos Padres da Companhia, porque nelles está mais segura que em Thezoureyros'.
[271] 'Carta de Fernão de Sousa a El-Rey", 10 February 1625, p. 322, 'pera dar rezidencia quando acabar, e deixar as contas findas cõ entrega do que carregar sobre os Thezoureyros que seruiraõ cõ elle, porque há de tornar pera o Reyno, e naõ ouzará fazer couza mal feita, e se a fizer será castigado, e naõ se siruirá V. Magestade mais delle'.
[272] 'A Carta de Fernão de Sousa à Mesa da Consciência' [A Letter of Fernão de Sousa to the Bureau of Consciousness] BAL, ms. 51-VIII-30, fl. 324–324v, 13 August 1625, p. 343, 'com esta será o jnuentario e mais papeis pertencentes á fazenda que ficou de Gaspar Alu[a] rez, que faíeceo no collegio da Companhia desta Cidade; cõ elles mando Simaõ de Niza prezo, que foy Thezoureyro dos defunctos e Manoel Paez que seruio de escriuaõ, Naõ vay Gaspar Ferras, que foy Prouedor, porque quando se deo a carta e ordê de V. Magestade pera o prender e embarcar, hera hido pera o Brazil. Em comprimento della foy precatório pera o prendere em Pernambuco, e ao Gouernador Mathias de Albuquerque escreuy que preso a bom recado o remetesse à Mesa da Consciência.'

The imprisonment of Simão de Niza brought the Gaspar Álvares scandal to its lowest point, demonstrating the lingering political and religious problems within Luanda and Kongo during the period and a political landscape that was mired in greed, jealousy, treachery and power struggles. The case of Niza only superficially highlights hidden issues about slavery in Angola, which so far has been brushed aside when researching the Atlantic slave trade. The case changes our ideas of what slavery was in relation to Central West Africa. Before leaving for his imprisonment in Portugal, Niza wanted to make clear that the corruption regarding Álvares's testament ran deep in the Society of Jesus in Luanda. During his hearing, he 'pulled out an instrument from the Judge of the Deceased',[273] with which he was intending to frame the Jesuits and shed light on their involvement in the scandal. 'Priests of the Society of Jesus knew of it, and that it was intended to discredit their religion, and they asked their lawyer to press charges against him, and obliged him with censures to show it, and by not obeying them he aggravated them, and declared it to priests.'[274] Niza confided in Fernão de Sousa as he sought protection from him against the priests who wielded great power in Luanda.[275] In order to aid him, Fernão de Sousa demanded that he show him the instrument in question. However, Niza refused, and 'persisted in his stubbornness and was sent [to Portugal] for excommunication'.[276]

On Christmas Eve, 1625, Fernão de Sousa concluded his enquiry into Álvares's scandal and sent a letter to the Crown in Madrid, stating: 'I have given an account to His Majesty on how I have proceeded in the case of the Deceased and Absents' wealth, and am sending in two ways the inventory of items that has been left by Gaspar Álvares, along with other things that belong to His Majesty.'[277]

---

[273] 'Carta do Governador Fernão de Sousa à Mesa do Paço' [A Letter of Governor Fernão de Sousa to a Bureau of the Palace], BAL, ms. 51-VIII-30, fl. 325v, 17 August 1625, p. 351, 'tirou hum estromento no Juizo dos defunctos'.

[274] 'Carta do Governador Fernão de Sousa à Mesa do Paço', p. 351, 'souberaõ no os Padres da Companhia, e que era em descrédito de sua Religião, e pedirão ao seu conseruador que procedesse contra elle, obrigando o cõ sensuras que o mostrasse, e por naõ obedecer a ellas as aggrauou, e declarou'.

[275] See the case of Ferras, who excommunicated him and sent him to the Island of São Tomé without consulting Fernão de Sousa, governor of Luanda. See 'Relaçaõ para o Ill.mo Sñr Collector'.

[276] 'Carta do Governador Fernão de Sousa à Mesa do Paço', p. 351, 'persistindo em sua contumácia [Obstinacy, stubbornness, insistence, rebellion] se resolueo em se embarcar excomungado'.

[277] 'A Carta de Fernão de Sousa a El-Rey' [A Letter of Fernão de Sousa to the King], BAL, ms. 51-VIII-30, fl. 328v, 24 December 1625, p. 405, 'tenho dado conta a V. Magestade de como procedy na arrecadação dos bens dos defunctos e auzentes, -e mandado por duas

1.8 KONGOLESE CAPTIVES RETURN FROM BRAZIL
(1623–1627)

Pressure to return the Kazanze and Bumbi captives to Angola and Kongo came predominantly from authorities within Kongo. The Kongolese king, Pedro II, demanded that justice be done and that Correia de Sousa return those he had sent to Brazil, São Tomé and the Spanish Indies. The Crown in Madrid sent a letter on 7 December 1622 ordering the governor of Brazil, Salvador and Bahia, Diogo Mendonça Furtado, to uncover the whereabouts of the captives:

> ... the Governor Diogo de Mendonça Furtado has been ordered to know the whereabouts of the *sobas* whom João Correia declares are free ... and if it is the case that from Brazil, there has been something written on this issue about the slaves, it will be considered soon. And I will be informed of what happens.[278]

On 9 December 1622, the Crown issued a letter to the governors of Portugal stating that a fact-finding meeting about what happened in Angola would be called, and subsequently the matter would 'be discussed in the state council' and the 'justification of the war and the truth behind the Blacks who were sent to Brazil' would be ascertained.[279] After obtaining the truth about the war, the Crown responded by ordering Correia de Sousa to return the Kazanze people and those from Bumbi as free agents. In addition, the cost of their return would be met by Correia de Sousa himself.

The authorities in Madrid were eager to find a solution to the issue of the captives and their illegal enslavement in Brazil. Pressure from Kongolese authorities would not dissipate until the captives were returned to their homelands in Kongo and Angola. On 17 December 1622, the Crown issued another letter to Diogo Mendonça Furtado, addressing him this time as 'friend' and asking him to enquire diligently about the captives and the important Kazanze and Mbumbi political figures among them.

---

vias o jnuentario da fazenda que ficou de Gaspar Alu[a]rez, e nas demais cousas tocantes ao real seruiço de V. Magestade'.

[278] 'Carta Régia ao Governador do Brasil' [A Royal Letter to the Governor of Brazil] AHU, Angola, cx. 1, doc. 321, MMA, VII, 7 December 1622, p. 65, 'ao gouernador Diogo de Mendo[n]ça Furtado se ordenará que saiba dos souas que João Correia declara que saõ liures ... e sendo caso que do Brasil se tenha escrito algua cousa sobre este ponto dos escrauos, se verá logo. E se me dará conta do que pareçer'.

[279] 'Carta Régia aos Governadores de Portugal' [A Royal Letter to the Governors of Portugal] AHU, Angola, cx. 1, doc. 321, MMA, VII, 9 December 1622, p. 64, 'uereis em conselho de estado, e aueriguandosse a justificação da guerra se fará consulta do que parecer assy acerca delia, como dos negros que se leuaraõ ao Brasil'.

The letter was signed by the Crown's secretary of state and tribunal justice, Christovão Soarez, who was among those summoned by Madrid to investigate the circumstances around the captives. The letter said:

... from Joao Correa de Sousa's, Governor of Angola's, letters I understood that among the number of Black captives whom he had sent in different vessels to this state came *sobas* and other persons who are declared on a paper, which you will be given, signed by Christovão Soarez, from my Council and my Secretary of State, Tribunal Justice [meaning unclear here]. And for the service of God and myself it is necessary that they are treated as free; it seems to me that on this occasion there should be ordered, as I do, that as soon as you receive them, find out from them whether they want to return to Angola.[280]

The Crown demanded that Correia de Sousa cover the cost of the captives' return, declaring: 'if they wish to return to Angola, he must send them as soon as possible, giving them their fares and subsistence, and whatever else they might need ... and giving them all good treatment'.[281]

Madrid was also informed of the political danger that the free Kazanze people in Brazil might pose to the governing authority there. In a letter to the governors of Portugal, the Crown declared that the captives were not to be allowed to come together in case they created an uprising. Their continuous separation from one another was vital; they were sent to different captaincies in Brazil including Maranhão: 'considering that they continue to separate Blacks [Angolans] that are present in Brazil, Maranhão or other parts, to ensure that being together does not inspire revolt'.[282] The captives were given the choice of returning to Angola or staying in Brazil.

Some were returned during the time of Bishop Frier Simão de Mascarenhas, who was interim governor of Luanda after Correia de Sousa's departure.[283] However, not all of them could be returned: as mentioned, the death toll had been enormous.[284] At the same time, the Dutch occupation of Pernambuco and Bahia may have made it difficult to determine the whereabouts of all the captives. Yet Madrid made demands

---

[280] 'Carta Régia ao Governador do Brasil' [A Royal Letter to the Governor of Brazil], AHU, Angola, cx. 1, doc. 321, MMA, VII, 17 December 1622, p. 66.
[281] 'Carta Régia aos Governadores de Portugal', p. 64, 'ao gouernador Diogo de Mēdo[n]ça Furtado se ordenou que saiba dos Souas que Joaõ Correa declara que saõ liures, se querem tornar para Angola e que querendo o fazer, os mande com a breuydade possluel, dandoselhe á custa de JoaÕ Correa, embarcação, mantimetos, e o mais de que tiuerem necessidade, fazendolhe[s] todo [o] bom tratamento'.
[282] 'Carta Régia aos Governadores de Portugal', pp.64–65.
[283] See Cadornega, *História Geral*, vol. III, p. 459.
[284] See Heywood and Thornton, *Central Africans*, p. 137.

for the return of the captives during the time of Correia de Sousa's government in Luanda and after.[285]

Pedro II wrote a letter to the Dutch authorities on 27 October 1623 requesting military aid and manpower. This could be interpreted as part of an African military effort to oust the Portuguese from Kongo, as Thornton and Heywood have argued.[286] However, the tone of Pedro II's letter of 7 December 1622 to the Hispanic Crown shows merely a desire to secure the liberation of the captives.[287] He demanded their return on the grounds that they had been unjustly captured and had not been for sale in the first place. This was an official plea to set free those who had never in fact been 'slaves'. What the letter indicates was that Kongo's authorities were ready to challenge the Portuguese on the issue of the illegal enslavement of Kongo's people, similar to the challenge made by Angola's Mbandi.[288] This was also not the first time that Kongo's authorities had fought for their people's liberty; indeed, they had fought for centuries for the liberation of their people. Afonso I of Kongo already had contested Portuguese trade and slave trade in his kingdom, demanding that it be stopped.

The Crown in Madrid sent three letters in December 1622: two letters to Diogo Mendonça Furtado, one on 7 December and another on 17 December; and one on 9 December to the Portuguese governors in Brazil. All the letters commanded the return of captives sent to Brazil and ordered that Correia de Sousa see to 'their fares, food, and any general needs they might have, to do everything for them and treat them well'.[289]

On 18 March 1624,[290] the Crown sent another letter to Furtado telling him that the captives had been declared free and should be sent back to Angola and Kongo. Having not received any news about their return from this first letter, the Crown issued a warning and demanded a further enquiry into the captives' whereabouts: 'until now I have not known

---

[285] Sousa's governance in Luanda began from 1621 and ended in 1623. See Cadornega, *História*, vol. III, p. 473.
[286] For Pedro II's letter sent to Dutch authority, see Heywood and Thornton, *Central Africans*, pp. 140–141; and John Thornton and Andrea Mosterman, 'A Re-Interpretation of the Kongo-Portuguese War of 1622 According to New Documentary Evidence', *The Journal of African History*, 51(2), 2010, pp. 235–248.
[287] Carta Régia ao Governador do Brasil [A Royal Letter to the Governor of Brazil] AHU, Angola, cx. 1, doc. 321, MMA, VII, 7 December 1622, p. 65.
[288] 'Relação de Fernão de Sousa a El-Rei'.
[289] 'Carta Régia aos Governadores de Portugal', pp. 664–666.
[290] 'Carta Régia ao Governador do Brasil' [A Royal Letter to the Governor of Brazil] AHU, Angola, cx. 1, doc. 323, MMA, vol. VII, 18 March 1624.

how the decree has been fulfilled; it seems to me necessary to issue it again.'[291] In Angola, Governor Fryer Simão de Mascarenhas was tasked with finding the captives, negotiating their release from captivity in Brazil and ensuring their safe return to Angola. However, Mascarenhas was dealing with an internal problem in Luanda, where the military junta faithful to Correia de Sousa was clinging to power. The junta disregarded Mascarenhas's instructions, and the Crown was forced to write instructing Pero Coelho de Sousa – the junta's leader – to turn the power of the military over to civilian authority so that the council could be run without interference. However, Pero Coelho de Sousa withheld any correspondence from Madrid from Mascarenhas, who remained ignorant of the Crown's instructions for six months after his arrival in Luanda on 9 August 1623. It was only on 13 January 1624 – by which time the junta's leader, Pero Coelho de Sousa, was dead[292] – that Mascaranhas received a letter from the king decreeing that de Sousa give up the government: 'On 13 January I received a letter that Your Majesty [was to] give new awards of royal offices to this government ... and consequently Your Majesty's decree to write to Pero Sousa Coelho that he give up the government. He has done it and the letter came into my hands [...] two days after confirming Pero Coelho de Sousa died.'[293]

On 3 February 1624, Mascarenhas informed the Crown of the outcome of his own enquiries in Brazil. He had managed to negotiate the release from Brazil of fifty-three people, including the duke of Bamba's cousin. Mascarenhas declared:

... with a satisfaction on the affairs of the Kingdom of Kongo and the war of Bumbi that was fought in the time of Governor João Correia de Sousa, I have written to you, Your Majesty, and to the King of Kongo of what has been done. For the people captured in that war [...] that have been scattered in that land, I made great effort and ordered that they were returned to the Duke of Bamba [...] Of the fifty-three people who came, one was the cousin [female] of the Duke.[294]

---

[291] 'Carta Régia ao Governador do Brasil', 18 March 1624, p. 'e porque ategora naõ tenho sabido de como se executou esta ordem, me pareceotornauolo a emcomendar por esta'.
[292] See Cadornega, *História Geral* vol. II, p. 567.
[293] 'Carta D. Fryer Simão de Mascarenhas', [A Letter of D. Fryer Simão de Mascarenhas], AHC, Angola, cx. 1, doc. 248, MMA, vol. VII, 3 February 1624, 'em 13 de Janeiro recebi a carta que V. Magestade [...] prouisam da noua Mercê deste Governo ... e pello cõseguinte man[dou] V. Magestade escrever a Pero de Sousa Coelho largesse [o] [Go]verno. Elle o auia feito e a carta ficou é minha mão [...] falecido dous dias antes que ella chegasse'.
[294] 'Carta D. Fryer Simão de Mascarenhas', 'em satisfação das couzas do reyno de Congo, e g [u]erra de Bumbe, que no tempo do Gouernador Joam Correa de Souza ouve, escrevi

However, Kongo continued to write letters, putting pressure on Madrid, because the number of captives who had returned from Brazil was far fewer than the number sent there. Madrid demanded that the governor of Brazil redouble his efforts to return them to Kongo, because 'being large, the number of Blacks whom João Correia de Sousa sent to Brazil, only very few of them have been sent back to Angola. And the governor wrote to say that he did not grant all of them freedom for he understood that some of them had come from the previous war.'[295]

Whilst diplomatic pressure exerted by Madrid on the Municipal Council of Luanda continued following the return of some of the captives, Pedro II was also conscious that Mascarenhas initially had limited power in Luanda, owing to the influence of the military junta who were still in control even after Pero Coelho de Sousa's death. He threatened to send his own ambassador to Madrid with complaints about Portuguese activities in the region if nothing was done to ensure the return of the remaining captives. Mascarenhas was aware of the political implications of not returning the captives, and sent two letters to Madrid explaining Kongo's stance and his attempts to dissuade Pedro II from sending his ambassador to Madrid:

> ... together with a letter that I have written to Your Majesty sent via São Tomé, there was also another [letter] from the king of Kongo that he sent me. He wanted to send an ambassador [to Madrid] with complaints. I have dissuaded him and I have been left calm. And I advised too that there is good treatment of the Portuguese there, including the restitution of [their] captured properties [...] that in the past was retained in his kingdoms [...], and that it is necessary that trade roots stay open [much freer] and that commerce continues with the king of Kongo.[296]

---

a V. Magestade e a El Rey [de Congo] o que convinha, e sobre a gente que na dita g[u]erra foi presa [...] que por esta terra se espalhou, mandei faser deligencia pera ser restituída, Ao Duque de Bamba [...] cinquoenta e tres pessoas, entrado neste numero [a] prima do Duque, [[[sé embargo desta [...]já mandado alguã pot vezes e na mesma [...] ou procedendo', MMA, vol. VII, pp. 199–202.

[295] 'Carta Régia ao Vice-Rei de Portugal' [A Royal letter to Voice-Royal of Portugal], AHU, cód. 295, fl. 80, MMA, vol. VII, 15 February 1624, p. 204, 'sendo grande o numero dos negros que Joaõ Correa de Sousa mandou ao Brazil, e muy poucos os que se tem enuiado a Angola, e escreuer o Gouernador (1) que ainda desses naõ deu liberdade a todos por ter entendido que algús naõ procederão como deuiaõ nas guerras passadas'.

[296] 'Carta de D. Fryer Simão de Mascarenhas' [A Letter of D. Fryer Simão de Mascarenhas] AHC, Angola, cx. 1, doc. 248, MMA, vol. VII, 3 February 1624, p. 200, 'em companhia de hua car[ta que por] uia de Sam Thomé escreui a V. Magestade hia outra de [el Rey] de Congo que me inuiou. Elle queria mandar Embaixador cõ queixas. Eu o desuadi e tenho socegado, e aduertido também do que hé licito e bom tratamento dos Portug[u]ezes, restituição da fazenda que prezam [...] passada lhes foi preza em seus Reynos [...] que cõuê os caminhos estam [mais liures] e o comercio se continua com o Rey de Congo'.

The political implications are evident in this letter. We cannot take for granted the importance of free-trade routes in giving access to the local markets in Angola and Kongo, which the Portuguese knew were important to their existence in Kongo and Angola. The free-trade routes could easily obscure the economic exploitation that took place in the region. Mascarenhas knew that the mission of Kongo's ambassador to Madrid would have made manifest the weakness of his authority in Luanda, as well as providing dangerous clarity on the heavy-handedness of Portuguese activity in Angola and Kongo and the illegality of the slave trade in the region.

Meanwhile in Salvador, Brazil, a new wave of political discourse was emerging to counter Madrid's decree to return the captured Angolans. This new argument presented an economic case for not returning the captives to Kongo, stating that not all captives sent to Brazil had been captured in an unjust war. As a result, not all of them should be returned to Angola and Kongo. After considering this argument, Madrid rebutted their claims opportunistically, asserting that if their presupposition of a 'just war' was correct and the captives had been captured legally, then Furtado needed to pay Brazil's royal fifth on the 1,211 enslaved people exported from Kazanze to Brazil. In this vein, Madrid sent a letter to Furtado on 15 February 1624:

... and considering that they came from a 'just war' and that until now there is nothing to indicate the contrary, it is important that my treasury does not lose the profit on these slaves. It seems to me necessary to give you the charge and decree that you confirm what you have heard and understood of what the governor of Brazil has done with them. Give him the order that it is necessary that he keeps what is for me, and that he sends the proceeds to this kingdom. It is important and there is a lot for you to answer for; take care to execute it without delay.[297]

According to my estimations, the royal fifth on 1,211 enslaved people worth roughly 60,550 cruzados would have been 12,110 cruzados. The documentary evidence shows that debate in Brazil about the return of captives from Kazanze was dropped altogether following the Crown's

---

[297] 'Carta Régia ao Vice-Rei de Portugal' [A Royal letter to Voice-Royal of Portugal], AHU, cód. 295, fl. 80, MMA, vol. VII, 15 February 1624, p. 204, 'E considerando que sendo a guerra justa e naõ constando ateegora do contrario, conuem naõ perder o proueito que minha fazenda pode ter destes escrauos, me pareçeo emcarregaruos e mandamos sque conforme ao que ouuerdes entendido que o Gouernador do Brazil tem feito delles, lhe deis a ordem que entenderdes que conuem para que se ponha em arrecadação o que me tocar, e se remetta o procedido a esse Reyno. E pois Vos hé prezente o muito que há a que acodir, tereis particular cuidado de fazer executar isto com toda [a] breuidade.'

demands, and instead the argument centred mainly on the captives from Bumbi. This was a political manoeuvre aimed at casting doubt on Madrid's claim that the captives sent to Brazil were illegal. The claim that the war waged on Kazanze had been just was designed to free the Bahian authorities from the burden of having to return the Kazanze captives, of whom there were many, to Angola; a much smaller number of captives were taken from Bumbi, and they were also of high status.

1.9 CONCLUDING REMARKS

Slavery did not exist in Angola and Kongo before the arrival of the Portuguese. Both the Angolan and the Kongolese authorities demanded the return of the people who had been taken to live in slavery in Brazil. They used their rights to exert pressure and demand freedom for these people, posing arguments based in Christianity, natural law, citizenship and humanity. This is why I am asking whether those taken to the Americas actually fitted into the category of 'enslaved people' or whether they were labelled 'slaves' in order to fit into the European merchants' commercial category. If enslaved people were being readily bought and sold, then it seems probable that the kings of Angola and Kongo, Mbandi and Pedro II, would have asked for the market price for these people rather than fighting for their return. In other words, we could extrapolate the argument and say that there were no enslaved people whatsoever in Angola in the light of this case. In commercial terms, these individuals would have had considerable market and labour value.[298] The difference between the authorities in Madrid, Angola and Kongo was their valuation of those taken to Brazil. For Madrid, if the return of the captives was not possible, on the assumption that they were caught from a 'just war', they demanded that reparations be paid to recoup their economic value, that is, one-fifth of the money accrued from the sale of the Kazanze sent to Brazil. Meanwhile, Kongo and Angola demanded a return of their subjects, regarding them as humans and not as objects of economic value or enslaved people.

The problem of runaway slaves in Angola, which was the reason given to wage war on the Kazanze and the Bumbi, also demonstrates that the model for modern slavery in Brazil could not work in Angola. It was possible to enforce slavery in a foreign country, when people are removed

---

[298] See Karl Marx, *Capital: A Critique of Political Economy*, vol. I, London: Lawrence & Wisehart, 1954.

from their own communities. However, the Angolans knew their own soil and laws and knew that they could not be enslaved for as long as the Africans who were taken to Brazil or elsewhere in the African continent, such as the island of São Tomé.[299] In Angola, of those captives who escaped or ran away from Portuguese captivity, some joined Queen Njinga to fight against the Portuguese. Brazil was new terrain, however, and it took time for the slave captives to familiarise themselves with the region before they could plan an escape. In Brazil, Native enslaved people were able to run away, because they knew their terrain well. In Ngugi wa Thiongo's terms, African slavery was possible because it was based on the removal of people from their own continent to be exploited in another.[300]

The governors in West Africa were not interested in adhering to Crown policy. This is very much reflected in their behaviour in Angola. They paid lip service to the Crown but largely ignored the rules it set. Nevertheless, the Council of Luanda came into conflict with the governors for seeking to benefit their own interests in how they enslaved Angolans. Often, council members used the Crown as leverage to gain the upper hand. The council depended on the good will of the African kings to maintain its interests in the region. Soldiers were very much a law unto themselves and were often manipulated by governors to work against the council. Diplomatic and trade policy set by the Crown was predominantly ignored by Portuguese soldiers, merchants and residents.

Demand for labour for Brazil's plantations or *engenhos* (sugar mills) created great incentives to wage war on the Angolans and Kongolese. The Angolan governors could go down two paths. They could ensure that such wars waged were 'just wars' and that the Crown received a fifth of all the booty derived from them, and that they, too, received their fifth. Alternatively, they could choose to wage wars unjustly and face the prospect of royal fines and having assets confiscated. To wage an illegal war, the governors needed the Municipal Council to support them so that no reports of war would be sent to the Crown in Madrid. The argument that any transactions between Africans and Europeans meant that there were sales taking place, and by extension that Africans were selling other

---

[299] In São Tomé in 1595, captive Africans rejected their status as slaves and staged one of the earliest slave revolts. For a detailed study of the slave revolt in São Tomé, see Seibert, 'São Tomé's Great Slave Revolt of 1595' and Rui Ramos, 'Rebelião e Sociedade Colonial: "Alvoroços" em São Tomé (1545–1555)', *Revista Internacional de Estudos Africanos* 4&5, 1986, pp. 101–136.

[300] See Ngũgĩ wa Thiong'o, Decolonising the Mind: The Politics of Language in African Literature, Nairobi: Heinemann, 1994.

Africans to the Europeans in markets is not sustainable. The existence of exchange or transaction of goods does not necessarily imply the buying and selling of people as slaves, i.e. an existing slave trade, and I would argue that the transactions that took place among Angolans were mainly for goods and produce, and rarely for human beings. The Kazanze case shows that there was no sale involved, just treachery.

Gaspar Alvarés's case demonstrates the Church's involvement in slavery, albeit with some protest against Correia de Sousa's unjustified war and kidnapping and stealing of the Kazanze and Bumbi people. The Church had used the slave trade to advance the Christian mission, while its own principles set the contradicting demand for universal freedom for humanity. Gaspar Alvarés's business was based on the slave trade and thousands of people from Angola who did not fit the category of slaves were shipped to Brazil by him. Yet, in contrast to Correia de Sousa, he was never criticised for his actions by the religious authorities in Luanda. This might be explained by the fact that Correia de Sousa was more aggressive and ruthless in obtaining enslaved people, and only interested in his own profit, without Alvarés's ties to the Church. Indeed, even after his death, the Church sought to continue Alvarés's business. Mendonça's revelations in the Vatican rested on the types of activities outlined in this chapter. Mendonça stated in the Vatican that Christian merchants were conducting their business illegally in Africa, and Africans were being *raided, kidnapped* and *stolen* through the mechanisms of *treachery* and *war*. The Municipal Council, Portuguese residents in Angola, governors and soldiers were all economically dependent on the slave trade for their survival. To achieve their ambition, they entered into the trade illegally by enslaving Africans and acquiring their land. In Chapter 2, I look at Dongo and its relations with Kongo in terms of political and social structures. I discuss Aidi Kiluanje, also known as Philipe I de Sousa or Dom Henrique Rei do Dongo, and as Samba a Ndumba in Angola, and his election to the throne of Pungo-Andongo. I will look at both his rivalry with Queen Njinga and his family ties with her, and how the Portuguese used his election to foster their trade relationships in Angola by transforming *baculamento* into a tax payment in enslaved people. It was this mechanism of enslavement that was at the heart of Mendonça's legal challenge in the Vatican in 1684.

2

Ndongo's Political and Cultural Environment: Alliance, Internal Struggle, Puppeteering and Decline

Academics, priests, journalists, soldiers and governors, as well as overseas councils in Europe, the USA and South America, contributed to the history and historiography of Ndongo's cultural, political and economic role in West Central Africa in the seventeenth century.[1] To a large extent this reflects concerns about Ndongo's historical position of power in the region, its diplomatic relations with Portugal, Spain and the Vatican, and its eventual decline. Birmingham's seminal work on the history of Pungo-Andongo as a vassal kingdom of Portugal in the latter part of the seventeenth century, and its subsequent destruction by the Portuguese, who had

---

[1] To name a few, Thornton, *Africa and Africans*; Heywood and Thornton, *Central Africans*; Miller, *Kings and Kinsmen*; Ferreira, *Cross-Cultural Exchange*; Candido, *An African Slaving Port*. See also Heintze, 'The Angolan Vassal Tributes of the 17th Century' and 'Luso-African Feudalism in Angola?'; Alfredo de Albuquerque Felner, *Angola: Apontamentos Sobre a Ocupação e Início do Estabelecimento dos Portugueses no Congo, Angola e Benguela Extraídos de Documentos Históricos*, Coimbra: Imp. da Universidade, 1933; Vansina, *Kingdoms of the Savanna*; Cadornega, História de Angola, vol. I and II, Benguela: Edição do Banco de Angola, 1948; Silvia Hunold Lara, 'Palmares & Cucaù: O Aprendizado da Dominação, Tese Apresentada para o Concurso de Professor Titular, Área de História do Brasil, Disciplina HH384 – História do Brasil I', Campinas, 2008, [unpublished thesis], etc. See Giovanni Antonio Cavazzi Montecúccolo, *Descrição Histórica dos Três Reinos do Congo, Matamba e Angola*, vols. I–II, trans. Graciano Maria de Leguzzano, Lisbon: Junta de Investigações do Ultramar, 1965. The pope sent a letter to congratulate Njinga on her baptism as a Roman Catholic; see the letter from Pope Alexander VII's Brief to the Queen Ana de Sousa Njinga, 'Carissimae in Christo filiae Nostrae Annae Reginae Singae Alexander Papa VII', AV, Epistolas ad Principes (EaP), vol. 64, fls. 70v–71, doc. 115, 19 June 1660; also Basil Davidson, *Black Mother, Africa: The Years of Trial*, London: Victor Gollancz Ltd, 1961. See also Cadornega, *História Geral*, vol. I, and, for overseas councils, Marcello Caetano, *O Conselho Ultramarino, Esboço da Sua História*, Lisbon: Agência-Geral do Ultramarino, 1943.

long been perceived as an ally, examines the fascinating development of Ndongo as a political player in the region. Birmingham states that 'in the fifteenth century, Kongo was the dominant power in the area, but by the sixteenth century the Mbundu Kingdom of Ndongo (or Angola) was rising to take its place before giving way, in turn, to the Kingdom of Kasanje'.[2] He highlights Ndongo's role beyond Central Africa and across the Atlantic when defining the remit of his research: 'The Mbundu have been chosen as the focus of attention partly because of their relationship to several larger Bantu groups and partly because of the continuity of their contact with the world outside Africa.'[3] In selecting this as his topic of research, Birmingham's intention was to 'alleviate the extreme paucity of historical writing on West Central Africa by indicating the direction in which future research might be conducted'.[4] However, he falls short of prescribing what this research might involve beyond African shores, particularly in Brazil. At the centre of his research is the destruction of Pungo-Andongo and the death of the last king, João Hari II, but he does not map the influence of the remainder of the royal family and their impact in the Atlantic, Brazil, Portugal, Spain and the Vatican. The exile of Ndongo's remaining royals as prisoners of war,[5] first to Salvador in Bahia, then to Rio de Janeiro and other captaincies in Brazil, and finally to Portugal, escapes his attention. The status of the Ndongo royals exiled after the death of João Hari II as prisoners of war needs to be distinguished from that of slaves who were labelled as 'war captives' as a pretext for selling them.[6] The exiled royals were considered 'special' prisoners, as the Portuguese continued to consider them allies. They were afforded houses, food and clothing, their expenses were covered by the Treasury of the Portuguese Crown and they were given the best education at the most prestigious institutions in Portugal at the time.[7] In particular, neither Birmingham nor any other researcher has

---

[2] Birmingham, *Trade and Conquest*, p. ix.   [3] Birmingham, *Trade and Conquest*, p. ix.
[4] Birmingham, *Trade and Conquest*, p. xiii.
[5] I call them prisoners of war in order to distinguish them from the war captives, who were Africans captured in wars, enslaved by the Portuguese and sold in the Americas. The princes were prisoners of war because they were sent to Brazil and Portugal for political reasons. They were not enslaved; rather they were taken care of by the Portuguese Crown and given freedom of movement.
[6] Candido, *An African Slaving Port*, pp. 155–156.
[7] See Consultas Mixtas, fl. 187; and Consultas Mixtas, fl. 301, and 'Carta do Rei D. Pedro II para o General de Alcobaça'. The same letter is reproduced in AHU-CU-Angola, cod. 168, fl. 355 and in Padre António Brásio, *Monumenta Missionaria Africana, África Ocidental (1666–1885)*, vol. XIII, Lisbon: Agência-Geral do Ultramar, 1952, p. 239.

addressed the journey of one of the prisoners, Prince Lourenço da Silva de Mendonça, from Angola to Salvador, Rio de Janeiro (Brazil), Portugal, Spain and the Vatican before now.[8]

José Matias Delgado's notes on *História Geral das Guerras Angolanas* are significant in charting the Ndongo royals' exile to Brazil.[9] While Gray has produced pioneering studies on Lourenço da Silva de Mendonça, he, too, does not connect Pungo-Andongo with Brazil, Portugal, Spain and the Vatican by examining the dialogue between Africans or New Christians in the Atlantic and runaway slaves in Quilombo dos Palmares in Brazil.[10] Mattos has made a comparison between Mendonça and Dias, but does not acknowledge Mendonça's family's connection with Ndongo. Silvia Lara, in her seminal work on Palmares and recently on princes of Ndongo, does not connect Mendonça with either Palmares or runaway slaves.[11] Heintze, writing on Ndongo's history and sources, as well as travellers' accounts in Angola, does not engage with Mendonça.[12] Miller

---

[8] See Birmingham, *Trade and Conquest*; Thornton, *The Kingdom of Kongo*. On p. 91, Thornton cites a reference to a Lourenço da Silva de Mendonça being the procurator of the confraternity of Our Lady of the Rosary in Luanda in around 1684. See also Lara, 'Palmares & Cucaù'.

[9] See Delgado, 'Notes', in Cadornega, *História Geral*, vol. II, pp. 544–554. Delgado offers detailed trajectories for the princes of Ndongo from Ndongo to Salvador, to Rio and to Portugal, and their distribution among different convents in Portugal; he was the first, in 1940, to chart their exile to Brazil and Portugal but he does not mention Mendonça as being part of this group. See also Silvia Hunold Lara, 'Palmares & Cucaú: O Aprendizado da Dominação, Tese Apresentada Para o Concurso de Professor Titular, Área de História do Brasil, Disciplina HH384 – História do Brasil I', Campinas, 2008, [unpublished thesis]. I had a long conversation with Lara about making a connection between Lourenço da Silva de Mendonça and Brazil and Palmares, but her view was that there was no connection.

[10] Gray, 'The Papacy', pp. 52–68.

[11] Mattos, '"Pretos" and "Pardos"'. See also Lara, 'Palmares & Cucaú' and Silvia Hunold Lara, 'Depois da Batalha de Pungo Andongo (1671): O Destino Atlântico dos Príncipes do Ndongo', *Revista de História*, 2016, pp. 205–225; also 'Carta de António da Costa de Sousa'. The first letter was about their distribution to different monasteries. The second was about their family line, i.e. who their parents were. The third scrap of paper, which contained details of their allocation to different monasteries, is clearly not part of the original; it was even written on different paper and was added after the initial letter from the king. It says: 'Repartiçaõ pelos Conventos de Lisboa, e Reyno. Princepez Pretos que uieraõ de Angolla, por ordê de S.A. e estaõ nesta Çidade' [First distribution to the Convents of Lisbon, and the Kingdom, Black Princes who came from Angola, by order of His Highness and they are in this city]. The fourth paper 'Memoria dos Principez pretos que uieraõ de Angolla' [The Memory of the Black Princes Who Came from Angola] is even odder: the A5 piece of paper lists their names and family ties to the king. Four of those sent to Peniche were illegitimate children of King Philipe and were a lot older than the rest.

[12] Heintze, 'Written Sources and African History'; and Heintze and Rieck, 'The Extraordinary Journey of the Jaga'.

on slavery in Angola and its hinterlands and Vansina on distance trading and Ambaca family's traditions do not make mention of Mendonça.[13] Heywood, in her majestic work on Queen Njinga's struggle against the Portuguese in Angola and tussle with her brother Philipe Hari I, Mendonça's aunt and grandfather, does not discuss Mendonça.[14] Thornton, who was the first person to detect Mendonça's document in the Vatican while undertaking research for his Ph.D. in the 1970s, could not make that link in the absence of further documentary sources.[15] Reginaldo, in her crucial research on the importance of Angolan Christians in Salvador, Bahia, and retention of their African practices, failed to make a connection with Mendonça.[16] Candido, in her crucial work on the common culture connecting Benguela and Brazil and on African agency, does not engage with Mendonça's struggle.[17] Similarly, Curto, Oliveira, Domingues da Silva, and Ferreira in their work on the role of individual and African agency do not engage with the royals in Brazil and Portugal, or with Mendonça.[18] This research unveils for the first time the answers to important questions about who Mendonça was, where his family and their nobility originated, and how his studies in Braga in Portugal led to positions of influence in Lisbon, the Royal Court of Madrid in Toledo and the Vatican.[19]

Mendonça, in his drive to secure freedom for and the integration of enslaved Africans in the Atlantic, Brazil, Lusophone Africa and Portugal, was necessarily forced to adapt his methods and strategy. His exile to Salvador, where he lived for eighteen months, was fundamental in shaping

---

[13] See Miller, *Kings and Kinsmen*; Miller, 'Capitalism and Slaving'; see also Vansina, 'Long-Distance Trade-Routes' and Vansina, 'Ambaca Society'.
[14] Heywood, *Njinga of Angola*.
[15] Thornton, *Africa and Africans in the Making of the Atlantic World*.
[16] Reginaldo, *Os Rosários dos Angolas*; and Reginaldo, 'André do Couto Godinho'.
[17] Candido, *An African Slaving Port*; Candido, 'O limite tênue entre a liberdade', and Candido, 'The Transatlantic Slave Trade and the Vulnerability of Free Blacks'.
[18] José C. Curto, 'Un Butin Illégitime'; Curto, 'Experiences of Enslavement'; Oliveira, 'Donas, Escravas e Pretas Livres'; Vanessa Oliveira, 'Devoção e Distinção Étnica na Irmandade do Homens Pretos do Rosário da Cidade de São Cristóvão-Sergipe', *Portuguese Studies Review*, 22(2), 2014, pp. 79–112; and Vanessa Oliveira, 'A África no Brasil: as Irmandades Religiosas como Símbolos de Resistência', *Caderno do Estudante*, 1, 2008, pp. 75–81. See also da Silva, *The Atlantic Slave Trade from West Central Africa*, and Domingues da Silva, 'The Kimbundu Diaspora to Brazil: Records from the Slave Ship Brilhante, 1838', *African Diaspora*, 8(2), 2015, pp. 200–219; Roquinaldo Ferreira, 'Slaving and Resistance to Slaving in West Central Africa', in David Eltis and Stanley L. Engerman (eds.), *The Cambridge World History of Slavery*, vol. III, Cambridge: Cambridge University Press, 2011, pp. 111–131.
[19] See APF, SOCG, vol. 490, fls. 140–140v, 1684.

his understanding of the dynamics of the lives and experiences of enslaved people, the culture of *engenhos*[20] (sugar plantations) and the relationship between enslaved people, and their masters in Bahian society. Above all, however, it allowed him to understand the wider struggle of the Mbundu people in Angola and then in Brazil. Later, in Rio de Janeiro, where he lived for approximately six months, he was exposed to a further dimension of the experiences, treatment, death and burial of enslaved Africans and the general cruelty that they endured.[21] In Braga, Portugal, where he studied for around four years, Mendonça's ideas were shaped further and he acquired the knowledge and tools to voice his views in a much wider arena.[22] These cumulative experiences helped him to assess the wider picture of the predicament of enslaved Africans in Brazil and Portugal. In Madrid, Mendonça was empowered further, and his influence spread from the Iberian Peninsula to the wider Atlantic, where he was able to contribute to discourses around the Native Brazilian question, which was about freedom and the liberty denied to the Native Brazilian population.[23] Later, his ideas were heard in the Vatican. It was here that the scope of his quest for the liberation of enslaved African and their integration into Portuguese, Spanish and Brazilian society was comprehensively defined. I will return to these issues in Chapter 4 and Chapter 5.

---

[20] Royal sugar plantations were large and dedicated only to sugar production. They employed up to 300 people. Smaller sugar plantations created different types of produce. See Arquivo da Santa Casa de Misericórdia da Bahia, Salvador [Archives of the Santa Casa da Misericórdia, Salvador, Bahia, ASCMB], liv. 2, Do Tombo, 1652–1685; liv. 3, Do Tombo, 1686–1829.

[21] For discussion of slave burials in the period in Rio de Janeiro and Salvador, Bahia, see Russell-Wood, *Fidalgos*; Júlio César Medeiros da Silva Pereira, *À Flor da Terra: O Cemitério dos Pretos Novos no Rio de Janeiro*, Rio de Janeiro: Garamond, 2007.

[22] See 'Sobre os Principes Negros do Dongo Unidos no Navio São Verissimo Capitania da Frota' and 'Carta de António da Costa de Sousa'. Villar de Frades Monastery was known as the Congregation of Secular Canons of St. John the Evangelist, founded in 566 AD by S. Martinho de Dume. It is also called the Blue Canons and the Congregation of the Lóios. The congregation sent priests to Angola in the seventeenth century. See also Joaquim Alves Vinhas, *A Igreja e o Convento de Vilar de Frades*, Barcelos: Junta de Freguesia de Areias de Vilar – Barcelos, 1998, and José Marques, *A Arquidiocese de Braga no Século XV*, Lisbon: Imprensa Nacional-Casa da Moeda, 1998. It was the first congregation to send priests to Kongo in the fifteenth and sixteenth centuries. Vilar de Frades had a history of receiving African and Indian students. On 22 April 1539, it received the nephews of the king of Kongo. See Brásio, *Monumenta Missionaria Africana, África Ocidental (1490–1508)*, vol. I, Lisbon: Agência-Geral do Ultramar, 1952, pp. 86–89, pp. 90–103, and on African and Indian students, see pp. 66–69.

[23] See Archivo General de Palacio, Madrid, [AGP], C° 869/45, Madrid, 8 March 1679, "Real Lorenzo Del, Lacayo dela Reina" [Noble Lorenzo, Servant to the Queen].

Mendonça's own experiences[24] in Ndongo, Brazil and Portugal allowed him to recognise that slavery was an Atlantic question and needed to be tackled as such. For this, Mendonça returned to the old strategy used by his predecessors in Ndongo and Kongo, which was to mobilise a wider network of distinct nations (ethnic groupings) in West Central Africa and in Europe in order to tackle Portuguese occupation of the region. King Álvaro II[25] of Kongo, Garcia II of Kongo and Queen Njinga had all implemented these strategies in their time.[26] Garcia II, for example, had allied with Spanish, Dutch and Catholics in Luanda.[27] In a letter to Philipe IV of Spain (1621–1640), he strongly criticised the Portuguese move towards independence from Spain and offered the Spanish Crown his support.[28] For Garcia, as long as Portugal remained within an Iberian alliance, Kongo and Angola had a strong ally in Spain. Garcia's allegiance with the Crown in Madrid shows his deep understanding of international politics and the need for diplomacy, cooperation and strategic alliances. A Portuguese exit from the Iberian union represented a return to what Green calls the 'monolithic and rigid senses of affiliation'[29] that underpinned the old Iberian world. For Garcia II, Portugal's independence represented a backward step for the economic development of the West Central African region. Continued development required institutions of

---

[24] See APF, SOCG, fls. 490, 140–140v, 1684.

[25] Álvaro II of Kongo sent his cousin Antonio Negrita as an ambassador to the Vatican in 1603 to argue the case for freedom for the Kongolese people and for West Central Africa in general.

[26] See 'Carta de D. Garcia II Rei do Congo a João Mauricio de Nassau' [A Letter of King Garcia II Sent with His Ambassador to João Mauricio de Nassau in the Netherlands], Algemeen Rijksachief (Haia) Raporten en Bricven: Congo 1642–1645, 1. W.I.C., Brazilie, n. 58, 12 May 1642, in Brásio, *Monumenta Missionaria Africana*, vol. VIII, pp. 584–587.

[27] 'Carta de D. Garcia II Rei do Congo ao Padre Reitor do Colégio de Luanda' [A Letter of King Garcia II of Kongo to Father Rector of the Society in Luanda], AHU–CU–001, cx 3, d. 335, Angola, 23 February 1643.

[28] For Garcia II's criticism of Portuguese independence from Spain, see 'Carta de D. Garcia II Rei do Congo a D. Philipe IV Rei de Espanha' [A Letter of King Garcia II of Kongo to the Father of the Society in Luanda], Arquivo Geral de Simancas [AGS], *Secretarias Provinciales*, maço 2639, 5 October 1646'; the same letter is also published in Brásio, *Monumenta Missionaria Africana*, vol. VIII, pp. 450–451, along with his petitions to Philipe IV of Spain to aid him with an army to take back Luanda, which was the centre of shell money. He also requested technical assistance with mining in his kingdom, 'Petições de D. Garcia II Rei do Congo a D. Philipe IV de Espanha' [King Garcia II of Kongo's Petition to King Philip IV of Spain], AGS, *Secretarias Provinciales*, maço 2639, also published in Brásio, *Monumenta Missionaria Africana*, vol. VII, pp. 452–453. On his relationship with the Dutch, 'Carta de D. Garcia II Rei do Congo a João Mauricio de Nassau'.

[29] Green, *The Rise of the Trans-Atlantic Slave Trade*, p. 150.

power to be inclusive[30] and markets to be liberalised. These policies were promoted both by the Spanish Crown and by Garcia II, as an internationally connected African monarch;[31] and, to express his faith in a liberalised market, Garcia offered the Spanish Crown a contract to begin mining in Kongo.[32] Meanwhile Queen Njinga's efforts to mobilise a network of distinct nations saw her ally with the Jagas group and the Dutch in her fight against the Portuguese.[33] She recruited supporters from many nations and, significantly, urged those who ran away from enslavement and who sought her protection to fight alongside her. This nexus of relationships between the enslaved people, their masters and those who protected them was replicated by Lourenço Mendonça before he presented his court case in the Vatican. This marked the beginning of his quest for freedom and integration for enslaved Africans. It was a truly Atlantic endeavour.[34] I will return to this in Chapter 4, but for now I will turn to the political and social structure of the Mbundu people in Angola.

The aim of this chapter is to argue that the destruction of Pungo-Andongo took place because Mendonça's family publicly challenged the centrality of the Portuguese Atlantic slave trade. I contend that Mendonça's struggle for freedom for enslaved Africans in Rome and his dialogue with the Indigenous Americans and the New Christians were inspired by his family background in West Central Africa. The next

---

[30] For a detailed historical understanding of the importance of institutions in providing the foundational stability of a nation's economy, see Daron Acemoglu and James A. Robinson, *Why Nations Fail: The Origins of Power, Prosperity and Poverty*, London: Profile, 2012.

[31] Incinha Té, the king of Bissau Island, adopted a free trade policy. On 25 May 1698, he sent a letter to the Portuguese Governor in Cabo Verde and to the King of Portugal Pedro II that foreign merchants must abide to his policy. See Lingna Nafafé, *Colonial Encounters*.

[32] For Garcia II's criticism of Portuguese independence from Spain, see 'Carta de D. Garcia II Rei do Congo a D. Philipe IV Rei de Espanha'.

[33] Giovanni Antonio Cavazzi da Montecuccolo, 'Missione Evangelica al Regno de Congo', MSS Araldi, Modena, vol. A, B, C (trans. John Thornton), 2008.

[34] See Mesquita, S.C. Africa fl. 486. As mentioned, the affidavit was signed by Gaspar da Costa de Mesquita in Lisbon on 15 February 1681. Mentioned in this affidavit, Lourenzo Del Real, known as Lourenzo De' Rè, was a Native American who supported Mendonça while both were residents in the Royal Court of Madrid. Monzon was also mentioned in connection with his post in the Royal Court of Madrid, see Archivo de Palacio Real de Madrid, Patrimonio Nacional, Archivo General [Archive of the Royal Palace, Madrid, General Archive], cx. 233, expediente n. 10, 'Jacinto Roxo Monzon que la algunos anos sirve el officie de Notario Mayor dela capilla. y el dem. Secretario de susticia con todos puntualidad y legalidad' [Jacinto Roxo Monzon that some years ago held the office Notary Major of the chapel and also a secretary of justice which he served with all punctuality and legality], 9 April 1677.

Ndongo's Political and Cultural Environment 145

section looks at the political, social and cultural structures in Angola, and how social stratification helps us understand the society in both Angola and Kongo and their system of governance.

This chapter thus focuses first on the discussion of the political and social structures of the culture of the Mbundu people, from which Lourenço Mendonça descended, and how they interconnected with the way of life in Ndongo. It gives special attention to the definition of the term 'slave' in Mbundu society. Then it examines the rise of Lourenço Mendonça's grandfather Philipe Hari I to the throne of Ndongo, and the role of the Mbundus' traditional tribute system of *baculamento*, which the Portuguese commandeered to secure a political contract with their vassal kings and *sobas*. The chapter also explores how the rise of Philipe Hari I was used by the Portuguese to dismantle regional alliances by dividing the existing kingdom of Old Ndongo into two, and thus creating rivalry between the royal houses of Ndongo and Matamba. While Philipe Hari I aligned himself with the Portuguese and their interests, Queen Njinga stuck to Mbundu-Matamba tradition. This rivalry only ended when the offspring of both houses were exiled to Brazil, an event that also brought about the kingdom's destruction. Finally, the chapter will also review the policies of the young governor of Angola, Francisco de Távora 'Cajanda', and the political challenges he faced with João Hari II's rise to power, a development that resulted finally in the turning of *baculamento* into a tax system. It will chart the destruction of Pungo-Andongo after João Hari II's claim for independence and the exile of the royal family to Salvador, Rio de Janeiro and other captaincies in Brazil, and finally to the confines of various monasteries and forts in Portugal.[35]

The chapter uses primary sources from the seventeenth century: Arquivo Histórico Ultramarino de Bélem (AHU); Biblioteca da Ajuda, Lisboa (BAL); Arquivo Público de Pernambuco, Recife, Brazil; Instituto Histórico e Geográfico de Alagoas, Maceió, Brazil; Coimbra (biblioteca de Coimbra), Portugal; Archivum Romanum Societatis Iesu (ARSI); Arquivo Municipal and Público de Salvador, Brazil; Arquivo Nacional do Rio de Janeiro, Brazil; and Padre António Brásio's *Monumenta Missionária Africana, África Ocidental*. This data fed into a proliferation of histories written in the eighteenth and nineteenth centuries on West Central Africa focused on 'debt', the 'judicial tribunal system' and 'pawns' as new methods for obtaining enslaved people in the region. However, the root cause underlying the emergence of these methods lies in the introduction in 1626 by the governor

[35] See 'Carta de Antonio da Costa de Sousa a Manuel Barreto de S. Paio'.

of Angola, Fernão de Sousa, of the tax system of *baculamento*. The primary sources show that enslaved Angolans captured in the wars – *kijiko* – who had escaped and returned to their homeland were given amnesty according to their laws. I have unearthed this new data, not used before, in both the Arquivo Distrital de Braga (ADB) and Biblioteca de Braga (BB). Let us now look at Angola (see Figure 8), its political, social and cultural structures, and how its social stratification helps us understand the society in both Angola and Kongo and their system of governance.

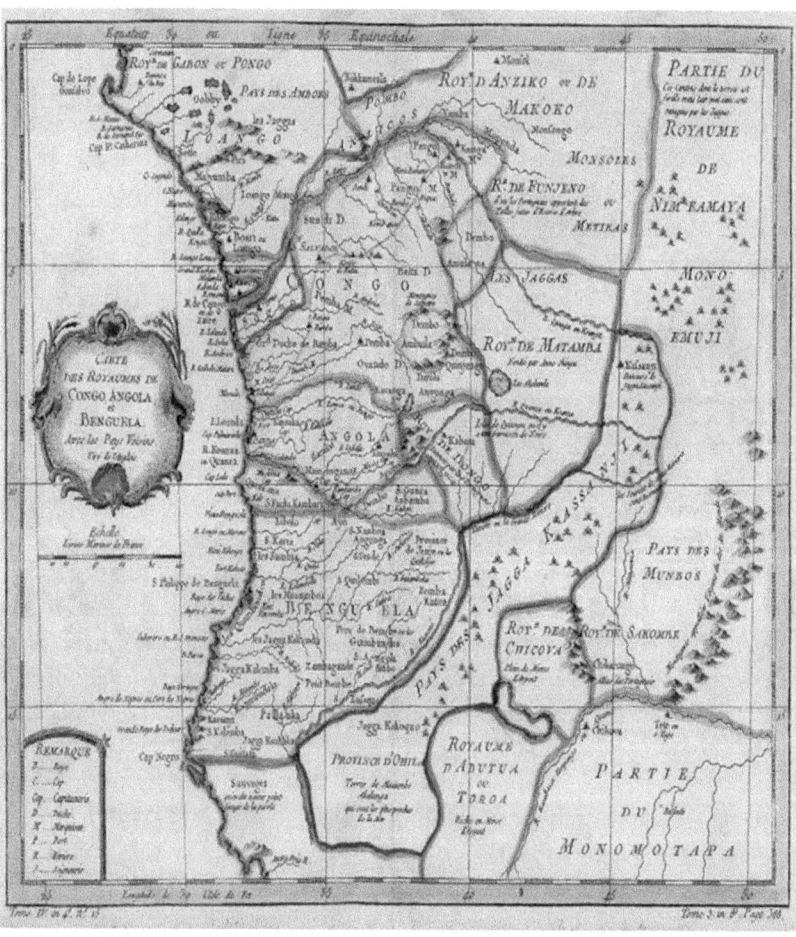

FIGURE 8 Map of Kongo, Angola and Benguela. Jacques Nicolas Bellin, 1747, Biblioteca Digital Luso-Brasileira (http://bdlb.bn.gov.br/acervo/handle/20 .500.12156.3/14333).

2.1 NDONGO'S POLITICAL, SOCIAL AND CULTURAL STRUCTURES

As explained in the Introduction, the Kingdom of Ndongo, also known in the seventeenth century as Dongo,[36] was a pre-colonial name for Ngola,[37] later called Angola by the Portuguese. The kingdom was named after the Mbundu monarch, Ndongo,[38] and the name became a succession title much like 'that of the Roman title, Caesar'.[39] Ndongo is a region in southern Kongo inhabited predominantly by the Mbundu people, who speak the Kimbundu language.[40] Kimbundu was widely spoken in the Atlantic in the seventeenth century, particularly in Salvador in Bahia, due to the large number of enslaved people transported there from Ndongo.[41] Ndongo included regions in the north such as the Kwanza River, Lukala and Bengo, and Old Ndongo (Ndongo originally also incorporated Matamba prior to the separation of the kingdoms by the Portuguese in 1626) had stretched further into territories such as Ilamba, Musseque and Quissama, all linked by Mbamba and unified into an area that came to be called Angola. The Mbundu people of northern Ndongo were termed

---

[36] See Freudenthal and Pantoja, *Livro dos Baculamentos*.
[37] For an etymological definition of the term, see Cadornega, *História Geral*, vol. I, p. 167. See also Amaral do Ilídio, *O Reino do Congo, Os Mbundu (ou Ambundos), O Reino dos 'Ngola' (ou de Angola) e a Presença Portuguesa, de Finais do Século XV a Meados do Século XVI*, Lisbon: Ministério da Ciência e da Tecnologia, Instituto de Investigação Tropical, 1996; Miller, *Kings and Kinsmen*; and Birmingham, *Trade and Conquest*.
[38] José P. Bayam, *Portugal Cuidadoso, e Lastimado com a Vida, e Perda do Senhor Rey Dom Sebastião, o Desejado de Saudosa Memoria: Historia Chronologica de Suas Accoens, e Successos Desta Monarquia em Seu Tempo; Suas Jornadas a Africa, Batalha, Perda, Circunstancias, e Consequencias Notaveis della*, Lisbon: Officina de A. de Sousa da Sylva, 1737, p. 382, 'Angolla he huma Monarquia na nova Ethiopia com este nome a intitullaraõ os Portuguezes accordando a terra o nome do Rey, que o dominava'.
[39] Bayam, *Portugal Cuidadoso, e Lastimado com a Vida*, p. 382, 'Angolla foraõ depois confervando feus fuceffores, como ... entre os Romanos o de Cezar'.
[40] Lawrence W. Henderson, *Angola: Five Centuries of Conflict*, Ithaca N.Y.: Cornell University Press, 1979.
[41] See 'Carta do Padre Antonio Vieira a Roque Monteiro Paim' [A Letter from Father Antonio Vieira to Roque Monteiro Paim], MMA XIII, Bahia, 2 July 1691, pp. 221–222. See also Margarida Petter, 'Línguas Africanas no Brasil: Vitalidade e Invisibilidade', in Ivana Lima Stolze and Laura Carmo (eds.), *História Social da Língua Nacional: Diáspora Africana*, Rio de Janeiro: FAPERJ, 2014, pp. 19–39; Jose Honorio Rodrigues, 'The Influence of Africa on Brazil and of Brazil on Africa', *The Journal of African History*, 3 (1), 1962, pp. 49–67. See also Ana Lucia Araujo (ed.), *African Heritage and Memories of Slavery in Brazil and the South Atlantic World*, Amherst, NY: Cambria Press, 2015; Hawthorne, *From Africa to Brazil*; and José C. Curto and Renée Soulodre-LaFrance (eds.), *Africa and the Americas: Interconnections During the Slave Trade*, Trenton, NJ: Africa World Press, 2005.

'Ambundu' and appeared often in the writings of Cadornega during the period. Meanwhile, southerners were called 'Ovimbundu'. Both groups spoke the same Kimbundu language.[42]

Ndongo was centrally ruled by a king of patrilineal succession and divided into 736 semi-decentralised political units administered by *sobas*.[43] The kings of Ndongo were subordinated to the kingdom of Kongo, and so Ndongo was technically a province of Kongo.[44] Thirty years after the Portuguese arrived there in the sixteenth century, the kings of Kongo were using their royal credentials in letters to their counterparts in Portugal. Afonso I of Kongo, known locally as Mvemba-a-Njinga or Mvemba ne Lumbu, addressed himself as 'the King of Manicongo, and the Lord of Ambundu'[45] in his correspondence with Dom Manuel, King of Portugal in 1512. In his letters to Pope Julius II in the same year, he informed the pope of his conversion to Christianity, and asked the Vatican to grant him royal credentials like his European counterparts:

Most Holy in Christ, Father, most gracious Lord our Julius II, by the divine providence of the Pontifical sumo. Your most devout son Dom Afonso, by the grace of God the King of Manicongo, and Lord of the Ambundu, command to kiss your most blessed feet with great devotion.[46]

Politically, Ndongo's system of governance was based on that of Old Kongo (which included Angola-Matamba), and even after Ndongo separated from Kongo in the seventeenth century, it still used the Kongolese political structure of *sobados*. This system of governance by proxy put central power in the hands of the king, while *sobas* were delegated administrative powers in their own provinces and granted a degree of autonomy. *Sobas* were of noble blood and were landowners with 'large portions of lands and vassals'.[47] They were in direct contact with their

---

[42] See Cadornega, *História Geral*, vol. I.
[43] See Elikia M'bokolo, *África Negra: História e Civilizações*, vol. I (até o século XVIII), Slavador: EDUFBA; São Paulo, Casas das África, 2008, pp. 185–205.
[44] See 'Carta do Rei do Congo à Cámara de Luanda' [A Letter of the King of Kongo to the Council of Luanda], AHU, Angola, cx.6, 14 November 1654.
[45] 'Rei de Manicongo & senhor dos Ambu[n]dos, 1512' [King of Manicongo and Ambundos], Damião de Góis, Crónica de D. Manuel, Parte III, cap. XXXVIII, see also parte III, cap. XXXIX.
[46] ATT, CC-II-30-I and Brásio, *Monumenta Missionaria Africana*, vol. I, p. 212, 'Sanctissimo em Christo, Padre, beatissimo senhor nosso Julio segundo, pela diuina prouidençia summo Pontifiçe. Vosso deuotissimo filho dom Afonso pela graça de Deos rei de Manicongo, & senhor dos Ambu[n]dos, manda beijar vossos beatíssimos pés com muita deuação, 1512'.
[47] Cadornega, *História Geral*, p. 27, 'Sovas que tem, com muitas dilatadas terras e Vassallos'; see also M'bokolo, *África Negra*.

communities and implemented local decisions on behalf of the king. Their authority was accepted and the people were bound by it.[48]

At the highest point in Ndongo's political hierarchy (see Figure 9) was the king, or *Ngola*. Beneath him was the *angolambole*, an army general who commanded 10,000 to 15,000 soldiers,[49] and the *camaristas*, the council of peace and war, whose members advised the king in the running of the kingdom. Beneath them were the *sobas*, noble administrators of provinces and villages. From the *soba* ranks the members of the council of elders, known as the *macota*, were appointed. The *macota* exerted a degree of control over the king.[50] The *tandala*, also appointed from *soba* ranks, were judicial figures who assisted the *macota* and were also the kingdom's politicians. They played the role of principal councillors and 'oversaw the entire lands and the politics of the kingdom'.[51] The *macunges*, who acted as ambassadors in realms outside the kingdom, were also drawn from among the *sobas*.[52] Finally, the *smiths* ensured the productivity of the kingdom and were regarded, through their innovation and toil, as the founders of the kingdom and the guardians of its myths.

Ndongo's political structure required close control and management to ensure its effectiveness as a system of governance, and the centrality of the king's power was crucial for the success of the kingdom. Indeed, while *sobas* were given some local power, the notion that they were autonomous administrators who could make decisions independently of the king is implausible and was invented by the Portuguese in their attempt to use *sobas* to destabilise the kingdom. If *sobas* did exercise independence in governing their provinces, it was the exception rather than the rule, and there was no principle of devolution embedded within the political structure of the kingdom. Instead, any independent action seen among the *sobas* who were vassals of the Portuguese was driven by their coercion

---

[48] Heywood and Thornton, *Central Africans*, pp. 68–98.

[49] John K, Thornton, 'The Art of War in Angola, 1575–1680', *Comparative Studies in Society and History*, 30(2), 1988, pp. 360–378. Philipe Hari I's army of 10,000 were used by the Portuguese; see 'Carta do Rei de Dongo a D. João IV' [A Letter of the King of Ndongo to D. John IV], AHU, Angola, cx. 5, 8 April 1653, and 'Consulta do Conselho Ultramarino' [Consultation of the Overseas Council], AHU, cód. 15, fl. 103v e 96v, Angola, cx. 5, 22 April 1654.

[50] See Heywood, *Njinga of Angola*; and Fernandes, *Description de la Côte Occidentale d'Afriqe*.

[51] Cadornega, *História Geral*, vol. I, p. 616, explains: 'governava todas suas terras e o politico de seu Reino'.

[52] Regarding *macumzes* (mukunji) (an envoy or ambassador), see Delgado's note in Cadornega, *História Geral*, vol. II, p. 90: the plural of *macumzes* is *mikunji* (ambassadors), but the Portuguese made it *makunzes*.

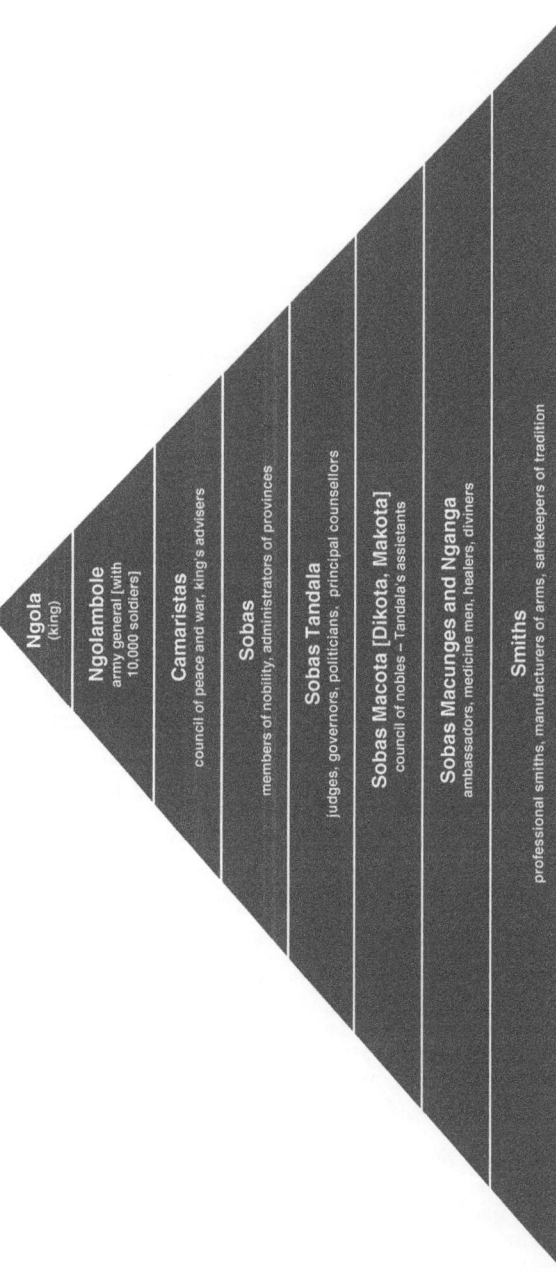

FIGURE 9 Ndongo's (Angola's) political structure, in the fourteenth to the seventeenth centuries. By the author, based on manuscripts and available literature.

by the Portuguese.[53] In particular, Queen Njinga struggled hugely to maintain her control of the *sobas*. The difficulties that her gender represented to Ndongo's royal patrilineage[54] were reinforced by Portuguese manipulation of the *sobado* through fresh claims of her illegitimacy to rule. However, it is clear that Ndongo had a defined and organised political system, and this challenges the traditionally held view that Africans did not have organised kingdoms prior to European contact and that their pre-existing political structures provided fertile ground for Atlantic slavery.[55] I will return to this issue in due course.

In addition to Ndongo's political hierarchy, there are social divisions to consider (see Figure 10). These were intertwined with politics and culture, and were played out in the political and social arena. The *Ngola* was at the top of the political and social hierarchy and he centralised and delegated power. *Sobas* governed the provinces, and the class still exists in Angola today. *Envala Ineni*, the *Ngola*'s first wife was in charge of all the *Ngola*'s wives. *Samba Angila* was the second wife of the *Ngola*, and *Mocama*, the third. The children of the *Ngola* were all of the noble class. However, distinctions between their succession rights were determined by the status of their mother within the royal household. The children of *Envala Ineni* were first in line to the throne, children of *Samba Angila*, second and so on. Philipe Hari I and Alváro II, both kings of Kongo, were sons of a *mocama*, a third wife, who was seen as little more than a household servant.[56] Outside of the royal household, *smiths* were the professional manufacturers of arms and a symbol of productivity and innovation and tradition.[57] *Murinda* were farmers and commoners and equal in status to *kijikos*, who were prisoners of war. The commonality in status between the *murinda* and *kijikos* indicates the nuances of social relations in Ndongo, nuances that the Portuguese, in labelling Ndongo's *kjikos* as *peças* (items), grossly misinterpreted. Ndongo's political structure and social divisions were, contrary to what is traditionally thought, not conducive to slavery.[58] It is my contention that there is no evidence to suggest that enslaved people had long been bought and sold, could be found in Ndongo's markets

---

[53] Heywood, *Njinga of Angola*. [54] M'bokolo, *África Negra*, pp. 426–427.
[55] See David Hume, *Essays, Moral, Political, and Literary, Part I, Essay XXI*, 'Of National Characters' (LF ed.) [1777], Indianapolis: Liberty Fund 1987, p. 28, footnote 10; and F. Hegel, *The Philosophy of History* (trans. J. Sibree), New York: Dover Publications, 1956, p. 18.
[56] On mistranslation of the Mbundu term 'wife' as 'concubine', see Miller, *Kings and Kinsmen*, p. 78.
[57] See Cadornega, *História Geral*, vol. I, p. 26.
[58] See M'bokolo, *África Negra* and Miller, *Kings and Kinsmen*.

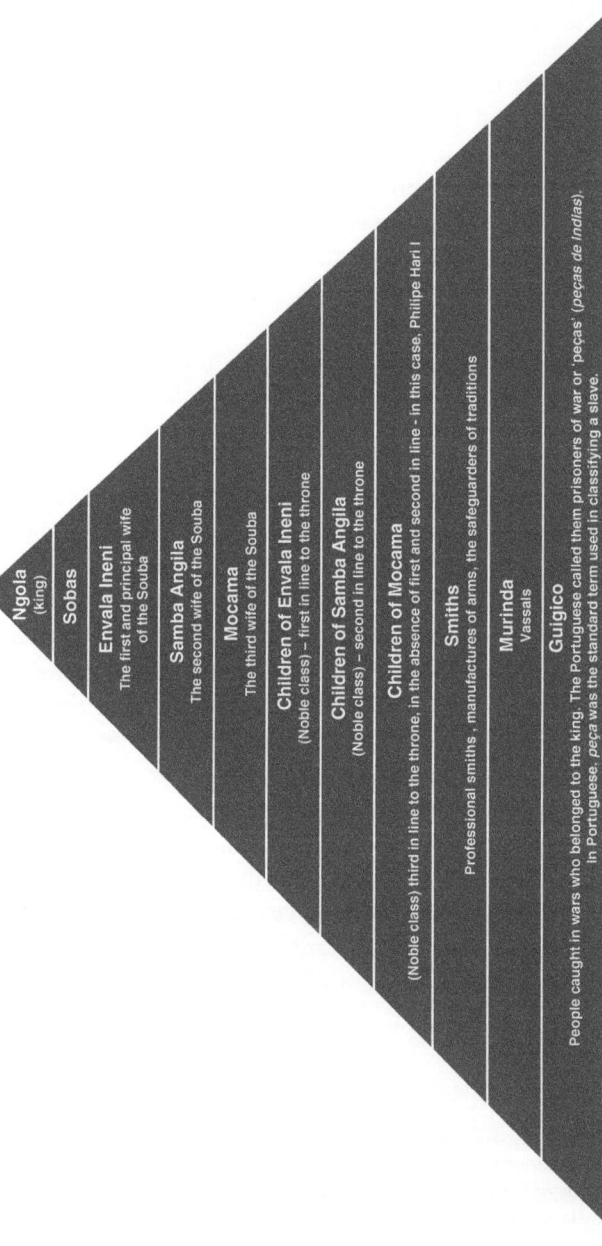

FIGURE 10 Ndongo's (Angola) social structure in the fourteenth to the seventeenth centuries. By the author based on manuscripts and available literature.

or were considered as currency.[59] As Mendonça's court case in the Vatican was to reveal in 1684, what was done to the Africans taken to the Americas as enslaved people was a crime against humanity because they were free people according to human, natural, divine and civil laws.

Let us now take a closer look at the use of the term 'slave' among the Mbundu people and see whether it resonates with the term used in the Atlantic slave trade. I would argue, as mentioned briefly in Chapter 1, that we are dealing with a term associated with completely different practices: servitude in Ndongo culture cannot be equated with slavery as the term was used in the Atlantic trade.

2.2 THE TERM 'SLAVE' IN NDONGO SOCIETY

The discourse around the inherited sense of guilt experienced by those regions that developed and operated the slave trade, including Islamic Asia, Europe and Africa, has often eclipsed other important issues within the wider debate. Arguments around the origins of the slave trade frequently imply that it was African political and social structures that were responsible for the establishment of Atlantic slavery.[60] However, the bishop of Cabo Verde, Santiago, was already arguing the opposite in the seventeenth century, claiming that it was the Europeans who in fact invented African Atlantic slavery.[61] Wadstörm, two centuries later, took the same view and contended that a need for labour in Brazil, following a failed experiment with Indigenous American labour, was the driving force of African slavery. In other words, it was the demand for labour in Brazil that was responsible for the introduction of slavery in Africa.[62] In

---

[59] See 'Carta do Irmão António Mendes ao Padre Geral' [A Letter of Brother António Mendes to Father General], Biblioteca Nacional do Rio de Janeiro [BNRJ], I-5, 2, 38, MMA II, Lisbon, 9 May 1563, pp. 495–509; and 'Carta do Padre Garcia Simões ao Padre Luis Perpinhão' [A Letter Father Garcia Simões to Padre Luis Perpinhão], BNL, ms. 308, fl. 221 v., MMA II, 7 November 1576, pp. 145–147; and see also Barreira, 'Informação Acerca dos Escravos de Angola', pp. 227–229.

[60] See A. L. Ferronha (ed.), 'Introdução', in Andre. A. de Almada, *Tratado Breve dos Rios de Guiné do Cabo-Verde, Feito peleo Capitão André Álvares d'Almada, Ano de 1594, Leitura, Introdução, Modernização do Texto e Notas*, Lisbon: Grupo de Trabalho do Ministério da Educação para as Comemorações dos Descobrimentos Portugueses, 1994, p. 9. See Jorge Fonseca, 'A Historiografia Sobre os Escravos'.

[61] 'Carta do Bispo de Cabo Verde a El-Rei' [A Letter of Cabo Verde's Bishop to the King], Biblioteca da Universidade de Coimbra [BUC], ms. 465, fls. 14–14v., in MMA, vol. V, [no date], século XVI [sixteenth century], pp. 442–445.

[62] See Wadström, *An Essay on Colonization*. Another example of that is slavery in the Atlantic islands of São Tomé and Madeira. São Tomé and Madeira's sugar plantations

the twentieth century, Rodney and Fage contributed significantly to the debate.[63] Rodney argued in support of Wadström and the bishop of Cabo Verde's views that African slavery came about through the Americas' demand for labour. Fage meanwhile took the opposite view, arguing that pre-existing African political structures had laid the ground for the European slave trade in Africa.[64]

Traditionally, servitude did exist in some African societies, but the nature of these systems was markedly distinct from that which took root in Europe and the Americas.[65] Africans had developed many forms of servitude that did not reduce those in servitude to chattel slavery. War captives in West Central Africa, for example, were often integrated into society and afforded opportunities for social mobility.[66] They were often employed as servants, concubines, soldiers and field workers. Captives even became holders of positions of high office, including King Álvaro II of Kongo, Dom Antonio Carrasco Ginga Amona of Matamba, and Philipe Hari I of Pungo-Andongo, in a multitude of roles.[67] In Angola, the term 'slavery', if it is to be applied at all correctly, encompassed a much broader and more complex system of servitude than was detected by European observers, as Stanley Engerman shows:

any definition of slavery has legal, cultural, political, and economic aspects, and it is often hard to know exactly where to draw the line among labour institutions as

---

did not last beyond the seventeenth century. São Tomé's sugar production had in fact already declined by 1595. For a detailed analysis of São Tomé and Madeira, see Philip D. Curtin, 'The Mediterranean Origins', in Philip D. Curtin (ed.), *The Rise and Fall of the Plantation Complex: Essays in Atlantic History*, Cambridge: Cambridge University Press, 1990, pp. 1–16, and Alberto Vieira, 'Sugar Islands: The Sugar Economy of Madeira and Canaries, 1450–1650', in Stuart B. Schwartz (ed.), *Tropical Babylons: Sugar and the Making of the Atlantic World, 1450–1680*, Chapel Hill, NC: University of North Carolina Press, 2004, pp. 42–84. Also see Gerhard Seibert, 'São Tomé and Príncipe: The First Plantation Economy in the Tropics', in Robin Law, Suzanne Schwarz and Silke Strickrodt (eds.), *Commercial Agriculture, the Slave Trade and Slavery in Atlantic Africa*, Oxford: James Currey 2013, pp. 54–78.

[63] As mentioned in Chapter 1, this discussion is found in Brásio's *Monumenta Missionaria Africana* and Carvalho's *Das Origens da Escravidão*.

[64] See Rodney, 'African Slavery'; Fage, 'Slavery and the Slave Trade'. For recent debate, see Heywood, 'Slavery and Its Transformation'.

[65] See Thornton, *Africa and Africans in the Making of the Atlantic World*.

[66] See E. E. Williams, *Capitalism & Slavery*, Chapel Hill, NC: University of North Carolina Press, 1994.

[67] King Álvaro II of Kongo's mother was the third wife of his father; he could have been regarded as an enslaved son – as could Philipe Hari I of Pungo-Andongo. Dom Antonio Carrasco Ginga Amona of Matamba was captured in the war by Queen Njinga. He became the king of Matamba after Queen Njinga's death. See also John Newton, *An Authentic Narrative*, Edinburgh: Chapman & Co, 1880.

legal slavery and the use of slavery as a metaphor for any form of human poverty and domination.[68]

Thornton shows that the status of *mubika*, those 'who were war captives, people enslaved judicially or were purchased ... is not described until the 1580s'.[69] This is significant because it opens up debate regarding the institutional practice of slavery in Ndongo society. It would not be an exaggeration to say that, with the arrival of the Portuguese in West Central Africa, the traditional system of servitude was transformed into a profit-making machine. External influences exerted considerable political, social and economic change on traditional African institutions. Ndongo's political and social structures were not exempt from this transformation.[70] Interestingly, by the 1580s, Portugal, as part of the Iberian Union, had appropriated a set of rules, already in use by Spanish explorers and settlers, that prescribed how they ought to behave in the Americas and other contact zones beyond the Iberian Peninsula. These were the long-established Laws of Burgos,[71] and while they may not have had any real impact on the ground, it remains thought-provoking to observe the changes in the language used in written reports following the Iberian Union. I will return to this in due course.

Thornton goes further to show that Ndongo society had a class of people called *kijikos*. He agrees with Cadornega, who said that *guigico* (*kijikos*) were war captives and belonged to the king. The *kijikos* were not the enslaved of Brazil, who were regarded as property and deprived of rights and human dignity. The *kijikos* were not enslaved in the European sense of the word. Cadornega tells us the *kijikos* were treasured by the king because he regarded them as his own biological children:

All [the king's] vassals were divided into two groups, some of whom were called sons of Murinda (commoners), who were taken as vassals, and some the sons of Guigico, who were those who had been taken in battle; and to the king, all were *peças* (slaves) and reputed by all as those of his own blood.[72]

---

[68] Stanley L. Engerman, 'Slavery at Different Times and Places', *The American Historical Review*, vol, 105(2), 2000, p. 481.
[69] Heywood and Thornton, *Central Africans*, p. 78.   [70] Elikia M'bokolo, *África Negra*.
[71] Ronald D. Hussey, 'Text of the Laws of Burgos (1512–1513) Concerning the Treatment of the Indians', *The Hispanic American Historical Review*, 12(3), 1932, pp. 301–326.
[72] See Delgado's note in Cadornega, *História Geral*, vol. II, p. 29, 'todos os seus Vassalos se dividião em dous generos, huns a que chamavão filhos de murinda que erão tidos por Vassallos, e os filhos de guigico por peças que erão os que tinhão apanhado nas guerras e para o Rey todos erão suas peças e reputados por esses e até os do seu proprio sangue'.

However, in equating the Mbundu word *kikijos* with the Portuguese word *peças* (literally pieces, used to mean 'slaves'), Cadornega set up an equivalence that did not reflect the reality of the *kikijos*' position, but that was uncritically accepted by his European readers. The political and social structure of the Mbundu people, however, tells a story of its own, one not reflected in Cadornega's language, showing that the acquisition, use and status of enslaved people was multilayered and more nuanced in Ndongo than the Western concept of slavery could encompass.

In a later source, Baltasar Barreira reported that enslaved people were sold in the market in Ndongo. His report takes an apologist stance and was written to defend the practice of slavery in Angola as natural to Mbundu's social and political structure. This document requires critical reading. It was written in defence of Novais's mission in Angola to curb the Laws of Burgos, which had driven foreign policy in Spanish America before the Iberian Union in 1580. Barreira was a Jesuit priest sent to Angola in 1576 following the death of his predecessor, Father Garcia Simões, as part of Paulo Dias de Novais's embassy. He later became advisor to Novais when the latter became the first governor of Luanda.[73]

On 19 September 1571, King Sebastião of Portugal instructed Novais, under 'his command, to subjugate and conquer the Kingdom of Angola'.[74] However, after the 1580s, Portugal's political landscape changed dramatically. The Philippine period heralded a different attitude towards the Portuguese captaincies in West Central Africa and Brazil, and Novais needed another inroad to gain the official support that would allow him to implement his policies in Angola.[75]

Following five years of imprisonment (1563–1568) at the hands of Ngola Kiluanje Kia Ndambi, from which he escaped thanks to his lover,[76] the *Ngola*'s daughter, Novais began a second period of administration in Ndongo that was less cooperative and more violent. It was driven by a personal desire for revenge. Freitas tells us that Novais 'swore and fulfilled a tremendous oath of revenge':[77]

In 1575, he landed in Luanda and conquered, by the sword and iron rod, as history tells us, the land of the unhappy Ambundu and Mbundu; and it opened a new cycle

---

[73] For a detailed study of Novais's embassy, see Amaral, *O Consulado de Paulo Dias de Novais*.
[74] 'Carta de Doação a Paulo Dias de Novais', pp. 36–51.
[75] See Birmingham, *Trade and Conquest*, pp. 48–55.
[76] For full detail, see Heywood, *Njinga of Angola*, pp. 18–34.
[77] de Freitas, *Reino Negro de Palmares*, p. 54, 'jurou e cumpriu a tremenda jura de vingança'.

of struggles, of blood, of death, and of shallow graves everywhere! Revenge was born of hatred and this hate opened graves! Whoever did not fall on the scorching earth followed as a slave to other lands never to have freedom again![78]

At the time when Barreira was writing in 1582, West Central Africa had already felt the devastating impact of slavery. Angola had emerged as the biggest market for enslaved people destined for Brazil as, by then, the Portuguese had been in the kingdom for forty years, having reached Kongo in 1484. In his report, Barreira indicated two pre-existing economic factors that were fundamental to the comprehensive exploitation of Angola: the local taxation system and a local slave trade that was accepted as a normative practice in Mbundu society. Since these practices were already legal and recognised in Mbundu society, the Portuguese were seen simply to be following the norm, in observance of the Spanish legal system of *encomienda*.[79]

For Barreira to galvanise support in favour of Novais's economic policy, he delineated three kinds of slaves in Angola, along with their market values:

Those who vassal lords [*sobas*] keep tilling their lands, those born out of them, and those who, through procreation, were inherited from their ancestors who took them from wars waged on those who did not recognise their authority. Others they themselves had taken from wars licensed by their king who had licensed the causes. Others were imprisoned for crimes for which they deserved death. Moreover, as it said, all three type of slaves move from one market to another,

---

[78] de Freitas, *Reino Negro de Palmares*, p. 54, 'em 1575 desembarcava em Luanda e conquistava a espada e a vara de ferro, como reza a história, a terra dos infelizes ambundos e mbundos e abriu um novo ciclo de lutas, de sangue e de morte e de covas rasas por toda parte! A vingança renascia o ódio e o ódio abria sepulturas! Quem não tombava na terra escaldante seguia como escravo para outras terras para nunca mais ter Liberdade!'

[79] The *encomienda* was used by settlers in Latin America to force conquered Indigenous people to provide labour for no reward. It was a slave's system first developed in the Iberian Peninsula during the period (722–1492) in which Spain was reconquering territories taken by the 'Moors' (Muslims) from North Africa. The Spanish Crown granted right to winners in war – be that a soldier or officer – to extract tribute from the Moors or other conquered peoples that lived in an area. For a detailed discussion of the reconquest of the Iberian Peninsula, see Francisco García Fitz, 'La Reconquista: un Estado de la Cuestión', *Clio & Crímen*, 6, 2009, pp. 142–215; on the *encomienda*, see Robert Stoner Chamberlain, 'Pre-Conquest Labor Practices' in John Francis Bannon (ed.), *Indian Labor in the Spanish Indies: Was There Another Solution?*, Boston: D. C. Heath and Co, 1966; see also Valencia, *The Encomenderos of New Spain*; Simpson, *The Encomienda in New Spain*; Altamira, 'El Texto de las Leyes'; and E. V. D. Costa, 'The Portuguese-African Slave Trade: A Lesson in Colonialism', *Latin American Perspectives*, 12(1), 1985, pp. 41–61.

and Blacks sell them to each other, partly for tilling their lands, partly for the taxes they pay to their king.⁸⁰

Barreira's take on the status quo was designed to demonstrate the legality of African slavery and the continued enslavement of those, and their descendants, who had been made to work the land by a vassal lord. In order to justify his claims, he referenced earlier documents relating to a 1548 inquest into the slave trade of São Tomé and Angola.⁸¹ The similarity between this earlier text and Barreira's is striking. Both cite three types of enslaved people in the Angolan marketplace, as distinguished above, and also assert that slavery was an ancient practice. Barreira's concluding remarks reiterated his position: 'the more we enter into the hinterland, dealing with the Blacks, the more we realise that in no part of Guinea can one buy *peças* more securely than in Angola.'⁸² In drawing a comparison between territories across West Africa, Barreira intended to lobby the Iberian Crown to implement the slave trade in the West Central African region. He also actively defended the violent actions and harsh policies that characterised Novais's governorship. Reminding the Crown of Novais's suffering at the hands of the kings of Angola, he remarked:

... and all the things that have been said combine to show that it is a very just cause that ours are now waging wars on theirs and enslaving them. Because four times their kings requested a priest to convert them, pretending always to keep them but robbing the Portuguese of their properties that they came with, as they did twice with diabolic pretentions at the time of past kings. And another when Governor Paulo Dias de Novais came with our priests for the first time, and another less than three years ago.⁸³

---

⁸⁰ Barreira, 'Informação Acerca dos Escravos de Angola', p. 228, 'as peças que se uendem saõ de tres sortes, huas que os Senhores de Vassalos tem em suas terras pera as cultiuar, nascidos e procreados de outros que seus antepassados tomarão em guerras e fizeraõ quando naõ reconheciaõ superior, outros que elles mesmos tomara nas guerras feitas com licença de seu Rey, o qual examina as cousas &c. Outros que foraõ comprehendidos em delictos, pelos quaes mereçiaõ [a] morte. E por que, como disse, todas estas tres sortes de peças andaõ de feira em feira, e as uendem hüs negros a outros, parte pera cultiuar suas terras, parte pera os tributos que pagaõ a seu Rey.'

⁸¹ See 'Inquirição Sobre o Comercio de S. Tomé com Angola Ordenado por D. João III' [Inquest into Slave Trade of São Tomé with Angola Decreed by D. John III], ATT, CC-I-80–105, MMA II, 12 November 1548, pp. 197–205.

⁸² Barreira, 'Informação Acerca dos Escravos de Angola', p. 228, 'quanto mais entramos pela terra, c tratamos dos negros, tanto mais experimentamos que de nhua parte de Guiné uaõ peças que se possaõ comprar mais seguramente que as de Angola'.

⁸³ Barreira, 'Informação Acerca dos Escravos de Angola', 'E a todas as cousas sobreditas se ayunta que hé muy iusta a causa porque os nossos lhe faze agora guerra, e os catiuaõ, por que quatro uezes pedirão aos Reis de Portugal Sacerdotes pera se conuerterem, pretendendo sempre retelòs, e roubar as fazendas dos Portugueses que com elles uinhaõ, como fizeraõ com inuençoes diabólicas duas uezes no tempo, dos Reis passados, e outra quando

From the Mbundu perspective, the people who entered the Atlantic slave market were not considered enslaved people. They were people of commoner status who came onto the market for sale for specific reasons, such as that they had been captured in 'just wars' or had been kidnapped. As has been emphasised, it is difficult to identify a distinct slave category in African society. King João II told Munzer that enslaved people were difficult to procure in Africa[84] and that other means were required to obtain them. African kings were certainly not ready to sell their own common people into slavery.[85]

Let us now look at how the Portuguese disrupted Ndongo's existing political structures with the election of Philipe Hari I, who subsequently aided them in advancing their economic interests in Ndongo. It may seem a cliché to suggest that the Portuguese exercised a policy of divide and rule. Nonetheless, Philipe Hari I's enthronement was a clear effort by the Portuguese to divide the House of Ndongo by rehashing old African rivalries surrounding power and gender within the royal family. Indeed, rivalries between royal siblings frequently resulted in royal factionalism.[86] Exacerbation of these rivalries, manipulated by the Portuguese, only intensified animosity between Njinga and Philipe Hari I.

2.3 KING PHILIPE HARI I OF PUNGO-ANDONGO (1626–1664)

The rise of King Philipe Hari I to the throne of Pungo-Andongo was the beginning of the dismantling of wider unity within the region that ultimately led to the Portuguese colonisation of Angola in the late nineteenth and early twentieth centuries. Philipe Hari I was a brother of Queen Njinga. They were born of the same father but different mothers. The sole source to document Philipe Hari I's bloodline was Cadornega,[87] who described Philipe Hari I's mother as *mocama*, the lowliest wife and seen as a household servant. Another source that gives us an indication of his family ties with Queen Njinga was Correia de Sá, who stated that Philipe

---

o Gouernador Paulos Dias de Nauaes ue[i]o cõ os nossos Padres a primeira uez, e outra há "menos de tres annos.'
[84] See Münzer, 'Itinerarium, De Inventione Africae Maritimae' and P. A. Brásio, *Munumenta Missionaria Africana 1342–1499*, Segunda Série, I Lisbon: Academia Portuguesa da História, 1958.
[85] See Fonseca, 'A Historiografia Sobre os Escravos'.
[86] See José Lingna Nafafé, 'African Orality in Iberian Space: Critique of Barros and Myth of Racial Discourse', *Portuguese Studies Journal*, 28(2), 2012, pp. 126–142.
[87] See Cadornega, *História Geral* vol. III, pp. 156–157.

Hari I was Queen Njinga's uncle.[88] When Philipe Hari I came to power, Cavazzi was not in Ndongo,[89] although he wrote extensively about Philipe Hari I's father, Ngola Quiluanji, and Philipe Hari I's grandfather, Ngola Mussuri.[90] Historians of Ndongo such as Birmingham, Miller, Vansina and, most recently, Lara have all neglected to investigate the blood ties between Philipe Hari I and Njinga. Heywood's recent, seminal biography of Njinga at least identified the connection.[91] Cadornega may not have been wholly reliable,[92] but he was a Portuguese soldier[93] and a New Christian[94] who fought many wars in Angola.[95] He lived in Angola in the same period as Philipe Hari I and Njinga, from 1639 until his death in 1690, and married an Angolan woman. In his later years, after leaving military service, he was appointed principal councillor of Luanda by Távora.[96] Of course, Cadornega was writing with the particular purpose of feeding information to the Portuguese Crown to justify the Portuguese conquest of Angola.[97] Nonetheless, in most cases his sources are reliable and verifiable against oral sources, and consistent with the accurate accounts he made of African practices he observed outside Angola.[98] Cadornega gives us great detail about the rivalry between Njinga and Philipe Hari I and the subsequent division of the House of Ndongo into the two Houses of Ndongo and Matamba.[99] He remarked that Philipe Hari I was of royal blood, though not of the highest nobility due to his

---

[88] See 'Carta de Salvador Correia de Sá'.
[89] Cavazzi came to Luanda in 1654 and lived in Angola as a missionary from 1654 to 1667 and again from 1673 to 1677. In 1667, he returned to Italy after the death of Queen Njinga in 1663. In 1673, he returned to Angola; by that time Pungo-Andongo had already fallen. See John Thornton, 'New Light on Cavazzi's 17th-Century Description of Kongo', History in Africa, 6, 1979, pp. 253–264. See also Montecúccolo, Descrição Histórica dos Três Reinos do Congo.
[90] Montecúccolo, Descrição Histórica dos Três Reinos do Congo.
[91] Heywood, Njinga of Angola, p. 92.
[92] For a detailed discussion of the use of Angola sources, Heintze and Rieck, 'The Extraordinary Journey of the Jaga'.
[93] See Charles R. Boxer, 'Background to Angola, Cadornega's Chronicle', History Today, 11 (1961): pp. 665–672.
[94] For a full discussion of Cadornega's background see Oliveira, 'As "Histórias" de Angola'.
[95] See Boxer, 'Background to Angola'. [96] See Boxer, 'Background to Angola'.
[97] See Oliveira, 'As "Histórias" de Angola'.
[98] Cadornega, História Geral, vol. III, pp. 255–261, 267–268. See Wilson Abreu; Margarida Abreu, 'Community Education Matters: Representations of Female Genital Mutilation in Guineans Immigrant Women', Procedia – Social and Behavioral Sciences, 2015, 171, pp. 620–628. See also A. Carreira, 'O Céu, Deus e a Terra', Boletim Cultural da Guine Portuguesa, 2(6), 1947, pp. 461–463.
[99] See Delgado's note in Cadornega, História Geral, vol. III, pp. 309–310.

mother's lower status: 'he was lord of Airi Province and Mauzondo, that he inherited, as well as the Rocks of the Mapungo'.[100] The rivalry between Njinga and Philipe Hari I intensified primarily as a result of his election to the throne of Ndongo, which was overseen by the Portuguese on 12 October 1626.[101]

During the reign of Ngola Mbandi (Queen Njinga's brother),[102] between 1617 and 1624, Portuguese attempts to establish peaceful relations with Ndongo proved disastrous.[103] Cadornega states that, like his father (Ngola Kia Samba) before him, Mbandi was not ready to accept settlement by the Portuguese in Luanda nor their advance south of Luanda towards Kissama. In addition, he was particularly reluctant to accept Portuguese interference in Ndongo's internal politics.[104] Successive governors of Angola, such as Luís Mendes de Vasconcelos (1617–1621)[105] and João Correia de Sousa (1621–1623), adopted aggressive policies towards Ndongo, as discussed in Chapter 1.[106] The Portuguese's ambition to build a fort in Mbaka caused unnecessary wars and made peace arrangements between Luanda and Kabasa, the seat of the kings of Ngola, impossible. Several peace treaties were signed but not honoured.[107] In one peace deal, under which the Portuguese were to abandon the fort of Nossa Senhora da Assunção de Ambaca in Mbaka in exchange for the return of Portuguese slave captives, neither side honoured the bargain. Both the Portuguese and Ngola Mbandi held their resolve. Mbandi's successor, Njinga, continued to refuse to return the captives, citing the illegality of such a demand since Mbundu laws did not allow the return of any runaway war captives to slavery. Tradition held that those who had escaped and reached their homeland were granted amnesty. As the governor Fernão de Sousa stated:

It is also necessary that Your Majesty send order to resolve this with Princess Ana [Queen Njinga] to oblige her to return the fugitive slaves, because they are His Majesty's slaves, and that the slaves being in her power, they are free and are not obliged to render service to their masters. Allowing that the majority of them came

---

[100] See Delgado's note stating that prior to becoming the seat of King Philipe Hari I, Pungo-Andongo was called Matadi Maupungo or Matadi ma Unpungu [Pedras altas ou Pedras de Altura] in Cadornega, *História Geral*, vol. III, p. 156, and p. 167.
[101] See Cadornega, *História Geral*. vol. III, pp. 156–157.
[102] Ngola Mbandi was Queen Njinga's brother.   [103] Birmingham, *Trade and Conquest*.
[104] Cadornega, *História Geral*, vol. I.   [105] Cadornega, *História Geral*, vol. I.
[106] Cadornega, *História Geral*, vol. I.
[107] See Caroline A. Williams, '"If You Want Slaves Go to Guinea": Civilisation and Savagery in the "Spanish" Mosquitia, 1787–1800', *Slavery and Abolition*, 35(1), 2014, pp.121–141.

from Ndongo [Dongo], and they were war captives from a war that was waged upon them; because, if they run away to their natural [place, home], they are free, their captivity will cease. And that is the reason to ask for them, and for obliging that they be returned by force. This is what I have been left with. His Majesty will decree for all and much more for His service.[108]

As Mbundu law held that war captives who escaped and reached their homeland were granted amnesty, Sousa furiously requested that the Crown in Madrid intervene and demanded proof from Njinga that all the fugitives in question had originally been captured during Ndongo's war. Sousa, interestingly, sent two almost identical letters to Madrid on the same day, differing only in their layout: one of them was laid out as bullet points,[109] the other as prose. Whether both were meant to be dispatched is unknown. That two letters were written, however, shows Sousa's desperation for the Crown to exercise sovereign power over the matter. Let us now examine the concept of *kijiko* in Mbundu society in Angola.

Runaway *kijiko* traditionally had two fates. Firstly, if a *kijiko* escaped captivity and returned to their original homeland, they were considered to be free.[110] Secondly, captives who ran away and joined a powerful lord or ruler who provided protection for them were also deemed to be free.[111] The Portuguese found this law difficult to comprehend and to abide by. Njinga was not willing to infringe on these internal laws and return to captivity those who had earned their freedom by escaping servitude.[112] Sousa was unsuccessful in his plea to overturn Njinga's legal argument and subsequently highlighted to the Crown the need to elect a Christian puppet king who would serve Portuguese interests. It was this appeal that led to the election of Philipe Hari I.[113]

This new analysis of Mbundu legal policies around slavery, which has so far not received adequate scholarly attention, is significant for our

---

[108] 'Carta de Fernão de Sousa a El-Rei', 22 August 1625, 'também conue mandar V. Magestade resoluer se te Dona Ana obrigação de entregar estes escrauos que foge, porque são catiuos dos vassalos de V, Magestade, e se em seu poder ficaõ liures e dezobrigados da seruidaó a seus senhores, presuposto que os mais deles vieraõ de Dongo, e foraõ catiuos na guerra que se lhe fez, porque se pela fogída pera o seu natural ficaõ forros cessará a causa, e a razaõ de lhos pedir, e de obrigar dalos por força; isto hé o que se me offerece. V. Magestade mandará em tudo o que for mais seu seruiço'.

[109] See Sousa's two letters at 'Carta de Fernão de Sousa a El-Rei' [Letter of Fernão de Sousa to the King], AHU-CU-001, cx. 2, d. 313, 7 March 1626.

[110] 'Carta de Fernão de Sousa a El-Rei', 7 March 1626.

[111] M'bokolo, *África Negra*; Thornton, 'The Kingdom of Kongo, ca. 1390–1678'.

[112] 'Carta de Fernão de Sousa a El-Rei', 7 March 1626.

[113] 'Carta de Fernão de Sousa a El-Rei', 7 March 1626.

understanding of the dynamics of runaway slaves in Angola and in Brazil, where they fled, for example, to Quilombo dos Palmares. It is also of tremendous significance in any analysis of Mendonça's discourse in the Vatican. Furthermore, it poses questions about the nature of the practice of slavery in Ndongo and what constituted a 'slave'. Historians of Ndongo have, until now, not addressed West Central African regional laws in relation to the Angolan slave trade in the seventeenth century. If there was indeed a normative, accepted practice of slavery, one must ask why enslaved people attempted escape at all. An obvious answer would be that they ran away because they did not consider themselves enslaved people: slavery was not in fact an accepted social norm within Mbundu society and therefore was not tolerated by those who had been captured. So who were these 'slaves' about whom so many documents were written, and why did they run away if slavery was a practice engrained in Mbundu society? Furthermore, if we accept that there was a group of people of 'slave' status, the number of enslaved people in the region would certainly have diminished significantly by the end of the sixteenth century because so many enslaved people were being shipped to the Americas. I will return to this issue when we examine the case of runaway slaves in Quilombo dos Palmares[114] and other places in Brazil in Chapter 4. First, let us examine Hari's election as a king allied to Portugal.

2.4 ELECTION OF PHILIPE HARI I AS PUPPET KING OF PORTUGAL

Philipe Hari I's election was influenced by the Portuguese in order to make it difficult for Njinga to rule Ndongo. Portugal's ability to wield so much power in the region by use of firearms meant that from 1626 the Ndongo kingdom had effectively become a Portuguese invention, and its spilt from the House of Matamba was designed to facilitate a Portuguese takeover of Angola. 'Africa', according to Mudimbe, was being invented, represented and interpreted in ways that did not reflect African reality.[115] Delgado asserts that the division of the houses of Matamba and Ndongo was indeed a Portuguese plot against Njinga, whom they mistrusted deeply and from whom they sought to withdraw their recognition as a queen of Angola:

The ancient kingdom of Angola, also called Ndongo, encompassed Matamba, which was where the ancient kings had originally come from. King Ngola

---

[114] See Cheney, *Quilombo dos Palmares*.   [115] See Mudimbe, *The Invention of Africa*.

Ambandi's succession belonged to his sister, Njinga, who we did not want to recognise, and so we sought to replace her with a *soba* who held our trust and to whom we gave the title of king of the Dongo and baptised him with the name of Philip. For us Portuguese, we ended the ancient kingdom of Angola, for Njinga and her successors were not for us kings of Angola. In their turn, they were entitled kings of Matamba. She made peace with us afterward and returned to the Catholic faith, leaving behind the life of the warrior. Succession then passed to D. Veronica, elected in 1681. The royal line after Njinga was weakened from king to king, and lost after the death of Veronica in the first quarter of the seventeenth century.[116]

Njinga refused to acknowledge that Philipe Hari had a legitimate claim to the throne of Ngola on the grounds that Philipe Hari I was a puppet king who had betrayed his family, people and traditions. Njinga accused Philipe Hari I of allying with the Portuguese after he had attended a clandestine meeting with the governor of Angola, Fernão de Sousa, in the fort of Ambaca.[117] Correia de Sousa, a predecessor of Fernão de Sousa, had already used Philipe Hari I in a war against Njinga. Soon after the meeting at the fort of Ambaca, Njinga sent her men to ambush Hari as he travelled home. During the ambush, three Portuguese soldiers were killed and six captives taken.[118] A letter sent to the king of Portugal on 7 March 1626 stated that two soldiers were killed and seven captives taken.[119] The Portuguese declared Njinga an illegitimate monarch on the grounds that a queen of Angola was unprecedented, so her gender

---

[116] Cadornega, História Geral, vol. III, p. 310, writes: 'O antigo reino de Angola, também chamado do Dongo, abrangia a Matamba, donde os antigos reis eram oriundos. Morto o rei Angola Ambandi, a sua sucessão pertencia a Irmã, à Jinga, que nós não quisemos recomhecer, substituindo-a por um soba de confianca, a demos o título de rei do Dongo, o batipzado com o nome de Philipe. Para nós, portugueses, acabava o antigo reino de Angola. À Jinga e os lhe sucederam não eram para nós reis de Angola. Por seu turno intitulam-se êles de referência reis da Matamba. Foi depois reconciliou connosco e voltou a fé católica, deixando a vida guerreira. À série vai até D. Verónica, eleita em 1681. Enfraquecidos de rei para rei, depois da Jinga, perde-se a série depois da morte de Verónica, no primeiro quartel de século XVIII.' See also note by Delgado on Kingdom of Pungo-AnDongo, 'o Novo reino por nós creado em 1626 – o Dongo – não chegou a durar meio século. Extingue-se com a tomada de Pungo-a-Dongo em 1671, contando apenas os dois reis, Philipe e João' (The New Kingdom of Dongo created by us in 1626, did not last for half a century. It fell later, the taking of Pungo-AndDongo in 1671, counting only with the two kings, Philipe and João), Cadornega, História Geral, vol. III, p. 310.

[117] 'Carta de Fernão de Sousa a El-Rei', 7 March 1626 and 'Carta de Fernão de Sousa a El-Rei', AHU-CU-001, cx. 2, D. 313, 21 February 1626, 'O soua Ayrequiloange, que o Gouernador Joaõ Correa de Sousa largou a Dona Anna pera correr cõ ella, mandey vir ao presidio da Embaça, por ser legitimo e verdadeiro sucessor do Rejno'.

[118] 'Carta de Fernão de Sousa a El-Rei', 21 February 1626.

[119] 'Carta de Fernão de Sousa a El-Rei', 7 March 1626.

precluded her from ruling Ndongo. Sousa remarked: 'she cannot be queen, because never before has a woman ruled this kingdom'.[120] Njinga, for her part, asserted that Philipe Hari I was illegitimate as ruler because he was a child of the third wife, who was therefore of housekeeper status. All Angolan sources at our disposal, in particular letters to Philipe IV of Spain, are silent on the issue, except for Cadornega, who states:

> Queen Njinga, heir to her father Angola Aquiluanji, king of this kingdom of Angola, wished to drink his [Hari's] blood for siding with the Portuguese, and she considered him not to be legitimate, because he was the son of a *mocama* [a servant or household woman], who was a concubine of the king. He was not of *Envala Ineni* or Samba Angila who were his chief women and whose children are reputed to be legitimate against those of his other wives and concubines, except in the absence of children from the first wives of whom we have spoken; in this way, Angola Airi Dom Philipe was of royal blood.[121]

Though claims of illegitimacy from both sides were justifiable, arguments determining who had the better claim to the throne appeared to favour neither of them. An outsider who was not familiar with the dynamics of Mbundu culture could easily misinterpret forms of social relationships and family ties. We see this struggle in Cadornega's writing, where *mocama* was described using three different concepts in the Portuguese language: *escravo* (slave), *criado* (houseworker) and *servente* (servant). Within the dynamics of the Ndongo household, these labels were not mutually exclusive. In the division of labour, there was little correlation between the concept of *mocama* and the over-simplistic meanings that Cadornega identified to translate the concept into Portuguese.

In the political structure of the Ngola court, female children could be brought into the king's compound or family home from within his circle of friends or from distant relatives. In most cases, it was a wife's relative or

---

[120] Both letters have the same information, word by word. 'Carta de Fernão de Sousa a El-Rei', 7 March 1626, and 'Carta de Fernão de Sousa a El-Rei', 21 February 1626, 'ella o nao poder ser, por naõ gouernar este Reyno molher'.
[121] See Cadornega, *História Geral*, vol. III, pp.156–157, 'Rainha Ginga, herdeira de seu pay Angola Aquiloangi, Rey deste Reino de Angola, que lhe desejava beber o sangue, por ser do partido dos Portuguezes, e ella o reputar por não legitimos, por ser filho de mocama [mucama – mukama was a servant or a household woman, not a slave], que erão as damas concubinas del Rey, e não da Envala Ineni [the first wife of *soba*, the principal of the mvala (concubine, Ineni – great], e Samba Angila [samba-njila, the second wife of the *soba*] que eraõ suas mulheres principaes, e dos filhos havidos nellas procedia a herança de seu reino, como reputados por legitimos, e naõ os das mais mulheres e concubinas, salvo em falta dos primeiros que havemos ditto; e como Angola Airi, Dom Phellipe, era do sangue real.'

friend who was brought in to help with household chores. There was an added cultural dynamic to this practice: female children could be brought into the household for the purpose of gaining social and political status. A similar tradition was also found among the Manjac people of Guinea-Bissau, hence the reason why kings had so many wives. As Cadornega put it:

> There was one of these Kings who had three hundred concubines, for his powerful noblemen prided themselves for having daughters who became the King's wives, for which he commanded them most jealously to his Court with great ceremony; they were very well treated and clothed in fine garments, given horses and servants to serve them.[122]

Relatives or friends of the queen could send their children to the king's compound to work and eventually become part of the king's household through marriage. These women were not enslaved (except perhaps in the sense that concubinage has an element of servitude associated with it). The king had the right to choose a second or third wife, but would do so only with the consent of his first wife, *Envala Ineni*. It was she who selected the right wife for the king and she commanded the full respect of all his new wives.[123] Once a marriage had taken place, the children born of his concubines became the representatives of their wider family interests before the king and in the case of any disputes. In legal disputes, they would stand as counsel on behalf of their relatives in the royal court. The description we have from Cadornega is rather alien to Mbundu social and political practices, and should be accepted with caution.

In Ndongo tradition, the first wife's son was the heir to the throne or the second wife's son when there was no heir from the first. The third wife's son was heir behind the sons of the first and second wives. Even so, Philipe Hari I should not have been elected as king while Njinga was still in power. His election was designed by the Portuguese to frustrate Njinga's rule because she had been uncompromising in her dealings with them.

---

[122] Cadornega, *História Geral*, vol. III, pp.156–157, 'Havia Rey destes que tinha trezentas concubinas, porque se prezavão os seus fidalgos Sovas poderosos terem filhas por mulheres do Rey para o que mandavão das mais geitiosas (p. 29) à sua Corte com grande apparato, ellas mui bem tratadas e vestidas a seu modo em rede a cavallo com serventes para as servirem e em cima com boas dadivas de peças e outras couzas de valor as quaes todas mandava acomodar dentro de seus muros em casas separadas cada huma com o estado de serventes.'

[123] Marina Temudo, 'Men Wielding the Plough: Changing Patterns of Production and Reproduction among the Balanta of Guinea-Bissau', *Journal of Agrarian Change*, 18, 2018, pp. 267–280.

Madrid had historically attempted to maintain strong ties with Angola by abiding by Angolan norms – as long as trade continued to flow. Portuguese governors on the ground in Angola, however, had other intentions and sought to establish trade monopolies, especially over the slave trade.

Nevertheless, once he had been appointed as governor of Luanda, Fernão de Sousa was given clear instructions by the Spanish Crown to ensure their mission in Angola was realised. Madrid did, however, question the motives of the Portuguese wars and the status of the resulting war captives in Angola, indicating that Sousa's predecessors in Angola had waged war without justification, as we saw in Chapter 1, and that this practice needed to be ended at all costs. These wars had achieved little except to strain relations between the Portuguese and the people of Angola. The Spanish Crown declared that the way forward for economic and political stability was peace, and remarked:

It is very important for my service that the door is closed to wars that have been caused by some governors of Angola without justified cause, from which there has been great damage. An express order is given to Fernão de Sousa who will go to that kingdom as a governor, so that he does not wage war, except a defensive one, or in case of an uprising that cannot be remedied by other means. And for those wars that have already been started, he must make peace so that they all cease.[124]

Sousa himself maintained that there was no use in waging war against Njinga unless she attacked the Portuguese settlement. The only way to topple her was to create a rival king born of a vassal *soba*. The new king would pay *baculamento*, a head tax of 100 enslaved people per year, to the Crown in Madrid[125] and would simultaneously open the market to allow free trade and commerce in Ndongo.[126] I will return to *baculamento* and its significance as a new Portuguese tax system in due course.

For Madrid, the foundation of the slave trade was based on production, and if there was no land to work thanks to the devastation of war,

---

[124] 'Carta de S. Magestade de 17 de Janeiro de 1624' [His Majesty's Letter, 17 January 1624], ATT, Colecção de S. Vicente [CSV], 24 January 1624, vol. XIX, fl. 188, MMA, vol. VII, p. 362, 'Jmporta muito a meu seruiço que se cerre a porta ás guerras que sem causa justificada tem feito algüs goucrnadores de Angola, de que se seguirão grandes danos; se dará ordem expressa a Fernão de Sousa que hora vay por gouernador àquele Reino para que não faça Guerra saluo se for defensiua, ou em caso de leuantamento que se não possa remediar por outros me[i]os. E que as guerras que achar leuantadas as componha e apazigue de modo que cessem de todo.'
[125] See 'Carta de Fernão de Sousa a El-Rei', 22 August 1625.
[126] See 'Carta de Fernão de Sousa a El-Rei', 22 August 1625.

enslaved people had no use. Sousa echoed Madrid's logic and intentions: 'I understand that waging war will bring trade to a standstill, even if it brought with it more slaves, because a land could not serve your Majesty without these heathens.'[127] In short, if war ruined the land for production, and consequently trade, there would be no need for enslaved people at all, and no supply of enslaved people if there was a need, since the local people would have fled or died.

Birmingham has pointed out that the Portuguese in Angola resorted to three means of acquiring enslaved people, the majority of whom came from Mbundu lands and neighbouring regions:

> The first was through tribute, which chiefs paid either to a Portuguese master or to the governor representing the Crown. The second method was direct warfare, a method officially discouraged but much favoured by governors who wanted to maximise their personal profit while on their short tour of duty in Angola ... common excuses for war were the recovery of runaway slaves or the punishment of tax defaulters. The third and probably most important means of filling the slave ships was trade with chiefs.[128]

In 1625, Sousa devised a plan to elect a new Christian king, thus creating an ally for Portugal. Sousa presented his strategy to the Crown as the best solution to the crisis between Queen Njinga and the Portuguese settlers in Luanda. The election of Philipe Hari I was therefore long in the pipeline because the Portuguese wanted to change the political structure of Ndongo in their favour.

> If it were possible to punish Dona Anna [Njinga] without much damage and to appoint a king, by your Majesty, delivering a hundred persons of baculation every year, and with an obligation to welcome the priests of the Society [of Jesus] and to give freedom to His vassals to receive the Holy Baptism, this would be convenient.[129]

Sousa's advice appeared sensible to the Crown in Madrid, and Philipe Hari I was elected in 1626. That the Crown accepted Sousa's proposal is, however, contrary to Cadornega's claim that Hari I's election was enacted

---

[127] 'Carta de Fernão de Sousa a El-Rei', 22 August 1625, 'entendo que dando guerra se acabará de todo o comercio, ynda que delia resulte peças, porque a terra naõ serue a V. Magestade sé gentio'.

[128] Birmingham, *Trade and Conquest*, p. 78.

[129] 'Carta de Fernão de Sousa a El-Rei', 22 August 1625, 'se se pudera dar hü castigo a dona Anna sem muito dano e nomear Rey por V. Magestade auassa[la]do com cem pessas de baculamento cada anno, com obrigação de fazer feira e dar entrada aos padres da Companhia e liberdade para seus vassalos recebere o santo baptismo, fora mui conueniente'.

without the permission of the Crown. There may be some truth in that, but we do not have Madrid's response to Sousa's letter and so have no evidence for the claim. Suffice to say that the Crown in Madrid accepted Philipe Hari I as king. In 1627, he was baptised, along with his wife and his first son, Francisco, in Luanda. He was given the name Philipe in honour of Philipe, king of both Portugal and Spain. Hari I's election left many of Ndongo's *sobas* bitterly disappointed, and some voted with their feet: Birmingham tells us that 'many chiefs were abandoning Ndongo to live elsewhere'.[130] Later, João Hari II, Hari I's son and successor, targeted these disenchanted groups and galvanised their support against the Portuguese. I will return to this issue in due course.

In 1658, Philipe Hari I reluctantly accepted the Portuguese demand for *baculamento*. However, he came to question it later and became involved in a dispute on the issue involving the Crown and the Portuguese Overseas Council that the latter eventually won.[131] It was a battle that Mendonça was to take up in the Vatican in 1684 and which he was to win there in 1686. Philipe Hari I's troops were used to wage wars against other *sobas* and his sons were soldiers in the Portuguese regiments, all of which gave him access to vital intelligence. Both his sons, Francisco and Ignacio da Silva (Mendonça's own father), died defending Portuguese interests in battles against the Dutch and Angolans respectively. In the next section, I examine how the Portuguese used the election of Philipe I to foster their trade relationships in Angola by introducing the *baculamento* tax system.

2.5 THE INTRODUCTION OF *BACULAMENTO* AS A TAX SYSTEM BY GOVERNOR FERNÃO DE SOUSA

The *kabakula* tribute, or *baculamento*, was viewed and understood by the seventeenth-century Mbundu in multiple ways. It was an African contract, specifically Mbundu, constructed over many generations and reimagined by the Portuguese so as better to navigate and exploit local tributary customs. *Baculamento* was a form of tribute paid to kings and lords of the land.[132] Angolan kings were subjects of the kings of Kongo

---

[130] Birmingham, *Trade and Conquest*, p. 95.
[131] See 'Carta de Hari I to Dom João IV' [A letter of Hari I of Ndongo to Dom João IV], AHU, Angola, cx. 5. See also Birmingham, *Trade and Conquest*, p. 118.
[132] For the use of the term, see Cadornega, *História Geral*, vol. I, p. 26 and p. 28. In the Kimbundu language, Luanda means parts or *baculamento*. It (Luanda) was a bank for the kingdom of Kongo because it was the island in which the shells used for currency were fished by divers or Kongolese employed by the king.

and they paid it as what Heywood terms 'tribute in kind'.[133] An analysis of the function of *baculamento* shows how these contracts were developed and demonstrates how the Portuguese used this tributary custom to their advantage, turning it into a tax. *Soba* vassals, although playing a very small role in this process, modified this traditional contractual concept to accommodate their new partnership with the Portuguese. Critically, however, the *sobas* continued to interpret *baculamento* differently to the Portuguese. Once they had agreed to pay *baculamento*, however, the contract was legally binding. What was once a symbol of the strength and unity of the kingdom became a burdensome form of taxation on Ndongo's rulers and their people as resources were redirected from the kingdom's constituencies to Portugal.

For us to understand the mechanism by which slavery became an economically productive source of commerce in Angola, we first need to address the very system used to achieve it: *baculamento*. For the Mbundu people *baculamento* was a contract based on friendship, recognition and mutual agreement, and was never enforced through violence. It was a contract of blood ties, a kind of covenant that subjects used as a means of paying respect to their superiors. Tax systems hardly existed in any African political and economic systems in the century. Kings generally inherited lands that had been left without an heir. *Sobas* were relatives of the kings, bound by ties of kinship, and the need to pay tax in the Portuguese sense of the word would have seemed preposterous: 'all had their place as children of the king and he gave them *libatas* (villages) and land for their livelihood'.[134] Lands were often leased or endowed to subjects but not for the purposes of generating taxes. The king leased arable land to labourers subject to their working it for crop production.[135] It is unthinkable that kings exploited their subjects through taxation systems.

The Portuguese misinterpretation of this pre-existing system of contract and its function indicates the stark disparity between African and

---

[133] Heywood, *Njinga of Angola*, p. 12.
[134] Cadornega, *História Geral*, vol. I, p. 30, 'os mais filhos tinhão o seu lugar como filhos do Rey e os accomodava com libatas e terras para o seu sustento'.
[135] Diogo Cão landed in Kongo in 1483, soon after Mani-Congo, king of Kongo, became a Christian. See Davidson, *Black Mother, Africa* p. 116 and also pp. 117–118: 'The story began in friendship and alliance. Within a few years of this visit to Mbanza, the "royal brothers" of Portugal and Kongo were writing letters to each other, which were couched in terms of complete equality of status. Emissaries went back and forth between them. Relations were then established between Mbanza and the Vatican. A son of the Mani-Congo was appointed in Rome itself as bishop of his country.'

Portuguese approaches to governance.[136] Birmingham posits that African élites believed their system to be more humane than that of the Portuguese. Gifts given to the kings, which were falsely interpreted by the Portuguese as taxes, were a symbol of one's success as a subject of the king. The giving of livestock was a symbol that regions were prospering. The Portuguese approach set out to acquire lands and to conquer the population and their leaders. By the mid-century, war had significantly depleted Portuguese resources, and Angola became an important source of taxes.[137] Taxation became a cornerstone of the Portuguese exploitation of Angola. However, corruption meant that *baculamento* served to line the pockets of Portuguese governors rather than bolster the economies of Spain and Portugal.

There was a considerable decrease in tax revenue sent to Portugal and Spain during Fernão de Sousa's governorship of Angola between 1624 and 1630. The amount registered on 10 June 1625 for 1624 was minimal; the certificate presented by the scribe António de Gouveia de Machado documented that *baculamento* paid comprised ninety-four enslaved people of varying ages, one of whom had died.[138] Therefore, in August 1625, King Philipe III decreed that all those contracted by the Crown in Madrid to trade in Angola and Cabo Verde would immediately pay outstanding taxes to the Crown in Madrid.[139] The *baculamento* system was acknowledged to have become a source of wealth accumulation for the few. On 6 October 1625, Governor Bento Banha Cardoso, who was governor prior to Correia de Sousa, sent a letter to the Crown complaining that the previous governors of Angola had made it impossible for *sobas* to open their markets to free trade. He insisted that to

---

[136] 'Carta do Rei de Dongo a D. João IV'.
[137] See 'Padre António Vieira – "O Problema de Escravatura"', [Padre António Vieira – The Problem of Slavery], in J. A. da Graça Barretto, *Monstruosidades do Tempo e da Fortuna, Diário de Factos que Sucederam no Reino de 1625 a 1780, até hoje Atribuído Infundamente ao Benedictino Fr. Alexandre da Paixão*, Lisbon: Tipografia da Viúva Sousa Neves – Editora, 1888, ms. p. 202, fl. 189 v. [1673]. Father António Vieira was a Portuguese Jesuit priest who worked in Salvador, Maranhão, Brazil and Cape Verde in the seventeenth century. He also served as a Portuguese diplomat, and member of the Royal Council during the reign of Dom João IV (1640–1656), the King of Portugal. He was born in Lisbon (Portugal) on 6 February 1608. At age of five years, he went with his parent to Salvador, Bahia, where his father, Cristóvão Vieira Ravasco, had been appointed as a registrar. In 1625, he entered priesthood training and became a figure of authority and celebraty in Brazil as well Portugal. His family was part of the Portuguese authority in Brazil. He died on 8 July 1697, in Salvador, Bahia.
[138] See AHU-CU-001, cx. 2, d. 184, 10 July 1625.
[139] See AHU-CU-001, cx. 2. d. 185, 9 August 1625.

demand that *sobas* pay *baculamento* would be impractical[140] without the Crown giving the governors more powers. His request reflected the fact that tax was traditionally voluntary among the Mbundu. He asked the Crown to enforce a lightweight tax that would act as an incentive for securing peace with the *sobas*. The only taxes due from the *sobas* would have been a light market tax.[141] Cardoso was reacting to a letter sent by Governor Sousa to the Crown two months earlier, in which he had suggested 109 *sobas* be ordered to pay all taxes owed. However, that order was impossible to implement without a strong military presence to enforce it.[142]

As stressed in the Introduction, the issue of *baculamento* has not received the scholarly attention it deserves in relation to the Atlantic slave trade in Angola in the century that this book examines. Historians of Angola such as, in historical order, Cadornega, Felner, Delgado, Birmingham, Miller, Vansina, Heintze, Heywood, Ferreira, Candido and Freudenthal, have not engaged with *baculamento* as a new tax system in tandem with slavery.[143] Heintze's examination of *baculamento* in Angola focuses on the early period of the century and does not mention Governor Fernão de Sousa's grand scheme to revamp *baculamento* as a tax system by which it became 'law *magna*' in Angola.[144] The weakness of her research on Sousa is that it focuses exclusively on the years 1617–1630,[145] prior to his crucial edict. Sousa made the announcement on 7 December 1631,[146] a year after he left his post in Angola and thus outside the period on which she worked. This seems to be the reason why she overlooked it. The scholars who followed the path she opened up and used the sources she had made available have equally fallen into this trap, particularly Freudenthal and Pantoja.[147] They described *baculamento* as a produce tax to be paid by *sobas* to the

---

[140] See 'Carta de Bento Banha Cardoso a El'Rei' [A Letter of Bento Banha Cardoso to the King], BAL, ms. 51, VII-30 fls. 315v-316, 25 January 1625.
[141] See AHU-CU-001, cx. 2, d. 191, 6 October 1625
[142] See AHU-CU-001, cx. 2, d. 313, 13 August 1625.
[143] See Freudenthal and Pantoja, *Livro dos Baculamentos*; Cadornega, *História Geral*, vols. I, II and III; Felner, *Angola: Apontamentos*; Delgado's note in Cadornega, *História Geral*; Birmingham, *Trade and Conquest*; Miller, *Kings and Kinsmen*; Vansina, *Kingdoms of the Savanna*; Heintze, 'The Angolan Vassal Tributes of the 17th Century'; and Heintze, 'Written Sources and African History'; Ferreira, *Cross-Cultural Exchange*; Candido, *An African Slaving Port*, and Heywood, *Njinga of Angola*.
[144] See 'Informação de Fernão de Sousa a El-Rei'; Heintze, 'The Angolan Vassal Tributes of the 17th Century' and Heintze, 'Luso-African Feudalism in Angola?'.
[145] See Heintze, 'Written Sources and African History', p. 78.
[146] See 'Informação de Fernão de Sousa a El-Rei'.
[147] See Freudenthal and Pantoja, *Livro dos Baculamentos*.

Portuguese, failing to detect Sousa's legislation because their study, again, does not extend beyond the year 1630. Green, who focuses on tribute in West Central Africa and its equivalent, *encomienda*, in the Latin American context in the seventeenth century, also missed Sousa's paradigm-shifting tax law regarding enslavement.[148] No one has seen so far that Sousa's imposition of taxation moved the meaning of *baculamento* away from the Mbundu economic understanding of it and that this had a profound impact on future generations of enslaved people in Angola, right up to the nineteenth century.

As described before, Sousa was the first Portuguese governor in Angola to introduce a system of taxation on the *sobas* that transformed *baculamento* from tax in produce (*encombos*) to a tax in enslaved people. Outlining his new tax, Sousa declared:

All tribute of *encombos* should be abated that are of goats and cows, because there are not any; those of dugout canoes, for which there is a lack of timber; of olio [palm oil], because of those sobas who do not have palm trees on their lands to make it; and of chickens, because of long travelling they bring them dead. That an edict of quality in enslaved be decreed, because all types of slave are called *peça*, and with such decrees, they will be relieved from paying tribute that they are obliged to, because they say they do not understand that it was forever, subsequently it be decreed to them in clear terms for which they are obliged to. They will continue to pay, and to all their successors as it is in the book where they are written, from my instruction that I will be handing over to the one Your Majesty has appointed.[149]

The *encombros* tribute paid by *sobas* to the Portuguese, which included produce such as cows, timber, palm oil and chickens, was thenceforth

---

[148] See Green, 'Baculamento or Encomienda?'
[149] Fernaõ de Sousa, 'Informação de Fernão de Sousa a El-Rei', 'Deuesse abater a todos o tributo dos *encombros,* que saõ chibarros e as vaccas, porque as naõ há; as almadias porque uaó faltando as madeiras; o azeite aos Souas que naõ tem em suas terras palmeiras de que se fas; e aos de longe as galinhas, porque as trazem mortas. Que se faça declaração na calidade das peças, porque a toda sorte de escrauo chamaõ peça, e cõ as ditas declaraçoens ficarão mais aliuiados pera pagar o tributo a que ficarem obrigados, porque dizem que naõ entenderão o ficauaõ pera sempre, posto que lhe[s] declararão nos asentos perque se obrigarão, o ficauaõ a pagar por sy, e por todos seus sucçessores, como consta do liuro en que estaõ asentados, na forma de minha instrução que tenho pera entregar a quem V. Magestade me ordenar.' Encombros or emcombas are muted goats, also known as *emponda* or *mponda*. These were a traditional gift given to a person of hierarchy to appease him or her or establish a friendship. Another example of the traditional friendship gift was the 'flour', 'chicken' and 'goats' that were given to Portuguese missionaries on their arrival in Ndongo in 1562. See 'Carta do Irmão António Mendes', BNL – CA, Ms. 308, 29 October 1562; also MMA vol. II, pp. 488–489.

stopped, and replaced by a tax paid in enslaved people. For Sousa, the tax in enslaved people was to be perpetual, that is, everlasting for succeeding generations of *sobas*. *Baculamento* was thus given a new meaning: tax payments in human beings became a substitute for the old *baculamento* paid in produce. Sousa's new tax system overhauled the tax system that had been put in place by Governor Bento Banha Cardoso (1611–1615) and continued by Luís Mendes de Vasconcelos (1617–1621), in which *sobas* were now obliged to 'pay an average 4 *peças de Indias* [slaves] each per annum'.[150]

Sousa's new tax system was put in place in 1626, the very year in which Mendonça's grandfather, Philipe Hari I, was elected king of Pungo-Andongo, and it boosted the slave trade in Angola. In the Portuguese interpretation, or Sousa's appropriation, of *baculamento*, human bodies became currency, and this change was the basis of Garcia II of Kongo's critique of it. He acknowledged that human bodies now replaced other commodities of exchange, such as shells, *nzimbos* and *patacas*, not only in West Central Africa, but also in the Atlantic world.[151] The commodification of human bodies as currency was the aim of the Atlantic slave trade. These African bodies, unlike the fragile bodies of cows, chickens and goat, could endure travelling long distances, as Sousa noted, becoming easily transportable currency. It was not surprising that João Hari II rejected the Portuguese alliance and declared independence in 1671.

Although Philipe Hari I willingly accepted *baculamento*, he insisted in the latter years of his reign that, as a king, he was not subject to *baculamento*.[152] It was an argument previously put forward in 1622 by Njinga in Luanda in support of her brother, Ngola Mbandi.[153] Njinga implored the Portuguese governor that Mbandi be seen as an allied king on an equal footing with other kings and not as a vassal of the Portuguese Crown.[154] If one returns to the political structure of Ndongo, one sees no tax collector within the range of political roles. Although Heywood and Thornton included *muuene kudya* (tax collector) as a category, it is not listed in Cadornega's description of Ndongo's political structure.[155] Each province was a self-sufficient unit that existed for the sustenance of its *soba* and his subjects. The aim of expanding the kingdom was to acquire

---

[150] See Heintze, 'The Angolan Vassal Tributes of the 17th Century', p. 61.
[151] Marx, *Capital*, pp. 125–333.   [152] See 'Carta do Rei de Dongo a D. João IV'.
[153] Montecuccolo, *Istorica Descrizione de Tre Regni Congo*, book 5.
[154] Montecuccolo, *Istorica Descrizione de Tre Regni Congo*, book 5.
[155] See Heywood and Thornton, *Central Africans*; Miller, *Kings and Kinsmen*, p. 77.

lands from provinces that already had enough to sustain their people. The aggressive nature of the Portuguese tax policy, which was accompanied by threats, violence, abuse and coercion of the *sobas*, was foreign to the traditional understanding of *baculamento*.[156]

In Sousa's letter from 1625, it is evident that the former governor, Bento Banha Cardoso was confronting two issues during his governance. Firstly, the bishop, Simão de Mascarenhas, was collecting one set of taxes from the *sobas* for the Church,[157] while the governor himself[158] was collecting another. This meant that *sobas* were being taxed twice. Secondly, there were not enough enslaved people in the provinces that could be paid as taxes.[159] The tax paid was based on the Judeo-Christian principle of paying a tithe, 10 per cent of one's earnings. This was the tax system that Sousa inherited from his predecessors, before his introduction of a tax paid in human beings in 1626, which he reported only in 1631. Regarding the situation he encountered, Sousa stated in 1625: 'I have given plots of land to the residents and they have been looking to till them, which will yield a major return of tithes to the treasury of Your Majesty.'[160] Labour was what was asked of Portugal's subjects in Angola at the time so that they would pay taxes in produce.

Bento Banha Cardoso, who died soon after Philipe Hari I came to power, was held responsible for Hari's election, which left the Crown in Madrid frustrated. The Portuguese could not provide substantial evidence of the legitimacy of Philipe Hari I's election, and for ten years they dragged out their explanation of why Philipe Hari I had been the winning candidate for the throne. He ruled Pungo-Andongo for thirty-eight years, between 1626 and 1664, one year less than Queen Njinga ruled Matamba (1624–1663). The monarchs remained rivals until Njinga's death. Their rivalry represented a traditional gender issue present in

---

[156] See Freudenthal and Pantoja, *Livro dos Baculamentos*.
[157] 'Carta de Fernão de Sousa a El-Rei', AHU-CU-001, cx. 2, d. 313, 13 August 1625, 'Tanto que cheguey comessey a puxar por isso, e porque o Bispo tinha cobrado alguás pessas dos Souas, fiz dliligensia com elle pellas arrecadar, para se entreguarem ao feitor sendo de baculamentos, ou pera as restituir aos Souas; respondeume que se eu as quizesse para mim que mas inuiaria. E por lhe não deffírir, conformandome com o que V. Magestade me manda em meu regimento, as não deu, dizendo que cu lhe não podia tomar conta disso, e que elle a daria quando V. Magestade lha pedisse.'
[158] 'Carta de Fernão de Sousa a El-Rei', 13 August 1625.
[159] See 'Carta de Bento Banha Cardoso a El'Rei'.
[160] 'Carta de Fernão de Sousa a El-Rei', 13 August 1625, 'tenho repartidas as terras pellos moradores, e procure se apliquem a semeallas, de que resultará maior rendimento de dízimos pera a fazenda de V. Magestade'.

much of African society as well as the inherited rivalry of their two mothers, which continued to be played out between their powerful children.[161] The next section explores the role of João Hari II, also known as Dom João de Sousa, the son who succeeded Philipe I.

2.6 NGOLA JOÃO HARI II, KING OF PUNGO-ANDONGO (1624–1671)

Ngola Philipe Hari I died in 1664 and his son Ngola João Hari II succeeded him. After a an alliance of thirty-eight years between Ndongo and Portugal, and the deaths of his father and brothers who had perished for the Portuguese project of conquest, João Hari II ended political, economic and cultural ties with Portugal. His father had left the economy of Ndongo completely broken as a result of Portuguese control and exploitation. In 1631 Dom Frei Francisco do Soveral, the bishop of Kongo, in his report in Latin to Pope Urban VIII, described Philipe Hari I as a miserable king whom the Portuguese had exploited. He declared:

> ... at the place called Dongo [Ndongo], where the most miserable king of Angola lives, captive of our Portuguese, vanquished and truly annihilated, devoid of empire or kingdom, two priests of the Society of Jesus help, that [families] with their families, dedicate themselves to everything that concerns the instruction and conduct of the Christian life.[162]

Birmingham claims that Philipe Hari I's relationship with Portugal, in particular with the Portuguese Overseas Council, went sour towards the latter part of his reign.[163] His treatment at the hands of the Portuguese Overseas Council had left the House of Ndongo disillusioned. João Hari II's hostile stance towards the Portuguese won him huge support among the Mbundu people, who were disenchanted with his father's vassalship to

---

[161] See Lingna Nafafé, 'African Orality'.
[162] See D. Frei Francisco do Soveral, 'Relatório de D. Frei Francisco do Soveral na visita "Ad Sacra Limina"', 'Jnfra scriptam relationem de statu Cathedralis ecclesiae Sancti Saluatoris transmittit ad Sanctissimum D. N. Vrbanú Papam Octauum et Sacram Congregationem Concilli Tridentini Prater Pranciscus de Soveral, Episcopus. Anno Domini"de"1631", p. 24, 'in loco vero qui vocatur Dongo, vbi habitat miserabilissimus ille Rex de Angola, a nostris Lusitanis captus, victus, ac nempe extinctus, suoque imperio et regno vix annihilatus, assistunt stunt duo Religiosi sacerdotes ex Societate Iesu, ad ilium instruendum, et cum sua familia, in omnibus quae ad christianam vitam pertinent dirigendum ac perficiendum. In hoc miserabilissimo statu praefatus Episcopus Franciscus suum Episcopatum inuenit.'
[163] See 'Carta do Rei de Dongo a D. João IV'; see also the Oversea Council's response to Philipe Hari I's complaint, 'Consulta do Conselho Ultramarino', 22 April 1654.

Ndongo's Political and Cultural Environment

the Spanish and Portuguese crowns.[164] In Cadornega's words, the House of Ndongo was viewed by the people of Matamba as a traitor to Mbundu traditions.[165]

The 1671 Portuguese victory over Pungo-Andongo in battle largely suffocated João Hari II's political and strategic goals for Ndongo and Matamba. Angola was not conquered by Portuguese effort alone; rather, it was the contribution and collaboration of the Angolans themselves that had allowed the Portuguese to gain dominion over their territories. The participation of many *sobas* and Philipe Hari I as vassals of Spain and Portugal, as well as the participation of *guerra preta*, undoubtedly aided the advancement of Portugal's interests in the region.

Birmingham and Delgado have paid little attention in their work on the period to João Hari II's political and economic plans.[166] When João Hari II succeeded to the throne in 1664, he set about settling scores, particularly with many *sobas*. He ordered that the *soba* Angolomem Acacombe, who had been his father's main rival and had consistently refused to follow his orders, be killed – and his remaining wealth used to finance the coronation.[167] In so doing, he made clear that the king's vassalship to the Iberian Crown had come to an end and signalled a return to traditional political processes, with the *macotas* forming the council who supported his government. His agenda involved a revival of Mbundu political and cultural traditions. The captain major of Ambaca, Luis Telles Barreto, was sent to Pungo-Andongo to assess the situation. He reported to Luanda that João Hari II had reneged on the alliance between Portugal and Ndongo, and that he 'had the loyal support from his subjects, the elders of his court and lords he had in his kingdom, and for that he desired nothing'.[168]

There are few written sources for João Hari II and his reign. This can be explained on two grounds: firstly, his reign was short-lived; secondly, unlike his father, he was not on good terms with the Portuguese Overseas Council. Most of the documents we have were written by critics

---

[164] Ibid.; see also [without author's name] *História de Angola*, Centro de Estudos Angolanos, Grupo de Trabalho História e Etnologia, Porto: Afrontamento,1975, pp. 61–71.

[165] See Cadornega, *Guerras Angolanas*, vol. II, p. 251.

[166] Birmingham, *Trade and Conquest* and Delgado's note in Cadornega, *História de Angola*, vols. I and II.

[167] See Cadornega, *Guerras Angolanas*, vol. II, p. 225.

[168] Cadornega, *História Geral*, vol. II, pp. 225-226, '... elle esta obedecido de todos os seus Vassallos e Grandes de sua Côrte que tinha em seu Reino e Senhores, que para isso havia mister mais nada'.

who did not bestow the same laudatory language on him as they had done on his father.[169] However, one can, with relative precision, extract João Hari II's economic and political plans from these same writings, particularly those produced by the new governor of Angola, Francisco de Távora 'Cajanda'.

2.7 FRANCISCO DE TÁVORA 'CAJANDA': PORTUGUESE GOVERNOR OF LUANDA (1669–1676)

Francisco de Távora 'Cajanda' was governor of Luanda between 1669 and 1676, during the reigns of Afonso VI and Pedro II of Portugal. The Luanda City Council had governed the Portuguese settlement for two and half years before he arrived,[170] and his predecessor, Tristão da Cunha, had only governed the region for one year, between 1666 and 1667.[171] In 1667, the policy of appointing governors to Luanda from Brazil changed, and henceforth governors were appointed directly from Portugal. Távora was the first to have been appointed from Lisbon since Salvador Sa, who arrived in Luanda in 1648. On 21 March 1668, Prince Regent Dom Pedro II appointed Távora as governor of Angola. Távora triumphed over nine rival candidates for the post: Jorge de Melo, Aires de Saldanha de Meneses e Sousa, Dom Pedro de Almeida, Dom António Lobo da Silveira, António Galvão, Manuel de Sousa Mascharanhas, Henrique Correia, Miguel Ferraz Bravo and Luís Velho.[172] The Portuguese Overseas Council deemed a wider pool of high-quality candidates necessary if the Angolan question and the challenges facing the Luanda City Council were to be effectively overcome.[173] Nonetheless, Távora's appointment at the age of 22 years raised eyebrows in Portugal, both because of his age and because people suspected his brothers, who had gained recognition for their part in the Portuguese Restoration Wars, influenced the election.[174] Like João Hari II, Távora appointed his brother (in this case Marques de Távora) as his army's chief

---

[169] For full detail on his contribution to the Portuguese project of conquest and his death, see Cadornega, *História Geral*, vol. II, pp. 224–227.
[170] See Cadornega, *História Geral*. vol. II, p. 259.
[171] See 'Consulta do Conselho Ultramarino', AHU_CU_001, cx. 10, d. 1149, and 'Carta Régia ao Governador de Angola' [A Royal Letter to the Governor of Angola], AHU, cód. 275, fls. 363v.-364, 18 October 1665; see also ATT, Chancelaria de D. Afonso VI, liv. 28, fl. 83 v., MMA, vol. XII, p. 574.
[172] See 'Consulta do Conselho Ultramarino', AHU_CU_001, cx. 10, d. 1149.
[173] See 'Consulta do Conselho Ultramarino', AHU_CU_001, cx. 10, d. 1149.
[174] M. J. Gabriel Saldanha, *História De Goa (Politica E Arqueologica)*, New Delhi: Asian Educational Services 1990.

of staff.[175] His other appointments included Third Field Master Francisco de Ledesma Torres and Lieutenant General João Pereira Caldas, both experienced men in their field, who brought infantry reinforcements from Salvador, Bahia.[176] On 5 March 1669, the Portuguese Overseas Council recommended to the Crown that key appointees needed to be highly experienced personnel in key areas such as infantry command, field warfare and fortification engineering. In addition, it was made mandatory that all were to serve in Angola for the duration of Távora's government.[177]

After Távora arrived in Angola, he wrote a letter, on 15 March 1670, informing the Crown and the Portuguese Overseas Council of what he observed in the region. He reported 180 *soba* vassals (those who had shown allegiance to Portugal or had been conquered by the Portuguese), among whom there was great political division.[178] This number may appear insignificant in comparison with the estimated 730 *sobas* in Ndongo and Matamba at the time. Indeed, in political and economic terms, the Portuguese had considerable support, although Candido has asserted that the stability of the *sobas*' vassalship fluctuated from time to time, depending on the terms of the agreements of allegiance that existed between them and Portugal.[179] African soldiers or *guerra preta* could be recruited from the regions controlled by cooperative *sobas*. Areas controlled by *soba* vassals were used for trading in goods as well as in slaves, and by 1664 these areas included Libolo, Dembos and Benguela.[180] Economically, each *soba* paid *baculamento* to the Portuguese, and with every change of governor in Luanda they were expected to gift a certain number of enslaved people.[181] Those *sobas* who could not afford to pay left the area,[182] abandoning their lands and property to search for new ones. Those who stayed were obliged to surrender their people, while others ended up giving babies, old men and even 'their wives and children to avoid similar punishment'.[183] These harsh

---

[175] See Cadornega, *Guerras Angolanas*, vol. II, pp. 260–261.
[176] See Cadornega, *Guerras Angolanas*, vol. II, p. 260.
[177] See 'Consulta do Conselho Ultramarino', AHU_CU_001, cx. 10, d. 1186.
[178] See Cadornega, *Guerras Angolanas*, vol. II, p. 545.
[179] See Candido, *An African Slaving Port*, pp. 76–87.
[180] AHU, Angola, cx. 8, doc. 69, 15 November 1664. For a detailed study of slavery in Benguela and its hinterland, see Candido, *An African Slaving Port*.
[181] AHU, Angola, cx. 10, doc. 26, 22 September 1670.
[182] 'Carta do Padre Gonçalo de Sousa em Nome da Câmara de Luanda' [A Letter from Father Gonçalo de Sousa Letter on behalf of Luanda Council], AHU, Angola, cx.1, 6 July 16.
[183] 'Carta do Vicário General de Angola, a El-Rei D. João IV' [A Letter of the General Vicar of Angola to King D. John IV, Vicar General Francisco Uāz de Rezende] AHU, Angola, cx. 3, ms., São Paulo de Asumpçaõ, 10 May 1653, 'danão molheres e filhos per se liurarem de semelhantes moléstias'.

terms resulted in some *soba* vassals rebelling against the *baculamento* that had been imposed on them.[184] In 1653, there was a real lack of enslaved people in regions where trade had been opened to the Portuguese.[185] All of this begs the question: who were the enslaved people in Ndongo, or even Angola for that matter? We will return to this issue in Chapter 4 when we consider Mendonça's discourse.

Some of the *sobas* who ran away to escape Portuguese taxation and *baculamento* joined powerful groups such as the Jagas.[186] Father Gonçalo de Sousa, in his letter to King João IV on behalf of the Luanda City Council, made a complaint that '*soba* vassals to His Majesty, cannot put up with the tributes of slaves [*baculamento*] or other taxes which they are obliged to pay, and they are withdrawing to the hinterland and are thrown together with the Jagas and other *sobas* that are not subjects of His Majesty.'[187]

Távora's strategy was to control trade and wage war against those regions unwilling to submit to the Portuguese. His wars against Conde de Sonho in Kongo, Dom António Jinga or Guzambambe in Matamaba and the *sobas* of Libolo, Cassanje and Kissama all ended in defeat. Távora wanted full control of the slave trade in the region, which he believed was in the hands of the Dutch in Lugano and Pinda. In his letter of 12 August 1670, he stated that the Dutch had taken 1,200 enslaved people from these locations to Curação.[188] Távora's policies included prohibition of *cachaça* (rum) production in Angola, arguing that the lack of dry wood would make it impossible to produce sugar in Angola. (The wood was needed to make fires for boiling sugar-cane juice to reduce it to sugar.) *Engenho* and its *cachaça* production was therefore left to Brazil,[189] but his actions demonstrated that the Portuguese policy was that Angola would simply be used to supply enslaved people for the Americas. Little was done to advance the economy in West Central Africa.

---

[184] AHU, Angola, cx.5, doc.101, 22 November 1652.
[185] AHU, Anaola, cx. 8, doc. 28, 26 September 1653.
[186] For a detailed study of Jagas, see Heintze and Rieck, 'The Extraordinary Journey of the Jaga'; Hilton, 'The Jaga Reconsidered'; Joseph C. Miller, 'Requiem for the Jaga', *Cahiers d'Etudes Africaines*, 11(3), 1981, pp. 385–423; Candido, *An African Slaving Port*, pp. 31–87.
[187] 'Carta do Vicário General de Angola, a El-Rei D. João IV', 'os sobas avassalados a V. Magestade cançados por naõ poderem aturar os tributos de escrauos a que estaõ obrigados, e por outras auexassoés se uáo retirando pera o sertaõ, e se lançaõ cõ os jagas e outros sobas que naõ saõ sogeitos a V. Magestade'.
[188] See Cadornega, *Guerras Angolanas*, vol. II, p. 545.
[189] For a detailed study of the relationship between enslaved people and alcohol, see José C. Curto, "Álcoól e Escravos: O comércio luso-brasileiro do álcool em Mpinda, Luanda e Benguela durante o tráfico atlântico de escravos (c. 1480–1830) e o seu impacto nas sociedades da África Central Ocidental", *Tempos e Espaços Africanos*, 2002, pp. 273–276.

Távora's policy for Angola grew out of Portuguese Restoration ideology, which aimed to recoup or reconquer the Portuguese lands in Europe, Africa, Brazil and Asia lost during the period of the Union of the Two Crowns (1580–1640). Many of his family had fought in battles for Portuguese Restoration and in the Spanish Succession Wars, and his method was to combat his African enemies with an iron fist. His military strategy included raising a strong army with a cavalry regiment; however, his plea to the Portuguese Overseas Council to establish cavalry in Angola was not met with approval initially, since a policy was already in place to prohibit cavalry. Despite this, Távora founded a company of cavalry, which was approved by the Crown on 9 May 1672.[190] Távora's introduction of fighting horses in Angola was intended to weaken João Hari II's formidable army, and Távora intended to increase the population of horses through breeding programmes. However, the Crown and Overseas Council overruled him, fearing that the Angolans would appropriate these military practices and begin breeding horses themselves.[191] Aside from Tavora's mentor, Salvador Correia de Sá e Benavides, a war hero and former governor of Angola and Rio de Janeiro, the Portuguese Overseas Council unanimously voted to ban horse-breeding in the region. Távora epitomised the hypocrisy of Portuguese Restoration ideology: while Portugal sought humanity, peace and freedom from Spain, it forced Angolans to accept a foreign yoke.[192] Meanwhile, Angolans were very well aware of Portugal's struggle for independence from Spain and the contradictions in its national ideology. João Hari II's claim for independence should be seen in the light of this as he sought to liberate Ndongo from the Portuguese yoke and a market economy based on the enslavement of the Mbundu people. The following section examines the destruction of Pungo-Andongo and the sending of the kingdom's princes and princesses, Queen Njinga's nephews and nieces, to Brazil.

2.8 JOÃO HARI II'S CLAIM OF INDEPENDENCE FROM PORTUGAL AND THE DESTRUCTION OF PUNGO-ANDONGO

João Hari II's scheme for separating from Portugal consisted of three central ideas. Firstly, he demanded that no payment of *baculamento* be

---

[190] See 'Carta para o Conselho Ultramarino', [Letter to the Overseas Council].
[191] Cadornega, *História Geral*, vol. II, pp. 542–543.
[192] See [without author's name] *História de Angola, Centro de Estudos Angolanos, Grupo de Trabalho História e Etnologia*, Porto: Afrontamento, 1975.

made to Portugal.[193] Secondly, he intended to take control of trade and to prevent Portugal retaining a trade monopoly.[194] Thirdly, he demanded that no wars be waged against the Angolan people.[195] This strategy was recorded in letters and documents written by critics of João Hari II, such as Cadornega,[196] Salvador Sá[197] and Miguel Manescal,[198] who reported the Portuguese victory over Pungo-Andongo on 29 November 1671.

Several other factors encouraged João Hari II to protest against Portugal's role in Angola and disregard the alliance with Portugal. These are worth considering when engaging in the wider narrative of the fall of Pungo-Andongo and João Hari II's desire for separation from Portugal and a return to Mbundu traditions. One of the contributing factors was the above-mentioned Portuguese Restoration and separation from the Iberian Union. A second was the mutiny in Luanda in 1668, in which the leaders of the Portuguese administration were challenged by unpaid Portuguese soldiers in Angola. The third factor was the unpopularity of the House of Ndongo with the Mbundu people.

João Hari II was defiant in the face of the Portuguese project of conquest and took further measures to cut diplomatic ties with Portugal by expelling priests and diplomats from his court and preventing Portuguese traders from engaging in commerce there.[199] This was not the first time that resistance of this nature had been expressed against the Portuguese in the region. In 1575, Álvaro I Nimi a Lukeni lua Mvemba, king of Kongo, informed Ngola Kiluanji Kia Ndambi, king of Ndongo, of

---

[193] 'Carta de Fernão de Sousa a El-Rei', 22 August 1625.
[194] See early Portuguese charts on trade monopoly in Senegambia; such rights were often extended to the new regions although they were implemented twelve years before the Portuguese reached Kongo in 1484 in 'Carta Régia de 8 de Fevereiro de 1472, concedendo aos habitants das ilhas de Cabo Verde e exclusive do comercio e resgate na Guiné desde o Senegal até Siera Leóa' [Royal Letter of Patent of the 8 February 1472, Granting to the Inhabitants of the Cape Verd Islands the Exclusive Privilege of Trading in Guinea, from the Senegal to Sierra Leone], in *Reply of the Portuguese Government to the Case in Support of the Claim of Great Britain to the Island of Bolama on the Western Coast of Africa and to a Certain Portion of Territory Opposite to that Island on the Mainland to be Laid Before the President of the United States of America as the Arbiter Selected to Decide the Question*, Lisbon: National Printing Office, 1869, pp. 175–177.
[195] See Cadornega, *História Geral*, vol. II, p. 246.
[196] See Cadornega, *História Geral*, vols. I, II, III.
[197] See 'Carta de Salvador Correia de Sá', 'Sobre o que escreve e Governador de Angola Fr. De tavora, acerca da v. q. alcansou delRey de Dongo, e forma qse deve ter có D. Philipe có e Irmaó do mesmo Rey ...'
[198] Relaçam/ Do FELICE SVCCESSO.   [199] See Cadornega, *História Geral*, vol. II, p. x.

a Portuguese plot to take over his land.²⁰⁰ Ndambi was told that: 'the Jesuits had come to see if Angola produced silver or gold, which would make it worthwhile for the Portuguese king to conquer his lands.'²⁰¹ Consequently, Ndambi expelled all Portuguese representatives in his kingdom, keeping nine as prisoners. Among these nine prisoners was Novais, the former governor of Angola mentioned above.

João Hari II attacked Dumbo Apebo, a *soba* vassal of Portugal from Latacao da Forte de Cambambe. According to Cadornega, João Hari II 'spoke outrageously and opprobriously of the Portuguese nation that had given him greatness and made him who he was'.²⁰² Távora sent Captain Major João Soares de Almeida to the fort of Mbaka to protect Dumbo Apebo. In the meantime, Diogo Gola Calanga,²⁰³ João Hari II's brother and captain general of his army was conducting assaults on distant territories. The Portuguese in Luanda demanded that João Hari II join them in battle against other Angolan regions, as his father had done, but he refused.²⁰⁴ Cadornega reported that:

Hari II did not respond to their call as he should, but rather answered them with contempt and haughtiness and entrenched the entrances of the fortress of Pungo-Andongo where his throne and residence were. And he had gathered many people for war from around the kingdom and lordships, who brought with them many firearms.²⁰⁵

The Portuguese were unable to match the power of Diogo Gola's army, and Captain Mayor João Soares de Almeida's forces were prevented from reaching the fort of Mbaka. Cadornega lamented that it was due to the

---

²⁰⁰ See 'Carta do Padre Garcia Simões para o Provincial'. In 1691 Ndembu, chief of Mbwila, expelled the Portuguese representatives from Kongo and Angola, cx. 10, 28 November 1691; for a detailed discussion, see also Birmingham, *Trade and Conquest*, p. 135.
²⁰¹ Birmingham, *Trade and Conquest*, p. 37.
²⁰² See Cadornega, *História Geral*, vol. II, p. 246, 'falando muitos desaforos e opprobrious da Nacao Portugueza que lhe havia dado a Grandeza e ser que tinha'. Similar language had also been used in the Lisbon report. See also Relaçam/ Do FELICE SVCCESSO.
²⁰³ Gola Calanga is Diogo Mbundu's name. At least this is how Cadornega has given us its spelling. On 1 May 1674, when João Hari II's heir was baptised in the monastery of Alcobaça, Diogo's name was also mentioned and his Mbundu name was spelt Cabangua. See 'Baptismo do Príncipe de Dongo' [The Baptism of the Prince of Dongo], BNL, ms. 7332, 1 May 1674, and Brásio, *Monumentum Memoria Africana*, vol. XII, pp. 297-298.
²⁰⁴ See Cadornega, *História Geral*, vol. II, p. 246.
²⁰⁵ Cadornega, *História Geral*, vol. II, p.246, 'a cujo chamado nao deferio como devia, antes respondeo com desprezo e altivez e foi intrincheirando as entradas da Fortaleza de suas Pedras on tinha sua morada e assent, e havia recolhido muita gente de Guerra de seu Reino e Senhorio com muita Armas de fogo'.

distance between Pungo-Andongo and Luanda that Diogo Gola Calanga was able to rebel against the Portuguese.

Távora was well aware of João Hari II's political intentions. For many, João Hari II 'and his father owed so much to Portugal'.[206] Cadornega described João Hari II's political resistance as ill thought out and claimed that Hari was 'not wanting to give anything away nor to satisfy what had been taken, and [was] therefore responding with displeasure and pride to what was written to him'.[207]

In order to wage war on Pungo-Andongo, Távora sought the approval of the Luanda Council of War and the Portuguese Overseas Council. He also sought support from the three main captaincies in Brazil: Salvador in Bahia, Rio de Janeiro and Pernambuco.[208] There was an economic justification, as 'the governor of Pernambuco, Fernão de Sousa Countinho concludes, that the conservation of Angola was also necessary for the State [Pernambuco], because factories [sugar plantations] would end up lacking the service of slavery, for the captaincy was dependent on Angola for its enslaved people'.[209] The personalities involved were experienced captains in the art of war in Brazil. Among them was João Fernandes Vieira, a military chief who had fought for the expulsion of the Dutch in Pernambuco and who later commanded the cavalry unit mentioned above. Among the soldiers were many Brazilians of Native American origin who would learn that the wars they had experienced at home mirrored those in Angola and that the Portuguese expansionist project extended beyond Brazil.[210] The war in Angola provided a platform for these soldiers to reflect on the experiences of the Native populations on

---

[206] Cadornega, *História Geral*, vol. II, p. 298, 'a quem elle e seu Pay devião tanto'. See also Relaçam/ Do FELICE SVCCESSO.

[207] Cadornega, *História Geral*, vol. II, p. 299, 'não querendo dar a nada descargo, nem satisfazer o que tomado tinha: antes respondendo com desaforo e soberba ao que se lhe escrevia'.

[208] See Cadornega, *História Geral*, vol. II, pp. 260–261.

[209] See F. A. Fereira da Costa, *Anais Pernambucanos* 4, Recife: Arquivo Público Estadual, 1951–1958, p. 43, 'que da conservação de Angola dependia também a dêste Estado, cujas fábricas acabariam faltando-lhe o serviço da escravaria, que dali se conduz para todo êle'. Távora's argument was that three captaincies of Brazil – Bahia, Rio de Janeiro and Pernambuco – were under direct threat, like Angola, if they did not participate in the war because of all were dependent on enslaved Angolans for their sugar production. This was a 'sugar war'. For further discussion, see Costa, *Anais Pernambucanos*, pp. 43–44.

[210] For a wider discussion of Brazil and Africa, see Luiz Felipe de Alencastro, *O Trato dos Viventes: Formação do Brasil no Atlântico Sul, Séculos XVI e XVII*, São Paulo, Brazil: Companhia das Letras, 2000.

Ndongo's Political and Cultural Environment

both continents and to begin to engage in a much deeper battle for liberation. Cadornega states:

... they came, after arriving at this port and city, as help from the city of Bahia, from the Governor Fernão de Souza Coutinho [governor of the captaincy of Pernambuco], to help the expedition of João Fernandes Vieira of Rio de Janeiro who was dispatched by the governor of the city of São Sebastião, Joao da Silva de Souza; all powerful ships, with captains skilled in the art of war, and reputable soldiers.[211]

There is little doubt that the Portuguese resorted to war against Pungo-Andongo, once regarded as an ally, as a direct response to João Hari II's decision to block the trade routes and his explicit efforts to build an economy more in line with the Mbundu way of life. The Portuguese Crown justified the waging of war not on the grounds that the Angolans refused to trade, but on their rejection of Gospel teaching. The minutes of the Portuguese Overseas Council meeting of 14 December 1652 recorded:

... there is a province or settlement of heathens that means a 'just war' could be waged, when they forbid the preaching of the Sacred Gospel; but not for rebuking trade in slaves, which ought to be sought by peaceful means and justification.[212]

In this period, evidence demonstrates that unscrupulous governors could wage war as a means of obtaining enslaved people. The Crown knew this, but wars were often rationalised as having other causes. The Portuguese Overseas Council passed laws to prevent governors in Angola from taking advantage of these situations, but very little was achieved. Governors often acted against natural law in order to achieve their slave-trading objectives. The Portuguese Overseas Council was well aware of these practices, its members having all been governors themselves prior to taking their roles within the Portuguese Overseas Council. Council documents stated that:

... the Council was in doubt that these were what the Judge was indicating; many times governors took honest pretexts for wars on heathens, but with little cause,

---

[211] See Cadornega, *História Geral*, vol. II, p. 545, 'vierao entao chegando a este porto e cidade, os socorros da Cidade da Bahia, expedidos pello Governador Fernão de Souza Coutinho [governador da capitania de Pernambuco], ajudando sua expedicao o Governador que foi destes Reinos João Fernandes Vieira ... do Rio de Janeiro despachado pello Governador daquella Cidade de São Sebastião, Joao da Silva de Souza; todos em Naos possantes, com Capitaens praticos nas couzas da Guerra, e Saldados de valor', pp. 300–301.
[212] See AHU, cód. 15, fls. 32v–33v, 14 December 1652, 'Consulta do Conselho Ultramarino', 'A huã prouincia ou pouoaçaõ de gentios se pode fazer a guerra justamente, quando prohibem a pregação do Sagrado Evangelho, mas naõ por recuzar o resgate de escrauos, que antes se deue procurar por meyos paçificos e justificados '.

apart from envy to capture and sell them, which went against natural laws, which was an unlawful thing in the eyes of the Supreme Pontiffs and lords and kings of this kingdom.[213]

Mendonça was later to engage in discussion around these laws during his crucial debate at the Propaganda Fide's Office in Rome on 18 March 1684.[214] We will return to this issue in Chapter 6.

Cadornega succinctly highlighted that João Hari II believed he was capable of liberating himself from vassalship by rescinding the loyalty he owed to those who had facilitated his accession to the throne: 'for the Kingdom of Ndongo was not his by legitimate inheritance. But, as the Lord of Airi Province, he was called Ngola Airui or Airi Aquiloanji and he thought he could be the lord of our fortress.'[215]

Távora wasted no time and consulted the Brazilian captaincies for guidance: 'Having examined what was seen, the governor dispatched from the state of Brazil all the cavalry, sending them from this city to the relief of the Mbaka, with some soldiers and residents, reputable persons and many of the slaves of their own free will.'[216] On 31 March 1671, the Overseas Council agreed to Távora's military proposal and granted him a petition to wage war on Ndongo. Afterwards, he sent two letters to the Overseas Council on 18 May and 27 July 1671, informing them of Hari II's insolence. Luiz Lopes de Sequeira (an Angolan-born army officer)[217] was already stationed in Mbaka and agreed to the war plan refined by the Portuguese Overseas Council. Sequeira was chosen to lead the Portuguese joint army, which included *guerra preta,* Angolan soldiers, as well as Brazilians, many of whom were Native American. Sequeira had risen to fame as a military strategist after he had led a successful offensive against

---

[213] See 'Consulta do Conselho Ultramarino', 14 December 1652, 'e duuida o Conselho de que o sejaõ estas que aponta o Prouedor, porque muitas vezes tomaõ os gouernadores onestos pretextos para fazer Guerra aos gentios, sem na realidade hauer outra cauza mais que a cobiça de cattiuallos, e vendellos, atropelando as leis da naturesa, cousa muy estranhada dos Sumos Pontífices, e dos Senhores Reys deste Reino'.

[214] See also Relaçam/ Do FELICE SVCCESSO.

[215] Cadornega, *História Geral*, vol. II, p. 299, 'pois aqulle Reino de Dongo lhe não vinha por legitima herança, mais o ser Senhor da Provincia do Airi, que por essa razão lhe chamavão Àngola Airi e outros Àiri Àquiloangi; prezumia e teve para sy, que se puderia senhorear da nossa Fortaleza'.

[216] Cadornega *História Geral*, vol. II, p. 299, 'o que visto examinado pello Governador despachou avizos ao Estado do Brazil, a todos Cavalhos, e mandou marchar desta Cidade ao soccorro da Enbaca, com alguns soldados e Moradores, pessoas de posses, e muita escravaria por sua livre vontade'.

[217] Relaçam/ Do FELICE SVCCESSO, p. 7.

Kongo's army at the Battle of Mbwila.[218] However, he died soon after at the Battle of Katole.[219]

From the perspective of Ndongo, the war was not one fought to preserve or further a king's interests. João Hari II galvanised forces from different constituencies in the region, from Matamba, Cansanje and Imbangala, as well as Ndongo, in a battle against a common enemy. It was an alliance that harked back to the unity of Old Ndongo (Ndongo and Matamba). According to Cadornega, after the death of Queen Dona Barbara (Queen Njinga's sister, who ruled Matamba), great factionalism arose in Matamba surrounding who would assume the throne.[220] João Hari II, acutely aware of the volatility of the situation, put pressure on the Portuguese-aligned *soba* vassals.[221] Pungo-Andongo itself was ready to apply more pressure on the new governor in Luanda. João Hari II sent Diogo Gola Calanga on a hunting trip to Quindonga, where Queen Njinga had lived following her defeat by the Portuguese on 7 July 1626, with the mission of determining the extent of the unity between Matamba and Ndongo. Cadornega interpreted Diogo's actions as election-seeking, but an assumption that Diogo aspired to the position as monarch is far-fetched. What is far more likely is that he was sent there by his brother to secure an alliance with Matamba against the Portuguese. Cadornega is right to say that the king of Ndongo was hated by Matamba. In the 1660s, the majority of the Mbundu population felt that the king of Ndongo was a puppet who had betrayed his people: 'his name and generation were so hated by all the people of that quilombo and kingdom, and were known for being opponents and rebellious traitors of the Crown'.[222]

Amona, king of Matamba, may have hated Diogo and his brother João Hari II, but in that moment, he recognised the need for an ally who was ready to fight for a united Angola. João Hari II aimed to reunite with Matamba and to form a wider confederation:

... the aforementioned king [João Hari II] seeing what was around him and could come forth, was aided by his friends and allies, such as the king of Matamba, Lord

---

[218] See Relação da Batalha de Ambuíla, MB, 29 October 1665, Addicional n.° 20.953, fls. 227–229 in MMA, vol. Xii, pp. 582–591 and see also Birmingham, *Trade and Conquest*, p. 125.
[219] Birmingham, *Trade and Conquest*, p. 130.
[220] See Cadornega, *História Geral*, vol. II, p. 250.
[221] See Cadornega, *História Geral*, vol. II, pp. 251–252.
[222] Cadornega, *História Geral*, vol. II, p. 251, 'sendo o seu nome e geração tão odiada de toda a gente daquelle Quilombo e Reino, reputados por contrarios e traydores rebeldes àquella Coroa'.

Quilombo of the Queen Ginga, Dom Antonio Carrasco Ginga Amona. Even though Amona was not fond of him, they were always fierce and tyrannous. They allied among themselves into one body against their persecution, and they sent him some of their Jagas flags with capable officers to help him in his offensive and for their defence. And the provinces of Aco and Libolo Gumza Ambandi and other *sobas* of his kingdom did the same and went with their best, and with luggage of their *vassallos* who were most condemned to our punishment.[223]

João Hari II refused to continue to be a Portuguese vassal king and to pay the *baculamento* that had burdened his father.[224] The Battle of Ndongo was the biggest and most demanding that the Portuguese had fought since the beginning of their conquest of Angola.[225] It was far from comparable to the Battle of Mbwila with Kongo, as Cadornega noted:

... for that arduous and difficult task is understood to have been one of the greater considerations that had been undertaken since the beginning of the conquest of these realms, because it was like a civil war, which took on a king so filled with everything, hidden and fortified in an eminence so strong by nature and inexhaustibly superior.[226]

The Battle of Pungo-Andongo was more complicated and nuanced than historians have historically led us to believe. It was a battle within what appeared to be a Portuguese-controlled zone in Angola. As such, it was difficult to win, and Ndongo's defeat ultimately came about due to the fighting power of the *guerra preta* who fought for the Portuguese project of conquest. The *guerra preta* had intimate knowledge of all things Native, of the *coisas da terra*, such as language and internal political dynamics. Their ability to infiltrate Ndongo ranks and procure vital intelligence

---

[223] Cadornega, *História Geral*, vol. II, p. 300, 'e antevendo o dito Rey o que se lhe apparelhava e podia vir, se prevenio de soccorros de seus Amigos e Alliados, como foi del Rey de Matamba Senhor Quilombo da Rainha Ginga, Dom Antonio Carrasco Ginga Amona, que ainda que o nao era seu de curacao, sempre pescadores e tirannos, se fizerao em hum corpo contra a perseguicao do justo e lhe mandou algumas Bandeiras de seus Jagas com Cabos de valor para ajudarem sua defensa e nossa offense, e o mesmo fizerao da Provincia de Aco e Libolo Gumza Ambandi e outros Sovas de seu Reino e partido com mulherio e bagagem daquelles seus Vassallos que estavao mais condenados ao nosso castigo'.

[224] See 'Carta do Rei de Dongo a D. João IV', 8 April 1653, and 'Consulta do Conselho Ultramarino', 22 April 1654.

[225] See Cadornega, *História Geral*, vol. II, p. 302.

[226] Cadornega, *História Geral*, vol. II, pp. 302–303, 'para aquella ardua e difficultoza empreza que se podia della entender era a de mayor consideracao que tinha havido depsois do principio da Conquista destes Reinos, porque era Guerra como Civil, e buscar hum Rey tao abastecido de tudo, recolhido e fortificado em huma eminencia tao forte por natureza, e superior pello inexpugnavel'.

informed the Portuguese military strategy and ensured a Portuguese victory.[227]

João Hari II was able to mobilise other provinces and create regional alliances, as had been done during the conflicts of 1590[228] and 1635.[229] He wanted *sobas* from the confederation to exert their authority and to proclaim their liberation and freedom from the Portuguese settlement in Luanda. Reports from Lisbon on the war claimed that João Hari II was 'stimulated by his brother D. Diogo, captain general of Ndongo's army who, with his natural and excessive ferociousness and intrepidity, incited all neighbouring kings and *sobas* (the name that describes potentates in those parts) that they went into the war and sought freedom.'[230] In Lisbon, João Hari II's actions were interpreted as a disease that would spread, and that had to be stopped before it infected the vassal *sobas* in Angola. Critically, justification for the war now extended beyond a Portuguese reaction to a trade blockade: the 'disease was growing in a way that could no longer be cured or curbed through lenient measures, but would have to be cauterised.'[231] It was clear that Portugal was operating from a post-Restoration ideological standpoint and not in the spirit of political partnership that had been the tone of earlier contact with the people in the region.[232] In seeking to free Ndongo and the wider region from the Portuguese, João Hari II revived strategies from the distant past. He demonstrated the power of the region when it united to confront a mutual enemy and overcome the suffering and pain of exploitation.

In 1671, the Portuguese response was to wage war on Ndongo. From 1668, trade in enslaved people had been blocked by João Hari II, which violated Portuguese-imposed trade regulations and opposed the spirit of free trade held as gospel in Europe. War was not only waged to resume

---

[227] For details of the war and how Hari II was betrayed by the Mbundu people who were fighting alongside the Portuguese army, see Cadornega, *História Geral*, vol. II, pp. 315–329.

[228] Delgado in *História de Angola*, vol. I and II. See also 'História da Residência dos Padres da Companhia de Jesus em Angola'.

[229] Delgado's note in Cadornega, *História Geral*, vol. I and II.

[230] Relaçam/ Do FELICE SVCCESSO, p. 10, 'estimulado de seu irmão D. Diogo Capitam General do seu exercito de natural feroz, & intrépido, cresceo de sorte nos excessos, que prouocou todos os Reys vezinhos, & os Souas (nome que explica naquellas partes os Potentados) a que rompessem a guerra, & procurasse a Liberdade'.

[231] Relaçam/ Do FELICE SVCCESSO, p. 6, 'enfermidade crescia de sorte, que jà se não podia curar com lenitiuos, se rezolueo a aplicarlhe cautérios'.

[232] See Boxer, 'Background to Angola'.

slave-trading, which was being hampered by João Hari II's resistance in 1671, but also to silence voices of dissent within the region:

> ... the wounds, which the heart receives, were not allowed to receive medicine. It was necessary that the siege of Black Stones [Pungo-Andongo] should be the hallmark to remind all, so that once the rebels vanished and hopes restored, that kingdom would flourish again with free commerce, that the king of Dongo was almost alone in devising.[233]

The war in Ndongo resulted in 2,000 deaths, and many people were taken prisoner. João Hari II fled with his family. However, he was later captured, and he and his queen decapitated. Documents reporting his death claim that João Hari II was not prepared to live under the Portuguese and had ordered his own death.[234] The remainder of his immediate family and closest relatives were exiled to Portugal and Brazil.[235]

João Hari II was not the only king in the region to be decapitated by the Portuguese. Antonio I, king of Kongo, was decapitated in 1665 and his head was buried in Luanda.[236] The Portuguese were known to have adopted African war practices to annihilate their African enemies, and decapitation or killing with iron was, in Mbundu tradition, deemed the worst crime one could commit against another human being. Specifically, Mbundu tradition held that a king should never be killed with a weapon made of iron.[237] João Hari II's head was not buried in Angola, unlike the heads of Antonio I and other kings before him. Instead, his head was transported to Portugal and buried there.[238] This incident is of particular significance as it raises important questions about African cultural

---

[233] Relaçam/ Do FELICE SVCCESSO, p. 12, 'Que assi como naõ admitem medicamento as feridas, que o coraçaõ recebe, era necesario, que o sitio das Pedras fosse aluo de todos os golpes, pera que de hũa vez se extinguissem nos rebeldes, as esperanças do remedio, & tornasse a florescer aquelle Reyno com a liberdade do comercio, que elRey de Dongo quasi totalmente diuertia.'

[234] See Relaçam/ Do FELICE SVCCESSO.

[235] See 'Carta de António da Costa de Sousa' and 'Carta de D. Pedro's II ao General of Alcobaça enviando-lhe D. Philipe, filho do Rei de Dongo para o fazer educar nas matérias da fé e em todas artes' [Letter of D. Pedro II, sending him Dom Philipe, son of the King of Dongo, to educate him in the matters of faith and in all arts], AtT, ms. Liv. n. 171 (83), PT/TT/MSLIV/0171/00083, 24 November 1673.

[236] See 'Descrição da Batalha de Ambuíla' [A Description of the Battle of Mbwila], BLN, Mercúrio Portuguez, 1666, Res. 110 (V), 20 October 1665, MMA, vol. XII, pp. 575–581; see also an account of the battle in 'Relação da Batalha de Ambuíla' [Report of Mbwila Battle], 29 October 1665, British Museum (BM), Additional n. 20.953, fls. 227–229, MMA, vol. XII, pp. 582–591.

[237] See Cadornega, História Geral, vol. II, p. 357.

[238] Barretto, Monstruosidades do Tempo e da Fortuna, p. 202.

Ndongo's Political and Cultural Environment

FIGURE 11 Seh Dong-Hong-Beh, a female soldier from Dahomey. Forbes, 1851.

practices, particularly those surrounding Mbundu's religion and politics. African tradition maintained that to truly kill a powerful enemy, decapitation was required (see Figure 11).[239] Without it, there was a risk that the enemy would come back to life. Indeed, decapitating an enemy meant appropriating his or her power. However, decapitation was not enough on its own, and the body parts also needed to be separated and buried in lands far away from each other, with seas and rivers dividing them. In

---

[239] Birmingham and Delgado have neglected to mention this in their works. See Birmingham, *Trade and Conquest* and Delgado's note in Cadornega, *História Geral*, vols. I and II. See Cadornega, *História Geral*, vol. II, pp. 542–557.

sending João Hari II's head to Lisbon, it seems that the Portuguese appropriated this practice.

João Hari II's family members were not the first high-profile Angolans to be sent to Brazil. In 1622, Sousa sent several *sobas* from Kissama to Bahia.[240] These earlier *soba* exiles were given the same privileges by the Portuguese Crown later bestowed on the princes of Ndongo, including lands, houses and servants. The earlier *soba* exiles were also given special dispensation to choose whether to remain in Bahia or return to Angola as they had constituted only a localised threat. João Hari II's influence, however, had extended across a huge region, so Mendonça's exiled family members were not given the same choice and were exiled for life.

2.9 CONCLUDING REMARKS

In the seventeenth century, West Central Africa was already a melting pot of strategic networks. The royals of Ndongo, who were exiled to Brazil and who included Mendonça himself, came from an environment characterised by complex politics and diplomatic relations. They also came from a tradition of competing regional voices, none of which were ready to accept Portuguese dominion over their lands and people. Kongo had forged historic allegiances with European countries, which contributed to maintaining the balance of power in the region. It had sought alliances with the Vatican, the Netherlands and Spain in order to check Portuguese economic and political pressure in the region. In 1605, Alvaro II, king of Kongo, had dispatched his ambassador to Spain and the Vatican to deal with matters relating to slavery, mining, religion and politics in his kingdom. Internally, confederation was sought to counter the Portuguese monopoly on trade.

In Chapter 3, I will address Mendonça's journey and that of his brothers, uncles, aunts and cousins as political exiles to Salvador and Rio de Janeiro. I will argue that his life there was shaped by his connections with the community of enslaved Africans and Indigenous Americans in Brazil who posed a threat to the Portuguese Crown, especially the Quilombo dos Palmares runaway enslaved people, who represented a new power in Brazil. The Palmarists not only had the support of the Indigenous Americans for their cause of freedom and liberation, but also of some quarters of the Brazilian-born élites of the time, who viewed them as economic partners.

---

[240] 'Carta Régia aos Governadores de Portugal', 9 December 1622.

3

The Journey of Mendonça: The Princes of Pungo-Andongo in Brazil

João Hari II, who ruled the House of Ndongo from 1664 to 1671, was a member of a generation who challenged the Portuguese alliance that their predecessors – that is to say, their grandfathers, fathers and uncles – had endorsed, though under coercion. They challenged the alliance because of the Portuguese enslavement of their people (Mbundu) and those of the wider region known today as Angola; they fought against opening their kingdom as a market for the Portuguese, and did not allow their soldiers to be part of the Portuguese contingent army,[1] the so-called *guerra preta* that was used to wage wars on Mbundu people during the reign of Philipe Hari I. The break from the alliance came at a critical juncture in Portuguese history – at a time when Portugal gained independence from Spain and withdrew from the Union of the Two Crowns in 1640,[2] a break acknowledged by Spain only in 1668.[3] My argument is that this first generation of rulers of the House of Ndongo, who were graduates of the Jesuit College of Luanda, sought a return to the tradition of their forefathers.[4] They sought fair trade that benefitted their people, and trade

---

[1] See Cadornega, *História General*, vols. I and II.
[2] See James Maxwell Anderson, *The History of Portugal*, London: Greenwood Press, 2000; David Birmingham, *A Concise History of Portugal*, Cambridge: Cambridge University Press, 1993, and António Pedro Vicente, *Espanha e Portugal: Um Olhar Sobre as Relações Peninsulares no Século XX*, Editorial: Tribuna de Historia, 2010.
[3] See Anderson, *The History of Portugal*.
[4] See Cadornega, *História General*, vols. I and II, and on return to traditions, see John K. Thornton, *The Kongolese Saint Anthony: Dona Beatriz Kimpa Vita and the Antonian Movement, 1684–1706*, Cambridge: Cambridge University Press, 1998, and Thornton, 'The Kingdom of Kongo, ca. 1390–1678: The Development of an African Social Formation', *Cahiers d'Études Africaines*, 22, 1982, pp. 325–342. See also Birmingham,

reforms that gave answers to the challenges of the region. This led to Portugal waging war against João Hari II as described in Chapter 2. I am using this evidence to showcase how the House of Ndongo's breaking of the alliance with Portugal led to the political exile of the House of Ndongo to Brazil (Lourenço da Silva Mendonça, his brothers, uncles, aunts and cousins) and Portugal (King Philipe Hari I's son, Dom Philipe Ngolamano, his uncle Diogo Cabangua, and Dom Ignaçio, Dom Antonio, Dom Sebastiam and Dom Deonizio). The aim of this chapter is to look at how the journey to Brazil threatened to shape the royals' antipathy towards empire, and how it informed Mendonça's thinking, in particular.

In the historiography of the Atlantic World, writing about Black men and Black women's experience has largely been dominated by historians whose work is geographically focused on enslaved people from Anglophone Africa being taken to the Americas; and it is focused on the eighteenth and nineteenth centuries.[5] One exception is Reginaldo's recent work on the free-born *pardo* man, 'André do Couto Godinho', though this is still a work about the eighteenth century.[6] None of this work has engaged with the seventeenth-century debate on freedom and movement of the Africans in the Atlantic region and Europe. Randy J. Sparks's article on 'The Two Princes of Calabar' (in modern southeastern Nigeria), Ancona Robin John and Little Ephraim John, recounts how two African princes fought for their freedom from slavery in the eighteenth century: captured in 1767, they were brought to England and then were able to free themselves and return to Calabar in 1777. They were royals like Mendonça and had gained a European education; the knowledge they had of the law made it possible for them to free themselves from slavery.

Trade and Conquest, and Heywood, *Njinga of Angola*; both authors claim that previous kings of Ndongo in the sixteenth century were not prepared to allow the Portuguese a stake in their kingdom, and Queen Njinga did likewise in the seventeenth century.

[5] See Luiz Mott, *Rosa Egipcíaca: Uma Santa Africana no Brasil*, Rio de Janeiro: Bertrand Editors, 1993; see also Luiz Mott, *Egipcíaca, Rosa (1719–1771)*, Oxford African American Studies Center, 2016 and online version 2017, https://oxfordaasc.com/view/10.1093/acref/9780195301731.001.0001/acref-9780195301731-e-73870; see also James H. Sweet, *Domingos Álvares, African Healing, and the Intellectual History of the Atlantic World*, Chapel Hill, NC: University of North Carolina Pres, 2011; Lisa A. Lindsay, *Atlantic Bonds: A Nineteenth-Century Odyssey from America to Africa*, Chapel Hill, NC: University of North Carolina Press, 2017; João José Reis, Flávio dos Santos Gomes and Marcus J. M. de Carvalho, *O Alufá Rufino: Tráfico, Escravidão e Liberdade no Atlântico Negro (1822–1853)*, São Paulo: Companhia das Letras, 2010; Reginaldo, 'André do Couto Godinho'; and Gilroy, *The Black Atlantic*.

[6] André do Couto Godinho was free-born. For further detailed discussion of Godinho, see Reginaldo, 'André do Couto Godinho'.

However, their case was a personal endeavour and not connected to the abolition movement in the Atlantic.⁷

João José Reis, Flávio dos Santos Gomes and Marcus J. M. de Carvalho analyse the life and journey of Alufá Rufino in the eighteenth eighteenth century, from the Oyo kingdom in modern Nigeria, where he was born and lived until he was captured at the age of seventeen years and taken to Brazil as an enslaved person. He learnt to read the Koran in Salvador, Brazil; and later gained his freedom. Then he moved to Rio de Janeiro where he was involved in the slave trade.⁸ He used his skills as a cook rise socially in Brazil. Nonetheless, Rufino's quest for freedom was an individual one and he was not seeking to win freedom for the wider enslaved community in Brazil. James Sweet is another wrtier to have engaged with Africans' movement in the Atlantic. In his work *Domingos Álvares, African Healing, and the Intellectual History of the Atlantic World*, Sweet demonstrates that Domingos Álvares was captured in Benin between 1728 and 1732; according to Sweet, Álvares was a victim of the military struggles of Agaja, the king of Dahomey, who enslaved him. He was sent to Brazil, but there used his knowledge of healing, a skill he brought with him from Dahomey, to liberate himself: 'in many respects, Domingos seized his own freedom' via medicinal *know how*.⁹ Similar is the work of Lisa A. Lindsay, whose book *Atlantic Bonds: A Nineteenth-Century Odyssey from America to Africa* is a study of James Churchill 'Church' Vaughan, a 'free black'¹⁰ American from South Carolina, who returned to Monrovia, Liberia (Africa) in 1853 and then went from there to Yorubaland, in modern Nigeria. Whilst in Liberia, Vaughan worked as a carpenter and served in a local militia; in Nigeria, he worked as a missionary. Lindsay uses Vaughan's journey from America to Africa to examine the intersection between the social, economic and political forces at play in the Atlantic world of the nineteenth century. Vaughan's experience in both Liberia and Nigeria demonstrates the complexity of how 'freedom' played out for an African descendant returnee from America to Africa. For Lindsay, Vaughan's social and political world was complicated in terms of the freedom he sought because in Lagos where he spent most of life people 'of all stripes held slaves, including the recently freed themselves'.¹¹

---

⁷ See Sparks, 'The Two Princes of Calabar'.
⁸ Reis, dos Santos Gomes and de Carvalho, *O Alufá Rufino*, pp. 52 and 69.
⁹ See Sweet, *Domingos Álvares*, p. 104.   ¹⁰ See Lindsay, *Atlantic Bonds*, p 259.
¹¹ Lindsay, *Atlantic Bonds*, p. 153.

This forged bonds between the practice of the Atlantic slave trade and Africa, and the pursuit of freedom in Vaughan's case is comparable in part with that of the Ndongo royals' circulation in the Atlantic. Mendonça argues in his court case that in the seventeenth century the enslaved Africans' freedom is an uncompromised value that cannot be sacrificed at the expense of the economic return pursued by the merchants and the enslaved owners. In this vein, Reginaldo follows the path of a free man of colour, André do Couto Godinho, who was born in 1720 in the Brazilian captaincy of Minas Gerais, in the town of Mariana, and died in the kingdom of Kongo as a missionary in 1790.[12] Godinho arrived in São Paulo de Assunção de Luanda, modern Angola, seat of the bishopric of Angola and Kongo, on 4 December 1779.[13] He travelled from Brazil to Portugal, where he studied, and for several years served at the Royal Court of Lisbon and then from there he was sent to Kongo.

In another recent work, '"Não tem Informação": Mulatos, Pardos e Pretos na Universidade de Coimbra (1700–1771)', Reginaldo recounts how Antonio de Souza Falcão, another free man of colour, had to fight to gain his doctorate from the Faculty of Medicine at the University of Coimbra, Portugal, because it was being denieds him on account of his skin colour.[14] Reginaldo uses Godinho's trajectory and Falcão's struggle as a strategy for engaging with wider issues of race and exclusion that free men of colour encountered in the Portuguese Empire during the second half of the eighteenth century, be it in the contact zones, Africa and Brazil, or in the imperial centre, Portugal. An interesting aspect of Godinho's work is that, a century later, his argument is harmonious with that of Mendonça in the Vatican. 'In his [Godinho's] famous sermon of the Rosary, he vehemently defended the unity of human nature'. For Godinho, humanity is not based on pigmentation which is an 'accident of colour'. For him 'slavery is not a natural consequence [of difference], but the result of crime, force, just or unjust war'[15]. Reginaldo uses Godinho to draw attention to social classifications, paying particular attention to the colour hierarchy and the emergence of an idea of race in

---

[12] Reginaldo, 'André do Couto Godinho', p. 173.
[13] Reginaldo, 'André do Couto Godinho', p. 142.
[14] Reginaldo, '"Não tem informação"'.
[15] Reginaldo, 'André do Couto Godinho', p. 170, 'em seu famoso sermão do Rosário defendeu com veemência a unidade da natureza humana que se sobrepõe ao acidente da cor, sendo, desse modo, a escravidão não uma decorrência natural, mas resultado do delito, da força, da guerra justa ou injusta'.

the Portuguese empire in the eighteenth century. However, she does not include in her debate the wider liberation message that informed Mendonça's court case in the seventeenth-century Vatican. Firstly, the central point in the historiography of the Atlantic circulation is to see this development as an intersection between freedom and the slave trade: that is, the liberated Africans return to the trade that once denied them their freedom. Secondly, the circulation is a space that allows Africans to gain their freedom by using internal knowledge of institutional practices in Europe: freedom expressed as triumphant individual agency. These works create a picture of Africans who proved integral to the Atlantic slave and contributed to maintaining it despite the freedom that they sought. However, the movement of the Ndongo royals – rather being another expression of the individual agency that has dominated the historiography of the eighteenth- and nineteenth-century Atlantic circulation – represented a robust collective challenge to the entire Atlantic project.

Tracing the Ndongo royals' trajectory in the Atlantic region gives us a sense of their wider message of freedom and abolition. This chapter brings the royals, free persons from Lusophone Africa, Angola, who were taken to Brazil, into the discussion; it is based on the new data I have discovered in the archives in Lisbon, Portugal, Salvador, Bahia, and Rio de Janeiro, Brazil[16]. The chapter pays particular attention to the ideas behind Lourenço da Silva Mendonça's subsequent message of freedom, which he delivered in the Vatican. The Ndongo royals' movements in the Atlantic region are distinguished by their engagement with the abolition of the enslavement of Africans in that region, rather than being an expression of an individual quest for freedom. Bringing the Ndongo royals' journey from Angola to Brazil into the discussion enables us to study abolition in relation to these other individual leitmotifs. Using new archival evidence, the chapter thus generates new knowledge about the circulation in the Atlantic that carries with it the message of hope for liberation for free and enslaved people's pursuit and practice of freedom. In so doing, it addresses gaps in the Atlantic scholarship on slavery, abolition and freedom, from the seventeenth century. The chapter is divided into eight subsections. The central argument is that the Ndongo royals' journey to Brazil deepened their knowledge of

---

[16] See AHU_CU_001, Cx. 11, D. 1272, 21 August 1672; see Francisco Gonçalves's letter, AHU_ACL_CU_005, CX2, D. 181, 24 May 1673, Brazil-Bahia, and 'Sobre os Principes Negros do Dongo Unidos no Navio Sao Verissimo'.

the Portuguese slave trade system and provided Mendonça with the evidence to challenge it in the Vatican.

The chapter first outlines the House of Ndongo's decision to move away from the alliance with Portugal, also looking at its role when it served Portugal loyally, providing soldiers known as *guerra preta* or as *quilamba* to fight on behalf of Portuguese interests against other Angolans. It also examines how João Hari II questioned the Portuguese economic model in a similar way to that of Palmares. The chapter then focuses on the Ndongo royals' experiences in Brazil, and on how their stay was shaped by the community of the enslaved Africans in Salvador and Rio de Janeiro; the royals' stay in Brazil allowed them to become acquainted with the predicament of these enslaved Africans and helped them establish political ties with Angolans in the city of Salvador who later mounted a protest against slavery in the Vatican.[17] It looks at how these experiences shaped Mendonça's discourse in the Vatican, discussed in detail in Chapter 5, and his court case against the Portuguese model deployed in Africa to enslave its people. It also examines the relationship between the Quilombo do Palmares, the early runaway community in the state of Pernambuco, and the Indigenous Americans. To understand the logic of running away from captivity in Brazil, I look at the Angolan legislation covering runaway enslaved people and argue that it was deployed against those who took refuge in Quilombo dos Palmares.[18] This clearly indicates that Palmares and the ideal of liberation it stood for was a question of political independence and power. Then I make a comparison between knowledge of the abuses suffered by the enslaved in Brazil that was published by the Italian Jesuit Antonil and the enslavement of Indigenous Americans after the Battle of Cayru, Bahia. I contend that Antonil's book might have been known to Mendonça and influenced his court case. The chapter also looks at how the community of Palmares forged a political and economic alliance with Cristovão de Burgos de Contreiras, known simply as Cristovão de Burgos, a Brazilian-born judge in the high court of Salvador who accepted the Quilombo dos Palmares community economic model – in contrast to many among the Portuguese governing authorities in Brazil. Indeed, this contrasted with

---

[17] See APF, SOCG, Series America Meridionale 1, fl. 309, and also APF, SOCG, vol. 490, fl. 138.
[18] For further discussion of asylum given to political refugees from Kongo in Sonyo (Sonho in Portuguese; this was a province of the kingdom of Kongo), see Thornton,'The Kingdom of Kongo'.

the way in which some members of the religious authority in Brazil, the Jesuits, particularly Father António Vieira, viewed and contested Palmares as an emerging colonial power, a contestation described at the end of the chapter.

The conclusions I draw are made possible by new data uncovered in archives in Brazil and Portugal, namely the Arquivo Público de Salvador, Bahia, Arquivo Público Estadual de Pernambuco, Recife, and Arquivo da Universade de Coimbra.[19] The data enabled me to understand that the Portuguese governing authorities in Brazil and the Portuguese Overseas Council believed at the time that the majority of enslaved Africans living in Palmares had come from Mendonça's home, Angola.[20] The documents reveal that the Portuguese Overseas Council was aware that the Palmarists, the enslaved Africans who lived in Palmares, knew Mendonça and his relatives, and that they spoke the same language as him, Kimbundu.[21] Palmares was both a political and a social space. It was not only a refuge for enslaved fugitives but also a place in which those born free came together and formed a community parallel to that of the Portuguese enslavers. It was an alternative power structure, with a different economic model. At the time, it was viewed as militant, and a menace to the Portuguese establishment in Brazil who attempted to destroy it by force of arms. Brazilian historiography has seen Palmares as an 'African state'[22] in

---

[19] See 'Atas da Camara' [City Council Minutes], fl. 23v, lhs. 1a10, 9 November 1672, p. 75, Arquivo Público de Salvador. See also 'Ordens Régias' [Royal Orders], cap. XXI, vol. VI, vol. IIa, 159v, n. 231, Arquivo Público Estadual de Pernambuco, Recife, and Arquivo da Universade de Coimbra.

[20] See AHU, cód. 17, fls. 59-59v, 21 August 1672.

[21] See AHU, cód. 17, fl. 59v, 21 August 1672, 'Consulta do Conselho Ultramarino', 'donde conheçidos dos negros delles, nos sejão mais prejudiçiaes'.

[22] Quilombos dos Palmares was established on the lines of a state in West Central Africa, so historians viewed it as an African state in Brazil. See Pitta, *Provincia da Bahia* and Nina Rodrigues, *As Sublevações de Negros no Brasil Anteriores ao Século XIX. Palmares' Os Africanos no Brasil* [1905], 5th ed., São Paulo: Companhia Editora Nacional, 2010, pp. 130–195. See also Mario Martins de Freitas, *Reino Negro de Palmares*; R. N. Anderson, 'The Quilombo of Palmares: A New Overview of a Maroon State in Seventeenth-Century Brazil', *Journal of Latin American Studies*, 23 (3), 1996, pp. 545–566; Charles R. Boxer, *The Dutch in Brazil, 1624–1654*, Oxford: Clarendon Press, 1973; C. E. Orser Jr., *A Historical Archaeology of the Modern World*, New York: Plenum Press, 1996; A. J. R. Russell-Wood, 'Black and Mulatto Brotherhoods in Colonial Brazil: A Study in Collective Behaviour', *Hispanic American Historical Review*, 54(4), 1974, pp. 567–602; S. B. Schwartz, 'Rethinking Palmares: Slave Resistance in Colonial Brazil', in Stuart B. Schwartz, *Slaves, Peasants and Rebels*, Chicago: University of Illinois Press, 1992, pp. 1294–1325; J. H. Sweet, *Recreating Africa: Culture, Kinship and Religion in the African-Portuguese World, 1441–1770*, Chapel Hill, NC: The University of North Carolina Press, 2003; R. Kent, 'Palmares: An African State in Brazil', *The Journal of African History*, 2,

Brazil. More recently there are those who viewed Palmares as creolised State.[23]

Based on that, I argue that Palmares created its own economy, which provoked the governing authorities in Bahia to reconsider the position of the Ndongo royals in the country, and prompted them to send the royals away from Salvador to Rio de Janeiro. The decision to remove the royals from Salvador demonstrated the governing bodies' fear that Palmares represented a new colonial power in Brazil and that the Palmarists' freedom movement had the support not only of Indigenous people but also of some quarters of the Brazilian-born élite (people of Portuguese descent born in Brazil), who viewed them as economic partners. I argue that even in Salvador and Rio de Janeiro the Ndongo royals' presence in continued to be connected with the revolutionary settlement of Palmares. This leads me to contend that the royals' journey to Brazil shaped their antipathy towards empire and informed Mendonça's thinking about the daily suffering of the enslaved in Brazil, which in turn shaped his court case in the Vatican.

3.1 THE HOUSE OF NDONGO: JOÃO HARI II AND DIOGO, THE FIRST GENERATION OF ALLIANCE BREAKERS

To understand why Mendonça, his brothers, uncles, aunts and cousins were forced to leave Angola, we need to look at former governor Salvador Correia de Sá's defence of the destruction of the kingdom of Pungo-Andongo.[24] Their exile to Brazil aided the royals in their struggle against the ideology

---

1965, pp: 161–175; Thornton, *Africa and Africans in the Making of the Atlantic World*; W. Hoogbergen, Palmares: A Critical View on its Sources, 2001, pp. 23–55: https://publ ications.iai.spk-berlin.de/servlets/MCRFileNodeServlet/Document_derivate_00001778/ BIA_070_023_055.pdf;jsessionid=888A9913152645 68BF28EA3C1CEB1192; Philip D. Curtin, *The Rise and Fall of the Plantation Complex*, and Carneiro, *O Quilombo dos Palmares*. For Nascimento, Palmares represented a pan-Africa in Brazil; see A. Nascimento, *O Quilombismo – Documentos de uma Militância Pan-africanista*, Petrópolis: Editora Vozes, 1980. For Palmares as a multicultural state, see Décio Freitas, *Palmares: A Guerra dos Escravos*, Rio de Janeiro: Graal, 1978; S. J. Allen, 'A "Cultural Mosaic" at Palmares? Grappling with the Historical Archaeology of a Seventeenth-century Brazilian Quilombo', in Pedro Paulo A Funari (ed.), *Cultura Material e Arqueologia Histórica*, Campinas: Unicamp (IFCH), 1998; R. Price, 'Palmares Como Poderia Ter Sido', in João José Reis and Flávio dos Santos Gomes (eds.), *Liberdade Por Um Fio: História Dos Quilombos no Brasil*, São Paulo: Companhia das Letras, 1995, pp. 52–59; and Clóvis Moura, *Rebeliões da Senzala*, São Paulo: Lech Livraria Editora Ciências Humanas, 1981.

[23] See Russell-Wood, 'Black and Mulatto Brotherhoods'.
[24] See AHU, cód. 17, fls. 59-59v, 21 August 1672.

of the Portuguese slave trade. Mendonça's stay in Brazil helped him to galvanise confraternities of Black Brotherhood in the city of Salvador, who later produced a *memorial*[25] with evidence that Mendonça used in his court case against the Vatican, Italy, Portugal and Spain.[26]

It is worth examining the idea that the exile of the Ndongo princes, first to Salvador in Bahia, then to Rio de Janeiro, by the governing authorities of the Municipal Council of Luanda, Bahia and Salvador respectively, arose out of concerns that their continued presence in Angola and then the possibility that they would join the community of African runaway slaves in Quilombo de Palmares could cause great danger to the establishment. Yet even though they were considered as a serious threat both to Brazil and to Portuguese interests in Angola, they still accrued benefits such as houses, food and clothing, and their expenses were covered by the Treasury of the Portuguese Crown.[27] Their treatment at the hands of Portuguese authorities begs several questions. In whose interest was their exile and who stood to benefit from it? Was there a conflict of interest between the Crown and the Portuguese governors, and their respective councils in Luanda, Bahia and Rio? Did the royals really pose a threat? Whose decision was it to wage war on Pungo-Andongo and to exile the royals?

A response to these questions requires an understanding of the regional politics as reflected in the local economic situation and the Portuguese interest in controlling the trade route in Angola.[28] Let me therefore return to the destruction of Pungo-Andongo of 1671. The letter from Sá, which I found in the Arquivo Histórico Ultramarino de Belém, has not been mentioned by any historian of Pungo-Andongo writing about the reasons for the kingdom's destruction.[29] In it Sá put forward reasons for the war

[25] A *memorial* is a document presented to a legislative body, or to the executive, by one or more individuals, containing a petition or a representation of facts. When such an instrument is addressed to a court, it is called a petition. See dictionary theLaw.com dictionary, https://dictionary.thelaw.com/memorial; see also Finlay, 'The Petition in the Court of Session'.
[26] See APF, SOCG, Series America Meridionale 1, fl. 309.
[27] See Consultas Mixtas, fl. 187, 28 November 1675; and Consultas Mixtas, vol. XIII, fl. 301, 18 July 1679.
[28] For detailed studies see Charles E. Nowell, *The Rose-Colored Map: Portugal's Attempt to Build an African Empire from the Atlantic to the Indian Ocean*, Lisbon: Junta de Investigates Científicas do Ultramar, 1982; R. Howes, 'The British Press and Opposition to Lord Salisbury's Ultimatum of January 1890', *Portuguese Studies*, 23(2), 2007, pp. 153–166; and Harold Livermore, 'The Anglo-Portuguese Crisis of 1890: Another Look at the Ultimatum', *Studia*, 2000, 56–57, pp. 23–59.
[29] See AHU_CU_001, Cx. 11, D. 1272, 21 August 1672.

and why the kingdom needed to fall. He defended in every way Távora's decision to send the royals to Brazil (1671–1673), making a political as well as an economic case for their exile. Sá was responding to a letter sent by the Crown to Távora a year earlier, on 12 August 1671, in which Távora was warned not to wage an offensive war on Angola and Kongo that could lead to civil war in the region.[30] Sá was of course a member of the Portuguese Overseas Council;[31] he was appointed on 28 November 1644, took office on 14 December 1644, and served until the end of the 1680s.[32] I will return in Chapter 6 to the Portuguese Overseas Council and its role. It is axiomatic that Sá was not in agreement with the Crown's ruling over the decision to wage war on Pungo-Andongo. The Portuguese Overseas Council had accepted the Crown's instruction and Sá had taken it on board in principle. However, he was subsequently free to vent his frustration with the Crown for their take on the Angola conquest. Sá was indeed known for his hardline thinking as a governor in Rio de Janeiro and in Luanda:[33] it was during his time as governor of Angola that the Dutch were expelled, and the more moderate Mbundu people (called *mansos* [tamed - conquered Mbundu]) who were living in Luanda at that time (see Figure 12) gave him the nickname *Nfumu etu, Làlânâ* (Our Lord, Liberator).[34] It appears that in 1671 he was worried about opposition to his political ideology – that is, the expansion of the Portuguese Empire through the conquest of Angola. He sought to persuade the prince regent of Portugal, Dom Pedro II, of his argument.

The justification for the conquest and destruction of Pungo-Andongo was its political alliances with Matamba and Conde de Sonho (in Kongo), which the royals could exploit to their advantage.[35] Sá was concerned that Africans in the region were keeping a close eye on the development of the Tristão da Cunha incident in 1667, during which the

---

[30] See King Pedro II's letter to Távora on 12 August 1671, AHU_CU_001, cx d. 1246.
[31] Sá was among the Overseas Council members that signed the letter that demanded the sending off the princes and princesses from Brazil to Portugal. See 'Carta de Salvador Correia de Sá'.
[32] For more detailed studies on the Portuguese Overseas Council, see 'Livro dos autos de posse dos Presidentes, Conselheiros e mais ministros do Conselho Ultramarino' [Book of Records of the Swearing in of Presidents, Councillors, and more Ministers of Overseas Council], AHU_CU_POSSES, cod. 2160. See also Erik Lars Myrup, 'To Rule from Afar: The Overseas Council and the Making of the Brazilian West, 1642–1807', unpublished Ph.D. thesis, Yale University, 2006; and Maria do Socorro F. Barbosa, et al. *Fontes Repatriadas: anotações de história colonial referenciais para pesquisa*.
[33] See Birmingham, *Trade and Conquest*.
[34] See Cadornega, *História Geral*, vol. II, p. 369.
[35] See 'Carta de Salvador Correia de Sá'.

FIGURE 12 Salvador Correia de Sá e Benavides (1648–1651). Museu de História Militar, Luanda, Angola. Photograph by the author.

Portuguese governor was ousted from power, and on how the Municipal Council of Luanda had handled it.[36] Sá believed that Africans knew that the Portuguese political regime in Luanda was weak and in turmoil.[37] Sá suspected that Angolans as well as Kongolese knew that Luanda was without a governor because of the power struggle between the military, the Municipal Council of Luanda and its Roman Catholic religious authorities.[38] He placed the blame for Cunha's exit from power on Angolans and Kongolese, who were taking advantage of the Cunha situation, he believed, to break away from the Portuguese alliance, as

---

[36] See 'Carta de Salvador Correia de Sá'.   [37] See 'Carta de Salvador Correia de Sá'.
[38] See 'Relação do Padre Mateus Cardoso'.

exemplified by the Pungo-Andongo revolt of 1671.[39] The revolt was a protest against the economic model, including the payment of *baculamento*, which opened the kingdom to the Portuguese as a marketplace, the recruitment of soldiers from the region as *guerra preta*, and the use of the Pungo-Andongo army to fight Angolans. It is clear from the sources available to me that the Portuguese governing authorities in Luanda were apprehensive that, if the situation were not contained, the entire region would follow the example of Pungo-Andongo[40] After the destruction of Pungo-Andongo, the Conde de Sonho was also to be destroyed in the same way as João Hari II.

There is no doubt that the Portuguese Crown had some misgivings regarding Pungo-Andongo,[41] but Sá urged the Crown to leave these aside and look at the wider picture of the conquest of Angola. For Sá, the significance of the war on Pungo-Andongo and its lesson for the other African kings in the region was clear:

> ... there is no doubting the zeal, prudence, and the worth with which Távora has proceeded with his government, and is worthy of receiving some great reward for the royal office from His Highness. His desire to be supported from the kingdom of Kongo and its king, to oppose count of Soyo, that rose against him, his natural Lord, and was able to happily defeat him and subjugate him.[42]

Sá went on to show that the Cunha event in 1667 had marked a change in politics in the region. The Africans had watched the event closely, and they had used it as a focal point for uniting against the Portuguese. Sá claimed that

> ... before Francisco de Távora became the governor of these kingdoms, Tristão da Cunha had already been expelled, and since those Black people observe unfolding events and are influenced by them, seeing that the Portuguese were becoming less obedient with respect to their governor, the vassals and confederated began to do the same.[43]

---

[39] See 'Carta de Salvador Correia de Sá'. [40] See 'Carta de Salvador Correia de Sá'.
[41] See 'Carta Sobre os Cativos do Dongo', MMA, vol. XIII, p. 185.
[42] 'Carta de Salvador Correia de Sá', 'Nao se pode duvidar do zelo, prodencia, e valor com q. Fran.co de Tavora ha procedido em seu governo, e ser digno, de q. V.A. lhe faca grandes merce; intentou meter de posse do Reyno de Congo ao seu Rey, oppondosse ao Conde de Sonho, q, se levantou contra elle, seu natural Senhor: e conseguindosse com felicidade o derrota lo, e mete lo de posse'.
[43] 'Carta de Salvador Correia de Sá', 'antes q. Franco. De Tavora fosse governar estes Reynos ja avia sucedido a expulsao de Tristao da Cunha: e como aquelles negros observao os sucessos, e por elles se governao, vendo que os Portugueses prevaricavao a obidiencia, e respeito ao seu g.or comessaram os geram vasalos, e confederados a fazerem o mesmo'.

Sá then explained to the Crown who King João Hari II and his brother, Dom Diogo Cabangua (Ngolambole), were, describing them both as the architects of Pungo-Andongo's break away from the Portuguese alliance. According to Sá, both were known to him while he was a governor of Luanda between 1648 and 1651, since their father, Philipe Hari I, the king of Ndongo, had asked Sá to have them educated by the Society of Jesus in Luanda: 'he brought with him these two children, Hari II, and this child of 10 or 11 years asking me, if I would send them to be taught by the Society of Priests while he is carrying out the army service, and that is how it was done'.[44]

João Hari II and Dom Diogo Cabangua were what we could call students of the Portuguese Empire; they were educated for the purpose of extending Portuguese interests in the region.[45] Birmingham equated the struggle that élites in Angola had for freedom in the seventeenth century with the struggle for independence in the region in the twentieth century; that is to say, that they wanted the same thing as their ancestors or forefathers had.[46] In other words, the struggle for freedom had not stopped since the inception of the Portuguese slave trade in Angola in the sixteenth century. João Hari II and Diogo were what Bhabha called 'mimic men' or 'hybrid men',[47] given the paradox of their being both part of the empire and part of the resistance to it. Following Bhabha's understanding, we can see them as Angolans who behaved according to the Portuguese manner. In my view, however, the Portuguese hoped that these Angolans and learned men of the empire would embody their grand narrative of political hegemony. João Hari II and Diogo were expected to carry on from where their father left off, so that the Angolans could be of further use in advancing Portuguese political and economic control in Angola. Yet, they were also a menace to the system that created them.

---

[44] 'Carta de Salvador Correia de Sá', 'trouxe comsigo estes dous filhos, o morto, e a este Infante de 10 ou 11 annos pedindome os mandasse doutrinar nos Padres da Comp.a em quanto elle andasse no exercito, e assi se fez'.

[45] See 'Carta de Salvador Correia de Sá'.

[46] See Birmingham, *Trade and Conquest*; also Raphaël Batsîkama and Patrício Batsîkama, 'Estruturas e Instituições do Kôngo', Revista de História Comparada, 5 (1), 2011, pp. 6–41.

[47] Homi Bhabha, *The Location of Culture*, London: Routledge, 1994, p. 88. For Bhabha, in their conquest of countries in America, Africa and Asia, European nations by necessity established local men or alliances to maintain control and dominance. On the one hand these local 'mimic men' supported European interests, but on the other they could be a menace to the system that created them. He asserts that: 'Mimicry conceals no presence or identity behind its mask ... the menace of mimicry is its double vision which in disclosing the ambivalence of colonial discourse also disrupts its authority.'

João Hari II and Diogo Cabangua were both part of the ruling system of Angola. They were groomed for the throne of Pungo-Andongo, but rebelled against the very system that shaped them. They were fighting to stop the Portuguese trade policy on commerce and slavery, and at the same time they were fighting to ensure that they never returned to the slave trade, via *baculamento*, that their father, Philipe Hari I, had been part of and which saw thousands of enslaved Angolans shipped to Brazil. Philipe Hari I would probably have paid 3,800 people if he had kept in line with his *baculamento* payments over the thirty-eight years of his rule as a king of Ndongo.[48]

Philipe Hari I had been loyal to the Portuguese project of conquest. He, and some of his sons, fought wars defending Portuguese interests: two of his sons died protecting Portuguese interests in Angola during the Dutch occupation, as we saw in the Chapter 2. Sá, who as governor of Luanda drove the Dutch out of Angola, remembered the contribution of Philipe Hari I to this endeavour. He stated:

> ... this King [João Hari II] and his brother [Diogo], are sons of a King [Philipe Hari I], the most loyal to His Highness that there was in those parts, in the seven years that the Dutch were Lords of that Kingdom ... [it was] with great loyalty that he assisted us in that Kingdom ... to the benefit of P. Cesar de Meneses and the other governors.[49]

Thus, the younger Ndongo royals, including Mendonça, were not killed because their grandfather had been loyal to Portugal; at least that is what Sá leads us to believe in his letter to King Pedro II.[50] Philipe Hari I is described as most loyal to the Portuguese Crown as king of Angola, and as someone who served Portugal's interests in Angola with great distinction and dedication. Cadornega tells us that Philipe Hari I was decorated with a medal of honour and was buried with pomp when he died.[51] He took on board all that was Portuguese and stayed loyal as a conquered king, even when he criticised the Portuguese slave trade from within.[52] In addition, he was not the only Angolan king or conquered political figure to be honoured for their loyalty to the Portuguese project of conquest.

---

[48] See 'Carta de Salvador Correia de Sá'.
[49] 'Carta de Salvador Correia de Sá', 'este Rey e o seu Irmao, sao filhos de hum Rey, o mais fiel a V.A. que ouve em aquellas partes, nos sete annos, que os Holandeses senhorearam aquelle Reyno ... comnossco co' m.ta lealdade, assistana ... favour de P.o Cesar de Meneses e dos mais governos'.
[50] See 'Carta de Salvador Correia de Sá'. [51] See Cadornega, *História Geral*, vol. II.
[52] See 'Carta de Rei Hari I para o Rei João IV' [King Hari I's Letter to King João IV], AHU, Angola, cx 5, 8 April 1653.

3.2 THE HOUSE OF PUNGO-ANDONGO'S ROLE AND FORMER LOYALTY TO PORTUGAL

Many *sobas* were rewarded by the Portuguese for their service. They were recompensed with prestigious positions and privileges that included land and education for their children. Among them was João Bango Bango, a *soba* who served Portuguese interests from a young age and for more than thirty years and was part of a *quilamba* contingent.[53] João Bango Bango's father, Faustino,[54] had also served Portugal's interests in Angola since the time of Paulo Dias Novais. Bango Bango was decorated with the Order of the Habit of Christ by Sá on 15 November 1647.[55]

Simão da Rocha Praça was another Black Angolan soldier who served Portugal for many years. As a soldier in the service of Portugal for nineteen years, he fought many wars against the Dutch on the River Bengo, against Nambuangongo, a powerful *soba* in Angola, and against Queen Njinga. He was promoted through the ranks from leader to sergeant to lieutenant and captain. On 17 October 1665, after participating in the Battle of Ambuila, one of the biggest battles in the region, he sent a letter to the Portuguese Crown requesting a promotion to the rank of captain major.[56] The role played by *guerra preta* or *quilamba* was crucial to Portuguese economic interests and their conquest of territories in Angola. However, their importance tended to be downplayed by the Portuguese governing bodies, and often only the negative aspects of their involvement – such as their rebellion against the economic system that forced them to be soldiers – was mentioned by historians.[57]

Let us return to the destruction of Pungo-Andongo. The governing authority in Luanda at the time, as represented in Sá's letter, tended to

---

[53] On *quilambas*, see 'Carta de Constantino Cadena a Fernão de Sousa' [A Letter from Constantino Cadena to Fernão de Sousa], AHU, Angola, cx. 2, 16 September 1626, and 'Relação do Governador dos Religiosos e Conventos Existentes no Reino de Angola' [Report from the Governor of Religious and Existing Convents in Angola], ASGA., *Livro de Registo de Ordens Régias*, Liv. 5, folios. 69 e sgs, Paiva Manso, *Historia do Kongo*, pp. 324–339, MMA, vol. XIII, 1693, pp. 330–46.

[54] For full detail on Faustino, see 'Mercê do Hábito de Cristo a um Quilamba Angolano' [Reward of the Habit of Christ to an Angolan Quilamba], AHA, 'Livro de Patentes do Tempo do Sr. Salvador Correia de Sá e Benevides' [Book of Patents of the Temple of the Sir Salvador Correia de Sá e Benevides], vol. 2.0, fl. 133 v.11 November 1647, MMA, vol. X, pp. 59–62.

[55] See, 'Mercê do Hábito de Cristo a um Quilamba Angolano'.

[56] See AHU_CU_001, cx. 5, d. 515, 17 October 1665.

[57] For a detailed discussion of the role of the *guerra preta* and their importance to the Portuguese conquest of Angola in the eighteenth century, see Carvalho, 'Guerras nos sertões de Angola'.

suppress any sense of Kongo-Angolan agency by employing a language of political and cultural caricature:

> ... the King of Ndongo [commonly known King of the Stones (of Pungo-Andongo)], João Hari II, was a young man with little experience of governance and had counsellors who were more interested in their ambitions, than in good governance. Being therefore ill advised, and with the title of the King, though still a vassal of His Highness, liked throwing insults, stealing from travellers, and there is talk that he killed some Portuguese, taking away their livelihood.[58]

It is intriguing that Sá accused João Hari II of stealing, considering the Portuguese's own staggeringly avaricious behaviour in Angola in taking lands illegally from Angolans and capturing and enslaving its people. Sá's language here implies deficiency on the part of the Africans and their actions; and, moreover, he silences African voices altogether. Given the claim made by Sá about the educational plan for João Hari II and Diogo, one can be left in no doubt that the Kongo-Angolan élite were taking their disapproval of the Portuguese economic model to a new level. They were aiming to channel their voices through official means within Portuguese institutions. The revolt of Pungo-Andongo in 1671 meant that the Angolans' intervention in that war was profoundly important in challenging the Portuguese political hegemony from the early period of the Angolan conquest. João Hari II's political focus was to repudiate the culture his father had been forced to accept and to adopt the stance that slavery was not the Angolans' problem, but a Portuguese one. João Hari II's challenge was to question the Portuguese trade agenda; time had moved on from his parents' generation's unquestioning acceptance of the Portuguese economic model. This was exactly the kind of political challenge the Africans deployed in Quilombo dos Palmares, and was the reason why the Portuguese authorities were fearful that the Angolan royals' presence in Brazil might lead to the formation of an African state.[59] Let us return to Sá's explanation of the Pungo-Andongo war

---

[58] AHU_CU_001, cx. 11, d. 1272, 21 August 1672, 'foy hum El Rey de Dongo [vulgarmente chamado o das Pedras] moco, e herdado de pouco, com huns conselheiros, mais inclinados a ambicao, que ao bom governo: sendo pois mal aconselhado, e co' o titulo de Rey, ainda q vassal de V.A. foi gostando de fazer insultos, roubando aos passageiros, e ha noticias q matara a alguns Portuguezes, por lhes tomar as fazendas'.

[59] On Palmares see Pitta, *Provincia da Bahia*. See also Cheney, *Quilombo dos Palmares*; Moura, *Rebeliões da Senzala*; Flávio dos Santos Gomes, Palmares: Escravidão e Liberdade no Atlântico Sul, São Paulo: Contexto, 2005; and Pedro Paulo A. Funari, 'Conflict and the Interpretation of Palmares, a Brazilian Runaway Polity', Historical Archaeology, 37(3), 2003, pp. 81–92.

and why it was in the interests of the Crown that the surviving members of the royals be spared, educated and integrated into Portuguese society.

Sá argued that both Philipe Hari I's son, Dom Diogo Cabangua, and his 10-year-old grandson, Dom Philipe, also known by the African names Golambano and Ngolamano, should be treated with fairness by the Crown because of Philipe Hari I's contribution. Philipe Hari I deserved recognition for his service to Portugal:

> Even though he [Philipe Hari I] knew that I was going to restore Angola, he came with ... [his] subject to help me against Queen Nzinga, King of Kongo and all those Dukes, Counts, and Marquesses of these Kingdoms, and all the free Lords that were following the Dutch with partiality. And there is no doubt, that this King, the grandfather of this child [Dom Philipe Ngolamano], deserves all the benevolence that Your Highness would decree that be used for his Nephew [Dom Philipe Ngolamano].[60]

In our terms, both Cabangua and Dom Philipe Ngolamano were protégés of Sá, who gave them a place to study in the Jesuit College of Luanda. Once they graduated from the College of Luanda they returned to Pungo-Andongo. Section 3.3 looks at the sending of the royals to Portugal and Brazil as political prisoners in order to prevent them from mobilising people in Angola to stage wars against Portugal after the destruction of Pungo-Andongo.

3.3 THE SENDING OF THE NDONGO ROYALS TO PORTUGAL AND BRAZIL AS PRISONERS OF WAR AND SÁ'S PLANS FOR ANGOLA

The Portuguese feared that they could lose Angola if they did not intervene, and decided to send Diogo Cabangua and the 10-year-old Dom Philipe Ngolamano, as members of the royal family of Pungo-Andongo, away from Angola to Portugal, and fourteen princes and two princesses to Brazil. The decision to send the royals away was not Távora's own; rather, it was made by the entire Municipal Council of Luanda, or at least the majority of the councillors accepted it. According to Sá, it was the responsibility of the Crown to offer Dom Philipe Ngolamano, the young heir to the throne of Ndongo, an education because of the service and loyalty his

---

[60] 'Carta de Salvador Correia de Sá', 'Tanto q. soube q. eu restasorara Angola, veyo co' ... vasalos a ajudarme contra a Raynha Ginga, Rey de Congo e todos os mais Duques, Condes, e Marqueses desses Reynos, e se.res livres q. seguiao a parcealidade dos Holandeses. E nao ah duvida em q. este Rey Avo deste minino, ha merecido toda a benevolencia que V.A. mandar se uze com este seu Netto'.

grandfather, Philipe Hari I, had shown to Portugal. It was Sá's suggestion that the 10-year-old Ngolamano be sent to Portugal to study and never return to Angola. In the letter, he defended Távora's policy and that of his government in Luanda. Moreover, Sá declined to address the internal problems of the Municipal Council of Luanda. What Sá failed to tell us was whether the soldiers who had mutinied against Cunha in 1667 in Luanda were all Portuguese or whether there had been Angolans among them – that is, whether Angolan soldiers were at the forefront of the mutiny. It is certainly possible, as prominent Angolans frequently fought alongside the Portuguese in Angola. As we saw above, Mendonça's own father, Ignaçio da Silva, his uncle, his grandfather Philipe Hari I, and Francisco and Bango Bango all fought for the Portuguese.[61]

Nevertheless, Sá used the Ndongo royals to cover up the mutiny, which was in fact instigated by influential military figures in Luanda, such as João Marques de Almeida, António Álves Correia, Atanásio da Costa, António Roiz d'Andrade and Captain João de Andrade, whose salaries had not been paid for two years.[62] Sá's verdict was to pronounce Ndongo's throne empty. Matamba was reorganising itself and returning to its roots and João Hari II wanted Ndongo to follow suit. It was this unity that Sá was ready to undermine and attempted to explain away, and it was this type of reorganisation around a political figure that Africans in Brazil were seeking.

Allowing the royals – who were capable of mounting a rebellion – to stay would have opened the floodgates for other kings and *sobas* in the region to do the same. If allowed to stay, they might have taken revenge similar to that in 1622 in Kongo, when the Kongolese tried to attack the Portuguese residents after Dom Paulo Affonso Nabangogo and other princes were forced out and sent to Brazil as prisoners of war by Correia de Sousa.[63] Angolan royals might well have taken similar action given the crimes committed by the Portuguese against many Angolan people during the war of Pungo-Andongo. Even if they had not themselves wanted revenge, the Angolan people would have demanded it of their leaders. The Portuguese Overseas Council said that the Ndongo royals could not

---

[61] On the sending of the royals to different monasteries, see 'Carta de António da Costa de Sousa'; and on Bango Bango, see 'Mercê do Hábito de Cristo a um Quilamba Angolano'.
[62] See Delgado's note in Cadornega, *História Geral*, vol. II, pp. 561–579. See also Caldeira, 'Dimensão Sociopolítica', p.51.
  See Delgado's note in Cadornega, *História Geral*, vol. II, p. 530; I am indebted to this. See also Caldeira, 'Dimensão Sociopolítica', p. 51.
[63] See 'Relaçaõ para o Ill.mo Sñr Collector', p. 514.

be permitted to stay in Angola because of the 'huge following they had there'.[64] The Angolan people supported the royals, and it was possible that they would follow whatever cause the royals wanted them to. Economically, by destroying Pungo-Andongo, Távora gained control of the trade routes and this would have given him the opportunity to control the market.[65] Sá tells us clearly the reasons for the destruction of Pungo-Andongo, but historians of Pungo-Andongo have so far failed to detect this.[66] It is worth nothing that even Boxer in his majestic work *Salvador de Sá and the Struggle for Brazil and Angola, 1602–1686* failed to discuss this issue, which should have been key to his book.[67] Sá in his letter, consisting of three and half pages, described in detail why the prince regent, Dom Pedro II, should support Távora 'Cajanda''s plan for war against Pungo-Andongo.[68] Its destruction was in line with the grand scheme of colonising West Central Africa. Sá's letter is without doubt central to understanding the ideology that led to the destruction of Pungo-Andongo, and there is no other source that provides such a profound insight from within Angola about the war.

Sá's proposal was based on his own lived experience in Angola, in which he became the embodiment of the Portuguese institution there, and its memory. Sá believed that he had a mission in Angola, and that he had been chosen by God for the Angolan conquest. He claimed to have lived up to an expectation laid on him by God, and King João IV of Portugal provided the means for the fulfilment of this mission when he appointed him both the governor of Rio de Janeiro (1637–1642, 1648, and 1659–1660) and subsequently of governor of Angola (1648–1651).[69] He claimed to have accomplished his mission and the weight of history was now on King João IV's successor, his son, Pedro II, to do likewise. Sá's letter was addressed to Dom Pedro II, and in it, he made clear that the destruction of Pungo-Andongo was necessary and that Távora must be supported.[70] The destruction of Pungo-Andongo paved the way for linking the Angolan trade route inland to Sofala, Mozambique. Even so, the Crown was unclear as to why the Pungo-Andongo war was necessary, and

---

[64] See Consultas Mixtas, vol. 13, fl. 301, 18 July 1679.
[65] See 'Carta de Salvador Correia de Sá'.
[66] See Birmingham, *Trade and Conquest* and Lara, 'Depois da Batalha de Pungo Andongo'.
[67] Charles R. Boxer, *Salvador de Sá and the Struggle for Brazil and Angola, 1602–1686*, London: Athlone Press, University of London, 1952.
[68] See 'Carta de Salvador Correia de Sá'.   [69] See 'Carta de Salvador Correia de Sá'.
[70] See 'Carta de Salvador Correia de Sá'.

Sá acted to defend the policy and convince the Crown to accept his interpretation of the destruction of Pungo-Andongo.[71]

Sá's vision was to build a fortress inland that would allow the trade routes from Sofala to Angola to be connected. This was to become a thorny issue in Portugal's relationship with Great Britain in the nineteenth century, known as the 'rose-coloured map'.[72] For Sá, a connection to the wealth of Mozambique and its trade made sense, and he argued that the next governor of Angola must be given the mission to accomplish it.[73] If the plan failed, the French – who were already trading with Angola – would take over. Sá clearly saw violence as the way to achieve his objective, and Birmingham says that the Portuguese appeared to favour 'evangelisation by sword'.[74] The conquest of Ndongo, with its relative proximity to Mozambique, and Sofala – which was an important commercial island that connected East African trade to India[75] – was essential to Sá's vision of a regional trading link that connected the Atlantic and the Indian oceans. It was indeed João Hari II's attempt to control this trade route that brought about his downfall. The Portuguese intention also was to have access to the mines of Monomotapa.[76] The Monomotapa mines were thought to be in what is today northern Zimbabwe and north-western Mozambique. Allowing the French control of the region would have meant ceding control of the trade route and the mines. Further light can be shed on the war by examining the royals' stay in Salvador and Rio de Janeiro after they left Angola and how their actions might have been shaped by what befell them in Brazil.

3.4 THE ROYALS' EXPERIENCES AND NETWORK IN BRAZIL

Mendonça and his relatives probably arrived in Brazil toward the end of December 1671, or at the beginning of 1672. The destruction of Pungo-Andongo took place in December 1671, and the Portuguese Overseas Council's correspondence shows that Mendonça, his brothers, uncles, aunts and cousins were already in Brazil at the beginning of 1672.[77] Mendonça's uncle, Diogo, and his cousin, Philip, the heir to the throne of Ndongo, arrived in Portugal in the latter part of 1672.[78] In the group

---

[71] See 'Carta de Salvador Correia de Sá'.
[72] See Charles E. Nowell, *The Rose-Colored Map*.
[73] See 'Carta de Salvador Correia de Sá'.   [74] 'Carta de Salvador Correia de Sá'.
[75] See Birmingham, *Trade and Conquest*, pp. 44–45.
[76] See Birmingham, *Trade and Conquest*, p. 45.
[77] See Lourenço da Silva Mendonça's petition in APF, 490, folio, 140.
[78] See Lourenço da Silva Mendonça's petition in APF, 490, folio, 140.

sent to Brazil were sixteen royals, including two princesses, and one nobleman, Dom Christovaõ. Not all of them were sent to the city of Salvador;[79] they were spread across different captaincies in Brazil, although there is no documentation that reveals anything about their time there apart from Salvador.[80] The instructions from the prince regent, Dom Pedro II, before the royals left Brazil for Lisbon, simply stated that they should be sent to the kingdom [Portugal].[81]

The royals arrived in Brazil as prisoners of war, but they were not the type of prisoners of war that could be categorised as enslaved people, as evidenced by Francisco Gonçalves, the minister charged with handing them over to the Secretary of the Portuguese Overseas Council. Gonçalves was rather ambiguous about their status, but soon clarified that they were not enslaved: 'I have received six slaves, I say Black Princes to hand in to the Secretary of the Overseas Council'.[82] They were political exiles with enough freedom of movement to make it possible to organise their escape and join the community of runaway enslaved people in Palmares, or at least to network with the enslaved Africans in the cities of Salvador and Rio de Janeiro. As mentioned, the possibility of their escaping to join the fugitive enslaved Africans in Palmares became a source of anxiety for the governing authorities in Bahia and Rio de Janeiro, as well as Portugal. Among the royals sent to Brazil and Portugal, some were a good deal older than Mendonça, and could have passed on their experience to the rest of the royals. Among those were the four sent first to the Royal Court of Lisbon (1672–1673), the three illegitimate sons of King Philipe Hari I – 'Dom Antonio, Dom Diniz, Dom Sebastião – and their servant Francisco Black',[83] who all ended up in Peniche after rebelling. I will return to them in Chapter 4.

The royals' stay in Brazil gave them invaluable experience and insight into the problems faced by enslaved people. This section examines their

---

[79] 'Carta de Sua Alteza Sôbre se embarcarem para Reino os parentes de El-Rei de Dongo que o Governador de Angola mandou para esta cidade' [A Letter from his Highness on the Travel to the Kingdom by the Family Members of the King from Dongo which the Governor of Angola sent to this city], Lisbon, 6 September 1672 in *Documentos Históricos, Cartas Régias, 1667–1681*, vol. LXVII, Ministério da Educação e Saúde, Biblioteca Nacional, Rio de Janeiro: TYP. Batista de Sousa, 1945, pp. 213–214.

[80] 'Carta de Sua Alteza Sôbre se embarcarem para Reino os parentes de El-Rei de Dongo'.

[81] 'Carta de Sua Alteza Sôbre se embarcarem para Reino os parentes de El-Rei de Dongo'.

[82] Francisco Gonçalves's letter, AHU_ACL_CU_005, CX2, D. 181, 24 May 1673, Brazil-Bahia, 'Rcebi seiis escravos, digo negros principes pera emtregar ao secretario de Conselho ultramarine'.

[83] See 'Carta de António da Costa de Sousa a Manuel Barreto de S. Paio'.

stay in Salvador and how they were able to make vital contacts with Black Brotherhoods and enslaved workers engaged in a variety of activities in the city who shared their knowledge of the region and the networks that the enslaved had already established.

The royals' stay in Salvador, Bahia, was not totally alienating, because there were many Africans, particularly Mbundu people from Angola, in the city at that time. The stay in Brazil was a true turning point for Mendonça's understanding of the predicament of enslaved Africans. Brazil's treatment of the enslaved Africans could not have gone unnoticed by the Ndongo royals in Brazil because:

> Bahia was a leading city in Portuguese America during the sixteenth and seventeenth centuries. Here was the seat of government, the only archbishopric in Brazil and the only High Court of Appeals [Relação]. The city was a flourishing commercial centre for imports and exports. In the eighteenth-century Rio de Janeiro gradually ousted Bahia from its position of supremacy.[84]

From its inception as a city in 1549, Salvador served as a link to Pernambuco, Paraíba and Sergipe in the north of the country and the isles, Porto Seguro, Espírito Santo, Rio de Janeiro, São Vicente and Buenos Aires in Argentina to the south. Ships from India, Angola, the Gold Costa, Guinea and Cape Verde, as well as England, France and Portugal all stopped in Salvador to trade, as Dampier, an English merchant reported in the seventeenth century.[85] The city was home to people from many different nations and included traders, enslaved Africans from West Central Africa, Angola and from elsewhere on the West African Coast, 'for the most part, in Senegambia and Guinea-Bissau and São Tomé and Príncipe'[86] (the so-called Guiné [Guinea] enslaved people)[87]

---

[84] Russell-Wood, *Fidalgos*, p.78.
[85] See Captain William Dampier, *A Voyage to New Holland Etc in the Year 1699, Wherein are described, The Canary Islands, the Isles of Mayo and St. Jago. The Bay of All-Saints, with the forts and town of Bahia in Brazil. Cape Salvador. The winds on the Brazilian coast. Abrolho Shoals. A table of all the variations observed in this voyage. Occurrences near the Cape of Good Hope. The course to New Holland. Shark's Bay. The isles and coast, etc. of New Holland. Their inhabitants, manners, customs, trade, etc. Their harbours, soil, beasts, birds, fish, etc. Trees, plants, fruits, etc. Illustrated with several maps and draughts: also divers birds, fishes and plants not found in this part of the world, curiously engraven on copper plates*, 3rd ed., London: Printed for James and John Knapton at the Crown in St. Paul's Churchyard, 1729.
[86] A. J. R. Russell-Wood, *The Black Man in Slavery and Freedom in Colonial Brazil*, Oxford in association with St Antony's College: Macmillan Press, 1993, p. 27.
[87] See Manuel Querino, *O Negro Na Bahia*, Livraria José Olympio Editor a Rua do Ouvidor: São Paulo, 1946. See also João José Reis, *Slave Rebellion in Brazil: The Muslim Uprising of 1835 in Bahia*, London: Taylor & Francis, 1995.

among its inhabitants. There were free people from Angola, who were there as soldiers, free Africans from the region of modern Guinea-Bissau, Cacheu, who were hired to work as carpenters.[88] Many of them were not employed in the sugar plantations, but as domestic workers, street hawkers, cooks and fishermen, while some of the women became wives or mistresses,[89] or transport workers who carried their masters through the streets of Salvador.[90] The nature of their work meant that both enslaved persons and the free constituted a powerful network throughout the city of Salvador and other regions of Brazil. They knew the city, knew the powerful, the wealthy and the poor, and knew to whom to sell, when and where. They also acquired the communication skills needed to sell or haggle for goods. In other words, they had the know-how of Salvador and Rio de Janeiro's communication networks, and economic and cultural sensitivities.[91] And this communication network was crucial for the royals to gain knowledge of what was going on in Bahia and Brazil, which made them suspicious to the authorities in Salvador and Rio, who feared 'they could connect with Palmarinos' and 'become a danger to Brazil'.[92]

The network of enslaved Africans in both Salvador and Rio de Janeiro was most evident in the work of *negros de ganho* (wage-earning enslaved African men). The *negros de ganho* had a considerable level of knowledge of the cities and countryside and were employed by their owners to carry out a particular role. They were present in many different Brazilian captaincies from the seventeenth century, particularly in Rio de Janeiro and Salvador, and were depicted in the work of both Johann Moritz Rugendas (1802–1858)[93] and Jean B. Debret (1768–1848), who lived in Rio de Janeiro between 1816 and

---

[88] Thirty carpenters from Cape Verde and Guinea-Bissau (Cacheu) were sent to Bahia to work in the shipbuilding industry. The issue was whether they should be exempted from paying tax and othe tax duties. They were not enslaved but free people with skills in carpentry. This demonstrates that not all Africans in Brazil were enslaved people, particularly those living in Bahia. See AHU, Baía, cx3, doc. 9; AHU_ACL_CU_005, cx. 2, D. 240, Brasil, Baía, 20 March 1694.

[89] Slave-masters often forced women to become their wives or mistresses. Their status as wives became apparent only when their masters wrote their wills, as in the above-mentioned case of Gaspar Álvares.

[90] See Dampier, *A Voyage to New Holland*.   [91] See AHU, Pernambuco, doc. 374.

[92] See AHU, cód. 17, fl. 301, 18 July 1679, '... ou meteremse com os negros dos palmares'; see also AHU, cód. 17, fls. 59-59v, 21 August 1672, 'que se pode seguir de buscarem mejo de fogirê para os *mocambo*, donde conheçidos dos negros delles, nos sejão mais prejudiçiaes'.

[93] See Johann Moritz Rugendas, *Viagem Pitoresca Através do Brasil*, São Paulo: Martins, 1972. This book was translated from German into Portuguese and was first published with the German title *Malerische Reise in Brasilien*, Paris: Engelmann, 1835.

1831.[94] *Negros de ganho* made hampers and baskets, and acted as messengers, carriers of chairs for the affluent, joiners, masons and smiths. They also hunted, gathered, undertook agricultural pursuits and travelled to the interior as muleteers or herdsmen. They acted as 'navigators, sailors, coachmen, and footmen'.[95] They also saved money earned from their activities to buy their own freedom and that of their fellow enslaved Africans, some of who were able to return to Africa.[96] According to A. J. R. Russell-Wood, in Peru *negros de ganho* could buy their freedom within seventeen months, while in Brazil in the seventeenth century it might take ten years to accumulate enough money.

Many enslaved Africans were used as sailors in the shipping trade in Bahia, and sailed from Salvador to other regions of Brazil and, presumably, parts of Africa.[97] There were high-profile African people (*sobas*) from Angola living in Salvador.[98] In 1584, thirty-five years after its foundation, Salvador's population was estimated to comprise of 3,000 Portuguese, 8,000 Indigenous Americans, termed 'tamed' Natives or Indigenous American Christians, and between 3,000 and 4,000 enslaved Africans, who were mainly from West Africa.[99] There were also a large number of enslaved Africans in Bahia, and by the 1620s many were free, having fought in the war against the Dutch in Salvador.[100] The Kimbundu language was widely used in Bahia, as well as Tupi (a Native American language).[101] Portuguese was the third language spoken in Bahia in the seventeenth century. Africans made up the majority of foreign migrants to Bahia: there were around 20,000 Africans and 10,000 Europeans or Portuguese in Bahia in the seventeenth century (see Table 3).[102] Angolan priests were also working in Salvador, and in Brazil at large,[103] and

---

[94] See Jean-Baptiste Debret, *Viagem Pitoresca e Histórica ao Brasil, 1834–1839*, Belo Horizonte: Itatiaia, 1978. The original was published as *Voyage Pittoresque et Historique au Brésil*, vol. II, Paris: Firmin Didot Frères, 1835.
[95] Russell-Wood, *The Black Man in Slavery and Freedom*, p. 35.
[96] See Paulo Cruz Terra, 'Free and Unfree Labour and Ethnic Conflicts in the Brazilian Transport Industry: Rio de Janeiro in the 19th Century', *Internationaal Instituut voor Sociale Geschiedenis* (IRSHo), 59, Special Issue, 2014, pp. 113–132.
[97] See Dampier, *A Voyage to New Holland*.
[98] Those who may have stayed in Salvador from the government of Correia de Sousa.
[99] This is an estimation by a Jesuit priest, Fernão Cardim, quoted by Russell-Wood, *The Black Man in Slavery and Freedom*, p. 27.
[100] See Hansen, 'Representações da Cidade de Salvador no Século XVII'.
[101] See Dias, *A Arte da Língua de Angola* and Luiz Vicencio Mamiami, *Arte de Gramatica da Lingua Brazilica da Nação Kiriri*, Rio de Janeiro: TYP, Central de Brown & Evaristo, 1877.
[102] See Stuart B. Schwartz, *Segredos Internos: Engenhos e Escravos na Sociedade Colonial*, São Paulo: Companhia das Letras, 1988.
[103] L. Azevedo, 'Cartas do Padre António Vieira a Roque Monteiro Paim', 2 July 1691, vol. III, Coimbra, Imprensa da Universidade, 1928, p. 620-621. See also MMA, vol. XIII, pp. 221–222.

prominent Angolan students at the Jesuit College in Salvador were being trained to take up work in Brazil.[104] Among them were influential directors of the Pernambuco college and the college in São Paulo.[105] Salvador was a multiracial, multi-ethnic, multilingual, multireligious, multicultural city. Yet Salvador's multiculturalism was not necessarily a Portuguese creation; it was

TABLE 3 *Number of houses (*fogos*) in each of the parishes (*freguesias*) and how many people (*almaj*) lived in each parish in the city of Salvador in the mid-eighteenth century. By the author, based on manuscripts*[106]

Parishes of the City of Bahia			
Parishes	Houses	Persons	
1 S Salvador na Se	1483	8946	
2 N Senhora da Conam da Prya	913	8017	
3 Santiso Sauamto do Pilar	416	4119	
4 S Antonio alem do Carmo	949	4060	
5 N Senhora das Brotas	159	1063	
6 Santiso Sauamto e S Anna	933	4070	
7 S Pedro	1132	6462	
8 Santiso Sauamento do Rozario	402	2004	
9 N Senhora da Vitoria	339	1522	
TOTAL	6.726	40.263	

---

[104] See Alexandre Almeida Marcussi, 'O Dever Catequético A Evangelização dos Escravos em Luanda nos séculos XVII e XVIII': http://www.historia.uff.br/7mares/wp-content/uploads/2014/04/v01n02a06.pdf, and Alexandre Almeida Marcussi, 'Cativeiro e Cura: Experiências Religiosas da Escravidão Atlântica nos Calundus de Luzia Pinta, Séculos XVII-XVIII', unpublished Ph.D. thesis, University of São Paulo (USP), 2015: https://bv.fapesp.br/pt/bolsas/134878/cativeiro-e-cura-experiencias-religiosas-da-escravidao-atlantica-nos-calundus-de-luzia-pinta-secul/. See also Serafim Leite, 'Jesuítas do Brasil, naturais de Angola', *Brotéria: Revista Contemporânea de Cultura*, 3(3/4), 1940, pp. 254–261.
[105] See Vaniclêia Silva Santos, 'As Bolsas de Mandinga no Espaço Atlântico: Século XVIII', unpublished Ph.D. thesis, State University of São Paulo, 2008, pp. 153–155.
[106] Iozé Antonio Cadas, 'Notícia Geral de Toda Esta Capitania da Bahia Desde o Seu Descobrimento Até O Prez.te Anno de 1759 por Iozé António Cadas' [General News on the Capitania of Bahia since its Discovery until the Present Jear of 1759 by Iozé Antonio Cadas]. The manuscript is housed in the Instituto Geográfico e Histórico de Salvador, Bahia, Brazil.

a multicultural and multilingual region among the different Native American peoples before the Portuguese arrived.

From the time sugar was introduced into Brazil in the sixteenth century, Salvador was one of its most valuable producers, along with other coastal captaincies such as Pernambuco, Rio de Janeiro and São Paulo.[107] The city of Salvador sits on the bay known as Bahia de Todos os Santos, in an area known as the Recôncavo, which covers approximately 10,400 square kilometres and is composed mainly of lowlands. Bahia de Todos os Santos is one of the largest bays in Brazil, covering about 750 square kilometres of salt water and about 190 kilometres of coastline.[108] Azevedo states that:

> ... the region's soil is of the massapé type [a clay soil that is almost always black]. Its fluvial net is comprised of the Paraguaçu, Açu, Subaé and Jaguaribe rivers, emptying into the bay, and by rivers Pojuca, Jacuípe and Joanes, that empty directly into the Atlantic Ocean. The first hamlets in the Recôncavo, dating from the sixteenth century, were installed in lowlands, around the Todos os Santos Bay, where sugarcane culture was concentrated. In the following centuries, they occupied the highlands, between the Paraguaçu and Jaguaribe rivers, where tobacco and subsistence crops were developed.[109]

The entire network of trade that ran through the towns of the Recôncavo was connected back to Salvador by rivers, making the transportation of agricultural goods easy. Some of its biggest *engenhos* (sugar mills) were in coastal areas, such as Victoria. The Recôncavo, hence Bahia, was run by the Municipal Council of Salvador. From the 1500s there were 25 *engenhos* in Bahia, by 1710 there were 146 *engenhos*, and by the end of the nineteenth century there were 855 *engenhos*, including those in Sergipe d'El-Rey, which was subordinated to Bahia de Todos os Santos (see Table 4).

To maintain their *engenhos* and productivity in sugar and tobacco, Salvador and the Recôncavo depended on a large number of enslaved Africans for labour. Antonil states that without the slaves it was not possible to do anything – 'preserve, and increase the farm, nor have a

---

[107] See Hansen, 'Representações da Cidade de Salvador no Século XVII', and Russell-Wood, *Fidalgos*.

[108] For a detailed study, see Milton Santos, *A Rede Urbana do Recôncavo*, Salvador: Imprensa Oficial do Estado, 1958, and Esterzilda Berenstein de Azevedo, *Engenhos do Recôncavo Baiano, Sugarcane Farms of Bahia's Recôncavo*, Brasília, DF: Iphan/Programa Monumenta, 2009.

[109] Azevedo, *Engenhos do Recôncavo Baiano*, pp. 23-24.

TABLE 4 *Number of sugar-cane mills in Bahia from the sixteenth to the nineteenth centuries. By the author, based on Berenstein de Azevedo (2009)*

Period	Quantity
16th century	25
17th century (1612)	50
17th century (1629)	80
17th century (1676)	130
18th century (1710)	146
18th century (1750)	172
18th century (1790)	200
18th century (1799)	400
18th to 19th centuries (1728–1827)	462
19th century (1834)	603
19th century (2nd half)	511
19th century (late)	855

current mill'.[110] Yet Salvador was a city with a confusing message on slavery: Jesuit priests were owners of slaves there, too,[111] and Father António Vieira's message on slavery was an ambiguous one.[112] The Salvador City Council was also famous for its political intrigue, involving Vieira's own family[113].

During his time in Brazil, Mendonça would have been well aware of severe problems concerning the well-being of the enslaved Africans in the country, and particularly of those in Salvador and Rio. High rates of mortality prevailed among enslaved Africans that disembarked in Rio from the seventeenth to the eighteenth centuries.[114] The stress levels of those working in sugar mills and issues of suicide, abuse, anxiety,

---

[110] Andreoni (Antonil), *Cultura e Opulência*, p. 19, 'Os escravos são as mãos, e os pés do senhor do engenho; porque sem elles no Brazil nao he possivel fazer, conservar, e augmentar fazenda, nem ter engenho corrente. E do modo, com que se ha com elles, depende te-los bons, ou mãos para o serviço'.

[111] See [no author] *A Quinta de Tangue, Um Monumento a Seriço da Cultura da Bahia*, Salvador: Publicações do Arquivo do Estado da Bahia, 1980.

[112] See 'Padre António Vieira – "O Problema de Escravatura"', [Padre António Vieira – The Problem of Slavery], in Barretto, *Monstruosidades do Tempo e da Fortuna*.

[113] See Schwartz, *Blacks and Indians*, and José Eisenberg, 'António Vieira and the Justification of Indian Slavery', *Luso-Brazilian Review*, 40(1), 2003, pp. 89–95.

[114] On the burial of slaves in Salvador, see *Livro 1º das Tumbas*, 1685–1709, Archives of the Santa Casa da Misericórdia in Bahia.

depression, harm, bullying, lynching, rape and abortion would have been apparent to him while in Brazil.[115] A Jesuit priest living in Salvador in the latter part of the seventeenth century, Antonil, reflected these issues in research that he carried out on the mill of Sergipe de Conde in Bahia in 1681. His findings resonate with the evidence Mendonça presented in the Vatican and indicate that reports of the mistreatment of the enslaved in Brazil were not based on probability or on far-fetched ideas, but on facts. I will return to the work of Antonil in due course.

We have scant information on Mendonça's own stay in Brazil beyond what the overseas and municipal councils in both Bahia and Rio said about the royals in general. Documents at our disposal indicate that he lived in Bahia, Salvador for eighteen months, and in Rio for six months.[116] What is certain is that while in Salvador, the royals formed a network with the Black Brotherhoods of the Rosary in the city. The crucial evidence, the *memorial*, used by Mendonça in the Vatican, including its condemnation of the slave trade in all of the Americas, came directly from the city's Black Brotherhoods. The *memorial* states that Atlantic slavery was a crime against humanity and that it should be abolished. I will return to this in Chapter 5.

Enslaved Africans in Brazil held an annual festival to elect a king and queen, usually of royal descent, to lead them.[117] Mendonça and his relatives would have fitted well into that category. It is not far-fetched to suggest that Mendonça's long stay in Bahia and Salvador would not have gone unnoticed by the free and enslaved Africans living in Salvador and Rio. The Municipal Council in Bahia and Salvador was aware of this impact, as prohibition was made to stop Africans gathering, as they did in

---

[115] Andreoni (Antonil), *Cultura e Opulência*. See also Jorge Benci, *Economia Cristã dos senhores no Governo dos Escravos*, São Paulo: Grijalbo, 1977: http://www.histedbr.fe.u nicamp.br/navegando/fontes_escritas/1_Jesuitico/benci_economia_crista_governo_escra vos.pdf. See also Dampier, *A Voyage to New Holland* and Russell-Wood, *The Black Man in Slavery and Freedom*, and Lourenço da Silva Mendonça's court case in the Vatican, in which he stated that he had lots of experience, APF, 490, fl. 140.

[116] For documents on Mendonça's stay in Salvador, see 'Recibo de Francisco Goncalves referente ao recebimento de negros escravos para entregar ao Secretario do Conselho'.

[117] See Russell-Wood, *The Black Man in Slavery and Freedom*, pp. 96–98. The process by which Africans selected their kings in Brazil is worthy of consideration. The Portuguese authorities kept a watchful eye on the process. It is not surprising that Mendonça and his relatives were not permitted to stay permanently in Brazil. See also comments by the Governor of Bahia, Afonso Furtado do Rio de de Castro de Mendonça, AHU, Brasil-Bahia, cx. 22, D. 2545-2546, no. 2545, 7 August 1673, and Bernardo Vieyra Ravasco, the brother of Father Antonio Vieira, AHU, Brasil-Bahia, cx. 22, d. 2545-2546, n. 2546, 8 August 1673.

the later colonial period – dancing was forbidden, the sound of drums at night was stopped. Some of these prohibitions extended to Mendonça's time. The documents state that the royals were already known by members of the fugitive community of Palmares. In fact, the fugitives not only knew them but also identified with them through their shared mother tongue – Kimbundu.[118]

The years Mendonça spent in Brazil (1672–1673) were a watershed in his life. There, he accumulated the evidence that he used in Rome to argue a case for the liberation of the enslaved Africans in Brazil.[119] These types of activity (celebrations)[120] in Brazil would have served as a link from the urban to the rural, making it possible that the royals might reach Quilombo dos Palmares.

The royals would thus have learned of the terrible lived experience of many enslaved Africans in the *engenhos* of the Recôncavo of the seventeenth century. The stories of these atrocities might have circulated through different mediums, via slaves themselves, daily conversations among slave-owners, soldiers, sailors, visitors and conversations among the general public conversations. The royals would have been briefed about numerous cases of the mistreatment of enslaved Africans in Brazil. Their own journeys by ship from Pungo-Andongo to Salvador, Rio de Janeiro and Lisbon, lasting weeks and months, most probably brought them into contact with news from sailors (among them Africans),[121] soldiers,[122] traders, visitors and ordinary travellers about the lives of enslaved Africans in Brazil.[123] In Salvador they would have met Angolan priests studying and working there, who would have served as a point of reference for them. Take, for example, the short stay of Antonio Manuel Negrita, a Kongolese ambassador, in Salvador in 1602, and his visit to the Vatican from the Kongo 1604. During his short stay in Salvador, he was briefed about the Kongolese prince, Pedro Morbala, who

---

[118] On the royals speaking the same language as the Palmarists, see AHU, cód. 17, Consultas Mixtas, 18 July 1679, fl., 301, and AHU, cód. 17, fls. 59–59v, 21 August 1672.
[119] See APF, 490, fl. 140.
[120] Enslaved Africans were engaged in activities such as selling, sailing and cooking to earn a wage in the cities in Brazil – and the city of Salvador was no exception; and they were also involved in hunting and herding on platations around these cities.
[121] See Andreoni (Antonil), *Cultura e Opulência*, and Benci, *Economia Cristã dos senhores no Governo dos Escravos*.
[122] See also Schwartz, *Blacks and Indians*.
[123] There were also Africans from Cape Verde and Guinea-Bissau whose skills were required in Brazil, but who were not enslaved and were paid for their work. See also AHU, Baía, cx.3, doc. 9; AHU_ACL_CU_005, cx.2, d.240, Baía, 20 March 1694.

had been kept as a slave in Pernambuco. Negrita helped to have him released from his captivity in Brazil.[124]

3.5 THE ROYALS' EXPERIENCES, THE SUGAR PLANTATION AND ANTONIL'S WHISTLEBLOWING WORK ON THE TREATMENT OF THE ENSLAVED AFRICANS IN BAHIA

We may not have the royals' own accounts of their experiences in Brazil. Nevertheless, we have at our disposal numerous documentary pieces of evidence and eyewitness accounts of the lives of enslaved Africans in Brazil, particularly in Salvador and Rio de Janeiro, from the seventeenth century. These eyewitness accounts include the work of Antonil and Benci, two Italian Jesuit priests who lived and worked in Salvador in a similar period to the royals' stay in Brazil; they were there nine years after the royals had departed in 1673.[125] Antonil's work sheds particular light on how the private life of the *engenhos* in Bahia could be thrown open for public scrutiny. Antonil wrote with the intention of informing European consumers that the sweetness of sugar, which he termed the 'drug', had more to it than people realised. He used the findings of his research to disclose the violence involved in sugar production in the mills. The royals would certainly have been in agreement with Antonil's assessment of the plight of enslaved Africans in Bahia. The similarity between Antonil's findings from the *engenho* Sergipe de Conde and the evidence presented in the Vatican by Mendonça is striking.[126] We will return to this issue in Chapter 5.

Antonil had been informed about life in the *engenhos*, the living conditions of enslaved Africans in Brazil and the relationship between masters

---

[124] Antonio Manuel Negrita [Archivio Segreto Vaticano, Miscellania, Armadio I (henceforward ASV, Misc., Arm I)], vol. 91, Collettione di Scritture di Spagna II, Papers of António Manuel, Certificate of Freedom, 25 Oct. 1604, vol. 91, fls. 124–158, fl. 126, 'Diogo Moniz declared: 'Certifico eu Diogo Moniz daCompa. De Jesus curado do Collegio de Pernambuco que he verdade que Pedro morbala natural de congo conteudo no aʃsima, he forro por que por elle dey sua valia a Belchior gracia [Garcia] rebelo cujo escravo era. Isto por ordem dos pes [padres] daCompa. Q reʃide em Angola pello [para o] mandar resgatar hû home q o tinha vendido ao ditto D.os [Domingios] gracia o qual o mandou resgatar por achar emI fora mal vendido por ser forro epor aʃsim paʃsar na verdade lhe dey esta por meu feito eaʃsinado no ditto Collegio a 10 de novembro de 1604. Diogo Moniz.' I am indebted to Professor John Thornton for his kindness in sending me this document.
[125] Andreoni (Antonil), *Cultura e Opulência*.
[126] See SOCG, vol. 495a, fls. 54-58, 60-61 and SOCG vol. 490, fl. 140 and 138. See also Andreoni (Antonil), *Cultura e Opulência*, and Jaca and Moirans, OFM Cap., *Servi Liberi*.

and the enslaved. To make a case about what he already knew, he went in search of evidence:

And because one day I was glad to see one of the most renowned [mills], which is in the Recôncavo on the seafront of Bahia, which they call the mill of Sergipe do Conde, moved by a praiseworthy curiosity, I searched for it in the space of eight or ten days, there it was, taking note of all that has made it celebrated and quite the king of the royal mills.[127]

Antonil used the *engenho* of Sergipe de Conde to openly call attention to the danger and precariousness of the lives that enslaved Africans led as they toiled to produce sugar. He talked to the administrators who had over thirty years of experience of running an *engenho*. He also interviewed other officials who held posts there. He drew his data from a rich pool of people with lived experience in the *engenho*:

And with the information that I have been given, by those who administered it more than thirty years with a well-known intelligence, and with the growth equal to the industry, and from the experience of a famous sugar master, who for fifty years occupied himself in this office with a happy success; and of the most official of the names, to which I briefly inquired to what each one belongs[128].

As for the *engenho* of Sergipe de Conde in Santo Amaro, Bahia, it was not the first time it had been under investigation. In 1625, Father André de Gouvêa, a Portuguese priest in Salvador, reported on the *engenho*. This document was sent both to the Jesuit College of Santo Antão in Lisbon,

---

[127] There is a distinction between *engenho real* (royal engenho) and *engenhoca/trapiche* (a small engenho). An *engenho real* was for sugar production and was operated on a water wheel, whilst an *engenhoca* was for making spirits and run by cows or horses. See Andreoni (Antonil), *Cultura e Opulência*, p. 8, 'Dos engenhos, uns se chamam reais, outros, inferiores, vulgarmente engenhocas. Os reais ganharam este apelido por terem todas as partes de que se compõem, e todas as oficinas perfeitas, cheias de grande número de escravos, com muitos canaviais próprios e outros obrigados à moenda, e principalmente por terem a realeza de moerem com água, à diferença de outros, que moem com cavalos e bois, e são menos providos e aparelhados, ou pelo menos com menor perfeição e largueza das oficinas necessárias e com pouco número de escravos, para fazerem, como dizem, o engenho moente e corrente"; "E porque algum dia folguei de ver hum dos mais afamados, que há no reconcavo á beira-mar da Bahia, á quem chamão o engenho de Sergipe do Conde, movido de hum louvavel curiosidade, procurei no espaço de oito, ou dez diaz aue ahi estive, tomar noticia de tudo o que o fazia tão celebrado e quasi rei dos engenhos reaes.'

[128] Andreoni (Antonil), *Cultura e Opulência*, p. 8, 'e valendo-me das informações, que me deu, quem o administrou mais de trinta annos com conhecida intelligencia, e com accrescentamento egual á industria: e da experiencia de hum Famoso mestre de assucar, que cincoenta annos se occupou neste officio com venturoso sucesso; e dos mais oficiaes de nome, aos quaes miudamente pergunteri o que a cada qual pertencia'.

Portugal, and to the Propaganda Fide's Archive in Rome.[129] Interestingly, the *engenho* of Sergipe de Conde belonged to the Jesuit College of Salvador, Bahia, in the seventeenth and eighteenth centuries (1622–1638 and 1643–1759).[130] Slavery and the Catholic Church in Salvador thus went hand in hand, explaining why priests were silent when it came to the condemnation of slavery as a practice. Their discourses in Salvador were about the treatment of enslaved Africans in the mills; they did not condemn slavery outright. That was left for Mendonça to take up.

When these people were conducting research into the *engenho* of Sergipe de Conde, why was slavery was not condemned in Bahia? Antonil's conclusions show that there were severe problems with how the enslaved Africans working there were handled, both in terms of their treatment and their relationship with the *engenho*'s administrators. It also shows that an *engenho*'s owner did not necessarily have to live there himself or administer it personally. The *engenho*'s owners could hand it over to different people to run. Priests were unlikely to take control of the running of sugar mills; as a result, they may have had little influence or control over its daily activities, particularly the relationship between the administrators and the slaves. Antonil wanted to show his readers that the sugar they valued so much came at a huge human cost:

I decide to leave in this blur all that might have been known, [because] my time is extremely short. However, I have gathered the information about [sugar] with care, and extended it with the same style, and with clear way of speaking, and about the soil that is used in the mills: so that those who do not know the cost of the sweetness relating to sugar, to those who produce it, that they know it, and that they feel more inclined to give it the price it deserves; and whoever again enters into the business of some sugar mill, should have these news, that they should be

---

[129] S. J. Serafim Leite, *História da Companhia de Jesus no Brasil*, vol. VIII, Rio de Janeiro: Imprensa Nacional, 1949, pp. 278–279, as cited by Pablo Antonio Iglesias Magalhães, 'A Relação do Engenho de Sergipe do Conde em 1625, *Afro-Ásia*, 41, 2010, pp. 237–264 (p. 239).

[130] Father Antonio Vieira was believed to have returned to Portugal on a diplomatic mission after Portuguese independence in 1641. However, there is new evidence from Magalhães that shows that Vieira also went to Portugal with his counterpart, Father Simão de Vasconcelos, for economic reasons. They made the trip to Portugal partly to deal with a dispute involving the *engenho* of Sergipe de Conde. See Magalhães, 'A Relação do Engenho de Sergipe do Conde em 1625'. It is important to note that the *engenho* of Sergipe de Conde was under the ownership of the count of Linhares e Mem de Sá, the Portuguese governor-general of Brazil (Salvador, Bahia) from 1558 to 1572. On seventeenth-century maps the location of the *engenho* was called Condessa de Linhares, see Figure 4.

directed to act with correctness; he who does it all for a living should desire to do it this way, and apply it.[131]

Antonil's book was censored in Portugal a few years after its publication, even though the Tribunal of Inquisition declared that it posed no direct threat or caused harm to the Christian faith. They saw it as a book of instruction for consumers of sugar about the dangers of its production: 'it is very worthy of a licence that it asks for: for this reason, those who want to go the state of Brazil will know, how very costly is the making of sugar, tobacco, and gold, that are more sweetly acquired in the Kingdom [Portugal] than they are dug in Brazil'.[132] I believe it was censored because it blew the whistle on the terrible lives of enslaved Africans in the *engenhos* in Brazil. The Crown was aware of the impact of the book on consumers and on those who were against slavery in Europe, coming as it did a few years after Mendonça made his statement in the Vatican about the ill treatment of enslaved Africans.

Antonil not only wanted to make consumers aware of the human cost of sugar before they bought it; he also wanted the book to become a manual for the *engenhos*. Yet he intended it to be an incomplete work that others, with more insight and 'a lighter feather, and well-trimmed', would bring to fruition:

For more clarity, and order, I have repeated in various chapters all that belongs to this drug, and to whom for which, and those that labour there, beginning, after reporting on the obligations of each, from the first origin of sugar in the cane, to their fitting perfection in the boxes, according to my limited means; which will at least serve, to give to others with better ability, and a lighter feather, and well-trimmed, with some perfect stimulus to this embryo. And if anyone wants to know the author of this curious [book], and useful work, he is a friend of the public good called: *Anonymous Toscano*.[133]

---

[131] Andreoni (Antonil), *Cultura e Opulência*, p. 8, 'me resolve a deixar neste borrão tudo aquilo, que na limitação do tempo sobredito apressadamente, mas com atenção ajuntei, e extendi com mesmo estilo, e modo de fallar claro, e chão, que se usa nos engenhos: para que os que não sabem o que custa a doçura do assucar a quem o lavra, o conheção, e sintão menos dar por elle o preço que vale: e quem de novo entrar na administração de algum engenho, tenha estas noticiais, dirigidas a obrar com acerto; he o que em toda a occupação se deve desejar, e intentar'.

[132] Andreoni (Antonil), *Cultura e Opulência*, p. 9, 'he muito merecedora da licença, que pede: porque por este este meio saberão os que se quizeram passar ao estado do Brazil, o muito que custão as culturas do assucar, tabaco, e ouro, que são mais doces de possuir no Reino, que de cavar no Brazil'.

[133] Andreoni (Antonil), *Cultura e Opulência*, p. 9, '... e para maior clareza, e ordem, reparti em varios capitulos tudo o que pretence a esta droga, e a quem por ella, e nella trabalha; começando, depois de relatar as obrigações de cada qual, desde a primeira origem do assucar na canna, até a sua cabal perfeição nas caixas, conforme o meu limitado cabedal;

Antonil summed up the enslaved Africans' treatment using three words beginning with 'p' (P. P. P.) in the Portuguese language: '... the work must also be kept moderate so that it is not more than their strength can bear. It is customary to say in Brazil that three P's are required for slaves, that is: *pão, páo* and *panno* [bread, a stick, and a piece of cloth].'[134] The punishment that the enslaved Africans endured was inhumane. He highlighted that enslaved Africans were treated worse than animals:

> Even when they start out with the stick, which means, of course, punishment, they should also offer proof to God that their food and clothing are as abundant as their punishment often is. Slaves are often falsely accused, and punishment is often inflected without much proof of guilt. And even when crimes are proved, the instruments they use to punish them with are too harsh, for they would not employ such devices against brute animals. Masters, in fact, sometimes give more care and attention to a single horse than they do to half a dozen slaves. The horse receives careful grooming; he has someone to bring him hay; he has a blanket when he perspires, a saddle, and gilded bridle.[135]

The disciplinary punishments that Mendonça revealed to the Propaganda Fide in 1684 were clearly still in use when Antonil carried out his research on the *engenho* Sergipe do Conde three years later, and even twenty-seven years later when his book was published:[136]

> Once their guilt has been established, they should be whipped moderately, or locked for a time in irons or in the stocks. But to punish with violence and vengeful spirit, with one's own hand and with terrible instruments, and to go at these poor people with fire or hot wax, or to brand them on the face, would not be tolerated among barbarians, much less among Catholic Christians.[137]

    que pelo menos servirá, para dar a outros de melhor capacidade, e penna mais ligeira, e bem aparada, algum estimulo de aperfeiçoar este embrião. E se alguem quizer saber o autor deste curioso, e util trabalho elle he hum amigo do bem publico chamado: o Anonymo Toscano.'

[134] Andreoni (Antonil), *Cultura e Opulência*, p. 20, '... e deve tambem moderar o serviço de sorte, que não seja superior ás forças dos que trabalhão, se quer que possão aturar. No Brazil costumão dizer, que para o escravo são necessarios tres P.P.P. a saber, pão, páo, e panno'.

[135] Andreoni (Antonil), *Cultura e Opulência*, p. 21 '... e posto que comecem mal, principiando pelo castigo, que he o páo; comtudo provera a Deus, que tão abundantes fossem o comer, e o vestir, como muitas vezes he o castigo, dado por qualquer cousa pouco provada, ou levantada; e com instrumentos de muitos por qualquer rigor, ainda quando os crimes são certos; de que se não usa nem com os brutos animaes, fazendo algum senhor mais caso de hum cavallo, que de meia duzia de escravos: pois cavallo he servido, e tem quem lhe busque capim, tem panno para suor; e sella, e freio dourado'.

[136] Mariza de Carvalho Soares, 'Engenho Sim, de Açúcar Não o Engenho de Farinha de Frans Post', *Varia História*, 25(41), 2009, pp.61–83 (p. 65).

[137] Andreoni (Antonil), *Cultura e Opulência*, p. 21, 'covencidos castigar-se-hão com açoutes moderados, ou com o metter em hum corrente de ferro por algum tempo, ou tronco. Castigar com impeto, com animo vigativo, por mão propria, e com instrumentos

Branding on the face was used to distinguish the enslaved, and they often bore the sign of their owners from the forts in São Tomé and in Minas, or of the different countries or regions from which they were brought to Brazil. There were thousands of different symbols of branding used in the slave trade. In the eighteenth century, the practice was extended to the Indigenous Brazilians.[138] In the early part of the century Afonso I, king of Kongo, complained about such practices: 'as soon as the captives are in the hands of white men they are branded with a red-hot iron'[139] (see Figure 13). For Antonil the inhumane treatment of enslaved Africans was not a necessity because the enslaved constituted the basic fabric of the Brazilian economy: 'the slaves are the hands and the feet of the *engenho*'s owner, because without them it is not possible in Brazil to do [anything], maintain, and develop a plantation, nor to have a functioning mill. And whether they are available for labour in good condition or not depends on how they are treated'.[140] The condemnation of slavery in Brazil may not have been Antonil's main concern. However, it was clear that he was horrified about the condition and treatment of enslaves in the *engenho* Sergipe do Conde.[141]

For Antonil, punishment was used as a form of education, and he wrote that 'after they made some mistake, as weak people are apt to do, they go voluntarily to their master to ask his pardon, or if they seek a protector to accompany them, it is the custom in Brazil in such cases to forgive them'.[142] He was describing African practices for resolving a feud and seeking reconciliation – such as was seen after the siege of Kazanze, as described in Chapter 1 – in which an intermediary bears the responsibility

---

terríveis, e chegar talvez aos pobres com fogo, ou lacre ardente, ou marcal-os na cara, não seria para se soffrer entre barbarous, muito menos entre christãos catholicos.'

[138] See Francisco Xavier de Mendoça Furtado and Marcos Carneiro de Mendonça (eds.), *A Amazôniana era Pombalina*, 2nd ed., vol. I (vol. 49a), *Correspondência do Governador e Capitão-General do Estado do Grão-Pará e Maranhão, Francisco Xavier de Mendonça Furtado, 1751–1759*, Edições do Senado Federal, pp. 387–389.

[139] 'Carta do Rei do Kongo ao Portugal Pedindo-lhe Físicos, Cirrurgiõ e Boticários com Competentes Boticas' [A Letter of the King of Kongo to Portugal Asking for Physician, Chirurgians and Boticarian with Competent Apotecaries] ATT, Corpo Cronológico, part 1, maç. 35, doc. n. 2, 28 Octcber 1526, 'e tanto que são em poder dos dittos homens brancos são logo ferrados e marcados com fogo'.

[140] Andreoni (Antonil), *Cultura e Opulência*, p. 19, 'os escravos são as mãos, e os pés do senhor do engenho; porque sem elles no Brazil nao he possivel fazer, conservar, e augmentar fazenda, nem ter engenho corrente. E do modo, com que se ha com elles, depende te-los bons, ou mãos para o serviço.' For symbols used in writing about enslaved Africans, see the manuscript in the Archive of Santa Casa in Salvador, Brazil, livro 9 do Bangve, 1792–1815.

[141] Andreoni (Antonil), *Cultura e Opulência*, p. 20.

[142] Andreoni (Antonil), *Cultura e Opulência*, p. 20.

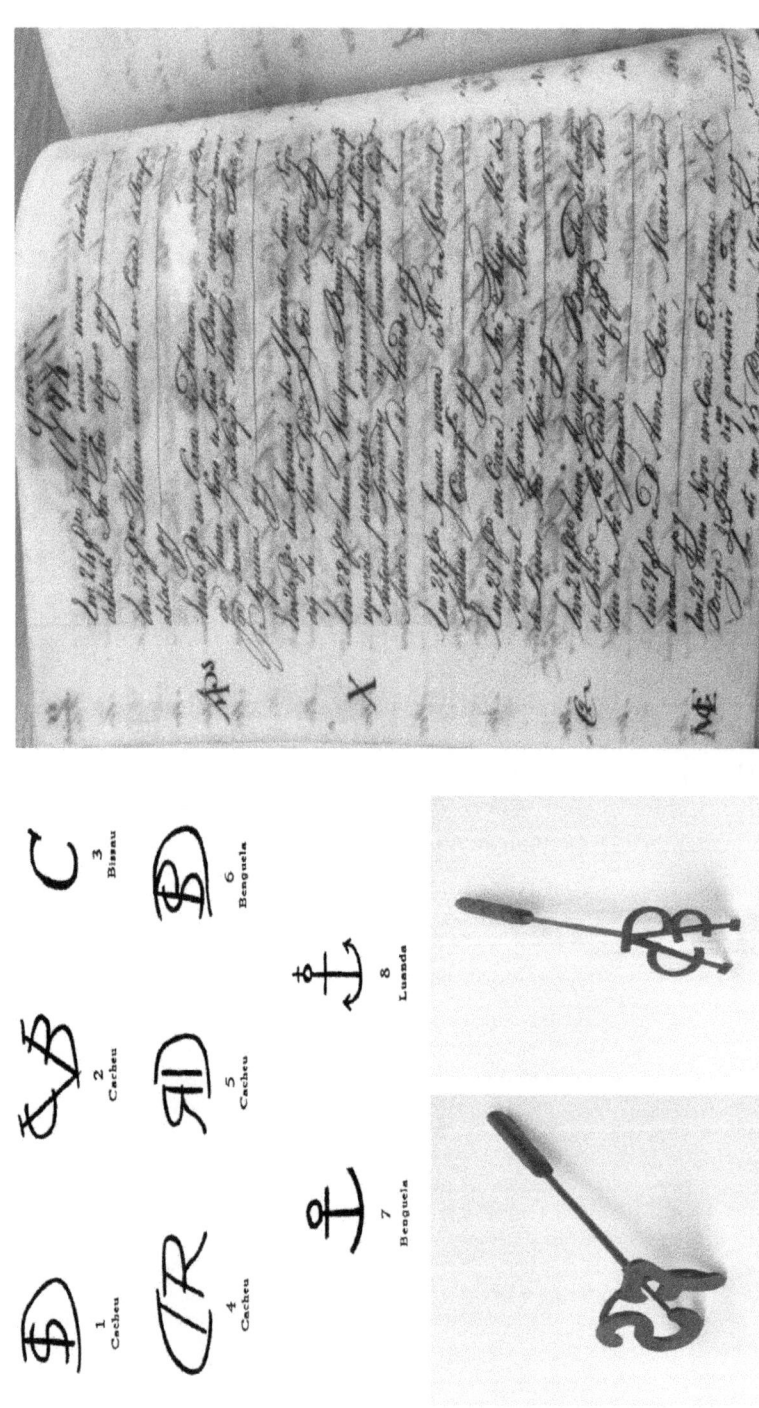

FIGURE 13 Branding symbols used to mark the forehead or the side of the face or arm, so that people knew who a slave belonged to. Livro de Banguê, Arquivo Santa Casa, Salvador. Photograph by the author.

for bringing both parties into amicable agreement. However, the contradiction was obvious in that slave-masters as well as governors saw the return of the fugitive enslaved as an opportunity to inflict their punishment on the slaves. If slaves sought reconciliation with their masters before they were punished, they were making a conscious choice not to join the runaway community in what was termed the *mocambo*,[143] another word for *quilombo*, that is, a runaway enslaved community. The choice they made was then to exercise their freedom to be part of the community.

Slaves had their own mechanism of getting back at their masters, through the practise of 'witchcraft', and Portuguese settlers were aware of its use for this purpose in Salvador.[144] The settlers used the Inquisition tribunals as a way of dealing with the threat of witchcraft, or responded to it with violence. Although appropriating the power of the deceased to cause harm to the community was prohibited in Angola, as we saw in Chapter 2, in Brazil, the slaves used such powers to curb the violence administered against them by the slave-owners:[145]

They are aware that here at least they possess some advantage, because otherwise they might flee to some runaway settlement in the forest, and, if recaptured, might take their own lives before their master can whip them. Or some relative might take revenge upon them, using either witchcraft or poison.[146]

Festivals in Brazil were necessary for the enslaved Africans, according to Antonil, as they provided the slaves with some form of psychological release from their conditions. These festivals were more than just a celebration or a day of rest from normal work and had their origins in African

---

[143] *Quilombo* and *mocambo* both come from the Angolan Kimbundu language: they mean a type of military camp. However, in Brazil the words came to be associated with resistance to enslavement: *quilombos* and *mocambos* went in tandem with slavery in a country where every captaincy had a community of runaway slaves – there were *mocambos* in Bahia, São Paulo, Minas Gerais, Mato Grosso, Goiás, Pernambuco, Alagoas, Sergipe, Maranhão and so on. In the sixteenth century *mocambo* was used to refer to communities of runaway enslaved people; in the seventeenth century it was used interchangeably with *quilombo*. See Moura, *Rebeliões da Senzala*.
[144] On African witchcraft in the city of Salvador, Bahia, Brazil, see Municipal de Salvador, 1640–1680, vol. 128, p. 71.
[145] Most enslaved Africans believed that witchcraft could be used to ill effect and that any person or group of people using sacred knowledge and power for personal gain or destructive purposes might be destroyed by the very power they attempted to manipulate. See Jacob U. Gordon, 'Yoruba Cosmology and Culture in Brazil, A Study of African Survivals in the New World', *Journal of Black Studies*, 10 (2), 1979, pp. 231–244.
[146] Andreoni (Antonil), *Cultura e Opulência*, p. 21.

practices. Prior to the arrival of the Portuguese, yearly festivals were held by many African societies.[147] They could also be announced either by the community or individuals if the need arose, such as for natural disasters like crop failure, pestilence, lack of rain, infant mortalities or an important occurrence akin to the swearing-in of a king.[148] During such festivals, an individual in the crowd or a priest might enter a trance, and this was taken as a good sign since it meant that a deity had 'possessed' or entered into the community and was demonstrating their presence.

According to Antonil, to totally deny the enslaved their leisure, their sole relief from slavery, was to wish them misery and melancholy, and an apathetic and sick body. For this reason, masters were better advised not to object when, on a few days each year, the slaves appointed their kings and sang and danced for a few hours, or when they sought some pleasure in the afternoon after they passed the morning celebrating the feasts of Our Lady of the Rosary of St. Benedict, the patron saint of the plantation chapel.[149]

The yearly festivals in Africa (both Angola and Nigeria) still aim to link the living with the dead, and to provide entertainment when a special occasion demands it. It is a way of keeping in touch with the ancestors – a circular and constant practice for most Africans. Through the festival the living seek to pacify or eliminate any evil influences arising out of witchcraft. The festival is also about social harmony. It seeks to ensure that all the reproductive processes are encouraged. Thus, human fertility is a vital concern, as is success in farming. Reconciliation and forgiveness are an essential ingredient, for example, of Gèlèdé in Nigeria – a festival that always tries to encourage the return of harmony in human relationships. Gèlèdé celebrates the power of others, and venerates female ancestors' spiritual power in the community.[150] For the enslaved Africans in Brazil, this was fundamental for a number of reasons. They could easily interpret their enslavement in Brazil as a misfortune that came about because the spiritual forces of their community in Africa were not in harmony with the living. Violence inflicted on them by their masters in Brazil could also be seen as punishment from the ancestors for this lack of harmony. Not

---

[147] Gordon, 'Yoruba Cosmology'.
[148] See John D. Y. Peel, *Religious Encounter and the Making of the Yoruba*, Bloomington, IN: Indiana University Press, 2003, and see also Gordon, 'Yoruba Cosmology'.
[149] See Gordon, 'Yoruba Cosmology'.
[150] See Babatunde Lawal, *The Gèlèdé Spectacle: Art, Gender, and Social Harmony in an African Culture*, Seattle, WA: University of Washington Press, 1996.

celebrating Gèlèdé's festival showed a lack of responsibility towards the spiritual world.

The Portuguese conquest of Bahia and Angola was full of contradictions. Some settlers were prepared to accept difference and live with conquered people as they were. Others were inclined to opt for Christianisation through education, hoping that the Indigenous people would abandon their worldview. Finally, there were those who were eager to combine both humane and spiritual practices of healing the body by applying Western conventional medicine while converting souls to the Christian God. In fact, the urban planning of Indigenous Brazilians' villages began with the intention of preventing their settlement in hinterlands, and with the aim that the Americans could be baptised, formed into communities of the Church and conditioned to the Portuguese way of life.[151]

However, to acculturate the Indigenous people of Brazil was never an easy task. The Indigenous people were not a *tabula rasa*, nor ready-made for the Portuguese way of life. They contested the new forms of living introduced by the Portuguese, whom they saw as *conquistadores* invading their land and meddling with their politics.[152] They resisted by attacking the newcomers' settlements.[153] The city of Salvador was under constant attack, and settlements on the outskirts of the city, such as Cayru, were hardest hit. The city-dwellers of Salvador hired infantry, particularly *bandeirantes*[154] from São Paulo, to resist the incursions of the Indigenous people.[155] Reinforcements were also sent from Lisbon. In 1669, three years before the arrival of the royals in Salvador, the

---

[151] Pitta, *Provincia da Bahia*, pp. 100–101.

[152] For a detailed study of Salvador settlement and the Natives reaction to it see Pitta, *Provincia da Bahia*.

[153] For the attacks on Portuguese settlements in Salvador and Pernambuco, see Guida Marques, 'Do Índio Gentio ao Gentio Bárbaro: Usos e Deslizes da Guerra Justa na Bahia Setecentista', *Revista Histórica*, 2014, 171, p. 22: http://dx.doi.org/10.11606/iss n.2316-9141.rh.2014.89006.

[154] *Bandeirantes* were Brazilian soldiers mainly from São Paulo who were used to fight wars in Brazil. Their role was similar to that of the *guerra preta* in Angola. For further discussion, Luiz Felipe de Alencastro, 'South Atlantic Wars: The Episode of Palmares', *Portuguese Studies Review*, 19(1/2), 2011, pp. 35–58, p. 36, 'in the second quarter of the 17th century two major regional armed forces emerged in Portuguese America: the *bandeirantes*, or *paulistas*, generally mestizo militias from São Paulo captaincy in the south, who launched slave hunting expeditions against the southern Indian tribes, and the Pernambuco and Paraiba volunteer forces who fought the Dutch occupation of Northeast Brazil from 1630 to 1654.'

[155] See Pitta, *Provincia da Bahia*, p.262.

governing authority of Bahia appointed Captain Manoel Barbosa de Mesquita to head a battalion to help quell the Indigenous peoples' insurgency. Yet, even with these reinforcements, Mesquita fell victim to the Indigenous people and was killed three months after his arrival in Salvador.[156]

As mentioned, the godfather of the royals was Afonso Furtado do Rio de Castro de Mendonça. He was appointed as governor a year before he received the royals in Bahia, on 8 May 1671,[157] and proved to be 'a governor that the position was seeking, not a man who was seeking to be governor ... his name was Afonso Furtado de Castro do Rio de Mendonça, which always for this state will be of glorious memory'.[158] He was born and bred in Bahia.[159] He knew the problems of the city and its dangers, and promised to free Bahia from the scourge of the Indigenous people when he was sworn in as governor of the city of Salvador: 'I say ... to you, noble ecclesiastics, distinguished secular gentlemen, royal magistrates of justice, gentlemen and good men of the city. My account consists ... to liberate your country from the indomitable barbarian.'[160] He asked for reinforcements from São Paulo and, in 1672, when the royals had spent a year in Salvador, he brought *bandeirantes* from São Paulo. A force comprising both Indigenous people and *bandeirantes* Paulistas, and led by João Amaro, an Indigenous individual born in Bahia, took Cayru, which was the Indigenous people's land, and handed it back to the Portuguese.[161]

Before his army attacked Cayru, Furtado de Mendonça met with Salvador's war council, which was composed of a group of leaders of soldiers and Apostolic missionaries, to seek their approval for the war. The war was approved, citing legislation on the already mentioned 'just wars', decreed by King João IV in 1655. The decree stated that in the case of a 'just war', the Indigenous people could be enslaved. In that case, the *encomienda*, or law of conviviality with the Indigenous people, was not to be followed. Cayru fell and its people were captured and sent into captivity or sold as slaves. Their value as slaves plummeted in the market in Salvador: 'they were sent into slavery in the City of Bahia, where they were sold for a derisory price, those with the best physical appearance were not

---

[156] See Pitta, *Província da Bahia*, p.262.
[157] See Cadas, 'Notícia Geral de Toda Esta Capitania da Bahia Desde'.
[158] Stuart B. Schwartz (ed.), *A Governor and His Image in Baroque Brazil: The Funeral Eulogy of Afonso Furtado de Castro do Rio de Mendonça by Juan Lopes Sierra*, trans. Ruth E. Jones, Minneapolis, MN: University of Minnesota Press, 1979, p. 45.
[159] Russell-Wood, *Fidalgos and Philanthropists*, p. 203.
[160] Schwartz, *A Governor and His Image*, p. 37.   [161] Pitta, *Província da Bahia*, p.262

sold beyond twenty cruzados, most of them were sold for less'.[162] Many of them died as they were, according to Pitta, not used to the work of *engenhos* and other farm work:

The majority was sent to Recôncavo to be sold for work in the sugar fields, mills and other *engenho* farms of ours. However, as the heathens of Brazil are not used to daily farm work, as are those from the African coast, and only till the land when in need, laze around when they have food to eat. They felt a new way of life, the forced labour, and not work done voluntarily, as they used to do of their own will, to which they have lost, and they hated it, and at the thought of enslavement, countless many have died.[163]

The Indigenous Cayru lands were divided up among the soldiers who fought the war. Here we see a war that reflected those in Angola; lands taken from the people of Cayru were given to the leaders of the soldiers and to other powerful people in the City of Salvador. João Amaro was rewarded by King Pedro II with the greatest parcel of land: 'he was given the right to build in those lands, where for the part of Bahia founded a veneration Town for Saint Anthony, commonly called João Amaro, less populated for its great distance'.[164] Although the Indigenous people's insurgency was given as the pretext for the war on Cayru, it was in fact driven by a desire to secure the precious metals believed to exist in the vicinity.[165] Economic interests drove the destruction of Cayru, just as they drove the destruction of Pungo-Andongo when João Hari II and Diogo refused to allow their kingdom to be used to enslave other Angolans.

At the time Cayru was taken, Bahia was suffering from a shortage of enslaved people from Africa.[166] Furtado de Mendonça had been forced to send a petition to King Pedro II asking for more African enslaved because

---

[162] Pitta, *Provincia da Bahia*, p.268, 'foraõ remettidos os cativos à Cidade da Bahia, onde eraõ vendidos por taõ inferior preço, que os de melhor feição naõ passavaõ de vinte cruzados, os mais por muito menos'.

[163] Pitta, *Provincia da Bahia*, p. 269 'a mayor quantidade se enviou para o Recôncavo a vender para o serviço das canas, Engenhos, e outras fabricas das nossas lavouras. Porém como os Gentios do Brasil naõ tem por costume o trabalho quotidiano, como os da costa de Africa, e só lavraõ quando tem necessidade, vagando em quanto tem que comer, sentiaõ de fórma a nova vida, o trabalhar por obrigaçaõ, e naõ voluntariamente, como usavaõ na sua liberdade, que na perda della, e na repugnancia, 'e pengaõ do cativeiro, morrendo infinitos'.

[164] Pitta, *Provincia da Bahia*, p. 269, 'concedeulhe faculdade para a edificar naquellas terras, onde para a parte da Bahia fundou o Villa da invocaçaõ Santo Antonio, chamado vulgarmente de Joaõ Amaro, pouco povoada pela grande distancia'.

[165] Pitta, *Provincia da Bahia*, p.270.   [166] See Schwartz, *A Governor and His Image*.

many were dying, and the town was growing.[167] Father Antonio Vieira also requested that enslaved people be sent from Angola to Bahia on behalf of the New Christians living in Bahia:

> ... it is Brazil that supports the commerce, and customs, and flame to our ports. These few foreign ships that we see in the ports, they had no unity in the River Plate. There is no money, and for the lack of Angolan slaves, soon there will be no sugar [in Brazil], because this year, if it does not reap more than half çafrã, and in the following years, it will forcefully be less each year. For lack of Blacks from Angola, it is not possible to supplement with slaves from other parts, because they are incapable of coping with the work of cane fields and sugar plantations.[168]

The Indigenous people sold to the sugar fields and mills, and other farms in Bahia, may have had a considerable impact on the enslaved Africans they worked alongside.[169] We must not underestimate the kind of network that may have existed among the enslaved Africans and the Indigenous people in the Recôncavo and how this may have increased the City Council of Salvador's anxiety about the possibility that the royals might join the fugitive community in Palmares. The Battle of Cayru may well have been a turning point in the royals' stay in Salvador. Indigenous people sent to work in the *engenhos* after the battle certainly came into contact with slaves who had been forced to move from Alagoas in Pernambuco – where the Palmares community was – to Bahia, particularly during the Dutch takeover of the

---

[167] See Furtado and Viera's plea for more enslaved people in Bahia, *Documentos Históricos dos Arquivos Municipal, Cartas do Senado 1673–1684*, vol. II, Prefeitura do Municipio do Salvador, Bahia, p. 20, and Padre Antonio Vieira 'Proposta de Vieira por parte dos Cristãos Novos a el Rey'.

[168] On Vieira's request for more enslaved people from Angola, see Graça Barreto, *Monstrusidades do Tempo e da Fortuna*, ms. 16, fl., 189 v, 'o Brasil que hé o que sustenta o commercio, e Alfandegas, e chama a os nossos portos, esses poucos navios estrangeiros, que nelles vemos, cõ a desunião do rio da Prata, não tem dinheiro, e cõ a falta de angola, sedo naõ terá assucar, porque já este anno, se não recolhe mais que meya çafrã, e nos annos seguintes será forçosamente caad ves menos, porque a falata de Negros de Angola, naõ se pode suprir cõ escravos de outra parte, por serem incapazes de aturar o trabalho dos canaviais, & engenhos.'

[169] In Table 3, we see the enslaved Africans and the Natives are working together in different farms in Pernambuco. There were three types of farmers – *lavradores de cana-livre* (who worked independently of the *engenhos*), *lavradores de cana-obrigada* (who worked for *engenhos* or obtained farmers to work for *engenhos*), and *lavradores arrendatários* (who used the lands that belonged to *engenhos* and hired lands to produce for *engenhos*) – and who were also called 'third', 'fourth' or 'fifth' parties in the terminology of the seventeenth century. These farmers retained about 3.5 per cent of the harvest; in general, farmers retained between 10 and 17 per cent. See *Documentos para a Hitória do Açúcar – Legislação*, Rio de Janeiro: Instituto do Açúcar e do Álcool, 1954, and Vera Lúcia Amaral Ferlini, 'A subordinação dos Lavradaores de Cana aos Senhores de Emgenho: Tensão e Conflito no Mundo dos Brancos', *Revista Brasileira de História*, 6(12), 1986, pp. 151–168, p. 161.

Mendonça's Journey: Princes of Pungo-Andongo in Brazil

FIGURE 14 View of St. Salvador. Artist unknown, Museu de Arte da Bahia (MAB), Salvador. Indigenous people are depicted in the foreground, roasting the limbs of their enemies before eating their flesh. Photograph by the author.

region between 1635 and 1638, when as many as 4,000 moved to Bahia.[170] This created a network of both Indigenous Americans and enslaved Africans with an easy connection to Palmares.

In an illustration of the period (see Figure 14), it becomes clear that the biggest threat to the security of the city of Salvador in the period were the Indigenous people, without eliding their collaboration with the enslaved Africans. The image depicts the Indigenous people literally devouring the Europeans. They gaze upon the city of Salvador from the Isle of Itaparica, separated only by the Bay of Todos os Santos. Significantly, the danger is not far away.[171]

Itaparica in the seventeenth century had a good number of *engenhos* (see Figure 15). On the right, on the Isle of Itaparica, there is Engenho de

---

[170] Stuart B. Schwartz, *Sugar Plantations in the Formation of Brazilian Society: Bahia, 1550-1835*, Cambridge: Cambridge University Press, 2010, p. 134.
[171] The gaze from the painting looks from Itaparica island towards the city of Salvador, the capital of Brazil at the time. Salvador was surrounded by protective walls.

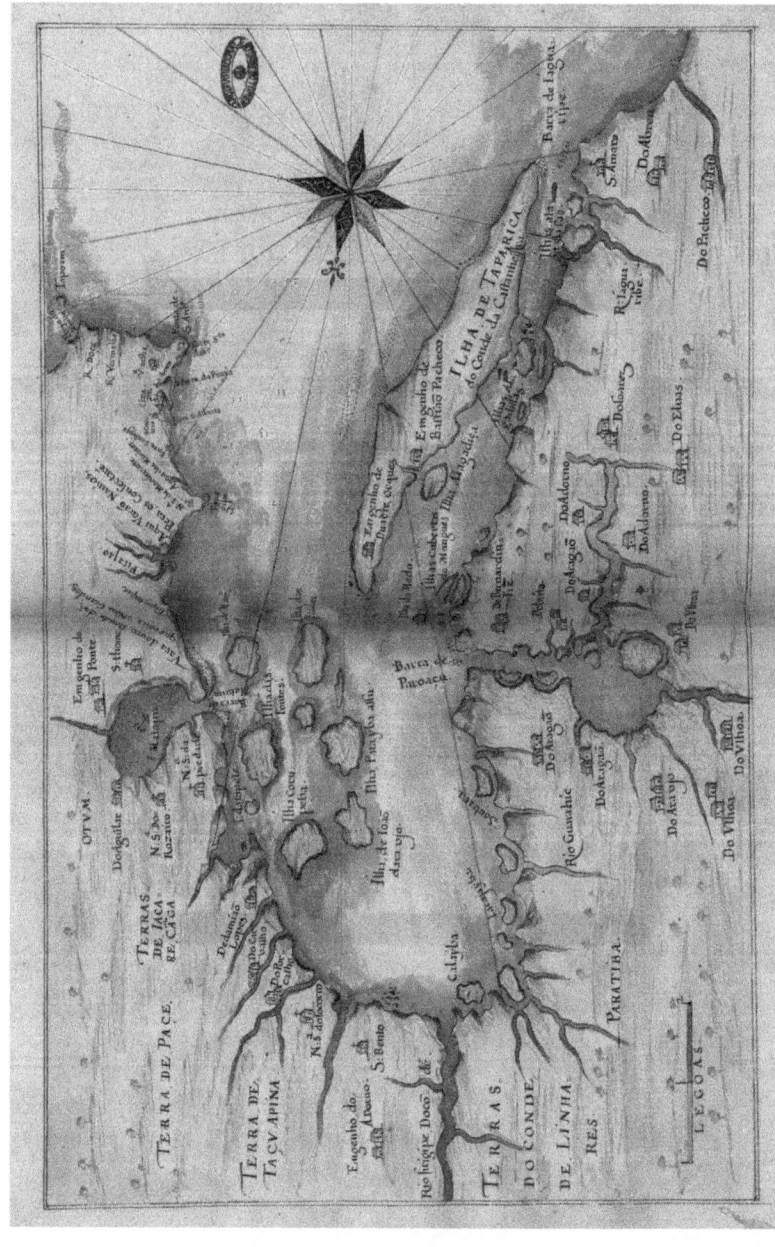

FIGURE 15 Map indicating *engenhos* in seventeenth-century Bahia. *Atlas Universal*, João Teixeira Albernaz (1640).

Duarte Orques and Engenho B. Utiaõ Pacheco. On the left there is Engenho Real, owned by Conde de Linhares, mentioned by Antonil. Above the river Sergipe Docõ, there is Engenho of A. Dorvo, In front is the city of Salvador. At the top there is Engenho de Ponte.

The city of Salvador was not a pleasant place for the colonial élite during the years of the royals' stay, threatened as it was by Indigenous people and fugitive enslaved Africans. The most important event of the war against the residents was also predicated on the idea that both enslaved Africans and Indigenous Americans joined forces to attack the city. The Indigenous Americans were associated with Africans of the Palmares, similar to those of Alagoas. The City Council of Salvador made a mention of this on 9 September 1672.[172] Historians have so far failed to detect this connection and conviviality between the Africans and Indigenous people in the hinterlands. The attack on the city was not unilateral, but rather bilateral, with the Africans joining forces with the Natives.[173] The threat from the Indigenous Americans and Africans worried the City Council, who associated it with Palmares, making the presence of the royals in Salvador unsustainable. There was no reason for the royals to stay in the city; their presence there was increasingly provoking suspicion. Furtado de Mendonça had to heed the voice of the City Council of Salvador and move the royals to Rio de Janeiro. Hence, he was fearful of the connection the royals might have with Africans in Palmares in 1673 and the prospect of the royals joining them. Palmares was equated with the violence that the 'non-tamed' or 'unseasoned - non conquered' Indigenous people usually carried out on the Portuguese settlements. The Africans of Palmares were believed to have a collaboration with the Indigenous people against the Portuguese. My contention is that Mendonça had to leave because the authorities in Salvador said he had similar goals to the Palmarinos.

On 9 September 1672, the City Council of Salvador requested support from the Crown in Lisbon to destroy Palmares:

... the cruelty we all suffer from the heathen of Angola that are in Palmares and as well those from surrounding land, your majesty will show your reward so that the

---

[172] See 'Atas da Camara' [City Council Minutes], fl. 23v, lhs. 1a10, 9 November 1672, p. 75. See also 'Ordens Régias' [Royal Orders], cap. XXI, vol. 6, vol. IIa, 159v, n. 231, Arquivo Público Estadual de Pernambuco, Brazil, Arquivo da Universade de Coimbra.

[173] The Indigenous Americans often rose to counter unfounded Portuguese attacks. The war against the Natives in the hinterland in Bahia intensified from 1660 onwards, after the expulsion of the Dutch from Brazil. Bahia continued to be attacked by the Natives, who had appropriated weapons from the Dutch. See Marques, 'Do Índio Gentio'.

Governor wages war on them as it deserves to your Royal Service as for the well-being of those who are in the Captaincy of Pernambuco, so these enemies can be obliterated.[174]

In Bahia, it was clear that the Indigenous people and the Africans were seen as threats to the interests of the settlers. So, the council's petition to the king of Portugal or regent was to ask for support, but also for the licence to eliminate the Indigenous people from Bahia: 'if you were to look at evil things that have been caused to the State of Brazil by the Natives, it was not only that they were made captives, but also to decree that they be eliminated once and for all'.[175] As Marques put it, the category of 'Indigenous' underwent a profound change; the Indigenous came to be described as 'barbarous', giving the *conquistadores* a right to make a claim that their actions against them were justifiable.[176] The desired elimination of the Indigenous people required a rhetoric that justified it, even while the real objective for repressing them was the appropriation of their resources.[177]

Fear of the Indigenous people and Africans revolting in Bahia had been a feature since the city's inception and this became more acute during the Dutch occupation of Brazil, when both Africans and the Indigenous Americans allied with the Dutch against the Portuguese. Thus, fear of revolt became a destabilising factor from the point of view of the Bahian governing authorities of the seventeenth century, as was the existence of Palmares, which was seen as a potential ally to the Indigenous people. In section 3.6 I look at the connection between the royals and the enslaved Africans in Palmares in the State of Alagoas. This section explores the ideology of the community of fugitive slaves at Quilombo dos Palmares and the idea of liberation as a question of power. I examine new data on Palmares and how the community of enslaved Africans there forged a political and economic alliance with Cristovão de Burgos de Contreiras (known as Cristovão de Burgos), a judge in the High Court of Salvador

---

[174] 'Atas da Camara', p. 75, 'A opreSsam que padecemos todos Com o gentio de Angola queaSsiste I nos palmares e bem odaterra CircumveSinho Representara VoSsa merce aSua Magestade pa- I ra que o Governador lhe faça Guerra aSsim pello que conv[e]m a[Se] Real Serviço como pellas I conveniencias que que se seguem a esta Capitania de Pernambuco emseextinguirem estes inimigos'.

[175] See Marques, 'Do Índio Gentio', p. 29, 'se bem se considerer os males que ao Estado do Brazil vieram causados pelos índios, não somente os derão por cativos mas também se mandarão acabar por hua vez'.

[176] Marques, 'Do Índio Gentio', p. 22.   [177] Marques, "Do Índio Gentio', pp. 19–20.

and a man at the heart of the Portuguese governing authority in Brazil who sympathised with the Palmarists' economic model.

3.6 THE QUILOMBO DOS PALMARES AND ITS ALLIANCE WITH THE INDIGENOUS PEOPLE

To assume that Angolans in Angola did not know about Palmares or that Angolans only came to know about Palmares when they were in Brazil would be to ignore the existing connections between the continents of Europe, South America and Africa at the time, what Green terms an 'Atlantic mobility'.[178] Ships going back and forth to Angola and movement from both sides would lead one to acknowledge that long before the Battle of Cayru connections had already been made and that Palmares had already become known to Angolans.[179] As we saw in Chapter 2, some Kongolese returned to Angola after being enslaved in Brazil during and after the short period when Correia de Sousa was governor of Angola. There were also Africans who were returned from Bahia to Angola because it was feared that they would unite with the runaway enslaved people in Palmares.[180] The Ndongo royals, however, were not allowed to return to Angola for fear that they might take revenge for what had happened to their relatives during the war. Coupled with that, they already knew about the existence of *mocambo* as a force of resistance in Brazil, and knew that they represented the ideology believed in by the first rebellious generation of the House of Ndongo.

Many historians have attempted to understand what Quilombo dos Palmares meant then; many interpret Palmares and the Palmarists in the light of contemporary politics in Brazil. These historiographies can be

---

[178] Green argues that there was a trading relationship between free Africans and people in the New World in the sixteenth and mid-seventeenth centuries. See Green, 'Beyond an Imperial Atlantic'. See also Green, *The Rise of the Trans-Atlantic Slave Trade*; Ferreira, *Cross-Cultural Exchange*; Candido, *An African Slaving Port*; Luis Nicolau Parés, 'A Formação do Candomblé: História e Ritual da Nação Jeje na Bahia', *Revista de História*, 158, 2008, pp. 309–314; João José Reis, Domingos Sodré, um Sacerdote Africano: Escravidão, Liberdade e Candomblé na Bahia do século XIX, São Paulo: Companhia das Letras, 2008; Alencastro, *O Trato dos Viventes*; Ana Lucia Araujo, 'Dahomey, Portugal and Bahia: King Adandozan and the Atlantic Slave Trade', *Slavery and Abolition*, 33(1), 2012, pp. 1–19. See also Cohen, *Global Diasporas*.

[179] Cape Verdean traders in West Africa were doing business between Africa, the Americas and Europe prior to the seventeenth century. See Green, 'Beyond an Imperial Atlantic', pp. 100–101. Free carpenters were brought from Cacheu in modern Guinea-Bissau to Salvador, see See AHU, Baía, cx3, doc. 9; AHU_ACL_CU_005, cx. 2, D. 240, Brasil, Baía, 20 March 1694.

[180] See Birmingham, *Trade and Conquest*.

grouped chronologically and thematically as follows: retention of African culture or African republic; agency; commercial exchange with neighbours; self-sustaining and dependent; spatial negotiation between Palmarists and the Portuguese governing authorities; proletarian struggle; Black consciousness; and liberation of the downtrodden.[181] By Palmarists, we refer to those enslaved Africans who ran away and lived in the Quilombo dos Palmares. They called their community 'Little Angola' (in Portuguese: *Angola Pequena*) – a term that emerged in the Palmares documents (Documento n. 54).[182] There are some who view Palmares as a 'multicultural state'[183]

---

[181] See Palmares Documents transcribed and edited by Ennes, Ernesto Ennes, *As Guerras dos Palmares (Subsídios Para a Sua Sistória), Domingos Jorge Velho e a 'Tróia Negra'*, vol. I, 1687–1700, Rio de Janeiro: Companhia Editora Naciona, pp. 133–181. There are 95 documents that have been transcribed without commentaries on them (hereafter: Palmares Documents). See Palmares Documents, 'Documento n. 54, Requerim.to que aos pés de VMag.de humildem.te prostrado fás em seu nome ... ', in Ernesto Ennes, *As Guerras dos Palmares*, p. 336, 'dev'era não excogitar obstaculos, mas antes defendellos nela', 'Requerim.to que aos pés de VMag.de humildem.te prostrado fás em seu nome, e em aqulle de todos os officiaies e Soldados do terço de Infantra São Paulista de que hê M. e de campo Domingos George velho, que actualm.te serve a VMag.de na Guerra dos Palmares, contra os negros rebelados nas capitanias de Perna.co'. The document is referred to, but not dated, in Carneiro, *O Quilombo dos Palmares*, p. 323.

[182] On the development of the historiography of Palmares, see Silvia Hunold Lara to whom I am indebted here: Silvia Hunold Lara, 'Palmares and Cucaú: Political Dimensions of a Maroon Community in Late Seventeenth-Century Brazil', Conference paper, 29–30 October, Yale University, New Haven, CT, 2010. See earlier work on Palmares as an African republic by the Bahian historian, Pitta, *Provincia da Bahia*. For more nuanced debate on cultural retention, see also Rodrigues, *As Sublevações de Negros no Brasil*; Arthur Ramos, 'O Espírito Associativo do Negro Brasileiro', *Revista do Arquivo Municipal*, 47(4), 1939, pp. 105–126; de Freitas, *Reino Negro de Palmares*. See also Cheney's recent work on Palmares as an African state in Brazil, see Cheney, *Quilombo dos Palmares*. See also Moura, *Rebeliões da Senzala* ; Décio Freitas, *Palmares: A Guerra dos Escravos* [1973], 5th ed., Porto Alegre: Mercado Aberto, 1984; Ivan Alves Filho, *Memorial dos Palmares*, Rio de Janeiro: Xenon, 1988; Gomes, *Palmares. Escravidão e liberdade no Atlântico Sul*. See also Funari, 'Conflict and the Interpretation of Palmares'. For a detailed study of commercial exchange, see Gomes, *Histórias de Quilombolas*. On 'dependent', see Márcia Amantino, "Sobre os Quilombos do Sudeste Brasileiro nos Séculos XVIII e XIX', in Manolo Florentino and Cacilda Machado (eds.), *Ensaios Sobre a Escravidão*, Belo Horizonte: Editora UFMG, 2003, pp. 235–262. For 'negotiation', see Lara, 'Palmares and Cucaú'. On 'proletarian struggle', see Moura, *Rebeliões da Senzala*; Carneiro, *O Quilombo dos Palmares* and 'Panteão da Liberdade e da Democracia', in *Coleção das Leis da República Federativa do Brasil*, Brasília: Imprensa Nacional, 1996, p. 5,726, and on 'liberation of the downtrodden', see Richard Martin, 'Zumbi dos Palmares: Um Novo Tiradentes?', *Clio – Revista de Pesquisa Histórica*, 2002, pp. 233–247.

[183] See Russell-Wood, 'Black and Mulatto Brotherhoods'; Thomas E. Skidmore, 'O Negro no Brasil e Nos Estados Unidos', *Argumento*, 1993, 1(1), pp. 25–45; Eugene D. Genovese, *From Rebellion to Revolution: Afro-American Slave Revolts in the Making*

composed of Africans, Indigenous Brazilians, Jews, Moors, people of dual heritage and Europeans.[184] A highly heterogeneous group formed the community of Palmares and lived with a shared objective of liberation. Funari in his recent archaeological study of Palmares concludes that the 'diversity of material evidence from Palmares does not seem to confirm purity or homogeneity, but there is no reason to deny its potential to challenge racial discrimination and hatred'.[185]

According to Sebastião da Rocha Pitta (1660–1738), a Bahian born in Salvador and a historian, the community at Palmares started when forty Guinean men, former enslaved people from Pernambuco, left for Palmares and formed a republic there.[186] Pitta was a contemporary of the Palmares War (1695). His father João Velho Gondim was a captain, although it is not known whether he took part in the conquest of Palmares. What is certain is that Pitta's account of the events at Palmares is the most contemporary one that we have. According to him, the men living there were former enslaved people, but they had not been ill-treated by their owners, which remains a moot point.[187] In other words, these were men who had voluntarily decided to form a republic of their own with other men with a similar vision to live 'free of any domination'.[188] Pitta saw their community as a robust republic that was not based on Greek principles or ideology,[189] but on their own African ideals, hence an African republic in Brazil.[190] The group at Palmares was a league of friends, family and relatives or *macamba* who established a community in which to live and engage in business with the local people (see Figure 16).[191] Indeed, the word *macamba* (meaning friends, family, relatives in Kimbundu) would be a more fitting name than *mocambo*, as there was no sense that the group set itself up as a military encampment, even though it became necessary for them to engage in armed fighting.[192] It would not be far-

---

of the Modern World, Baton Rouge, LA: Louisiana State University Press, 1981; Stuart B. Schwartz, 'Mocambos, Quilombos e Palmares: A Resistência Negra no Brasil Colonial', *Estudos Econômicos*, 1987, 17, pp. 61–88. Here I am indebted to Funari.

[184] See Clóvis Moura, *Sociologia do Negro Brasileiro*, São Paulo: Ática, 1988.

[185] Funari, 'Conflict and the Interpretation of Palmares', p. 88. See also Genisete de Lucena Sarmento, *A Ocupação das Terras do Quilombo dos Palmares e a Criação de Vilas, Introdução à Hitória de União dos Palmares*, Maceió: CBA Editora, 2019.

[186] See Pitta, *Província da Bahia*.   [187] See Pitta, *Província da Bahia*, pp. 323–344.

[188] See Pitta, *Província da Bahia*, p. 324, 'viver isentos de qualquer dominio'.

[189] See Pitta, *Província da Bahia*.   [190] See Pitta, *Províincia da Bahia*, p. 324.

[191] For the use of the term *macamba* (friends), see Dias, *A Arte da Língua de Angola*, p. 4. Pedro Dias was a Jesuit priest who composed a Kimbundu grammar in seventeenth century.

[192] Querino, *O Negro Na Bahia*. Querino argues that Palmares was formed for the purpose of living in peace with its neighbours.

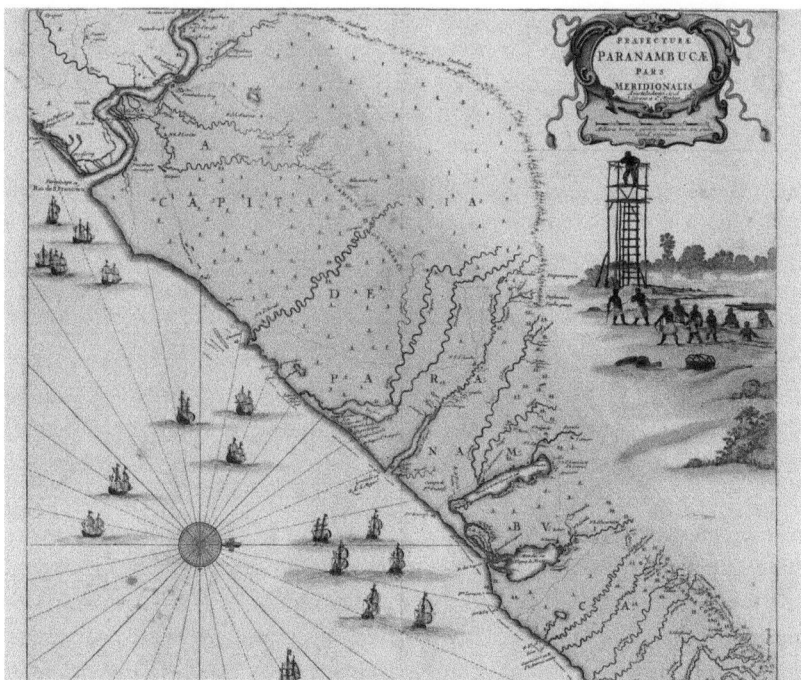

FIGURE 16 Map of Palmares, in the south of the Captaincy of Pernambuco, by Barleus (1647). There are no contemporary paintings of Palmares and Barleus's work is perhaps the only one available that shows Palmares. Public domain.

fetched to suggest that it was the Portuguese who used the term *mocambo* rather than *macamba* to describe the community for political reasons and to encourage support and justify their war against it.

Histories of Palmares have so far made no connection between members of Palmares with their homes in Africa and with the Brazilian-born political élites. What is known is that former enslaved Africans inhabited Palmares and formed a community there. Neither has the movement of enslaved Africans returning from Palmares, other *mocambo* or *quilombos*, or from Brazil more broadly, to Angola been established, nor has the Palmares community's economic partnership with Brazilian-born élites been researched. The documents that I uncovered suggest that Palmarists, or those with potential connections to Palmares, did return to Angola.[193]

---

[193] The documents show that some of men who rebelled against the Portuguese authorities were caught and exiled to Angola. See 'Ordens Regias' [Royal Decrees/Orders], Capitulo

In other words, Palmares was known in Africa, and Africa in Palmares. The case of the rebellion in the district of Camamú, in the Captaincy of Ilheus, could demonstrate that there was a network that linked enslaved Africans in Bahia with Palmares, even though the *mocambo* that is referred to here may just be a *mocambo* local to Bahia. Nonetheless, to discount the royals' potential connection with Quilombo de Palmares would be a bold move.

António Luís Coutinho da Câmara, the governor of Bahia from 1690 to 1694, and later a viceroy of India, considered it his key mission to destroy the existing *mocambo* or *quilombos* in the region. He informed Pedro II, king of Portugal, about the links connecting runaway enslaved people and the continuing danger and threat posed by the *quilombos*. Coutinho da Câmara sought help from the *bandeirantes*, as had his predecessors. The enslaved Africans in the district of Camamú, the Captaincy of Ilheus, staged a rebellion against the governing authority there: 'the Blacks were committing such crimes, that neither the Captain Major dared to come out of his house and Court Officials were not able to operate. Killing anyone whom they met, sacking all their goods, and finally making destruction, and committing tyrannies.'[194] *Bandeirantes* were called in, but even then, the rebellion continued. They were caught and brought to the High Court of Appeals in Bahia, and there they were found guilty: 'The High Court of Appeals sentenced five of them for being the main culprits, others who were more than thirty were exiled to Angola'.[195] Camamú's revolt exemplified the resistance of the most famous *quilombo* of all – Quilombo dos Palmares. The attack on the *quilombo* leaders was similar to that on Camamú. Like Camamú, Palmares was destroyed in 1695 because it posed a constant and very serious threat to the Portuguese authorities' economic interests in the region.

The measures taken by the Portuguese authorities in Brazil, as well as by Portugal, to prevent the Ndongo royals from staying in Brazil warrants a specific analysis accompanied by an examination of the histories of Palmares rooted in the ideology of runaway enslaved people in Angola.

XXI, vol. IIa, [159v] n°231, Arquivo Público Estadual de Pernambuco, Brazil (Arquivo da Universade de Coimbra).

[194] 'Ordens Régias'.

[195] 'Ordens Régias', 'obrando taes excessos, que nem o Capitáo mor se atrevia asahir fora de sua caza, nem os officiaes da Justiça apodiáo administrar matando aquem lhesparecia; soquestrandolhe osbens, efinalmente fazendo insolencias, etiranias ... ena Relaçam della foráo sentenciados sinco delles; por serem os principaes agressores, justiçados, eos mais que passaráo detrinta degradados para Angolla'.

In particular, this involves addressing the question of why enslaved people ran away in Brazil if slavery was, as many historians have claimed,[196] a normative practice in Africa. Indeed, an examination of the law regarding war captives in Angola, particularly in Mbundu society, throws light on the dynamics of runaway enslaved people in Brazil. As mentioned in Chapter 2, there was amnesty law used in Mbundu society in the seventeenth century and Angolan customary practices were underpinned by three principles: the Principle of Return or the Principle of Mucuâ; the Principle of Safe Haven; and the Principle of Asylum.

First, the Principle of Return or Mucuâ was based on the law of liberty, and on the ability of captives to exercise their liberty to gain independence, with the protection of the law. In his Kimbundu grammar, published in 1697, the Jesuit priest Pedro Dias[197] translated the term *mucuâ* into Portuguese as *abode*, which means a place of habitation. Thus the Principle of Return, that is, of returning home, was not simply about having the independence to achieve freedom, but about having the legal resources to free one's self when there was a legal precedent to achieve it.[198] This legal framework was the original place, a place of citizenship, home – *mucuâ* – and guaranteed *nbata rinène* or 'a great house' or community[199] to which an enslaved could return. According to Thiongo, home is a place of being, where we are taught the values of our legal system, philosophy, history, economy and our identity, in other words, who we are.[200] Accordingly, *mucuâ* is a site of Mbundu identity, which is not based on the Cartesian philosophy of being, *cogito ergo sum* ('I think, therefore I am')[201], but on the African philosophy 'I think, therefore we are'[202]. Crime was dealt with in this original place. If an accused was found guilty, his or her sentence and punishment were dealt with locally, and the guilty would repair the damage of the crime by either serving the plaintiff or giving gifts to make up any

---

[196] For a detailed discussion of Africa as a slave society, see Carvalho, *Das Origens da Escravidão*; Brásio, *Monumenta Missionaria Africana*. See also Boxer (ed.), *South China in the Sixteenth Century*, p. 152; Miller, *Kings and Kinsmen*; Heywood, *Njinga of Angola*. See Holl, 'Slavery and Suffering', and M'bokolo, *África Negra*.
[197] Dias, *A Arte da Língua de Angola*, p. 4.
[198] See the debate between Queen Njinga Mbandi and Fernão de Sousa, 'Carta de Fernão de Sousa a El-Rei', 22 August 1625; see also Pitta, *Provincia da Bahia*, pp. 324–344.
[199] See Dias, *A Arte da Língua de Angola*, p. 4, 'Nbata Rinène "Cafa grande", a great house'.
[200] See Thiong'o, *Decolonising the Mind*.
[201] See René Descartes, *Discourse on Method and Meditations on First Philosophy*, Oxford: Basil Blackwell, 1986, p. 65. René Descartes, *Specimina philosophiae*, Amsterdam: Elzevier, 1644.
[202] See John S. Mbiti, *African Religions & Philosophy*, London: Heinemann, 1969.

losses.²⁰³ The *soba* ensured that any punishment was fair for both parties. This legal system has survived in Angola until today.²⁰⁴

Second, the Principle of Safe Haven details the amnesty that applies to a fugitive who finds refuge with a powerful lord or a king. The fugitive may feel that legal process had not been followed in events leading to his or her capture or that the legality of his or her capture had not been proven. Seeking amnesty is fundamental to the captive achieving freedom, and amnesty could be sought from a powerful lord, who would use his power to protect the fugitive.²⁰⁵

Third, the Principle of Asylum covers cases where the accused could seek to leave his or her community after being found guilty or simply after being accused if there was not enough evidence to support his or her prosecution. The accused might leave his or her original location and move to another province, in which case amnesty would also apply, but she or he could never return to the location where she or he were accused of the crime, particularly in cases of crimes such as murder and witchcraft.²⁰⁶ Running away in such circumstances is not based on personal whim; there must be protection and a legal network in place to achieve it. If a fugitive did not know a powerful lord directly, she or he needed to be introduced to one by a representative.

In Brazil, the Principle of Safe Haven and the Principle of Asylum were applied by the runaway enslaved people through the formation of *quilombos* or *macambos*, which entailed the use of these principles. Thus, to run away from one's captivity was not done in a vacuum; one needed a safe haven. The first principle appears to have been used more frequently than the last in Brazil. Antonil noted that enslaved people, once guilty, could run away or commit suicide, but they normally sought reconciliation with the owners by reuniting with them.²⁰⁷

Quilombo dos Palmares could not have existed as a safe haven for as long as it did (1607–1695) without some form of legal space allowing for it. I argue that Brazil, in particular Palmares, was not a *terra nullis* ('unowned

---

²⁰³ See Fu-Kiau, *African Cosmology of the Bantu-Kongo*.
²⁰⁴ According to my interview with an Angolan Ph.D. student at Wolverhampton University. See also Batsîkama and Batsîkama 'Estruturas e Instituições' and Batsîkama, 'O Poder Político'. I obtained ethical clearance prior to the interview.
²⁰⁵ For further detail on asylum in Kongo, See Thornton, 'The Kingdom of Kongo'; Heywood, 'Slavery and Its Transformation', see also M'bokolo, *África Negra*.
²⁰⁶ See Isak Niehaus, *Witchcraft and a Life in the New South Africa*, Cambridge: Cambridge University Press, 2012.
²⁰⁷ See Andreoni (Antonil), *Cultura e Opulência*.

land'), nor was it *res nullis* ('unowned things'); it was not a kind of 'nobody's land'.[208] On the contrary, it belonged to the Indigenous Brazilians, who befriended Africans in the region. If it were not for their alliance with the Indigenous Brazilians, who allowed Palmares to exist, there would not have been a safe haven for Africans at Palmares. *Mocambos* were never a threat to the Indigenous people, who may have seen them as extensions of their own resistance. *Mocambos* represented a form of maintaining the Indigenous people's claim to the land. *Quilombos* would not have existed if they were not afforded protection from the so-called 'untamed' Indigenous people, the 'Indios Bravos' also known as 'Tapuyas Bravos – Pira-Tapuia'.[209]

There were also groups of Indigenous people who joined forces to protect themselves from the Portuguese attacking from Pernambuco. There were two particularly fierce groups of Native fighters in the region – the Cupinharôz and Precatiz. These Indigenous Brazilians could have fought against the Africans in Palmares if they wanted, but they never did; at least we do not have documentary sources to suggest that they did. For the Portuguese they, nevertheless, posed a threat:

> Cupinharôz and Precatiz ... are those who caused more harm to the settlers, and the Precatiz who hid themselves underground in wait for White settlers and with their bellies tied with robes, and they run much faster than horses, and they do not touch the ground, except with their toes. There are many other nations of the Natives that are around this ward that are not known by name. Those aforementioned above are those that we have been given names, or that at present wage constant wars against us.[210]

What is interesting is that the so-called untamed Tapuyas never saw Quilombo de Palmares or Africans in general as their enemies[211]. Instead

---

[208] See Sarmento, *Ocupação das Terras do Quilombo*.
[209] See Funari, 'Conflict and the Interpretation of Palmares'.
[210] See 'Documento n. 65', 'Dezcripção do certão do Peauhy Remetida ao Illm.o e Rm.o S.or Frei Francisco de Lima Bispo de Pernam.co.[Peauhy 2 de Março de 1697]', pp. 371–389, in Ernesto Ennes, *As Guerras dos Palmares (Subsídios Para a Sua Sistória)*, Domingos Jorge Velho e a "Tróia Negra", vol. I, 1687-1700, Rio de Janeiro: Companhia Editora Nacional, 1938, p. 389, 'Cupinharôz e Precatiz ... são os que tem feito mayores danos nesta povoação, e os Precatiz que se meterrão debaixo da terra pa. fazerem esperas aos brancos e com a barriga amarrada, com cordas correm mais, do que cavallos, e não tocão a terra senão com az pontas dos pez outras m.tas naçoens há no sercuito desta frag.a de que senão sabe nome, as asima ditas são as que nos derão, ou de prez.te dão guerra mais viva &c.' Ennes transcribed the documents that are termed 'Documents de Palmares' [hereafter Palmares Documents] in the archive in Portugal and they form part of his book's appendix. Thanks to him, these documents are now available to us.
[211] Tapuyas or Pira-Tapuia was a people group that lived in the region of Palmares. See Jean Léry and Janet Whatley, *History of a Voyage to the Land of Brazil, Otherwise Called America*, Berkeley, CA: University of California Press, 1990.

they turned their attacks on the Portuguese residence in Peauhy[212] and other areas of Pernambuco. Indigenous people and Africans lived together in Canindê.[213] They supported each other in a fight for survival; they worked together in the fields, herding cattle and trading.[214] The Africans, as well as the Portuguese, were being Tapuyanised. They lived like the Indigenous people, adopting their clothing, marriage and cultural practices.[215] Concomitantly, this intersection between the Indigenous people, Africans and White Europeans was not new in Bahia. In the late sixteenth century the *Santidade* movement arose in Jaguaripe.[216] This was described by Ronaldo Vainfas as an Indigenous movement or sect created in response to Portuguese violence in the region. As a movement, it was political as well as religious. It resisted Portuguese ideology that marginalised both Indigenous and Africans in Bahia. Vanifas states that: 'the *Santidade* movement was looming in plain sight in its haven in Jaguaripe, inciting revolts, setting Bahia on fire'.[217] As a movement its members included fugitive enslaved Africans and White Europeans. Vanifas declares: 'there is still no shortage of news about the adhesion of Blacks from Guinea, Mamelukes and even White people who converted to *Santidade* and practiced their ceremonies'.[218]

In Canindê and Peauhy, there were 112 farms out of a total of 129 farms in the region of Palmares.[219] Enslaved Africans worked on these farms alongside their Indigenous counterparts. There was also a dual

---

[212] See 'Documento n. 65'.
[213] See 'Documento n. 65'. Canindé was part of the Captaincy of Pernambuco; it currently belongs to the State of Ceará.
[214] See 'Documento n. 65', and Philip D. Curtin 'Sugar Planting: From Cyprus to the Atlantic Islands', in Curtin, *The Rise and Fall of the Plantation Complex*, pp. 17-28.
[215] See 'Documento n. 65'.
   See 'Documento n. 65'.
[216] For a detailed discussion of the *Santidade* movement in Jaguaripe, Bahia, see Ronaldo Vainfas, *A Heresia dos Índios: Catolicismo e Rebeldia no Brasil Colonial*, São Paulo: Companhia das Letras, 2010. See also Laura de Mello e Souza, *Diabo e a Terra de Santa Cruz: Feitiçaria e Religiosidade Popular no Brasil Colonial*, São Paulo: Companhia das Letras, 1987, and Carlos Carvalho and Moraes Sato, 'Geoprocessando as Relações Sociais na Cidade da Bahia – Século XVI', in Carlos Valencia Villa and Tiago Gil, *O Retorno dos Mapas: Sistemas de Informação Geográfica em História*, Porto Alegre: Ladeira Livros, 2016.
[217] Vainfas, *A Heresia dos Índios: Catolicismo*, p. 97, 'a Santidade se agigantava a olhos vistos no seu refúgio de Jaguaripe, incitando revoltas, incendiando a Bahia', p. 97.
[218] Vainfas, *A Heresia dos Índios: Catolicismo*, p. 97 'Não faltam notícias, ainda, sobre a adesão de negros da Guiné, mamelucos e até brancos que se converteram à santidade e praticaram suas cerimônias'.
[219] See 'Documento n. 65'.

heritage composition in the intake of enslaved on some of the farms: 13 per cent of those 112 farms had enslaved Africans and Indigenous Brazilians working and living together on these farms; 1 per cent of the farms owned four slaves; 1 per cent owned five slaves; 1 per cent owned six slaves; 1 per cent owned seven and only 1 per cent of the farms had a maximum of twelve slaves. The farms formed a trade network in the region that exchanged goods in Pernambuco, Maranhão and the Spanish Indies.[220] As we can see from these numbers (see Table 5), there was conviviality between the enslaved Indigenous Americans and Africans. They lived and worked together and married each other. This demonstrates the kind of solidarity that Mendonça was able to tap into when he was galvanising support from different constituencies in the Atlantic for his court case.

The ethnic composition of the Tupi-Indigenous Americans in the region supports my claim that Palmares was a heterogeneous community (see Table 6)[221]. It reveals that while the farms were created by Europeans, they were cultivated by a diverse range of peoples drawn from the region.

In Canindê and Peauhy enslaved Africans and enslaved Indigenous people were put together to work on different farms owned by different Portuguese or Paulista owners.[222] Among these enslaved labourers, there was a great degree of conviviality, and the owners appeared to exercise less control over the enslaved working on these farms. The closeness with which the enslaved Africans and Indigenous Americans lived and worked together must indicate that they shared an understanding among themselves. It was this kind of shared meaning that created a network between the Indigenous Americans and the enslaved Africans that in turn attracted the fugitives enslaved Africans in the region to Palmares. Sarmento argued recently in her book, *A Ocupação das Terras do Quilombo*, that Jorge Velho, the captain charged with destroying Palmares in 1695, lived in Peauhy for a while. It was from there that he gathered knowledge from the Indigenous Americans that helped him destroy Quilombo dos Palmares.[223]

The analysis of the composition of the farms from Caninde and Peauhy in the seventeenth century serves to illustrate the type of lives that fugitive

---

[220] See 'Documento n. 65'.
[221] These thirty-seven different people groups of Indigenous Americans in Brazil never waged war on Palmares.
[222] Sarmento, *A Ocupação das Terras do Quilombo*.
[223] See Sarmento, *A Ocupação das Terras do Quilombo*.

TABLE 5 *The 129 farms in Canindé and Peauhy, Palmares. By the author, based on 'Documento n. 65'*

Farm's numbers	Farm's name	Farm owner's name	Slave's name	Slave's ethnicity	Gender	Status	Number of owners per Farm	Number of slaves per Farm	Leagues
	New Ward of Our Lady of Vitoria in the hinterland of Peauhy - Canindé = (Itaim Merim) North and South of Itaim								
1	Alagoa das Itariz	Manoel da Silva Soares	Natives		Females	Slaves	1	3	
2	Alagoa do Jaquaré	Christovão de Pinto Brito Sam Payo	Blacks		Males, female	Slaves	1	2	
3	Alagoa do Susuapara	Constatino Ferreira e Faria	Blacks		Male and female	Slaves	1	8	
4	Aldea	Jullião Gomes	Black		Male	Slaves	1	3	
5	Alegrete	Manoel da Rocha	Blacks		Male and female	Slaves	1		
6	Algodoins	Sebastiam Cardoso de Araujo and Alexandre Ferra	Blacks and Indigenous		Males	Slaves	2+1 = 3	2	
7	Almas Sanctas	Silvestre Gomez married to an Indian woman with 2 children	Native		Male	Slaves	1	13	
8	Angicos	Miguel Miz	Black and Indigenous		Males	Slaves	1	4	
9	Anta	Manoel Gonçalves Palha	Black		Male	Slaves	1	2	
10	Asusuapara	Capt. Major Andre Dias da Costa	Blacks		Male and female	Slaves	1	3	
11	Atalhada	Belchoir Gonçalves	Black		Male	Slave	1	2	
12	Barra	Andre Barbosa Correia and Raphael Barboza	Blacks		Male and female	Slaves	1	2	
13	Barreiras	Gregorio de Barros	Black		Male	Slave	1	2	
14	Batalha	Manoel Barboza	Black		Male	Slave	1	3	
15	Berlengas	Dionizio Dias Pera	Black		Male	Slave	1	5	
16	Bigode	Francisco Mendes	Black		Male	Slave	1		
17	Bitorocdira	Capt. Major Bernardo de Carvalho	Blacks		Male and female	Slave	1	2	
18	Boa Cea	Antonio Luiz	Black		Male	Slave	1	4	
19	Boa Vista	Gonçallo Nunes Teyxeira	Blacks		Male and female	Slaves	1	2	
20	Boa Vista	Luiz Mourinho	Black and Indigenous		Males	Slaves	2	2	
21	Boqueirão	Manoel Alves	Blacks			Slaves	3	6	

249

TABLE 5 (cont.)

22	Boqueirão	João de Soouza, Captain Alexandre Rebello de Sepulveda (Owner)	Blacks	Male and female	Slaves	2	2	2
23	Boqueirão	Paulo Affonso do Monte	Blacks	Male and female, female Natives	Slaves	1	3+4 = 7	2
24	Borotis	Franisco Antunes	Black	Male	Slave	1	1	2
25	Buraco	Antonio da Silva	Blacks	Male and female	Slaves	1	2	2
26	Cabeça do Tapuya	Ignacio Barboza da Gama	Black and Native	Males	Slaves	1	2	2
27	Cachoeira	Henrique Valente and Antonio Lopes				2		5
28	Campo Grande	Antonio Bento	Black	Male	Slaves	1	1	5
29	Campo Largo	João Rebello and João Ferreira das Neves	Black and dual heritage	Males and female	Slaves and female married to a slave	2	3	2
30	Cana Branca	Egaz Moniz de Seya Barreto	Blacks	Males and Females	Slaves	1	3+2 = 5	3
31	Canavieira	Francisco Cardozo de Amaral	Blacks	Male and female	Slaves	1	2	2
32	Carnahiba	Damazo Pinhro	Black	Male	Slave	1	1	2
33	Castello	Antão da silva	Black	Male	Slave	1	1	3
34	Catarenz	Manoel Pinto de Carvalho and Antonio Roiz Calvo	Blacks	Male and female	Slaves	1	2	4
35	Citio da Cruz	Francisco Affonso e Christovão Barboza Pra	Blacks	Males and female	Slaves	1	3	
36	Citio das Flores	D.os Barbosa	Natives	Males	Slave	1	2	
37	Citio das Manganas	Alvaro velho	Black	Male	Slave	1	1	20
38	Citio das Pedras	Miguel Gomez	Blacks	Male and female	Slave	1	2	2
39	Citio das Pimentas	Alferes João da Rua Siqueiros	Black and Native	Males	Slaves	1	2	3
40	Citio de Catherina	An. to Gomez, and Andre Gomez (owner) with a Native woman	Portuguese, Native and Blacks	Male and female; Indigenous	Slaves	1	3	
41	Citio de Cobra		Blacks (no white)	Male and female	Slaves?		2	3
42	Citio Debaixo	Franc.co Moniz	Black	Male	Slave	1	1	2
43	Citio do Mendes	João de Versa	Blacks	Male and female	Slaves	1	2	3
44	Citio Real	Miguel Rib.ro	Black	Male	Slave	1	1	
45	Corrente	Alferes Christovão Alz's da Palma, and Manoel Roiz	Blacks	Males and female	Slaves	2	3	
46	Craibas	Antonio Cunha Sotto Mayor	Black	Males and females	Slaves	1		2
47	Craibas	Luis da Silva	Blacks	Males and females	Slaves	1	3	2
48	Cural do campo	Manoel da Costa	Blacks	Male and female	Slave	1	2	10
49	Dor de Barriga	Gaspar Ferniz Salgado	Black	Male	Slave	1	1	3

250

50	Espinheiros	Fran.co da cunha		Blacks	Male and female	Slaves	1	2
51	Estereito	Simão Da Costa					1	3
52	Estereito	Manoel da Costa Farjado		Black	Male	Slave	1	2
53	Fazenda de Barra	Manoel Antunes trigo		Black	Male	Slave	1	
54	Fazenda de Egoas	Capt. Major D.os Affonso Certão (owner)	Fran.co	Black and Native	Male with his Native wife +5 daughters	Slave (an Accountant)	1	3
55	Fazenda grande	Antonio Gomez Pera		Black and Native female	Male and female	Slaves	1	5
56	Forta	Captain Major Antonio de Antas de Azevedo, Bar da Gama de Azevedo, and Fernando Velho da Gama		Blacks	Males and females	Slaves	3	2
57	Franqueira	André da Fraga		Black	Male	Slave	1	2
58	Gado Bravo	Franc.co Meyrelles		Black	Male	Slave	1	4
59	Gameleiras	Fran.co Machado Guimaraiinz		Indigenous female and Blacks	Males and female	Slaves	1	4
60	Gamelleira	Antonio Antunes		Black	Male, male and female	Slaves	1	2
61	Ginipapo	Francisco Gil do Reis		Blacks	Males and females	Slaves	1	2
62	Ginipapo	Miguel Pinheiro de Carvalho		Blacks	Male and female	Slaves	1	4
63	Goribas	Manoel Dias Braga		Black	Male	Slave	1	3
64	Gracioza	Francisco de Quadros					1	4
65	Ilha	Cribonies Cadeira					1	2
66	Inhingas	João Lobo		Blacks	Male and female	Slaves	1	2
67	Jacaré	Manoel Miz		Blacks	Male and female	Slaves	1	4
68	Jardim de S. Cruz	D.os de Aguiar and wife Mariana Cabral (the only married white man), and D.os da Silva		Natives	Males and females	Slaves	3	3
69	Jatobã	Alferes Lourenço de Souza Meirelles		Black	Male	Slave	1	
70	Jouzeiro	Manoel Barreto		Black	Male	Slave	1	2
71	Lagoa do Jacaré	Ant.o Affonso		Black	Male	Slave	1	
72	Lagoa Gr.de	Antonio dos Santos and Luiz Roiz Viana		Black	Male and female	Slaves	2	2
73	Maravilha	Gonçallo de Alm.da e Francisco de Alm.da		Blacks	Male and female	Slaves	1	2
74	Matto	Fran.co de Barros		Black	Male	Slave	1	
75	Mocaitã	Capt. Major Joseph Garcia Páz (owner) and Manoel Leitã		Portuguese, Native males and females, Blacks and mulatto	Males and females	Slaves	1	1+4+2+4+1 = 12	4
76	Mocambo	Domingos Lopez de Carvalho		Black and Indigenous	Male and female (Tapuye)	Slaves	1	2	2

TABLE 5 (cont.)

#	Place	Owner	Ethnicity	Gender	Status			
77	Olho da Agoa	João Barboza	Black and Indigenous	Males	Slaves	1	2	2
78	Onsa	Manoel de Araujo Velho	Black	Male	Slave	1	1	2
79	Os Espinhos	João Fran.co de Oli.vra	Blacks	Males, female and male	Slaves	1	2	3
80	Passagem	João Carneiro da Foneua	Blacks	Male and female	Slaves	1	2	2
81	Piedras	Sabatiam Pereira	Black	Male	Slave	1	1	2
82	Pico	D.os Gonçalves	Black	Male	Slave	1	1	2
83	Pobre	Pedro Alves de olivr.a	Black and Indigenous	Males	Slaves	1	2	4
84	Poçoinz de S. Miguel	Captain Major and Antonio Nunes				1		5
85	Porto Alegre	Francisco Cardozo da Rosa and Antonio de Sousa Branco	Tapuya	Male	Slave	1	1	3
86	Poty	Antonio Gonçalves	Blacks	Males and females	Slaves	1	4	3
87	Retiro	Antonio Fernandes	Black	Male	Slaves	1	1	2
88	Riacho	Joseph Freire de Andradde	Blacks	Males and females	Slaves	1	2	1
89	Rio Grande	Fran.co Frz de Lima	Blacks	Males and female	Slaves	1	3	7
90	S. Antonio	Domingos Antunes	Indigenous, Columinz and Tapuyas	Male and female	Slaves	1	2	
91	S. Antonio	Gonçallo Carneiro and Gaspar da Cruz	Blacks	Male and female	Slaves	2	2	3
92	S. Antonio	João Roiz	Black	Male	Slave	1	1	
93	S. Cosme	Manoel Ribeiro	Native	Male	Slave	1	1	
94	S. Franc.co de Xavier	Franc.co da Cunha and Ant. Payva	Natives	Males and females	Slaves	2	4	3
95	S. João das Flores	Balthesar Machado	Indigenous	Male and female	Slaves	1	2	
96	S. Matheus	Joseph Nunes Ferreira and Manoel de Vale	Blacks	Males and females	Slaves	2	4	3
97	S. Niculao	Salvadord João	Blacks	Male and female	Slaves	1	2	10
98	S. Pedro	Domingos de Carvalho	Natives	Male and female	Slaves	1	2	3
99	S. Vicente	Manoel Alz Quaresma	Blacks	Males and females	Slaves	1	4	3
100	Saco	Gonçalves Antunes	Blacks	Male and dual heritage	Slaves	1	2	
101	Saco	D.os Affonso Preto married to a dual heritage woman	Black	Male	Slave	2	1	1
102	Salinas	Ignacio Gomez, Alferes Silvestre da Costa Gomes de Abreu (owner) with an Indian and African women	Blacks	Males and females	Slaves	1	4+2 = 6 concubines	
103	Salinas	João vaz	Blacks	Male and female	Slaves	1	2	6
104	Salinas	João vaz	Blacks	Male and female	Slaves	1	2	6

252

105	Salinas	Manoel Per.a		Blacks	Males and females	Slaves	1	1	3
106	Sam Lazaro	Joseph Ribr.o de Castor		Natives	Males	Slaves	1	1	3
107	Sam Vitor	João Pinto		Blacks	Males, female, male, female	slaves	1	2	4
108	Sambahiba	Lucas va Vasquez Barboza		Black	Male	Slaves	1	1	3
109	Sambambaya	Aleixo de Barros Galvão, Alferes Bezerra Correia (owner)		Indigenous	Male, female Tapuyas	Slaves	2	3	2
110	Santa Roza	João Ferreira de Barros		Blacks	Male, male and female	Slaves	1	2	
111	Serra	Estevão Borges e Antonio Nunes		Blacks	Dual heritage, female, male, female	Slaves	2	3	3
112	Serra	Pedro Alves Pereira		Nativa	Male	Slave	1	1	2
113	Serra	Lourenço da Costa vellozo		Blacks and a dual heritage woman	Males and Female	Slaves	1	3	2
114	Serra Negro	Rodrigo		Blacks	Male and female	Slaves	1	2	
115	Serra vermelha	João feliz and M.el Lopez		Black	Male	Slave	1	1	3
116	Sobrado	Manoel Pinto		Blacks	Male and female	Slaves	1	2	1
117	South of Itaim	South of Itaim	South of Itaim	South of Itaim	South of Itaim	South of Itaim	South of Itaim	South of Itaim	South of Itaim
118	Susuapara	Maneul Travassos Borges		Blacks	Male and female	Slaves	1	2	2
119	Susuapara	M.el de araujo Costa		Blacks	Male and female	Slaves	1	2	2
120	Taboleiro Alto	Manoel dos Santos		Blacks	Male and female	Slaves	1	2	5
121	Tabua	Paulio Ferreira de Azavedo		Blacks	Male and female	Slaves	2	2	2
122	Tapera	Simão Da Costa and M.el Simoinz		Blacks	Males and female	Slaves	1	2	
123	Tapera	Fran.co Varella		Blacks	Male and female	Slaves	1	2	2
124	Tatú	Salvador Carneiro		Blacks		Slaves	1	2	
125	Tocano	Antonio Bezerra		Black and Indigenous	Male and female	Slaves	1	2	
126	Torre	Manoel Pereira		Black	Male	Slave	1	1	4
127	Tranqueira	Antonio Soares Touguia and D.os Alfonso Serra		Blacks	Males and female	Slaves	2	2+1 = 3	3
128	Varzea Branca	Barnabe de Araujo		Black slave and Tapuya	Male and female	Slaves	1	2	3
129	Vitoria	Antonio Alz		Blacks	Male and female	Slaves	1	2	

253

TABLE 6 *Unconquered Tapuyas who were at war with New Parish of N. S. da Victoria, Palmares. By the author, based on 'Documento n. 65'*

Names	Where they lived	Weapons
1 Aroachizes	Top end of Parnahiba	
2 Carapotangas	Top end of Parnahiba	
3 Aroquanguiras	Savauhy with entry to Parnhiba	
4 Preecatiz	Yrusuy with entry to Parnhiba	
5 Curuás	Top end of Goruguca	
6 Rodeleiros	Top end of Goruguca	(Discs)
7 Beiçudos	Top end of Goruguca	
8 Bocoreimas	In Goruguca	
9 Cupequacas	In Goruguca	
10 Cupicheres	In Goruguca	
11 Gutamez	On the River Mearim	
12 Goyias	On the River Mearim	
13 Anicauz (eat White people)	Top end of River Preto	
14 Aranhez	On the River Paranahiba	
15 Corerás	On the River Paranahiba	
16 Ayitetus	On the lower part of River Paranhiba	
17 Abetiras	On the much lower part of River Paranhiba	
18 Beirtés	On the lowest part of River Paranhiba	
19 Goaras	On the River Paranhiba	
20 Macamasus	On Moni and Igoará	
21 Nongazes (eat White people)	At the entrance of Para	
22 Tramambés (at peace with White people)	At the entrance of the River Paranhiba	
23 Anassuz and Alongâz (fear White people)	At the hinterland of Guapada	
24 Arûas (in peace with White people)	On the River S. Victor	
25 Ubatês	At the hinterland of Araripe	

(continued)

TABLE 6 *(continued)*

Names	Where they lived	Weapons
26 Meatanz	At the hinterland of Araripe	
27 Corsiâs	At the River Goroguea	
28 Lanseiros	At the River Goroguea	
29 Arayez	At the top of Peauhy	
30 Acumez	At the top of Peauhy	
31 Goaratizes	At the top of Canindê	
32 Jaicôs	At the top of Canindê	
33 Jendoiz	At the top of Canindê	
34 Ycos	At the top of Canindê	
35 Uriûs	At the hinterland of Araripe	
36 Cupinharôz (made many attacks on the residents)	At Canindê	
37 Precatiz (made many attacks to the residents)	At Canindê	

Africans and the Indigenous Americans that befriended them might have lived in the region and also in Quilombo dos Palmares. It can be assumed that the inhabitants of Palmares shared a variety of cultures, reflecting the multi-ethnic demographic of the region. They lived in peace among themselves or at least had an interdependent relationship with the neighbouring communities.[224] From both Table 5 and Table 6 we can glean the Palmarists' possible mode of living. At a time when Indigenous Brazilians were constantly revolting and battling against European invasions by the Portuguese and Dutch, it is significant that there is no record of conflict between the African inhabitants of Quilombo dos Palmares and the Indigenous Brazilians. Carvalho claims that 'in the private spheres of daily life, the colonists shared an identity that was much closer to that of the Palmarists than to the farm owners and other local

---

[224] For a full discussion of multiculturalism in Palmares, see Stuart B. Schwartz, *Slaves, Peasants, and Rebels: Reconsidering Brazilian Slavery*, Urbana, IL: University of Illinois Press, 1996; Funari, 'Conflict and the Interpretation of Palmares'; Cheney, *Quilombo Dos Palmares*; Aline Vieira de Carvalho, 'Archaeological Perspectives of Palmares: A Maroon Settlement in 17th Century Brazil', *African Diaspora Archaeology Newsletter*, 10(1), 2007, pp. 1–18.

elites'.²²⁵ And Anderson notes that 'the trade with Palmares was such that many colonists opposed war with the Palmarinos'.²²⁶

3.7 THE QUILOMBO DOS PALMARES, CRISTOVÃO DE BURGOS AND THE ROYALS OF NDONGO

In the region of Palmares, the Portuguese or white residents were called *colonos*, and they were seen as lawless by those loyal to the cause of the Portuguese Crown. They were accused of being an enemy of the people, and hence of the grand scheme of Portuguese conquest in Brazil, for 'their ambition made them the colonies of Blacks, and enemies of the people'.²²⁷ They were dependent on Africans for trade and security, and needed 'Africans to consent to allow them to settle on such lands [where] they [residents] were paying taxes of tools, gunpowder, lead, firearms and everything else that they have asked them'.²²⁸ Some of the residents could not meet these demands and had to leave. 'Those who left Palmares, did so because of the lack of these things [paying taxes], or loyalty that they already had shown them, and not because of the rebellion of the Blacks'.²²⁹ Palmarists afforded their subjects protection from their enemies.

Judge Cristovão de Burgos and his friend Manoel de Souza were among those accused of being *colonos*²³⁰ by a *paulista* and Captain of the *campo* [Field], called Domingos Jorge Velho, who was given the task of destroying Quilombo dos Palmares. Velho inculpated Burgos of paying taxes to Palmarists to allow him to set up a cattle farm near the runaway enslaved Africans in Palmares. The land Burgos wanted to retain in Palmares was an important meeting point for other trade routes in the region, and the best in the country. Velho argued that settlers who abandoned their farms did so because they were disloyal to the Palmarists, their 'Black masters',²³¹ and defaulted on their tax payments. Velho saw there were many settlers in this predicament: 'as many others were found in that

---

[225] Carvalho, 'Archaeological Perspectives of Palmares', p. 8.
[226] Anderson, 'The Quilombo of Palmares'. [227] 'Documento n. 54', p. 335.
[228] 'Documento n. 54', p. 335.
[229] See 'Documento n. 54', p. 335, 'Requerim.to que aos pés de VMag.de humildem.te prostrado fás em seu nome ... sua ambição os fazia ser colonos dos negors, e jnimigos dos povos; por.to pa que os taes negros os consentissem povoár em taes terras lhes pagavão tribute, de farram.tas de polvora, chumbo, de armas, e de tudo o mais q. ells lhes pedião: e q.do as largarão hera porq. Os taes Colonos faltavão com estas couzas, ou a lealdade, q. com ells professavão, e não p.la mera rebelião dos negros.'
[230] See 'Documento n. 54'. [231] See Cheney, *Quilombo dos Palmares*, p. 169.

similar situation, defaulting on their customary payment left them fearing the Blacks' retributions'.[232]

Judge Cristovão de Burgos 'was an octogenarian and a very wealthy man with plenty of land',[233] indeed the Salvador City Council described him as 'the wealthiest man in the country',[234] and it is significant that he was accused by Velho of preventing the conquest of Palmares for his personal gain and for conniving to derail conquest, which had already cost the Portuguese Treasury dearly in funding the fight against the Quilombo.[235] He was also charged with obstructing justice by interfering in the distribution of the lands that were to be given to the soldiers in the war on Palmares: 'rather than causing obstacles [to superintendents], he should have first defended them himself before justice'.[236] Velho made a direct complaint to King Pedro II, to stop Burgos for what he saw as the 'unjust ambition of one Bachelor, whose services are very less inferior to the supplements for many reasons'.[237] Burgos was born in Bahia, 'probably between 1615 and 1618'. He was sent to Coimbra, Portugal, for his education, where he gained 'a bachelor's degree in civil law; in 1644 he entered the royal employ. After a tour of duty as *juiz de fora* of Ponta Delgada in the Azores, he returned to Brazil, where he married widow Helena da Silva Pimentel[238] and thus married into a sugar mill family that was part of the City Council of Salvador's élite. In 1654, Burgos was appointed high court judge of Bahia and of Brazil for that matter. His appointment as a Brazilian-born judge did not go down well with the Portuguese Overseas Council, who did not want him in Bahia 'where he is a native'.[239]

It was significant that Burgos was accused by Velho of preventing the conquest of Palmares and of being one of the *colonos*, as these crimes

---

[232] 'Documento n. 54', p. 335.
[233] 'Documento n. 54', p. 336, 'octuagenario, e m.to rico' (eighty years of age and very wealthy).
[234] See Stuart B. Schwartz, *Sovereignty and Society in Colonial Brazil: The High Court of Bahia and its Judges, 1609–1751*, Berkeley, CA: University of California Press, 1973, p. 354.
[235] 'Documento n. 54', p. 317, 'q- em as m.tas expedições q- no espacio de quasi quarenta annos os Governadores de Pern.co mandarão com consideraveis poderes, a conquistallos, nunca poderão'.
[236] See 'Documento n. 54', p. 336, 'dev'era não excogitar obstaculos, mas antes defendellos nela'.
[237] See 'Documento n. 54', p. 337, 'serão postos a injusta ambição de hû Bacharél, cujos serviços são m.to inferiors ao dos supp.tes por muytas razoins'.
[238] For a detailed study of Cristovão de Burgos, see Schwartz, *Sovereignty and Society*, p. 353.
[239] As cited by Schwartz, *Sovereignty and Society*, p. 354. See also Consulta CU, 8 August 1656, AHU, Bahia, papeis avulsos, Caixa 8 (2nd series non-catalogued).

would constitute high treason. Palmares was not new to Burgos: thirty-five years before the final war on Palmares in 1694, 'he had received a large land grant on the São Francisco River in 1659 but his major property holdings were in the Recôncavo parishes. Besides land which he owned in Santo Amaro de Pitanga, Burgos controlled three sugar mills, two in the parish of Paripe and the other in Passé.'[240] He was accused of greed and opportunism for wanting to gain lands in Palmares at any cost. According to Velho, Burgos was 'not happy with others [lands] and lots of land that he has in the hinterland, which he acquired against all justice'.[241]

If Velho's claim is to be taken seriously, then Burgos might well have been a long-term partner of the Palmarists, and might have viewed them as counterweights to the Portuguese Crown's political and economic interests in Brazil. In 1675, the City Council of Salvador charged Burgos with non-payment of taxes. He probably used his power to avoid paying taxes, or his refusal to pay, it could be argued, demonstrated a form of opting-out from the Portuguese Crown's claims on Brazil. It also shows that his loyalty lay elsewhere, perhaps with the Palmarists' claim for independence as an African republic.[242] The Palmarists taxed their subjects, who in return were offered protection from their enemies. Palmares's neighbours or people who lived in the area of Palmares were given a mark so that they could be distinguished from other people who were not from there. Burgos's economic and political interests in the region would have been protected by the Palmarists. His dispute with the governing authorities in Bahia, and his connection with Palmares is politically significant because of the link made with the royals of Ndongo with Palmares and the Brazilian authorities' fears about their stay. If the royals really represented a threat to Brazil, perhaps Burgos would have seen them as the perfect allies for maintaining his business interests in Palmares.

When the royals arrived in Salvador, there was already political turmoil and resentment generated by the Brazilian-born élite – the very élite to which Burgos belonged – who were being excluded from power sharing in Brazil. They were excluded from running for political office in the City Council of Bahia, particularly the role of supreme judge in the Court of Salvador, which was the seat of the Supreme Court of Brazil. Four months

---

[240] Schwartz, *Sovereignty and Society*, p. 354

[241] See 'Documento n. 54', p. 336, 'o qual não se contentando com outras m.tas sesmarias, q. logra neste sertão, contra toda a justiça'.

[242] Schwartz, *Sovereignty and Society*, pp. 354–355, states that 'Cristóvão de Burgos was not only a judge of the high court of Bahia, but a wealthy, well-connected *senhor de engenho* with slaves and dependents.'

before the royals arrived in Salvador, the Brazilian-born élite in the city protested to demand that the City Council revoke the decision to exclude them from office. Lima states that 'these brave patriotic individuals, without lack of due respect to the Majesty Throne'[243] sought justice, and that it was their rights as citizens to serve the Crown in their country. On 14 August 1671, a letter of protest was sent to the Crown in Portugal expressing in the strongest terms their disapproval of the decision to prevent them from being appointed as supreme judge.[244] The letter was signed by four prominent Bahians, excluding Burgos: 'the Judge Manoel da Rocha, Municipal Councillor Thomé Pereira Falcão, Francisco Sutil de Siqueira, and the Procurator João de Matos Aranha'.[245] By that time Burgos had already completed one stint as a high court judge in Brazil. However, he returned to the post four years later, two years after the royals left the city, when he was reappointed as a high court judge by default after the previous appointee, Augostinho de Azevedo Monteiro, died suddenly in 1675.[246] One could postulate that in spite of his reappointment, he was not happy with his treatment at the hands of the Salvador authorities and instead opted to expand his business in Palmares. One might also speculate that he was looking for an alternative way for Brazil to be run politically. Such sentiments would probably have been shared by all those who were denied the right to take up political positions.

We do not, yet, have at our disposal written evidence that the royals went to Palmares or that they met Burgos in person. However, the correspondence between the overseas councils and the Crown in Lisbon and the governors of Angola, Bahia and Rio de Janeiro indicates that there was a real concern about the threat posed by Palmares and a fear that the royals would join the community.[247] On the basis of this evidence, it is also possible to suggest that the royals made some form of contact about

---

[243] See José Ignacio de Abreu Lima, *Synopsis ou Deducção Chronologica dos Factos Mais Notaveis da História do Brazil*, Pernambucco: Na typographia de M. F. De Faria, 1845, p. 133, 'dirigindo ao Monarcha o seguinte officio, dictado pelo mais corajoso patriotismo, sem faltar ao respeito devido a Magestade do Throno'.

[244] The full letter is cited by Lima. See Lima, *Synopsis ou Deducção*, pp. 133–134.

[245] See Lima, *Synopsis ou Deducção*, p. 133. The Brazilian-born élites' protest to overturn the ban dragged on until the end of the seventeenth century, see Brasil, Baía, doc. 2734, 1 September 1676 and Brasil, Baía, doc. 2699, 29 February 1676 in "Documentos Avulsos da Capitania da Bahia", 1675–1677, cx. 22–23, n. docs. 2660–2787.

[246] See F. Burges de Barros, *Á Margem da História da Bahia*, Salvador: Mamia Imprensa Official do Estado, Praça Municipal, 1934, p. 203.

[247] See See AHU, cód. 17, fl. 59v, 21 August 1672, 'Consulta do Conselho Ultramarino', 'nos sejão mais prejudiçiaes' (they will be a danger to us). See also AHU., Cód. 17,18 August 1679, 'Consultas Mixtas', fl. 301, 'de modo que nos fosse de grande prejuizo, e no Brasil

joining Palmares with either the enslaved Africans in Salvador, the Indigenous Americans or Brazilians like Burgos, who were tired of paying taxes to the Portuguese Crown that were not then invested in Brazil. It makes no sense that the Brazilian and Portuguese authorities would have raised the alarm about the royals' stay in Brazil had there not been a real possibility that they would run away to join their brothers and sisters in Palmares or 'little Angola'.[248]

It is certainly clear where Burgos's political allegiance lay, as he stopped paying tax to the Crown. He also owned land in Palmares on which he paid tax to the Palmarists. This allegiance was only revealed by Velho twenty-four years after Burgos first befriended the Palmarists, when he disagreed with the state's policy of waging war on Palmares. As an old man, he was perhaps able to stand up against the system without fear of repercussions. The prohibition on the Brazilian-born engaging in politics is telling regarding the royals' stay in Salvador and the uneasiness felt by the governing authorities in Bahia about their presence in Brazil. The Brazilian-born found in the royals a partnership and a common goal to frustrate Portuguese economic interests in Brazil.

3.8 THE QUILOMBO DOS PALMARES AND FATHER ANTÓNIO VIEIRA

Issues of politics are intrinsically bound up with questions of religion and power, and in the seventeenth century this became more blatant as far as Palmares was concerned. Western Christianity provided a supporting framework for political legislation that was largely a product of those who were at the forefront of the mission to the unconverted, mainly the priests. The religion enabled them to appear to be living a good life even while they were denying the rights of humanity to others. Mendonça's court case in the Vatican was to call attention to this disparity and to demand that enslaved Africans be treated equally as members of the Universal Church.

On 28 January 1689, Pope Innocent XI sent a letter of approval to Father Antonio Vieira to take the 'blessings of Christ to Palmares'.[249] We

---

hauia o mesmo' (In this way, they would be of great danger to us, and in Brazil it would be the same).

[248] See 'Documento n. 54', p. 325. Velho believed that Palmarinos called their settlement in Palmares 'Angola janga' or 'Angola pequena': 'como elles chamavão' (as they were called).

[249] For current debate on Palmares, see Cheney, *Quilombo dos Palmares*, p. 70

do not have Vieira's response to Innocent XI, but we know that he opted not to take Christ's forgiveness to Palmares, and, justifying his view on economic and theological grounds, refused to do what Innocent XI asked him. The timing of Innocent's letter to Vieira is interesting, given that it was sent three years after Mendonça presented his second discourse to the Propaganda Fide in Rome in 1686. While reconciliation with the Palmarists was central to Innocent XI's demand, the events leading to Mendonça's influential court case have to be seen as playing an important role in this quest for freedom and the abolition of Atlantic slavery.[250] Mendonça, his brothers, uncles, aunts and cousins were identified by the governing authorities in Bahia as being sympathetic to the Palmarists' cause.

In 1691, three years before the destruction of Palmares in 1694, Pedro II was advised by his councillors to opt for a more dialogue-based approach to Palmares as the best way to achieve a resolution that would allow Palmares 'to explore the possibility of some kind of truce'.[251] His approach was to use the Christian missionaries to achieve this, and Padre Antonio Vieira was called in to look into the proposal, but he rejected it. He believed that approaching the Palmarists via Christian missions was not viable, in particular because the Italian priest[252] whose idea it was to engage in such a mission was too young and inexperienced.

Vieira believed that the king's letter, despite its good intentions, levelled criticism at the Society of Jesuits, to which he belonged. In other words, he felt Pedro II was overlooking the Jesuits' achievements and comparing their work with other religious orders who were prepared to look at the case of Palmares in another way and seek a peaceful solution. Vieira took Pedro II's letter as a personal attack on the Jesuits:

> I give grace to Your Mercy, and not without great confusion of mine and ours, of the concept that Your Grace has of the spirit of the Society. So, God will separate, like that of Moses, whom Your Grace have compared us with, the zeal and desire I have of all of us to use ourselves, and with all our might, in this very proper work of our institute. However, not everyone by their hidden judgements grants God the same aspirations, not all, even those dressed in the same Habit, that we are for everything[253]

---

[250] See SOCG, vol. 495a, fl 393.   [251] Cheney, *Quilombo dos Palmares*, p. 70.
[252] The Italian priest that Vieira referred to could well have been Antonil, who had arrived in Bahia in 1681, the same year Vieira returned to Bahia from Maranhão, or Benci, who arrived in 1683.
[253] 'Dou a V. M.cê as graças, e não sem grande confusão minha e nossa, do conceito que V. M. cê tem do espírito da Companhia. Assim repartirá Deus, como o de Moisés, a quem V. M.cê nos compara, o zelo e desejo que eu tenho de que todos nos empregássemos, e com todas as forças, nesta obra tão própria do nosso instituto . Mas nem a todos por seus ocultos juízos

It seems clear that there was tension between the competing missionary orders in Brazil at the time. Indeed, Vieira was highly critical of other orders when he was in Maranhão,[254] particularly with regard to the enslavement of the Indigenous people. The older orders such as the Jesuits had established ideas about their mission in Brazil, for example, favouring the creation of hamlets for conquered Indigenous people. This thinking was challenged by men like Antonil, who suggested that Jesuit priests were becoming too comfortable in their missionary approach to the Indigenous Brazilians.[255]

The traditional philosophy of the Jesuits regarding the 'tamed hamlet' was that the Indigenous Brazilians were to be brought to live in a hybrid space, segregated from their own society. As Nóbrega put it in a letter to Father Miguel de Torres in 1558:

> The law, which they are to be given, is to prevent them from eating human flesh and waging war without a licence from the Governor; to make them have one woman, to dress, for they have plenty of cotton, at least after being Christians, to take away their sorcerers, to ensure they behave justly among themselves and with Christians; to make them live tamely without joining other groups elsewhere, unless it is among other Christians, having enough land divided among themselves, and with these Fathers from the Society to indoctrinate them.[256]

'Tamed hamlets - conquered hamlets were created for the purpose of facilitating the Jesuits' mission in Brazil. According to Dias, these hamlets were administered by Jesuits and the Indigenous peoplewere taken out of their social landscape and placed in a neutral space where they were then given Christian instruction. They were prevented from living their customary lives and encouraged to live a European style of life.[257] Thus, they were

---

concede Deus as mesmas isnpirações, nem todos, posto que vestidos do mesmo hábito, somos para tudo.' Azevedo, 'Cartas do Padre António Vieira', pp. 620–621.

[254] See Vieira's critique of other orders in Azevedo, 'Cartas do Padre António Vieira a Roque Monteiro Paim', pp. 620–621. See also MMA, vol. XIII, p. 221–222. On slavery in Maranhão, see also Daniel B Domingues da Silva, 'The Atlantic Slave Trade to Maranhão, 1680–1846: Volume, Routes and Organisation', *Slavery & Abolition*, 29 (4), 2008, pp. 477–501.

[255] See Andreoni (Antonil), *Cultura e Opulência do Brazil*, pp. 14–15.

[256] Here I am indebted to Vaniclėia Silva Santos, 'As Bolsas de Mandingas', p. 113, 'A lei, que lhes hão-de dar, é defender-lhes comer carne humana e guerrear sem licença do Governador; fazer-lhes ter uma só mulher, vestirem-se, pois têm muito algodão, ao menos depois de cristãos, tirar-lhe os feiticeiros, mantê-los em justiça entre si e para com os cristãos; fazê-los viver quietos sem se mudarem para outra parte, se não for para entre cristãos, tendo terras repartidas que lhes bastem, e com estes Padres da Companhia para os doutrinarem'.

[257] See Mariza de Araújo Dias, 'Os Jesuítas e a Escravidão Africana no Brasil Colonial: Um Estudo Sobre os Escritos de Antonio Vieira, André João Antonil e Jorge Benci (sécs. XVII

to work for themselves and for the living expenses of the Jesuit missionaries. The colonists and priests were often at odds over who should administer the *Índios Mansos* or conquered Indigenous people. Different missions in Bahia in the eighteenth century built hamlets in different towns and wards for the Natives in order to 'tame' them (see Table 7)[258]. For example, in Ipitanga, three groups of Indigenous people –Tupis, Goiaras and Potigazes – lived together in the same hamlet. The biggest hamlet was Reys Magos, which had 300 inhabitants, and the second largest was Riritiba; the smallest one was Siriahem, with 16 inhabitants.

Vieira rejected Pedro II's proposal regarding freedom for Palmares and opted for the creation of a traditional 'tamed hamlet - conquered hamlet', in which, like the Indigenous people in such hamlets, they would work to sustain the living of the priests and pay their tribute. There was an obvious flaw in Vieira's rationale, for this was the life the enslaved people in Palmares had lived before and it made no sense for them to return to it.

For Vieira, there was no such thing as negotiation with Palmarists for their salvation or for their blessing: 'I very much admire (that such is the same zeal in which His Majesty has for saving everyone!) that, without further information from the superiors of this Province, in which there were an offer of a private priest to go to the Palmares'.[259]

To sustain his argument, Vieira gave five reasons why Palmarists should not be allowed to be citizens of the Portuguese Empire. Firstly, as the missionary approach was not viable, it 'would have been the Angolan Native priests that we have, whom they trust, and believe, and understand them, as the language they use is of the same country. However, all of them agree that it is a matter beyond the control of all grounds and hope.'[260] Secondly, 'for Palmarists in this particular instance, they will not trust anyone, for they believe that they are all governors' spies, who will

---

e XVIII)', unpublished Master's thesis, State University of São Paulo, 2012: https://repositorio.unesp.br/bitstream/handle/11449/93370/dias_ma_me_assis.pdf?sequence=1.

[258] These tame villages were run by Jesuits (among the the largest priests' society to create them in Bahia were: Jesuits, Franciscans, Carmelites with Shoes 'Calsado'); among them were Italian priests and some clerics.

[259] Azevedo, 'Cartas do Padre António Vieira a Roque Monteiro Paim', pp. 620–621, and MMA, vol. XIII, p. 221, 'Muito me admiro (mas tal é o mesmo zelo em S. Magestade de salvar a todos!) que, sem outra informação dos superiores desta Província, houvesse por bem a oferta por um padre particular em ir aos Palmares'.

[260] Azevedo, 'Cartas do Padre António Vieira a Roque Monteiro Paim', pp. 620–621, and MMA, vol. XIII, p. 221, 'primeira: porque se isto fosse possivel havia de ser por meio dos padres naturais de Angola que temos, aos quais crêem, e deles se fiam e os entendem, como de sua própria pátria e língua; mas todos concordam em que é matéria alheia de todo o fundamento e esperança'.

TABLE 7 *Conquered Indigenous people in Bahia, Brazil, in their respective villages and the missionary societies that set them up. By the author, based on 'Documento n. 65'*

General Map of All Missions or Villages of 'settled gentiles' (mission of Brazilian Indigenous people)

General Map of All Missions or Villages of Brazilian Indigenous people that there are in this governance	Villages with their names	Parishes which they belong	Types of Missionary (priests) Societies that administer in them	New Villages that were set up	Prayers from Missions or Parishes	Dioceses to which they belong	Capitances	Districts	Extension of land for each village	Houses, or Souls in each one	Types of nations that live there	Distance in leagues for each of them from this City	Notes of when each Village was set up by the Jesuits
Iuru	Lagarto	N. Sra dos Campos do Rio Real	Jesuits	Tavora	N. Sra do Socorro	Bahia	Serge' d'ElRei	Serge' d'ElRei	-	Cazais 60	Kiriris	50	
Saco dos Morsegos	Itapicuru	S. Ana dos Tucanos	Jesuits	Mirandela	Acensao de Xpo	Bahia	Bahia	Bahia	Bastes	90	Kiriris	65	
Canabrava	Itapicuru	S.Joao do Girimuabo	Jesuits	Pombal	S. Thereza	Bahia	Bahia	Bahia	Poucas	100	Kiriris	60	
Natuba	Itapicuru	N.Sra de Nazareth do Itapicuru	Jesuits	Souza	N. Sra da Concam	Bahia	Bahia	Bahia	Mto Pouca/	110	Kiriris	50	
Ipitanga	Bahia	S. Amaro da Ipitanga	Jesuits	Abrantes	Espirito Sto	Bahia	Bahia	Bahia	6 legas 4	40	Tupis ou Tupina'bas com mista de Goiaras e Potigazes	70	Em 8 de abro de 1758
Sirahem	Camamu	N. Sra da Asu'cao do Camamu	Jesuits	Santarem	S. Mig le S. Andre	Bahia	Ilheos	Bahia	Bastes	16	Paiará	30	
Escada dos Ilheos	S. Jorge dos Ilheos	Sta Crus dos Ilheos	Jesuits	Olivensa	N. Sra da Escada	Bahia	Ilheos	Bahia	Bastes	130	Tabajaras ou Tupinaquis	50	
Marahiu	Camamu	S. Sebastiam do Marahiu	Jesuits	Barcelos	N. Sra da/ Ca'deia/	Bahia	Ilheos	Bahia	Bastes	86	Tupinaquis	30	

Grens	S. Jorge dos Ilheos	S. Crus da Va de S. Jorge	Jesuits	Almada	N. Sra da Concam	Bahia	Ilheos	Bahia	Muitas	86	Grens	60
S. Joao dos Tupis	Sta Cruz	N. Sra da Pena	Jesuits	Trancozo	S. Joaó	Rio de Janro	Porto Seguro	Bahia	Muitas	120	Tabajaras ou Tupinaquis com mista de Tupinambas	70
Patatiba	Sta Cruz	N. Sra da Pena	Jesuits	Va Verde	Espirito Sto	Rio de Janro	Porto Seguro	Bahia	Muitas	80	Tupyraquiſ c'o mysta de Pondantus	80
Reritiba	Guruparim	N. Sra da Conceisam	Jesuits	Benavente	N. Sra da Asu'sam	Rio de Janro	Espirito Sto	Espirito Sto	12ls	250	Tupinambas	150
Reys Magos	Va da Vitoria	N. Sra da Serra	Jesuits	Almeida	Sto Reis Magoſ	Bahia	Espirito Sto	Espirito Sto	Muitas	300	Tupinambas	120
Itapicuru de sima	Itapicuru	N. Sra de Nazareth	Franciscans	Almeida	S. Anto eN. Sra da Saude	Bahia	Bahia	Bahia	Menos d'l lga	Cazais 80	Tupinambas	45
Masacara	Itapicuru	S. Joao de Girimuabo	Franciscos	Almeida	Sma Trindade	Bahia	Bahia	Bahia	1 legua	200	Kiriſ Caimbes	60
Bom Jesus da Jacobina	Jacobina	S. Antonio	Franciscos	Almeida	Bom Jesus	Bahia	Bahia	Jacobina	Mto pouca	100	Kiriſ Caimbes	80
Sahi	Jacobina	S. Antonio	Franciscos	Almeida	N. Sra das Neveſ	Bahia	Bahia	Jacobina	1 legua	150	Kiriſ Caimbes	80
Boaneiro	Jacobina	S. Antonio	Franciscos	Almeida	N. Sra daſ Brotas	Bahia	Bahia	Jacobina	1 legua	100	Kiriſ Caimbes	100
Rodelas	Pambú	Sto Anto do Pambu	Italian	Almeida	S. Joaó Bapta	Bahia	Serg. d' ElRei	Jacobina	1 legua	Almas 200	Poreás	170

TABLE 7 (cont.).

Porto da Folha	Va Nova Real	S. Anto do Urubu de bx.	Italian	Almeida	S. Pedro	Bahia	Serg. d' ElRei	1 legua	250	Unumarús	124
Pacatuba	Va Nova Real	S. Antonio	Italian	Almeida	S. Telis	Bahia	Serg. d' ElRei	½ legua	466	Caxago	106
Una do Cairú	Va do Cairú	N. Sra do Rozo	Italian	Almeida	S. Fidelis	Bahia	Bahia	1 legua	160	Tupinambas	16
Aldeia do Rio Real	Va da Abadia	N. Sra da Abadia	Carmelites with shoes	Almeida	Jesus Ma Joze	Bahia	Serg. d' ElRei	Mto pouca	Cazais 8	Kiriris	52
Iaparatuba	Va da Abadia	Jesus Ma Jose S. G Pe do banco	Carmelites with shoes	Almeida	N. Sra do Carmo	Bahia	Serg. d' ElRei	Mto pouca	12	Boimé	65
Maserandupio	StaLuzia	S. Amaro da Ipitanga	Carmelites with shoes	Almeida	S. Antonio de Arquim	Bahia	Bahia	6 leguas	Cazais 50	Tupis ou Tupinambas	22
Conquistada Pedra Brca	Cachoeira	N. Sra do Desterro Oiteiro Redondo	Carmelites with shoes	Almeida	S. Antonio de Arquim	Bahia	Bahia	Mto pouca	Cazais 20	Kiriris	28
Outra do mesmo sitio	Cachoeira	N. Sra do Desterro Oiteiro Redo	Carmelites with shoes	Almeida	S. Antonio de Arquim	Bahia	Bahia	Mto pouca	Cazais 17	Sapuias	29
Poxino	S. Jorge	S. Boaventura de Poxin	Clergyman	Almeida	S. Antonio de Arquim	Bahia	Porto Seguro	Mto pouca	Cazais 17	Sapuias	29

Aramaris	S. Joao de Aguas	Espirito Sto do Inhambupe	Clergyman	Almeida	S. Antonio de Arquim	Bahia	Bahia	Bahia	Mto pouca	Cazais 15	Kiriris	40
Manguinhos	S. Joa ode Agua Fria	Espirito Sto do Inhambupe	Clergyman	Almeida	S. Antonio de Arquim	Bahia	Bahia	Bahia	Mto pouca	20	Caramurú	35
S. Ant. da Aldeia	Maragogipe	S. Bartholomeo	Clergyman	Almeida	S. Antonio	Bahia	Bahia	Bahia	Mto pouca	20	Caramurú	35
Jiquirisá	Boipeba	S. Antonio	Clergyman	Almeida	N. Sra dos Prazeres	Bahia	Bahia	Bahia	Mto pouca	20	Caramurú	35
Agua azeda	Boipeba	S. Antonio	Clergyman	Almeida	N. Sra dos Prazeres	Bahia	Serge d' ElRei	Serge d' ElRei	Mto pouca	20	Caramurú	35
Jaguaze do Rio da Alda	Jaguaripe	N. Sra dNazareth	Clergyman	Almeida	Nazareth	Bahia	Bahia	Bahia	Mto pouca	20	Caramurú	35
Aldeia do Salitre	Sto Anto do Urubu	S. Antonio	Clergyman	Almeida	N. Sra da Madre de D.	Bahia	Bahia	Jacobina	Mto pouca	20	Caramurú	35

internally advise them secretly how to conquer them'.[261] Thirdly, 'for Palmarists, least of these suspicions, or in all or in some, will suffice to kill them with venom, as they discreetly and secretly do to one another'.[262] Fourthly, 'for even if they cease from the assaults they make on the Portuguese village, they will never stop allowing those of their nation to run away'.[263] The fifth argument Vieira put forward was based on theological grounds. For Vieira, the Palmarists' sin made them incapable of salvation. Their way of life represented the opposite of Christian values: they were in a state of damnation 'because being rebels and captives, they are and remain in continuous and in present sin, that they cannot be absolved of, nor receive the grace of God, without returning to the service and obedience of their masters, which they will not do'.[264] Thus, Vieira determined the only option for the Palmarists was that they lived in the fashion of the Indigenous people in hamlets for the conquered: 'there was only one effective and efficacious way of truly reducing them, that was his majesty and all his masters conceding to them spontaneous, liberal and secure freedom, living at these sites as other Indigenous, free people and that then the priest could have his parishes and indoctrinate them like the others.'[265] Palmarists were the new colonisers of Brazil, and if they were afforded freedom, this 'would be the total destruction of Brazil, since the other blacks knowing that through this means they could be free, each city,

---

[261] Azevedo, 'Cartas do Padre António Vieira a Roque Monteiro Paim', pp. 620–621, and MMA, vol. XIII, p. 221, 'segunda: porque até deles neste particular, se não hão-de fiar por nenhum modo sempre que são espias dos governadores, para os avisarem secretamente de como podem ser conquistados'.
[262] Azevedo, 'Cartas do Padre António Vieira a Roque Monteiro Paim', pp. 620–621, and MMA, vol. XIII, p. 221, 'terceira: porque bastará a menor destas suspeitas, ou em todos ou em alguns, para os matarem com peçonha, como fazem oculta e secretissimamente uns aos outros'.
[263] Azevedo, 'Cartas do Padre António Vieira a Roque Monteiro Paim', pp. 620–621, and MMA, vol. XIII, p. 222, 'quarta: porque ainda que cessassem dos assaltos que fazem no povoado dos portugueses, nunca hão-de deixar de admitir aos de sua nação que para eles fugirem'.
[264] Azevedo, 'Cartas do Padre António Vieira a Roque Monteiro Paim', pp. 620–621, and MMA, vol. XIII, p. 222, 'quinta: fortíssima e total, porque sendo rebelados e cativos, estão e perseveram em pecado continuo e actual, de que não podem ser absolutos, nem receber a graça de Deus, sem se restituirem ao serviço e obediência de seus senhores, o que de nenhum modo hão-de fazer'.
[265] Azevedo, 'Cartas do Padre António Vieira a Roque Monteiro Paim', pp. 620–621, and MMA, vol. XIII, p. 222, 'só um meio havia eficaz e efectivo para verdadeiramente se reduzirem, que era coneedendo-lhe S. Magestade e todos os senhores espontânea, liberal e segura liberdade, vivendo naqueles sitios como os outros indios e gentios livres, e que então os padres fossem seus párocos e os doutrinassem como aos demais'.

each town, each place, each sugar mill, would soon become other Palmares, fleeing and going to the forests with all their stock, that is nothing more than their own body'.[266]

Vieira's arrogant sermon preached the damnation of the Africans, but claimed at the same time that they could be saved. His sermon was paradoxical and showed that his own understanding of Scripture was as confused as his position on the enslaved Africans. At the heart of his contradictory sermon was our common humanity, which had been abused in Brazil, where the enslaved were brutally dehumanised. The predicament of the enslaved Africans in the Americas exposed the injustice of slavery and opened it up to questioning, condemnation and abolition. However, Vieira was not willing to take that debate into a public arena and instead explained it away. For him, Atlantic slavery was necessary for the Africans to achieve salvation in the afterlife. Bringing the enslaved Africans to Brazil provided them with an opportunity to gain salvation through their labour:

... there is no slave in Brazil, and when I see more of these miserable lots [Africans], which is not something for me to profoundly think about it. I compare the present with the future, the time with eternity, and what I see and with what I believe, I do not understand; that God who made these men in his image and likeness, like others, would predestine two hells, one for this life, and the other for next. Notwithstanding, today when I see such devotions and festivals before the altars of the Lady of Rosary, all brothers among themselves, as children of the same Lady, then I am convinced myself, without doubt that the captivity of the first transmigration [slavery] is ordained for his mercy for the freedom of the second.[267]

Africans had received the Christian Gospel before Europeans arrived on the continent, and Africans such as Augustine of Hippo were among the

---

[266] Azevedo, 'Cartas do Padre António Vieira a Roque Monteiro Paim', pp. 620–621, and MMA, vol. XIII, p. 222, 'porém esta mesma liberdade assim considerada seria a total destruição do Brasil, porque conhecendo os demais negros que por este meio tinham conseguido o ficar livres, cada cidade, cada vila, cada lugar, cada engenho, seriam logo outros tantos Palmares, fugindo e passando-se aos matos com todo o seu cabedal, que não é outro mais que o próprio corpo.'

[267] Padre António Vieira, Sermões, Porto: Lello, 1959, p. 330, 'não há escravo no Brasil, e mais quando vejo os mais miseráveis, que não seja matéria para mim de uma profunda meditação. Comparo o presente com o futuro, o tempo com a eternidade, o que vejo com o que creio, e não posso entender, que Deus que creou estes homens tanto à sua imagem e similhança, como os demais, os predestinasse para dois infernos um n'esta vida, outro na outra. Mas quando hoje os vejo tão devotos e festivais diante dos altares da Senhora do Rosário, todos irmãos entre si, como filhos da mesma Senhora, já me persuado, sem dúvida, que o cativeiro da primeira transmigração é ordenado por sua misericórdia para a liberdade da segunda.'

great theologians to have influenced Western theological thought.[268] Their Christianity was not based on the colonial power that Vieira came to enjoy and represent in Brazil. It did not come with the sword and firearms, but was based on the less aggressive Egyptian and Ethiopian branches of Christianity and on Saint Thomas's Christianity, which reached Asia before the Portuguese arrived there.[269] The Africans' Christianity was not imbued with the power that Western Christendom came to enjoy. For Vieira, salvation for the Africans came about through slavery. He thought slavery was a positive experience because it gave Africans a chance that their fathers in Africa had not had to enter the gates of heaven: 'You must give infinite grace to God for giving you knowledge of himself, and for taking you out of your lands, where your fathers have lived as heathens; and he has brought you to this country [Brazil], where you have been instructed in faith, to live as Christians, and you will be saved.'[270] Vieira's Christianity thus offered militancy rather than a message of salvation. It had an economic message based on the Portuguese idea of God rather than on the benevolent God that the Africans knew before the Portuguese arrived.

3.9 CONCLUDING REMARKS

The royals from Ndongo were moved swiftly out of Brazil because they represented legitimacy for the *quilombos*. If they had decided to join the runaway communities, especially Palmares, it would have been difficult to deal by force alone with the communities' claims to legality. Instead, the Crown would have had to concede certain concessions. It would have been problematic if the Palmarists had direct contact with a recognised political figure. The Portuguese authorities feared the formation of a parallel empire, created with the Indigenous people, that would make

---

[268] See Lewis Ayres, *Augustine and the Trinity*, Cambridge: Cambridge University Press, 2010; see Augustine, *City of God*.

[269] For a detailed discussion of Saint Thomas, the apostle of Christianity in India centuries before the arrival of the Portuguese, see A. Mathias. Mundadan, *History of Christianity in India*, vol. I, Bangalore, India: Church History Association of India, 1984; Leslie Brown, *The Indian Christians of St. Thomas, An Account of the Ancient Syrian Church of Malabar*, Cambridge: Cambridge University Press 1956, and Placid J. Podipara, *The Thomas Christians*, London: Darton, Longman and Tidd, 1970.

[270] Vieira, *Sermões*, 1951, p. 303, 'deveis dar infinitas graças a Deus por vos ter dado conhecimento de si, e por vos ter tirado de vossas terras, onde vossos pais e vós vivíeis como gentios; e vos ter trazido a esta, onde instruídos na fé, vivaes como christãos, e vos salveis'.

Brazil something of an African state. This was the fear expressed in Vieira's letter to the Crown in which he proposed that Africans, rather than the Portuguese, would be the colonisers of Brazil. The Palmarists not only knew about the royals, for some of their members were enslaved Angolans, but also shared a language and culture with them. As royalty, Mendonça's family could also demand recognition by the Portuguese governing authorities. The Palmarists were feared by the Portuguese in Brazil for creating political rivalry. If allowed to stay, the royals would have become a point of reference or a point of contact for the authorities, the Africans in Brazil and in Africa, and the Indigenous people . And the Portuguese feared that they would join forces with the Indigenous Brazilians. Waging war against them would have needed legal justification.

Palmares was *macamba* and not *mocambo*, it became *mocambo* by necessity. The intention of its forty founding runaway enslaved people was to form a community and not a military camp, and any military side to the community was only meant to be temporary and for a specific purpose. The claim that Palmares was *mocambo* was made by the Portuguese to justify a 'just war' aimed at its destruction. A *mocambo* was formed for the purpose of war and not as a permanent state. Palmarists did not see themselves as *mocambo*, but rather as *macamba*. Palmares might possibly have survived as an independent state in Brazil, however, had it not been for Vieira's interpretation of it and the theologically infused economic/moral case he made against it. Vieira's interpretation and understanding of Palmares has not been considered in Brazilian historiography. The focus has been on Palmares as an African republic and as a multiracial polity in Brazil.[271]

The *mocambos*, including Palmares, arose as attempts to find a solution to the brutality of slavery in the *engenhos*.[272] Palmares exposed the arbitrary nature of the rule of the colonial or *conquistador* class, who saw the enslaved as savages.[273] Negotiation lay at the heart of Palmares: they negotiated with the Natives they considered their *macamba* or friends and with the Portuguese residents in the neighbourhood.[274] The Indigenous Brazilians would have viewed the Africans as fighting a common battle, and did not consider them enemies. Palmares was a refusal to submit to

---

[271] See Rodrigues, 'As sublevações de negros no Brasil'; Lara, 'Palmares and Cucaú', and Funari, 'Conflict and the Interpretation of Palmares'.
[272] Andreoni (Antonil),*Cultura e Opulência*.   [273] 'Documento n. 54'.
[274] 'Documento n. 54'.

the Portuguese, a declaration of independence, and a symbol of insubordination. Resistance provided a space for negotiation as it created an absence in the balance of power between Palmares and the Portuguese Crown. Palmares's resistance to Portugal's economic interests was only an option because there was no scope for negotiation. The Palmarists opted for a non-negotiable relationship with the Portuguese. Palmares was a rejection and at the same time an inversion of the colonial values around slavery and the treatment of enslaved people as non-human. However, the Palmarists pursued other things in Palmares, exploring resources, power, wealth, control, collection of taxes and protection. The region of Pernambuco provided the Palmarists with alternative ways to pursue the kind of life that they knew best, the African way of life, with the flexibility to adapt to the local Brazilian environment in which they found themselves.

King Pedro II's letter about Palmares highlighted the existing tensions between the Crown and officials overseas, both political and religious, who appeared to harbour different ambitions and goals.[275] Power might have been with the Crown, but the real decision-makers were often those who were left to implement policy. Pedro II contested Vieira's established thinking. Nonetheless, Vieira was not ready to budge from his position and took a more militaristic approach to Palmares, perhaps on the advice of his brother Bernardo Vieira Ravasco, who was secretary of state and war in Brazil from 1649 onwards.[276]

The Palmarists were not just about gaining their freedom. They were also trying to make Brazil a living space for themselves based on the realities on the ground. They used the resources available to them – the land, natural resources and minerals such as gold and silver – to make a

[275] Dom Pedro II's letter to Padre António Vieira is not available. However, Vieira's response provides a clue about the existing tension between Dom Pedro II's advisors [Overseas Council] and Vieira. See Azevedo, 'Cartas do Padre António Vieira a Roque Monteiro Paim', pp. 620–621 and MMA, vol. XIII, p. 222, 'só um meio havia eficaz e efectivo para verdadeiramente se reduzirem, que era coneedendo-lhe S. Magestade e todos os senhores espontânea, liberal e segura liberdade, vivendo naqueles sitios como os outros indios e gentios livres, e que então os padres fossem seus párocos e os doutrinassem como aos demais'. On the Brazilian-born élites' protest, see Lima, *Synopsis ou Deducção*, p. 133. See also Brasil, Baía, doc. 2734, 1 September 1676 and Brasil, Baía, doc. 2699, 29 February 1676 in 'Documentos Avulsos da Capitania da Bahia', 1675–1677, cx. 22–23, n. docs. 2660–2787. For Jorge Velho's camp as loyal to the Portuguese Crown, see 'Documento n. 54'. The Portuguese Overseas Council objected to the appointment of Burgos as a judge. See also Consulta CU, 8 August 1656, AHU, Bahia, papeis avulsos, Caixa 8 (2nd series non-catalogued).
[276] See Schwartz, *A Governor and His Image*.

living. They mirrored what the Portuguese did in Brazil. Like the Portuguese, they appropriated the natural resources available to them, using the gold they found to build a republic. This was what the Portuguese were aware of and afraid of.

There were those, like Burgos, who were prepared to accept Palmares's vision of widening their relationships within Brazil to include even those at the heart of Portuguese interests and power, and for whom the conquest of Palmares was a contradiction. Burgos preferred to ally with a so-called enemy of the state, and many of the wealthy in Brazil were not interested in the destruction of Palmares. In the end, its destruction came about because of a war between two parties within the Portuguese establishment – the Brazilian-born who wanted representation and those loyal to the Crown. The destruction of Pungo-Andongo, as we saw in Chapter 2, resulted from conflict between forces loyal to Portugal – the *guerra preta*, in which Sequeira played an important role – and those backing King João Hari II, who were in favour of Angolan independence. Similarly, as we have seen, Burgos's allegiance with Palmaristas set him against those loyal to the Portuguese Crown, including Velho and those around him.[277]

Vieira argued that by resisting in Palmares, the Africans there evaded the Brazilian political space. For Vieira, though, there were incongruent modes of operation between the Portuguese ideology of demonisation and the ideology of Palmares. In other words, these ideologies could not be reconciled in Brazil; either one had to give in, or the other had to be totally annihilated. In his view, the very fact of Palmares's existence in Brazil implied an African culture that refused to be tamed. The Palmarists' resistance and constant challenge to Portuguese power was in itself a refusal of the ways of God that amounted to a mortal sin for which there was no salvation. Vieira saw their obliteration as the only justified course of action.

The journey of the royals from Pungo-Andongo to Salvador, Bahia, and Rio de Janeiro provided Mendonça with an enlightening experience

---

[277] See Cadornega, *História Geral*, vol. II, pp. 300, 315–329. João Hari II galvanised forces from different constituencies in the region, from Matamba, Cansanje and Imbangala, as well as Ndongo. João Hari II was betrayed by Mbundu people who were fighting alongside the Portuguese army, see Cadornega, *História Geral*, vol. II, pp. 315–329. On *guerra preta*, see 'Carta de Constantino Cadena a Fernão de Sousa', AHU – Angola, cx. 2., 16 September 1626; MMA, vol. XIII, pp. 479–481 and 'Carta do governador de Angola a El-Rei de Portugal', AHU – Angola, cx. 2., 9 de Março de 1643; MMA, vol. IX, pp. 28–38. Luiz Lopes de Sequeira (an Angolan-born army officer) played a crucial role in the Battle of Pungo-Andongo. See Relaçam/ Do FELICE SVCCESSO.

from which he built his court case about the suffering of the Indigenous Americans and enslaved Africans whose liberty had been denied in the Atlantic region. His engagement with the Indigenous population in Brazil and his connection with the fugitives in Palmares brought him an increased awareness of their common search for freedom. This engagement was a catalyst for him to not only argue in the Vatican for the liberation of Africans but to argue also for the freedom of the Indigenous Americans who had stood alongside their Africans counterpart in Palmares. It is the aim of the Chapter 4 to address Mendonça's struggle for the freedom of enslaved Africans in the Atlantic region and his attempts to tackle it not only as a regional problem but as a wider Atlantic issue.

4

Mendonça's Journey to Portugal and Spain, and the Network of the Hebrew Nation and Indigenous Americans

This chapter further broadens the debate about the Ndongo royals' awareness of the abuses that they learned of during their time in Salvador and Rio de Janeiro, which connected them with the enslaved Africans and the Indigenous Brazilians whose violent treatment on the Brazilian plantations caused untold deaths, abuse and suffering.¹ The royals' exile to Brazil had been intended to silence them, or at least make them politically inactive.² However, their stay there actually provided them with another space for political activities and allowed them to extend their influence. The political space in Brazil provided fertile ground for making their voices heard among the African constituency there and the Indigenous Brazilians who, like the West Central Africans, were being suffocated by the Portuguese in the seventeenth century.

Whilst in Portugal, the Ndongo royals came to realise that the denial of humanity they experienced was a wider problem in the Atlantic region: it was not just Africans and Indigenous Brazilians who were treated as subhuman, but the New Christians, too. It was in Lisbon, at the centre of the empire, that the mechanism of their dehumanisation was designed, legitimised and

---

¹ For a detailed treatment of the enslaved people on sugar plantations in Brazil, see Andreoni (Antonil), *Cultura e Opulência*. See also Carlos Alberto Santos Costa, et al., Fabiana Comerlato and Cinthia da Silva Cunha, 'Arqueologia do Baixo Sul da Bahia: Engenho Rio de Contas, Itacaré, Bahia, Brasil', *Revista de Arqueologia*, 31(2), 2018, pp. 256–281; Freyre, *Casa Grande & Senzala*, and Maria Adelina Amorim, '*Questões Jurídicas sobre os Índios do Brasil*' com José Maria Mendes, in *Cadernos de Literatura de Viagens*, n° 2, *Subsídios para o Estudo dos Índios das Américas*, Lisbon: CLEPUL/ Coimbra, Almedina, 2010, pp. 25–49.
² See 'Consulta do Conselho Ultramarino Sobre os familiars do Rei do Dongo" and MMA, vol. 13, pp. 507–508, 'com o sequito que timnhão."

constituted. Awareness of the ill-treatment of these different groups at the centre of the Portuguese Empire played a crucial role for the royals in enabling them to grasp the broader issue that united the disparate groups in their struggle for their freedom. For Mendonça, in particular, the relationship between anti-slavery discourse and the critique of the Inquisition/persecution of Jews and New Christians was a key element that widened his solidarity with these constituencies. The interaction of and contact between Indigenous Brazilians, New Christians and Africans in Africa has nevertheless been, until now, one of the less studied topics of Atlantic history.[3]

Geographically, politically, culturally and religiously, New Christians, Black Africans and Indigenous Brazilians are different social groups. At least, that is how they appear at the superficial level, creating the notion that they are mutually exclusive groups. In the Portuguese Empire from its inception in the fifteenth century, these groups were understood as having distinctive cultural characteristics, particularly in Portugal.[4] In 1541, Francisco Machado stated that 'where there are Moors, Blacks, Indians, Jews, it is inevitable that each one follows his own path and sect'.[5] However, there were those from within Europe who have lumped these groups, particularly the Jews and Black Africans, together.[6] Tudor Parfitt shows that Jews were thought of as Blacks in medieval Europe; and, according to him, this perception of the Jews as Blacks persisted in the period of the European Enlightenment. He demonstrates that West Central Africa had a flourishing community of Black Jews in Loango in the eighteenth century.[7]

---

[3] For further studies of the relationship between enslaved Africans and the Indigenous Brazilians, see Stuart B. Schwartz and Frank Salomon, 'New Peoples and New Kinds of Peoples: Adaptation, Readjustment, and Ethnogenesis in South American Indigenous Societies (Colonial Era)', in Stuart B. Schwartz (ed.), *Cambridge History of Native Peoples of the Americas*, vol. III, Cambridge: Cambridge University Press, 1999, pp. 467–471. See also Mary W. Helms, 'The Cultural Ecology of a Colonial Tribe', *Ethnology*, 8(1), 1969, pp. 76–84.

[4] See Jonathan Schorsch, *Jews and Blacks in the Early Modern World*, New York: Cambridge University Press, 2003. See also Brian Pullan, *The Jews of Europe and the Inquisition of Venice, 1550–1670*, Oxford: Basil Blackwell, 1983.

[5] As quoted in Schorsch, *Jews and Blacks*, p. 112, and see Mildred Evelyn Vieira and Frank Ephraim Talmage (eds. and trans.), *The Mirror of the New Christians (Espelho de Christãos Novos) of Francisco Machado*, Toronto: Pontifical Institute of Mediaeval Studies, 1977, p. 323.

[6] For further discussion of Jews and Black Africans on Jews and Black Africans as a unified category, see Fray Prudencio de Sandoval, *Historia de la Vida y Hechos del Emperador Carlos V, Biblioteca de Autores Españoles*, vol. 82, Madrid: Ediciones Atlas, 1955.

[7] See Tudor Parfitt, *Hybrid Hate: Conflations of Antisemitism and Anti-Black Racism from the Renaissance to the Third Reich*, Oxford: Oxford University Press, 2020.

Jonathan Schorsch has recently argued that in the early modern period Catholic Iberian discourse attempted to link Jews with Africans, or Blacks as marginalised groups.[8] They were bracketed together as one group because of their distinctive religious beliefs. However, Conversos (Jews converted to Christianity) and Sephardic Jews of the sixteenth through the eighteenth century reacted against this discourse that associated them with Blacks to construct their own identity.[9] Schorsch states that 'those born as New Christians on the Iberian Peninsula or in Spanish and Portuguese colonial territories, reflect both the variety of concerns Blacks raised for Europeans and often concerns specific to Jews'.[10] For Schorsch, Black Africans' social visibility in Portugal and elsewhere brought out this tension, which had been heightened through the Conversos' wanting to see themselves as distinctively different from Blacks. This tension between Conversos and Blacks, resulting in 'conflating anti-Christian and anti-Black feelings',[11] arose during the seventeenth-century Inquisition period in Iberia. Inquisition records show cases in which New Christians were accusing Blacks of being anti-Jewish and vice versa.[12] Nonetheless, and in spite of these individual sentiments in the Iberian Peninsula, there was a nuanced relationship at a political level that Schorsch is not able to articulate in his interesting analysis. Examples of this can be found in West and West Central Africa from the end of the

---

[8] Here I am indebted to Schorsch. For further discourse on Catholic Iberian that connected Black with New Christians. See Fray Prudencio de Sandoval, *Historia de la Vida y Hechos del Emperador Carlos V*, Biblioteca de Autores Españoles, vol. 82, Madrid: Ediciones Atlas, 1955; see also Elias Lipiner, *Izaque de Castro: o Mancebo que veio Preso do Brasil*, Recife: Fundação Joaquim Nabuco/Editora Massangana, 1992, and Judith Laikin Elkin, 'Colonial Origins of Contemporary Anti-Semitism in Latin America', in David Sheinin and Lois Baer Barr (eds.), *The Jewish Diaspora in Latin America: New Studies on History and Literature*, New York: Garland Publishing, 1996, pp. 127–141.

[9] Jonathan Schorsch, 'Blacks, Jews and the Racial Imagination in the Writings of Sephardim in the Long Seventeenth Century', *Jewish History*, 2005, 19, pp. 109–135. See also Schorsch, *Jews and Blacks*.

[10] Schorsch, 'Blacks, Jews and the Racial Imagination', p. 109.

[11] Schorsch, 'Blacks, Jews and the Racial Imagination', p. 109.

[12] For a full discussion of these issues in which Conversos and Blacks were scorning each other, see Elvira Pérez Ferreiro, *El Tratado de Uceda contra los Estatutos de Limpieza de Sangre: Una Reaccíon ante el Establecimiento del Estatuto de Limpieza en la Orden Franciscana*, Madrid: Aben Ezra Ediciones, 2000; David M. Gitlitz, *Secrecy and Deceit: The Religion of the Crypto-Jews*, Philadelphia: Jewish Publication Society, 1996; António Baião, *A Inquisição em Portugal e no Brasil, Subsidios Para a Sua Historia, A Inquisição no Século XVI*, Lisbon: Edição do Arquivo Historico Portugues, 1921, and Boleslao Lewin (ed.), *Confidencias de dos criptojudíos en la Cárcel de la Inquisición*, Buenos Aires: Tall. Gráf. J. Kaufman, 1975.

fifteenth century to the eighteenth century. New Christians were serving African rulers in different roles, such as ambassadors, lawyers and scholars. African kings were afforded some protection from Iberian Catholic persecution.[13] Tension might have existed between these groups in the Iberian Peninsula. However, this does not diminish their common interest in freedom. Despite their differences, New Christians, Black Africans and Indigenous Brazilians showed that they shared an experience of violence and expulsion that brought them together creatively and formed more of a network than we have been led to believe.[14] They all suffered exploitation and enslavement in the Atlantic region. New Christians and Black Africans were both enslaved in São Tomé,[15] whilst Indigenous Brazilians and Black Africans were enslaved together in Brazil.[16] The Indigenous Brazilians and Africans worked together and married each other as we saw in chapter 3[17] The New Christians lived and worked together with Africans in Africa[18] and in Portugal they supported Mendonça's court case for the abolition of the Atlantic slave trade[19].

This chapter first explores the arrival of the Ndongo royals in Portugal and how the process of education involved attempts to silence their voices in Lisbon. We will then look at Mendonça's studies in Vilar de Frades, Braga, Portugal, and his appointment as an Attorney of the Confraternity of Our Lady Star of Black Men in Lisbon and in the Royal Court of Madrid, Toledo[20]. Crucially, it examines Mendonça's alliance with

---

[13] For further debate on New Christians' inteligencias, see 'Carta Régia ao Cardeal de Borja'; see also MMA, vol. VI, pp. 323–325. See also Lingna Nafafé, *Colonial Encounters*.
[14] See Lingna Nafafé, *Colonial Encounters* and Green, 'Masters of Difference'. See also Parfitt, *Black Jews in Africa*. Tudor Parfitt, *The Lost Tribes of Israel: The History of a Myth*, London: Weidenfeld and Nicolson, 2002; Tudor Parfitt and Yulia Egorova, *Genetics, Mass Media and Identity: A Case Study of the Genetic Research on the Lemba and Bene Israel*, London: Routledge, 2006.
[15] Seibert, 'São Tomé's Great Slave Revolt of 1595'.
[16] On the Indigenous Americans' enslavement in Brazil, see Hawthorne, *From Africa to Brazil*. For further legal debate, see Amorim, 'Questões Jurídicas sobre os Índios do Brasil'.
[17] See "Documento n. 65""Documento n. 65'.
[18] For further debate on Jews and Africans or Black Jews in Africa, see Parfitt, *Black Jews in Africa*. Parfitt, *The Lost Tribes of Israel*; Parfitt and Egorova, *Genetics, Mass Media and Identity*.
[19] See Mezquita, S.C. Africa vol. I, fl. 486.
[20] See APF, SOCG, fl. 486, Lisbon, 15 February 1681; and 'Carta de Giacinto Rogio Monzon'. See also Gaspar's imprisonment, ANTT, Inquisição de Lisboa, 'Processo de Gaspar da Costa Mesquita' [The Court Case of Gaspar da Costa Mesquita], TT/TSO-IL /028/01240, Tribunal do Santo Ofício, Inquisição de Lisboa, proc. 1240, auto 44, maço 4, n. 1, cópia microfilmada, Torre do Tombo, mf. 3474, 23 April 1682–23 August, 'Acordão os Inquisitores, Ordinario, eDeputados deSanta Inquisisão, que vistos estas, culpas

Indigenous Peruvians in Toledo, which he established in the course of his education in Vilar de Frades in Braga and the confraternity of Toledo.[21]

We thus thoroughly examine the inhumane treatment of other constituencies, such as the New Christians, and how the other constituencies saw parallels in Africa with their own experiences in Europe. I demonstrate that in spite of this rejection of their humanity and culture, the Ndongo royals also had hope, garnered from the legal resources that were made available to them through the confraternities' rights and the idea of one constitution for all confraternities, that they could resist domination and obtain the freedom of the enslaved Africans and other marginalised groups in the Atlantic region. I show how the royals were separated as an attempt to prevent them from uniting among themselves, and how each group continued to fight to express their freedom and to retain their humanity. I look at how the royals who arrived in Portugal from Brazil were divided and sent to different monasteries, and how two groups of the royals who were sent directly from Pungo-Andongo to Portugal resisted the culture that was imposed on them and fought for their freedom, humanity and economic rights.

The process of the Ndongo royals' integration into Portuguese society through education did not run smoothly and was accompanied by intrigue and political cynicism. While some of the royals reacted to this behaviour assertively, others – such as Mendonça – opted to use the social resources available to them to protest non-violently at their treatment and that of others. My key argument here is how threatened the Portuguese Overseas Council felt by the royals and the complex measures they used to isolate them because of fear about the potential for political upheaval, as a result of the abusive situations they had witnessed both in Angola and Brazil. Critically, I argue for the crucial relationship between anti-slavery discourse and the critique of the Inquisition/persecution of Jews and New Christians in their quest for freedom and liberation as equal members of human society.

In the first section, I explore the attempt to silence the Ndongo royals and prevent them from uniting in their efforts against the Portuguese establishment by sending them to different monasteries.

---

e confessos de Gaspar DaCosta de Mesquita, christão novo, banqueiro, natural emorador destaCidade deLisboa': http://digitarq.arquivos.pt/details?id=2301127.

[21] For discussion of slave burials in the period in Rio de Janeiro and Salvador, Bahia, see Russell-Wood, Fidalgos; Júlio César Medeiros da Silva Pereira, À Flor da Terra: O Cemitério dos Pretos Novos no Rio de Janeiro, Rio de Janeiro: Garamond, 2007.

4.1 THE NDONGO ROYALS: FROM BRAZIL TO PORTUGAL AND THEIR DISTRIBUTION TO DIFFERENT MONASTERIES

The Ndongo royals were not the first Africans to study in Portugal, although their education was an imposition rather than a voluntary undertaking. Afonso I, king of Kongo, sent many students to Portugal, including members of his own family, during his reign (1509–1542).[22] They were sponsored by means of the sale of ivory, and those who could not continue their studies or gain a degree were ordered to enter the priesthood and continue their studies rather than return to the Kongo without formal qualifications.[23] Students from Angola were sent in 1676 to study in other countries in Europe, particularly Italy and the College of Propaganda Fide in Rome.[24] The nature of Africans' presence in Portugal in this period warrants a new study in its own right. Suffice to say here that it was against this background that the Ndongo royals were sent to various monasteries to study.

The Pungo-Andongo royals – twenty princes and two princesses with three servants – were sent to Portugal in four different stages after the war of 1671 (see Figure 17). Historians such as Delgado, Birmingham and particularly Lara have not detected this detail in their work.[25] Groups II and III were sent from Angola to Brazil in 1671 and then to Portugal in 1673. Group I – Dom Philipe (Ngolamano) and Dom Diogo (Cabangua) – were sent under the charge of António de Castro de Sousa, who was a scribe at the Portuguese Royal Treasury in 1648 and a senior crown judge in Luanda, Angola, in 1665.[26] Group IV consisted of four illegitimate sons of Philipe Hari I – Dom Ignaçio, Dom Antonio, Dom Sebastiam

---

[22] See 'Carta do Rei do Congo a D. João III' [A Letter by the King of Kongo to King John III], ATT, CC-I-32-99, 25 August 1526, MMA, vol. I, pp. 483–484, 'Item. Senhor, nós temos muyto marfym e cada dia nos vem, o quall desejamos mãdar e vossos navyoos a esses reynos, pera cõ elle escusarmos as despesas que v A. cõ nossas coussas faz'.

[23] See 'Carta do Rei do Congo a D. João III' and 'Despesas Com os Estudantes Indios e Pretos em Lisboa' [Expenses with Black and Native Students in Lisbon], ATT, ms. 186, 3 March 1538 to 7 May 1543, MMA, vol. II, pp. 66–69.

[24] See 'Carta de Fra Griostomo de Genua' [A Letter of Fra Griosostomo from Genoua], APF, SOCG, Rome, vol. 30 di Genaro 1676, MMA, vol. XIII, pp. 391–396, p. 394.

[25] See Cadornega, *História Geral*, vol. II, pp. 547–548; Birmingham, *Trade and Conquest*; and also Lara, 'Depois da Batalha de Pungo Andongo'.

[26] See Cadornega, *História Geral*, vol. II, pp. 588–589. Sousa returned to Luanda, Angola, with Governor Aires de Saldanha de Meneses e Sousa on 27 August 1676. While in Portugal he was appointed colonel of an infantry regiment for Angola on 26 June 1675. He died in Angola on 16 May 1680. See also 'Carta de António da Costa de Sousa a Manuel Barreto de S. Paio' and 'Sobre os Principes Negros do Dongo Unidos no Navio Sao Verissimo'.

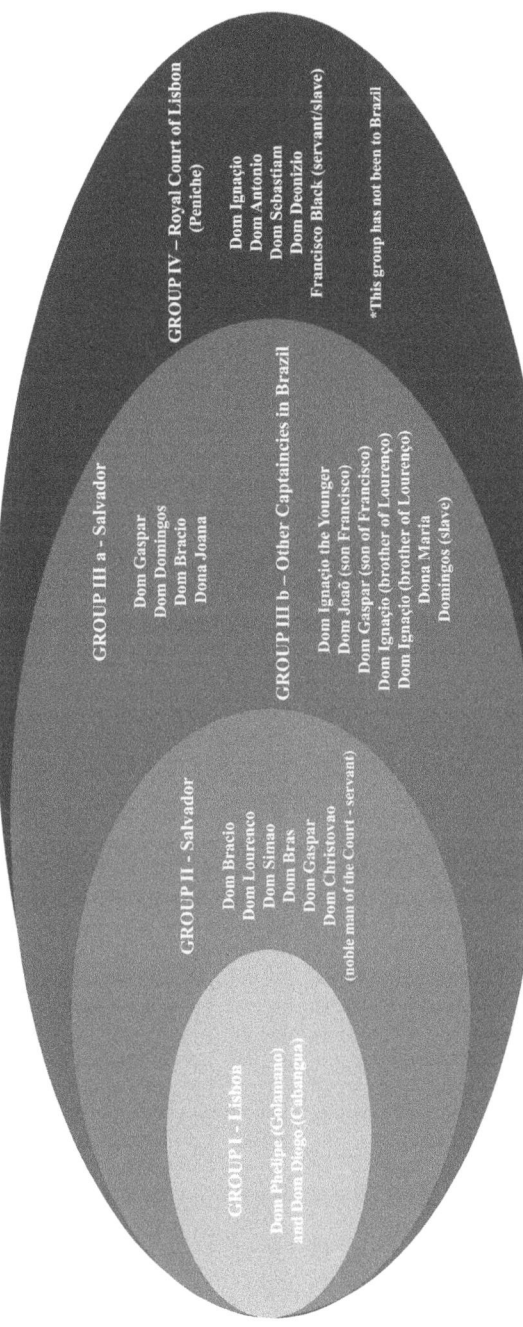

FIGURE 17 Graph illustrating the arrival of the four groups of royals in Portugal. By the author, based on manuscripts.

and Dom Deonizio – who were sent to Peniche, where they stayed with a certain Ferráz (an officer charged with looking after them), although it is unclear when they arrived in Portugal. Sixteen royals plus a nobleman called Domingos, who was described as a royal servant, were sent initially to Brazil. In Group II and III there were ten royals who were sent to Salvador in the Bahian captaincy, including Mendonça, one of his brothers, Simão, and several cousins.[27] Group IIIb consisted of six people, including Princess Maria, and two of Mendonça's brothers – both named Ignácio[28] – who were sent to other, unknown, captaincies in Brazil. Of Group IV, only the youngest, Ignacio, was not sent to a monastery in Portugal. Twelve royals out of eighteen were sent to monasteries in Portugal.[29]

The first group sent to Portugal after the war of Pungo-Andongo was the 10-year-old heir to the throne of Ndongo, Dom Philipe (Ngolamano), and his uncle, the chief of the army 'Ngolambole' of Pungo-Andongo, Dom Diogo (Cabangua). They were sent directly to Portugal as prisoners of war.[30] On the afternoon of 21 August 1672, almost three months after Cabangua and Ngolamano's arrival in Lisbon, the president of the Portuguese Overseas Council convened an emergency meeting on the orders of the regent, by then His Highness Pedro II.[31] The agenda of the meeting

---

[27] According to the governor of Bahia, 'Carta de Afonso Furtado do Rio de Castro de Mendonça' [A Letter by Afonso Furtado do Rio de Castro de Mendonça] AHU, Brasil-Bahia, cx. 22, d. 2545-2546, n. 2545, 7 August 1673, and the brother of Father Antonio Vieira 'Carta de Bernardo Vieyra Ravasco' [A Letter by Bernardo Vieyra Ravasco], AHU, Brasil-Bahia, cx. 22, d. 2545-2546, n. 2546, 8 August 1673.

[28] See 'Carta de Bernardo Vieyra Ravasco'.

[29] These figures are based on the draft of a letter I recently uncovered at the Public Archive of Salvador, Brazil. I was able to trace the final, and legible, version of the letter to the Arquivo Historical Ultramarino de Belém in Lisbon. The letter, which is dated 9 November 1673, shows that the group of ten royals (Groups IIIa and IIIb) that were sent to Brazil were the last group to leave Brazil for Portugal. The letter also indicates that the group almost lost their lives, presumably for lack of health care while aboard the *S. Verissimo* in the harbour in Lisbon, where they were waiting for a decision from the Overseas Council as to where they would be sent. The letter also shows that Mendonça's group (Group II) had been in a similar predicament when they arrived in Lisbon six months earlier. See 'Recibo de Francisco Gonçalves referente ao recebimento de negros escravos para entregar ao Secretario do Conselho' [Receipt of Franciso Gonçalves in Relation to the Received Slaves from the Secretary of the Council], AHU-Bahia, cx 2. doc. 92, AHU_ACL_CU_005, cx.2, d. 181, Reſcebi seiis escravos, digo negiors principes pera emtregar ao secretario do consleho ultramarino, Bahia dia 24 de maio 1673'. Gonçalves had confirmed that he had received six princes.

[30] See Felner, *Angola: Apontamentos*, and MMA, vol. XIII, pp. 297-298.

[31] 'HisHighness' was the term used to refer to Pedro II before he become king, after which the title His Majesty would have applied. 'Consulta do Conselho Ultramarino', AHU, cód.

was to decide what precautionary measures were needed to handle the stay of Ngolamano and his uncle Dom Diogo Cabangua and where they would be sent in Lisbon. On 2 September, almost two months after the first meeting, the Portuguese Overseas Council decided to send Ngolamano to the Royal Monastery of Alcobaça, where he was baptised in 1674, and Cabangua to the Fortress of São Julião de Barra in Lisbon. In the margin of the letter dated 2 September 1672, the Portuguese Overseas Council also stated that all of the king of Ndongo's relatives sent to Brazil should be sent to Portugal: 'Dom Philipe, I order to be sent to Alcobaça and Dom Diogo to the Forte of São Julião da Barra. To those relatives [of the King] that have been sent to Brazil, the Council [Overseas Council] has given the necessary orders that they be sent to the Kingdom [Portugal].'[32]

While in the Fortress of São Julião de Barra, Cabangua was not allowed to work, as that risked him creating a network with those he might encounter and passing on information – including accounts of war, slavery, injustice, the Portuguese Overseas Council and the Portuguese relationship with the people of Angola[33] – about the Angolan political landscape and the Portuguese activities there. Cabangua was a highly educated figure who would have been able to articulate the reasons for the war in Angola and the political stance of the people in the region. There may well have been a group in Lisbon interested in Angola and the Portuguese political position there.[34] Fra Girolamo Merolla da Sorrento, for example, arrived in Lisbon in November 1682 on his way to the Kongo, and was well received by Kongo Christians living there. There were certainly people in Lisbon with a strong interest in what was going on in West Central Africa. There were Angolans and Angolan priests at the Royal Court of Lisbon, and confraternities in the city who would have wanted to know the truth of what was going on in Angola.[35] Cabangua

17, fls. 59–59 v, 'o Duque Presidente ordenou Da parte de vA. que esta tarde se abrisse o Conselho'.
[32] 'Consulta do Conselho Ultramarino', 'A Dom Phelipe mando para Alcobaça e a Dom Diogo para a Torre de São Julião; pello que toca aos parentes que forão para o Brazil o Conselho passe as ordens neçessarias para uirem para o Reyn'.
[33] See letters from Pedro II, See 'Dom Pedro por Graça de Deos'.
[34] See Gray, 'The Papacy'.
[35] See 'Carta de António da Costa de Sousa a Manuel Barreto de S. Paio'. Princess Joanna stayed at the Court. She was not sent to the monastery since she was considered too attractive: 'a Princeza Dona Joanna por ser mossa formoza, parecendo á Raynha Nossa Senhora tella em seu seruiço ficará nelle'. See also 'Consulta do Conselho Ultramarino', 'O Duque P. / Saluador Correa de Sáa j Benauides / Antonio Paes de Sande / Feliciano Dourado / Joaõ Falcaõ de Sousa / Pedro Alueres Seco de Macedo'.

was said to have died of smallpox while in prison in the Fortress of São Julião de Barra in Lisbon, but we cannot say for certain whether his death was natural. Smallpox was certainly a disease that killed many people in both Angola and Bahia at the time.[36] However, Cabangua was in Portugal to serve his sentence, as a document from August 1672 indicates: 'the uncle [of Dom Philipe of Dongo] was the General of the armed forces, he was imprisoned at the Fortress of S. Gião [São Julião da Barra], so that he will be indicted [prosecuted] for his crime, and punished for the crime he deserved'.[37] He was viewed by the Portuguese governing authorities as a highly dangerous figure to Portuguese interests in the region, who might well have served as a source of information for the abolitionists,[38] confraternities, New Christians and anti-Inquisition groups in Lisbon.

On 7 May 1673, the 10-year-old Ngolamano was sent to Alcobaça in the care of Paschoal de Azevedo Freyre, Officer Major of the Secretary of

---

[36] Smallpox had been registered in the seventeenth century as a killer disease in Angola and Salvador, Bahia. See 'Carta do Clero de Angola ao Nuncio Apostólico', APF, SRC, Angola, Kongo, vol. 2, fls. 127–128, 17 October 1687, MMA, vol. XIII, pp.70–72, 'e aos Missionários nos mattos sempre socorrendo com o prouimento opportuno; no tempo que heraõ as bexigas nesta Cidade, mal que matou muyta gente andaua o dito Padre correndo as ruas todas da Cidade com huã campainha O nas maons uisitando quem necessitauaõ dos santos Sacramentos da Igreia; era em tudo perfeitíssimo e digno de imitação, exemplo e doctrina'. See also documentos de Camara de Bahia. For a detailed study of Angolan disease in the period, see José Pinto de Azeredo, *Ensaios Sobre Algumas Enfermidades D'Angola (1799)*, Luanda: Luanda, Instituto de Investigação Científica de Angola, 1967.

[37] Barretto, *Monstruosidades do Tempo e da Fortuna*, p. 202, 'o tio que era General do exercito, o mandou meter na torre de S. Giaõ, para se lhe processor a culpa, e castigalo pelos merecimentos do processo', and, for latter, 'entrou em Lisboa o Monte Negro cõ as tres naos da índia; e na mesma maré entrou hü navio de Angola cõ a cabeça del Rey de Dongo, e das Pedras, rebelado, e vencido em batalha, e prisioneiro seu jrmaõ d. Diogo, e hü filho del Rey chamado d. Phelippe de poucos annos, a o qual S.A. mandou doutrinar a o Mosteiro de Alcobaça, e o tio que era General do exercito, o mandou meter na torre de S. Giaõ ('), para se lhe processor a culpa, e castigalo pelos merecimentos do processo' (The *Monte Negro* arrived in Lisbon [harbour] with three other ships from India; and in the same tide another ship arrived from Angola with the head of the King of Dongo, and of Pedras [Stones] who had rebelled, and has been defeated in the battle, and his brother, the prisoner, d. Diogo, and one son of the King, called d. Phelippe of a few years of age, the one His Majesty has sent to the Monastery of Alcobaça to be instructed, and the uncle [of Dom Philipe of Dongo] who was the General of the armed forces, was imprisoned at the Fortress of S. Gião [São Julião da Barra], so that he will be indicted (prosecuted) for his crime, and be punished for the crime he deserved.'

[38] Gaspar says people talked to him about the slavery case. Mesquita, S.C. Africa vol. 1, fl. 486; on Angolan priests in the Royal Court of Lisbon see AHU, Angola, cx. 10, fl., 678v, 24 August 1673.

the Overseas Council.[39] Ngolamano being of high profile, heir to the throne of Pungo-Andongo, the majority of the Portuguese Overseas Council members needed to attend the meeting. The members of the Overseas Council – Duque Nuno Alvares Pereira de Melo (Duque de Cadaval), the president; Saluador Correa de Sá Benauides; Antonio Paes de Sande; Feliciano Dourado; Joaõ Falcaõ de Sousa; and Pedro Alueres Seco de Macedo (the obvious absentees from the meeting were Francisco Malheiro and Rui Teles de Meneses)[40] – had made a unanimous decision to send Ngolamano to Alcobaça. On 24 November 1673, Pedro II summed up the Crown's position with regard to the plan for Ngolamano in a letter he sent to the principle general of the Convent of Alcobaça: 'I have decreed to consider the best part for his education, where he could learn, and be endowed with quality in those areas that could make him apt …'[41]. Pedro II made it clear that it was a political decision to send Ngolamano to Alcobaça and to have him instructed in a way that would dissuade him from revisiting the past of his parents and people:

I have decided that there was no convent ultimately more suitable than that of Alcobaça, where I hope, that with the instruction of the priests and with the doctrine, and that of art, among which he could learn. He will be able to achieve my desired will I have for remedying him, and for that I have entrusted you with a great deal that you pay particular attention. I have decreed that you take care of his wellbeing, not only that he be instructed in the stuff of faith, also in all good art, and commending him to be taught by whom you judge will do this with greater wisdom.[42]

---

[39] See 'Consulta do Conselho Ultramarino', 'Paschoal de Azevedo Freyre, official mayor da secretaria deste Conçelho'.
[40] See 'Consulta do Conselho Ultramarino'. Both Francisco Malheiro and Rui Teles de Meneses were appointed members of the Portuguese Oversea Council from 1664 and 1667 and continued to serve until 1687, see 'Consulta do Conselho Ultramarino Sobre o Bispo de S. Tomé', AHU, S. Tomé, cx. 3, doc. 86, Lisbon, 17 October 1687, MMA, vol. XIII, pp. 68–69.
[41] ATT, miscelânia, cód. 171, fls. 483–484. Repetido no cód. 168, fl. 355, 'Carta do Regente d. Pedro ao Superior de Alcobaça', vol. XIII, Lisboa, 24 November 1673, MMA, vol. XIII, p. 239, 'mandando eu considerar a parte maiz conveniente pera a sua educaçaõ, donde podesse aprender, e dotarsse daquellas partes que o fizessem [alem de ser filho de hum Rey] hábil, para lhe poder fazer mercê'.
[42] ATT, Miscelânia, cód. 171, fls. 483–484. Repetido no cód. 168, fl. 355, 'Carta do Regente d. Pedro ao Superior de Alcobaça', Lisbon, 24 November 1673, MMA, vol. XIII, p. 239, 'resolvi, que em nenhuã parte poderia maiz vtilmente aproveitar-se, que nesse Convento de Alcobaça aonde espero, que com a communicaçaõ dos Religiozos e com a doutrina, e artez, que entre ellez pode aprender, se poderá comseguir o dezejo que tenho de o poder remediar, e assy voz encommendo muito que com particular attençaõ mandeiz ter cuidado de sua pessoa, pera que naõ só, que seja instruhido naz materiaz da fé, maz em

The choice of Alcobaça was fundamental from Pedro II's ideological viewpoint. Alcobaça was a royal monastery[43] and Pedro II's selection of priests to instruct Ngolamano demonstrated that his intention was to control him. He wanted Ngolamano to be instructed in the social and political environment of Portugal. Most importantly, the priests at Alcobça monastery were to change Ngolamano's world-view so that he became sympathetic to Portuguese political and economic interests in the Atlantic region, including the conquest of Africans. Severim, a Portuguese economist writing in the seventeenth century, argued that to make Africans happy and friendly towards the Portuguese, Portugal had to invest in their education and give them an education in Portugal.[44] If Portugal were to achieve its mission of retaining its territories overseas in the face of encroachment by other European countries, Africans had to be included in the grand plan of the empire by acculturating them in Portuguese customs and state apparatus and giving their children scholarships. For Severim, Portugal did not have the means or military capability to conquer its European enemies, hence they needed Indigenous Africans to help. The price for that was to educate them in all things Portuguese. According to Severim, religion, that is, Western Christianity, was a tool that could be used to domesticate the Africans. In his view, history had taught that through culture you could conquer people. He argued that there was a need for the Portuguese to carry out a mission of peace in Angola because the Angolans were powerful, and any attempt to conquer them by force would not benefit Portugal's interests in the region.[45] The colonial project was based on the annihilation of other cultures and, by implication, the imposition of European culture. Denying people their culture and values made them dependent on the colonisers' values.

Returning to the Ndongo royals' education in Portugal, they were educated with the aim of making them abandon their culture and values, which constituted their identity. As we saw in the case of Ngolomano, the monasteries to which they were sent were again chosen carefully. The royals' Portuguese education was an attempt to reduce them to dependence on Portuguese values. Severim would have been well placed to remember that the Portuguese ideology for converting the African élite

todaz as boaz artez, emcommendando o seu ensino a quem julgardez, que o fará com maior acerto'.
[43] See Manuel Vieira de Natividade, *O Mosteiro de Alcobaça*, Coimbra: Imprensa Progresso, 1885.
[44] See Manuel Severim de Faria, ARHM, Salazar y Castro, ms. B-4, fls. 95–105 v.
[45] See Manuel Severim de Faria, ARHM, Salazar y Castro, ms. B-4, fls. 95–105 v.

in West Central Africa and West Africa was a 200-year-old strategy. Afonso I, king of Kongo, had graduated from the Jesuits' college in the Kongo in the fifteenth century, and he became a defender of the Catholic faith and made Christianity a state religion: 'and he was the son of the same King, that was called D. Affonso, he was a dedicated Catholic, that embraced the faith, he burnt all his idols, making their practice as idolatry, a great preacher and vehement defender of Catholic faith'.[46]

The Portuguese Crown and the missionary societies' intention to educate Africans on the Western model was in line with the resolutions of the Council of Trent on the education of the Indigenous people in Africa, the Americas and Asia. The council's recommendations focused on providing Indigenous people with the knowledge that would enable them to teach Christianity to the non-believers. It was an education guided by the desire to missionise African, Asian and Indigenous American people. The decrees of Trent on education were in practice implemented by those countries heavily involved in the Atlantic project in the sixteenth century, 'such as Italy, Spain, the kingdom of Portugal'.[47]

Like Cabangua, Ngolamano was to be kept away from other Angolan students in Portugal for the fear that he would influence them by giving them information about the political situation in Angola and what had happened to his parents, King João Hari II and his wife Camasa.[48] As we saw in Chapter 2, both were brutally killed, and João Hari II's head was carried to Portugal for burial, although we do not know exactly where.[49] Ngolamano might well have constituted a danger to the establishment.

---

[46] See *Arquivo das Colónias*, n. 34–38 (2 November 1678), Outubro-Dezembro de 1931, p. 471, 'e um filho do mesmo Rey, a que chamavaõ d. Affonso, se fez taõ Catholico, que abrazou, e queimou todos os idolos, fazendo-se de idolatra, grande pregador e acérrimo defensor da fé Catholica]'. See also the 'Report from the Governor of Religious and Existing Convents in Angola', 1693, ASGA, *Livro de Registo de Ordens Régias*, liv. 5, fls. 69 e sgs., Paiva Manso, *Historia do Kongo*, pp. 324–339, MMA, pvol. XIII, p. 330–346.

[47] Faria, ARHM, fls. 95–105 v, p. 685 'em Itália, Hespanha e neste Reyno de Portugal'.

[48] See Felner, *Angola: Apontamentos* and MMA, vol. XIII, pp. 297–298, p. 297.

[49] See See 'Baptismo do Príncipe de Dongo' [Baptism of Prince of Dongo], 'o tio que era General do exercito, o mandou meter na torre de S. Giaõ, para se lhe processor a culpa, e castigalo pelos merecimentos do processo'. See also Barretto, *Monstruosidades do Tempo e da Fortuna*, p. 202, 'entrou em Lisboa o Monte Negro cõ as tres naos da India; e na mesma maré entrou hum navio de Angola com a cabeça del Rei de Dongo, e das Pedras, rebellado, e vencido em batalha, e prisioneiro seu irmão d. Diogo, e hum filho del Rey chamado d. Filippe, de poucos annos, a o qual S.A. mandou doutrinar a o Mosteiro de Alcobaça, e o tio que era General do exercito, o mandou metter na torre de S. Giaõ, para se lhe processor a culpa, e castigá-lo pelos merecimentos do processo.'

Before his baptism in Alcobaça, he was constantly mindful of what he had experienced in Angola, which one priest described as the 'devil experience' and which in Kimbundu language might have been described using the term *kuxaketa* (to invoke a devil).[50] Ngolamano's knowledge of the horrific experience of his parents' deaths, and the loss of his uncle in Portugal, would have stayed with him for the rest of his life. He may have been with his parents when they were executed in Angola, or Cabangua may have told him what had happened. We cannot underestimate the sense of injustice and loss to a young man, who probably had no chance to say goodbye to his parents in a ceremonial way. He was denied the opportunity to be supported by family who, in the traditional African way, would have encouraged the grieving to be *vakola pupa* (strong at heart).[51] The young man had to deal with the loss in the way he found fit, but, at the same time, he had to deal with the suspicions of those who did not understand him and accused him of undertaking rituals in Portugal, which priests then decried as devilry.[52] From the point of view of the chief priest of Alcobaça, Ngolamano should not have been baptised, but this was to fail to recognise the enormous trauma that the young man had endured, nor to acknowledge the fact that, in spite of all he had been through, Ngolamano asked to be baptised because he was ready to fulfil his civic role.

Both Ngolamano and Cabangua were politically active and constituted a direct danger to the Portuguese establishment in Portugal. They had first-hand experience and were part of the political epicentre of Ndongo. It was little wonder that they were imprisoned as they were. The available sources, however, do not reveal Ngolamano's fate in Portugal.[53]

The Ndongo royals of the second group (Group IV) were sent directly to the Royal Court at the Ribeira Royal Palace (Palácio Real da Ribeira) in Lisbon, Portugal. They were highly political figures and used their experience to resist the Portuguese establishment following their arrival in Portugal in 1671. Three of them – Dom Antonio, Dom Sebastiam and

---

[50] See Cadornega, *História Geral*, vol. I, p. 620. He used the word *sacalamento* that came from the Kimbundu verb *kusakala*, to invoke.
[51] See Cadornega, *História Geral*, vol. I, p. 613.
[52] See Felner, *Angola: Apontamentos*, pp. 468–469; Documento n. 43.
[53] The difficulty with finding out more about the royals is that only their first names appear in the documents we have, such as the letters from Bahia and that of 24 August 1673. Mendonça was exceptional in this regard, as his surname appears in the Vatican documents, enabling us to make the connection back to Pungo-Andongo. See 'Carta de António da Costa de Sousa a Manuel Barreto de S. Paio' and 'Sobre os Principes Negros do Dongo Unidos no Navio Sao Verissimo'.

Dom Deonizio – were described as *grandes* (older) than the last, Ignacio the younger, and had some knowledge of how politics worked in Portugal.⁵⁴ Dom Antonio, Dom Sebastiam, Dom Deonizio and Ignacio all arrived in Lisbon in 1671, although the exact date in the year is unknown; there they met their sister, Dona Joana, who was already a resident at the royal court (see Figure 17).

They were separated from the Bahian group and they appeared from the outset to be politically engaged and to be voicing their views. Whilst in the royal court, they were seen as a threat that could have a direct political impact on the Portuguese. At least that was the view expressed by Francisco Gonçalvez Ferráz, who warned a royal servant, António da Costa de Sousa, about the political assertiveness of the prisoners. Costa de Sousa passed the message on to the royal secretary, Manuel Barreto de S. Payo, who put considerable pressure on the Portuguese Overseas Council to take measures to tame them before the members of the general public who might want to know about the war and Portuguese political manoeuvres in Angola got in touch with them. Payo succinctly states: 'I am of the opinion that in order to avoid explosive situations or a public scene, they [Dom Antonio, Dom Sebastiam and Dom Deonizio] should be sent to the House of Catechism⁵⁵ and be instructed in the Ministries of faith to best enable them for the service.'⁵⁶ Payo further advised the Portuguese Overseas Council to find an 'Angolan Jesuit priest resident at the Royal Court of Lisbon or look for somebody who has the knowledge of their language [Kimbundu]'⁵⁷ who would be charged with indoctrinating them. However, they were instead sent from the court to the house of Francisco Gonçalvez Ferráz in Lisbon. We do not know how long Ferráz kept them in his house, but the advice he gave to the Portuguese Overseas Council demonstrates that he knew them well enough to form a strong opinion about them. In his receipt, he acknowledged that he had received six slaves or Black princes to hand over to the Overseas Council (see Figure 18).⁵⁸

---

⁵⁴ See 'Carta de António da Costa de Sousa a Manuel Barreto de S. Paio'.
⁵⁵ For the House of Catechism, see Saldanha, *História de Goa*, pp. 238–239
⁵⁶ See 'Carta de António da Costa de Sousa a Manuel Barreto de S. Paio', 'estes sugeitos sou de parecer por iuitar estrondos ou nota, se recolham á Caza dos Catacumenos e nella os instruam nos Mistérios da fee, e para os capacitarem milhor."
⁵⁷ See 'Carta de António da Costa de Sousa a Manuel Barreto de S. Paio', 'se saberá se há na corte algum relegiozo da Companhia filho de Angola, ou se buscará outro que lhe saiba a lingua'.
⁵⁸ See 'Recibo de Francisco Goncalves referente ao recebimento de negros escravos para entregar ao Secretario do Conselho'.

FIGURE 18 Francisco Gonçalvez Ferráz's letter, Arquivo Público de Salvador, Bahia. In the letter he talks about six slaves, then corrects himself by saying he had received six princes. Photograph taken by the author.

How long Dom Antonio, Dom Sebastiam and Dom Deonizio stayed at the Royal Court of Lisbon is not stated in the Overseas Council's correspondence. They were resistant to the court, and to the attempt to send them to the House of Catechism and to Brazil. They were ultimately sent to Peniche, a small town 100 kilometres away from Lisbon, where they stayed until at least 1695, since we do not have documents relating to them after this.[59] They spent at least twenty-seven years there.

The length of the stay of the three older princes in Ferráz's house is not stated in the document sent to Manuel Barreto de S. Paio, but it is clear from the correspondence between the Portuguese Overseas Council and the Crown that they were not actually dispatched to the different monasteries listed in the letter of 24 August 1673, nor were they sent to the House of Catechism to be indoctrinated in the ideology of the Portuguese Empire.[60] Instead, the Portuguese Overseas Council fought hard to have them sent to Maranhão, Brazil, and to have them enlisted in the army

---

[59] See AHU_CU_Reino, cx. 60, pasta 36, 9 July 1695, 'Osprincipes pretos que por ordem de sua Mag.de estao na Villa de Peniche'. Another letter, AHU_CU_Reino, cx.60, Pasta 36, 9 July 1695, 'Ostres Principes Pretos fizeram peticao a VMg.de poreste Conselho, em que dizem, que por ordem de VM.de estao na Villa de Peniche aonde VMg.de por sua Real grandeza lhe fas merce mandar lhe dar a cada hum quatro vintens por dia para o seu sustento'.

[60] See 'Carta de António da Costa de Sousa a Manuel Barreto de S. Paio', 'auendo ocaziaõ para a índia, se remetaõ para lá seruirem a S.A.'.

there, where there were fewer Angolans than in Bahia and Pernambuco and where the princes' influence would be limited.[61] Dom Antonio, Dom Sebastiam and Dom Deonizio must have served in the army that their brother, João Hari II, raised against the Portuguese, and were not ready to give up their struggle for freedom. For this reason, they were seen as a great danger to the empire. It would appear from António da Costa de Sousa's letter to Manuel Barreto de S. Paio that they may not have had a formal Portuguese education like that of the third group, but they were knowledgeable and well-informed about politics. The princes clearly rebelled against the system that was used to deny them their liberty. In fact, they were accused of not being good citizens of the kingdom (Portugal) because they did not comply with its laws, and were clearly unwilling to become what was expected of them, and were sent to Peniche: 'Black men and relatives of the King of Ndongo that had come to this Kingdom and resided in this court, for having transgressed the orders, they were sent to the Fortress of Peniche.'[62] Peniche would limit the Ndongo royals' contact with Angolans, as only ships from Bahia arrived there, but not those from Angola.[63]

In Peniche, they were 'handed over to Lieutenant General Simaõ Matheus, who was the governor of the Fortress'.[64] They later moved from the fortress in Peniche to houses provided by the Portuguese Crown in the town,[65] and probably married Portuguese women and had families. Although there are no sources that confirm this, their demand in

---

[61] See 'Provisão sobre escravos para Brasil', AHA, aa. 1937, Documentos Antigos Registados em 1799, fl. 25v, p. 15, 18 March 1673, see MMA, vol. XIII, pp. 218–219. Angolans were sent to Maranhão to be used as slaves in place of Indigenous Brazilians. For statistics on slaves in Maranhão in that period, see Hawthorne, *From Africa to Brazil*, pp. 40–41. The number of slaves sent from Angola to Maranhão in 1673 was 950. See also See AHU_CU_Reino, cx.60, pasta 36, 9 July 1695. However, the Portuguese underestimated the level of communication between the regions in Brazil at the time: documentary sources from the period show that Natives from the Palmares region were trading with Pernambuco and Maranhão. See Palmares Documents, pp. 133–181.

[62] See,'Consulta do Conselho Ultramarino Sobre os familiares do Rei do Dongo' and MMA, vol. XIII, pp. 381–382, 'os pretos e parentes de ElRey de Dongo que tinhaõ uindo a este Reino e assitão nesta corte por terem feito desmandos, se emuiassem para a fortaleza de Peniche'.

[63] Padre Antonio Vieira travelled from Bahia to Peniche in 1641, see Schwartz, *A Governor and His Image*.

[64] See 'Consulta do Conselho Ultramarino Sobre os familiares do Rei do Dongo' and MMA, vol. XIII, p. 381, 'onde ficaraõ entregues ao thenente general Simaõ Matheus qua a gouerna'.

[65] See AHU_CU_Reino, cx.60, Pasta 36, 9 July 1695, and AHU_CU_001_cx. 13, d. 1505, 12 June 1682.

the documents for an increase in their salary every year and for clothing every two years indicates this. The last time we hear about them is in 1697.[66] By then their household expenses were costing 'close to twenty-five thousand Reis, and in each year, in the carrying out of inspections, it exceeds a hundred thousand Reis'.[67] In 1673, the princes were paid 1,088,560 reis by the Crown Treasury; by 18 July 1679, the figure was 100,000,000 reis;[68] and by 1682, it was 162,600,000 per annum. At that point, the Overseas Council stepped in and capped their expenses to 162,600,000 per annum, on the grounds that a soldier received less than the amount each was getting per year. The princes appear to have remained in Peniche for more than twenty-seven years, and it remains unclear whether the right opportunity ever came for them to be sent to Brazil.[69]

The fate of the younger prince, Dom Ignacio, who had been studying before he left Angola, was that he was sent from Peniche either to Évora or Coimbra,[70] although we do not know which city, nor do we have any evidence about him staying in Peniche. The Portuguese Overseas Council's discussion of the princes' futures focused entirely on Dom Antonio, Dom Sebastiam and Dom Deonizio and on whether to send them out of Portugal to Brazil or to have them educated in Portuguese culture.

What is clear is that the Peniche group was as active as the Bahian group (groups II, IIIa and IIIb), many of whom were sent to monasteries in Portugal and that they were figures who, like Mendonça, were determined and conditioned, or enabled, by historical and social forces that lay outside of their control to appropriate the social resources available to them to create a space in which to voice their concerns for freedom. As we saw in Chapter 3, the Bahian contingent constituted a danger to Brazil for their potential to connect with runaway enslaved communities in Bahia

---

[66] AHU_CU_Reino, cx.60, Pasta 36, 9 July 1697.
[67] AHU_CU_001_cx. 13, d. 1505, 12 June 1682, 'cujo sustento emporta cada mes com casas pagas e outros gastos, que fazem perto de uintem e sinco mil reis, e em cada anno, em formação da uistoria passante de sem mil reis'.
[68] In 1682, the cost of living for each of them was 80.00 reis per day, 29,200,000 each per annum – a total of 87,600,000 per annum. Inspections costs were 25,000,000 for each prince each year, making at total of 75,000,000. Altogether the cost was 162,600,000 per annum. See AHU, Angola, cx. 11, 12 June 1682.
[69] See the document, AHU_CU_Reino, cx.60, Pasta 36, 9 July 1695, and the other letters on Peniche.
[70] See 'Carta de António da Costa de Sousa a Manuel Barreto de S. Paio', 'o pequeno (pareçendo que estuda) se mandará a Euora, ou a Coimbra'.

and in Brazil at large.[71] They served as a reminder to the Portuguese establishment that slave communities in Brazil were seeking a form of empowerment and a focal point for unity through a political leader.

As mentioned above, the Bahian group arrived in Portugal in two stages. Mendonça's group (Group II) arrived first, and a second cohort (groups IIIa and IIIb) arrived in Lisbon from Rio de Janeiro on 9 November 1673. There, they were left onboard the ship for nearly two months in poor conditions and without clothing or enough food; indeed, they almost died.[72] The Crown's instruction to the Portuguese Overseas Council to send the Ndongo royals to various monasteries, both those in the kingdom and those belonging to the Portuguese Court, was not immediately heeded. A letter sent by the Portuguese Overseas Council to the Crown on 9 November 1673 in response to the Crown's letter of 24 August 1673 indicates that the council was well aware of the royals' predicament, but failed to act promptly. This suggests that the council's intention was that the royals should meet their death, and there may well have been a complaint made to the Crown, which forced the council to act.[73] The Portuguese Overseas Council opted out of the royals' care, and argued that they did not have the money to support them, it having been spent on the earlier arriving Angolans: 'and if the Council had had means to help these, they would have done. Notwithstanding, other money that you have given, has been spent on the first Blacks that came, as they were dying too'.[74]

The Crown's letter of 24 August 1673 – which stated that the princes should be sent to the wealthiest monasteries in the country, including the monasteries that belonged to the Crown, such as that of Alcobaça, and that on concluding their studies they should serve the Crown domestically, that is to say within Portugal rather than overseas – sheds important light on who actually made the journey from Brazil. The Municipal Council of Luanda's letter of 9 November confirmed that all of the ten royals that Furtado listed as having been sent to Portugal[75] were aboard the *São*

---

[71] See 'Carta de Antonio da Costa de Sousa a Manuel Barreto de S. Paio'.
[72] See 'Sobre os Principes Negros do Dongo Unidos no Navio Sao Verissimo', Lisboa, A.H.U, Códices do Brasil, 17, fls., 9 November 1673, p. 129-130.
[73] See 'Sobre os Principes Negros do Dongo Unidos no Navio Sao Verissimo'.
[74] 'Sobre os Principes Negros do Dongo Unidos no Navio Sao Verissimo', 'e se o Conselho tivera alguns efeitos para assistir a estes o fizera. Porem, algum dinheiro que havia de sua reparticao se dispendeu com os negros primeiros que vieram, por estarem tambem perecendo'.
[75] See the Governor of Bahia, Afonso Furtado do Rio de de Castro de Mendonça, AHU, Brasil-Bahia, cx. 22, d. 2545-2546, n. 2545, 7 August 1673, and 'Carta de Bernardo Vieyra Ravasco'.

Verissimo in Lisbon.[76] Lara has claimed that 'Dona Joanna may have stayed in Salvador',[77] but she may not have been aware of this detail; I would argue that Dona Joanna's status would have made it impossible for the Portuguese to leave her in Brazil. Moreover, an inspection of the actual documents housed in the Arquivo Histórico Ultramarino de Belém, rather than the version of the Crown's letter transcribed and published by Brásio,[78] reveals that this was not the case. The letter was accompanied by a list outlining which of the royals should go to what monastery. The list includes all ten of the Ndongo royals who were sent to Salvador, including Dona Joanna.[79] In Brásio's version, the letter and list are presented as one document – suggesting that both were written before the royals arrived in Lisbon from Brazil. However, the original documents reveal that the Crown's letter was written in one hand and the list, a handwritten note filed with the letter, was in another. This suggests that the list outlining where the royals went was written at a later date and was in fact not a list of where they might go, but a list of where they did go, and is thus proof that Dona Joanna also made the journey to Lisbon.

The monasteries' group consisted of King Philipe Hari I's sons and illegitimate sons, and the children of his sister and of his sons Francisco – the heir to the throne of Ndongo who died fighting a war against the Dutch – and Ignacio da Silva – the father of Lourenço da Silva Mendonça who died in Quissama fighting for the Portuguese project of conquest as a *kilamba* (or *quilamba* captain) of *guerra preta*.[80] Dom Christovão, an ordinary nobleman, though referred to as a servant, was also part of the group.[81] A servant called Domingos (who belonged to the royal family of Ndongo) was also taken with the group, and a servant called Francisco *o negro* [the Black] accompanied the Peniche Group I. They were distributed among the monasteries as follows (see Table 8):

Sending the royals to different monasteries was intended to silence them. It was carried out to weaken the chances that the royals would galvanise themselves to mount any form of political resistance. It was seen

---

[76] See A.H.U, Codices do Brasil, 17, fl.s, 129–130, 'Sobre os Principes Negros do Dongo Unidos no Navio Sao Verissimo', Lisboa, 9 November 1673.
[77] Lara, 'Depois da Batalha de Pungo Andongo', p. 212.
[78] Brásio, *Monumenta Missionaria Africana*, vol. X.
[79] See 'Carta de Afonso Furtado do Rio de Castro de Mendonça' and 'Carta de Bernardo Vieyra Ravasco'.
[80] See Cadornega, *História Geral*, vol. I, p. 620. *Quilambas* were captains of *guerra preta* and were salaried.
[81] See 'Carta de Antonio da Costa de Sousa a Manuel Barreto de S. Paio'.

TABLE 8 *Distribution of the Ndongo royals to different monasteries. By the author, based on 'Carta de António da Costa de Sousa a Manuel Barreto de S. Paio'*

Distribution of the royals to different monasteries. B, by the author, based on 'Carta de António da Costa de Sousa a Manuel Barreto de S. Paio'	
Dom (Prince) Gaspar (son of King Philipe Hari I of Ndongo)	To Nossa Senhora de Graça de Lisboa, Lisbon
Prince Domingos (son of King Hari I of Ndongo)	To Santo Elói de Lisboa, Lisbon
Prince Ignacio (bastard son of King Philipe Hari I)	To São Vicente de Lisboa, Lisbon
Ignação the Younger (son of the King Philipe Hari I's sister)	To São Vicente de Lisboa, Lisbon
Prince Antonio (the bastard son of King Philipe Hari I)	To Colégio de Padres da Companhia de Santo Antão de Lisboa, Lisbon
Prince Diniz (bastard son of King Philipe Hari I)	To Monastério da Ordem de Cristo, Tomar
Prince Sebastião (bastard son of King Philipe Hari I)	To Convento de Santa Cruz, Coimbra
Prince João (Dom Francisco's son, King Philipe Hari I's son who died at the time of Dutch invasion of Angola). Dom Francisco died in the war against the Dutch.	To Colégio da Companhia de Coimbra
Prince Gaspar (the son of Dom Francisco mentioned above)	To Monastério de Tibans, Braga
Barga: Prince Simão (son of Dom Ignação da Silva, who was the son of King Philipe Hari I, brother of Prince Lourenço)	To Monastério de Basto
Prince Lourenço (Lourenço Mendonça da Silva, son of Dom Ignação da Silva, who was the son of King Philipe Hari I) who went to Rome	To Monastério de Vilar de Frades
Prince Ignacio (son of Dom Ignação da Silva, who was the son of King Philipe Hari I, brother of Prince Lourenço)	To Monastério de Moreira, Braga
Prince Ignacio (son of Dom Ignação da Silva, who was the son of King Philipe Hari I, brother of Prince Lourenço)	To Monastério de Selzedas, Braga
Prince Christovão (an ordinary noble)	To Monastério de Selzedas, Braga
Princess Dona Joanna	To stay with Princess the wife of the Regent Dom Pedro II of Portugal (for being beautiful)
Princess Dona Maria	To Carnide, Lisbon

as a positive decision after the failure in Brazil to provide the necessary political framework to tame them. Their time in the monasteries was meant to control their political activities and season them in a way that their stay in Brazil had not; it was also meant to provide them with different cultural and political resources. After all, this was a kingdom where the political milieu and the mechanisms to tame them were available. If Angola and Brazil were both regarded as politically chaotic and disordered, Portugal was the opposite. The distribution of the royals to different monasteries was a well-executed plan by the Crown and the Portuguese Overseas Council, in which siblings – including Mendonça and his brothers – were not sent to the same monasteries.

Let us return to Mendonça's particular case, his journey from the monastery of Vilar de Frade in Braga to Lisbon and his subsequent appointment and stay in Toledo. We will examine what kinds of cultural, economic and political resources were given to him and how he appropriated these to make his claim for the liberation of the enslaved Africans in Africa, Brazil, Portugal and Spain, as well as other constituencies in the Atlantic.

4.2 LOURENÇO DA SILVA MENDONÇA IN VILAR DE FRADES, BRAGA, C.1673–1677

I have carried out extensive research in the Archive of Braga District concerning Mendonça's studies at Vilar de Frades, and have visited the monastery itself. Most of the monastery has been converted into a psychiatric hospital (see Figure 19), although the main church is still in use. Only an incomplete tile painting (see Figure 20 and Figure 21) and chapel benches made from the Brazil wood of the period remain from the sixteenth and seventeenth centuries. A monastic community was established on the site in the eleventh century, and in the fifteenth century the monastery passed into the hands of the Order of Loios.[82] The Order of Loios had a tradition of receiving students from Africa and Indigenous Brazilians going back to the sixteenth century. In 1539 Vilar de Frades received students from the kingdom of Kongo and also Indigenous Brazilians.[83] So Mendonça would have

---

[82] See 'Carta de António da Costa de Sousa a Manuel Barreto de S. Paio'. For more on the history of the monastery, see Marques, *A Arquidiocese de Braga no Século XV*; C. A. Ferreira de Almeida, 'Arquitectura Românica Entre Douro e Minho', unpublished Ph.D. thesis, University of Porto, 1978. See also Manuel de Aguiar Barreiros, *A Portada Românica de de Vilar de Frades e o Seu Symbolico*, Braga: Marques Abreu, 1920.

[83] See 'Despesas Com os Estudantes Indios e Pretos em Lisboa'.

FIGURE 19 Igreja e Mosteiro de Vilar de Frades/Mosteiro de São Salvador, where Lourenço da Silva Mendonça studied for three to four years. Public domain.

certainly met students from different parts of Africa and Brazil, and particularly Indigenous Brazilians, at Vilar de Frades. It was also a monastery that was involved in the sale of enslaved people.[84]

Vilar de Frades was an interesting monastery that was critical of Catholic teaching and praxis.[85] It was also favoured by several popes,[86] including Innocent XI, to whom Mendonça addressed his court case. Favours, pardons, exemptions and privileges were also granted by Gregory VII, Eugenius IV, Leo X, Pius II, Alexander VI, Clement VII, Pius V, Sixtus V, Clement VIII, Innocent XI and Alexander VIII.[87] Pope Gregory XII was one of the patron saints of the Congregation

---

[84] See 'Despesas Com os Estudantes Indios e Pretos em Lisboa', p. 67, a slave was sold for 1450 reis bj [40].
[85] See Vinhas, *A Igreja e o Convento de Vilar de Frades*.
[86] See Vinhas, *A Igreja e o Convento de Vilar de Frades*.
[87] See L. Elliott Binns, *The History of the Decline and Fall of the Medieval Papacy*, London: Archon Books, 1967; Joseph Brusher, *Popes Through the Ages*, Whitefish MT: Van Nostrand, 1959, and Gail Marzieh, *The Three Popes: An Account of the Great Schism*, New York: Simon and Schuster, 1969.

FIGURE 20 Pope Gregory XII, without papal hat. Vilar de Frades Chapel, Braga, Portugal. Photograph by the author.

(Figure 20 and 21). He rose to power during the Great Schism (1378–1417) in Western Europe, a crisis that brought division among clerics, royals and practitioners of the Catholic faith for many years. During his reign, two other popes competed for the same Catholic authority, and only Gregory's resignation brought about a compromise that ended the Schism. Gregory was subsequently made bishop of Porto, Portugal. He used the Vilar de Frades Congregation in Braga as a platform for voicing his criticisms of the Catholic Church's

Mendonça's Journey to Portugal and Spain 299

FIGURE 21 Pope Gregory XII, with papal hat. Vilar de Frades Chapel, Braga, Portugal. Photograph by the author.

practices.[88] The teachings and critiques of Pope Gregory XII would have not gone unnoticed by Mendonça and those responsible for the Church's influence in Western society and involved in its power struggles.[89] If there was a lesson to be learnt from the Great Schism, it was that issues needed to be tackled at the root and not at the peripheries. Mendonça must have understood that the Church held the key to the problem of slavery: it was Rome that needed to make the headway, and not Portugal or Spain.

---

[88] See Vinhas, *A Igreja e o Convento de Vilar de Frades*.
[89] For detailed studies, see Walter Ullman, *The Origins of the Great Schism: A Study in Fourteenth Century Ecclesiastical History*, Hamden, CT: Archon Books, 1967; John Holland Smith, *The Great Schism: 1378*, New York: Weybright and Talley, 1970, see also Brusher, *Popes Through the Ages*.

In the Archive of Braga District is an enrolment book for Vilar de Frades that covers the period from 1575 to 1648. It does not show the fees paid, but does list the students' names and the subjects they studied, including: Mission, Gospels and Epistles. Courses were run for three to four years.[90] Unfortunately, details of students enrolled from 1648 to 1678 are missing. We also have the names of the directors of Vilar de Frades from the period of Mendonça's stay in Braga.[91] In the following section, I explore Mendonça's life in Lisbon, his appointment to the role of attorney general and the legal resources made available to him via the confraternities' constitution.

4.3 MENDONÇA AND THE CONFRATERNITY OF OUR LADY OF ROSARY OF BLACK MEN IN PORTUGAL

We know that Mendonça came to Lisbon for the first time on 23 August 1673, although Gray claimed that 'we do not know how or when he reached Lisbon'.[92] We also know that he returned to Lisbon for a second stay in 1681, or at least that he was already living and working in Lisbon by then (the exact date of his return to Lisbon is not stated in Mesquita's letter).[93] He might well have arrived in Lisbon for his second period from Vilar de Frades, where he was being educated. Indeed, he almost certainly did move from Vilar de Frades back to Lisbon, unless we assume that he travelled outside Portugal, to Brazil, after finishing his studies, as the letter of 26 March 1686 from the Propaganda Fide in Rome perhaps indicates: 'Lourenço da Silva de Mendonça from the Kingdom of Kongo in the Indies [Brazil]'.[94]

Mendonça's work in Lisbon appears to have been centred on the confraternities of Our Lady of Rosary of the Black Men, of which there were many in Portugal (Évora, Alentejo, Algarve), São Tomé, Angola, Kongo and Brazil.[95] By 1526 the confraternities had been granted the right, via their *compromisso* or constitution, to liberate their members from slavery or buy them from captivity. Many enslaved and free Africans joined the Confraternity of Rosary of S. Domingos in Lisbon in the sixteenth century,

---

[90] See Arquivo Distrital de Braga [ADB], Barcelos Fontes, Matriculas, XIII, 1575–1648.
[91] To name a few: Cristovao Do Espirito Santo (1671–1672), Francisco da Conceicao (1673), Antonio da Conceicao (1674–1676), Jose do Anjos (1677–1679), Cabangua dos Anjos (1680–1682), Bernado da Madre de Deus (1683–1685), Diogo do Espirito Santo (1688–1688), and Francisco dos Santos (1689–1692). See ADB, ms. 924 fl.s. 268 and 773–778.
[92] See Gray, 'The Papacy', p. 52.   [93] See S.C. Africa, vol. I, fl., 486.
[94] See SOCG, vol. 495a, 393, 'Lorenzo deSilva de Mendoza delRegno diCongo nell' Indè."
[95] See Russell-Wood, *Fidalgos and Philanthropists*.

and there was also a confraternity of Évora.[96] However, in 1550 an internal conflict between those of African descent and white Christian members of the Confraternity of Rosary of S. Domingos, which included 'Whites and Blacks, owners of enslaved people and enslaved people themselves',[97] which led to the closure of the confraternity a few years later, in 1565.[98] In 1518, the Crown had given privileges to the Confraternity of Rosary of S. Domingos that would appear a contradiction to Portuguese society because it was already an enslaving society. The privileges meant that Africans were given the right by law to gain their freedom from slavery, instead of maintaining them in bondage already at the beginning of the sixteenth century.[99] By 1518, Africans were in the majority in the Confraternity, and were thus able to elect those of African descent to the council of the Confraternity's *Mesa* (table), or board of guardians.[100]

There has been a good deal of research on confraternities of Black peoples that focuses primarily on their internal organisation, disputes and privileges in terms of their right to a place of burial.[101] However, there has been little research devoted to the legal arguments and the rights set out in the confraternities' constitutions around the liberation of enslaved Africans. Even Russell-Wood in his seminal work did not pay attention to this question.[102]

---

[96] Here I am indebted to Lahon, 'Da Redução da Alteridade'.
[97] See Lahon, 'Da Redução da Alteridade', p. 59, 'brancos e negros, donos e escravos, encontram-se no mesmo recinto para rezar num pé de igualdade'.
[98] Lahon, 'Da Redução da Alteridade', *Projecto História*, p. 60, "Em Lisboa, o ingresso das populações africanas escravas ou libertas na instituição instalada no Mosteiro Dominicano da cidade, é atestado a partir da primeira década23 do século XVI e durante a seguinte em Évora. Se, nesta cidade a coabitação entre irmãos negros e brancos, mas, sobretudo, entre donos e escravos, parece não provocar conflito, tal não é o caso em Lisboa.'
[99] Lahon, 'Da Redução da Alteridade', p. 60, 'Com efeito, por razões nunca explícitas, mas que contradizem aparentemente a lógica mesmo de qualquer sistema escravagista, o poder real atribuiu, logo no início do século XVI, aos confrades negros da confraria do Rosário de Lisboa, uma série de privilégios que reforçavam os fracos direitos dos escravos que entraram rapidamente em conflito com o poder dos donos'.
[100] Lahon, 'Da Redução da Alteridade', p. 60, 'Pois, sendo cada vez mais numerosos na confraria, os irmãos negros conseguiram eleger vários, dentre eles, a lugares-chave da Mesa da instituição'.
[101] See Brásio, *Os Pretos em Portugal*, pp. 53–83; see also Russell-Wood, *Fidalgos and Philanthropists*. For recent work on confraternities, see George J Fonseca, *Religião e Liberdade: os Negros nas Irmandades e Confrarias Portuguesas (séculos XV a XIX)*, Lisbon: Papelmunde, V. N. Famalicão, 2016; see Gray, 'The Papacy', pp. 52–68, and Lucilene Reginaldo, 'Rosários dos Pretos, "São Benedito de Quissama": Irmandades e Devoções Negras no Mundo Atlântico (Portugal e Angola, Século XVIII)', *Studia Historica, Historia Moderna*, 38(1), 2016, pp. 123–151 and Reginaldo, '"África em Portugal"'.
[102] Russell-Wood, *Fidalgos and Philanthropists*.

The right to freedom in the constitution of 1526 is often interpreted as the right of the confraternities to buy enslaved people rather than to buy the freedom of enslaved. This argument is used to demonstrate that there was something inherently undesirable in the way in which confraternities' rights were used. Thus, the quest for freedom from slavery appears to be incidental and impossible to achieve. There are even those who advocate that confraternities operated nominally in societies in which the idea of slavery was enshrined.[103] However, to understand Mendonça's liberation argument one needs to engage with the specific clauses of the confraternities' constitution that allowed members to gain their freedom by exercising these rights. Furthermore, to comprehend the membership of the confraternities, there is a need to recognise the privileges that the constitution awarded them, in terms of belonging, legal rights and their relationship with the political and religious authorities in the lands in which they were situated.

At the centre of the confraternities was the legal framework, the *compromisso* or constitution that allowed the confraternity members to belong to the community of the free, liberated them from slavery and allowed them to engage in business transactions. By virtue of their membership of a confraternity, members were freemen; the act of becoming a member of a confraternity was an act of freedom. By joining confraternities members exercised their right to freedom. The confraternities were clubs for the free, regardless of their status – be they Africans, Indigenous Brazilians, White Europeans, Blacks, male, female, Jews, Moors – all could be members. The privileges, particularly those around freedom, afforded to the confraternities via the constitution provided the legal framework in which Mendonça was operating. By not engaging with the legal aspects of the confraternities' constitution, researchers have failed to address Mendonça's legal argument in his court case in the Vatican. Even Gray, with his profound knowledge of Mendonça's intervention in Rome, failed to address the fundamental point of Mendonça's legal argument in the Vatican on *natural, human, divine, civil* and *canon* law. I will return to this debate in Chapter 5.

Many enslaved Africans were brought to Portugal. Even in the fifteenth century, Jérôme Münzer, a German medical doctor who visited Portugal from 26 November to 1 December 1494, claimed that he 'saw an enormous forge with many ovens, where anchors and columns were made', and that 'there were a great many Negroes working near these ovens that he believed they

---

[103] See Lahon, 'Da Redução da Alteridade' and Gray, 'The Papacy', pp.52–68; and Russell-Wood, *Fidalgos and Philanthropists*.

were between Cyclops and Vulcano'.[104] Indeed, there were so many Blacks in Lisbon, that he exclaimed: 'O! how large the number of Negro slaves in Lisbon these days brought out of Ethiopia'.[105] On 26 March 1535, a Flemish priest, Nicholas Clenardo, wrote from Évora to his friend Látimo that:

> ... the slaves swarm in every part. All the work is done by captive Negroes and Moors ... I believe that in Lisbon male and female slaves are more than the free Portuguese. It is difficult to find a house where there is not at least one of these female slaves ... the wealthier have slaves from both sexes, and there are people who make good profit with the sale of the slaves' children born in the house.[106]

Resende, a Portuguese historian and chronicler, was critical of the number of enslaved Africans in Portugal: 'we bring to this kingdom a growing number of captives and if the Natives go, that is, if it goes this way, they will be more than us, in my opinion'.[107] By 1550, in Lisbon alone there were 10,000 Africans, constituting 10 per cent of the population. By the mid-eighteenth century 15–17 per cent of Lisbon's population was of African descent, and 800,000 Africans had been brought to the Iberian Peninsula (see Figure 22).[108] So there were many Africans living in Portugal before Mendonça reached the country, and among them were both enslaved and free Africans who had gone to Portugal on their own initiative as students, ambassadors, priests and businessmen.[109] These groups constituted the members of the confraternities, the first of which – the Confraternity of Our Lady of the Rosary of Black Men – was created in Lisbon at the Monastery of São Domingos[110] on

---

[104] Münzer, 'Itinerarium', p. 17, 'tot erant laborantes nigri in suis caminis ut Ciclopas et Vulcanum crederes'.
[105] Münzer, 'Itinerarium', pp. 19-20, 'o quam magnus numerus sclavorum nigrorum in dies ex Aethiopia Lisbonam apportantur'.
[106] M. Gonçalves Cerejeira, *O Renascimento em Portugal*, Clenardo, Coimbra: Imprensa da Universidade, 1918, II, pp. 14–5, 'Os escravos pululam por tôda a parte. Todo o serviço é feito por negros e mouros cativos ... estou em crer que em Lisboa os escravos e as escravas são mais que os portugueses livres de condição. Dificilmente se encontrará uma casa, onde não haja pelo menos uma escrava destas ... os mais ricos teem escravos de ambos os sexos, e há indivíduos que fazem bons lucros com a venda dos filhos das escravas nascidos em casa.'
[107] Miscelania e Variedade de Histórias, 1545, as quoted by Brásio, *Os Pretos em Portugal*, p. 14, 'Weemos no reyno metter tantos captiuos crescer & yrem se hos naturaes que se assi for, serem mais elles que nos, a meu ver'. See also Maxwell, *Slavery and the Catholic Church*, pp. 44–50, and Saunders, *A Social History of Black Slaves and Freedmen*, p. 45.
[108] See Lahon, 'Da Redução da Alteridade', p. 54 and 55.
[109] See Lingna Nafafé, *Colonial Encounters*.
[110] Lahon, 'Da Redução da Alteridade'; see Isabel Castro Henriques, *Os Africanos em Portugal História e Memória Séculos XV-XXI, Inauguração da Exposição*, Lisbon: Torre de Belém, 2011, and Fonseca, *Religião e Liberdade*.

FIGURE 22 *Chafariz d'el Rey em* Lisboa. Artist unknown, 1570–1580. Interracial depiction of the city of Lisbon. Public domain.

14 July 1496, forty years after the Portuguese had arrived in the region of modern Guinea-Bissau, Sierra Leone and Senegal.[111]

By the seventeenth century there were many confraternities, or Brotherhoods of Black people, in Portugal (see Figure 23). According to Gray,[112] they were seen as 'a respectable alternative to the revolutionary quilombos or settlements formed by slaves',[113] which were more militant in outlook. The confraternities were the centres from which enslaved Africans and free Blacks, whether born or liberated, living in Portugal could voice their concerns about their position in Portuguese society.

The *compromisso* or constitution of 9 July 1526 requested by the confraternity of São Tomé on the Atlantic coast of West Africa stipulated that it should have the same privileges and freedoms as those given to the confraternities in the city of Lisbon by King Manuel I of Portugal.[114] These were legal and binding rights founded on religious principles and

---

[111] For the debate on the arrival of the Portuguese in the region of Guinea-Bissau and their integration into the local culture, see Lingna Nafafé, *Colonial Encounters*.
[112] Gray, 'The Papacy', pp. 52–68.   [113] Gray, 'The Papacy', p. 55.
[114] See 'Carta de El-Rei D. João III', ATT, Chancelaria de D. João III, liv. 12, fl. 134 v, 9 July 1526, 'sam taes como os que ellRey meu Senhor e padre', MMA, vol. I, p. 472.

FIGURE 23 Cover of the Confraternity's *compromisso* (constitution) of Our Lady of Rosary of Black Men. Biblioteca Nacional de Portugal. Photograph by the author.

these rights were intended 'for being something in the service of Our Lord'.[115] The case of São Tomé is significant: it was the location of the first confraternity of the Rosary created on the African continent. The first Portuguese contact with São Tomé was in 1471, when João de Santarém and Pêro Escobar arrived. The two men named São Tomé in honour of Saint Thomas, as they had arrived there on his feast day. In 1485 King João II (1481–95) and the Portuguese Crown granted the island to João de

---

[115] 'Carta de El-Rei D. João III', 'por ser cousa do serujço de noso Senhor', MMA, vol. I, p. 472.

Paiva (1485–90). The attempt to settle the islands began, but it soon failed as the settlers were not able to produce food and were unable to cope with the tropical diseases in the area. In 1512, a royal decree ordered that all enslaved African women who had married the first white settlers on the island, along with their dual heritage offspring, should be given manumission.[116] Five years later, in 1517, another royal decree manumitted all enslaved African males who had arrived on the island with the first colonists. In 1520, a royal charter allowed free dual heritage people or *mulattos* to hold public office if they owned property and were married. However, this measure failed to even out the asymmetrical social relations that existed on the island. Hence, the need arose for the constitution granted in 1526. In the following years, more enslaved Africans were brought to the island, mainly from Benin, Kongo and Angola, to work on the sugar plantations. The relationship between the free, the plantation owners and enslaved Africans was fragile, and culminated in a large slave revolt led by Amador in 1595.[117]

I am not going to enter into a detailed discussion of the history of São Tomé, but it is vital that we place the history of the confraternity's constitution in the context in which it emerged on the island in the sixteenth century when slavery was at its height. In essence, on 6 March 1684, Mendonça was demanding a return to the terms of the constitution given to the confraternities of Our Lady of Rosary of Black Men in both Lisbon and São Tomé. His argument for the use of legal proceedings was a strategy to secure the inclusion of enslaved Africans in the life of metropolitan Europe, Africa and the Americas, where the confraternities had made their contribution felt.

The constitution demanded that all the enslaved who were members of the confraternities should gain their freedom and legally challenge any authority that was not in favour of their liberation. It was the responsibility of the *Mesa*, particularly the attorneys of the confraternity, to take the initiative, either individually or in conjunction with other attorneys, to use the resources available to them to liberate their members. Freedom for the members of the confraternity was an entitlement, intrinsic to their membership, and it was expected.

Let us look at some of these legal clauses embedded in the *compromisso*. The liberation of confraternity members, according to the constitution, was to be publicly disclosed through a legal action to 'bestow them

---

[116] See Seibert, 'São Tomé's Great Slave Revolt of 1595'.
[117] See Seibert, 'São Tomé's Great Slave Revolt of 1595', pp. 29–50.

rights and grant them all privileges and freedoms'.[118] As a public action, this could be carried out legally through sale, which included the *Mesa* buying off the enslaved Africans in order to secure their freedom. The purchase of enslaved Africans for their liberation needed to be accompanied by a certificate of freedom, *carta de alforria*. The Constitution stated:

... thereto, it pleases me that Black men and Stewards of the said Confraria, could by themselves and with their attorneys to petition [judicially] and oblige freedom and manumission with the certificate of freedom of any Black men and women that may be members of the Confraternity of Our Lady of Rosary.[119]

In cases where there might be a dispute with previous owners regarding the current status of a liberated enslaved African, the dispute was to be resolved by evaluating the price of the slave in question:[120] 'Thereto, it pleases me that if there is any testament left declaring any slave as manumitted [with certificate], [they] should immediately be set free, giving payment for the one that may not have been manumitted, the heirs that he belonged to should look at his worth [in order to set a price to free them]'.[121] Moreover, justice was to be applied to their homes: 'thereto and pleases me that manumitted Blacks of the said Island [São Tomé] that might have houses, they should not be aggrieved by judicial Officer and Governors or other people, except when laws have required them to do so'.[122] The constitution was legally binding, and the expectation was that the local authorities would abide by its terms:

... for these privileges and rights, I wish, and it pleases me that the said manumitted men and Blacks that would be members of the said confraternity will enjoy and please and also fully as this letter of mine has declared. Therefore, I decree that the captain, supreme judge, judges, and district judges of the said island that are now there and those that will be and any other oficers and people that this my letter is

---

[118] 'Carta de El-Rei D. João III', 'privileges comceder e outorgar todos os priujllegios e ljberdades', MMA, vol. I, p. 472.

[119] 'Carta de El-Rei D. João III', 'outro sy me praz que os homees pretos e mordomos da dita Comfraria, posam por sy e por seus procuradores demãdar e obrigar a ljberdade e allforria de quaésquer pretos e pretas que forem comfrades', MMA, vol. I, p. 473.

[120] For further discussion of the topic, see Brásio, *Os Pretos em Portugal*.

[121] 'Carta de El-Rei D. João III', 'Outro sy me praz que tamto que é allgum testamento ficar decrarado allgum espravo por forro, seja logo posto e sua ljberdade, damdo fiamça que senão podese ser forro os erdeiros a que pertemce poderé aver sua vallia', MMA, vol. I, p. 473.

[122] 'Carta de El-Rei D. João III', 'outro sy quero e me praz que os pretos forros da dita Ilha que casas teuerê, no sejam vexados pellos homees do meyrinho e allcaydes ou outras allguas pessoas, salluo quamdo pellas Justiças lhe for mamdado que o façaõ', MMA, vol. I, p. 473.

shown to and the knowledge of it remains, that they should let these said Blackmen and women of the said confraternity, use and enjoy the said privileges and rights above declared[123].

As a legal document, the constitution of the confraternity, as inherited from Manuel I, made its privileges intelligibly an ethical question and morally manageable: 'and in all it is to be complied with and obeyed, and ensured that it is abided to'.[124] Central to the constitution was that it was up to individuals to take action to ensure that the constitution's principles were respected. In particular, there was an expectation that the local authorities (municipal councils) would implement the terms of the constitution without undue pressure from the members: 'without doubt, not with any embargo to be put on it, as this is my mercy'.[125] The responsibilities of the authorities were embodied in the law, which in turn held them accountable for their actions before the confraternity members.

The confraternity of São Tomé, like its counterpart in Lisbon, acted as a centre for voicing Blacks' concerns, and it addressed themes of freedom, integration and the right to trade. This search for freedom was not seen as an individual quest, but as part of a notion of belonging that allowed for being part of the society in which they found themselves, be that in São Tomé, Angola,[126] Portugal, Spain or Brazil. Within the sphere of enslaved Africans, the theme of integration assimilated other leitmotifs within Africa, Portugal, Spain and Brazil, such as burial and liberation. Integration was a way of acknowledging the fundamental principle of the enslaved person's human rights, his or her right to attain freedom. It relates to the traditional way in which taking war captives within African societies was a way of expanding a community and integrating outsiders through kinship and relations of dependence – the opposite of the practice of chattel slavery in the Atlantic region. This kind of integration is not just

---

[123] 'Carta de El-Rei D. João III', 'dos quaes priujllegios e ljberdades quero e me praz que hos ditos ditos ome[n]s foros e pretos que forē cõfrades da dita Comfraria gouuaõ e gozem asy e tam jmteiramēte como nesta mjnha carta hé decrarado. Porem mamdo ao capitão, corregedor, juizes, vereadores da dita Ilha que ora saão e ao diamte foré e a quaesquer outros ofiçiaes e pessoas a que esta mjnha carta for mostrada e o conhecimento della pertécer, que leixē aos ditos pretos e pretas comfrades da dita cõfraria, vsar e gouujr dos ditos priujllegios e ljberdades acjma decrarados', MMA, vol. I, pp. 473–474.
[124] 'Carta de El-Rei D. João III', 'E em tudo lhe cumpraõ e guarde e façaõ compryr e guardar esta mjnha Carta, como nella hé cõtheudo', MMA, vol. I, p.474.
[125] See 'Carta de El-Rei D. João III', 'sem duuyda nê ebargo allgũ que a elo seja posto, por que asy hé mjnha mercê', MMA, vol. I, p. 474.
[126] Outside Portugal, the first confraternities were established in São Tomé in 1515, then in Angola, and subsequently in Brazil.

individual freedom or the freedom to live in isolation, but the freedom to 'belong' to a family of human beings.[127]

The constitution also gave the São Tomé confraternity the right to trade and to raise funds to liberate their members from slavery. It was allowed to raise funds via ships licensed to trade in West Africa by the Portuguese Crown and heading to Guinea and Mina (Ghana, Togo, Benim and Nigeria). Most of the ships were trading in enslaved Africans. Money could be raised by various means on the ships. Some was raised via merchants buying candles that had been made or purchased by the confraternities of Our Lady of Rosary of Black Men. Money also came from charitable donations made by the traders and passengers on the ships, who were often informed about the confraternities of Our Lady of Rosary of Black Men by the captain. Any money raised for the confraternities was to be given to the ship's captain in front of his scribe; it was then given to the stewards and the officials of the confraternity, and its scribes were responsible for the receipts.[128] This reflects Brásio's assertion that confraternities in Portugal were given the right to participate in commerce in Lisbon. They could also raise funds from within the churches where their members worshipped: 'Stewards and members of the confraternity, should by themselves, or people who they might ordain, could ask for offerings for the said confraternity within the church while the mass is going on and not on any other occasion'.[129] In São Tomé free female members of the confraternity were given the right to be retailers: 'free African women of the island of the said confraternity should be trading, buying and selling anything they like without imposed taxes'.[130] These privileges were fundamental to Mendonça's work as a general attorney, to which we now return.

The only document that gives us any information about Mendonça's second stay in Lisbon is the letter of recommendation provided by

---

[127] See Brásio, *Os Pretos em Portugal*.
[128] 'Carta de El-Rei D. João III', 'as quaes esmollas seraõ êtregues aos capitães das ditas caravellas peramte seus espriuães, pera que tãto que tornare á dita Ilha as emtregaré aos mordomos e oficyaes da dita Comfraria e pello espriuaõ della lhe serem carregados e receyta', MMA, vol. I, p. 473.
[129] 'Carta de El-Rei D. João III', 'E asy mesmo me praz que os mordomos e Comfrades da dyta Comfraria, posam per sy ou per as pesoas que pera jso ordenaré, pedir esmollas pera a dita comfraria demtro na jgreja, emquamto diserê a mjsa somente e naõ em outra parte', MMA, vol. I, p. 473.
[130] 'Carta de El-Rei D. João III', 'outro sy me praz que as pretas forras da dita Ilha, que forem comfrades da dita comfraria, posam ser regateyras e côprar e vender quaésquer cousas que quiserê, sem embargo de quallquer proujsam e mãdado que acerqua diso aja em comtrairo', MMA, vol. I, p. 473.

Mesquita on 15 February 1681.[131] In it, Mesquita confirms Mendonça's appointment as attorney general in Lisbon for the confraternities of Our Lady of Rosary of Black Men: 'I confirm that Lourenço da Silva Mendonça, a pardo man and natural of this kingdom of Portugal[132] is now working in this city of Lisbon'.[133]

Mesquita's statement appears to indicate that Mendonça may have taken a position of attorney general soon after his arrival in Lisbon, where he stayed until 15 February 1681, when he departed for the Royal Court of Madrid, Toledo. If he was appointed to the position of attorney general in Lisbon, it could not have been long after he left Vilar de Frades in around 1677–1679. If this was the case, then it would imply that Mendonça came from elsewhere to Lisbon and was elected as member of the *Mesa*, the board of guardians of the Confraternity of Our Lady of the Rosary of Black Men. Yet, Mesquita's letter shows that Mendonça was already on duty in Lisbon as a procurator general for all Black people in Portugal, Brazil and Castile prior to 1681.[134] This is also a possibility considering that there was a plan to send his three uncles from Peniche to Maranhão or Pará, Brazil.[135] The process of Mendonça's naturalisation in the kingdom is unclear. Indeed, it is unclear if he even needed naturalisation, given that his grandfather was an ally of Portugal and in 1605, King Álvaro II of Kongo had offered naturalisation to all Portuguese residents in his kingdom after seven years' residence.

His years in Lisbon provided Mendonça with the necessary means to carry his ideas to Rome. In itself, membership of the Confraternity of the Rosary of Our Lady of Black Men gave him the legal platform for doing so, regardless of his personal status, and as a member of the board or *Mesa*. He may have been a political prisoner, but there was no legal framework to prevent him from being part of the association, and he was not a slave. In other words, the confraternity was a perfect fit for him as he honed his arguments regarding freedom. Lahon may have argued that confraternities were at odds with the culture of enslaving societies like that of Portugal at the time and that Mendonça was

---

[131] S.C. Africa, vol. I, fl., 486.
[132] 'Kingdom of Portugal' in the seventeenth century referred only to Portugal; Portuguese contact zones in Africa, Asia and Brazil were not included. 'Natural of the Kingdom' could imply someone born in Portugal from a Black enslaved person. However, this was not applicable in Mendonça's case. See Lahon, 'Da Redução da Alteridade'.
[133] S.C. Africa, vol. I, fl., 486.   [134] See S.C. Africa, vol. I, fl. 486.
[135] See 'Consulta do Conselho Ultramarino Sobre os Familiares do Rei do Dongo' and MMA, vol. XIII, pp. 507–508.

contained because of the existing political and religious situation,[136] but this is a view that ignores the legal framework laid down in the constitution of the confraternities.

Mendonça sought support from within the confraternities, particularly from the members of the *Mesa*, such as Lorenzo de El Real and Mesquita, who represented the tradition of the Council of Trent from which the constitution emerged.[137] There may have been other voices from Portugal that condemned slavery, but they did not do so from the universal point of view of the liberation that Mendonça sought for the enslaved Africans in Africa, Brazil, Portugal and Spain, and the Indigenous Brazilians and New Christians. Mendonça, by exercising the legal side of the confraternity's constitution, would set himself up for success where others before him had failed.[138] He used the constitutional rights of Black Brotherhoods within the legal framework of the time; legally, he was not demanding anything new from Western Christendom: he simply deployed the existing legal framework to liberate enslaved Africans. His role as an attorney gave him the leverage to deal with the legal side of liberating the confraternity members.[139]

Mendonça's work for the confraternities in Portugal did not represent anything new. In Angola, there were already confraternities in Luanda and Quissama.[140] Both of his uncles were students at the Jesuit College of Luanda, from where a letter was sent by the Confraternity of the Rosary of Our Lady of Black Men of Luanda, Angola, to Rome on 29 June 1658.[141] Mendonça might have been aware that the confraternity of Luanda had struggled for its rights within the Church in Angola, even though they were members of the Catholic Church. Indeed, he could well have been a member of the confraternity of Luanda. The ideas associated with resistance would not have been alien to him, nor would the requisite procedures.

In the Atlantic, and in Brazil in particular, there were different confraternities, such as those of the Mulattoes and Black Men.[142] Mendonça appeared to have represented both of these constituencies in the Vatican.[143] In the seventeenth century in Salvador, Bahia, which he visited, there were various confraternities, and they often had complicated interests

---

[136] See Lahon, 'Da Redução da Alteridade'.   [137] See S.C. Africa, vol. I, fl. 486.
[138] See S.C. Africa, vol. I, fl. 486.   [139] See Reginaldo, *Os Rosários dos Angolas*.
[140] Reginaldo 'Rosários dos Pretos'.
[141] See SOCG, Africa 6, Congo 250, 29 June 1658, fl. 248.
[142] See Russell-Wood, *Fidalgos and Philanthropists*.
[143] See SOCG, 490, fl. 140 and Gray, 'The Papacy', pp. 52–68.

of their own.¹⁴⁴ Let us look now at Mendonça's wider network with the New Christians in Portugal and the Indigenous Brazilians in Braga and in Toledo.

4.4 MENDONÇA'S NETWORK WITH NEW CHRISTIANS IN PORTUGAL AND THE INDIGENOUS PERUVIANS IN TOLEDO, 1674–1681

Mendonça's stay at Vilar de Frades coincided with the papacy of Clement X (1669–1676), during which there was no Inquisition against New Christians in Portugal. Yet at the same time those imprisoned in the 1660s for practising Judaism were not released, and the battle for power between the Inquisitors, Prince Regent Dom Pedro II and Pope Clement X's representatives continued.¹⁴⁵ The New Christians continued to be accused of practising Judaism in the period of Clement X's papacy; indeed, anti-New Christian sentiment intensified in Portugal after 1670. On 2 June 1671, New Christians were victims of an accusation of sacrilege that took place in Odivelas. On 5 September 1673, a month after Mendonça's arrival in Portugal, there was a royal decree that demanded that those New Christians found guilty must abandon the country with their family and leave behind any minors aged seven and under.¹⁴⁶

After Clement X's death in 1676, Cardinal Benedetto Odescalchi became Pope Innocent XI with the support of Louis XIV of France, although he later struggled with the pretensions of the French king. Innocent XI brought financial and social reform to the Roman Catholic Church. He favoured more evangelical styles of preaching, and 'stressed the importance of rigorous instruction in the Catholic faith ... Christian education ... social justice and public decency'. He was in fact a charitable pope 'to the needy'.¹⁴⁷ Like his

---

¹⁴⁴ See Russell-Wood, *Fidalgos and Philanthropists*.
¹⁴⁵ See Lucia Silva da Mota, 'A Família Mesquita em Portugal e em Terras de Piratininigas', unpublished Master's dissertation, University of São Paulo, 2008.
¹⁴⁶ See Anita Novinsky, 'Padre Antônio Vieira, a Inquisição e os Judeus', *Jewish History*, 6 (1–2), 1992, pp. 152–162, 'O movimento anti-semita em Portugal nesse início da década de 70 tinha se intensificado, e apresentava as mesmas características que o anti-semitismo em todos os tempos. Mas um acontecimento local agravou a situação: os cristãos-novos foram responsabilizados por um sacrilégio ocorrido em Odivelas, em 2 de junho de 1671. Como represália, um decreto real denominado'Lei do Extermínio', datado de 5 Setembro de 1673, determinou que todos portugueses cristãos-novos, confessos no crime de judaísmo, saíssem de Portugal com suas famílias, mas deixando seus filhos menores de 7 anos.'
¹⁴⁷ Graham Darby, 'Pope Innocent XI: The Saviour of Christendom?' *History Today*, 61(5), 2011, p. 19.

predecessors, he also favoured the monastery of Vilar de Frades.[148] Thus, it was perhaps no surprise that Innocent XI was open to Mendonça's request for freedom for the enslaved Africans. Yet, in spite of opposing 'the violence against Protestants' and not believing in 'forcible conversion',[149] Innocent XI re-established the Inquisition in Portugal around the end of 1681 or the beginning of 1682.[150]

While in Lisbon, Mendonça met and formed a strong relationship with Gaspar da Costa Mesquita, an apostolic notary who gave him a letter of reference for the Vatican. Mesquita was a New Christian from a line of New Christians going back beyond his parents' generation.[151] To date, no one has published details of Mesquita's background as a New Christian and his connection to the Inquisition in Portugal; even Gray in his seminal work has overlooked Mesquita's history.[152] On 23 April 1682, Gaspar was condemned to prison by the Holy Office or the Inquisition Office, having been denounced by members of his own family; he was imprisoned on 25 April 1682[153]: The verdict of Inquisitors, Ordinaries, and Deputies of the Holy Inquisition, who have seen these faults and confessions of Gaspar Da Costa de Mesquita, a New Christian, a banker, a natural and resident of this City of Lisbon, have agreed to his guilt'.[154] He had given Mendonça the letter of recommendation of 15 February 1681.[155] When he was accused or practising his Jewish faith, he was arrested and imprisoned for a year. We do not know the political reasons for his denunciation, as these reasons were not always clear. His crime was somehow connected with religion, but it is unlikely to have been to do with religion only.[156] As Novinsky has identified, the targeting of the New Christians in Portugal was a case of ethnic rather than religious discrimination.[157] It was also clear that those with money were targeted and that members of their family were used to denounce them.[158] The accusation of practising Judaism was used as cover for the real aims of the Inquisition.

---

[148] See Vinhas, *A Igreja e o Convento de Vilar de Frades*.
[149] Darby, 'Pope Innocent XI?', p. 21.   [150] See Mota, 'A Família Mesquita'.
[151] ATT, Tribunal do Santo Ofício, Inquisição de Lisboa, proc. 1240, auto 44, maço 4, n.º 1, cópia microfilmada. Portugal, mf. 3474.
[152] Gray, 'The Papacy'.   [153] See 'Processo de Gaspar da Costa Mesquita'.
[154] 'Processo de Gaspar da Costa Mesquita', 'acordão os Inquisitores, Ordinario, eDeputados deSanta Inquisisão, que vistos estas, culpas e confessos de Gaspar DaCosta de Mesquita, christão novo, banqueiro, natural emorador destaCidade deLisboa'.
[155] See Mesquita, APF, SOGC, Series Africa, Angola, Congo, vol. 1, fl., 486.
[156] See Green, 'Matters of Difference'.   [157] Novinsky, 'Padre Antônio Vieira'.
[158] See 'Processo de Gaspar da Costa Mesquita'.

Once accused, Mesquita was free to be interrogated by the Inquisition officer about his possessions, his business, his commercial network and his finances.[159] Among his possessions were items relating to trade with Brazil, Italy and India. Mesquita was a banker, a profession followed by his forebears. His father, Manoel da Costa, was a powerful merchant who, according to Silva da Mota, was the only one to own five ships at the turn of the seventeenth century.[160] Silva da Mota points out that in 1602 'the Inquisition Office accused New Christians of controlling the slave trade and of being the holder of money from trade contracts and of major power in the Kingdom [Portugal]'.[161] However, it would be naive to assume that New Christians' influence in Portugal was limited to commerce and the slave trade; their sphere of influence extended to other sectors of Portuguese society, such as governance, politics and religious leadership within the Catholic Church[162]. On 16 November 1682, Mesquita made his confession before the Inquisition Tribunal, after seven months in prison.[163] Intriguingly, in his confession he named eighty-six people, among them one particularly familiar name – Francisco de Távora. This might well be another Távora, and not the former governor of Angola responsible for sending the royals to Brazil and Portugal. However, documentary sources indicate that Távora did return to Portugal and left from there to become viceroy of India in 1681, the same year Mendonça left for Madrid. It could well have been him named on the list. Távora may have been complicit in Mesquita's arrest, possibly after learning about his relationship with Mendonça. After his confession, Mesquita was released from prison on 8 August 1683 in the Terreiro do Paço, in Lisbon, in front of members of the royal family and nobility, including religious leaders.

The case of Odivela[164] and the experiences of Mesquita should not overshadow our view of seventeenth-century Portugal as a complex cultural and political landscape. The accusation made about Odivela is an example of the political rhetoric used at the time, yet conviviality between the New Christians and the Old persisted alongside the official prohibition

---

[159] See Mota, 'A Família Mesquita', p. 72.   [160] See Mota, 'A Família Mesquita', p. 81.
[161] Mota, 'A Família Mesquita', p. 82.
[162] José Gonçalves Salvador, 'Os Cristãos-novos nas Capitanias do Sul. (Séculos XVI e XVII). Os Cristãos-Novos do Sul e Suas Relações com a Igreja', *Revista de História*, 25(51), 1962, pp. 49–86.
[163] See 'Processo de Gaspar da Costa Mesquita'.
[164] See Jorge Martins, *O Senhor Roubado a Inquisição e a Questão Judaica*, Lisbon: Heuris – Europress, 2002.

of the Jewish lifestyle. Many New Christians served the Crown, as Mesquita did, and there were some priests who came to persecute the New Christians. To take the view that New Christians were involved in enslaving Africans and that, as a result, they were not capable of being involved in working for their liberation, would be to fail to take into account how politics functioned. Some Africans were involved in slavery, too, but that did not prevent other Africans from seeking to free the enslaved. According to Novinsky, New Christians played an important role in Portugal: some were financiers of the king, particularly during the Portuguese restoration, and helped provide the capital to liberate Portugal from Spain and subsequently from the Dutch. For example, the merchant Duarte da Silva was a financier of Dom João IV[165] and invested a large amount of capital for the Portuguese project of conquest. In general, many New Christians contributed to the running of the Portuguese Empire, and their contribution was recognised in some quarters in Portugal.

In 1643, Father Antonio Vieira, who so severely harassed the Palmarists, as we saw in Chapter 3, had pleaded with Dom João IV to change course regarding the New Christians, and to ensure that those who had left Portugal for fear of the Inquisition be asked to return.[166] Vieira not only asked for the return of the New Christians to the kingdom, but also that João IV 'exempt them from physical payment, eliminate a distinction between New Christians and old, to allow mixed marriages, and yet to ask the pope for a general pardon of those Judaising'.[167] From 1669 to 1675 Vieira was in Rome attempting to persuade Clement X to pardon the New Christians. This means that he presented the New Christians' case in the Vatican in 1669 a decade before Mendonça arrived in Rome.

While in Lisbon, Mendonça lobbied Mesquita about the liberation of the enslaved Africans. The conclusion of that conversation saw Mendonça travel to Toledo in the first instance, and, subsequently, to the Vatican. Mesquita's own experiences in the Atlantic, gathered through his travels to Rio de Janeiro, Bahia, India and Rome, led him to support Mendonça's intervention regarding the liberation of the Africans and the correlation between the Africans' plight and that of the New Christians.[168] Mesquita believed in Mendonça's project and stated that many people had spoken

---

[165] See Novinsky, 'Padre Antônio Vieira'.   [166] See Novinsky, 'Padre Antônio Vieira'.
[167] Novinsky, 'Padre Antônio Vieira', pp. 151–152.
[168] See Mesquita, S.C. Africa, 1, fl., 486, Lisbon, 15 Feb. 1681.

to him about the horrific suffering of the enslaved Africans, which he also experienced first-hand:

> ... competent procurator of all the Mulattoes throughout this kingdom, as in Castile and Brazil, so that he might obtain a papal brief concerning a certain matter for which they are petitioning. For me as a notary it has been brought to me by many mulatto men from various parts about the same matter that for a long time they have been petitioning the Roman curia. For which I can confirm that it owes a lot to the said Lourenço da Silva. For worthy cause he petitions the matter through all venues so that he could reach out and reveals the truth.[169]

He declared that Mendonça had the necessary credentials to present the case for the liberation of the enslaved Africans in the Vatican. For Mendonça, seeing the Inquisition of the New Christians brought to a standstill in Portugal might have been a watershed moment in his liberation discourse: the New Christians' plight was comparable to that of the enslaved Africans, and the work of Viera in the Vatican to gain their pardon may have given him hope.

The relationship between the New Christians and the Africans went back to the end of the fifteenth century, when many Jews left Spain and subsequently Portugal because of the Inquisition. Many went to the west coast of Africa (in present-day Sierra Leone, Senegal and Guinea-Bissau), where they were protected by the African ruling classes.[170] The African kings told the Portuguese zealots who followed the Jews to Africa that religion was not to be used as a platform for persecution. They vehemently told the Catholics that they could not use their creed to make judgements on those of a different faith.[171]

In Angola and Kongo, New Christians established relationships with the élites through marriage. They were often accused of running for high office, particularly in the Church, where some of them went into the priesthood, but they were also often charged with blasphemy.[172] They were also accused by the Portuguese Overseas Council of favouring the kings of Kongo and Angola over Portuguese interests, and of providing Kongo's élites with legal aid in the courts against the

---

[169] Mesquita, S.C. Africa, 1, fl., 486, Lisbon, 15 Feb. 1681, 'p.que seja emteligente noproCurar hum Breve do Papa p. certo negocio que solicitao ha mim notario me consta p. m.tos homens pardos de varias partes me virao falarsobreomesmo neg.cio que ha tempo sesolecita naCuriadeRoma q outrosim sey que selhe deve m.to aditto Lourenco DaSilva pello Bem que solecita este negocio protodas as vias que pode alCansar eporverdade'.

[170] See Lingna Nafafé, *Colonial Encounters*. See also Green, 'Masters of Difference'.

[171] See Lingna Nafafé, *Colonial Encounters*.   [172] See AHU, Códice 554, fl.s 31 v. 32.

Church.[173] In fact, Angolans and Kongolese élites used New Christian lawyers to defend their interests in the courts against the Portuguese. The connection between the New Christians and the Africans was not only apparent in Africa and the Americas, but also in Lisbon, where contacts were made through shared religious, cultural and economic experience. New Christians and free and enslaved Africans often established contact through membership of the churches.[174]

In Portugal, it remains unclear how long Mendonça knew Mesquita and how they were connected. They may have become acquainted with each other during Mendonça's stay in Brazil, but I have recently discovered documents that show that Mesquita's father was trading in Angola and possibly had contact with Mendonça's grandfather, Philipe Hari I.[175] So their connection may have had its roots in Angola.

Mendonça needed official credentials from Portugal, where he had already been appointed as an attorney, to support his intervention in the Vatican. He was not given them, so he went to the Royal Court of Madrid in Toledo to obtain a letter of reference. It was significant, because Mendonça had expected to get a letter of recommendation from the head of state in Portugal, the prince regent, Dom Pedro II. Since he did not have the legal power to provide it because he was only the Regent and had imprisoned his brother, King Afonso VI who reigned from 1656 to 1683, Mendonça travelled to Toledo, where he waited for eighteen months to be appointed as procurator (attorney) of the *Mesa* for the Confraternity of the Rosary of Our Lady of the Star of Madrid.

In Toledo, Carlos II, king of Spain, also appointed Mendonça as attorney general for the confraternities of Rosary of Our Lady of Star for the Black Men.[176] It was an international role that transcended the frontiers of the kingdom of Portugal to include Portugal, Spain, Brazil and the colonies in Africa and Asia. Mendonça represented the confraternities of Black Men in the four continents – Africa, America, Asia and Europe – in which Christianity was fully practised. As a Christian kingdom and one of the superpowers of the period, Spain symbolised political, economic and spiritual power in the seventeenth century, and Mendonça's appointment

---

[173] See APF, SOCG, Africa 6, Congo 250, 29 June 1658, fl. 248.
[174] See Lahon, 'Da Redução da Alteridade'. See also Jonathan Schorsch, 'Blacks, Jews and the Racial Imagination'.
[175] See AHU_CU_001, cx. 11, d. 1272, 21 August 1672.
[176] See 'Carta de Giacinto Rogio Monzon'.

as an international attorney reflected Spain's political and cultural dominion.[177]

Mendonça was empowered in the Royal Court of Madrid by the archbishop of Toledo, Luis Manuel Fernández de Portocarrero y de Guzman (1678–1709), who, before serving as archbishop, had been cardinal protector of Spain in Rome, and had served as an interim viceroy of Sicily and a counsellor of state. Mendonça's appointment was endorsed by influential and powerful figures at the Royal Court of Madrid in Toledo. Among those that nominated Mendonça were Enun.o Cardinal Dabarco,[178] a vice-chancery (cardinal vice-chancellor) in the Royal Court of Madrid in Toledo, and Dom Lorenzo dé Rè (Del Real), a 'councillor of Christ, master of music and a guardianship porter of His Majesty, Dom Carlos II, King of Spain'.[179] Del Real was a Native of the city of Lima in the kingdom of Peru, and resident at the Royal Court of Madrid, Toledo. In his letter of support for Mendonça, Del Real called him his elder brother.[180] The letter also gives an intriguing description of Del Real that suggests he was of a dual heritage or Native Peruvian background. The city of Lima in Peru in the sixteenth century was a dynamic city in which enslaved Angolans worked alongside their Indigenous counterparts in domestic work. By the seventeenth century, it was a transnational city where the majority of the population was Black Africans. A census commissioned in 1636 by the viceroy of Peru, Marquis of Chichón, showed the extent to which the city was a transnational space. José R. Jouve-Martín asserts that:

... in 1651, Lima had become a predominantly Black city, a feature accentuated by the forced relocation of most of its Indigenous population to the nearby parish of Santiago del Cercado in 1590. The Black population peaked as proportion of the total probably around 1636, when a census ordered by the Marquis of Chichón showed that the capital of the Viceroyalty of Peru had a total of 10,758 Spaniards compared to 13,620 individuals classified as negroes and 861 as mulattoes.[181]

In the seventeenth century, Lima was also home to well-to-do free Black Africans who had some influence in the city. Many of those wealthy

---

[177] See 'Carta de Giacinto Rogio Monzon'.   [178] See 'Carta de Giacinto Rogio Monzon'.
[179] 'Carta de Giacinto Rogio Monzon', 'Conselliero dell' ordine di Christo Maestro della Musica di S.M. et portinero de guardamazzieri di S.M. naturale nesta città di Lima nelregno del Berù, et residente nesta corte'.
[180] See 'Carta de Giacinto Rogio Monzon'.
[181] For further discussion of the topic see, José R. Jouve-Martín, 'Death, Gender, and Writing: Testaments of Women of African Origin in Seventeenth-Century Lima, 1651–1666', in McKnight and Carofalo, *Afro-Latino Voices*, pp. 105–125.

Africans, particularly the women, left their wills as part of their religious obligations in the *Tribunal de bienes de difuntos* (Colonial Tribunal of Property of the Deceased), which was legally bound to administer the wills for the heirs. In Lima, wealthy former enslaved African descendants acquired knowledge of the existing law in Peru and were able to use it in the tribunal cases to their advantage, particularly African women who might not have had legal resources available to them.[182] One might speculate that the success story of these women's cases in Lima could have been brought to the attention of Mendonça in his conversation with Del Real prior to him leaving for Rome. These cases might have been familiar to Del Real who would have passed them to Mendonça in Toledo. In the seventeenth century, the Royal Court of Madrid was already a transnational space before Mendonça arrived in the city. From documents I have discovered in the General Archive of the Royal Palace of Madrid, Lorenzo Del Real also oversaw a choir for the Royal Court of Madrid, which was composed of male and female Black youth singers.[183] Del Real was in a confraternity with Mendonça, and Mendonça may have been appointed as a member of its *Mesa*. Generally, such a confraternity would have been attached to the local church, which might have been in Toledo itself, although I have not been able to locate documents in Toledo to this end.

Mendonça's appointment in Madrid, as endorsed by Del Real, demonstrates that there existed a confraternity of Black people in the city. This is despite claims that there was no Black Brotherhood in Madrid in the period.[184] I have found documents in the General Archive of the Royal Palace of Madrid that indicate the existence of two such Brotherhoods in Madrid: the Brotherhood of Saint Andrés and the Brotherhood of Our Lady of Assistance.[185]

---

[182] See Jouve-Martín, 'Death, Gender'. See also David Barry Gaspar and Darlene Clark Hine (eds.), *Beyond Bondage: Free Women of Color in the Americas*, Urbana, IL: University of Illinois Press, 2004; and Susan Kellogg and Matthew Restall (eds.), *Dead Giveaways: Indigenous Testaments of Colonial Mesoamerica and the Andes*, Salt Lake City, UT: University of Utah Press, 1998.

[183] Archivo General del Palacio Real de Madrid [AGPRM], Archivo Palacio Real Sección Administarivo [APRSA], leg. 650, Negros y Negras, 1679, Carlos II. See also Niñas y Niños Cantores (coleg.), empleos de Casa Real, Nodizas 1700–1799; Niñas y Niños Cantores (coleg.), empleos de Casa Real, Nodizas ó Annos de Cria 1660 á 1669; Niñas y Niños Cantores (coleg.), empleos de Casa Real, Nodizas ó Annos de Cria 1650 á 1659.

[184] Gray, 'The Papacy'.

[185] See AGPRM, Sección Reinados Caja 130, Carlos II, 1665–1684, Casa Real Cuentas de los Mayordomos de las Hermandades de San Andrés y Nuestra Señora de la Assistencia, signatura Antiga, Historia 169.

Mendonça's appointment was also endorsed by the apostolic notary in the Court of Madrid, Giacinto Rogio Monzon,[186] and by Antonio Ceipo de Vales and Antonio Lopez Wllanero (Valeriano), who were newly arrived in the Royal Court of Madrid in Toledo.[187] We do not have full details of their roles in Toledo or of how their arrival came to coincide with Mendonça's appointment. Nevertheless, their names show that they were Portuguese, and they might have been invited to attend the appointment of the attorney general, who was empowered to create confraternities of the Rosary in any part of Christendom, and to catechise members in every kingdom in which Christianity was to be found.

4.5 CONCLUDING REMARKS

The Portuguese Crown brought the Ndongo royals to Portugal in groups and dispersed them to separate monasteries for fear of their possible political impact on other Africans and the general public if they stayed together. Important figures such as the heir to the throne of Pungo-Andongo, the 10-year-old Ngolomano, and his uncle, Dom Diogo Cabangua, were isolated in order to silence them. Four other royals who came directly from Angola – Dom Antonio, Dom Sebastiam, Dom Deonizio and Ignacio – ended up in the small town of Peniche for the same reason: they were viewed as a threat to Portuguese society given their direct knowledge of the Portuguese political pretensions and manoeuvres in Angola, which they had witnessed and experienced themselves, and because thet were seen as being capable of inspiring resistance in the Royal Court in Lisbon.

We have little information on the returning group from Brazil, with exception of that of Mendonça himself who appropriated resources available to him by galvanising various confraternities in Portugal, Spain, Brazil and around the world through different networks. First, his study in the monastery Vilar de Frade, a traditional place for educating African and Indigenous American students informed his thinking about their common struggle and goals. It was a place close to the heart of many popes, particularly Innocent XI, because it represented the best of the

---

[186] 'Carta de Giacinto Rogio Monzon', 'Antonio Ceipo de Vales, Gios Ceipo Valdes, et Antonio Lopez Wllanero freschi in questa corte, et d. Lorenzo de' Rè alla presente dime Giacinto Rogio Monzon Notario Secretario. Et in ill desta Giacinto Rogio Monzon Notario Apostolico'.

[187] See 'Carta de Giacinto Rogio Monzon'.

spirit of universal Christianity that resonated in the different constituencies of Christianity in Africa, Asia and the Americas. It was a monastery of international standing, capable of impressing on its students the spirit of radical thinking. Mendonça was no exception.

On finishing his education in Vilar de Frades Mendonça returned to Lisbon, where he entered the Confraternity of Our Lady of Rosary of Black Men. The confraternities were important political and spiritual institutions because they could voice their members' desire for freedom based on the privileges given to them by the constitution. The constitution of 1526 guaranteed the right to personal freedom from slavery and the possibility of fighting for it legally. Mendonça was appointed attorney general for Portugal, Brazil and Castille by the Confraternity of Our Lady of Rosary of Black Men. This gave him the platform to lobby the religious and political authorities responsible for the slave trade in the Atlantic region. Since he could not get the complete support in Lisbon from the prince regent, Dom Pedro II, his next step was to go to Toledo to continue to lobby the authorities there. He became attorney for the Confraternity of the Rosary of Our Lady of the Star of Madrid and then universal attorney for all confraternities in Toledo, appointed by the Spanish king, Carlos II, and Archbishop Luis Manuel Fernández de Portocarrero y de Guzman.

Having been exiled to Brazil and then given an education in Portugal, Mendonça acquired the knowledge and the skills to find his way within the religious and political hierarchies of the Portuguese and Spanish empires. What is more, he formulated his quest for freedom as a supranational issue that needed to be dealt with internationally. He partnered with the New Christians and Indigenous Americans in this quest. The New Christians were accused of heresy, while their wealth was confiscated; the Indigenous Americans and Africans were forced by unjust wars, taxation and kidnapping to give up their resources of land and people. The cumulative resources of the New Christians, Indigenous Brazilians and Africans – their economic capital, their labour, lands and precious metals – became the property of the few, and the reasons for their oppression were explained away. Mendonça, who had himself suffered oppression in Angola and had witnessed the lives of enslaved Africans, New Christians and Indigenous Americans in Brazil, Portugal and Spain, was able to make a connection with them and appropriated their existing networks. He used their experiences in the Atlantic region to make his liberation discourse on African slavery a supra-Atlantic message.

The fact of Mendonça's appointment to an international role gave him the power to voice his liberation message, and to include not only the enslaved Africans but also the New Christians and the Indigenous Americans across the Atlantic who professed Christianity. In his study, Gray overlooked the importance of the legal role of attorney general given to Mendonça, which allowed him to question the Atlantic slavery system in its entirety,[188] contending instead that Mendonça's aim was not to debate the liberation of enslaved Africans as an international issue but only as a localised one.[189] The relationship between the persecution by the Inquisition of the New Christians and the enslavement of the Africans and Indigenous Americans, as well as their resulting common search for liberty and details of how the denial of religious freedom was implicit in the denial of enslaved Africans' humanity are factors that have also not been considered in scholarship on the Atlantic region. Although there is copious literature both on New Christians and on the Black population groups in the Atlantic region, very little of it has attempted to place the two in dialogue. The New Christians' religious freedom has received a great deal of attention, but in isolation from the enslaved Africans' search for freedom. Moreover, the paucity of research on Mendonça, and on the 'abolition and integration' of the enslaved and the wider network of New Christians and the Indigenous Americans constitutes a serious gap in our knowledge and our understanding of the intricate dynamics of the power relations in the Atlantic and Europe in the seventeenth century. In Chapter 5 I will look at Mendonça's court case in the Vatican, and how he challenged Pope Innocent XI to end Atlantic slavery.

---

[188] See Gray, 'The Papacy'.   [189] See Gray, 'The Papacy'.

5

Mendonça's Discourse in the Vatican: Liberation as a Wider Atlantic Question

This chapter explores the presentation of Mendonça's court case in the Vatican on the abolition of Atlantic slavery and practices of freedom for the enslaved Africans. As we have seen, there are a wide range of inter-related issues in West Central Africa such as institutions or institutional practices, an individual challenge to slavery and the pretexts used by European merchants to capture Africans that need to be brought together in the context of his case.[1] We have seen how these contexts themselves have long histories.

The immediate concern of Mendonça's court case is the crime committed against enslaved people in the Atlantic region and how the Vatican had been implicated in the long history of European conquest in the area by issuing bulls that gave Iberian kings a monopoly over Africa and the Americas, which empowered them to enslave people with impunity in these regions.[2] The abuses and violence that Iberian governing authorities (kings, governors, captains, bishops, priests and merchants) committed were consistently justified in the service of

---

[1] On the development of slavery in the state see Thornton, 'The Kingdom of Kongo', Heywood, 'Slavery and Its Transformation', Curto, *Enslaving Spirits* and Curto, 'Experiences of Enslavement'. On individual resistance to slavery, see Candido, *An African Slaving Port*, pp. 1–29, and pp. 143–236; for detailed studies of individual challenges to slavery in the eighteenth century, see the work of the two Africans, Equiano, *The Interesting Narrative*, and Cugoano, *Thoughts and Sentiments*. On strategy deployed by the merchants to capture Africans, see the High Court of Appeal 'Relação de Antonio Bezerra Fajardo', see also See Frei Melchior da Conceicam, 'Alvaras, Cartas, Provizioes, Regimentos', and Wadström, *An Essay on Colonization*.

[2] For Pope Nicholas V's bull dated 8 January 1454, Brásio, *Monumenta Missionaria Africana*, vol. I, p. 281. See, *Bulls Eximiae Devotionis and Inter Caetera*, May 3, 1493.

Christianity.[3] All these individuals were formally under the authority of the Roman Curia, whose responsibility it was to ensure that their actions were kept in check.[4] Mendonça's case questioned the legality of the pope's power, and his right to issue death warrants for those people who did not profess the Christian faith.[5] The worst was that the warrant also included those who formerly declared themselves members of the Christian Church, that is, Africans, Indigenous Americans and the New Christians[6]. By questioning the justness of the pope's bulls, Mendonça's court case cuts deep into the subsequent historiography of West Central Africa. He directly challenged the accepted wisdom on 'market', 'war' and 'slavery' that would come to dominate modern understanding of these practices in Kongo and Angola.[7]

There is no consensus in the historiography of West Central African society about the existence of slavery prior to the Europeans' arrival. Individual narratives of enslaved Africans in the Atlantic in the eighteenth century suggest that slavery was alien to African society. These narratives would support Mendonça's claim about the injustice of the enslavement of the Africans.[8] I will use two of these cases to endorse Mendonça's case. First, Cugoano's narrative of how he was kidnapped corroborated Mendonça's evidence presented in the Vatican a century earlier. Cugoano stated: 'I was early snatched away from my Native country, with about eighteen or twenty more boys and girls, as we were playing in a field.'[9] His testimony and exhibits on the Atlantic

---

[3] For the chain of responsibility from the Luso-Iberian governing authorities back to the pope, see Jaca and Moirans, OFM Cap., *Servi Liberi*. See Luis de Molina, *De Iustitia et Iure: Opera Omnia, Tractatibus Quinque, Tomisque Totidem Comprehensa*, Coloniae Allborogum: Sumptibus Fratrum de Tournes, 1759. Also Faria, 'Sobre a Fundação de Seminários'.

[4] See Jaca and Moirans, OFM Cap., *Servi Liberi*. See Molina, *De Iustitia et Iure* and Faria, 'Sobre a Fundação de Seminários'.

[5] See Jaca and Moirans, OFM Cap., *Servi Liberi*. See also Molina, *De Iustitia et Iure*.

[6] For New Christians' inquisition, see Pullan, *The Jews of Europe and the Inquisition*; Novinsky, 'Padre Antônio Vieira'. For African Christians brought to inquisition in Portugal, see Green, 'Masters of Difference'.

[7] See Thornton, 'The Kingdom of Kongo'; Miller, *Way of Death*; Curto, *Enslaving Spirits*; Heywood, 'Slavery and Its Transformation'; Curto, 'Experiences of Enslavement'; Heintze, 'Ngonga a Mwiza'; Heintze, *Angola nos séculos XVI e XVII*; Candido, 'Conquest, Occupation, Colonialism and Exclusion'; Candido, 'O Limite Tênue entre a Liberdade e Escravidão'.

[8] See Cugoano, *Thoughts and Sentiments*; Equiano, *The Interesting Narrative*, and Baquaqua, *Biography of Mahommah*.

[9] See Cugoano, *Thoughts and Sentiments*, p. 120.

Slave and Slavery are revealing of the methods used to capture Africans.[10] He described his raptors as Africans: 'I was first kidnapped and betrayed by some of my own complexion.'[11] What Cugoano did not know was that his abductors were conquered people who were in the service of the British captains-major and their governors in the Gold Coast, similar to that of Angola.[12] As Blackburn claims, 'the slave-holders of the main Atlantic states – Portugal, Spain, the Netherlands, England, France, and the United States'[13] emulated each in their practices. Second, similarly, Equiano states that he was kidnapped at age 11 and taken to the Americas. He declared:

... in this way I grew up till I was turned the age of 11, when an end was put to my happiness in the following manner ... ere long it was my fate to be thus attacked and to be carried off when none of the grown people were nigh. One day, when all our people were gone out to their works as usual and only I and my dear sister were left to mind the house, two men and a woman got over our walls, and in a moment seized us both, and without giving us time to cry out or make resistance they stopped our mouths and ran off with us into the nearest wood.[14]

---

[10] Cugoano was born in Agimaque or Ajumako in present-day Ghana, on the coast of Fantyn. See Cugoano, *Thoughts and Sentiments*, pp. 120–127.

[11] See Cugoano, *Thoughts and Sentiments*, p. 126. Conquered African kings were reduced to being men of war fighting on behalf of Portugal or Spain. They were the army of their conquerors and the machine that captured and enslaved other African people on behalf of Portugal or Spain. Conquered African kings' subjects were used to extend the conquest in the region in the service of Portugal, Spain, England, Holland or France. Philipe Hari I, Mendonça's grandfather, was an example. The conquered Africans paid their tax in enslaved people per year as long as they lived; if they did not comply with these rules, they were killed or sold with their families into slavery. This law was applied by the European empires during the Atlantic slave trade. We need to grasp this when discussing African participation in the Atlantic slave trade. See 'Informação de Fernão de Sousa a El-Rei', 7 December 1631, BAL - Ms. 51-VIII-31, folios 5–9 v. and Frei Melchior da Conceicam, 'Alvaras, Cartas, Provizioes, Regimentos'. On common European practice in the Atlantic, see Blackburn, *The American Crucible*. See also 'Carta do Governador Geral de Angola a EL-REI D. João IV', AHU – Angola, cx. 4, 17 September 1655, and 'Carta do Padre Pedro de Barchi ao Prefeito da Propaganda', APF., SRCG, vol. 420, fls. 452–453 v., 30 January 1668, Dongo, Regno, il cui Rè è Cristiano, tributário del Rè di Portugallo [The Kingdom of Dongo, whose King is Christian, pays his tribute to the King of Portugal]; MMA, vol. XI, pp. 70–75, p. 73.

[12] For further discussion of British activity in the region, see Sylvanus John Sodienye Cookey, *King Jaja of the Niger Delta: His Life and Times, 1821–1891*, New York: Nok Publishers, 1974. For a detailed discussion of the validity of Cugoano's narrative, see Gunn, 'Creating a Paradox'.

[13] See Blackburn, *The American Crucible*, p. 21.

[14] Equiano, *The Interesting Narrative*. Equiano was born around the year 1745 in 'Eboe' in present-day Nigeria.

In 1766 Equiano was able to buy his own freedom. He argued for the abolition of the Atlantic slave trade, as a Native of Africa.[15] In his narrative, he demonstrated that abolition was not only an ethical matter but also one of metropolitan economic interest.[16] Equiano's *Narrative* entails, prior to that of Thomas Buxton's[17] and David Livingstone's works,[18] the 'legitimate trade' argument, i.e. the idea of exporting commodities and establishing commerce with African people as a step on the way to an international division of labour that was not based on slavery but a legitimate trade between the two continents of Europe and Africa, and in this case specifically between Britain and Africa. He declared: 'it is trading upon safe grounds. A commercial intercourse with Africa opens an inexhaustible source of wealth to the manufacturing interest of Great Britain, and to all which the slave-trade is an objection.'[19] Equiano, like Mendonça, wanted a fair society based on equality. His testimony confirmed the method deployed to capture Africans. The work of Wadström in the eighteenth century demonstrated the continuing use of the same method even though it was a century after Mendonça's court case.[20] Christopher Ehret states that: 'despite common assumptions to the contrary, few sub-Saharan Africans had ever been enslaved before the rise of the first Islamic empire.'[21] According to him, it was from the eighth century that the slave trade was to be introduced in the sub-Saharan region, after the arrival of Islam.

Luis de Molina (1535–1600), a Portuguese Jesuit priest and jurist, argued that the Christian mission to Africa ought to be carried out through a different means than slavery. Those whose ambition is to make economic gain in Africa should do other business in the region.[22]

---

[15] See Wadström, *An Essay on Colonization*. In the appendix, there is list of subscribers who received a copy this work [An Essay on Colonization]. Wadström called him 'Guftavus Vaffa, a native of Africa'. There is a debate as to whether Equiano was actually born in South Carolina – see Vincent Carretta, *Equiano, the African: Biography of a Self-made Man*, New York: London: Penguin Books, 2006 and James H. Sweet, 'Mistaken Identities? Olaudah Equiano, Domingos Álvares, and the Methodological Challenges of Studying the African Diaspora', *The American Historical Review*, 114(2), 2009, pp. 279–306.

[16] See Equiano, *The Interesting Narrative*.   [17] Buxton, *The African Slave Trade*.

[18] Seaver, *David Livingstone*; Jeal, *Livingstone*; Livingstone and Macnair (eds.), *Livingstone's Travels*.

[19] Equiano, *The Interesting Narrative*, p. 356.   [20] Wadström, *An Essay on Colonization*.

[21] See Christopher Ehret, *The Civilizations of Africa, A History to 1800*, Oxford: James Currey, 2002, p. 342.

[22] See Henrique Joner, 'Impressions of Luis de Molina about the Trade of African Slaves', *Patristica et Mediaevalia*, 36, 2015, pp. 39–50: https://core.ac.uk/download/pdf/322579935.pdf. Accessed on 16/04/2021.

According to Molina, judicially, all conflicts carried out in Africa 'were more robberies than wars', hence illegal.[23] These claims made by Molina in the mid-sixteenth century resonated with Mendonça's ones a century later in 1684. On wars waged against Africans and their illegal enslavement, Molina declared:

> ... very rarely are they presumed to be fair. Those who consider themselves more powerful invade and oppress others; and those are who most export slaves, supporting the injustices of others and unjustly taking from the enslaved their freedom ... It follows how rarely it is presumed to be just the war between Africans.[24]

Fajardo and Melchior listed cases of abuse in Kongo and Angola. These cases could not be justified on the ground of just war.[25] Methods used by Portuguese governors and their captains were based on their own economic interest as we have seen in Chapter 1. Meanwhile, Melchior listed cases in which sobas were being given 'forced gifts' or 'buttering-up gifts' in order to be provided with enslaved people. Melchior stated: 'together these officers start to pursue them, to pay them for their [bansos composed of] shoes, and the work on the roads, and if they do not give them what they ask, they arrest the *sobas*, and put them in irons to take them to the Captain-Mores of the outposts.'[26]

If there were slave practices in the Kongo and Angola, clearly Mendonça would have made this explicit in the Vatican. The evidence he presented in the Vatican refutes the claims made above that slave markets already existed in West Central Africa before the era of Atlantic trade.[27]

As stated in the Introduction, research on the abolition of slavery in the Atlantic region tends to focus on the eighteenth and nineteenth centuries,

---

[23] See Joner, 'Impressions of Luis de Molina', p. 47, 'potius ilia esse latrocinia, quam bella'.
[24] As quoted by Joner, 'Impressions of Luis de Molina', p. 47, 'Sane quam rarissime praesumendum est ea iusta esse. Etenim, qui se inter eos potentiores arbitrantur, alios iniuste invadunt, & opprimere conantur atque hi sunt, qui maiores mancipiorum venalium praedas asportant, aliis iniuriam sustinentibus, mancipiisque ipsi suam libertatem amittentibus [...]. Ex quibus patet, quam raro praesumendum sit esse bella iusta inter Aethiopes.' See Molina, *De Iustitia et Iure*, Apud Sessas, Venetiis, 1611. '40 II, 35, col. 172'.
[25] See High Court of Appeal 'Relação de Antonio Bezerra Fajardo' and see Frei Melchior da Conceicam, 'Alvaras, Cartas, Provizioes, Regimentos'.
[26] See Frei Melchior da Conceicam, 'Alvaras, Cartas, Provizioes, Regimentos', 'juntamente os começão estes officios apreseguir, que lhes paguem os seus sapatos, e o trabalho dos caminhos, e se lhes lhe não dem o que lhe pedem os prendem, e metem em ferros para os levar aos Capitains Mores dos presídios'.
[27] See Miller, *Kings and Kinsmen*; Thornton, 'The Kingdom of Kongo', and Heywood, 'Slavery and Its Transformation'.

with selective reference made to previous centuries and figures such as Buxton, Equiano, Cugoano, Livingstone, Wilberforce and Nabuco in Brazil.[28] Mendonça should be just as important in these debates, especially since he took the debate back as early as the seventeenth century and included the New Christians and Indigenous Americans.[29] No one has so far examined the highly organised, international-scale liberation attempt headed by Mendonça in the Vatican court on 6 March 1684. Discourses about abolition have not engaged with Mendonça's claim for the freedom and integration of enslaved Africans in Africa, Portugal, Spain and the Americas.[30]

The court case presented by Mendonça arguing for the abolition of slavery included different organisations, Black Brotherhoods and interest groups of 'men', 'women' and 'young people'[31] of African descent in Spain, Portugal, Brazil and Africa. It also included other constituencies such as the New Christians and the Indigenous Americans.[32] The scale of this international initiative led by Africans in the Atlantic region themselves has not been fully researched since the inception of European slavery in the Atlantic in the fifteenth century.[33] This finding is substantiated with new data I have uncovered in the Overseas Historical Archive of Belém, Portugal, Royal Palace of Madrid, and Archive of Propaganda Fide, which links Mendonça's activity to that of the New Christians and the Indigenous Americans and the abolition of the Atlantic slave trade in its entirety – Africa, Brazil and the Americas (Latin America and Caribbean).

This chapter shows how Mendonça's court case challenges and refutes the established historiography on the seventeenth century, and particularly that on the eighteenth and nineteenth centuries, which asserts that Africa was a slaving society that aided the European Atlantic slave trade.[34] His evidence demonstrates how the Atlantic slave trade operated as

---

[28] Buxton, *The African Slave Trade*; see Equiano, *The Interesting Narrative*; for discussion of Livingstone, see Seaver, *David Livingstone*; Jeal, *Livingstone*; Livingstone and Macnair, *Livingstone's Travels*. For a detailed discussion of Wilberforce, see Ackerson, *The African Institution*; Bayne, *Men Worthy to Lead*; and Belmonte, *Hero for Humanity*; see also Bethell, *Joaquim Nabuco*; Nabuco, *The Life of Joaquim Nabuco*; Vieira, *Obras Escolhidas*; Vieira, *Sermões*.

[29] See APF, SOCG, vol. 490, folio, 140. [30] See APF, SOCG, vol. 490, folio, 140.

[31] See SOCG, vol. 495a, fl. 58, 'tante huomini, come feminine, e ragazzi'.

[32] See APF, SOCG, vol. 490, folio, 140.

[33] For discussion of Africans and Indigenous people in Brazil, but not of international organisations, see Schwartz, *Blacks and Indians*.

[34] S.C. Africa, 1, fl., 486, Lisbon, and SOCG, 490, fl. 141r-v.

a machine that used violence as a strategy to maintain its existence in Africa.[35] Fundamentally, Mendonça's intervention leads us to return to the issues discussed in Chapter 1 about the injustices and brutality used to enslave people in West Central Africa through raiding and kidnapping. It also returns to the main question of the book: that is, to ask how the debate Mendonça initiated on abolition opens up new understandings of the broader questions about slavery in the Atlantic region, and how this engagement produces new insights into the study of African slavery and its abolition in Brazil, the Americas (Latin America and the Caribbean), Spain, Portugal and Africa. Following from this broader question, it interrogates the extent to which Africa was a slaving society and whether those Africans brought out of Africa fitted, in fact, another category of slavery altogether. It also asks whether those enslaved by Europeans were truly slaves in the legal sense. Were there any legal grounds at all on which Atlantic slavery could be based? Responses to these questions can be found in the evidence Mendonça presented, with which historians of the Atlantic have not engaged. That Mendonça's quest for freedom was not an isolated endeavour is further substantiated by another new piece of data I have found, from King Garcia II (1641–1661) of Kongo. He questioned how Africans were being enslaved by Europeans, and wrote to Pope Innocent X in 1648 to protest, almost forty years before Mendonça presented his court case in the Vatican.[36] Also, Afonso I, king of Kongo, had challenged as early as 1526 the enslavement of his people, including his own family, despite the claim made (see Chapter 1) about his involvement in the slave trade.[37]

My key argument in this chapter is that Mendonça's presentation in the Vatican was a court case, and not a petition as Gray has led us to believe, and that the accused were the Vatican, Italian, Portuguese and Spanish governing authorities. As noted in the Introduction, the documents for Mendonça's court case were organised into three categories, based on the order in which they were presented and their importance: (A) Mendonça's presentation of the first case as an attorney; (B) the accused's responses, that is, the responses from the governing authorities in Italy, Spain and Portugal and the slave-masters in Spain, Portugal and Brazil; and (C) the

---

[35] See 'Carta de d. Garcia II Rei do Congo ao Padre Reitor do Colégio de Luanda', and SOCG, vol. 490, fl. 54.
[36] APF, Eminetissimi e Reuerendissimi Signori, SRCG, vol. 247, fl.s, 165–165 v., 9 May 1648
[37] See Miller, *Kings and Kinsmen*; Heywood, 'Slavery and Its Transformation'; and Thornton, 'The Kingdom of Kongo'.

plaintiff's cases or the voices of the Africans from different organisations, confraternities and interest groups, including the constituencies of men, women, and young people within the confraternities themselves.[38]

Mendonça's presentation prompted the Vatican to ask for eyewitnesses, whose evidence was given by Moirans, Jaca and another priest.[39] The Vatican decided to punish wrongdoers, but Portugal, Italy and Spain attempted to overturn the Vatican's verdict.[40] The authorities in Italy and Spain claimed that the Vatican was not being informed about the truth of what was happening to the enslaved Africans in the Americas, Spain and Portugal. Portugal stated that enslaved Africans in the Americas were not badly treated.[41] Black confraternities around the world then appealed to the Vatican about the delay to the announcement of its verdict, as they believed that the justice ministers had decided in their favour after hearing Jaca and Moirans' accounts of the violations of their basic human rights.[42] Indeed, both Jaca and Moirans demanded that justice be done.[43] Black constituencies subsequently flooded the Vatican with complaints after the defendants' responses, because the Vatican was sitting on the fence about the case to end slavery.[44] The confraternities insisted that there was no place for slavery in the Christian community: freedom and redemption were for all human beings, and the wrongdoers or guilty parties should be punished.[45]

Accordingly, the chapter presents initially the African voices of protest that contested slavery before Mendonça's court case, namely the Kongolese kings Garcia II and Afonso I. Then I present in detail Mendonça's presentation from 1684 in the Vatican and its political implications, impact and reactions. I focus especially on his challenging of the infractions in *natural*, *human*, *divine* and *civil* law. Finally, I discuss the final statement he lodged in 1686, as well his argument both in the presentation of the court case and its concluding statement. Yet in order to understand his intervention we must first turn first to those Africans who preceded him in protesting against slavery. He may have been forgotten by history, but he was not the first.

---

[38] See SOCG, vol. 495a, fl. 58.
[39] See APF, SOCG, vol. 490, fl. 138, 'da tre sacerdoti, due Spagnoli, et un Portoghese'.
[40] See APF, SOCG. vol. 495a, fl. 57.   [41] See APF, SOCG. vol. 495a, fl. 57.
[42] See Jaca and Moirans, Propaganda Archives, 'series: Acta de anno 1685', no. 26, March 12, fls. 35–37, and see also John M. Lenhart, 'Capuchin Champions of Negro Emancipation in Cuba, 1681–1685', *Franciscan Studies*, 6, 1946, pp. 195 (195–217).
[43] See Jaca and Moirans, Propaganda Archives, 'series: Acta de anno 1685'.
[44] See confraternities response, SOCG, vol. 495a, fl. 62.   [45] See SOCG, vol. 495a, fl. 62.

5.1 AFRICAN VOICES OF PROTEST BEFORE MENDONÇA'S DISCOURSE IN THE VATICAN

Historians of the slave trade in the Atlantic have given no voice to Africans in the quest for the abolition of the slave trade in the Atlantic before the eighteenth and nineteenth century. The contribution of Africans to the debate on abuses in the slave trade has been driven into the background, particularly in the sixteenth and seventeenth century. If there is debate, it centres first on the voices of protest from within Portuguese society, and only then looks beyond to African societies.[46]

For example, in his analysis of Father Fernando Oliveira's critique of the Portuguese Atlantic slavery in the sixteenth century, Livermore contends that Oliveira was among the few to openly criticise the practice. He states that Oliveira 'devoted an entire chapter to a violent denunciation of the slave trade',[47] and suggests that Oliveira was robust in his criticism by demonstrating that 'there was no such thing as a "just war" against Muslims, Jews or heathens who had never been Christians and who were quite prepared to trade with the Portuguese'.[48] For Livermore, no work is equal to Oliveira's, and he boldly asserts that 'Africa had produced no one since St Augustine with the ideas of Oliveira to limit their [European slave owners'] greed.'[49] This is quite an assertion, especially given that prior to Oliveira's writing, as noted above, Afonso I, king of Kongo, had already criticised the Portuguese slave trade.[50] We will return to this issue in due course.

It should be no surprise to anyone that voices of protest were frequently raised against the Atlantic slave trade, and Africans engaged in violent and non-violent resistance against their enslavement by Europeans. Enslaved Africans would often revolt aboard the ships carrying them to the Americas, as has been documented by David Richardson in his study *Shipboard Revolts* (2001).[51] Who would not have revolted if they had been violated in the most inhumane way possible? Richardson shows that although slave revolts were commonplace, 'the voices of those who were its [slavery's] victims are rarely heard when one looks for evidence or

---

[46] See Maxwell, *Slavery and the Catholic Church*, and Saunders, *A Social History of Black Slaves and Freedmen*, and Boxer, *The Church Militant*.
[47] Livermore, 'Padre Oliveira's Outburst', p. 22.
[48] Livermore, 'Padre Oliveira's Outburst', p. 22.
[49] Livermore, 'Padre Oliveira's Outburst', p. 23.
[50] See 'Ruious Remetente: Del Rey de Manycõgo', ATT-CC-I-35-21, 18 October 1526, pp. 489–490, and see 'Carta do Bispo de Cabo Verde a El-Rei'.
[51] See Richardson, 'Shipboard Revolts'.

explanations of shipboard slave revolts. Occasionally, explanations attributable to slaves are to be found.'[52] Richardson goes on to demonstrate that 'of the 392 insurrections, 353 (90 per cent) took place in the period from 1698 to 1807'. However, he explains that 'given gaps in records and the paucity of evidence on revolts for ships other than those of the French, Dutch, and British, it is difficult to determine the proportion of slave ships that experienced an insurrection'.[53]

Earlier voices of protest against the enslavement of Africans included those of African kings, African communities and European priests working in Africa.[54] According to our documentary sources, Africans began to speak up against the Europeans soon after the first Portuguese encounters with West Africans in the mid-fifteenth century and with the West Central Africans at the beginning of the sixteenth century.[55] In the seventeenth century, Lourenço da Silva Mendonça himself took a court case.[56] In fact, many Africans spoke out; few were heard or taken seriously. This view is echoed by J. M. Lenhart, who claims that 'only from time to time the humanitarian world heard a few protests like that of the two Capuchins [Francisco de Jaca and Epiphane de Moirans] who were imprisoned in Havana because of their condemnation of the planters' failure to provide for the religious instruction of the Negroes'.[57] African protests fell on deaf ears or, at least, into an environment that was not prepared to listen to them.[58]

However, one of the earliest records of African protest can be found in the chronicle of Luís de Cadamosto, an Italian merchant employed by Henry the Navigator (1394–1460), duke of Viseu, Portugal, on his second voyage (1456) to River Senegal, or the West African River, in the region known today as Senegal, Guinea-Bissau and the Gambia.[59] Cadamosto spoke with Africans who told him that they did not want to engage in any

---

[52] Richardson, 'Shipboard Revolts', p. 4.   [53] Richardson, 'Shipboard Revolts', p. 7.
[54] See 'Carta do Bispo de Cabo Verde a El-Rei, Bibioteca da Universidade de Coimbra'.
[55] For further detailed discussion of West Africa protest, see, Cadamosto, *Navegações de Luís*. For West Central Africa, Afonso I, 'Ruious Remetente: Del Rey de Manycõgo'; 'Carta de D. Garcia II Rei do Kongo ao Padre Reitor do Colégio de Luanda'; see Philipe Hari I's protest in AHU – Códice. 15, fl. 103 and 96v, and that of King Ngola Mbamdi in 'Relação de Fernão de Sousa a El-Rei'.
[56] See Mendonça's case, APF, SOCG, vol. 495a, fl. 392; see SOCG, vol. 495a, fl. 54, and APF, SOCG. vol. 495a, fl. 58.
[57] See also Lenhart, 'Capuchin Champions of Negro Emancipation'.
[58] See 'Carta de D. Garcia II Rei do Kongo ao Padre Reitor do Colégio de Luanda'.
[59] Cadamosto, *Navegações de Luís*. For detailed studies of the River Senegal and its three headstreams from the Fouta Djallon in modern Guinea Conakry, which borders Guinea-Bissau and drains into the Atlantic Ocean, see Louis Papy, 'La Valée du Sénégal: Agriculture

business with him or his men. He asked them through an interpreter to give him a reason why they did not desire peace, because he had come a long way to bring presents to their king:

> The response was that, in the past, they had received news about our coming and of our trade with the Negros of Senegal, who could not seek our friendship unless they wanted to be bad men, for they certainly believed that we Christians ate human flesh [*che noi Cristiani mangiavamo carne umana*], and that we only bought Negroes to eat them; for this reason they did not want our friendship on any terms, but wanted only to slaughter us all, and then gift our possessions to their lord, who they said was a three-day journey away.[60]

Cannibalism was attributed to the Africans in the seventeenth century, particularly in Western Central Africa to the Jaga people group of Angola, who, as we saw in Chapter 1, were accused of eating the flesh of their captives.[61] The Europeans accused Africans of racticing cannibalism as a part of a strategy to justify slavery. They argued that they were saving Africans from death by enslaving them rather than letting them be killed and eaten by each other.[62] Internal Africans wars, which supposedly led to killing and cannibalism, were used to give licence to Atlantic slavery.[63] However, on the West African coast, it was Africans making accusations of cannibalism: they accused Cadamosto and his men of kidnapping Africans to take to Europe to eat. This contradicts the view – voiced by

---

Traditionnelle et Riziculture Mécanisée', *Les Cahiers d'Outre-Mer*, 4(16), 1951, pp. 277-324.

[60] Cadamosto, *Navegações de Luís de Cadamosto*, p.68, 'La risposta sua fu che pel passato di noi aveano avuto qualche notizia, e del nostro praticare con li Negri di Senega: e quali non potevano esser salvochè cattivi uomini, in voler nostra amistà; perchè eglino tenevano per fermo che noi Cristiani mangiavamo carne umana; e che non comperiamo li Nigri slavochè per mangiarli; e che per questo non volevano nostra amistrà per alcun modo: ma che ne volevano ammazzar tutti; e dappoi delle cose nostre fariano un presente al suo signore, il qual dicevano esser lontano tre giornate.'

[61] For further discussion of Jaga, see Hilton, 'The Jaga Reconsidered' and Cadornega, *História Geral*. On cannibalism in West Central Africa see Beatrix Heintze, 'Propaganda Concerning "Man Eaters" in West Central Africa in the Second Half of the Nineteenth Century', *Paideuma*, 49, 2003, pp. 125-135; Mariana P. Candido, 'Jagas e Sobas no "Reino de Benguela": Vassalagem e Criação de Novas Categorias Políticas e Sociais no Contexto da Expansão Portuguesa na África Durante os Séculos XVI E XVII', in Alexandre Vieira Ribeiro, Alexsander Lemos de Almeida Gebara and Marina Berther (eds.) *África: Históricas conectadas*, Niterói: PPGHistória-UFF, 2014, pp. 39-76; Jared Staller, *Converging on Cannibals: Terrors of Slaving in Atlantic Africa, 1509-1670*. Athens, OH: Ohio University Press, 2019.

[62] For detailed discussion of saving Africans from death see, Molina, *De Justitia et Jure*.

[63] See Mendonça's legal challenge, SOCG, vol. 495a, fls. 54-55, see also 'Instrutione Gagisterno Cybo', Molina, *De Justitia et Jure*, and Cadornega, *História Geral*, vol. III.

Brásio,[64] Molina,[65] Carvalho[66] and Thornton and Miller on the idea of 'wealth in people'[67] – that it was the Africans' societal structures that formed the foundation for the institution of the Atlantic slave trade.[68] As we saw in Chapter 2 and Chapter 3, evidence on *baculamento* suggests that African society was not at the root of the Atlantic slavery. This is not to say that Africans were not involved in the slave trade in the subsequent period of its history with European slave-traders through coercion and violence.[69] However, as Mendonça showed when he presented his criminal case in the Vatican, the Africans and those being enslaved continued to abhor the inhumanity of the Atlantic slave trade. Likewise, an anonymous priest in 1612 sent a letter to King Philipe III of Spain to complain about Atlantic slavery, declaring that enslaved African people were 'shocked by the way the Portuguese make slaves of them against the law of their land'[70] and against human law, to which we will return in due course.

On 1 May 1684, the Vatican nuncio in Lisbon, Mesquita's successor, raised awareness of the established African interpretation of the slave trade, which was that the enslaved thought they were taken to Portugal and Brazil to be turned into oil. At the same time, he also negated any sympathy the Vatican officials in Rome may have felt for the enslaved by placing the slave trade in the realm of myth: 'neither Blacks in Brazil nor in the Kingdom [Portugal], turn out to be desperate, because they do not find the evil as they believe they will when they leave Angola or other parts of Africa, where they are informed that they are taken to Brazil or to the Kingdom to be turned into oil'.[71] However, it is evident that Africans

---

[64] See Brásio, *Monumenta Missionaria Africana*.   [65] Molina, *De Justitia et Jure*.
[66] Carvalho, *Das Origens da Escravidão*, p. 45, 'não inventámos a escravidão dos Negros; encontrámo-la formando a base daquelas sociedades imperfeitas'.
[67] Miller, *Way of Death*; Miller, *Kings and Kinsmen* and Thornton, 'The Kingdom of Kongo"; Thornton, 'The Origins and Early History' and Thornton, *Africa and Africans in the Making of the Atlantic World*.
[68] António Luís Ferronha, 'Introdução', in André de Almada, Tratado Breve dos Rios de Guiné do Cabo-Verde, Feito peleo Capitão André Álvares d'Almada, Ano de 1594, Leitura, Introdução, Modernização do Texto e Notas, Lisbon: Grupo de Trabalho do Ministério da Educação para as Comemorações dos Descobrimentos Portugueses, 1994, p. 9.
[69] Frei Melchior da Conceicam, 'Alvaras, Cartas, Provizioes, Regimentos', and Heywood and Thornton, *Central Africans and Cultural Transformations*.
[70] 'Proposta a sua Magestade sobre a escravia das terras da Conquista de Portugal', Document 7,3,1, n. 8, Seção de Manuscritos, Biblioteca Nacional, Rio de Janeiro, in Conrad, *Children of God's Fire*, p.15.
[71] See the Vatican Nuncio's letter from Portugal, dated 1 May 1684, APF, SOCG. vol. 495a, fl. 57.

knew the truth of their predicament in Brazil, since, as we saw in Chapter 1 and Chapter 3, there were those who returned from Brazil to Africa, and to Angola in particular.[72]

Questions about the nature of Africans' own practices of slavery, and discussion of the status of the so-called slaves in Africa by Europeans and some African historians[73] justify the new research approach adopted here. In the view of Miers and Kopytoff, 'African slavery' was 'an Institution of Marginality' and was distinct from the institution of Atlantic slavery.[74] For Africans, 'the New World type of slavery, far from being a norm, was in fact a rather unusual historical creation'.[75] As we saw in Chapter 1 and Chapter 2, many *sobas* and kings in West Central Africa were coerced into trading in slaves with the Europeans.[76] This early period of Portugal's encounter with West Africa and West Central Africa requires a critical examination of the practice of slavery, and an investigation into whether we are dealing with completely different understandings of war 'captives' from the European and African points of view. It provides scope for rethinking how we engage with the nature of servitude or giving service to another person among West Central Africans.

King João II of Portugal (1481–1495) was hailed as a perfect prince, who masterminded the Portuguese expansionist project overseas after taking over from Prince Henry the Navigator.[77] In 1494, he confirmed to Jerome Münzer, a German medical doctor in Évora, that the procedure for obtaining enslaved people from the Africans was tedious, which might imply it involved legal proceedings and political negotiation. Boasting of his own astuteness, he claimed that only a crafty European king could find ways to buy 'African captives' from the African kings. As Münzer succinctly put it: 'our ingenious King at present, however, buys slaves from a victorious King and through his

---

[72] See 'Relaçaõ para o Ill.mo Sñr Collector'.
[73] See M'bokolo, *África Negra*. For him, Kongo was an enslaving society.
[74] For further debate on the issue, see Miers and Kopytoff, 'African "Slavery" as an Institution'.
[75] Miers and Kopytoff, *Slavery in Africa*, p. 59.
[76] For further discussion of the capture of slaves in the eighteenth century, see Candido, *An African Slaving Port*, and António Carreira, *As Companhias Pombalinas de Navegação Comércio e Tráfico de Escravos entre Africana e o Nordeste Brasileiro*, Bissau: Centro de Estudos da Guiné Portuguesa, 1969. Also Freudenthal and Pantoja, *Livro dos Baculamentos*, and Heintze, 'The Angolan Vassal Tributes of the 17th Century'.
[77] See Elaine Sanceau, *The Perfect Prince: A Biography of the King Dom Joao II*, Porto: Livraria Civilização-Editora, 1959, and Anthony R. Disney, *A History of Portugal and the Portuguese Empire*, vol. II, New York: Cambridge University Press, 2009.

interpreters'.[78] There may have been thirteen of these interpreters, among whom was a nobleman called Adamum, who had been kidnapped by the Portuguese from West Africa. The king of Portugal had then ordered that they be instructed in the Portuguese language in order to become interpreters.[79] Münzer's statement serves as a reminder that Africans' involvement in slavery in this period was far from being the full-blown process that came to be accepted in the seventeenth and eighteenth centuries, and nor was the slave trade a unified endeavour. Faria, in his defence of the Africans in the seventeenth century, stated that 'our Portuguese in those parts ... so often they are those without fear of God ... they carry out great deceptions, robberies and extortions by unjustly capturing Natives in order to satisfy their covetousness'.[80] Rodney later called this a process of warfare, trickery, banditry, kidnapping and social violence.[81]

In 1526, less than a generation after the Portuguese established their relationship with West Central Africa, Afonso I, the king of Kongo, issued

---

[78] Jérome Münzer, Itinerarium Hispanicum Hieronymi monetarii (1494–1495), Manuscript 431, Munich, Bayrische Staatsbibliothek, p. 248, 'rex autem noster ingeniosus iam schlavos a rege victore emit, et per suos interpretes'. Slave trade became a profitable business in which all European institutions were involved. Later on, the Portuguese Crown made a contract with Bartolomeu, a wealthy man, who was selling slaves in Spain and Italy, under which the king received 40,000 docados every year, 'admisit item cuidam Florentino ditissimo domino Bartholomaeo, etiam dentes, schlauos et alia preter aurum, qui, certo pacto cum rege habito, omnes nigros in sua manu habet, et eos per omnem Italiae et Hispaniae oram vendit, et dicunt regem ex eo quotannis plus quadraginta milibus ducatorum habere', p. 246.

[79] Münzer, *Itinerarium hispanicum Hieronymi monetarii*, p. 227, 'Qui euntes noctu in terram sub diluculo probe puteum inuenerunt homines cum utribus, captisque 13 animabus reuersisunt in nauem. Jnter quos quidam noblis Adamum nominatus, Ethiops. Reursi igitur Portugaliam cum gaudio. Jnformatus igitur Rex hos nigros fecit discere linguam Portugalie'.

[80] M. S. Faria, 'Discyrso Sexto, Sobre a Propagaçam do Evangelho nas Provincias de Guiné, Das Condições, com que os Summos Pontifices deraõ Reys de Portugal Senhorio de Guiné', in *Noticias de Portvgal*, Lisbon: Na Officina Craesbeeckiana, 1655, pp. 228–229, 'os noſſos Portugueſes naquellas partes ... muitas vezes eftes ſaõ os que ſem temor de Deos fazem ... grandes enganos, roubos, & extorſoës, por cativarem os naturais contra juſtiça, & ſatisfazerem a ſua cobiça'.

[81] See Walter Rodney, *How Europe Underdeveloped Africa*, p. 104. For an example of Portuguese trickery in the sixteenth century in West Africa, see A. Donelhas, 'Outra Relação em 14 Capítolos que fez Andre Donellas, ao Governador e Capitão Geral Fr. de Vaz Concellos da Cunha; Sobre a Serra Leoa, Reys e Senhores que a Habitão, e Secunvezinhos,Ritos, Costumes e Todas Variedades de Rios, Portos, Arvores, Animais Aves Pexes com os Proveitos que Dela se Tirão", Ms. 51-IX-25, in Palácio de Ajuda, Lisbon, 1625, ch. 14, fols. 177–178. For a detailed discussion of the trickery in the sixteenth century of Sad Life (a Portuguese migrant), see Lingna Nafafé, *Colonial Encounters*, pp. 81–84. See also, A. Á. Almada, 'TratadosBreue dosRejnos deguine docaboverde' [Treaty of the Kingdoms of Guiné and Cape Verde], in Biblioteca Nacional de Lisboa, 1594.

a letter to Dom João III containing serious complaints about the slave trade taking place in his kingdom.[82] Kidnapping[83] was the recurrent theme in Africans' complaints to the Portuguese, the Vatican and Hispanic authorities throughout the period of the Europeans' establishment of their presence in Africa. Indeed, Mendonça began his presentation with that very point. Afonso I stated in his letter that the slave trade was destroying his kingdom, since adults and children were being kidnapped and taken to be sold in Europe. Portugal was not providing his kingdom with the agreed education and skills. Instead, it had broken the terms of the agreement by prioritising the illegal slave trade in his kingdom.[84] He declared:

> ... each day the traders are kidnapping our people, children of this country, sons of our nobles and vassals, even people from our own family. This corruption and depravity is so widespread that our land is entirely depopulated. In this kingdom we need only priests and schoolteachers, and no merchandise, unless it is wine and flour for Mass. It is our wish that this Kingdom should not be a place for the trade or transport of slaves. Many of our subjects eagerly lust after Portuguese merchandise that your subjects have brought into our domains. To satisfy this inordinate appetite, they seize many of our black free subjects ... They sell them. After having taken these prisoners [to the coast] secretly or at night ... As soon as the captives are in the hands of white men, they are branded with a red-hot iron.[85]

This does not suggest that the new consumer culture was in itself unacceptable. It leads us to ask not so much what Western products did to the Kongolese but rather what the Kongolese did with their people to obtain the products. Molina stated that Africans became caught up in slave-trading because of their desire for Portuguese goods.[86] However, he also stated that:

---

[82] See 'Ruious Remetente: Del Rey de Manycõgo'.
[83] See the discussion of 'kidnapping' in Benguela, Angola, in Candido, *An African Slaving Port*.
[84] See 'Relação que faz o Capitão Garcia Mendes Castelobranco, do Reyno do Congo' [Report of the Captain Garcia Mendes Castelobranco, from the Kongo Kingdom], BAL, ms. 51-VIH-25, fls. 63–67v, 16 January 1620, MMA vol. VI, pp. 437–444. The king did not allow slaves to be taken from his kingdom, or even to pass through it.
[85] 'Ruious Remetente: Del Rey de Manycõgo', 'Outro sy Senhor em nossos Reynos há outro grande emcomueniente e de pouco serujço de Deus, o quall hé que mujtos nossos naturães, pollo dessejo mujto que tem das mercadarias e coussas desses Reynos, que os vossos a estees tragem, e a esta coussa e por satysfazerem seu desordenado apetito, furtam muitos dos nossos naturaees forros e jsemtos. E muytas vezes se comteçe furtarem fidallgos e filhos de fidallgos, e parentes nossos, e os leuam a vender aos homes brancos que em nossos Reynos esta; e lhos trazem esscõdidos e outros de noyte, por nam serem conhecidos. E tamto cjue sam em poder dos ditos homês brancos, sam logo fer[r]ados e marcados cõ fogo. E ao tempo que os leva pera ébarquar sam lhe per nossas guardas achadas; e alegam que os cõpraram e nã sabem dizer a que, pello quall nos eomvem fazer Justiça, e restytuyr os lyures, a sua liberdade. E assy o vam cramãdo.'
[86] See Molina, *De Iustitia et Iure*.

'if there were no Portuguese traders in the region, the problems of that society would be greatly reduced, since they would not have [access to trading partners] to whom to sell the slaves.'[87] For Afonso I, the Kongolese consumers of Western goods were a political threat to the kingdom itself. He claimed that these consumers were becoming wealthy and, through their accumulation of goods, were able to acquire levels of power that threatened the kingdom of Kongo:

> Lord, Your Highness will know how our kingdom is going to be lost in such a way that it is convenient for us to provide it with the necessary security, to a great ease in which your trading-station stewards and officers allow men and merchants to come to this Kingdom and to settle with stores, goods, and things for our maintenance, which are dispersed all over our kingdoms and provinces in such abundance that many vassals, from whom we had their obedience, arise from it [they stop being obedient], because they have abundantly more than us. Before, we had them contented and subject to us and entirely under our vassalage and jurisdiction. This is a great harm, both to the service of God and to the security and peace of our Realms and state.[88]

Afonso I was aware of the dangerous power that these goods were giving to some of his vassals and the claim that they were making for political independence from Kongo. This was dangerous for both the security of the kingdom and its relationship with Portugal. However, unlike his predecessors, particularly his father, Afonso I fell short of breaking the alliance with Portugal. He was unable to do so because he had only come to power with the support of the Portuguese.[89] It was one thing to condemn certain actions, and another to take action against an oppressive system.

---

[87] See Molina, *De Justitia et Jure*, II, 35, col. 17 4, C. As quoted by Joner, 'Impressions of Luis de Molina', p. 47.

[88] António Luís Ferronha, *As Cartas do 'Rei' do Congo, D. Afonso*, Lisbon: Grupo de Trabalho do M. da Educação para as Comemorações dos Descobrimentos Portugueses, 1992, pp. 56–57, 'Senhor: Vossa Alteza saberá como nosso reino se vai a perder em tanta maneira que nos convém provermos a isso com o remédio necessário, o que causa a muita soltura que vossos feitores e ofciais dão aos homens e mercadores se virem a este Reinos assentar com lojas, mercadorias e coisas muito por nós defesas, as quais se espalham por nossos reinos e senhorios em tanta abundância que muitos vassalos, que tinhamos à nossa obidiência se levantam dela, por terem as coisas em mais abastança que nós, que com as quais os antes tínhamos contentes e sujeitos e só nossa vassalagem e juridição que é um grande dano assim para o serviço de Deus como para segurança e sossego de nosso Reinos e estado.' See a similar argument in J. Boulegue, *Le Grand Jolof, XIIIe-XVIe siècle (Les Anciens Royaumes Wolof)*, Paris: Diffusion Karthala, 1987. Also Ivana Elbl, 'The Horse in Fifteenth-Century Senegambia', *The International Journal of African Historical Studies*, 1991, 24(1), pp. 85–110.

[89] See Georges Balandier, *Daily Life in the Kingdom of the Congo from the Sixteenth to the Eighteenth Century*, London: Allen & Unwin, 1968; see also Haywood and Thornton, *Central Africans*, and Fromont, *The Art of Conversion*.

At the beginning of the seventeenth century, the bishop of Cabo Verde contested the established thinking of the time in a letter in which he asserted that African social, economic and political structures were conducive to slavery.[90] His critique was levelled at those who assumed that interethnic conflict in Africa lay behind the capturing of slaves and their transport to Portugal. On the contrary, the evidence shows that in this early period the Europeans waged war on Africans or used treachery in order to procure slaves, as we saw in Chapter 1. Many of the people the Europeans claimed were already enslaved were not enslaved at all.[91] According to the bishop, if there were true slaves in Africa, they were too few to be counted. The bishop's words bring an historical situation to our attention about which other priests remained absolutely silent:

... because humanly, there are too many ways in which they have unfairly been captured to detail. For some have been stolen by force or deceived, others blamelessly condemned to captivity, as are women, children and relatives through the fault of the parents, others were taken from unjust wars, because they are not bought legally, but more from will of those who captured them. Others sold by their parents without enough need; others were captured with a fraudulent art of a dead man who discovers the murderer's hut, when they want to capture some of his family, and others by other improper ways. So the practitioners say that out of a thousand slaves who come to the Kingdom, nine hundred are barely captives.[92]

Brásio dates the bishop's protest to the beginning of the seventeenth century, but from its internal evidence I would argue for a date in the mid-seventeenth century, if not around the time when Mendonça was preparing his court case. The bishop touches on enslavement of Africans when the Dutch were present in West Central Africa: he mentions the relationship between the Dutch and African élites, perhaps referring to the situation in the 1640s, when Queen Njinga of Matamba and Garcia II were allies of the Dutch.[93] The letter began with

---

[90] See 'Carta do Bispo de Cabo Verde a El-Rei'.
[91] See Azevedo, 'Cartas do Padre António Vieira a Roque Monteiro Paim', pp. 620–621.
[92] 'Carta do Bispo de Cabo Verde a El-Rei', 'porque humanamente se não pode atalhar aos muitos modos cõ que iniustamente os catiuaõ. Porque hús saõ furtados por força ou engano, outros condenados sem culpa a catiueiro, como são as molheres, filhos e parentes pola culpa dos paes, outros tomados en guerras intustas, porque naõ traraõ de *iure*, senão de que mais pode. Outros uendidos por seus paes, sem necessidade bastante; outros cõ híí artefiçio fraudulento de homé morto que descubra a caza do matador, quando querem catiuar algü con toda sua familia, e outros por outros modos iniustos. De sorte que dizem os practicos que de mil escrauos que ué ao Reyno, os noueçentos saõ mal catiuos.'
[93] 'Carta do Bispo de Cabo Verde a El-Rei'.

a demand that Portugal change the law to allow enslaved Africans to gain freedom on the basis of *favore fidei* (benevolent faith). In other words, it demanded that Portugal grant freedom both to those who had converted to Christianity while still in Africa and those who converted after their enslavement. His critique of the Portuguese economy, culture and readiness to use war to procure African enslaved people was endorsed by his contemporaries, particularly King Garcia II of Kongo (see Figure 24), who – as mentioned above – complained to the Portuguese and the Vatican authorities about the slave trade being

FIGURE 24 Garcia II, king of Kongo/Nkanga a Lukeni, Albert Eckhout, 1641. Public domain.

carried out in his kingdom by Portuguese merchants from the Angolan settlement of Luanda.

Garcia II saw the Portuguese slave trade in Luanda as an alien trade imposed on West Central Africans. Although some Africans were caught up in it, it was unknown in the region prior to the arrival of the Europeans, particularly the Portuguese. For him the slave trade ran counter to all that West Central Africa had been built upon – the exchange of goods or produce among its peoples rather than the sale of human beings. In a letter to the principal of the Jesuit College in Luanda, he asserted:

There is nothing that harms men more than ambition and pride. This reigned in this City of Luanda. And as it was, so there could be no peace with this Kingdom, instead of gold and silver and other goods which function elsewhere as money, the trade and the money are persons, who are not gold, nor in cloth [which Kongo was known for], but who are creatures. It is our disgrace and that of our predecessors that we, in our simplicity, have given the opportunity to do many evils in our realm, and above all that there are people who pretend that we were never lords over Angola and Matamba. The inequality of arms has lost us lands over, and where there is violence, rights are lost.[94]

Garcia II of Kongo's outrage at Atlantic slavery is clear. For 159 years, since the Portuguese arrived in Kongo in 1484, they had destroyed the economic structures that had served Kongo for generations, in which 'shells' or *sinbos* were the currency.[95] The Portuguese introduced an economic model in the region based on enslaved people.[96] To combat the slave trade and its economic model, Garcia II was prepared to die for his people: 'and believe me, and the Lord we trust and confess, that my will

---

[94] 'Carta de D. Garcia II Rei do Congo ao Padre Reitor do Colégio de Luanda', 23 February 1643, 'naõ há couza que mais danifique os homens que a ambição e soberba. Essa reinou nessa Cidade da Loanda. E asim fosse naõ podia nuca auer pazes com este Reino, porque en lugar de ouro, prata e outras couzas que serue de moeda em outras partes, o trato e moeda saõ pessas, que naõ saõ de ouro ne de panos, senão creaturas. Nossa desgracia, e a dos meus antepassados que cõ a nossa simplicidade demos lugar a que crecece tantos males en nossos Reinos, e sobretudo que aia homés que afirme[m] que numca fomos Senhores de Angòlla e Matamba. A desigoaldade das armas nos fizerao perder tudo, que ahonde há forssa, direito se perde.'

[95] Pacheco Pereira states that 'the Negroes of these islands [Angola] pick up small shells (of the size of pine-nuts in their shell) which they call "zinbos." These are used as money in the country of Mani-Congo; fifty of them buy a hen and three hundred a goat and so forth': Pacheco Pereira, Durate Pacheco Pereira, *Esmeraldo de Situ Orbis*, Series II, LXXXI, London: Hakluyt Society, 1892, p. 145. Anne Hilton argues that Kongo's tax and transactions were based on produce: 'salt, together with *nzimbu* shell money, formed the principal item of Mbamba and Sonyo's political tribute and economic exchange': Hilton, 'The Jaga Reconsidered', p. 193.

[96] 'Carta de D. Garcia II Rei do Congo ao Padre Reitor do Colégio de Luanda'.

is not anything else than to let my land be taken away from me and this is my firm intended purpose, that even if thunder and lightning fall, I will die to liberate my people'.[97] Garcia II outlined his firm intention not to allow his people to be taken into slavery, and not to honour his treaty with Salvador Correia de Sá, which declared he should pay *baculamento* of 1,000 slaves to Portugal per year or face invasion.[98] There was no doubt in Garcia II's mind that he would not compromise the lives of his people; they were far more tenacious than the Portuguese, who called them 'fools and beasts', seemed to believe.[99] He went on to assert that Queen Njinga Mbandi of Matamba (1624–1663), his contemporary and firm ally, was a good Catholic up to the point when she was forced to abandon Christianity because the Portuguese wanted to take her land and enslave her people.[100]

Garcia II harked back to the example of his people's ancestors and to a way of life that should be an example for the living to follow.[101] This way of life was devoted to serving the community, and he contrasts this to life after they adopted Christianity, which in his experience endorsed other values, including the use of violence against its own members, and had little regard for human dignity, particularly that of the Africans. Garcia II's protest is important for us because it shows the different levels at which Africans engaged with Atlantic slavery and its inhumanity, and the ways in which they challenged it through the centuries, to the seventeenth century and beyond.

Two years after writing to the principal of the Jesuit College in Luanda, Garcia II lodged a second complaint, this time written in Italian and addressed to the Vatican. In this document, he attacked the Portuguese slave trade in Kongo and in the wider region for the cruelties, made possible by the Portuguese use of firearms, levelled against the people there. He reiterated his earlier complaint to the governing authorities in

---

[97] See 'Carta de D. Garcia II Rei do Congo ao Padre Reitor do Colégio de Luanda', 'e creyame, pello Senhor que cremos e cõfessamos, que o meu animo naõ hé senaõ de que se me despeg[u]em as minhas terras e esse hé o meu intento propozito firme, que ainda que cayam rayos heide morrer por libertar o meu'.

[98] See 'Carta de D. Garcia II Rei do Congo ao Padre Reitor do Colégio de Luanda'.

[99] 'Carta de D. Garcia II Rei do Congo ao Padre Reitor do Colégio de Luanda', 'nos chamare de paruos e bestas, pois ouue en nós tanta cõfiança, do que outros apelidos'.

[100] See 'Carta de D. Garcia II Rei do Congo ao Padre Reitor do Cológio de Luanda'. Garcia II created a united front with Njinga Mbandi during the seven-year war between the Dutch and the Portuguese in Angola. See 'Chancelaria de D. Afonso VI', ATT, liv. 25, fls. 144v., MMA, vol. X, pp. 502–503.

[101] Lingna Nafafé, *Colonial Encounters*.

Portugal. He mocked Portuguese Christianity, at the time engaged in the ethnic cleansing of New Christians, claiming that the behaviour of the Portuguese Christians in West Central Africa meant they could hardly be called Christians at all since they were not preserving and respecting Christian values.[102] He asserted that:

> ... the Portuguese who lived there, who were the newest Christians – that means that they were Christians only by name, but they were in fact Jews – they have been tyrannical and cruel to the people of Kongo, in ways that cannot be said. Using the force of firearms, they kidnapped men and women, loaded them on ships, and sent them to Brazil to produce sugar; without being moved to pity by their weeping and sorrows from fathers and mothers whose own children were taken away, or by the grieving of those who were being imprisoned.[103]

His complaint had a second theme – the damage caused to Christianity by the violence used to enslave Africans. This was a theme Mendonça also used when he showed the consequences of so-called Christians using a militant approach to capture Africans in the name of the Christian God. For Garcia II, such behaviour also had consequences for the Portuguese migrants living in his kingdom:

> I will say no more, because I do not want to bore Your Eminence, but these and other tyrannies could be told, which every year caused so much hate against the Portuguese inside the kingdom of Kongo and throughout the neighbouring kingdoms. It is so much that I will not be able to say any more.[104]

Garcia II went on to substantiate his claim about the 'hatred' that slavery provoked in the Africans against the European Christians by reiterating the point he had made in the letter to the College in Luanda that Queen

---

[102] See Robert Warren Anderson, 'How to Expect the Portuguese Inquisition', Unpublished Ph.D., George Mason University, Fairfax, Virginia, 2011, and L. M. E. Shaw, *Trade, Inquisition and the English Nation in Portugal, 1650–90*, Manchester: Carcanet Press, 1990.

[103] 'Garcia II, Eminetissimi e Reuerendissimi Signon', APF-SRCG, vol. 247, fl.s. 165–165 v., 9 May 1648, MMA vol, X, pp. 139–144. 'a Li Portoghesi in quelle parti, come che sonó per il piü christiani nouelli, che altro non uuol diré in buon linguagio che christiani di nome, e giudei di fatti, hanno usato tirannie e crudeltá indeibili in quei popoli del Congo, á forza d'armi, rubando huomini e donne per cancarne le naui, e mandarli al Brasile per fare il zuccaro, senza mouersi punto á pietá, ne per li gridi e clamori che i padri e madri dauano in uedersi togliere i proprij figli, ne per il pianto di quei che da loro erano fatti prigioni.'

[104] 'Garcia II, Eminetissimi e Reuerendissimi Signon', 'queste et altre simili tirannie si porriano diré, quali si tralasciano per non tediare l'Eminenze Vostre, le quali tutte hanno causato si grand'odio in quei [Regni] del Congo, e ne' popoli circonuicini contro i Portoghesi, che non li possono sentir nominare'.

Njinga Mbandi was a devout Christian until the Portuguese wanted to take her land and enslaved her people: 'Queen Njinga, whose country borders with Kongo, was a Christian before but she rightly abandoned her faith because of the cruelty she saw in the Portuguese, in their way of cruelly waging war, only to take possession of her kingdom.'[105] Garcia II's critique of militant Christianity went to the heart of Western Christendom. In the fifteenth century, papal bulls were sent to the Iberian kings allowing them to wage war on the infidels in the name of Christianity. In a bull dated 8 January 1454, Pope Nicholas V said that Africa was to be occupied and the infidels reduced to perpetual slavery:

Our each and every solemn prayer having been sent with the great King Alfonso, thinking and awaiting that he and his successors will be able to acquire provinces, islands, ports and seas, whatever kingdoms, duchy, principality, lordships, possessions and movable or immovable goods and whatever they have seized or possessed by invasion, conquest, purging, cleansing and subjection from Saracens, pagans and other enemies of Christ, and reduction of their persons to perpetual servitude, so he will possess what he has acquired and acquires in the future from Cape Bojador and Não right up to Guinea and beyond along that southern coast.[106]

The Christianity sanctioned by Nicholas V was violent, enforced through the sword and exclusive. It favoured one messenger, the Portuguese, and there were no grounds for dialogue. By contrast, the Christianity that entered North Africa in the second century came with a message of peace.[107] The Portuguese kings also persuaded the pope that the enslavement of the Africans helped finance wars that would expand Christianity.[108] It was this type of Christianity that Mendonça sought to

---

[105] 'Garcia II, Eminetissimi e Reuerendissimi Signon', 'La Regina Zinga, che confina con il Congo, quale era prima Cattolica, ha abandónate la Fede, non per altro, che per hauer ueduto la crudeltá de Portoghesi in mouergli crudel guerra, solo per impossessarsi del suo Regno'.

[106] Brásio, *Monumenta Missionaria Africana*, vol. I, pp. 281, 'nos premissa omnia et singula debita meditatione pensantes et attendentes quod cum olim prefato Alfonso Regi quoscunque Sarracenos et Paganos aliosque Christi inimicos ubicunque constitutos ac Regna, Ducatus, Principatus, dominia, possessiones et mobilia ac imobilia bona quecumque per eos detenta ac possessa inuadendi, conquirendi, expugnadi, debelandi, et subiugandi illorumque personas in perpetuam servitutem redigendi ... ipse Alfonsus Rex eiusque successores ... acquiri poterunt Provincias, Jnsulas, portus et maria ... iam acquisita et que in futurum acquiri contigerit ... a Capitibus de Bojador et de Nam usque per Guineam et ultra versus illam meridionalem plagam extendi.'

[107] See Kwame Bediako, *Christianity in Africa: The Renewal of a Non-Western Religion*, Edinburgh: Edinburgh University Press, 1995.

[108] Reginaldo, '"África em Portugal"'.

challenge in the Vatican. The historiography of Africans selling their own people to the European merchants only emerged from apologetic texts in the seventeenth century, and subsequently became the norm for reading African political structures.[109] Mendonça's discourse was to counter this essentialist and exclusive take on Christianity by revealing that the Atlantic slave trade was introduced by European Christian merchants in Africa.[110] This echoed a sentiment expressed by Father Oliveira in 1555, in his work *Art of Naval War* or *Arte da Guerra do Mar*, that 'we [Portuguese] were the inventors of such a vile trade, never previously used or heard of among human beings'.[111]

5.2 MENDONÇA'S CRIMINAL COURT CASE PRESENTATION IN 1684

Mendonça arrived in the Vatican not as a slave but as a free person with experience of the enslaved Africans in Angola, Brazil, Portugal and Spain. He was an attorney with an international pedigree, and had represented confraternities in Brazil, Portugal, Spain and elsewhere in Christendom.[112] The message he carried in the court case he presented in the Vatican contained profound questions about the status, predicament, and death of

---

[109] As we saw in Chapter 1, Afonso I was armed and was also given aid by the Portuguese Crown, which demanded payment in slaves in return for its investment. In economic terms, these were not gifts without terms of agreement or strings attached to them: The military aid Afonso received from the Portuguese Crown was to be paid back according to the criteria set by the Crown. Clearly, he paid back what he owed Portugal in enslaved people on 5 October 1514. How long the term of the agreement was, we do not know. These terms need to read in tandem with other tax payments – *baculamento* set by Fernão de Sousa in seventeenth century discussed in Chapter 1. All African Christian conquered kings were subject to *baculamento*. Those who were not Christians and were not conquered were hardly involved in the slave trade. We have numerous examples of kings selling war captives in Angola (Mendonça's grandfather included) and then later in the eighteenth century in Dahomey and on the Gold Coast. However, these cases have not been studied in conjunction with their status as conquered kings with an obligation to the counterparts in Europe and taxes they were required to pay in enslaved people. See 'Carta do Rei do Congo to D. Manuel' and 'Regimento de D. Manuel a Simão da Silva (1512)'. See also 'Informação de Fernão de Sousa a El-Rei', and see Frei Melchior da Conceicam, 'Alvaras, Cartas, Provizioes, Regimentos'.
[110] SOCG, vol. 490, fl. 140.
[111] Fernando Oliveira, *A Arte da Guerra e do Mar*, Lisbon: Biblioteca National, 1937, pp. 23–25. As cited by Boxer, *The Church Militant*, p. 33. For further debate about the Portuguese introduction of the Atlantic slave trade in Africa, see Maria do Rosário Pimentel and Maria do Rosário Monteiro (eds.), *Senhores e Escravos nas Sociedades Ibero-Atlânticas*, Lisbon: CHAM, 2019.
[112] See S.C. Africa, vol. 1, fl. 487r-v.

the enslaved and forcibly made the case that after conversion and baptism in the Roman Catholic Church they should be integrated into the Christian community.[113] And it linked the enslavement of Africans to the oppression of New Christians and the enslavement of the Indigenous Americans.

Mendonça brought to the Vatican evidence of the cruelties and abuses used against the enslaved Africans in the Americas described in Chapter 1, Chapter 2 and Chapter 3. His intervention was first disclosed to Pope Innocent XI, who passed it on to the Office of Propaganda Fide or 'General Congregation', which was charged with dealing with any issues arising overseas. Mendonça may have been aware that it would be difficult to get his demands met by sending the court case directly to the Propaganda Fide, as the Propaganda Fide 'made it a practice not to answer simple missionaries ... [and] asked that their petition be presented directly to the pope'.[114] On 6 March 1684, Mendonça presented his criminal court case in the Vatican. There, he stated in clear terms the cruelties inflicted on enslaved Africans in Brazil, outlining not only their predicament in Brazil but also the methods deployed by Christian merchants to have them captured in Africa. The case articulated and delineated three steps or modes of operation used by Europeans: (1) the capture of African boys and girls from their mothers and their sale to Christian merchants, who in turn sold them in Europe like cattle; (2) the hunting of Africans as one would hunt animals, putting them together to procreate and the subsequent sale of their offspring; (3) the claim that 'Blacks are sometimes at war against each other and eat their prisoners, in such cases the Christian merchants save them from death by buying them; and they are also sold together with their children who are going to be born from them as perpetual slaves'.[115] Mendonça's court case uncovered before the Vatican numerous lies that had been told about the existence of slavery as a practice in Africa prior to the Europeans' arrival.[116]

---

[113] See SOCG, vol. 490, fl.140.
[114] See Lenhart, 'Capuchin Champions of Negro Emancipation'.
[115] SOCG, vol. 495a, fls. 54 and 55, and 138, 'l'uno di quelli pigliati da Ladroni, che per lo più rubbano fanciuli e fanciule con violenza dall'istefse Madri, e conducendoli alle Navi sono comprati da quei Mercanti per portarli a vendere come animali in Europa. L'altro comprandoli dalli stefsi Christiani, che vanno à caccia di quella gente, come di animali, e li tengono afsieme anco come tali à far generazione per rendere la vendita più copiosa. Il 3°. Che solendo tallora li Negri guerreggiare trà di loro, e mangiarsi li Priggioni, in simili cafi li Mercanti Christiani li salvano dalla morte con il comprarli, e se li vendono afsieme anco con gli figli che vengono à nascere da efsi perpe-tuame^te: schiavi.'
[116] See S.C. Africa, vol. I, fl., 486. See also Barreira, 'Informação Acerca dos Escravos de Angola'.

From his first presentation of the case, Mendonça called into question what African slavery constituted, if it existed at all. He presented what was later to become the fundamental debate on whether there were precedents for slavery in Africa, as we saw in Chapter 1 and Chapter 2. The Vatican officials and the political governing authorities in Italy, Spain and Portugal were expecting the usual rhetoric about benign treatment of the enslaved Africans in the Atlantic region,[117] instead they heard shocking revelations about the abuses suffered by the enslaved, the atrocities committed in the process of enslaving them and the enforced procreation – in effect, institutionalised prostitution – endorsed by the nobility in Portugal and the slave-masters in Brazil that drove the sale of child slaves. To an extent, Mendonça's disclosure of the abuses committed against the enslaved Africans in the Atlantic was not entirely new. What was new was that the Vatican had not heard it before from the Africans themselves, the very people against whom these crimes were being committed.

Mendonça's case was presented with evidence corroborated by confraternities in Brazil, Portugal and Spain.[118] The case thus provided first-hand accounts of the methods used for capturing the Africans, the maintenance of the enslaved people for procreation, and the African warfare that have been accepted in the historiography of the slave trade as producing captives who were then sold to European merchants.[119] Exploring these three axes as presented by Mendonça gives us an understanding of the history of the early Atlantic slave trade not from the perspective of a fixed or settled interpretation, but rather as a configuration of multiple layers of possibilities that need to be revisited, so that the current historiography can be revised. This is not simply presenting historical evidence in order to tell the history of slavery differently but rather an archaeological return, in the Foucauldian sense, to the sources.[120] This is to say that I use the documents available as sources for a more profound understanding of the episteme – the historical, a priori or strategic apparatus of the Portuguese and Spanish empires as well as the Vatican's mindset – that made the slave trade possible

---

[117] See Reginaldo, '"África em Portugal"', and 'Viaggio Del Carinale Allessandrino Legato Apostolico Alli Ser Re Di Francia, Spagna e Portogallo 1571' [Journey of the Cardinal Allessandrino Legato Apostolic to the King of France, Spain and Portugal], BAL, 46-IX-3.

[118] See SOCG, vol. 495a, fl. 54.

[119] For further detail on the Portuguese Crown's use of enslaved people for procreation in sixteenth-century Portugal, see Cardinal Alexandrino, 'Relazione del Viaggio, Fatto Dall Ilmo'.

[120] Michel Foucault, *The Order of Things: An Archaeology of the Human Sciences*, London; New York: Routledge, 2002.

and was behind its maintenance over the centuries. Let us return to the case and look at the logic of Mendonça's engagement and how it was handled.

Mendonça organised his case on a wider scale than we have been led to believe and than has been recognised before. It was a concerted effort that drew on evidence from around the Lusophone, French and Hispanic Atlantic world, from Africa, the Americas (including Brazil and the Caribbean and other parts of the Americas) and Europe. Gray, for example, did not detect several documents in folio 54 labelled *Sommario*, the summary of the evidence presented by Mendonça and Cardinal Savio Millini's defence on behalf of the governing authorities in Italy and Spain filed together in (A): 'The Saint Congregation of the Propaganda Fide, Oriental Indies [Brazil], A, Lourenço de Silva Mendonça, from the Kingdom of Kongo in Brazil'.[121] Nor did he spot the file in (B) labelled 'Oriental Indies'[122] (Brazil and Americas), consisting of responses from the governing authorities themselves about their interests in Brazil and Latin America. Finally, filed in (C) is a document, 'to the Saint Congregation of Propaganda Fide, for the Black people and born in Brazil, Portugal and Spain,' that details the response from the constituencies of Black people and from those born in Brazil, Portugal and Spain (see Figure 25).[123]

This was not a case presented by one Brotherhood or one lawyer working on behalf of a Brotherhood. Rather, it was a collective case, probably prepared over many years, in which many Brotherhoods of enslaved Africans united to defend their rights and protest against their treatment. Back in Brazil, Portugal and Spain, these organisations and Brotherhoods monitored the progress of Mendonça's case in the Vatican. They constituted a well-organised group with one aim: to challenge the Vatican as the bearer of law. They also saw as the Vatican as the *mens rea* (the guilty mind) that had passed the bulls that allowed for the enslavement of the Africans. They demanded that the Vatican give them their freedom in the ranks of human society.[124] In other words, Pope Innocent XI and his predecessors were no less guilty than the European merchants in the Atlantic or the sellers and buyers of slaves: while the merchants committed *actus reus* (the guilty act), the popes committed *mens rea*. In the eyes of the law, they were all guilty of crimes against the Africans and the Indigenous people in Brazil; and thus,

---

[121] SOCG, vol. 495a, fl. 54, 'Alla Sacra Cong.ne DePropaganda Fide Indie Orientali A Lourenzo DeSilva de Mendoza DelRegno diCongo nell' Indie'.

[122] SOCG, vol. 495a, fl. 60b, 'Inde Orient.le'.

[123] SOCG, vol. 495a, fl. 60c, 'Alla Sacra Congregato.ne d. Propaganda Fide Per la Gente Nere e Parde nati nel Brazile, Portugalle, e Spagna'.

[124] See SOCG, vol. 495a, fl. 54.

FIGURE 25 Mendonça's criminal court case and documents classification A, B, C. By the author.

more generally, against humanity. For Molina what happened in the Atlantic was a crime against justice of which the merchants were guilty, declared that 'all who exercise this deadly sin place themselves in a situation of eternal damnation, unless they can be excused because of an invincible ignorance. But I never knew of any in this condition.'[125]

Mendonça's classification of the three different types of document used in his case reveal the different constituencies involved and their take on Atlantic slavery. The documents in (A) and (C), the plaintiff's case and Mendonça's account, were intended to disclose the ill-treatment of the enslaved Africans in the Americas, Africa, Portugal and Spain. In (A) and (C), slavery was presented as an illegal practice that needed to be outlawed by the Vatican. The defendants' documents in (B) deployed an economic and political strategy to conceal the evil of slavery. (B) presented lies and inaccurate information that were deliberately intended to deceive the Vatican, suggesting that Atlantic slavery was spiritually beneficial for the enslaved Africans and that their treatment was in line with their low cultural status as Africans, while also claiming that the Natives required

---

[125] See Molina, *De Justitia et Jure*, II, 35, col. 171, C. As quoted by Joner, 'Impressions of Luis de Molina', p. 53.

punishment to educate them into working. (A), which included Millini's response,[126] exposed the lies told in (B) to cover up the crimes being committed against Africans and Indigenous Americans; it showed that the enslaved were captured by force, and against their will and their laws, which were known by their European captors and buyers.[127] Hence the Portuguese acted in contravention of both natural and human laws. Mendonça thus demonstrated that no transaction took place between Africans and the European merchants who governed the market, thereby ruling out the notion that Africa was a marketplace for enslaved.[128] The Portuguese captured Africans by fraud and tricks.

Mendonça presented his case with evidence, as Vieira once encouraged New Christians to do before the pope on their petition against the inquisition of 'Sanctum Officium' or 'Holy Office'. (B) contains the documents of the governing authorities in Italy, Spain and Portugal, their responses to Mendonça's discourse and their efforts to contradict and rebut his case. There was, however, also an attempt from these authorities, especially the Italians and Spaniards, to repair the harm caused and to stop the sale of Christians, and particularly their children, into slavery. The documents in (C) represent the sophisticated activism and protests of enslaved Africans against the governing authorities in Portugal, Spain and Italy.

In brief, (A) documents are the first evidence Mendonça presented, which was about the unjust methods used to capture Africans. Documents in (A)

---

[126] See SOCG, vol. 495a, fl. 54.

[127] People captured in wars belonged to the king whose army had captured them; these war captives could not be sold, since they belonged to the king. The idea that Africans secured slaves by capturing their fellow countrymen in wars and then selling them was simply wrong. For Africans, *kitanda* (markets) were for the peaceful exchange of goods between parties, not places of violence and certainly not a venue for the exchange of human beings. Even the use weapons in marketplaces were forbidden by Africans. See Fernandes, *Description de la Côte*, fol, 120, '... esta feyra se faz çinco leguas do porto do mar e desta feyra ao ryo de Casa Māsa ha sete leguas pello ryo de dētro...vem a esta feyra muyta gēte de 15 e 20 leguas em derrador e ordenaçã delrey da terra he q enguē emtra nest feyra cõ armas e se alguē emtra cõ ellas perdeas...vem a esta feyra sete e oyto mil pessoas e trazē de todallas cousas pera esta feyra q ha em suas terras pera vender e assi daquellas q vem de Portugal' (There is a market in this land, which is five leagues from the sea port and from this market to the Casamance river it is seven leagues from the river to the interior...many people come to this market from fifteen and twenty leagues around and the King of the land decrees that no one may enter this market with weapons and if anyone is caught he loses them. Seven and eight thousand people come to this market and they bring everything that there is in their land to sell in this market and likewise those that come from Portugal). See also Lingna Nafafé, *Colonial Encounters*, pp. 75–77.

[128] For a discussion of market and transaction, see Acemoglu and Robinson, *Why Nations Fail*.

and (C) constitute the bulk of his final statement presented in 1686, whilst (B) constitutes the bulk of its questioning, including an anonymous letter[129] addressed to Alderano Cybo (1613–1700), an Italian cardinal, written before Mendonça presented his final statement. In (C), confraternities and different organisations and pressure groups from the enslaved Africans corroborated their experience and collectively denounced the problems of slavery that resulted from the contradictions inherent in the economic and legal model of the Atlantic world. This was a protest that went well beyond the militant Palmarist resistance – the community in Palmares having been forced to take up arms in the struggle to protect their existence. In Mendonça's case, the protest was made through legal routes, approved by the religious and political authorities of the time.

Like other contemporary cases in the courts of law, Mendonça first presented a statement of claim, giving a concise summary of the nature of his claim. Second, he presented the people involved, the Christian merchants. Third, he presented the remedies he was seeking, which were, firstly, the abolition of the Atlantic slave trade and, secondly, the punishment of the perpetrators, that is, the prosecution by the Inquisition Tribunal of those accused of the crime of enslaving the Africans. His summary claims:

> In the General Congregation of 6 of March 1684 a report has been read given by the Sanctity of Our Lord, in which were reported the cruelties practised in the Indies against the Blacks and the unjustified methods used to enslave them, from which results the loss of countless Souls; this is because when they [the Blacks] saw that not only themselves but also their own children, even if white and baptised, must stay in perpetual slavery, they kill themselves. Moreover, it was considered by the same congregation that the Christian Merchants were buying those people in three ways.[130]

Mendonça's claim caused a huge backlash from the political authorities in Italy, Spain and Portugal, and a vigorous response from enslaved African constituencies in Madrid, Lisbon and Salvador, Brazil.[131]

---

[129] An anonymous letter that refuted the arguments Mendonça made in his court case and addressed to Alderano Cybo was sent to the Vatican. See 'Instrutione Gagisterno Cybo', *Scritt Riferite nei Congressi Africa Angola Congo Senegal Isole dell'Oceano Atlantico da 1645 al 1685*.

[130] SOCG, vol. 495a, fl. 54.

[131] See SOCG, vol. 495a, fl.s 54 to 63. On the cover of page 63, 'Indie Orientali, Sig. Card. Azzolino', and 'Indie Orientali, Die 19 Jannuarij 1686, Signitures. Cardinal Azzolino was experienced in politics and law. He was awarded a doctorate in philosophy, law and theology from the University of Fermo, Italy. See Gianvittorio Signorotto and Maria Antonietta Visceglia (eds.), *Court and Politics in Papal Rome, 1492–1700*, Cambridge: Cambridge University Press, 2002.

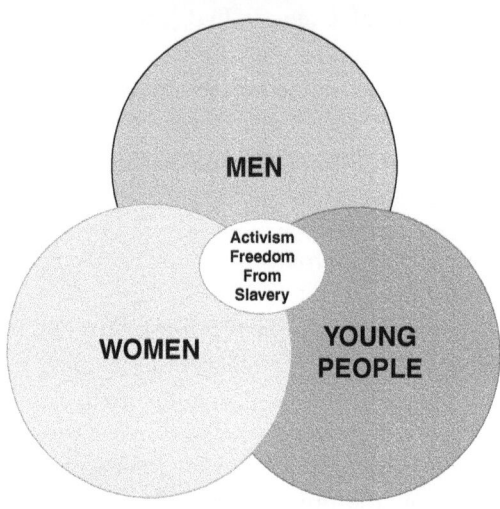

FIGURE 26 Activism of 'men', 'women' and 'youth' from confraternities in Brazil, Portugal and Spain. By the author.

The verdict from the Vatican on Mendonça's court case regarding the wrong of the Atlantic slavery was sealed and signed on 19 January 1686 by an Italian priest, Cardinal Decio Azzolino, and contains several signatures from other cardinals in the Vatican.[132] The responses from enslaved Africans in (B) were organised under three headings – 'men', 'women', and 'youth' (see Figure 26) – and came from Spain, Portugal and Brazil.[133] Each of these groups made their voices heard in the Vatican.[134] They called on Pope Innocent XI to overturn the Vatican's verdict on Mendonça's case in their favour, according to the evidence presented by Mendonça on 6 March 1684.

They demanded that justice be served, and the accused be punished according to the letter of the law.[135] Furthermore, they presented the solution to the problem of Atlantic slavery and requested that the Vatican issue reparations for the Atlantic slavery.

> ... it has been requested to repair such abuses and it has been established by [l'Ill. mo V.V] to write to the nuncios of Spain and Portugal to effectively raise the issue

---

[132] See SOCG, vol. 495a, fls. 54 and 55.   [133] See SOCG, vol. 495a, fl. 58.
[134] See SOCG, vol. 495a, fl. 54.   [135] See SOCG, vol. 495a, fls. 54 and 55.

Mendonça's Discourse in the Vatican 353

to the majesties of those kings [kingdom] in order to forbid the aforesaid inconveniences, which impede the spread of the faith and [invoke] hatred in these people against the Christians who treat them so cruelly.[136]

The evidence presented pointed a finger directly at the European Christian merchants and their respective governing authorities as the root cause of Atlantic slavery.[137] The Christianity of enslaved Africans was not being taken into account with regard to their mistreatment. Lenhart's analysis of slave critiques in Havana, Cuba, between 1681 and 1685 aired the view that 'the colonists had never considered the Negro as belonging to the pale of Christianity'.[138] I will now examine the response from both the Spanish and Italian governing authorities.

5.3 REACTIONS TO MENDONÇA'S COURT CASE

After Mendonça presented his first evidence-based case, Cardinal Millini was charged by the Vatican with gathering a response to the case from the Spanish and Italian authorities about the criminal court case Mendonça presented in the Vatican on 6 March 1684. He approached the marquise d'Astorga and the prince of Gonzaga. The marquise of Astorga and Great Spain was Antonio Pedro Sancho Dávila y Osorio (1615–1689), a nobleman with military connections, and a man in the service of Phillip IV of Spain and King Carlos II of Spain. He was the governor of the palace of North Africa, Oran and Mazalquivir, and was also the ambassador of Spain in Rome.[139] The prince of Gonzaga was Vincenzo Gonzaga Doria, duke of Mantua and Montferrat (1602–1694).[140] He came from a powerful family that ruled northern Italy from the fourteenth century to the beginning of the eighteenth

---

[136] SOCG, vol. 495a, fl. 54.   [137] See SOCG, vol. 495a, fls. 54 and 54.
[138] See Lenhart, 'Capuchin Champions of Negro Emancipation'.
[139] Vicente de Cadenas y Vicent, *Revista Hidalguia, La Revista de Genealogia, Nobleza y Armas*, 6, 1954, p. 423.
[140] Gonzaga had enormous power on issues relating to the Atlantic slave trade in the seventeenth century, during the time Mendonça arrived in the Vatican to present his court case before the Vatican. Vincenzo Gonzaga Doria was born in 1602 in Italy and died in 1694. He was a soldier and lived in Spain. He was captain general of Galicia in 1652. Served as viceroy of Catalonia in 1664–1667, then was appointed viceroy of Sicily in 1678. A gentleman of the chamber of Carlos II, king of Spain, he took over the governorship of the Council of Indies role in the absence of Enríquez de Ribera who was 8th duke of Medinaceli, who served in the post from 1671 to 1691. See Francisco Xavier de Garma y Durán, *Theatro Universal de España: Descripcion Eclesiastica y Secular de Todos sus Reynos y Provincias*, tomo IV, Barcelona: En la Imprenta de Mauro Martí, 1753, p. 118, 'D. Vicente Gionzaga, Comendador de Villa-franca en la Orden de Calarrava, Gentil-Hombre de la Camara de S. M. Governador de Galicia,

century. Gonzaga was an interim governor of the Consejo de Indias (Council of Indies) in the absence of the duke of Medinaceli, Juan Francisco de la Cerda y Enríquez de Ribera, from 1680 to 1685. The Council of the Indies was an extremely important office of the Spanish overseas administration for the Americas, which advised the king on executive, legislative and judicial matters.[141] Millini made an effort to speak to Gonzaga in person.[142] He stated: 'I also talked to the prince of Gonzaga who is the governor of the Council of the Indies'[143]. After hearing what Millini told him about the brutal treatment of enslaved Africans and the crimes committed against them, Gonzaga concluded that the pope was being misled (B). He asserted: 'His Blessing was wrongly informed about the mistreatments that were presumed to be used against Blacks after they become Christians, because this was not sustainable.'[144] Gonzaga was also convinced that the pope had not been briefed about the continuing sale of enslaved Africans who were Christians.[145] He issued a decree to remedy the ill treatment of the enslaved Africans and to stop the sale of those who were Christians: 'the proper commands were given, and they were going to be carried out in order to repair such disorder'.[146]

After speaking to Gonzaga, Millini wrote to Dávila y Osorio, who at the time occupied an important post as Spain's 'gvernor of the council of the Indies',[147] in a letter dated 9 March 1684, and disclosed to him the initial conversation he had had with Gonzaga: 'I informed him that I had written to the Lord Marques and that Lord Gonzaga approved the fact that I acted with such diligence.'[148] Dávila y Osorio's response to Millini was similar to that of Gonzaga regarding the incorrect information on slavery:

... [he] believed that His Blessing was wrongly informed about the supposed bad treatments against the Blacks after they become Christians, because this was not

---

Virrey de Scilia, y Governador del Conſelo de Indias'. See also Gonzaga, Vincenzo in 'Dizionario' Biografico, trecani.it., p. 354.

[141] See J. H. Parry, *The Spanish Theory of Empire in the Sixteenth Century*, Cambridge: Cambridge University Press, 1940; María Isabel Cabrera Bosch, *El Consejo Real de Castilla y la Ley*, Madrid: Emprensa en España, 1993 and Silvio Zavala, *Las Instituciones Jurídicas en la Conquista de América*, 3rd. ed., Mexico City: Porrúa, 1935.

[142] See SOCG, vol. 495a, fl. 54. For a detailed discussion of the House of Gonzaga, see Selwyn Brinton, *The Gonzaga, Lords of Mantua*, London: Methuen, 1927. See also Alessandro Cont, 'Sotto Tutela: Il Sovrano Bambino in Italia (1659–1714)', *Rivista Storica Italiana*, 124(2), 2012, pp. 537–581.

[143] See SOCG, vol. 495a, fl. 56. [144] See SOCG, vol. 495a, fl. 54.

[145] See SOCG, vol. 495a, fl. 55. [146] See SOCG, vol. 495a, fl. 55.

[147] See a Letter by Cardinal Millini, SOCG, vol. 495a, fl. 56, Madrid, 20 April 1684.

[148] See SOCG, vol. 495a, fl. 56.

sustainable; but he believed that some inconvenience about their sale was still going on; however, the right orders were given to remedy (repair) such disorder, and they were going to be carried out immediately.[149]

The two noblemen's responses are not surprising given that the kings of Portugal had always informed the Vatican that they intended to ensure that the enslaved Africans who converted to Christianity were cared for.[150] Indeed, the passing on of constitutions to the Black confraternities was to ensure that there was a scope for enslaved Africans to be protected in Portugal, Spain and in the contact zones. However, it was one thing to pass laws, and quite another to enforce those laws.

Both Italian and Spanish political authorities believed that action needed to be taken about the abuse levelled against the enslaved Africans in Latin America. Nonetheless, they continued to assert that the pope was being misinformed about the treatment of the enslaved Africans in the Atlantic. The Portuguese governing authorities gave their response to Mendonça and the Black confraternities' claims via the papal nuncio, Mesquita's successor, on 1 May 1684.[151] They claimed firstly that it was impossible to separate the enslaved Africans captured in a 'just war' from those who continued to be sold even though they were Christians,[152] and went on to state that the king abhorred 'enslaving the Blacks through fraud and bad deeds'.[153] King Pedro II may have abhorred the injustice of slavery, but he fell short of making it illegal. We do not know what action he had taken to support Mendonça's case before the latter left for Rome. He may have questioned the destruction of Pungo-Andongo, but I have found no evidence that he took affirmative action to abolish slavery. His sympathy had no meaning for the enslaved Africans in Brazil and Portugal. The Portuguese nuncio's argument that it was 'impossible to separate those who have been bought legally ... from those born in slavery',[154] was unsustainable. Enslaved people who had been legally bought were taxed, and 20 per cent of that value went to the king, demonstrating that those bought legally – if one could ever use this expression – could easily be identified. Moirans argued that all Africans who were taken out of Africa as slaves were not in fact slaves, because the process by which they were obtained was against the

---

[149] See SOCG, vol. 495a, fl. 56.   [150] See Lahon, 'Da Redução da Alteridade'.

[151] The Vatican nuncio's name from Portugal did not appear on the letter of 1 May 1684. However, it is stated that it came from Portugal. A list of the nuncios can be found in Liisi Karttunen, *Les Nonciatures Apostoliques Permanentes de 1650 a 1800*, Geneva: E. Chaulmontet, 1912.

[152] See SOCG, vol. 495a, fl. 56.   [153] See SOCG, vol. 495a, fl. 57.

[154] See SOCG, vol. 495a, fl. 57.

law.[155] Indeed, the majority of those taken out of Africa were illegally enslaved, as we have seen from witnesses such Garcia II and the bishop of Cabo Verde. Afonso I, king of Kongo, had sought to separate those enslaved Africans bought legally from those being illegally taken out of his kingdom by placing his own officers in the custom office to ensure that those leaving his kingdom were legal slaves. Kongo was a Christian kingdom, and therefore there should not have slave trade from there; it was illegal to carry out a trade in human beings there.[156]

The nuncio's account shows that there was no will among the Portuguese governing authorities to do away with slavery. This attitude was reflected in Pedro II's legislation regarding improvements to the shipment of slaves from Africa to Brazil, drafted on 18 March 1684 while Mendonça was in the Vatican presenting his evidence on the cruelties of slave trade.[157] The nuncio from Portugal also tried to make an economic argument for the slave trade, claiming that 'if the Portuguese in Brazil were not receiving the service of the Blacks they would not be able to cultivate [the land], nor [dig the mines] that they have obtained'.[158] It scarcely needs to be pointed out that the economic case presented by the Portuguese authorities should not have been used as a framework for enslaving Africans. Molina argued that since the Portuguese Christian missions in Africa lost all spiritual objective, then the trade monopoly that was passed on to them by Pope Nicholas V (*Dum diversas*) in 1452 lost its purpose.[159] The need for a labour force does not entitle some human beings to enslave others,[160] and it was this thinking that Mendonça challenged in his closing statement in the Vatican. The nuncio also claimed that it was necessary to treat slaves harshly to ensure that they worked: 'if they [Blacks] are not slaves, because [they] are people who abhor work and they do not undertake it unless they fear punishment'[161]. The punishment of the enslaved Africans in the Americas defied human logic, yet the abuse was kept hidden by many priests and governors in Brazil, as well as elsewhere; only Moirans spoke out against it.[162]

---

[155] See Jaca and Moirans, OFM Cap., *Servi Liberi*.
[156] For further discussion of the illegality of slave trade in mid-sixteenth-century Kongo, see Molina, *De Justitia et Jure*.
[157] See all three letters: AHU_CU_001, cx. 13, d. 1554; AHU, Arquivo de Cabo Verde, livro 42, fls 29v-32v, cód. 544, fl. 50v, 28 March 1684; 'Lei sobre a arqueação dos navios', [Law on the Tonnage of Ships], Arquivo de Angola, 1936, vol. 13, 28 March 1684, pp. 321–322.
[158] SOCG, vol. 495a, fl. 57.   [159] See Molina, *De Justitia et Jure*.
[160] See Jaca and Moirans, OFM Cap., *Servi Liberi*.   [161] SOCG, vol. 495a, fl. 57.
[162] See Jaca and Moirans, OFM Cap., *Servi Liberi*.

After presenting the argument that punishment was necessary to make the enslaved Africans in Brazil work, the nuncio turned his attention to the Indigenous Brazilians. He reiterated an old stereotype used against them – that they were less industrious – to defend the need for enslaved Africans in Brazil. He depicted the Natives as people associated with nature and argued that 'they do not have any worries and they need little, since in Brazil they go naked and sustain themselves hunting, fishing and with other fruits that the land produces by itself and they do not worry about working'.[163] As we saw in Chapter 4, the Indigenous Brazilians presented difficulties for the Portuguese in the country because they tended to become ill or run away. The perceived failings of the Natives were used as a pretext for continuing to enslave Africans. Vieira and De Las Casas used a similar argument.[164] Of course, this was no ground for maintaining the slave trade. The nuncio downplayed the dehumanising and harrowing treatment that was evident in Brazil, where there were no laws to protect the enslaved and their 'life expectancy at birth was approximately twenty-three years, or twelve years less than that of an American slave in 1850'.[165] The nuncio stated: 'I have heard that the treatment that the Portuguese give to them, in particularly in Brazil, is harsh but everybody [endeavours] to keep them alive and healthy because they buy each of them at 100 pieces and more, and if they are without Blacks they cannot cultivate their lands.'[166] His claim made it clear the enslaved Africans' complaints were not to be taken seriously.

The nuncio went on to claim that slaves were treated better in Portugal than in Brazil: 'here in the kingdom [Portugal] Black slaves are treated sufficiently well; rather, many fear losing their masters when their masters die and they are freed, because they remain in a worst condition than before'.[167] Documentary evidence that supports this claim is very difficult to come by. In fact the evidence suggests that enslaved Africans in Portugal were ill-treated and, in contradiction of the nuncio's claim, wanted their freedom as much as slaves anywhere else. Father Oliveira declared that the

---

[163] SOCG, vol. 495a, fl. 57.
[164] See António Vieira, *Escritos Sobre os Índios*, Lisbon: Temas & Debates, 2015. On De Las Casas' debate about the Natives, see Anthony Pagden, *The Fall of Natural Man: The American Indian and the Origins of Comparative Ethnology*, Cambridge: Cambridge University Press, 1982; and Lewis Hanke, *The Spanish Struggle for Justice in the Conquest of America*, Boston, MA: Little, Brown, 1965.
[165] David Brion Davis, *Inhuman Bondage: The Rise and Fall of Slavery in the New World*, Oxford: Oxford University Press, 2006, p. 117.
[166] SOCG, vol. 495a, fl. 57.   [167] See SOCG, vol. 495a, fl. 56.

deaths of Blacks in Portugal were numerous (although the numbers are unknown), that they were buried without clothes and that lime was poured on their corpses to help them decompose quickly.[168] The nuncio's claim about the enslaved Africans wanting to remain in slavery in Portugal runs counter to the evidence presented by the confraternities in the Vatican,[169] to which I will return in due course. To accept the nuncio's and Portugal's argument would be to disregard the suffering of the enslaved Africans in the Atlantic region and dismiss Mendonça's case in the Vatican.

After the response from Portugal was received in the Vatican, the news went out to Africa, Portugal, Spain and Brazil that the enslaved people's claim for freedom was in doubt because the Portuguese governing authorities had raised issues about their treatment and their case. Through their representative Brotherhoods, the enslaved Africans responded: 'after receiving his replies, the Blacks have complained again to this congregation, raising the same grievances and pleading to provide to their miserable condition as in the paper C'.[170] They resisted the laws that dehumanised them. They knew that changes were not going to come if they did not air their voices in protest about the slave trade and its system of perpetual slavery.

The Black Brotherhoods, particularly from Spain, Portugal and Brazil, complained that there was little truth in what the nuncio and the Portuguese had said, and that their suffering was being ignored. They urged the pope to take punitive action against the 'sellers' and 'buyers' of Africans, and to demand that orders be given to the overseas officials in Africa to prohibit the slave trade in those regions: 'It is suggested that to repair the situation first, the following is to be done: ministers of Guinea are to order that the sale of kidnapped Black Brotherhoods or those taken from the fields with fraud be prohibited.'[171] The kidnappers were deploying various tactics to acquire slaves, including capturing them from agricultural fields. Kidnappers went to these places knowing that the Africans would be exposed and an easy target for slave-traders. The Blacks' statement demonstrates the injustice of the slave trade in seeking captives through easy means, rather than through the alleged wars that were believed to be the legal source of the enslaved.

Furthermore, the Vatican was expected to demonstrate that the pope was committed to ending slavery, issuing terms that would allow the

---

[168] Oliveira, *Elementos para a História do Município de Lisboa*, p. 509.
[169] See SOCG, vol. 495a, fl. 62.   [170] SOCG, vol. 495a, fl. 54.
[171] SOCG, vol. 495a, fl. 55.

respective religious authorities in the different regions of the Atlantic region to chastise those guilty of slave-trading: 'His Majesty was to allow the bishops to publish the excommunications against buyers and sellers ... Furthermore, to publish in his dominion that, if such criminals are caught, they will be punished.'[172] The means of their punishment was to be religious Inquisition, by which their property would be confiscated, and they would be imprisoned and, if found guilty, burnt alive. The Black Brotherhoods went to the root of the problem, claiming that both the sellers and buyers needed to be punished if slavery was to be stopped. The enslaved Africans clearly knew what it would take to abolish slavery: not a substitution for labour as was proposed by late eighteenth-century abolitionist organisations, such as the Bulam Association,[173] but rather the punishment of the sellers and buyers who were the reason why slavery lasted for so long. They also put forward another argument: that slavery should never be for life, that in Africa being an enslaved person was only a temporary state, used to punish those, for example, caught in an illegal act, and it only involved a sense of service and never enslavement.

The proposals set out by the enslaved Africans from different constituencies in (C) is badly filed in the Vatican archive. Folio 55 v should have followed from folio 55 r. However, the end part of 55 v becomes folio 62 v, making it difficult for the researcher to piece together the ending of folio 55 v. This is perhaps why their proposals escaped Gray's attention. The enslaved African activists also argued that the children born from the enslaved Africans should not be enslaved as they were born in another dispensation and should not be included in the system: 'Second, although the Blacks who are sold legally as slaves to cultivate the land must be perpetually slaves, it is not reasonable that their children must also be perpetually slaves.'[174]

In order to end Atlantic slavery, the solution proposed by the different confraternities of the enslaved Africans in Brazil, Portugal and Spain came up with a compromise that would allow the accused, the civil authorities in northern and southern Europe and the slave-owners to recover their losses:

Thus, if it is not possible to resolve the matter for those who keep the children of Blacks as slaves, at least it must be provided for the future, declaring that from now

---

[172] SOCG, vol. 495a, fl. 56.
[173] The Bulam Association was a British abolitionist organization created in 1791.
[174] SOCG, vol. 495a, fl. 62. Heywood and Thornton, *Central Africans*, p. 312 contend that 'the definition of slavery as a lifetime, heritable servitude would develop only with the Plantation Generation'.

on – in Brazil as well as in the dominion of the Catholic King [Spain], in that of Portugal and for those taken into Europe – the children born from Christian slaves should not remain slaves; so that in the purchase everyone will know that they are buying only the life of the present man or woman.[175]

Here they were prepared to offer some concessions in order to secure the freedom of future generations. They clearly understood the economic mechanisms of the Atlantic region: it may have been difficult to release all those sold into slavery, but in the new dispensation there could be freedom for all. Here is evidence also that Mendonça proposed a total end to slavery, contrary to Gray's claim that 'he did not attempt to question the institution of slavery itself'.[176]

Slavery was a crime against the Christian principles of *jus canonico*[177] and, despite their concessions over current slaves, the Black confraternities urged the pope to take his cue from the French *Engagé*, who had declared slavery to be only temporary and not for life: 'moreover, this is against the Canon law [*jus canonico*] which is practised in the French islands of America where after some time slaves are freed again'.[178] After serving their term of servitude, the protesters and activists of the documents in (C) demanded that the enslaved should be made free and integrated into society so that they could serve their communities. Slavery did not mean exclusion from society: there were mechanisms to restore them to the society after they served their time.[179]

Indentured servants in the French Caribbean *Engagé* were tied up to their masters for labour only for three years. The French law had it that after three years' service 'the said indentured servant shall be declared free and paid by the master of that which they had agreed until the day he left his service; the master of the house [case] will have the responsibility of administering to his indentured servants, Negroes and Negresses when they are sick.'[180] This is the fair treatment that Mendonça wanted in Brazil and elsewhere to reduce the death toll. As Taber remarks: 'the French state made servitude a more attractive option for potential migrants but it also reduced masters' control over their servants'.[181]

---

[175] SOCG, vol. 495a, fl. 62.
[176] Richard Gray, *Black Christians and White Missionaries*, London and New Haven, CT: Yale University Press, 1990, p. 17.
[177] See SOCG, vol. 495a, fl. 62.   [178] SOCG, vol. 495a, fl. 62.
[179] See SOCG, vol. 495a, fl. 62.
[180] See de Tracy, 'Réglement de M. de Tracy', pp. 119–120, 'ledit Engagé sera réputé libre et payé par le Maître de ce qu'ils sont convenus jusqu'au jour qu'il sortira de son service; le Maitre de Case aura soin de faire panser ses Engagés, Negres, et Négresses lorsqu'ils seront maladies'. As quoted by Taber in '"To Strengthen the Colonies"', p. 12.
[181] See Taber, '"To Strengthen the Colonies"', p. 14.

The above response from the confraternities about *Engagé* demonstrates that the Blacks were working across the Atlantic to find out about what went on with enslaved Africans and how they were treated by the different countries that were engaged in the slave trade. The practice of giving freedom to indentured servants referred to in the Vatican documents was indeed the practice among Jews. It is based on the laws codified in the Torah. The protesters and activists of the documents in (C) opted for it as a solution for the enslaved Africans.

The notion that the human violence that we came to know of in the Atlantic slave trade emerged in Africa and was transported to the Americas is not grounded in historical sources so much as myth.[182] For Moirans, all men were free by *natural law*.[183] On 12 March 1685, both Francisco José de Jaca and Epifanio de Moirans testified before the Vatican on the atrocities committed against enslaved Africans. They gave evidence in eleven clauses, from which I have selected nine that clearly demonstrate the impact of their evidence:

1. That illicitly, by force and fraud, they [the enslavers] made the Blacks enslaved.
2. That illicitly the enslavers buy and sell these Blacks.
3. That ... these Blacks that are unfairly taken are put together with others to [procreate] are then sell them.
4. That buyers are under no obligation to investigate the right or unfair title [whether caught legally or not] of these being enslaved.
5. That the owners of such Blacks or other savages ... [fraudulently captured] are not required to set them free.
6. Neither are the owners and buyers required to compensate them for their harm caused on these Blacks enslaved.
7. That it is unlawful for the owners ... to injure and kill the aforementioned Blacks or others enslaved.
10. That it is unlawful to keep [Blacks] enslaved in bondage even after baptism, whether they are rightly or unjustly taken.
11. That it is unlawful to buy Negroes immediately [when they were not sure of their status] or not from heretics and then sell them to merchants.[184]

---

[182] See Heywood and Thornton. *Central Africans and Cultural Transformations*.
[183] See Jaca and Moirans, OFM Cap., *Servi Liberi*.
[184] Jaca and Moirans, Propaganda Archives, 'series: Acta de anno 1685', no. 26, March 12, fls. 35–37. '1.Che sia lecito con forza e fraude far schiavi li negri, et altri selvaggi; 2.Che sia lecito venderé e comprare tali negri, o selvaggi fatti schiavi con la forza; 3.Che quando

The following is my critical assessment of the evidence they presented regarding the most relevant points. Jaca and Moirans's case was heard before the justice ministers in the Vatican. Their demand that Atlantic slavery be abolished concerned both the Indigenous Americans and the enslaved Africans, who were presented as subjects of the pope. They declared: 'as the ministers of justice in the kingdom of Holy Faith, and those in other provincesuch as India [the Americas], to those under the pretext that the poor Indians [the Natives] are vassals of His Catholic Majesty'.[185] For them, there were no enslaved people in Africa. The manner in which the Africans were captured demonstrated the illegality of the trade, as they were obtained 'with fraud and deception, and sometimes war being deployed with that end'[186]. Jaca and Moirans's evidence was based as much on their own experiences in the Americas as on the accounts of other witnesses who had worked in Africa; they drew on their own experiences to claim that that 'the Capuchin missionary Fathers in the Americas and Africa represent the various and unjust ways with which the Negroes are enslaved in those parts.'[187] According to them, the injustices inflicted on Africans were not confined to the African continent alone, but equally present in the Americas, where 'the slave-masters were inhumanly treating the enslaved Africans'[188] to the extent that legal intervention from the pope and his justice ministers in the Vatican was needed. Absorbing what Mendonça's case was about, Jaca and Moirans demanded that the justice ministers take legal action to eradicate Atlantic slavery, and they proposed in the above points that the enslavers be

tali negri presi ingiustamente sono mescolati con altri giustamente vendibili; 4.Che li compratori non sono obligati investigare del titolo giusto o ingiusto delle loro servitù; 5. Che li possessori di tali negri, o altri selvaggi presi con dolo e fraude non sono tenuti a dimetterli; 6.Ne meno sono tenuti li possessori e compratori a compensare li loro danni; 7.Che sia lecito alli medesimi possessori ... di morte, ferire et ammazzare li suddetti negri o altri schiavi; 10.Che sia lecito tenere in servitù li schiavi anco dopo il battesimo siano giustamente o ingiustamente presi; 11.Che sia lecito comprare li negri mediatamente o immediatamente da gli eretici, e venderli ad essi.' For further detailed study see Lenhart, 'Capuchin Champions of Negro Emancipation', to whom I am indebted here.

[185] Jaca and Moirans, Propaganda Archives, series: Acta de anno 1685, no. 14, March 12, fol. 35-37, 'come li ministri di Giustitia nel regno di Santa Fede, et altre provincie nell' India, sotto pretesto che li poveri Indiani sono vasalli di Sua Maestà Cattolica'.

[186] Jaca and Moirans, 'series: Acta de anno 1685', p. 213, 'con fraude et inganno, et alle volte con occasione di guerra mossa a questo fine'.

[187] Jaca and Moirans, 'series: Acta de anno 1685', p. 213, 'li Padri Capuccini missionarii nell' America e nell' Africa, rappresentano li varii et ingiusti modi con li quali si fanno schiavi li negri in quelle parti'.

[188] Jaca and Moirans, 'series: Acta de anno 1685', p. 213, 'li loro padroni da quali sono trattati inhumanamente'.

'prohibited under the penalties and ecclesiastical censures'.[189] Let us take a closer look at each of their points.

Points 1–2 reveal that the Atlantic slave trade was illegal from the outset. Violence and firearms were deployed to achieve its goals. The use of force to acquire the enslaved in Africa rules out the notion that there was a transaction and that there was an existing market in Africa through which slaves were sold and bought. Jaca and Moirans's statement supports Mendonça and the confraternities' claim that the Africans taken to the Americas as enslaved were not already slaves and that the slave trade was illegal, and that the Vatican needed to eradicate the entire Atlantic slave trade.

Point 3 exposes the mechanism applied to multiply the number of the enslaved in order to meet the demand in the Americas. It confirmed the contention in Mendonça's court case that Africans were forced to reproduce human bodies to serve the economic interests of the enslaved people's owners.

Point 4 uses the language of the buyers who want to obtain 'goods' in the market, and deals with the fact that the origin of the enslaved should be made known. The authors claim that knowing where enslaved people are from is the threshold behaviour for a ' reasonable buyer or merchant': buyers should not neglect to perform an action expected from a reasonable buyer.[190] However, this had already been ruled out, and they point to the complete silence about how the enslaved people were acquired: 'after [Africans] being enslaved in the aforementioned ways, they are bought by merchants, without taking account news about their capture and of their just or unjust servitude, the merchants then transport them from Africa to America'.[191] This meant that the buyers or merchants were guilty before the law of being in possession of illegal 'goods'. The call here was for the Vatican to review laws that they had passed to the kings of Portugal and Spain about enslaving the heathens if they rejected the preaching of Christian Gospel. The claim of point 4 was that the law was not being applied and the correct procedure not being followed. The

---

[189] Jaca and Moirans, 'series: Acta de anno 1685', p. 213, 'prohibiré sotto le pene e censure ecclesiastiche le seguenti propositioni'.

[190] See Hyman Gross, *A Theory of Criminal Justice*, Oxford: Oxford University Press, 2005, and H. L. A. Hart, *Punishment and Responsibility*, Oxford: Oxford University Press, 1968.

[191] Jaca and Moirans, 'series: Acta de anno 1685', p. 213, 'dopo fatti schiavi nei modi sudetti, sono comprati da mercanti, senza prender a kuna notitia della loro giusta o ingiusta servitù, che li trasportano dair Africa nell' America'.

capture of Africans for enslavement was not based on religious grounds, that is, the rejection of Christianity, but on economic grounds.

In points 5–7, Jaca and Moirans demanded 'freedom' for the enslaved Africans and 'reparation' for the damage done to them. This was in line with civil laws, from which European criminal laws derived. The harm to the enslaved Africans' rights to health and humanity was as much a crime in civil as in criminal law.[192] The illegality of the Africans' enslavement was not based on the merchants' ignorance of the law, but on the same merchants' willingness to break it. Therefore, their actions in Africa were unlawful, and a crime against humanity.[193] The merchants were not only guilty of being careless and negligent in their duty of care towards the Africans and the Natives; their crime was reasonably foreseeable. In other words, it was a preventable crime, but they had nonetheless decided to cause injury to the enslaved. According to Molina, all merchants knew facts about the unfair process that was used to capture Africans. He remarked 'that there is not a single merchant who did not know of these injustices, that even being aware of the illegal status of some bought them as slaves without worrying about the necessary titles and just did not care about the morality of these purchase'.[194]

As mentioned above, documents (C) brought together active African voices proclaiming the need to put an end to slavery. They demanded that the Vatican come clean and inform the confraternities about the true outcome of their case after Francisco José de Jaca and Epifanio de Moirans gave their evidence on 12 March 1685.[195] If the Vatican did not have a solution to the problem, they had a solution of their own:

> 6. Mons. Secretary says that to provide against such illegal contracts it was proposed by the zeal of some Capuchin missionaries to declare wrong and to forbid, under punishment ... some propositions which were sent to the Saint Office, but it is not known which decision has been taken about them.[196]

After the statement from the two men was received, the Vatican delayed announcing the verdict. In legal terms, Mendonça's evidence was found

---

[192] See Simon Deakin, Angus Johnston and Basil Markesinis, *Tort Law*, Oxford: Oxford University Press, 2003; Michael Gorr and Sterling Harwood (eds.), *Controversies in Criminal Law*, Boulder, CO: Westview Press, 1992; Hart, *Punishment and Responsibility*.

[193] See Ernest van den Haag, *Punishing Criminals: Concerning a Very Old and Painful Question*, Chicago, IL: University of Chicago Press, 1978.

[194] See Molina, De Justitia et Jure, II, 34, col. 157–159. As quoted by Joner, 'Impressions of Luis de Molina', p. 43.

[195] See APF, n. 26, fl. 35–37.   [196] See SOCG, vol. 495a, fl. 62.

insufficient: there was uncertainty and doubt about his statement. It is not clear whether the impasse was created by Millini's report to the Vatican, since both Gonzago and Dávila y Osorio's statements were presented in similar terms, suggesting Millini had a hand in putting them together. It seems reasonable to argue that he attempted to downplay the ill-treatment of the enslaved Africans in the Atlantic for the Vatican's officials in order to favour the political authorities from Spain and Italy. Millini was certainly acquainted with the abuses suffered by the enslaved Africans, as he was familiar with the claims made by Francisco José de Jaca and Epifanio de Moirans in Havana, two years before Mendonça's first presentation in the Vatican.[197] But, in that case, too, he attempted to suppress those that sought to highlight the abuse. In 1682, whilst an apostolic nuncio in Madrid, Millini had been given charge of Jaca and Moirans, who had openly criticised slave-owners in Cuba and demanded liberation for the slaves, with compensation for their labour.[198] Moirans put forward four arguments in his book arguing for the liberation of enslaved Africans: (1) 'Nobody can buy or sell any of the Black slaves of Africa, as they are commonly called'; (2) 'all those who own some of them are obliged to manumit them under penalty of eternal damnation'; (3) 'their masters are obliged to manumit them, to remunerate them for their work and to pay them compensation'; and (4) 'the Blacks who live in places of the Americas, working in family properties, called *sucreries* by the French, or *ingenios* by the Spaniards, must by divine obligation of the natural law leave and look for territories in which they attend to their eternal salvation'.[199]

Both Moirans and Jaca were aiming to secure the abolition of African slavery in the Atlantic region. As a result, they were deported from Cuba and incarcerated in Spain. Millini attempted to dismiss their case and, in his report to the Vatican, remarked that the cardinals ought to consider the embarrassment to the king caused by the commotion in America.[200]

---

[197] See Lenhart, 'Capuchin Champions of Negro Emancipation'.
[198] See Lenhart, 'Capuchin Champions of Negro Emancipation', and Jaca and Moirans, OFM Cap., *Servi Liberi*, as cited by Lenhart.
[199] Jaca and Moirans, OFM Cap., *Servi Liberi*, fl. 2, '1. Neino potest emere aut vendere Nillum ex mancipiis affrica Nigris Conniuriter Nuneupatis; 2.Onines qui possident quadom ex illis tenentur Manumittere sub Pena damnationis a'terna; 3.Tenetur domini eorum Manumitten do resttituere eis Labores eorum & Soluere pretium. 4.Tenetur Nigri morantes in locis Indiarum Laborantes in rebus familliaribus dictis a gallis Sucreries, & ab hispanis Ingenios innaqairbus vendotur Mancipia, Divino Iure naturali abire et petere loca in quibus Curent de Salure Sua a'terna.'
[200] Lenhart, 'Capuchin Champions of Negro Emancipation in Cuba'.

He contacted the political authorities of both Gonzago and Orsorio to look at their case.[201] The two priests were detained in Valladolid, Spain, for two years and later released. On 2 March 1685, they appeared in the Vatican to present their evidence on the abuse of enslaved Africans in the Atlantic region.[202] They were later nominated by the enslaved African constituencies to testify against slavery and its abuses in the Atlantic in support of Mendonça's case.[203] However, Millini was not prepared to put the Spanish economic business in the Americas at risk by supporting Jaca and Moirans or Mendonça. Instead, he opted to stay on the side of the power and economics, as did the Vatican. To do that, he withheld vital information that could have strengthened Mendonça's court case. He might have also been constrained by the Council of the Indies, to which Dávila y Osorio was a minister. In 1685, intriguingly, Millini accepted a post as apostolic nuncio and returned to Spain, where he had previously served as nuncio, and subsequently resigned just before Mendonça's closing statement took place in 1686. There might have been pressure on Millini, as the Vatican cardinals who responded to Jaca and Moirans's case demanded that the nuncio in Madrid write to the authorities in the Indies about the abuses committed in the Indies.[204]

The problem of the global economy was of interest to Portugal, Italy and Spain, and shows why there is a need to go beyond the traditional focus on single colonial powers to examine the interconnected histories within the Atlantic. For example, Italian merchants were among the first foreign merchants to be employed by the Portuguese Crown for the exploration of West Africa.[205] Antonio de Noli, an Italian merchant and nobleman from Genoa, was appointed the first governor of Cape Verde by King Afonso V. The Italians' commercial activities can be found in River Plate, Argentina.[206] In the fifteenth century, many Italian merchants in

---

[201] See SOCG, vol. 495a, fl. 54.
[202] See APF, n. 26, fl. 35–37. Here I am indebted to Lenhart, 'Capuchin Champions of Negro Emancipation'.
[203] See APF, act 75.   [204] See Lenhart, 'Capuchin Champions of Negro Emancipation'.
[205] See Cadamosto, *Navegações de Luís*, and Hall, *Before Middle Passage*.
[206] See Bernard Vincent, et al., *Estudios en Historia Moderna desde una visión Atlántica Libro Homenaje a la Trayectoria de la Profesora María Inés Carzolio*, La Plata: Universidad Nacional de La Plata, 2017. On Italian merchants in Argentina, see Nahuel Cavagnaro, 'Los Hombres de Negocios: las Redes Genovesas en la Edad Moderna', in Bernard Vincent et al. (eds.), *Estudios en Historia Moderna* desde una visión Atlántica Libro Homenaje a la Trayectoria de la Profesora María Inés Carzolio, La Plata: Universidad Nacional de La Plata, 2017, pp. 582–603. See also Girolamo Benzoni, *History of the New World, by Girolamo Benzoni, of Milan. Shewing His Travels in*

Lisbon worked as bankers who invested heavily in Portuguese expeditions to Africa and India. Tognetti states that 'in the Portuguese capital, some Florentine merchants of high status operated on behalf of the [Cambini] bank, both as agents and as partners (*accomandatari*). They are documented many times in Portuguese archives; Bartolomeo di Iacopo di ser Vanni, Giovanni di Bernardo Guidetti and Bartolomeo di Domenico Marchionni are the most famous.'[207] Merchants such as Bartolomeo Marchionni 'at the beginning of the 16th century ... participated in financing of the voyages of "discovery" and trade led by captains of the Portuguese navy of the calibre of Pedro Álvares Cabral and Afonso de Albuquerque, realising fabulous profits'.[208] Their capital was invested not only in the expedition but also in the slave trade, and they became slave-owners themselves. Bartolomeo Marchionni, for example, invested a large amount of his capital in buying slaves: 'from 1493 to 1495, the registers of Casa dos Escravos in Lisbon recorded 1,648 slaves belonging to Marchionni, and between 1489 and 1503 he would send 1,866 black enslaved Africans from Lisbon to the kingdom of Valencia'.[209] The centre of the Atlantic slave trade may have been in Portugal or Spain, but it was indeed a European project.[210] It was this economic force – Europe – that Mendonça's intervention in the Vatican aimed to challenge. Yet, given the dimensions of the task, he failed to achieve his immediate desired outcome.

5.4 MENDONÇA ON NATURAL, HUMAN, DIVINE AND CIVIL LAWS IN HIS CLOSING STATEMENT IN 1668

There were those in the Vatican – and particularly in the Office of Propaganda Fide – who doubted Mendonça's experience on the issue

---

America, from A.d. 1541 to 1556: With Some Particulars of the Island of Canary, trans. W. H. Smyth, London: Printed for the Hakluyt Society, 1857.
[207] Tognetti, 'Trade in Black African Slaves', p. 216.
[208] Tognetti, 'Trade in Black African Slaves', p. 222.
[209] Tognetti, 'Trade in Black African Slaves', p. 222.
[210] See Bernhard Wadström *Observations on the Slave Trade: And a Description Of Some Part of the Coast of Guinea, During a Voyage, Made in 1787, and 1788, in Company with Doctor A. Sparrman and Captain Arrehenius, by C.B. Wadstrom, Chief Director of the Royal Assay and Refining Office; Member of the Royal Chamber of Commerce, and of the Royal Patriotic Society, for Improving Agriculture, Manufactures, and Commerce in Sweden*, London: Printed and sold by James Phillips, George-Yard, Lombard-Street, 1789. For the Italian project on Cabo Verde, see Hall, *Before Middle Passage*. See also Ferreira, *Feiras e Presídios*, pp. 11–22.

and even questioned his African identity. It was a doubt plainly expressed in the final statement in 1686 from the defendants' representatives, who claimed that Mendonça had been misinformed about the treatment of the enslaved Africans in the Americas. The statement accused him of being a reductionist for his lack of understanding of the complexity of the economic mechanisms at work in the Atlantic region and claimed that to abolish slavery as Mendonça was hoping was not viable for the Americas.[211] Mendonça had to demonstrate to the Vatican's officials that he had experience in the matter, and to ensure that his African identity was not in doubt. His claim to share the royal blood of the kings of Kongo and Angola might be viewed as political, but it was in fact a claim made to silence those in the Vatican who doubted his African credentials.[212] Revealing his identity, particularly tracing his bloodline back to the kings of Kongo, from whence Matamba or Angola came, gave Mendonça a platform for his message. His ancestors had already witnessed the plight of the enslaved. A letter sent to Rome on 29 June 1658 by the Confraternity of Luanda, Angola, invoked the rights of man, stating 'for in the service of God we must all be equal',[213] to make clear that they wanted proper recognition and equality. While Mendonça's ancestry may explain his commitment to the abolition of slavery, it also raises interesting questions about the role of the African confraternities in Iberian society, and more particularly about their status and prestige in Portugal.

Mendonça, apart from being of 'the royal blood of the kingdoms of Kongo and Angola,' was also a 'highly educated figure'[214]. He was a 'legal councillor' and thus well placed to address the issue of slavery. His cultural heritage was the precondition that added weight to his case about the injustices that he observed among enslaved Africans. He felt duty-bound to inform Innocent XI about the tyrannical cruelty with which they were treated.[215] Above all, he wanted to 'tell the truth' about their predicament.[216]

Mendonça stated that the cruelty and brutality employed against the enslaved Africans involved the use of 'wax from Spain, fat with sap, human excrement and high materials'.[217] Such cruelty went beyond common limits to become, for Mendonça, a crime against every 'divine and

---

[211] See SOCG, vol. 490, fl. 141, 'Instrutione Gagisterno Cybo', paragraphs 4 and 5.
[212] See Millini's claim in SOCG, vol. 495a, fl. 54.
[213] Africa, 6, Kongo, 250, fol. 248, 1658, 'pois no serviço de Deus devemos todos ser iguais'.
[214] SOCG, 490, fl. 140r, 'e di molte altre educationi'.   [215] See SOCG, 490, fl. 140r.
[216] See S.C. Africa, vol 1, fl. 486.   [217] SOCG, 490, fl. 140r.

human law'.[218] Such cruelty was not used even in the time of the early Church.[219] What was worse, in Mendonça's view, was that the enslaved themselves were Christians: the slave-owners, who by law were obliged to protect and defend the enslaved, were the ones committing acts of such tyrannical cruelty. It is axiomatic in both human and divine law that those in authority are to use their position to protect those who are most vulnerable. By openly accusing the Vatican, Italy, Spain, Portugal and the Christian merchants of *actus reus* in the process of enslaving Africans, Mendonça established a position from which he could question and dismantle the entire grounds upon which the institution of Atlantic slavery stood. Mendonça explicitly questioned the institution of slavery, and argued from the positions of *human, natural, divine* and *civil* laws.

Firstly, he argued that slavery contravened human law – that is, the law of the land as laid down by particular groups of people. Human law is derived from 'human nature'[220] – it is law that humans make to organise their societies; they agree among themselves to abide by its principles. Human law is the set of principles that govern human interactions in different parts of human societies. For Thomas Aquinas (1225–1274) all human beings can know the difference between right and wrong without being introduced to Christian ethics, and it is human law that makes this possible.[221] Embedded in this is the idea of the eternal law – that is, God's laws for creation, by which nature is governed. Human laws are general principles of law applicable to all societies, what Anthony J. Lisska calls a 'mutual forbearance and respect'[222] for other human beings. In H. L. A. Hart's terms, human law is a 'core of good sense'[223] that allows people to govern themselves based on 'the common good'.[224] In Mendonça's interpretation of human law, slavery was a violation of the Africans' and the Indigenous Americans' human rights, since it treated them as though they were not human beings, but rather 'mere means'[225], that is, mere objects that existed only to be used by others for their own benefit. Mendonça drew on human law to demand that the dignity of all of

---

[218] SOCG, 490, fl. 140r, 'usano contro ogni legge Diuina, et humana'.
[219] See Conrad, *Children of God's Fire*.   [220] Hart, *The Concept of Law*, p. 20
[221] See Lisska, *Aquinas's Theory of Natural Law*.
[222] Lisska, *Aquinas's Theory of Natural Law*, p. 4.
[223] Hart, *The Concept of Law*, p. 19.
[224] Jacques Maritain, *Man and the State*, Chicago, IL: University of Chicago Press, 1951, pp. 91–100.
[225] James Luchte, *Kant's Critique of Pure Reason: A Reader's Guide*, London, New York: Continuum, 2007.

those, both 'Blacks and whites'[226], caught in the Atlantic slave trade be respected. He attempted to restore to the enslaved the human value that had been lost through their enslavement:[227] for Mendonça, the enslaved people's rights as human beings had been taken away from them by the slave-masters in Brazil, Portugal and Spain. In being denied their rights, the enslaved were denied the basic prerequisite for living their lives with dignity.

Secondly, Mendonça argued that slavery was against natural law. According to Aquinas, natural law derived from creation itself and the idea that God the creator wants all human beings to have good things or basic goods.[228] Among these basic goods are, first, 'life', that is, the drive to sustain life itself. To have a good life also entails respect for the lives of others, 'the individual rights of a person',[229] and hence that all human beings be treated as equal. For they are 'human being as well as our next of kin'.[230] To sustain life is the human instinct of preservation, namely, to preserve the lives of other people. Second is the admonition to 'seek God', that is to say, that as creatures created by God, or what Richard Swinburne called the 'Ground of our being',[231] we are required to have knowledge of God and to aspire to live in accordance with His will. Third, we are enjoined to 'avoid offence', that is, to live a life that does not alienate other human beings. In Aquinas's view, natural law derives from all of these.[232] Natural law is an attainment of the 'right act' or 'purposive activity'.[233] Natural law is the 'morality of aspiration'.[234] For Aquinas, natural law is 'nothing else than the rational creature's participation in the eternal law'.[235] Natural law is said to give us reason to be moral. Using reason allows us to derive the natural law, or, in John Finnis's terminology, 'natural rights' from the natural law.[236]

---

[226] SOCG, 490, fl. 140r.   [227] Jaca and Moirans, OFM Cap., *Servi Liberi*.
[228] See Lisska, *Aquinas's Theory of Natural Law*.
[229] Lisska, *Aquinas's Theory of Natural Law*, p. 4.
[230] See Molina, *De Justitia et Jure*, II, 35, col., 171, C. 'qua homines et proximi sunt'. As quoted by Joner, 'Impressions of Luis de Molina', p. 53.
[231] Swinburne, *The Coherence of Theism*.
[232] See Lisska, *Aquinas's Theory of Natural Law*.
[233] Martin P. Golding, *Philosophy of Law*, Englewood Cliffs, NJ: Prentice-Hall, 1975, pp. 30–33.
[234] F. Lon Fuller, *The Morality of Law*, New Haven, CT, London: Yale University Press, 1964, pp. 96–99.
[235] Lisska, *Aquinas's Theory of Natural Law*.
[236] John Finnis, *Natural Law and Natural Rights*, Oxford: Oxford University Press, 1980, p. 40.

Thirdly, Mendonça contended that slavery had been practised against divine law or God's law, in this case as expressed through Church or canon law (*jus canonico*),[237] which regulated the behaviour of the followers of the Christian God and their relations with their neighbours – that is, with other human beings – with whom they share common humanity and towards whom they ought to behave with the same 'internal morality of law'.[238] *Jus canonico* entails a conjugation of relationships that preserve the dignity of other human beings.

Fourthly, Mendonça argued that slavery was incompatible with civil law. Civil law is stated explicitly and is clear and known to everyone. It is based on codes, for example legislation on human rights. Civil law gives individual permission for most actions. However, one's freedom to act is limited, and responsibility is equated with liability. One is considered guilty if one acts irresponsibly. For Mendonça, the 'sellers', 'buyers' and the 'lawgivers' were irresponsible and lacking in their duty of care towards the Africans, even though they knew the legal system of the Africans and that of the constitution of the Brotherhoods. The confraternities of Black people wanted a return to the basics of the law as given by the Vatican. Law is order and good order is good law. For this reason, Mendonça had taken his defence to the Vatican, because it had the jurisdiction to hear his case. In Moirans's term, there was a chain of legal relationships linking what happened in the Atlantic region back to the pope: 'Governors in the Indies [Brazil and Latin America] are subjects of a Catholic king and kings are subjects to the pope.'[239] The Vatican was the source of laws and the institution under which those laws operated.

5.5 MENDONÇA'S ARGUMENT IN HIS COURT CASE IN 1684 AND IN HIS CLOSING STATEMENT IN 1686

Mendonça stated that 'humanity is infused with the spirit of God',[240] maintained that 'the colour of Black and white people is an accident of nature'[241] and argued that we share a common humanity, a quality that makes us people. Therefore, there were no grounds for enslaving the Blacks as if they were irrational. Besides which, among the enslaved were Black Christians or members of the Christian community and their

---

[237] See SOCG, vol. 490, fl.s 54–56.   [238] Fuller, *The Morality of Law*, pp. 38–40.
[239] Jaca and Moirans, OFM Cap., *Servi Liberi*, fl. 5.
[240] SOCG, 490, fl. 140r, 'alla quale col suo fiato infuse Dio l'anima'.
[241] SOCG, 490, fl. 140r, 'solo per un minimo accidente di Negro, ò Bianco'.

children. Mendonça's contention was that, if laws were binding, slavery was 'unnatural'[242] to human existence.

On the basis of his own 'experience',[243] Mendonça said that it was impractical and unreasonable to accept slavery as the norm. He highlighted that nowhere 'in the scripture'[244] did it say that our differences, our Blackness or whiteness, were grounds for selling Blacks into slavery, and claimed that for the sake of 'benefit enslaved Africans were sold to perpetual slavery'.[245] The result of this cruelty, according to Mendonça, was that slaves lost hope and committed 'suicide'.[246] He declared that it was Pope Innocent XI's responsibility to liberate enslaved people from this cruelty. Previous popes, he said, might have issued many 'briefings', but they failed to fulfil their duty of care by putting a stop to this cruelty. On the one hand, they had no interest and on the other no will to look into reports of these cruelties. The historical evidence I found has shown that they popes were in favour of and even encouraged slavery. Mendonça clearly put Pope Innocent XI on trial: he was on the same footing as the slave-owners and merchants. The pope represented the very institution, the Vatican, which had passed bulls to the Iberian kings (of Portugal and Spain), enjoining them to conquer Africans in the name of the Christian God. Molina declared that 'the responsibility for the slave trade is not theirs alone, and that this was the bishops', priests' and rulers' responsibility, that they should issue a law against it'.[247]

Several bulls to this effect had been sent to the Portuguese Crown in the fifteenth century. There was the aforementioned bull of 1452 issued by Pope Nicholas V, *Dum diversas*. In 1455, Pope Calixtus III confirmed the grants to conquer and enslave in *Romanus Pontifex*, which also granted monopoly over all lands in Africa to King Afonso V of Portugal. On 3 May 1493, Pope Alexander VI issued the *Inter Caetera* bulls, granting the West Africa region, and also Brazil, to the Portuguese monarchy, and the Americas to Spain. The boundaries between Portugal and Spain were then settled at the Treaty of Tordesillas on 7 June 1494.[248] All the bulls gave both Spain and Portugal the legal right to capture and enslave

---

[242] SOCG, 490, fl. 140r, 'irraggioneuole'.   [243] SOCG, 490, fl. 140r, 'scortta'.
[244] SOCG, 490, fl. 140r, 'non so in qual legge trouino'.
[245] SOCG, 490, fl. 140r, 's' habbia à vendere p[er] intere*f*se in perpetua schiauitù'.
[246] SOCG, 490, fl. 140r, 'uccidono'.
[247] See Molina, *De Justitia et Jure*, II, 34, col. 153, A. As quoted by Joner, 'Impressions of Luis de Molina', p. 49.
[248] See Bulls *Eximiae Devotionis and Inter Caetera*, May 3, 1493, as quoted by Maxwell, *Slavery and the Catholic Church*, p. 56.

Africans at will. Münzer stated clearly that when the Portuguese returned from their sixth expedition to Guinea, they brought with them about 653 enslaved, some of whom they sold in Portugal, while others were given as a present to the pope and the remaining were given to other people.[249] Mendonça declared 'although the predecessors of Your Blessing have sent several Briefs against it, because of convenience they[250] [the popes, eventually the Kings and their governing authorities, that is, the governors] have never implemented them. Thus, the sore has not been cured but largely corrupted'.[251] He thus said that not only were the pope and the governing bodies not interested in remedying the situation, they even made it worse. Metaphorically, Mendonça compared it with a 'wound';[252] 'rather than curing it, on the contrary, they aggravated it', they made it 'chronic'.[253] He proposed a solution to the problem, which was to excommunicate all those involved in the crime. He demanded that Pope Innocent XI issue a decree to punish those who took part in what Mendonça saw as a crime against Christian principles and the law.[254]

He went to Rome to challenge the pope's position, which was intentionally geared to facilitating access to justice for African enslaved people, and to persuade Pope Innocent XI to take action and support the enslaved people's right to judicial oversight of appeal for their liberation, 'that he as the supplicant marks this as a matter of such importance that it should be given remedy'.[255] For Mendonça, full judicial scrutiny of the papal bulls that promoted slavery was necessary to ensure that those involved in the trade fulfilled their Christian obligations. His final statement was that the power to adjudicate 'should be given to the Holy Office or the Propaganda

---

[249] See Münzer, *De Jnventione* ... op. cit., p. 231, 'Adductique cum eis sunt 653 schalaui, quos Portugalie partim vendiderunt, partim Pape et alljs dono derunt'. The envoys sent by the Portuguese Crown on this expedition were Gil Eanes, Lançorete, Gonçalo de Sintra and Nuno Tristão.

[250] 'The 'they' to whom Mendonça is referring is inclusive of the chain of relationship that Moirans talks about that lays the responsibility for the suffering and abuse inflicted on enslaved Africans in the Americas on the pope's shoulders. See Jaca and Moirans, OFM Cap., *Servi Liberi*.

[251] SOCG, 490, fl. 140r, 'E benche gli Predeceſsori diV.B.^{ne} habbiano sopra ciò spedito diuerſi Breui atteso l'intereſse che gliene prouiene non gli hanno mai uoluto dar esecut.^{ne} onde non s' é curata la piaga piu tosto corrotta maggiormen.^{te}'

[252] SOCG, 490, fl. 140r, 'piaga'.

[253] SOCG, 490, fl. 140r, 'onde non s'é curata La piaga, ma piu tosto corrotta maggiorm.te."

[254] See Mendonça's argument, SOCG, 490, fl. 140r-v, and Jaca and Moirans, OFM Cap., *Servi Liberi*.

[255] SOCG, 490, fl. 140r, 'ricorre il supplicante accio in una materia di tanta importanza si dia remedio'.

Fide'.[256] Both offices were to enforce the new laws that would bring to an end the entire institution of slavery. They were also in the position to inform the pope about the suffering of the slaves and what befell them, 'one of which [the abuses] we hope will be represented at the Curia'[257]. In other words, Pope Innocent XI could not claim to be ignorant about the enslaved people's plight.[258] These offices knew and had knowledge of what had been happening to the enslaved Africans.

Mendonça carried a message of death to the Vatican: death for the enslaved Africans was not a question of if, but when. The death that Mendonça was talking about was not what one could view as a necessary component of being a mortal creature, that is, this was not death by natural causes, but rather death that was imposed on enslaved Africans for being marked as slaves, as someone's property. In his court case in the Vatican, Mendonça made it clear that the enslaved Africans in Brazil and elsewhere were living between the threat of violence and the loss of hope of a proper human existence. Their lives were swept away by violence and by suicide, which they often took upon themselves as a way to end their suffering. He encapsulated their suffering in the Latin dictum *mors certa est*, translated into Spanish as *Morir Es Lo Mas Cierto* (Death is certain).[259] (see Figures 27

FIGURE 27 Coat of arms of Propaganda Fide surrounded by the text *Morir Es Lo Mas Cierto*, drawn by Gaspar da Costa de Mesquita in his recommendation letter. Image created by the author.

---

[256] SOCG, 490, fl. 140v, 'si degni rimettere questa materia alle sacra Congregatione del S. Officio, ò à quella di Propaganda fide'.
[257] SOCG, 490, fl. 140v, 'una delle quali si spera rappresentarà alla S.ria Vra'.
[258] See 'Carta do Bispo de Cabo Verde a El-Rei', and Jaca and Moirans, OFM Cap., *Servi Liberi*.
[259] See S.C. Africa, vol. 1, fl. 486.

FIGURE 28 Original coat of arms of Propaganda Fide surrounded by the text *Morir Es Lo Mas Cierto*. Image created by the author.

and 29). It was an inscription that featured on the coat of arms of the letter of recommendation that the papal nuncio in Portugal, Gaspar de Mesquita, gave him(see Figure 29), and this can still be found on top of the Propaganda Fide building in the Vatican.[260]

No historian, including Gray, has so far detected these nuances in both the letter and the Propaganda Fide's coat of arms. The significance of the phrase *mors certa est* or *Morir Es Lo Mas Cierto* is telling, because it sums up Mendonça's claim about the violence committed against the enslaved Africans. The complete phrase is *mors certa est, at eius hora incerta est* or 'Death is certain, its hour is not'. By removing *hora incerta est*, Mendonça was challenging the deep-seated human fear of death, what Martin Heidegger captured in the phrases 'the end of the world – is death' and 'being Existence lies in fear'.[261] Jerade argues that 'for the mortal the *hora mortis* [hour of death] is the *quod* [time] of the mystery'.[262] Whereas for Mendonça the *quod*' or when was no longer a mystery because for those enslaved in the Atlantic the *tempus incertum* (the 'time uncertain') had been removed: death was the daily companion of the enslaved Africans, the New Christians and the Indigenous Americans.[263]

---

[260] See S.C. Africa, vol. 1, fl. 486.
[261] Martin Heidegger, *What is Metaphysics?* trans. Siavash Jamadi, Salisbury: Phoenix Publishing, 2014, pp. 302 and 299.
[262] Miriam Jerade, 'Mors Certa, Hora Incerta: Derrida on Finitude and the Death Penalty', *The New Centennial Review*, 17(3), 2017, p. 104.
[263] On the Inquisition of New Christians see Novinsky, 'Padre Antônio Vieira'; for the Africans, see SOCG, vol. 495a, fls. 54–56, 60–62, on the Natives' death see, BAL, 50-X-37, 1604.

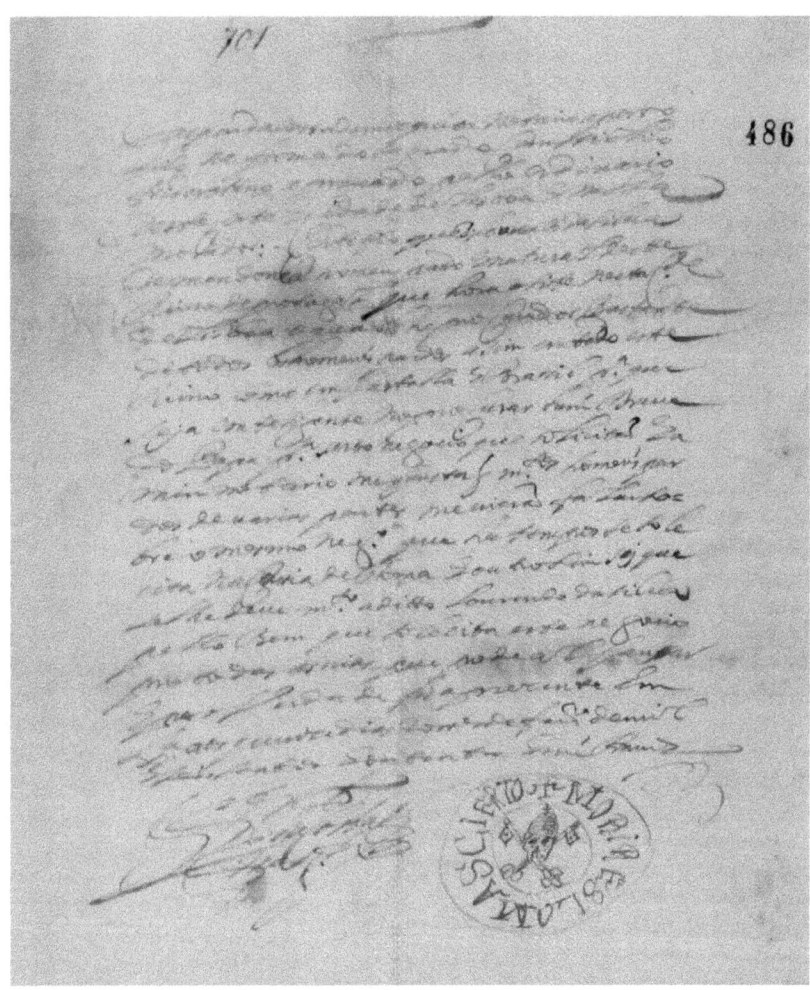

FIGURE 29 Signature and Propaganda Fide coat of arms with text *Morir Es Lo Mas Cierto* on the recommendation letter by Gaspar da Costa de Mesquita. Photograph by the author.

Thus, Mendonça argued in the Vatican that: (1) to be human is to know that death is certain, even though we do not know its hour, and it is this knowledge that, in part, distinguishes us from the immortal Gods and also from other animals that aren't aware of their own mortality; (2) enslaved Africans are subject to such extreme and continuous violence and terror that they live in the very hour of death – they are, in effect, the living dead; (3) because slavery removes the uncertainty of the hour of death in this way, it removes the enslaved from the category of humanity. It was an intriguing approach, in which he drew directly on Greek mythology,[264] and implicitly on Judaeo-Christian ideas about suicide. In so doing, he based his argument on European Christian precepts that were, at that time, similar to those shared by Angolans. Mendonça was an Angolan from the kingdom of Pungo-Andongo, where missionisation was implemented and his family was Christianised; he himself was part of the civilising mission and believed in the European vision of Christian community. These Angolans akin to other Africans in the Central and West African Coast were Christians and were baptised in the Roman Catholic Church. Nonetheless, that did not spare them from being rounded up and enslaved.

An example of Angolans continuing to be enslaved even after their conversion to Christianity was, as already mentioned, that of the subjects of Queen Njinga Mbandi.[265] After her second conversion to Christianity, Father Giovanni Antonio Cavazzi da Montecuccolo, her confessor and an ambassador to the Vatican, returned and gave a glowing account of Njinga's kingdom, people and fame in Angola. The outcome of that report was sent to her on 19 June 1660 by Pope Alexander VII (1655–1667), and never used by historians until now. In it, Alexander VII declared Njinga Mbandi's membership of the Catholic faith, and that of her people:

... our beloved daughter in Christ, I greet you. Clearly with an immense joy, the conversion of Your Majesty to the Pontifex spirit, the universal Church and the Holy faith is undoubtedly complete. Therefore, recognising the truth of the Christian religion, it is with all diligence that we congratulate your heroine for your great fame and glory, and for having gained the salvation of the soul in the name of paternal love.[266]

Alexander VII blessed and granted Njinga and her entire kingdom the benefits that came with membership of the Universal Church, meaning

---

[264] Time has been debated as far back as Plato's era. See Plato, *Gorgias*, trans. W. Hamilton, Harmondsworth, Middlesex: Penguin Books Inc., 1960, p. xx. Pluto, the Greek god complained about time, 'so Pluto ... came to Zeus and complained that people were arriving at both destinations [after life] contrary to what they deserved'. As a result, Zeus said, 'I will put an end to this. At present verdicts are wrongly given.' To end such confusion among judges and prevent further concerns about people being judged on the day of their death, Zeus decided that he 'is to take from mortals the knowledge of the hour of their death ... Prometheus has been given orders to bring this to end.' Hence, we have the phrase in Latin that sums up Zeus's verdict for men's knowledge about the day of death *mors certa est, at eius hora incerta est* or 'death is certain, its hour is not'. See also Jerade, 'Mors Certa, Hora Incerta'.
[265] For a detailed analysis see Cadornega, *História Geral*.
[266] 'Carissimae in Christo filiae Nostrae Annae Reginae Singae Alexander Papa VII'.

that Angolan people should not have been enslaved. He stated: 'thus, through him [Cavazzi], we bestow, with all our love, an Apostolic blessing to Your Majesty. By repeating anew this blessing, we join with commitment and wholeheartedly not only to Your Royal Person of God our Lord, but also to the faithful subjects of Your Kingdom'.[267] Yet, even though Angolans were Njinga's subjects and many were Christians – 'we have heard that, in imitation of such an example, most part of your Court, with many others, were purified by the Holy Baptism'[268] – they continued to be taken into captivity against their will, hence against natural law. Alexander VII's brief was in stark contrast with previous bulls that were sent to Luso-Hispanic kings in the fifteenth century, and superseded them, but the promise that Njinga's subjects would be protected for being part of the Christian faith was ignored. Mendonça's court case brought the betrayal of those that the faith was meant to protect before the Vatican.

On the rejection of Mendonça's first court case, anti-slavery protests from across the world intensified. Mendonça marshalled these different constituencies of enslaved Africans to put their complaints in writing. The Vatican received many protests as the document classified (C) (the second complaint) stated:

> ... meanwhile everybody ... men as well as women and young people write to Your Lord as Father and ... of all the people and creatures baptised to provide remedy [reparation] to such abuse and contracts of baptised bodies by the white Christians themselves.[269]

This level of organisation among the confraternities was new in the history of the Atlantic slave trade and had been unheard of since its inception. In his closing statement, Mendonça brought a message of universal freedom for all people, races and ethnicities. Written evidence was sent to Pope Innocent XI by young people, men and women, and not just those who were already feeling the impact of slavery and its brutality. In other words, Africans took action. They took ownership of their situation, and the onus was on them to determine their destiny. Mendonça's court case made use of the available connections that

---

[267] 'Carissimae in Christo filiae Nostrae Annae Reginae Singae Alexander Papa VII', 'tarnen per eum Apostolicam benedictionem amantissime Maiestati Tuae largiti sumus. Hanc autem denuo repetentes qua Regiae Personae Domnique Tuae, qua cunctis istius Regni fidelibus ex omni corde prorsus impertimur'.

[268] 'Carissimae in Christo filiae Nostrae Annae Reginae Singae Alexander Papa VII', 'imitationi tanti exempli sicut Aulae Tuae maiorem partem cum alijs permultis iam Sacro baptismate ablutam audiuimus'.

[269] See SOCG, vol. 490, fl. 62.

already existed in the Atlantic in order to expose the tyranny of the Atlantic slave trade, which the merchants and their respective governing authorities had attempted to explain away by masking its illegality and attempting to use Christianity to conceal the suffering of the enslaved.

Mendonça and the constituencies of enslaved Blacks expected that the Vatican would act on the evidence presented and demanded that the governing authorities abide by any decision made by the pope to abolish slavery. Pope Innocent XI indeed made a partial decision to abolish slavery in agreement with the confraternities. The confraternities were aware that there had been differing opinions within the governing authorities in Italy, Spain and Portugal over how far the liberation of the enslaved should go, given the impact it would have on the Atlantic economy.

On 26 March 1686, a closing statement was made to confirm that Atlantic slavery was a crime against human, natural, divine and civil laws, to expose the lies that had been used to deny the inhumanity of slavery and to rebut the governing authorities' claims about the suffering being endured by enslaved Africans. A letter dated 26 March 1686 stated that Mendonça had been in Rome several times.[270] This suggests that he was also in Rome for the closing statement.

Mendonça used the final statement to launch his universal message of liberation, which encompassed all those caught up in the Atlantic system, including the New Christians – who by 1686 were once more facing the Inquisition in Portugal – and the Indigenous Brazilians. The punitive action taken by the Inquisition authorities against the New Christians was based on the idea that their faith – Judaism – was different from that of Christendom and, hence, unacceptable. Mendonça believed that people should be judged not on the basis of their ethnicity – for example, as Jews – or who they were, but on who they were before God: they should be judged not as Jews, pagans or heathens but by their faith in God. While Jews or New Christians, those whom Mendonça called Occult Jews, were involved in the Atlantic slave trade, he defended the vast majority of New Christians, who were not involved in slavery:

... the seal of holy baptism, not being of Jewish race nor pagans, but only those following the Catholic faith, like any and every Christian, as is known to all. No one who has received the water of holy baptism should remain and those who have

[270] SOCG, 495a, fl. 58.

been born or would be born to Christian parents should be free, under pain of excommunication ... remembering that God sent his son to redeem humanity and that He was crucified.[271]

The Vatican accepted the evidence of Mendonça's case and, acting on what had been presented to them, accepted the solution proposed by African descendants from the different confraternities. The ministers of justice from the Propaganda Fide demanded that Spain and Portugal change their treatment of enslaved Africans in the Atlantic region. The Vatican sent warning letters to the nuncios in Spain and Portugal to ask both countries to abide by the Vatican's decision. The Spanish and Portuguese authorities were expected to instruct their respective governors overseas to stop the cruelties associated with slavery and were warned that they would be punished if they did not do so.[272] We will return to the action taken by Portugal regarding the Vatican's verdict in Chapter 6. The Vatican did not add anything new to the case, except to ask the authorities to respect the view proposed by the confraternities in Europe and in the Atlantic region. Christianity was expected to provide protection to enslaved African Christians from abuse by the *engenhos*' masters and slave-traders.

On his coat of arms, Mendonça included the scales of justice, which for many people around the world represent order and fairness. It is worth remembering that scales were used as a symbol of justice long before Portugal's contact with the African continent; indeed images of the scales of justice have been found from the third century BC in Egypt (see Figure 30).[273]

---

[271] SOCG, 495a, fl. 58, 'Seconda reclamazione a Nro Sige et alla Sta Mre Chiesa alla Sta Mre Chiesa reclamando Giustizia' [Complaint to the Holy Father and to Holy Mother Church Demanding Justice']. Here I am indebted to Gray for the transcription of the title.

[272] See 'Lettere della Santa Congregazione' [A Letter of the Holy Congregation], APF, 73, fls. 9v-10; see also 73, fls. 10v-11v.

[273] The Last Judgement of Hunefer: Ammit (Ammut or Ahemait), a composite animal with the face (head) of a crocodile and the body of a lion and hippopotamus, is the devourer of the who dead appears in the final scene of the final judgement. Anubis, taking care of the scales of justice, weighs the deceased person's heart with the goddess Ma'at. Ammit is ready to devour the body of any deceased person who does not pass the judgement; on the right-hand side, Ammit is waiting to eat the deceased. If the deceased is found to have lied, committed wrongdoing or if he recites the negative confession and does not pass the judgment, he is eaten by Ammit. In this scene, the deceased is Ani, here with his wife. The god Thoth is writing the verdict, after which, if it is negative, Ammit will devour the deceased. See Siegfried Morenz, *Egyptian Religion*, Ithaca, NY: Cornell University Press, 1973; see also Barbara S. Lesko, *The Great Goddesses of Egypt*, Norman, OK: University of Oklahoma Press, 1999; Donald B. Redford, *Ancient Gods Speak: A Guide to Egyptian Religion*, Oxford, New York: Oxford University Press, 2002; Richard H. Wilkinson, *The Complete Gods and Goddesses of Ancient Egypt*, New York: Thames & Hudson, 2003

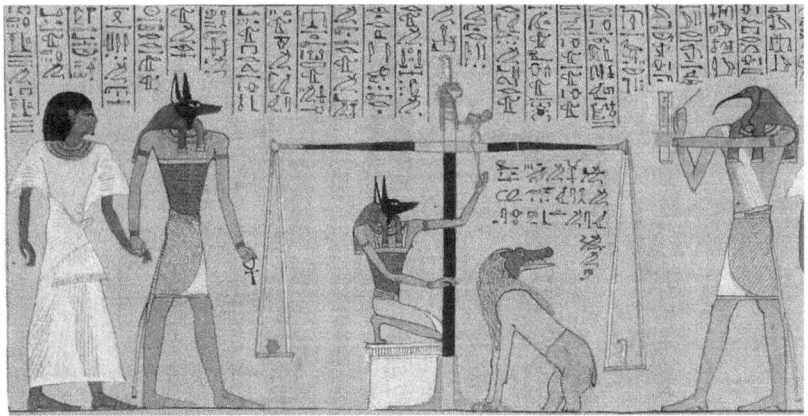

FIGURE 30 Last Judgement of Hunefer with scales of justice, Book of the Dead, c.1275 BCE, papyrus, Thebes, Egypt (British Museum). Public domain.

Mendonça's use of the scales reminded Pope Innocent XI of his responsibility for justice, which was being denied to the Africans, the Indigenous Americans and the New Christians, even though they were part of Christendom. In the confraternities' understanding, the pope was obliged to act as a lawgiver and unbiased judge to all people, regardless of their creed, race or ethnicity. Mendonça and the confraternities of Black people around the world were demanding that Innocent XI be impartial with regard to the decision to abolish Atlantic slavery, and that he fairly weigh up all the evidence in support of their case as presented by Mendonça. It was imperative that Innocent XI understood the crimes of deceit and treachery towards Africans in the Atlantic region perpetuated by the governing authorities and their merchants in Portugal, Spain, Italy and the Americas, and to bring those responsible to justice. In other words, the pope's decision was to be measured according to his ability to find balance between the conflicting versions of the plight of the enslaved as presented by those who suffered and those who bought and sold them.

and Raymond O. Faulkner, Ogden Goelet, Eva Von Dassow and James Wasserman, *The Egyptian Book of the Dead: The Book of Going Forth by Day: Being the Papyrus of Ani (royal scribe of the divine offerings), Written and Illustrated circa 1250 B.C.E., by Scribes and Artists Unknown, Including the Balance of chapters of the Books of the Dead Known as the Ban Recension, Compiled from Ancient Texts, Dating Back to the Roots of Egyptian Civilization*, San Francisco, CA: Chronicle Books, 2008.

5.6 CONCLUDING REMARKS

The idea that Africa was an enslaving society that sold its own people, thus making Atlantic slavery justifiable, is an argument that favours the European powers and sanitises the history of slavery. We should not forget that the Atlantic slave trade was part of the conquest that sustained slavery and that the slave trade did not exist in isolation. There was no slave trade in West Central Africa or West Africa of any magnitude before the European expansion. This rhetoric came from the discourses of nineteenth-century anti-abolitionists. Mendonça's discourse in the Vatican raises questions about slavery and the laws as they were followed then – namely, the *natural, human, divine* and *civil* laws. The theme of abolition was central to his debate, which he placed in the wider context of liberation in the Atlantic region. The facts of slavery have implications for natural law, which is intrinsic to our understanding of core human values such as 'natural necessities'.[274] Lisska in his analysis of Hart's work on natural law concludes that 'survival ... is the central linchpin in human existence and the "necessity" that in principle cannot be overridden by the law'.[275] He argues that salient facts about the human species (that is, the human condition) make moral and legal systems comprehensible and necessary.

In the criminal case he presented to the pope in 1684, Lourenço Mendonça da Silva helped initiate the debate about the treatment of Black African enslaved people by marshalling a set of arguments in favour of liberating Christians and their children. He was particularly concerned with the enslaved as victims of circumstances that were invariably beyond their control. These views were perfectly in keeping with the laws of the time, which he used to his advantage. Mendonça's intention was to bring the suffering of the enslaved to the pope's attention. His argument was that justice should be available to all humanity. What seemed unacceptable to Mendonça was that previous bulls reduced the rights of the enslaved and that they had no protection. These bulls had no place in an arena of law where issues of life and liberty were at stake.

The thrust of his argument was to show that he knew that to effectively liberate enslaved Africans it must be accepted that Africans' freedom included the freedom of all of those who had been on the receiving end of the Atlantic injustice. He knew that geographical distance might

---

[274] Hart, *The Concept of Law*, p. 19.
[275] Lisska, *Aquinas's Theory of Natural Law*, p. 4.

separate them, but their oppression was the same: the Indigenous Brazilians, New Christians and enslaved Africans shared common ground in their search for liberty. In Chapter 6 I will examine Mendonça's tussle with the Portuguese Overseas Council, which tried to overturn his court case on the abolition of the Atlantic slave trade and sent an anonymous letter to nullify it. The chapter deals with Mendonça's psychological struggle to cleanse his family name from the stain of having been coerced into participating in the slave trade by the Portuguese authorities.

6

Mendonça's Quest for Abolition and the Tussle between the Portuguese Overseas Council and the House of Ndongo

Historians have generally not seen the Portuguese Crown's slavery legislation of 18 March 1684 as a response to Mendonça's court case in the Vatican. They have generally viewed it as an attempt to regulate the length of the slave trade journey from West Africa and West Central Africa (Angola and Cape Verde) to Brazil. According to Boxer, the law set out to limit the number of travel days from Luanda: to Recife, to an average of thirty-five days; to Bahia, to an average of forty days; and to Rio de Janeiro, to an average of two months.[1] Boxer argues that the legislation demonstrated the Portuguese Crown's humanity: it was humanitarian legislation brought forward against the background of abusive treatment of the enslaved Africans in Angola and Brazil.[2] Miller made the point that a longer journey meant that more enslaved Africans died on board the ships, for reasons including the poor diet afforded to the Africans.[3] I will return to that issue in due course.[4] Those who hold the view that the legislation was designed to manage the journey across the Atlantic have argued that it was introduced to protect enslaved Africans so that they 'would arrive alive and safe'.[5] José G. Salvador states

---

[1] See Boxer, *Salvador de Sá and the Struggle for Brazil and Angola*.
[2] Boxer, *Salvador de Sá and the Struggle for Brazil and Angola*, p. 251.
[3] See Miller, *Way of Death*.
[4] On the debate about the reason for the legislation, see Miller, *Way of Death*, Luís Viana Filho, *O Negro na Bahia*, Rio de Janeiro: Martins Editora, 1976 and Maria do Rosário Pimentel, 'Aspectos do Quotidiano no Transporte de Escravos do Século XVII: do Sertão africano à Costa Americana', *Estudos Ibero-americanos*, 25(2), 1999, pp.233–244.
[5] See Nireu Oliveira Cavalcanti, 'O Comércio de Escravos Novos no Rio Setecentista", in Manolo Florentino (ed.), *Tráfico Cativeiro e Liberdade (Rio de Janeiro, Séculos XVII–XIX)*, Rio de Janeiro: Civilização Brasileira, 2005 (pp. 15–77), p. 19, 'chegariam vivos e com saúde'.

Mendonça's Quest for Abolition and the Tussle   385

that it was passed in order to deal with the brutality of the slave-traders: 'thus, in 1684, Dom Pedro II, concerning the problem, renewed and expanded the legislation of 1609 and that of 1664 that succeeded it'.[6] Recently, however, Wesley Salles has argued that the legislation followed the discovery of metal in Brazil and that an increased demand for labour might have been the cause behind it.[7]

Several pieces of legislation were passed after 1684 in attempt to stop the ill treatment of enslaved Africans. On 24 September 1808, Prince Regent João VI of Portugal passed another law following that of 1684.[8] Ana Viotti argues that the legislation was there to regulate merchant fraud. She states: 'if any seaman or merchant wanted to circumvent the fee payment scheme, fraud would occur in the tonnage'.[9] Furthermore, in 1813 John VI passed a new law that also included clauses from the law of 1684.[10]

Although historians' general interpretation of the 1684 legislation is accurate, I suggest that we can interpret it more effectively if we link it to the court case that Mendonça presented the same year.

This chapter makes the case that the Crown's slavery legislation of 18 March 1684 was a response to Mendonça's court case in the Vatican. It argues that the debate about the freedom of enslaved Africans was a tussle between Mendonça and the Portuguese Overseas Council, part of a long debate initiated by his grandfather Philipe Hari I in 1658 and continued by his uncle, João Hari II, from the 1660s onward. It looks at the Portuguese Overseas Council's lack of jurisdiction over the internal affairs of the kingdom and its undermining of its own role in attempting to overturn Mendonça's court case verdict in the Vatican through a discreet anonymous letter. It then examines how Mendonça marshalled his legal argument

---

[6] José G. Salvador, *Os Cristãos Novos e o Comércio no Atlântico Meridional*, São Paulo: Pioneira, 1978, p. 100, 'assim, D. Pedro II, em 1684, renovou e ampliou o alvará de 1609 e os sucedâneos de 1664, acerca do problema'.

[7] Wesley Dartagnan Salles, 'Lei das Arqueações de 1684: Por uma Nova Interpretação', *Oficina do Historiador*, 4(2), 2011, pp. 75–95.

[8] For further dicussion of the 'regimento' of 1808, see Ana Carolina de Carvalho Viotti, 'As Proposições de Antonio de Saldanha da Gama para a Melhoria do Tráfico de Escravos, "Por Questões Humanitárias e Econômicas"', *História, Ciências, Saúde*, 23(4), 2016, pp.1169–1189.

[9] See also Viotti, 'As Proposições de Antonio de Saldanha da Gama', p. 1171, 'se algum navegador ou comerciante quisesse burlar o esquema de pagamento de taxas, a fraude ocorreria na arqueação'.

[10] See Cartas de Lei Alvarás Decretos e Cartas Régias. 45. Alvará – de 17 de Novembro de 1813. Collecção das Leis do Brazil de Biblioteca da Camara dos Deputados183, Rio de Janeiro: Imprensa Nacional, 1890, No. 621-30, pp. 48–55.

to uphold the verdict for his case against the pulling power of the Portuguese Overseas Council. Next, it analyses the political struggle between the Overseas Council and the House of Ndongo, examining also the Portuguese Crown's attempt to deal with the impact of Mendonça's court case and Mendonça's tussle with the Overseas Council.

As stated above, I argue in this chapter that the Portuguese Crown's slavery legislation of 1684 was a direct response to Mendonça's court case. Before this book, historians of West Central Africa have been unable to explain fully the political background to the legislation since they failed to connect it with Mendonça's court case.[11] The historical focus has been on issues of slave mortality on board ships, but not on the legislation and its political makeup. For this reason, Pedro II's law has not received the scholarly research that it deserved. I also argue that the anonymous letter was actually written by the Portuguese Overseas Council itself to counter Mendonça's argument in the Vatican, and not by the Spanish authorities, as Gray has led us to believe.[12] It is my contention that the Portuguese Overseas Council, as a tribunal that dealt with issues overseas, sent an anonymous letter to the Vatican, because Mendonça's court case was outside their jurisdiction and it was the only way that it could interfere. My position is that Mendonça took his criminal court case to the Vatican to seek the abolition of the Atlantic slave trade for the enslaved Africans, and liberty for the Indigenous Brazilians and New Christians, while also not forgetful of the burden and stigma of his own family's involvement in the slave trade, for which he wanted to make amends. He succeeded in winning the legal argument against the Portuguese Overseas Council where his family had been unsuccessful. Yet I conclude that the Portuguese Crown's positive response to Mendonça's court case failed to address the case for radical abolition that Mendonça and the Black confraternities made. Let us now look at the tussle between the Portuguese Overseas Council and the House of Ndongo.

6.1 THE PORTUGUESE OVERSEAS COUNCIL AND THE HOUSE OF NDONGO

The Bragança dynasty that came to power in 1640 sought to restructure Portuguese political power, particularly as manifested overseas. The

---

[11] See Russell-Wood, *Fidalgos and Philanthropists*, Birmingham, *Trade and Conquest*, and Heintze and Rieck, 'The Extraordinary Journey of the Jaga'.
[12] Gray, 'The Papacy'.

Crown replaced the administrative model created during the Iberian Union. Among the first major reforms, following the creation of councils of war, finance and international relations, was the formation of the Portuguese Overseas Council in 1642.[13] It was based on the extinct Council of the Indies, instituted by King Philipe III in 1604, which had lasted until 1614. The Portuguese Overseas Council was subordinated to the Secretary of State for the Affairs of the Navy and Overseas domains. Its exclusive role was to deal with the affairs of overseas colonial administration. On 14 July 1642, King João IV of Portugal issued a decree in which article 6° clearly stated the terms on which the Portuguese Overseas Council was to govern and its jurisdiction:

> for the said Council for the good, belongs all matters and business of whatever character, in respect of such States of India, Brazil and Guinea, the Islands of S. Thomé and Cape Verde, and all the most overseas parts, excluding the Azores and Madeira Islands, and places of Africa. For that the Admonitive Treasury of the said states will be administered from Portugal [the kingdom].[14]

From its inception the Portuguese Overseas Council was composed of four members. '[It] consisted of a president (generally a count or marquis), two councillors from the landed or military aristocracy (capa e espada), and a third councillor with a degree in either canon or civil law (letrado).'[15] The two councillors were members of the Portuguese nobility. Apart from these members, there was another contingent: 'a non-voting secretary and various scribes, porters, and other lesser functionaries who were responsible for running errands, receiving and delivering paperwork, and carrying out other lesser assignments'.[16] By the late seventeenth century the number of councillors had increased to six.[17] Myrup states that: 'like

---

[13] The difference here between the remit of the International Relations Department and that of the Portuguese Overseas Council was that the former was political and dealt with non-colonial states abroad, whilst the latter was a tribunal, which dealt with overseas issues – these may also have been political in colonial states. For further discussion, see Caetano, *O Conselho Ultramarino*, p. 39.

[14] Caetano, *O Conselho Ultramarino*, p. 118, 'ao dito Conſelho virão dirigidas todas as materias, & negocios, de qualquer calidade que forem, tocantes aos ditos Eſtados da India, Braſil e Guiné, Ilhas de S. Thomé, & Cabo Verde, & de todas as mais partes Ultramarinas, tirando as Ilhas dos Açores e Madeira, & Lugares de África, & por elle ha de correr a adminiſtração da fazenda dos ditos Estados, & a que delles vier ao Reyno, ſe adminiſtrara pelo Conſelho da fazenda'.

[15] See Myrup, 'To Rule from Afar', p. 93.   [16] Myrup, 'To Rule from Afar', p. 93.

[17] See 'Consulta do Conselho Ultramarino', 'Conde de Val de Reis (the President of the Council), Salvador Correia de Sáa J Benauides, Francisco Malheiro, Ruy Tellez de Menezes, Feliciano Dourado and Carlos Cardoso Godinho'.

other royal tribunals, the council consisted of lawyers (letrados) and aristocrats who worked together to resolve disputes, determine jurisdictional authority, and, more generally, advise the crown in colonial matters.'[18] Some of the prominent members were former governors in Angola, Brazil and India, such as Salvador Sá, Távora and Silva, to name but a few. These were members with political and economic interests in these regions, as we have seen in Chapter 1 and Chapter 3. They were also believed to have the requisite knowledge about the people and politics of the region; this was certainly the case with Salvador Sá, as we saw in Chapter 3. Their advice to the Crown was important as they already had knowledge of the overseas territories.

As shown in Chapter 1, the Portuguese Overseas Council wielded considerable power and was often in conflict with governors and city councils overseas. They also dealt with a range of issues emerging from Africa, Brazil and India, and there were many. On 17 November 1645, it was decided that the council would meet six days a week, Monday to Saturday, in order to deal with the emerging issues from overseas: (i) on Mondays, Tuesdays and Wednesdays they dealt with issues concerning India; (ii) on Thursdays and Fridays, they dealt with business to do with Brazil; (iii) on Saturdays, they dealt with issues regarding Guinea (Africa), Cape Verde, Angola, Mozambique, São Tomé and other parts of the world.[19] The Portuguese Overseas Council functioned as an intermediary between the Crown and overseas affairs. They acted as a tribunal that took decisions that related to military, economic and family affairs, including those of African allies.[20] The council wielded 'tremendous influence over the crown's decisions, the Overseas Council presided over an extensive network of patronage and paternalism.'[21] They could veto the Crown's decisions as well as those of city councils overseas and of those based in Africa and allied to the African kings, in the case of Philipe Hari I. I will return to this in due course.

Concomitantly, the Overseas Council handled Angolan issues, either by bypassing the Muncipal City Council of Luanda or sometimes along with it. On its creation, on 13 February 1642, it took over the role played by the 'Conselho da Fazenda' (Council of the Treasury), founded in 1591 during the reign of Philipe II, the Hapsburg king of Spain who also ruled Portugal and united both Crowns. The Overseas Council's jurisdiction

---

[18] See Myrup, 'To Rule from Afar'.
[19] For further details see Caetano, *O Conselho Ultramarino*, p. 48.
[20] See AHU, cód. 14, fls. 339–339v, 5 October 1651.
[21] See Myrup, 'To Rule from Afar', p. 20.

restricted the power of veto from the city councils overseas to a certain extent, an example being the case of Philipe Hari I, king of Pungo-Andongo, discussed in Chapter 2. On 8 April 1653, Philipe Hari I wrote to his counterpart King João IV on issues relating to the military threat to his kingdom, mainly from his sister Njinga of Matamba. Philipe Hari I asked for help from the Crown of Portugal as an ally. He also complained about his relationship with the Overseas Council, particularly that its jurisdiction reduced his power and left him as a nominal king only. According to Philipe Hari I, his own *sobas* and 'vassals' were being enslaved and taken from his kingdom by his son-in-law, António de Teixeira Mendonça, who he said had stolen 10,000 people, enslaved them and taken them to work on his estates.[22]

Furthermore, Philipe Hari I asked the Crown to give him a special dispensation that exempted him from *baculamento* and to stop him being pressurised by governors to enslave his people as part of vassalship to Portugal. Sousa stated on Philipe Hari I's coronation that 'the king of Dongo [Philipe Hari I] will have to pay [*baculamentos*] per year for being the vassal king of His Majesty, which will be written on the reproduction copy and vassalship that Your Majesty command.'[23] For Philipe Hari I, this was not the way to treat an ally. He made it clear that he had been a loyal king to the Portuguese project of conquest in Angola to the point of losing his heir to the throne during the Dutch war defending the Portuguese interest. Birmingham states that his treatment by the Portuguese had left some members of his family from the Court of Ndongo very unhappy, as we have seen in Chapter 2.[24] Philipe Hari I's complaint was typical of the problems Angolan rulers faced under the Atlantic slave trade.[25] This issue began with Afonso I of Kongo and continued up until the eighteenth century.[26] Philipe Hari I's complaint epitomised the issues encountered in the Angola of the time.[27] Candido argues that slaves were not often taken from distant territories, as we have been led to believe, and instead were taken from within the territories of Portugal's Angolan allies.[28]

---

[22] See 'Carta de Hari I de Ndongo para Dom João IV' and Birmingham, *Trade and Conquest*, p. 118.

[23] BAL, ms. 51-VIII-30, fls. 235–235v, 'que ElRej de Dongo [h]ade pagar cada anno, sendo vassalo de sua Magestade, como se verá no treslado da escritura do feudo e vassalagê que mando a S. Magestade'.

[24] Birmingham, *Trade and Conquest*.

[25] See 'Carta de Hari I de Ndongo para Dom João IV'.

[26] Candido, *An African Slaving Port*.   [27] See Conrad, *Children of God's Fire*.

[28] Candido, *An African Slaving Port*.

Regarding the issue raised by Philipe Hari I, he was first supported by the Overseas Council, which ruled that his men – nobles and *sobas* – should be returned to him.[29] A year later, the council changed its mind after the intervention of one of its councillors, Salvador Sá, who provided an insight into the issue and advised the Crown not to return the men to Philipe Hari I, but to send them back to their respective places, for they were Dom João IV's subjects rather than Philipe Hari I's. The council then argued unanimously that those subjects were not his, but belonged to Portugal.[30] Philipe Hari I lost the case on the grounds that what was his belonged to the Crown. He continued to pay *baculamento*, probably until the end of his reign in 1664.[31] The change to the previous decision came about because of Teixeira's widow's complaint to the Crown and the Overseas Council that the aforementioned subjects belonged to her husband and not to King Philipe Hari I.[32] The action of restitution was often accompanied by violence, but in this case Sá advised João IV not to allow captains of the *presidio* to use violence against Philipe Hari I.[33] The case shows that slavery in Angola was not what the Portuguese thought it to be.[34] It confirms the relevance of questions that have been central to this book, especially regarding the issue challenged in the Vatican by Mendonça, who rejected the established view that slavery was an ancient practice in West Central Africa.[35]

When Dom João Hari II, the son of Philipe Hari I, came to power, he had the same cloud hanging over him –the requirement that he pay *baculamento*. He decided to reject the Portuguese requirement, at great cost to his life, throne and family.[36] All the heirs to the throne of Ndongo, including Mendonça, were exiled to Brazil and Portugal.[37] When they were sent into exile, the members of the House of Ndongo were brought face to face with the pain of Angolans enslaved in Brazil, Portugal and elsewhere; this was particularly the case for Mendonça.[38] Enslaved Africans were carried off to Brazil by force, but Mendonça could not

---

[29] See AHU – Códice. 15, fl. 103v., e 96v, 22 April 1654.
[30] See AHU, cód. 15, fl. 103v and 96v.
[31] Philipe Hari I was obliged to pay *baculamento*, see BAL, ms. 51-VIII-30, fls. 235–235 v, 30 January 1627, and, on his complaint about paying later during his reign, AHU, cód. 15, fl. 103 and 96v.
[32] See AHU, cód. 15, fl. 103v and 96v.   [33] AHU, cód. 15, fl. 103v and 96v.
[34] Barreira, 'Informação Acerca dos Escravos de Angola'.
[35] See Barreira, 'Informação Acerca dos Escravos de Angola' and MMA III.
[36] For Ndongo's war see, Relaçam/ Do FELICE SVCCESSO and Cadornega, *História Geral*, vol. II.
[37] Birmingham, *Trade and Conquest*.   [38] See Pereira, *À Flora da Terra*.

overlook the role his family played in the slave trade.[39] His own father, Ignaçio, contributed to the banishment of people when he took part in wars alongside the Portuguese.[40] As the governor of Angola of the time Luis Martins de Sousa Chicorro (1654–1658) declared in his report to the king of Portugal, the House of Ndongo was part of the contingent that joined the Portuguese army in fighting in Quissama. He stated 'all those that are *sobas*, and have names of Your Majesty's vassals, are obedient, and have been with their people in the war of Quissama, and also the king of Dongo [Ndongo] came with his elder son, called Dom Ignacio.'[41] It could be argued that Mendonça's family were coerced into being involved by the Portuguese vassalship agreement imposed on his grandfather.[42] However, this would not have diminished the psychological effect of this knoweldege on Mendonça, particularly after his stay in Salvador, Rio, Braga, Lisbon and Toledo.[43] According to our documentary sources, Mendonça was ill by the time he got to Rome. The nature of his sickness is not mentioned in the document, but it was this on which 'he has spent most of his money while in Rome'.[44] The possibility that he was burdened by the knowledge that he and his family had contributed to enslavement and suffering of his own countrymen cannot be ruled out entirely.[45] These experiences accumulated to shape his court case in the Vatican. He also informed the officials of Propaganda Fide that he was experienced in dealing with these affairs.[46]

The destruction of Pungo-Andongo led to the capture and enslavement of a large number of Africans. Seven hundred enslaved people were given to the regent of Portugal, Pedro II, as his fifth, another 700 slaves were the governor's fifth and an undisclosed number of captives were divided among the army officers who took part in that war. In monetary terms,

---

[39] See 'Informação de Fernão de Sousa a El-Rei', 7 December 1631, BAL - Ms. 51-VIII-31, folios 5–9 v.
[40] According to the Governor of Angola, 'Carta de Luís Mendes de Sousa Chichorro para Dom João IV' [A Letter by Luís Mendes de Sousa Chichorro to King John IV], AHU, Angola, cx. 4, 17 September 1655.
[41] "Carta de Luís Mendes de Sousa Chichorro para Dom João IV', 'todos os mais que saõ souas, e tem nomes de vaçallos de v Magestade estaõ obedientes, e andaõ com a sua gente na guerra da Quiçama, a que veyo também o Rey de Dongo com seu filho mayor, por nome d. Ignacio'.
[42] See Freudenthal and Pantoja, *Livro dos Baculamentos*, and 'Informação de Fernão de Sousa a El-Rei', 7 December 1631, BAL - Ms. 51-VIII-31, folios 5–9 v.
[43] See S.C. Africa, vol. I, fl. 487r-v; S.C. Africa, vol. I, fl. 486; and SC Africa, Angola, Congo, Senegal, vol. II, fl. 393.
[44] See SC Africa, Angola, Congo, Senegal vol. II, fl. 392.
[45] See SC Africa, Angola, Congo, Senegal vol. II, fl. 392.   [46] See SOCG, vol. 490, fl.140.

by 1652 a slave's tax cost 4,000 reis each. So 4,000 x 700 slaves is equal to 2,800,000 reis plus 2,800,000 adds up to 5,600,000.[47] As described in Chapter 2, the war of Pungo-Andongo was condoned by the influential councillor of the Portuguese Overseas Council, Salvador Sá[48]. When Mendonça began his legal struggle in the Vatican, it was on behalf of wider Atlantic constituencies such as enslaved Africans, New Christians and Indigenous Brazilians. Anger at the destruction of Pungo-Andongo was of course also part of his motivation; but in taking up this struggle this anger was subsumed in the representations he made on behalf of these constituencies. Accordingly, in his opening statement in the Vatican he did not explicitly mention the Pungo-Andongo war. Notwithstanding this, I would argue that this event was understood in his discourse to be underlying the wider picture.[49] Let us now look at Mendonça's impact.

6.2 THE PORTUGUESE CROWN AND MENDONÇA'S IMPACT AT THE VATICAN

On 18 March 1684, after Mendonça presented his court case, the Portuguese Crown began one of the biggest slave trade shipment reforms in the history of the Atlantic slave trade, which to date no historian has linked to Mendonça's discourse and intervention in the Vatican.[50] His presentation of his court case in the Vatican and its impact was felt in the Luso-Hispanic dominion of the seventeenth century, as we saw in Chapter 5. Boxer claimed that Dom Pedro II, king of Portugal, and his counterpart, Carlos II of Spain, wanted to abolish African slavery, but their own advisers – the Overseas Council, ministers of the Indies, priests – thought differently and they persuaded them against taking that action.[51] However, he does not develop this issue further, nor does he indicate the sources he used to substantiate this interesting claim. I can now show that it was the impact of Mendonça's court case that brought such changes from both kings, Dom Pedro II and Charles II. Boxer states:

... in the 1680s, both Charles II, 'the bewitched,' of Spain, and Pedro II of Portugal had some misgivings about the validity of the West African slave trade; but their scruples of conscience were stiffed by the conviction of their ministers (and

---

[47] See AHU, Angola, cx. 4.   [48] See AHU_CU_001, cx. 11, d. 1272.
[49] See SOCG, vol. 490, fl. 140.
[50] See SOCG, vol. 495a, fls. 54–55; and SOCG, vol. 490, fl. 140.
[51] See Boxer, *The Church Militant*.

perchance of their confessors?) that if this trade was abolished, their respective American empires would no longer be economically viable.[52]

Both kings wished to support Mendonça's case, as we have seen from Toledo's letter in Chapter 5, and the reform decree I will discuss in due course.[53] The original copy of Pedro II's 'regimento' 'brief' or reform provisions is housed in the National Archive of Rio de Janeiro and a transcribed copy of it is held by the Arquivo Historical Ultramarino de Bélem in Lisbon.[54] I located this during my research in Rio de Janeiro. It is a long brief, containing twenty-three chapters or articles.

In 1684, soon after coming to the throne, King Pedro II decided to consider a proposal to improve the conditions of the enslaved African shipments in the Atlantic slave trade. central to his deliberations were the mortality rates of the enslaved on board and their safety while being transported. The law, which we may call 'Dom Pedro II's Atlantic Slave Trade Law of 1684',[55] was codified after Mendonça's court case presentation in the Vatican. Mendonça directly accused the Luso-Hispanic authorities of involvement in the African slave trade and the inhumane treatment that went with it.[56] Pedro II was pressurised to take action on the slaves' treatment in Brazil soon after Mendonça's case was brought to the attention of the Vatican officials in Rome.[57] Russell-Wood states that: 'in 1688 he had ordered the governor of Rio de Janeiro to investigate all allegations of cruelty by masters against their slaves, and to take legal action against the masters if these allegations were shown to be true.'[58] There is good evidence to support my argument that Mendonça's intervention in the Vatican led to the changing of laws in Portugal regarding the condition of the enslaved Africans on vessels to Brazil. The speed with which the legislation was implemented shows that it was carried out under pressure to make a change. Dom Pedro II declared:

... as there is no time available to publish, print and send a copy of it under my seal to the counties of this kingdom and its conquests [overseas] in the form of that style, because the ships are setting sail to the said conquests. The said copies will be

---

[52] Boxer, *The Church Militant*, p. 35.
[53] See Carlos II's support of Mendonça, S.C. Africa, vol. I, fl. 487r-v, and Dom Pedro II's reform law 'Dom Pedro por Graça de Deos Rey de Portugal e dos Algarves daquem e dalém mar" [For the Grace of God, Dom Pedro the King of Portugal and of Algarve and of that Overseas], AHU_CU_001, cx. 13, d. 1554, Angola, 18 March 1684.
[54] See 'Dom Pedro por Graça de Deos' and Russell-Wood, *Fidalgos*, p. 385.
[55] 'Dom Pedro por Graça de Deos' and SC Africa, Angola, Congo, Senegal vol. II, fl. 393.
[56] SOCG, vol. 495a, fls. 54–55.   [57] SOCG, vol. 495a, fls. 55–56.
[58] Russell-Wood, *Fidalgos and Philanthropists*, p. 222.

sent by my Overseas Council so that governors, senior crown judges, [ombudsmen], commissioners of the Treasury to comply with it and enforce it, without lacking to its said solemnities and of its fulfilment to the contrary.[59]

The final article, article 23, demonstrates Mendonça's impact. Pedro II urged its compliance without delay and the normal protocol of signing the document with the seal and sending it to each governor was not followed. Notwithstanding, he urged the Portuguese Overseas Council to send it on ships that were leaving for Africa, Brazil and India. The tone of it, and urgency with which it was sent, gives a clear indication that pressure was being exerted from outside. It was the biggest slave trade law and it would shape eighteenth- and nineteenth-century Portugal, if not all of Europe. It took England almost a century to call for similar regulation in the late 1780s when Parliament agreed to act to protect the health and improve the mortality rate of enslaved people; a piece of 'Legislation, known as Dolben's Act' or 'The Regulated Slave Trade Law of 1788'.[60]

In the preamble, Pedro II's law dictated the remit of the regulation. He addressed it to all Portuguese trade contact zones overseas: 'Africa, Guinea, Conquest [Overseas], Navigation, Ethiopia, Arabia, Persia and India ... I make it known to those that this law seen as desired to all Dominions of my Crown and for all vassals and subjects that they keep the dictates of the reason of this law and that of Justice.'[61] He declared:

... they be informed that in taking the Black captives from Angola to the State of Brazil, masters and those charged to take them on ships endeavour on violence of bringing them so tight and close to one another that they are not only lacking necessary breath for life to which preservation [of life] is common and natural to all be they free or slaves. However, the cramming that they come under, succeeds

---

[59] 'Dom Pedro por Graça de Deos', 'como naõ há tempo para se poder publicar, imprimir e enviar a copia della sob meu Sello e seu signal ás Comarcas deste Reyno e suas Conquistas na forma do estilo por estarem de partida os navios que para as ditas Conquistas fazem viagem se enviaraõ a ellas as ditas copias pelo meu Conselho Ultramarino para que os Governadores, Ouvidores, Provedores da Fazenda a cumpraõ e dêm á execuçaõ sem embargo de lhe faltarem as ditas solemnidades e da Ordenaçaõ em contrario'.

[60] For further debate on William Dolben's Act, see James LoGerfo, 'Sir William Dolben and "The Cause of Humanity": The Passage of the Slave Trade Regulation Act of 1788', *Eighteenth-Century Studies*, 6(4), 1973, pp. 431–451, see also Clarkson, *History of the Rise, Progress and Accomplishment*.

[61] 'Dom Pedro por Graça de Deos', 'em Africa, Senhor de Guiné e da Conquista, Navegaçaõ, commércio da Ethiopia, Arabia, Pérsia e da Índia &c ... faço saber aos que esta Ley virem que desejando que em todos os Domínios da minha Coroa e para com todos os Vassallos e súbditos della se guardem os dictames da razaõ e da Justiça'.

in ill-treating them in a way in that many die. Those who remain alive arrive impiously pitiful.[62]

The slave trade in Angola became central to Pedro II's law. If the sixteenth century was Guinea's century for the slave trade – Sierra Leone, Guinea-Bissau, Senegal, the Gambia, Guinea-Conakry, Ghana and Benin, 'modern Nigeria'; the seventeenth century was the Angolan century, as we saw in Chapter 1, Chapter 2 and Chapter 3[63]. In the seventeenth century an increased number of enslaved people were taken to Brazil, where many died and were buried in shallow graves. In Rio de Janeiro there is evidence that confirms the the fact that many people died crossing the Atlantic or on arrival in Rio, all as a result of the terrible voyage, from sickness arising from the long journey or as a result of the ill treatment they suffered on board.[64] Other captaincies of Brazil at the time, such as Bahia, Pernambuco, Maranhão may come to reveal similar mass cemeteries for enslaved Africans in the near future. Vieira and Furtado, governors of Brazil in Bahia during the time Mendonça arrived there, both claimed that many enslaved Africans were dying, but that they were needed for production.[65] Dom Pedro II went even further and stated that:

I have taken to resolve this from now that there cannot be carried any Blacks on ships and any other shipments without first in all and each one of them that they consider the capacity of tons that they can take with respect to wrapping cloths and covers for them, the basement for fresh water supply for sea travel and food in the following way.[66]

---

[62] 'Dom Pedro por Graça de Deos', '... sendo informado que na conducçaõ dos Negros captivos de Angola para o Estado do Brasil obraõ os carregadores e mestres dos navios a violência de os trazerem taõ apertados e unidos huns com os outros que naõ sómente lhes falta o desafogo necessário para a vida cuja conservaçaõ hé commua e natural para todos ou sejaõ livres ou escravos, mas do aperto com que vêm succede maltrataremse de maneira que morrendo muitos chegaõ impiamente lastimosos os que ficaõ vivos'.

[63] See BADE, cód. cxvi/1/33, fls. 168–168v, and MMA vol. III.

[64] See Pereira, À Flora da Terra, and Russell-Wood, Fidalgos and Philanthropists.

[65] See Furtado and Viera's plea for more slaves in Bahia, Documentos Históricos dos Arquivos Municipal, Cartas do Senado 1673–1684, vol. II, Prefeitura do Municipio do Salvador, Bahia, p. 20, and 'Proposta de Vieira por parte dos Cristãos Novos a el Rey', in Barretto, Monstruosidades do Tempo e da Fortuna.

[66] 'Dom Pedro II's Atlantic Slave Trade Law of 1684', AHU_CU_001, Cx. 13, D. 1554, Angola, 18 March 1684, 'fui servido resolver que daqui em diante se naõ possaõ carregar alguns Negros em navios e quaesquer outras embarcações sem que primeiro em todos e cada hum delles se faça arqueaçaõ das toneladas que podem levar com respeito dos agasalhados e cubertas para a gente e do poraõ para as agoadas e mantimentos tudo na forma seguinte:'. See also Pereira, À Flora da Terra, and Russell-Wood, Fidalgos and Philanthropists.

Pedro II wished to ensure that the new law was followed by the slave-traders, governors, customs officers, judges, vessel masters, stevedores and the Portuguese Overseas Council to reduce the evils of the slave trade; the law was to remedy with immediate effect loss of lives in the Atlantic. When enslaved Africans were transported from Africa to various parts of the Atlantic, Brazil in particular, they were crammed on board ships, and each had very limited room in which to move. Those able to cope with the lack of air and appalling sanitary conditions may have died after falling ill. As LoGerfo claims: 'these egregiously indecent conditions generated fatal diseases, the effects of which in close quarters spread the contagion prodigiously and required the disposal of corpses on an almost daily basis'.[67]

Pedro II's legislation involved rigorously observing seven major themes: (1) Tonnage or arching were to be set by measuring the capacity of cargo space on board the vessel for enslaved persons. On the larger part of the deck, there were to be seven persons on tons of two cubes spaces, which had windows to allow them to breath. On vessels without small windows, there were only to be five per person for the two-ton cubes. On the larger deck there could be packed five young persons for each ton.[68] (2) Regarding food provisions, the enslaved were to be fed three times a day and given sufficient fresh water to drink 1.4 litres or 0.58 English gallons per day until they reached their destination. The amounts needed were to be calculated on the basis of the length of the journeys from Angola to Brazil: thirty days journey from Angola to Pernambuco, forty days to Bahia and fifty days to Rio de Janeiro.[69] (3) In terms of health care, those who were sick were to be separated and given medication in separate rooms and be treated with the 'love of your neighbour'.[70] (4) There was to be a priest on board the ship to assist those dying and for conversation – many priests, Africans in particular, did not want to take this job.[71] (5) Governors were obliged to build reception houses in the African ports in which the enslaved could rest while waiting for the journey. However, this was more of an optional requirement.[72] (6) There was to be auditing, meaning vessels were to be given logbooks and certificates, which they were to produce at each

---

[67] See LoGerfo, 'Sir William Dolben and "The Cause of Humanity"', p. 431.
[68] See 'Dom Pedro por Graça de Deos', chapters I-VI, XII-XII, XIII.
[69] See 'Dom Pedro por Graça de Deos', chapters VII, XIII, IX.
[70] See 'Dom Pedro por Graça de Deos', chapter X.
[71] See 'Dom Pedro por Graça de Deos', chapter XI.
[72] See 'Dom Pedro por Graça de Deos', chapters XV and XVI.

destination of their journey.⁷³ (7) Punishment was to be inflicted on those who were not complying with rules, according to the laws set in this regulation. Ship captains who did not comply with the law were to be exiled to Brazil.⁷⁴

It was often difficult to enforce compliance by governing authorities overseas with laws passed by the Crown, as we saw in Chapter 1. The extent to which Pedro II's slave trade law of 1684 was implemented remains a moot point. Russell-Wood is of the opinion that 'letters from the king to his governors and archbishops rarely produced practical results. Nevertheless, they were evidence of strong royal concern for the living conditions of slaves in Brazil.'⁷⁵ Towards the end of the seventeenth century there was a substantial change of policy within the white confraternities, which were given the monopoly for burials in the cities, particularly those of Rio de Janeiro and Salvador. 'On 4 October 1693 the *Mesa* of the Misericórdia of Bahia had established the *banguê* for the burial of slaves.'⁷⁶ This demonstrates a clear reform to the way things were done before Mendonça's presentation in the Vatican. The *Mesa* of the Misericórdia of Bahia of Santa Casa of the city of Salvador was tasked in the same period with reducing the fee of 800 reis to 400 reis for burials, so the enslaved could afford proper burials. Pressure was exerted by the bishop of Brazil on the white confraternities to carry out this task: 'If the *Mesa* failed to comply, the burial monopoly of the Misericórdia would end.'⁷⁷

In May 1694, similarly, Dom Pedro II gave instructions to the governor of Rio de Janeiro, Dom João de Lencastre, to ensure proper burials were possible for the enslaved population. He declared: 'I order you very specially for what I understand of slaves, they ought to be buried with Christian decency. For that you work all that is necessary that they would continue any longer. An improper deed is so contrary to love, which for all; Blacks and Whites must be equal.'⁷⁸ The Misericórdia of Rio de

---

⁷³ See 'Dom Pedro por Graça de Deos', chapter XXI.
⁷⁴ See 'Dom Pedro por Graça de Deos', chapters, XVI, XVII, XVIII-XIX and XXIII.
⁷⁵ Russell-Wood, *Fidalgos and Philanthropists*, p. 222.
⁷⁶ Russell-Wood, *Fidalgos and Philanthropists*, p. 222. *Banguê* is a Kimbundu word. It means stretcher or wheelbarrow.
⁷⁷ Russell-Wood, *Fidalgos and Philanthropists*, p. 222.
⁷⁸ Russell-Wood, *Fidalgos and Philanthropists*, p. 223. See also 'Carta do Rei para o Governador' [A letter of the King to the Governor] ANRJ, códice 952, vol. 7, fl. 18, 23 January 1694, 'vos ecomendo muito especialmente a do q' se entendeo conveniente para q' os escravos possão ser enterrados com a decencia de Christãos; sobre o q' obrareis tudo o q' for necessario para q' se não continue mais tempo algum, hũa acçã imporpria, e tão

Janeiro had accepted Dom Pedro II's order to do so but was still charging 960 reis per head. Notwithstanding this, he ordered Lencastre to reach an agreement with the Misericórdia of Rio de Janeiro and to bring fees in line with Salvador, Bahia, to 400 reis. After a year, agreement was reached and the fee for burial was levied at 400 reis.[79] Dom Pedro II efforts to ameliorate the living conditions of the enslaved and improve their burial in Brazil suggests that he might have been under pressure from the Vatican, following Mendonça's intervention focusing on the death rate and ill-treatment in the Atlantic region. The Vatican nuncio in Lisbon, after sending his response to the Vatican, was anxious to hear what the next step was going to be for the governing authority in Portugal. He said: 'I will wait for the orders of the S. Congregation and Your Eminence.'[80]

Pedro II sent a decree to the Portuguese governors of Rio de Janeiro in Brazil, Angola and Cape Verde containing twenty-three chapters, and to the governor of Cape Verde one of twenty-eight chapters.[81] He had to take action with regards to this large and important reform of slave-shipping.[82]. The Reform Law strongly recommended that the preservation of life is part of human rights and that all human beings, be they 'enslaved' or 'free', need to be provided with the essentials of life.[83] This indicates that Pedro II knew about the verdict on Mendonça's court case in the Vatican and acted in anticipation of the Vatican's demand to the Iberian kings.[84] Pedro II then wrote a personal letter to the governor of Cape Verde, Ignacio de França Barboza, on 30 March 1684, informing him that he ought to abide by the regulations that had been sent to him two days earlier, on 28 March 1684. He declared, 'I, the king, salute you. Wishing in all dominion of my crown with all my vassals that they abide

contraria a caride q' para com todos, negros e brancos, deve ser igual', and for the agreement see Códice 952, vol. 7, f. 148 and vol. 8, f. 7.

[79] For further detail on the discussion of burial see, Russell-Wood, *Fidalgos and Philanthropists*, pp. 222–259.

[80] See SOCG, vol. 495a, fl. 57.

[81] See all three letters: AHU_CU_001, cx. 13, d. 1554; AHU, Arquivo de Cabo Verde, livro 42, fls 29v-32v, cód. 544, fl. 50v, 28 March 1684; 'Lei sobre a arqueação dos navios' [Law on the Tonnage of Ships], Arquivo de Angola, 1936, vol. XIII, 28 March 1684, pp. 321–322.

[82] See AHU, Arquivo de Cabo Verde, livro 42, fls. 29v-32v, códice 544, fl. 50v.

[83] See AHU, Arquivo de Cabo Verde, livro 42, fls. 29v-32v, códice 544, fl. 50v, 'Lei sobre a arqueação dos navios', 28 March 1684, 'que não somente lhe falta o dezafogo necessário para a vida cuja conservação hé commua, e natural para todos, ou sejão livres ou escravos'. See also MMA, vol. XIII, pp. 503–510, p. 503.

[84] AHU, Arquivo de Cabo Verde, livro 42, fls. 29v-32v, códice 544, fl. 50v, 'Lei sobre a arqueação dos navios', 'para se dar de comer aos ditos negros, tres vezes no dia'.

by the laws of reason, and that of justice.'[85] On the same day, the President of the Overseas Council, Conde Val de Reis, wrote a similar letter to the governor of Angola, Luis Lobo da Silva, urging him to abide by the code of the decree.[86] The difference here was that from Luanda, then an island and the departure point or slave shipments, and from the subsequent islands (Cape Verde and São Tomé), the enslaved people were taken to the state of Brazil and specifically to Maranhão.[87] Lobo da Silva was strongly warned about his conduct, if he were to be found guilty of defying the orders he had been given 'and when you are found guilty in any of the orders or in any other, I will order in accordance to the law to proceed against you for being disobedient to my orders'.[88] This is indicative that the Crown was aware of the danger of not acting on the recommendation from the Vatican regarding the slave trade in the Atlantic. Mendonça's claim about the ill-treatment of the enslaved Africans was not new. As we saw in Chapter 1, Chapter 2 and Chapter 3, the Portuguese Crown was informed of what was going on in Africa and Brazil. However, after the Vatican's verdict on Mendonça's case, the Portuguese authorities in Lisbon wanted to show that they were cooperating. The legal argument presented by Mendonça could not be brushed aside.

Joseph Miller has focused on the death rate on board ships rather than on legislation to reduce it, particularly in the seventeenth century from the regions where the Portuguese were operating.[89] He has argued that the enslaved Africans' death rate on board the vessels was very much part of an abolitionist debate. I am in agreement with Miller and would certainly place Dom Pedro II in the abolitionist camp. For Miller, death rates on ships carrying enslaved Africans to Brazil were closely related to

---

[85] AHU, Arquivo de Cabo Verde, livro 42, fls. 29v-32v, códice 544, fl. 50v, 'Carregamento de escravos para o Brasil', 'Eu El Rey vos emvio muito saudar. Dezejando em todos os dominós de minha Coroa com todos os vassallos se guardem os ditames da razão, e da justiça'.

[86] Arquivo de Angola, 1936, vol. 13, 'Carta régia sobre a arqueaçao dos navios negreiros', Luis Lobo da Silva. Ev El Rey vos envio muito saudar. Dezejando que em todos os dominios da minha Coroa, e para que com todos os vassallos e súbditos della se goardem os dictames da rezam, e da Justiça.' See also MMA, vol. XIII, p. 566.

[87] See Arquivo de Angola, 1936, vol. XIII, 'sendo informado, que na condução dos negros captivos, que v em dessas Ilhas para o Estado do Brazil e Maranhão'. See also MMA, vol. XIII, p. 566.

[88] See Arquivo de Angola, 1936, vol. XIII, 'e quando a encontreis em algum cazo, ou de alguã qualquer maneira, mandarei proceder contra vós como dezobediente ás minhas ordens'. See also MMA, vol. XIII, p. 567.

[89] See Joseph C. Miller, 'Mortality in the Atlantic Slave Trade: Statistical Evidence on Causality', *Journal of Interdisciplinary History*, 13(2), 1981, pp. 317-329.

'tight-packing'.[90] However, this type of analysis obscures other factors that are equally important for understanding the death rates on board the ships. Miller argues that the high death rate may have been caused as much by existing physical deficiencies and disease in the enslaved people deriving from poor soil and diet in Africa as the immediate condition of the vessels. To take this view is to discount the slavers and the sellers, as if they were separate groups with separate interests. The slavers and sellers worked in tandem with each other.[91] If there were no ships taking the enslaved people to Brazil, then other causes of death might have been registered and as a result changed the way we analyse Pedro II's involvement. Both Pedro II and Mendonça blamed the enslaved Africans' deaths on human actions and not on a sequence of epidemics that might have originated in Africa.[92]

The African origin of the diseases that occurred intermittently on board the vessels carrying enslaved Africans to the Americas has been used to defend the slave owners' economic case.[93] It is an argument used to evade responsibility for the deaths and to suggest that the vessels were economically healthy, viable spaces, so giving the insurer of the vessels a free pass.[94] If the argument is taken at face value, the condition of Africans at the point of their capture needs to be looked at. The geographical location from which they were kidnapped and the long distance they travelled to reach their point of embarkation might have weakened them and this might have contributed to the death rate on board the ships.[95] What is more, they were starved to make them weak in order to prevent them from rebelling against the ships' masters and crew. By the time they arrived at

[90] Miller, 'Mortality in the Atlantic Slave Trade'. For further detail on mortality see Silva, 'The Atlantic Slave Trade to Maranhão'.
[91] See SOCG, vol. 495a, fl. 54.
[92] See 'Dom Pedro por Graça de Deos', and Katherine Arner, 'Making Yellow Fever American: The Early American Republic, the British Empire and the Geopolitics of Disease in the Atlantic World', *Atlantic Studies*, 2010, 7(4), pp. 447–471.
[93] For debate on Atlantic diseases see Arner, 'Making Yellow Fever American', Wilbur G. Downs, 'History of Epidemiological Aspects of Yellow Fever', *The Yale Journal of Biology and Medicine*, 1982, 55, pp. 179–185; and Frantz Tardo-Dino, *Le Collier de Servitude: La Condition Sanitaire des Esclaves aux Antilles françaises du XVIIe au XIXe siècle*, Paris: Éditions Caribéennes; Agence de Coopération culturelle et technique, 1985.
[94] See Kenneth F. Kiple and Virginia Himmelsteib King, *Another Dimension to the Black Diaspora: Diet, Disease and Racism*, Cambridge: Cambridge University Press, 2003.
[95] On the enslaved's death caused by starvation and long-distance travel, 'Carta de Padre Gonçalo de Sousa por parte do Conselho Municipal de Luanda' [A Letter from Father Gonçalo de Sousa on Behalf of Luanda City Council, Angola], AHU, Angola, cx. 1, 6 July 1633.

their vessels, many did not have the resistance left to survive. As Father Gonçalo de Sousa, who wrote on behalf of the Luanda City Council, Angola, warned the Portuguese Crown, many of the enslaved brought to Luanda's harbour were dying of hunger after a long journey to board the ships and their deaths were caused by the long journeys they had endured.[96]

The Crown opted for the betterment of their conditions in Brazil and failed to make much difference. Russell-Wood states that 'numerous decrees were issued to protect the Negro, such as those aimed at reducing the mortality in the slaving ships (appropriately enough known as *tumbeiros* or pall-bearers) by lessening the numbers of slaves kept below decks, punishment of slave-owners found guilty of cruelty, as well as measures to ensure that every slave received a decent burial'.[97] In fact, Christian masters in Brazil owed a duty of care to the enslaved Africans on the grounds of their membership in the confraternities and thus to the community of the Church. However, it was clear that those whose responsibility it was to protect them were in fact their abusers. Effective protection depended on the law-making authorities ensuring that subjects complied with the legislation. A letter issued by the Vatican confirmed agreement with Mendonça's statement about death toll in the Atlantic:

> ... to this is added an even greater grief on hearing how they are then so cruelly tormented that this results in the loss of innumerable souls, who are rendered desperate by such maltreatment perpetrated by those same Christians who should indeed protect and defend them; and, by the hatred which this conceives, the progress of the missionaries in spreading the holy faith remains impeded.[98]

Regardless of the response by Pedro II to the initial scandal of the enslaved people's treatment in Brazil, the Vatican wanted the governing authorities in these places to take preemptive action that ensured that the abuse was stopped. Despite this response from the Crown, some officials such as those in the Portuguese Overseas Council were still smarting from the Crown's rushed decision to issue the 1684 legislation. They wanted to retain the old practice of slavery in Brazil. The Portuguese Overseas Council's task was to protect the interests of the state rather than the reputation of Christendom, which was a central concern for the Vatican and for Mendonça. Their response was discrete, as they did not want to be seen to deal with issues outside of their jurisdiction.[99] They sent an

---

[96] See 'Carta de Padre Gonçalo de Sousa por parte do Conselho Municipal de Luanda'.
[97] See Russell-Wood, *Fidalgos and Philanthropists*, pp. 139–140.
[98] As quoted by Gray 'The Papacy', p. 60.   [99] SOCG, vol. 490, fl. 140.

anonymous letter to the Vatican to challenge the claims about abuse and the enslaved Africans' lack of freedom.

6.3 MENDONÇA'S TUSSLE WITH THE PORTUGUESE OVERSEAS COUNCIL

When Mendonça made his claim in the Vatican, one of the guilty parties was the Portuguese Overseas Council. Their members, as we have seen, included ex-governors of Angola, Brazil and India. They were directly involved in the processes of hunting down Africans to enslve them and in the acts of violence being committed against them. They were part of the decision-making regarding wars and the so-called just wars.[100] They were receiving one-fifth of the revenue coming from just wars in terms of Africans captured in these wars.[101] They were part of distributing lands to soldiers, and captains.[102] They owned plantations in Brazil, Africa and India. Their labourers were enslaved Africans or Indigenous Brazilians.[103] The Council's position was undermined by Mendonça's reporting of violence and abuse in the slave trade.[104] To protect their interests and maintain their hold over the slave trade, its members needed to act.[105] To do so, they used discreet methods to respond to the Vatican's actions.[106] The Vatican being outside of their jurisdiction, they had to take action without showing their faces. The Vatican nuncio stated that the issue of Brazil was a matter for the Portuguese kings, an issue that tied in with the Portuguese Overseas Council's jurisdiction as least as far as their providing knowledge about it.[107] With Europe not being the space of their operations, they had to use the nuncio in Portugal and also hide behind the anonymous letter, to which we must now return. I argue that the anonymous letter was written by the Portuguese Overseas Council rather than the Spanish authorities, as Gray stated.[108]

---

[100] See Jaca and Moirans, OFM Cap., *Servi Liberi*.
[101] See 'Carta Régia ao Governador de Angola'.
[102] See the Kazanze case in BNL, ms. 241, FG, fls. 174, 182–183, 18–189 v.
[103] See BAL, cartografia, MS. [Topografia (...) Provincia da Quissama} Angola, CA 1622, ARM. Met. X 51-IX-20 (fl. 2) and 'Relação do Padre Mateus Cardoso', and MMA, vol. VII, p. 177.
[104] See SOCG, vol. 495a, fls. 55–56.   [105] See AHU_CU_001, cx. 11, d. 1272.
[106] SOCG, vol. 490, fl. 141.
[107] See AHU_CU_001, cx. 11, d. 1272, and, on the war of Pungo-Andongo, see Relaçam/ Do FELICE SVCCESSO.
[108] Gray, 'The Papacy'.

The anonymous letter, addressed to Cardinal Cybo, had three main points of focus: (i) social disorder, (ii) the Africans' culture and (iii) labour and the reward of the Christian faith. Firstly, relating to social disorder: the argument presented was that there is no legal precedent for the crime committed and that the civil authorities could not comply with this new demand. 'I am of the opinion that for the ministers to give a new law concerning grave and terrible things presented by the Procurator of Indies of the Blacks' congregation will cause disorder; from experience in obtaining briefings on this topic, the result has been superfluous.'[109]

The second argument was to question the credibility of Mendonça's information and allege that African culture was inherently evil: 'you must be aware that the person who brought this information was not informed about the truth concerning the culture of these barbarous [people]'.[110] Mendonça, in order to rebut the Portuguese Overseas Council's claim, revealed his identity and the fact that he had the blood of the kings of Kongo and Angola in his veins.[111] In other words, he was descended from the region in which both Kongo and Angolan kings had been defending their subjects from slavery.[112] As mentioned in Chapter 5, both Afonso I and Garcia II had protested to the kings of Portugal. The Vatican had also received a complaint from the Kongo about their subjects being hunted and kidnapped.[113] On 25 October 1617, Dom Alvaro III of Kongo complained to Pope Paul V about the Portuguese attack on his kingdom, in which his people were being hunted by the Portuguese and taken into slavery.[114]

The third argument was based on monetary considerations, especially on the price of the enslaved people: 'you must know that a Black is bought for 600 or more Spanish dollars; since a Black cost so much, one must take care of him, as if he is his own son, and his owner governs him with a great deal of meanness.'[115] Enslaved Africans were costly and as a result it made sense for their owners to care for them; the enslaved people's economic

---

[109] 'Instrutione Gagisterno Cybo', *Scritt Riferite nei Congressi*, paragraph 1.
[110] See 'Instrutione Gagisterno Cybo', *Scritt Riferite nei Congressi*, paragraph 2.
[111] SOCG, vol. 490, fl. 140.
[112] See Afonso I's criticism of the slave trade, Ruious 18–10–1526, Remetente: Del Rey de Manycõgo, ATT-CC-I-35-21., pp. 489–490, and 'Carta do Bispo de Cabo Verde a El-Rei'; 'Carta de D. Garcia II Rei do Kongo ao Padre Reitor do Colégio de Luanda'; Philipe Hari I's criticismo in AHU – Códice. 15, fl. 103 and 96v, and that of King Ngola Mbamdi in 'Relação de Fernão de Sousa a El-Rei'.
[113] Vatican Library [VL], cód. VL, 12516, fl. 66, 25 October 1617.
[114] VL, cód. VL 12516, fl. 66.
[115] See 'Instrutione Gagisterno Cybo', *Scritt Riferite nei Congressi*, paragraph 3.

value made it impossible for the owners not to look after them. However, as we saw in Chapter 3, Antonil had questioned the slave-masters in Brazil about their duty of care towards enslaved Africans and many were given no care at all. According to Antonil, animals were better cared for than the enslaved Africans.[116] The Portuguese Overseas Council argued that the enslaved were generally well cared for, but that because of the Africans' violent nature the slave-masters sometimes had to use force to punish them; thus, in order for the owners to be protected, if any of the enslaved Africans reacted in a 'beastly manner against his owner, it is necessary to punish him severely in the most violent manner with the burning highly used for animals otherwise he would kill his lord, as has happened many times, such punishment is therefore inevitable'.[117] The council attempted to cast doubt on Mendonça's court case by claiming that 'if Blacks behave humanly well, it is false to state that they are been treated inhumanly, because of their high cost one must seriously take care of them'[118]. However, some priests who had worked in Brazil, including those who visited it, were shocked to see the levels of cruelty against the enslaved Africans. They claimed the violence used against the enslaved people was not comparable to that used against the Christians by the Moors.[119] In 1701 in the city of Salvador, where Mendonça had stayed, the treatment of the enslaved Africans was described as a 'barbaric, cruel, and bizarre way that the majority of masters treat their unfortunate working slaves'.[120] Other visitors were less empathetic. French merchant Louis-François de Tollenare, who lived in Brazil from 1816 until 1818, thought the issue of the enslaved Africans not worth considering as a subject of analysis, nor even categorising them as human beings, because they were not regarded as such, but were 'cattle'.[121]

Another further argument was developed from the third, taking the criterion of 'nature' as its justification. The economic case was used to

---

[116] See Andreoni (Antonil), *Cultura e Opulência*.
[117] See 'Instrutione Gagisterno Cybo', *Scritt Riferite nei Congressi*, paragraph 3.
[118] See 'Instrutione Gagisterno Cybo', *Scritt Riferite nei Congressi*, paragraph 3.
[119] See Conrad, *Children of God's Fire*.
[120] See Luis dos Santos Vilhena, *Recopilaçã de Noticias Soterpolitanas e Brasilicas Contidas em XX Cartas que da Cidade de Salvador, Bahia de Todos os Santos, Escreve hum a Outro Amigo em Lisboa*, Salvador: Imprensa Official do Estado, 1921–1922, II, pp. 187–189, as cited by Conrad, *Children of God's Fire*, p. 61.
[121] See Louis-François de Tollenare, *Notas Dominicaes Tomadas Durante uma Residencia em Portugal e no Brasil nos Annos de 1816, 1817 e 1818, Parte Relativa a Pernambuco*, Recife: Empreza do Jornal do Recife, 1905, pp. 78–87, 93–96, as cited by Conrad, *Children of God's Fire*, p. 63.

justify the enslavement of the Africans in Brazil. Wadström stated that once the project of enslaving the Indigenous Americans failed, the focus was on the Africans.[122] The weakness of the Indigenous Americans was used as an excuse to justify and normalise the Africans' enslavement. The Indigenous Americans, they said, had no interest in the land and as a result their land could be taken away from them, whilst the Africans for their part were interested in the land but were people accustomed to slavery; and their experience of the African climate helped them survive hard work in the Americas. The Africans, being from a slaving society, could be enslaved:

You must be aware that America has great need of Negroes, either for irrigating the land or for mining, for no one can cope with such heat and the painful jobs, and I hope that either the kingdom of Spain or that of Holland is continuing to go to Guinea to buy a large number of barbarous Blacks and idolatrous and subsequently sell them in the American harbours.[123]

Enslaved Africans were the backbone of the Brazilian economy. They were the 'feet' and 'hands' of the slave-owners in Brazil. Slavery, as the bishop of Cape Verde put it, helped create the Portuguese class society; or at least it helped establish it on a firm footing. According to him, many Portuguese shunned manual labour and got the enslaved Africans to do it.[124] As we saw in Chapter 2, Vieira relied on the Philippine ideology according to which without enslaved Africans there could be no Brazil.[125]

Christianity was presented as the reward for the enslaved Africans' toil in Brazil. Their bodies became the embodiment of labour. Their culture was considered antagonistic to Western Christendom, so converting them to Christianity was viewed as a way of domesticating them. As Vieira put it, the heavens must be theirs after their toils on Earth.[126] The Portuguese Overseas Council declared that Christianity offered a better solution for them: 'they are to be baptised, and to be indoctrinated in the Christian doctrine, and at the end they are more docile than Native Americans, and better Catholics, and the end result is very good for the soul and body.'[127] Their suffering was justified by their future reward in heaven. Cruelty was normalised and unleashed according to how submissive they were to their masters. As Bogle notes, enslaved Africans in North American plantations

---

[122] Wadström, *Observations on the Slave Trade*.
[123] See 'Instrutione Gagisterno Cybo', *Scritt Riferite nei Congressi*, paragraph 4.
[124] 'Carta do Bispo de Cabo Verde a El-Rei'.
[125] By Philipine, I mean the ideology associated with the rule of the kings of Spain who ruled Portugal at the time of the Union of the Two Crowns.
[126] See Vieira, *Sermões*.
[127] 'Instrutione Gagisterno Cybo', *Scritt Riferite nei Congressi*, paragraph 4.

were classified by submissiveness: 'Toms' were good slaves and submissive, whereas 'Bad Bucks' were those considered big, strong and violent types.[128] In the matter of religion, the Africans showed a better disposition in accommodating to Christian values than the Indigenous Brazilians; this was a reason why they were enslaved in the Americas. The argument was that enslavement eliminated the deficit inherent in their culture – part of which was the accusation that they practised cannibalism.[129] The Africans' supposed inhumanity was used to justify treaing them like animals.

The Jagas of Angola, as a group of people, were described as cannibals, because of their non-domestication to Western culture. They resisted the Portuguese influence in Kongo.[130] On 1 May 1594, a priest's report from Angola stated that 'there were forty wealthy Portuguese men who lived on this island [Luanda], they came from the kingdom of Kongo, because of the Jacas [Jagas], ferocious barbarians who fed themselves on human flesh'.[131] Jaga became a synonym for cannibal and was generalised as a term to cover most Africans. The Overseas Council used the myth to undermine Mendonça's complaint in the Vatican: 'Whilst in their countries they were butchering each other, like beasts among themselves and feasted on such meat.'[132]

The process of taming the Africans in the Atlantic region was used as an argument that the price for their liberation must be taken into account, along with the investment in them – their market price and the other costs of making them part of human society. All these costs needed to be included in the debate about their liberation. The liberty of enslaved people was outweighed by the costs incurred in educating them and providing them with skills. Slavery had it benefits in promoting Christianity, and because it cost less than making the enslaved into good citizens:

> ... you need be aware that it is impossible to practise the restitution of freedom for the service of 10 years, taking into account that they are very expensive since it would seem a vanity, for the first price is 600, and it may cost the first more than

---

[128] See Donald Bogle, *Toms, Coons, Mulattos, Mammies and Bucks: An Interpretive History of Blacks in American Films*, New York: Continuum, 1989.

[129] See Cadornega, *História Geral*, vol. III; Hilton, 'The Jaga Reconsidered'; Miller, 'Requiem for the Jaga' and Candido, *An African Slaving Port*.

[130] See Hilton, 'The Jaga Reconsidered'.

[131] 'História da Residência dos Padres da Companhia de Jesus em Angola, e Cousas Tocantes ao Reino, e Conquista', MMA, vol. IV, p. 554, 'nesta ilha moravão quarenta homens portugueses muito ricos, que se tinhão recolhido do Reyno de Congo por causa dos Jacas, ferocíssimos barbaros que se mantém de carnehumana, e tinhão destruido, e comido todo aquele Reyno', and Birmingham, *Trade and Conquest*, pp. 43–48.

[132] 'Instrutione Gagisterno Cybo', *Scritt Riferite nei Congressi*, paragraph 4.

1000 pesos to buy the slave. There are other costs to bring him up in the faith, and to teach him skills.[133]

The economic argument was thus used to downplay Atlantic slavery, which was presented as an investment in the Africans' integration into Western human society. The author(s) of the anonymous letter thus made the perverse claim that the effects of abolishing slavery on the economy of the Luso-Hispanic regions mattered more than the freedom the Africans would gain if they were liberated from slavery. Standard taxes of 20 per cent of all enslaved Africans taken to the Americas would be lost as a result of abolition. The problem of the financial difficulties that would arise is succinctly stated, 'however, this will be momentarily difficult because His Majesty gains great sums in taxes from such sales [and he] won't prejudice this through such change'.[134]

The economic argument was extended to the children of the enslaved people, given that their freedom would depend on the price ratio of their parents – if parents werte brought cheaply the children were held in captivity for less time than if parents were brought more expensivley: 'In the future it could be ordered that children remain free and, in this way, they would buy the fathers at a lower price.'[135] This argument was aimed at postponing the harmful economic loss involved in freeing the Africans and at maintaining the institution of the Atlantic slave trade, enabling it to survive in Africa and Brazil for another 204 years, until 1888, when it was finally abolished in Brazil. It was argued: 'It is well possible to give freedom to their children as born from a baptised father; but this will be difficult to obtain because sometimes the father is bought old, and [they] will gain dividend through the slavery of their children.'[136] The 'free womb law' that allowed children born of enslaved parents to be freed did not come into effect in Brazil until 1871.[137]

The author(s) of the anonymous letter set out to demonstrate a Christian attitude by involving Cardinal Millini, who could write to the king of Portugal to alleviate the ill treatment of the enslaved Africans: 'anyway, it could be written to Cardinal Millini to recommend to His Majesty that the

---

[133] 'Instrutione Gagisterno Cybo', *Scritt Riferite nei Congressi*, paragraph 5.
[134] 'Instrutione Gagisterno Cybo', *Scritt Riferite nei Congressi*.
[135] 'Instrutione Gagisterno Cybo', *Scritt Riferite nei Congressi*.
[136] 'Instrutione Gagisterno Cybo', *Scritt Riferite nei Congressi*.
[137] Sidney Chalhoub, 'Interpreting Machado De Assis: Paternalism, Slavery, and the Free Womb Law' in Sueann Caulfield, Sarah C. Chambers and Lara Putnam (eds.), *Honor, Status, and Law in Modern Latin America*, Durham, NC: Duke University Press, 2005, pp. 87–108.

Blacks who become Catholics are well treated'.[138] Since the Crown acted on Millini's recommendation, their action fell short of the expectation of the confraternities,[139] and was reduced to the slave ship reform.

6.4 CONCLUDING REMARKS

Pedro II had missed the central point raised by Mendonça, that the slave trade should be abolished. Mendonça was arguing not that the enslaved people's conditions be improved and that they be treated better, but rather that they should be made free persons as members of the Christian community. Clearly their suffering was one of the many issues to address. Cardinal Cybo, the addressee of the anonymous letter by the Portuguese Overseas Council, summed up what already was in Mendonça's court case, namely that 'they [the enslaved] are burnt with flames and the fat used to cook the roast on the fire is poured on them. So many kinds of impious tyrannical behaviour weigh on them that many of the so-called Blacks, suffocate themselves by despair, holding their breath to the point of asphyxiation, or they suffocate themselves with their own hands when their hands are let free. Many of them run into the sea to drown, when they are free to do so.'[140] For Mendonça the problem of enslaving the Africans lies at the point of hunting them downand kidnapping them, and in the use of violence to capture them from their homes and fields in Africa. This is the root of the problem that the Crown ought to tackle: if they were to get rid of slavery, they must begin in Africa. To achieve this, they need to aim at rooting out the buyers and sellers who, in Mendonça's view, were European Christian merchants.[141] Then the Crown must ensure that the slave-masters gave proper treatment to those already enslaved in Brazil. Nonetheless, their status as enslaved persons must not last beyond seven years, similar to that of the biblical liberation of the Old Testament.

However, to do justice to Mendonça's impact on the Portuguese Crown, the Portuguese authority took action to remedy the situation of the enslaved Africans in Angola, Cape Verde and Brazil, after the Vatican sent a letter to nuncios in both Portugal and Madrid requesting them to talk to governing authorities in Lisbon and Spain respectively.[142] Cardinal

---

[138] 'Instrutione Gagisterno Cybo', *Scritt Riferite nei Congressi*.
[139] See SOCG, vol. 495a, fls. 55–56.   [140] SOCG, 490, fl., fol. 138 and fl. 145.
[141] See SOCG, vol. 495a, fl. 54.
[142] See APF, 'Lettere della S. Congregazione' [A Letter of the Holy Congregation], 73, fls. 9v-10 and fls. 10v-11v, 6 March 1684.

Cybo wrote to Cardinal Millini urging him to act on behalf of the Holy Office in Rome regarding the plight of Africans enslaved in Brazil or in the 'Indies, ... on seeing that there still continues in those parts such a detestable abuse as to sell human blood, sometimes even with fraud and violence'.[143] Summarising Mendonça's presentation, Cybo stated that such a practice in Brazil 'involves a disgraceful offence against Catholic liberty, by condemning to perpetual slavery not only those who are bought and sold, but also the sons and daughters who are born to them, although they have been made Christians'.[144] Mendonça's intention was to end the institution of slavery entirely – his was a demand for justice and an advocacy of human rights.

My argument is that the Portuguese Overseas Council was involved in the decision-making on slavery and that this was an issue that fell within their grasp. Their positioning made them unlikely to engage seriously with a policy change that might benefit Africans and threaten the Crown's interests. However, the confraternities' right to seek justice and freedom for their members empowered them to challenge the actions of the council. The legitimacy of the confraternities' operations within the world of Christendom, affording them a legal platform for freedom and expression of justice, granted them the right to take action against the force that was propelled to annihilate them.[145]

Central to the response from the Portuguese Overseas Council was the depiction of the Black African enslaved as backwards, helpless and unimaginative.[146] Black African humanity was presented as different and strange, the embodiment of the Other and incontrovertibly inferior to Iberian culture.[147] The conception of African humanity that appeared in the anonymous letter was composed of a system of presentations and representations encoded by the same set of economic, political and cultural forces that had brought the slave trade into the consciousness of the Iberian Peninsula, and later of the Americas.[148] Is it not intriguing that Jagas enslaved in Brazil or in the Americas would cease to consume human flesh, abandoning a practice for which they were notorious?[149] It is worth noting that many slave-masters were killed by those they enslaved, but we have no record of the killers feasting on their flesh. If they were cannibals,

---

[143] Gray, 'The Papacy', p. 60.   [144] Gray, 'The Papacy', p. 60.
[145] See 'Carta de El-Rei D. João III'.
[146] See SOCG, vol. 490, fl. 141 and SOCG, vol. 495a, fls. 56–57.
[147] See the 'Carta do Nuncio do Vaticano'.
[148] See Oliveira, *A Arte da Guerra et do Mar*.   [149] See Cadornega, *As História Geral*.

they would certainly have maintained such a ritual practice in the Americas, as evidence has shown the level of their cultural retention in Brazil in areas such as music, religion, gastronomy, technology, arts and language was strong.[150]

In the Portuguese Overseas Council's view of the slave trade, enslaved Africans were framed in a binary-opposition power relation between dominant and dominated – masters and enslaved people – and the links between culture and power.[151] The relationship between slave-owners and enslaved people was a relationship of power, of domination and of varying degrees of complex hegemony.[152] I contend that the Atlantic space became a site of description and the Portuguese Overseas Council used descriptions that seemed best suited to their purpose, these becoming the language of learning and knowing for the people who lived in these regions of the world. As Rorty argues, 'most oppressors have had the wit to teach the oppressed a language in which the oppressed will sound crazy'.[153] The confraternities' struggle with the Portuguese Overseas Council was over a distorted description of the former that the council wanted the Vatican to accept, but they wanted to bring to light their Atlantic plight and disseminate it into the wider public domain of Luso-Hispanic society of the seventeenth century.

Slavery was justified by the supposed deficits and evils of African culture and religion.[154] Western Christendom was a moral and civilisational yardstick against which to measure African culture and religion.[155] The absence of meaningful translations of concepts from African cultures by which the rulers of Christendom could understand them helped make defensible the culture that supported the slave trade.[156] Cruel treatment of the enslaved was explained away on the basis of this deficit in their culture.[157] African cultures were judged as violent, subhuman and cannibalistic.[158] The Africans' right to justice was denied and, when accepted, was measured by reference to Christian values, hence Western

---

[150] See Rodrigues, 'As sublevações de negros no Brasil'.
[151] See Russell-Wood, *Fidalgos and Philanthropists*.
[152] See Said, *Orientalism* and Stuart Hall, *Representation*, London: Sage, 2013.
[153] Richard Rorty, 'Feminism and Pragmatism', in Russell S. Goodman (ed.), *Pragmatism: Critical Concepts in Philosophy*, New York: Routledge, 1995, pp. 1–35 (pp. 3–14).
[154] SOCG, vol. 490, fl. 141.   [155] Cadornega, *As História Geral*, I, II and III.
[156] For the pope's bull, see Brásio, *Monumenta Missionaria Africana*, vol. I, fl. 28, pp. 277–286.
[157] see Brásio, *Monumenta Missionaria Africana*, vol. I, ffl28, pp. 277–286.
[158] SOCG, vol. 490, fl. 141.

Christendom.[159] Their enslavement was seen as a natural process, even though they had accepted membership of the Christian community.[160]

Mendonça challenged the Portuguese Overseas Council's interpretation of African culture and questioned their ideology. He challenged the Iberian or Luso-Hispanic economic scheme and its colonial foundation.[161] His case in the Vatican was a direct challenge to the Iberian decision-makers, hence the Portuguese Overseas Council and the Council of Indies.[162] He interrogated the very scheme to which his family was subjected and the validity of the economic model and the power of the Portuguese Overseas Council,[163] who were the rulers of the empire.[164] He also challenged the fabric of the Atlantic project. Notwithstanding this, the Portuguese Overseas Council attempted to change the Vatican's verdict in their favour. They used economic arguments as the basis for their relationship with African élites. Mendonça's taking the case to the Vatican implicitly defied the Portuguese Overseas Council to admit that their stance on African politics and economics was not viable. The case of his family's allegiance to Portugal was part of the Portuguese-wide strategic allegiances in the Atlantic.[165]

The fundamental difference between Mendonça and the Portuguese Overseas Council lies, I argue, in the different values each ascribes to Christianity and membership of the Church.[166] According to Mendonça, attachment to Christianity and the confraternity forms part of legal justice. Such a confraternity's right to justice is therefore an essential part of common humanity. According to Moirans, natural law makes all persons free and autonomous:

> ... of this essential freedom that resides formally in the will of man, [natural law] is immutable by eternal, immovable law. Natural freedom of man is deduced, that is, natural law is autonomous. Since, therefore, all men by eternal law have freedom in their will, by natural law, he is a free person from any man and remains autonomous[167].

---

[159] See the letter by the dean of the Jesuits Society in Angola stating that the Kongolese were deemed Christians, but they should be treated equally to Angolans who were subjects of the king of Portugal. 'Carta de Manoel Fernandes Curado a El-Rei' [Carta de Manoel Fernandes Curado to the King], AHU, Angola, cx. 8, 29 July 1665.
[160] See Vieira, Sermões.   [161] See Acemoglu and Robinson, Why Nations Fail.
[162] See Birmingham, Trade and Conquest, p. 153; and SOCG, vol. 495a, fls. 54–55.
[163] See Cadornega, As História Geral.
[164] See Caetano, O Conselho Ultramarino; Myrup, 'To Rule from Afar'.
[165] All the king's alies were liable to pay baculamento, see Freudenthal and Pantoja, Livro dos Baculamentos.
[166] Faria, 'Sobre a Fundação de Seminários'.
[167] Jaca and Moirans OFM Cap., 'Servi Liberi', p. 199.

Fostering membership for the common good is therefore among the most important contributions Mendonça made to the life of the enslaved Africans; in this he departs significantly from the Portuguese Overseas Council.[168] The council denied that Christian membership implied common humanity and denied that meaningful ties of Christendom could develop the right to justice. This interpretation of the differences between the Portuguese Overseas Council and Mendonça points to an important understanding of natural law, and thus to the conceptual understanding of human value. Moirans, in his defence of the Africans against their enslavement, claimed that 'Blacks are enslaved against natural law and it must also be considered that they have been made slaves against positive divine law.'[169]

I argue that the letters of apologetics, which priests and governors of Angola alike addressed to the Crown and notably the local city council during 1623–1671, cannot bear the interpretation usually put upon them. That is to say, that Angolans were a slaving society and that they were preventing governors and merchants from trading in the so-called Angolan markets. It was a period marked by the climaxes of the governor-sponsored and military suppression of Angolans. In 1623, a special mission had arrived in Angola led by the Judge (Syndicante) of the Crown to closely look at how matters were developing in Angola.[170] As we saw in Chapter 1, political tension that led to several arrests of members of the Muncipal City Council of Luanda and some Jesuit priests, and to the deaths of Kazanze leaders, may have broken out in the same year, in which 1,200 people including children and old men were illegally sent to Brazil as enslaved people by Correia de Sousa. By 1671, Pungo-Andongo was destroyed, with the rest of the royals sent to Brazil and subsequently to Portugal. It should not be surprising, therefore, that Mendonça had taken a criminal court case to the Vatican and presented a firm stand on the issue of kidnapping, coercion, violence and abuse of Africans.

In his early years in Angola, Mendonça would have been aware of the situation of his family and their coercion into paying *baculamento*, endorsed by all Portuguese governors and former governors of Angola who were then members of the Portuguese Overseas Council, and he had seen his grandfather fighting them regarding slavery. Mendonça wished to

---

[168] See Jaca and Moirans, OFM Cap., 'Servi Liberi', p. 207.
[169] See Jaca and Moirans, OFM Cap., 'Servi Liberi'.
[170] See High Court of Appeal 'Relação de Antonio Bezerra Fajardo', and 'Padre Mateus Cardoso's High Court of Appeal'.

take the initiative at this crucial moment when the opportunity was presented to him through his appointment as an international lawyer for the Black confraternities, in Africa, Brazil, Portugal and Spain, and elsewhere in the world of Christendom.[171] He followed a legal procedure and set almost all his grievances aside, as he offered to portray the plight of the enslaved majority.[172] He felt justified in letting the world know their side of the story. With such a platform at the Vatican, he presented explosive issues regarding how Africans were being enslaved. For the confraternities and enslaved Africans, the most explosive issues had been the use of force and violence, the retention of children born in captivity as enslaved people and the barbaric crimes committed against Africans by the Christian kingdoms, their governors, priests, buyers and sellers in the process of enslavement.[173] The art of public speech would have suited him, such as represented by his presentation of a criminal court case. He came from a tradition, that of the Kimbundu, in which rigorous training for public speech was fundamental, particularly for those like him who took up the role of *Machungy*; a position of ambassador and lawyer.[174] His court case in the Vatican was a greater condemnation of Atlantic slavery than we have up until now been led to believe. However, the court case he presented cannot exhaust the sense of injustice that he himself had gone through and witnessed. He was an international lawyer par excellence.

---

[171] S.C. Africa, vol. I, fl. 487.   [172] S.C. Africa, vol. I, fl. 486.
[173] See SOCG, vol. 495a, fls. 54–55.   [174] Cadornega, *As História Geral*, vol. I, II and III.

Conclusion

Considerable scholarship has traced the flows of captives from West Central Africa, especially the Kongo and Angola areas, and the Bights of Benin, Biafra and the Upper Guinea Coast. However, this book is the first work to consider the movement for the abolition of slavery in the seventeenth century as a unified endeavour in both the Old and New Worlds. This book has engaged with African abolition and the wider Atlantic network, including not only enslaved Africans but also New Christians and Indigenous Americans in the mid-seventeenth century. Anglophone and Lusophone scholars have paid little attention to the Black Atlantic abolitionist movement beyond the Americas, a topic that has been considered in depth here. Let me summarise my main findings.

I have examined in great detail Mendonça's court case regarding the abolition of slavery, which he presented before the Congregation of Propaganda Fide, the office charged with missionary work in Africa, Asia and the New World, that is, the Americas, in the Vatican, Rome, Italy on 6 March 1684. I have argued that it was not a petition, as Gray in his erudite article on *The Papacy and the Atlantic Slave Trade* has led us to believe.[1] Rather, it was a criminal court case, brought against the Vatican, the governing authorities of Italy, Portugal, Spain and Christian slave merchants for their involvement in the Atlantic slave trade.[2]

Mendonça began his criminal court proceedings on the basis of four principles contravened by the enslavement of the Africans: human, natural, divine and civil laws. To bolster his legal case, he demonstrated how

---

[1] See Gray, 'The Papacy'.
[2] SOCG, vol. 495a, fls. 54–55; SOCG, vol. 495a, fls. 62 and SOCG, vol. 490, fls. 140–141.

the enslaved Africans were captured in Africa before being brought to Europe and the Atlantic to labour. I have contended that Mendonça advanced his intervention in the Vatican by exhibiting three major cases and *modus operandi* deployed in securing and enslaving the Africans: (i) abduction/kidnapping; (ii) raiding/hunting and (iii) salvaging, that is, saving Africans from death. Firstly, he demonstrated that African boys and girls were abducted from their mothers and sold to Christian merchants who in turn sold them in Europe in a manner akin to cattle. Secondly, he explained that Africans were hunted and raided from their fields and farms, as one would hunt animals, put together to procreate, and their offspring then put up for sale at auctions for profit. Thirdly, he elucidated that it is a false affirmation that Africans who were at war with each other, ate their captives or sold them to merchants.[3] Wadström, in his account to the British Privy Council in 1792 on the British abolitionist debate, noted that inter-ethnic wars in Africa rarely took place, and in most cases were instigated by European merchants, who often coerced their African allies.[4] According to Moirans and Jaca's evidence in the Vatican, this salvaging of war captives was seen as a lesser crime.[5] Abduction and raiding were the most significant crimes committed against the Africans.

Mendonça's court case in the Vatican revealed the truth[6] about Atlantic slavery and its injustices as endorsed by the Vatican's bulls and implemented by the Italian and Luso-Hispanic governing authorities and their priests, merchants, buyers and sellers in Africa, the Americas and Europe. I have claimed that Mendonça accused the Vatican of being involved in *actus reus*, of being negligent and lacking a duty of care to the enslaved Africans who were Christians, as were the Indigenous Americans and the New Christians. The Vatican was acting in contravention of laws that it was meant to uphold and was thus implicated in the crimes committed against the enslaved in the Atlantic region. The pope was to be considered guilty of the same crimes as the merchants, governors and ships' captains in the Atlantic and in the New World. All knew the suffering of the enslaved people, but deliberately or intentionally decided to ignore it. In so doing, they were committing a crime against humanity. Mendonça advocated that the Vatican, instead of curing their wounds, that is alleviating the enslaved people's suffering, was aggravating them. Ill-treatment of the enslaved Africans was not helped by the Vatican's

---

[3] See SOCG, vol. 495a, fls. 54–55.   [4] See Wadström, *An Essay on Colonization*.
[5] See Jaca and Moirans OFM Cap., 'Servi Liberi'.   [6] See S.C. Africa, vol. 1, fl. 486.

bulls, which were passed on to the Portuguese Crown in the fifteenth century, as we saw in Chapter 5. As Moirans put it, what was happening in the Atlantic was undertaken with the full knowledge of the governors, and the governors were responsible to the Catholic kings and the Catholic kings were responsible to the pope.[7]

In order to contextualise the court case and explain his pioneering claims I have meticulously traced the trajectory of Mendonça's life journey and his background in Angola, his work in Salvador, Rio de Janeiro, Braga, Lisbon, Toledo and the Vatican as a student and as an attorney for the Black Christian Brotherhood in the Atlantic. I have examined his claims for abolition, in which he argued for the freedom of those enslaved from their 'captivity after seven or ten years of service' and condemned the entire foundation of Atlantic slavery.[8] I have challenged the established interpretation of Mendonça's presentation in the Vatican, which saw him as seeking only that the Holy Office deal with the suffering of enslaved Africans in the Atlantic and liberate the enslaved African Christians and their offspring. Instead, I have suggested that he was arguing for a universal condemnation of slavery. I have argued that Mendonça defied the Vatican to examine its own position, as passed via papal bulls to the Luso-Hispanic crowns between the fifteenth and seventeenth centuries, and to condemn and abolish Atlantic slavery in its entirety. And I have proposed that Mendonça's universal condemnation of Atlantic slavery and demand for the abolition of the slave trade and liberation of enslaved Africans came about because of his role as an attorney for the Black Christian Brotherhood, a role conferred on him by the king of the Christian Kingdom (Spain), Carlos II, and the archbishop of Toledo, Luis Manuel Fernández de Portocarrero y de Guzman. His abolition claims thus transcended Luso-Hispanic frontiers to include other non-Iberian empires in Africa, the Americas and Europe, and enabled him to take his criminal court case to the Supreme Court of Christendom in an attempt to overturn Nicholas V's bull, which was the foundation of perpetual Atlantic slavery.[9]

To understand the historical setting and background of the court case, I have explored the Atlantic slave trade by examining cases in Angola and Kongo. I have looked at the case of the wars against Kazanze and Bumbi, which reveal the need to reassess our understanding of Atlantic slavery and see clearly the unlawful strategies of enslavement by the Portuguese.

---

[7] See Jaca and Moirans OFM Cap., *Servi Liberi*.   [8] See SOCG, vol. 495a, fls. 54 to 55.
[9] See 'Carta de Giacinto Rogio Monzon'.

The king of Kongo, Pedro II (1622–1624), showed no interest in the tax returns that his counterparts, the Luso-Hispanic kings such as Philipe IV (1621–1640) in Madrid, were entitled to for the enslaved Kongolese sent to Brazil by the governor of Angola, Correia de Sousa. While Philipe IV demanded a tax rebate for the captives sent to Brazil, Pedro II simply wanted his people returned to the Kongo.[10] Furthermore, when Afonso I (1509–1543), king of Kongo, sent students to Portugal to study, he paid their fees with ivory and not with the revenues from slavery.[11] In order to obtain enslaved people, Portuguese governors in Angola had used *guerra preta*, Angolan contingent soldiers trained to fight alongside the Portuguese. Most of the recruited Angolans came directly from the region in which *sobas* or Angolan provincial governors allied to the Portuguese project of conquest were stationed.[12] *Guerra preta,* such as Sequeira, Bango Bango, King Philipe Hari I (1626–1664; Lourenço Mendonça da Silva's grandfather), Dom Inacio da Silva (Lourenco Mendonça da Silva's father) and Dom Francisco (Lourenco Mendonça da Silva's uncle) were thus used to advance the Portuguese project of conquest in Angola,[13] and were promised rewards and lands in Angola from the conquered territory.[14] Their use became part of the pattern of the Portuguese expansion, and they were the most committed warlords in the Portuguese conquest of Angola. Their participation helps explain the Portuguese attitude to coercion, abduction, kidnapping and pillage in the region. Such actions at the local level plainly suited the governors' interests, as well as those of most of the resident traders in Luanda.[15] The Portuguese tactics hardly encouraged the so-called enemies to initiate negotiations, rather they prompted explosive reactions from the Africans, who were not prepared to give in to Portuguese demands, such as Queen Njinga.[16] This inevitably led to war being waged against those Africans who resisted the coercive alliance with Portugal. For the governors, the obvious solution to the crises that they had, in general, instigated, was the use of military force;[17] as the Angolan oral tradition has it, the Europeans who arrived in

---

[10] Philipe IV asked for a return of enslaved Angolans send to Brazil in 'Carta Régia ao Vice-Rei de Portugal', AHU, cód. 295, fl. 80.
[11] See AHU, Angola, cx. 2. [12] See Candido, *An African Slaving Port*.
[13] See Cadornega, *História Geral*.
[14] See 'Carta João Correia de Sousa ao Marquês de Frecilha', and 'Relação do Padre Mateus Cardoso'.
[15] See 'Relação do Padre Mateus Cardoso', 'Carta João Correia de Sousa ao Marquês de Frecilha'.
[16] On Ndongo's war see, Relaçam/ Do FELICE SVCCESSO.
[17] See Relaçam/ Do FELICE SVCCESSO.

the region 'spat fire' on their ancestors, meaning that they used firearms on them.[18]

The period from 1617 to 1667 marked one of the peaks of the Portuguese practices of suppression, war, violence and abuse of the Kongolese and Angolan people in West Central Africa. Politically and economically motivated violence took place in both Angola and Kongo during the period.[19] As Cadornega, a contemporary historian from the period, confirmed, about 1,000,000 people from Angola had been enslaved and sent to Brazil by the end of the seventeenth century.[20] The kidnapping of old people, women and children and their sending to Brazil as enslaved people was common practice.[21] In one case I have examined how the governor, Correia de Sousa, kidnapped 1,200 people in 1623 from Kazanze, half of whom died on board the ships that were taking them to the city of Salvador, Bahia, and a life of slavery.[22] In the same year, the Philippine administration in Spain, in one of its biggest scandals, sent a crown judge, Fajardo, to investigate numerous cases in the region, including Correia de Sousa's case. The Kongo authorities appealed to the Vatican and Madrid to take action against Correia de Sousa to prevent retaliation from the people in Kongo, who had already threatened to take the issue into their own hands and had accused the king of Kongo of protecting the country enemies.[23] In 1671, an outbreak of violence, spearheaded by the governor of Angola, Távora, destroyed the kingdom of Pungo-Andongo in Angola. As a result, more than 2,000 people were sent to Brazil as enslaved people, including Mendonça and his brothers, uncles, aunts and cousins, all exiled as prisoners of war. I have used these cases to refute the established thinking that Africans were willing participants in the Atlantic slave trade ('Africans themselves were active participants in the slave trade and because slavery was widespread in Africa')[24] and the idea that markets for enslaved Africans already existed in Africa

---

[18] For a detailed discussion of the oral tradition of the region, see G. L. Haveaux, *La Tradition Historique des Bapende Orientaux*, Brussels, 1954, pp. 35–37 and 46–47. Here I am indebted to David Birmingham.

[19] See Mbwila's war, 'Relação da Batalha de Ambuíla', [Report on the War in Ambuíla], MB, Addicional n. 20.953, fls. 227–229, 29 October 1665, and in MMA, vol. XII, pp. 582–591.

[20] See Cadornega, *História Geral*.

[21] For a detailed discussion of Benguela's captives, see Candido, *An African Slaving Port*.

[22] See 'Carta João Correia de Sousa ao Marquês de Frecilha'.

[23] See Mbwila's war of 1665, 'Relação da Batalha de Ambuíla', and Heywood and Thornton, *Central Africans*.

[24] See Thornton, *Africa and Africans in the Making of the Atlantic World*, p. 74.

before the Portuguese conquest.[25] In the book I have revisited these legends in light of the Vatican's bulls and the *baculamento* imposed by Portuguese governor Fernão de Sousa on African allies in Angola, which required them to make tax payments in enslaved people. I have shown that this was a turning point in because it shaped the operation of the slave trade in the region as well as its normalisation in the the eighteenth and nineteenth centuries.

It follows that it was no surprise that Mendonça took a court case to the Vatican that explicitly referred to issues of violence, kidnapping and coercion.[26] Indeed, if we are to engage critically with the attitude of the Portuguese governing authorities in Luanda, we should look at the immediate problem of what the governors hoped to achieve in the seventeenth century and beyond in capturing Africans.[27]

Before reaching the Vatican, Mendonça had galvanised the support of confraternities of Black Brotherhoods of enslaved and free people of African descent in Brazil, Portugal and Spain, where he had travelled and lived, and had formed within different organisations of 'men', 'women' and 'youth'.[28] These organisations formed pressure groups, sending letters to the Vatican that urged Pope Innocent XI to take action to abolish Atlantic slavery. All the confraternities of Black Brotherhoods in the Americas gave evidence in support of Mendonça's case in the Vatican through their representatives in the City of Salvador, Bahia, Brazil.[29] I have argued that Mendonça mobilised this activist movement against slavery in the seventeenth century, and that the movement achieved greater international solidarity even than the anti-slavery movements of the eighteenth and nineteenth centuries. It was a global and inclusive endeavour undertaken by Africans themselves. I have argued that the court case Mendonça presented called for the liberation not only of Africans but also of other Atlantic constituencies such as New Christians and the Indigenous peoples of the Americas. His claim for

---

[25] See Boxer, *Portuguese Seaborne Empire*, Thornton, *Africa and Africans*, p. 6. Padre Baltasar Barreira, who was Novais's confessor, claimed that there was an African slave market: see 'Informação Acerca dos Escravos de Angola'. In Barreira's terminology, Africans here would mean people from regions we now call Angola, Kongo, Guinea, Sierra Leone, Ghana and Nigeria (Benin). After all, the category Africa, which included the political geography of demarcation, came later. As Mudimbe shows, the category of 'Africa' did not really exist until the eighteenth century. See Mudimbe, *The Invention of Africa*.

[26] For further detail see SOCG, vol. 495a, fls. 54 and 55.

[27] See Birmingham, *Trade and Conquest*.   [28] See SOCG vol. 495a, fl. 58.

[29] See APF, SOCG, Series America Meridionale, vol. 1, fl. 309.

freedom was a universal one. I have contended that Mendonça moved beyond a victim-master model of the relationship between Africa and the rest of the world, without simply offering a critique of that model. Crucial to my research is the question of how Mendonça provokes us to rethink our methodological engagement in studying the African diaspora's agency and freedom, not as a localised endeavour, but rather as a global issue.

I have maintained that Mendonça's network with Indigenous Americans and New Christians was based on their shared search for freedom. Their common ground was their oppression. The Indigenous Americans and New Christians were in solidarity with Africans and vice versa. They formed a united front against the injustices done to them in Africa, Brazil, Spain and Portugal.[30] Mendonça, in his final appeal, delivered a message of liberation for all, whether 'Jews, pagans or Christians', based on their legal rights: they belonged to the ranks of human society, which were based on inclusive membership. I have argued that he saw the enslavement of the African people in Brazil and the Americas as an Atlantic issue that needed to be tackled collectively, along with the Inquisition of the New Christians in Portugal and Brazil, and the enslavement of the Indigenous Americans. This in many ways anticipated later discourses on human rights and humanitarianism. I would even argue that the relationship between the Africans' abolition discourse, the Inquisition of the New Christians and the plight of Indigenous Americans, as well as their common search for liberty, and how the denial of religious freedom was implicated with the denial of enslaved Africans' humanity are strands of dialogue that have not so far been considered together in the historiography of the Atlantic slave trade.[31] I have argued that engaging with this dialogue has given us a better understanding of how those whose liberty had been denied sought

---

[30] See André Á. Almada, 'TratadosBreue dosRejnos deguine docaboverde' [Treaty of the Kingdoms of Guiné and Cape Verde], BNL, chapter 2, fl. 16v, 1594. Ganagoga is an African term, from Guinea-Bissau, used by the Beafada people to describe a New Christian network in the region in the sixteenth century. In the Beafada language it means a person who transcends cultures or is able to adapt to a different culture, 'chamado pellos negros ho ganagoga q querdizer nalinguados Beafares homē qfallatodas as linguas comodefeito asfallam. E pode este homē atravesar todo o sertao do nosso guine dequaes quer negros quesaja' ['a man who speaks all languages, as they do, he can cross the whole of hinterland of our Guinea and [talk] to whatever Negroes there may be'].

[31] See Oliveira, *Elementos para a História do Município de Lisboa*; Maxwell, *Slavery and the Catholic Church*, and Saunders, *A Social History of Black Slaves and Freedmen*. See also the recent work by Gray, 'The Papacy', and the discussion in Brazil by Andreoni (Antonil), *Cultura e Opulência*.

to overcome their oppression by allying with different constituencies in the Atlantic.[32] The idea that the enslaved people and African kings in general were passive about the Atlantic slave trade must therefore be countered with robust recognition of the fact that they resisted their enslavement everywhere they were taken and used the Black Brotherhoods in Angola, Brazil, Portugal and Spain to articulate their abhorrence of the system that was designed to deny them their humanity.

Mendonça's legal case in the Vatican demonstrates what Benton terms 'global legal regimes'.[33] She argues that the local legal system played an important role in shaping Western legal theory through the 'conscious efforts' made in the contact zones 'to retain elements of existing institutions and limit legal change as a way of sustaining social order'.[34] Mendonça stretched the limits of Western legal jurisprudence beyond this by contesting it not only in the contact zones, as his grandfather did, and in the tribunal centres of Europe, such as that of the Portuguese Overseas Council, but at the Supreme Court of Western Christendom, the Vatican. Following Benton, by bringing a case that had not been given a proper hearing in his own country, we can see that Mendonça's legal challenge transformed the Vatican's jurisprudence through the court case process, so that it included other world legal systems.[35] In other words, Mendonça's court case was provoked by external circumstances and phenomena common in seventeenth-century Angola and Kongo, countries that were subject to external pressures, from the Portuguese governors in Angola, that had evolved imperceptibly over a long period of time.[36]

I have also argued that the Portuguese Crown's response to Mendonça's criminal court case was positive but fell short of the abolition that the confraternities of Black Brotherhoods in Africa, Brazil, Portugal and Spain hoped for. An anonymous letter that I argue was written by one or more members of the Portuguese Overseas Council gave perverse economic and civilisational arguments in support of slavery and of the

---

[32] See Schwartz, *Blacks and Indians*. [33] Benton, *Law and Colonial Cultures*, p. 3.
[34] Benton, *Law and Colonial Cultures*, p. 3.
[35] For further detail on the New Christians' network with the Africans in Kongo and Angola, see AHU, cód., 16, fl. 170, 12 August 1665. It is easy to isolate Mendonça's case against slavery by treating it purely in terms of the case he made to the Vatican. It is said that Mendonça criticised slavery, but not as a universal crime. This interpretation is insufficient for many reasons. It throws no light on the nature of and sources related to Mendonça's court case and his engagement with the wider network in the Atlantic.
[36] See on Kazanze, 'Carta João Correia de Sousa ao Marquês de Frecilha' and 'Relação do Padre Mateus Cardoso'.

slave trade. Thus, when we engage with Mendonça's court case, we have had to go beyond the accepted arguments used in the justification of African slavery, such as the inferiority of African culture.[37] We have attempted to deconstruct those arguments at a deeper level by rereading Mendonça's sources as shaped by his own, distinctive evidence and life experience.[38] Such an endeavour requires us to rethink the possible difference between African thought and experience and that of Europeans. The Atlantic slavery discourse often appears too sophisticated in relation to the inhumanity of the slave trade; it can seem as if slavery was the Africans' doing, and that this diminished, if not removed, the complicity of Christian merchants. However, when seen in relation to the blunt and unambiguous language of Mendonça's criminal court case against slavery, the flaws of the discourse on African slavery become apparent.[39] Historians must recast their prejudices about African involvement in slavery and apply different methods and tools to seize the full implications of Mendonça's explicit statements in the Vatican. In doing so in this book, we can see his case as a door into the political and economic landscape of this crucial period, when the slave trade in the region fulfilled nothing more than Portuguese economic ambitions.

Mendonça accused the 'buyers' and 'sellers' of enslaved people of a wretchedly inhumane treatment of enslaved Africans, particularly pointing the finger at Italy, Spain and Portugal. Merchants from these countries were the most active in the Atlantic slave trade from the fifteenth to the seventeenth centuries.[40] The Vatican officials knew the modus operandi of the Atlantic project, thus Cardinal Millini was charged with contacting the authorities of Italy, Spain and Portugal to find out about the relationship between enslaved Africans and their Christians owners in the Americas and how they were being treated.[41]

Mendonça's court case was not the only case to be presented at the Vatican in these years. According to Gaspar de Mesquita, the papal nuncio in Lisbon who gave Mendonça a reference letter in 1681 to take to the Vatican, many people in the past had come to talk to him about the enslaved Africans and their plight in the Atlantic.[42] Yet, for undisclosed reasons, they failed to bring their cases to fruition. Mendonça was able to bring these

---

[37] For a detailed discussion of African slavery, see Fage, 'Slavery and the Slave Trade'.
[38] See SOCG, vol. 490, fls. 140–141.   [39] See SOCG, vol. 495a, fls. 54 to 55.
[40] See Tognetti, 'Trade in Black African Slaves', pp. 213–224 and SOCG, vol. 490, fls. 140–141.
[41] See SOCG, vol. 495a, fl. 54.   [42] See S.C. Africa, 1, fl. 486.

failed cases together and supplement their evidence with contributions from different confraternities or Black Brotherhoods in Brazil, Portugal and Spain.[43] Mendonça's case also included the voices of distinct constituencies of men, women and youth from within these groupings, each demanding a verdict from the Vatican.[44] In Mendonça's court case against slavery, he drew on the Ndongo royal critique of slavery and colonialism, which referred to the relationship of power between the Europeans and Africans. He also drew on his battle with the Portuguese Overseas Council on the question of abolishing slavery in Brazil, Portugal and Africa.

Mendonça involved the families of Mantua and Gonzaga in his discourse on Atlantic slavery by accusing Italy and Spain of the crimes against enslaved Africans. These families included the prince of Gonzaga, Vincenzo Gonzaga Doria (duke of Mantua and Monferrato), and the marquis of Astorga in Italy, Antonio Pedro Sancho Dávila y Osorio in Spain, and the Vatican nuncio in Portugal. Mendonça thus connected the Atlantic project to its foundations, namely the European origin of the Atlantic slave trade. It was not one country or empire's project; rather, it was inter-European.[45] The centre may have been in Portugal or Spain, but the slave trade was a wider European endeavour.[46] Spain was a Christian kingdom, Italy was the seat of Christendom and Portugal was a Catholic nation, and these were the leading proponents of the Atlantic slave trade.[47]

We should not think in terms of a period of slavery in Africa giving way to a period of colonisation. The two were inextricably linked: enslavement of Africans was part of the European project of conquest. Slaves were a product of wars waged on Africans by Europeans, who used their conquered allied kings, as Birmingham has put it: 'a large part of the supply of slaves undoubtedly came from the expansionist wars of the Ngolas'. The oral tradition of the Pende people of Angola has it that when Europeans arrived in Angola, they exchanged goods such as 'eggs and chickens for cloth and beads'.[48] Then 'the white men came yet again. They brought us maize and cassava, knives and hoes, groundnuts and tobacco. From that time until our day the Whites brought us nothing but wars and miseries.'[49]

---

[43] See SOCG, vol. 495a, fl. 54.   [44] See SOCG, vol. 495a, fl. 54.
[45] See Wadström, *Observations on the Slave Trade*.
[46] On the Iberian Union, see Oliveira, *History of Portugal*.
[47] See Tognetti 'Trade in Black African Slaves'.
[48] See Birmingham, *Trade and Conquest*, p. 24.
[49] Haveaux, *La Tradition Historique*, p. 47, and the letter that the dean of the Jesuits Society in Angola, Manoel Fernandes Curado, sent to the king of Portugal on 29 July 1665, AHU, Angola, cx. 8.

The governors in seventeenth-century Angola followed a fixed format in creating false wars, using the pretext that Angolans were stealing their property.[50] They would often wait until provoked by some alleged incident committed against the Portuguese residents by Africans, then launch a military campaign against the Africans responsible, with the intention of hunting down, kidnapping and capturing the civilians and turning them into enslaved people.[51] They would often set conditions, such as the return of alleged runaway slaves to Luanda, for negotiations. Any refusal to return slaves was met with the implication that this would justify the Portuguese using force, regardless of whether there were runaway slaves or not.[52] Cases were then reported to the administration in Madrid, with the implication that the Africans were the guilty party.[53] The governors imposed shape and meaning on these events in which they were so deeply implicated. So, we need to understand that Mendonça was arguing from a different starting point to the Portuguese authorities, in particular the Portuguese Overseas Council, and that he was reflecting a different climate of opinion, which led him to very different conclusions from those of the council.[54]

Atlantic slavery was viable because the majority of the people used for forced labour were not from the region where they were deployed. Where slaves were deployed in their region of origin, they would often run away. In Africa, African enslaved returned to their homes. In Brazil and São Tomé Island, the Indigenous American slaves formed runaway communities. It must be noted that by removing people from their land in Africa, the colonisers also effectively depopulated the land and made it available for new settlers, as in the case of the Kazanze in Angola whose land was given to the Portuguese war veterans.

The term 'slave' or 'slavery' is one of the most murky and ill-defined concepts in the entire history of the Atlantic slave trade as far as African servitude is concerned; its apparent meaning remains buried in the culture and traditions of the African people who came into contact with the Portuguese in West Central Africa and Africa in general. To equate them with the European understanding of these terms, is taking a considerable

---

[50] Correia de Sousa, Sousa, Bishop of Kongo, Linda
[51] See 'Carta João Correia de Sousa ao Marquês de Frecilha', Mateus' sreport, 'Relação do Padre Mateus Cardoso', and 'Informação de Fernão de Sousa a El-Rei', 7 December 1631, BAL - Ms. 51-VIII-31, folios 5–9 v.
[52] See Heywood, *Njinga of Angola*.
[53] See 'Informação de Fernão de Sousa a El-Rei', 7 December 1631, BAL - Ms. 51-VIII-31, folios 5–9 v.
[54] See SOCG, vol. 490, fl. 141.

risk that does not do justice to African practices.⁵⁵ The historian of West Central Africa is in constant danger of taking slavery or so-called African slavery for granted. The fate of the enslaved Angolans, the place of governors in Angolan and Brazilian society, indeed, the whole direction of the Portuguese conquest was intimately linked with the kidnapping, raids and wars waged against Africans whom the Portuguese saw as pagans, but who possessed wealth that should not be allowed to accrue to them.⁵⁶ The use of violence and force, aided by the papal bulls, gave the Portuguese licence to pursue their ambitions in the name of the Christian God. Thus, Africans were recast as enslavers who had so-called ready markets for slaves, in which they were already trading slaves among themselves. Europe's image of an enslaving society became enmeshed with that of African society, so that it seemed as if slavery was innate to African culture.⁵⁷

The institution of Atlantic slavery was justified by the governing authorities in Portugal and Spain on the basis that it acted as *paedagogos* (from the Greek παιδαγωγός), an instructor for the enslaved Africans, teaching them to be Christians and good citizens fit for unpaid labour. They were exploited, abused and killed in the name of Christendom.⁵⁸ However, Mendonça's intervention in the Vatican was to reveal that behind the hidden agenda of *paedagogos*, violence was used to reinforce the establishment of the institution of slavery in Brazil. For Mendonça, Christianity could not be used as a moral yardstick for the development of the Africans and the Indigenous Americans.⁵⁹ Christian values were to be lived by all human beings regardless of their creed.⁶⁰ Most importantly, according to Christian values, all people belonged to the same 'ground of our being'.⁶¹ To take an understanding of Christianity that endorsed violence against its members was contradictory to the values Christianity promoted. The apologetic letters written and addressed to the Crown, bishops and local councils by priests and governors, in particular from the period soon after the Union of the Two Crowns and thereafter, between 1580 and 1640, cannot bear the usual interpretation.⁶² Portugal was confronted with

---

[55] See Frei Melchior da Conceicam, 'Alvaras, Cartas, Provizioes, Regimentos'.
[56] See on Kazanze and their land destributed to the Portuguese war vetarans 'Carta João Correia de Sousa ao Marquês de Frecilha'.
[57] See Gray, 'The Papacy'; Barreira, Informação Acerca dos Escravos de Angola'; and Painter, *The History of White People*.
[58] Cadornega, *História Geral das História Geral*.   [59] See SOCG, vol. 490, fls. 140–141.
[60] See SOCG, vol. 490, fls. 140–141.   [61] Swinburne, *The Coherence of Theism*.
[62] See 'Carta de Doação a Paulo Dias de Novais' and Barreira, 'Informação Acerca dos Escravos de Angola', p. 229.

a situation in which it had to reform its laws in line with Spain's. It wished to take the initiative in this situation without incurring the odium of appearing to be an aggressor and an enslaving society. Thus, its early correspondence with the Spanish Crown and bishops was marked by all the ponderous courtesy of a great civilising nation unmasking the brutality that was going on in the Atlantic.[63]

The fact that Europe was a slaveholding society does not necessarily mean that Africa was the same. Nor does the observation that slavery was an ancient practice imply that it was a universal practice.[64] The debt-based legal system of holding a person in service seen in Africa is not comparable to the slave system as practised in the West or in the Atlantic region, nor is it justifiable to think of it as normal practice across the entire continent.[65] Moreover, members of some groups of Africans in the region of West Africa, such as the Balanta and the Bijogos, committed suicide rather than be taken into slavery in the Americas, and this demonstrates that slavery was not a normative practice among these people.[66]

To deal with the issue of slavery, Mendonça incorporated all those who were on the receiving end of the project, such as Indigenous Americans, Africans, New Christians and White European children or their descendants who were being enslaved. He approached the issue through strictly legal channels, because the Vatican would then have no option but to hear his case. In his discourse he inflamed Vatican officials, including members of the Propaganda Fide and the political authorities, who heard his shocking disclosure of the methods deployed to capture Africans. It was a case that involved highly placed participants from constituencies of different confraternities, and it was the biggest case of activism with regard to the Atlantic slave trade since the inception of early modern slavery in Africa by Europeans. The activist groups involved were victims of Atlantic slavery, and among them were some of those who had recently gained their freedom.[67]

Mendonça's court case connected historical events and the European political and commercial space[68] in the sense that he went beyond the traditional practice of focusing on a single colonial power and its operations. Although focusing on a single colonial power has often proved very useful in classifying and describing colonial situations, the approach

---

[63] See SOCG, vol. 495a, fl. 57.   [64] See Gray, 'The Papacy'.
[65] For further debate see Rodney, 'African Slavery'.   [66] See Rodney, 'African Slavery'.
[67] See APF, Series America Meridionale 1, fl., 309.
[68] See Birmingham, *Trade and Conquest*.

is limited because it precludes the possibility of understanding the connections between different powers and their global operations.[69] Mendonça's engagement with other constituencies in the Atlantic slave trade came from the backdrop of regional resilience and confederation that shaped his engagement in striving for the freedom of the enslaved Africans in Angola, Brazil, Portugal and Spain. It also served as a springboard for his network with the Indigenous Americans and New Christians in the Atlantic region, Portugal and Spain. This intersection between slavery and freedom, and networks between the Portuguese 'Hebrew Nation', the Indigenous Americans and Africans seeking their freedom in the Atlantic region is also a new discovery. I have argued that engaging with this dialogue will give us a better understanding of how those whose liberty had been denied sought to overcome it by allying with different constituencies in the Atlantic region. Mendonça's journey from Pungo-Andongo to Salvador, Rio de Janeiro, Braga, Portugal, Toledo, Madrid and the Vatican provided him with a collegial experience through which he could deal with the suffering of those whose liberty had been denied. After being appointed by Charles II, king of Spain, and the archbishop of Toledo as an international legal procurator for the confraternities of Blacks in Portugal, Brazil and Spain and many other parts of the world where Christianity was to be found, Mendonça felt duty-bound to use his position to liberate those suffering from oppression in the Atlantic region.[70] Following Mendonça's visit to the Vatican, Portugal and Spain made a concerted effort to abolish slavery in the seventeenth century.[71]

However, in the fifteenth century, Pope Nicholas V, in his bull of 8 January 1454, conferred an explosive right on the Portuguese Crown when he sanctioned the perpetual slavery of all Africans considered infidels.[72] The Portuguese hierarchy thought well of the pope's plan, and

---

[69] See Wadström, *Observations on the Slave Trade* and Earle and Lowe, *Black Africans in Renaissance Europe*.

[70] See both Lisbon and Toledo's affidavits, S.C. Africa, vol. I, fl., 486, and S.C. Africa, vol. 1, fl., 487.

[71] See Brásio, *MMA*, vol. I, pp. 277–86, ff.281

[72] Brásio, *MMA*, vol. I, pp. 277–286, 'nos premissa omnia et singula debita meditatione pensantes et attendentes quod cum olim prefato Alfonso Regi quoscunque Sarracenos et Paganos aliosque Christi inimicos ubicunque constitutos ac Regna, Ducatus, Principatus, dominia, possessiones et mobilia ac imobilia bona quecumque per eos detenta ac possessa inuadendi, conquirendi, expugnadi, debelandi, et subiugandi illorumque personas in perpetuam servitutem redigendi ... ipse Alfonsus Rex eiusque successores ... acquiri poterunt Provincias, Jnsulas, portus et maria ... iam acquisita et que in futurum acquiri contigerit ... a Capitibus de Bojador et de Nam usque per Guineam et ultra versus illam meridionalem plagam extendi.'

sought to get his permission to eliminate the human rights of the Africans. The bull gave the Crown a licence to kill, to use violence against people who were never found guilty before any law, human, natural, divine or civil. Nevertheless, it was death sanctioned by the Supreme tribunal of Christendom, the Vatican, so the House of Aviz requested from Pope Martin V (1417–1431) the right to an indulgence from the Church for those that might die implementing the verdict and securing the conquest of Africa. (This meant that those who died in pursuing this cause would go straight to heaven, according to their beliefs.)[73] To legitimise the verdict, justification was necessary and the justification used was that Africa was a slaveholding society and that such practices were natural to Africans.[74] Coupled with this was the Africans' alleged non-Christian nature, which left them vulnerable to the charge of being infidels. Thus, they could be hunted, raided and abducted without trial under the pretext that they were the enemies of Christendom. As Heywood puts it, 'many of the victims were kidnapped on the roads, being free, without being guilty of any crime and made slaves'.[75] Through Nicholas V's verdict, thousands lost their land and their right to be human. Countless lives were lost across the Atlantic Ocean, in Brazil, Africa and in Europe. Africans were seen as existing in a simple state of nature, whilst the Indigenous Americans were the embodiment of the primitive. Africans were seen as incapable of the refinements of Western civilisation. The social and political subordination of Black people was represented as part of the inescapable God-given order of the universe.[76]

I have argued that Mendonça's presentation of the evidence and his speech shows that slavery was not a practice that could be argued to be natural to Africans, as we have been led to believe. The methods used to capture the Africans demonstrated that we are dealing with a trade that was alien to the Africans. If there were so-called slaves created from traditional or legal practices in the region where the Portuguese were operating, then they were left behind. The majority of those who were

---

[73] J. Barros, *Década I*, Lisbon: Sá da Costa, 1932, chapter 7, 'E pera aquelles q na tal cõquista perecessem jndulgëcia plenária pera suas álmas' ('those who would die in such conquest plenary indulgence for their souls').

[74] See other priests' documents in Kongo referred to in the letter from 1660. See 'Carta do Secretário da Propaganda Fide ao Secretario dos Breves', 14 September 1660, APF., Lettere, vol. 43, fls. 37v.-38, MMA, vol. XII, p. 300.

[75] Heywood, *Central Africans and Cultural Transformations*, p.21.

[76] Stuart Hall, 'The Spectacle of the Others', in Stuart Hall (ed.), *Representation*, London: Sage, 1997.

taken, to Europe first and subsequently to the Americas, were ordinary people, captured from their fields while doing their work.[77] Most of them were unprepared for war, carrying work tools, not weapons. A second group among the enslaved were young people kidnapped from their mothers who were then used for procreation and eventually sold to the markets in Europe and the Americas.[78] Father Oliveira claimed that the Atlantic slave trade was the invention of the Portuguese, and that no other European nation did what they did.[79] The bishop of Cape Verde asserted that the Atlantic slave trade helped created Portuguese class society.[80] Garcia II, king of Kongo, said that Atlantic slavery changed the trade landscape of Kongo and Angola, making human beings the currency.[81]

All the Portuguese and Spanish kings were beneficiaries of the Atlantic slave trade. They were entitled by their own laws to receive 20 per cent of enslaved people or of taxes on sales of all the enslaved people sold in Africa, Brazil and the Americas under 'just war' laws.[82] For this reason, slavery in Africa, whether supported by people being captured, kidnapped, stolen or otherwise, could be justified as long as it could be argued that they were being held under the terms of 'just war'. It was enough that such actions were deemed legitimate for the Luso-Hispanic kings to be paid their 20 per cent. This tax system needs to be considered in tandem with debates regarding Atlantic slavery. The standpoint, particularly of Lusophone historiography, is often fixed on African kings who were said to be selling their own people.[83] Yet, Birmingham declares that 'the trade in slaves was advantageous to the Portuguese Crown, not only because it established a rich sugar colony in São Tomé, but also because the slave trade was taxed and so provided direct revenue'.[84]

I have argued that Mendonça's battle in the Vatican for the abolition of the slave trade was also a battle to clear his family's name of their involvement in Atlantic slavery, since his grandfather, father and uncle were actively involved through their alliance with the Portuguese in Angola. However, their involvement was carried out under pressure from the Portuguese Crown. They, too, resisted and tried to stop slavery, but they were unable to do so, under pressure from the Portuguese

---

[77] See SOCG, vol. 495a, fls. 54 and 55.
[78] See Cardinal Alexandrino 'Relazione del Viaggio, Fatto Dall Ilmo'.
[79] Oliveira, *A Arte da Guerra e do Mar*.
[80] 'Carta do Bispo de Cabo Verde a El-Rei', p. 442.   [81] AHU, Angola, cx. 2.
[82] See 'Carta Régia ao Vice-Rei de Portugal'.
[83] See Fonseca, 'A Historiografia Sobre os Escravos'.
[84] Birmingham, *Trade and Conquest*, pp. 24–25.

Overseas Council. That battle was lost, leaving Mendonça's other two uncles, João and Diogo, to declare the independence of Pungo-Andongo from Portugal, losing their lives and destroying the kingdom as a result. To win that battle, Mendonça needed to bypass the Portuguese Overseas Council and the Spanish Council of Indies, which were directly involved in Atlantic slavery.

Mendonça's argument in his criminal court case contradicts European justifications of the Atlantic slave trade that claim that Africans sold their own people. This argument arose in Europe as a perverse strategy to justify the institution of slavery and subsequently colonialism. Indeed, Mendonça tried to move beyond the traditionally simplistic binaries of Black and White to instead locate the difficulties of Black people, New Christians, Indigenous Americans, freemen and enslaved people, whose fates were connected, within the socio-political, religious and economic context of the time. His contributions to understanding the nature of Atlantic slavery and arguing for its abolition, to the general context of the regional alliance in West Central Africa, to creating networks among its victims and to arguing the legal case on the basis of novel legal principles make him a truly ground-breaking figure.

The legacy of this truly outstanding African abolitionist of the seventeenth century consists in showing to us that Atlantic slavery was a European project whose cruelty and unlawfulness were known, licensed and given the seal of authority by all its rulers: popes, king and overseas governors, including those in Angola, Brazil and India.

Bibliography

[without author's name] *A Quinta de Tangue, Um Monumento a Seriço da Cultura da Bahia*, Salvador: Publicações do Arquivo do Estado da Bahia, 1980.

[without author's name] *História de Angola, Centro de Estudos Angolanos, Grupo de Trabalho História e Etnologia*, Porto: Afrontamento,1975.

[without author's name] *Reply of the Portuguese Government to the Case in Support of the Claim of Great Britain to the Island of Bolama on the Western Coast of Africa and to a Certain Portion of Territory Opposite to that Island on the Mainland to be Laid Before the President of the United States of America as the Arbiter Selected to Decide the Question*, Lisbon: National Printing Office, 1869.

Abreu, Wilson and Margarida Abreu, 'Community Education Matters: Representations of Female Genital Mutilation in Guineans Immigrant Women', *Procedia – Social and Behavioral Sciences*, 2015, 171, pp. 620–628.

Acemoglu, Daron and James A. Robinson, *Why Nations Fail: The Origins of Power, Prosperity and Poverty*, London: Profile, 2012.

Ackerson, Wayne, *The African Institution (1807–1827) and the Antislavery Movement in Great Britain*, Lewiston, NY: E. Mellen Press, 2005.

Akyeampong, Emmanuel, 'Africans in the Diaspora: The Diaspora in Africa', *African Affairs*, 13, 2000, pp. 183–215.

Alencastro, Luiz Felipe de, *O Trato dos Viventes: Formação do Brasil no Atlântico Sul, Séculos XVI e XVII*, São Paulo: Companhia das Letras, 2000.

'South Atlantic Wars: The Episode of Palmares', *Portuguese Studies Review*, 19 (1/2), 2011, pp. 35–58.

Alexandrino, Cardinal, 'Relazione del Viaggio, Fatto Dall Ilmo, e R.mo Fr. Michelle Bonnello, Cardinal Alexandrino Del Tit: di S. Ma. Sopra Minerva, Nipotte di Pio V, Legato Alli Serenis.mi Re, Di Franca, Spangna, e Portogallo, Colle Annotarioni delle Citta, Terre, e Luoghi, Descritto Da Mes.r Gio: Battista Ventu: Rino da Fabriano, l'anno 1571', BAL, 46-IX-3.

Alfagali, Crislayne, *Ferreiros e Fundidores da Ilamba: Uma História Social da Fabricação do Ferro e da Real Fábrica de Nova Oeiras (Angola, segunda metade do século XVIII)*, Luanda: Fundação Agostinho Neto, 2018.
Allen, S. J. 'A "Cultural Mosaic" at Palmares? Grappling with the Historical Archaeology of a Seventeenth-Century Brazilian Quilombo', in Pedro Paulo A Funari (ed.), *Cultura Material e Arqueologia Histórica*, Campinas: Unicamp (IFCH), 1998.
Almada, André Á, 'Tratadosbreue dosRejnos deguine docaboverde' [Treaty of the Kingdoms of Guiné and Cape Verde], BNL, 1594.
Almeida, C. A. Ferreira de, 'Arquitectura Românica Entre Douro e Minho', unpublished Ph.D. thesis, University of Porto, 1978.
Altamira, R., 'El Texto de las Leyes de Burgos de 1512', *Revista de Historia de América*, 4, 1938, pp. 5–79.
Amantino, Márcia, 'Sobre os Quilombos do Sudeste Brasileiro nos Séculos XVIII e XIX', in Manolo Florentino and Cacilda Machado (eds.), *Ensaios Sobre a Escravidão*, Belo Horizonte: Editora UFMG, 2003, pp. 235–262.
Amaral, Ilídio do, *O Consulado de Paulo Dias de Novais: Angola no Último Quartel do Século XVI e Primeiro do Século XVII*, Lisbon: Ministério da Ciência e da Tecnologia, Instituto de Investigação Científica Tropical, 2000.
Amorim, Maria Adelina, '*Questões Jurídicas sobre os Índios do Brasil*' *com José Maria Mendes, in Cadernos de Literatura de Viagens, n° 2, Subsídios para o Estudo dos Índios das Américas*, Lisbon: CLEPUL/ Coimbra, Almedina, 2010, pp. 25–49.
Anderson, Robert Warren, 'How to Expect the Portuguese Inquisition', Unpublished Ph.D., George Mason University, Fairfax, Virginia, 2011.
Anderson, James Maxwell, *The History of Portugal*, London: Greenwood Press, 2000.
Anderson, Robert Nelson, 'The Quilombo of Palmares: A New Overview of a Maroon State in Seventeenth-Century Brazil', *Journal of Latin American Studies*, 23(3), 1996, pp. 545–566.
Antonil, Antonio Andreoni (ou André João Antonil), *Cultura e Opulência do Brazil por suas Drogas, e Minas, com Varias Noticias Curiosas do modo de fazer o Assucar; Plantar, & Beneficiar o Tabaco; Tirar Ouro das Minas & Descubrir as da Prata; e dos grandes Emolumentos, que esta Conquista da America Meridional dá ao Reyno de Portugal com estes, et Outros Generos, et Contratos Reaes* (1717), Lisbon: Conselho Nacional de Geografi, [1717] 1963.
Araujo, Ana Lucia, 'Dahomey, Portugal and Bahia: King Adandozan and the Atlantic Slave Trade', *Slavery and Abolition*, 33(1), 2012, pp. 1–19.
Araujo, Ana Lucia (ed.), *African Heritage and Memories of Slavery in Brazil and the South Atlantic World*, Amherst, NY: Cambria Press, 2015.
Arner, Katherine, 'Making Yellow Fever American: The Early American Republic, the British Empire and the Geopolitics of Disease in the Atlantic World', *Atlantic Studies*, 2010, 7(4), pp. 447–471.
Augustine, St., *The City of God Against the Pagans*, in R. W. Dyson (ed.), Cambridge: Cambridge University Press, 1998.

Ayres, Lewis, *Augustine and the Trinity*, Cambridge: Cambridge University Press, 2010.
Azeredo, José Pinto de, *Ensaios Sobre Algumas Enfermidades D'Angola (1799)*, Luanda: Instituto de Investigação Científica de Angola, 1967.
Azevedo, Esterzilda Berenstein de, *Engenhos do Recôncavo Baiano, Sugarcane Farms of Bahia's Recôncavo*, Brasília: Iphan/Programa Monumenta, 2009.
Azevedo, L., 'Cartas do Padre António Vieira a Roque Monteiro Paim', 2 July 1691, vol. III, Coimbra: Imprensa da Universidade, 1928.
Baião, António, *A Inquisição em Portugal e no Brasil, Subsidios Para a Sua Historia, A Inquisição no Século XVI*, Lisbon: Edição do Arquivo Historico Portugues, 1921.
Balandier, Georges, *Daily Life in the Kingdom of the Congo from the Sixteenth to the Eighteenth Century*, London: Allen & Unwin, 1968.
Baquaqua, Mahommah Gardo, *Biography of Mahommah G. Baquaqua, a Native of Zoogoo, in the Interior of Africa (a convert of Christianity), with a Description of that Part of the World, Including the Manners and Customs of the Inhabitants*, Chapel Hill, NC: University of North Carolina, [1854] 2001.
Barbosa, Ignacio de Vilhena, *As Cidades e Villas da Monarchia Portugueza que Teem Brasão d'Armas: Volume I*, Lisbon: Typographia do Panorama 1860.
Barker, Charles, *Cultural Studies, Theory and Practice*, London: Sage, 2003.
Barreiros, Manuel de Aguiar, *A Portada Românica de Vilar de Frades e o Seu Symbolismo*, Braga: Marques Abreu, 1920.
Barretto, J. A. da Graça, *Monstruosidades do Tempo e da Fortuna, Diário de Factos que Sucederam no Reino de 1625 a 1780, até hoje Atribuído Infundamente ao Benedictino Fr. Alexandre da Paixão*, Lisbon: Tipografia da Viúva Sousa Neves – Editora, 1888.
Barros, F. Burges de, *Á Margem da História da Bahia*, Salvador: Mamia Imprensa Official do Estado, Praça Municipal, 1934.
Barros, J., *Década I*, Lisbon: Sá da Costa, 1932.
Barros, M., *Litteratura dos Negros: Contos, Cantigas e Parabolas*, Lisbon: Typographia do Commercio, 1900.
Batsîkama, Patrício, 'As Origens do Reino do Kôngo Segundo a Tradição Oral', *Sankofa, Revista de História da África e de Estudos da Diáspora Africana*, 3 (5), 2010, pp. 94–113.
Dona Beatriz Nsimba Vita, São Paulo, Ancestre, 2021.
'O Poder Político Entre os Mbûndu', *Sankofa*, 9(16), pp. 96–134.
Batsîkama, Raphaël and Patrício Batsîkama, 'Estruturas e Instituições do Kôngo', *Revista de História Comparada*, 5(1), 2011, pp. 6–41.
Bayam, José P., *Portugal Cuidadoso, e Lastimado com a Vida, e Perda do Senhor Rey Dom Sebastião, o Desejado de Saudosa Memoria: Historia Chronologica de Suas Accoens, e Successos Desta Monarquia em Seu Tempo; Suas Jornadas a Africa, Batalha, Perda, Circunstancias, e Consequencias Notaveis della*, Lisbon: Officina de A. De Sousa da Sylva, 1737.
Bayne, Peter, *Men Worthy to Lead; Being Lives of John Howard, William Wilberforce, Thomas Chalmers, Thomas Arnold, Samuel Budgett, John*

Foster, London: Simpkin, Marshall, Hamilton, Kent & Co. Ltd, Reprinted by Bibliolife, 1890.
Bediako, Kwame, *Christianity in Africa: The Renewal of a Non-Western Religion*, Edinburgh: Edinburgh University Press, 1995.
Belmonte, Kevin, *Hero for Humanity: A Biography of William Wilberforce*, Colorado Springs, CO: Navpress Publishing Group, 2002.
Benci, Jorge, *Economia Cristã dos senhores no Governo dos Escravos*, São Paulo: Grijalbo, 1977: https://purl.pt/24731/1/index.html#/18/html.
Benton, Lauren, *Law and Colonial Cultures: Legal Regimes in World History, 1400-1900*, Cambridge: Cambridge University Press, 2002.
Benzoni, Girolamo, *History of the New World, by Girolamo Benzoni, of Milan. Shewing His Travels in America, from A.d. 1541 to 1556: With Some Particulars of the Island of Canary*, trans. W. H. Smyth, London: Printed for the Hakluyt Society, 1857.
Bethell, Leslie (ed.), *The Cambridge History of Latin America*, Cambridge: Cambridge University Press, 1984.
Bethell, Leslie and Murilo de Carvalho (eds.), *Joaquim Nabuco, British Abolitionists, and the End of Slavery in Brazil: Correspondence, 1880-1905*, London: University of London Press, 2009.
Bhabha, Homi, *The Location of Culture*, London: Routledge, 1994.
Binns, L. Elliott, *The History of the Decline and Fall of the Medieval Papacy*, London: Archon Books, 1967.
Birmingham, David, *A Concise History of Portugal*, Cambridge: Cambridge University Press, 1993.
  Empire in Africa: Angola and Its Neighbors – Research in International Studies, Africa Series, Athens, OH: Ohio University Press, 2006.
  Trade and Conquest in Angola, Oxford: Clarendon Press, 1966.
Blackburn, Robin, *The American Crucible: Slavery, Emancipation and Human Rights*, London: Verso, 2011.
Bogle, Donald, *Toms, Coons, Mulattos, Mammies and Bucks: An Interpretive History of Blacks in American Films*, New York: Continuum, 1989.
Bosch, María Isabel Cabrera, *El Consejo Real de Castilla y la Ley*, Madrid: Emprensa en España, 1993.
Bostoen, Koen, Odjas Ndonda Tshiyayi and Gilles-Maurice de Schryver, 'On the Origin of the Royal Kongo Title Ngangula', *Africana Linguistica*, 2013, pp. 53–83.
Botero, Giovanni, *Relations, of the Most Famous Kingdoms and Commonweals, Through the World Discoursing of Their Situations, Religions, Languages, Manners, Customes, Strengths, Greatnesse, and Policies*, London: Printed by Iohn Hauiland, and are to be sold by Iohn Patridge at the signe of the Sunne in Pauls Church-yard, 1630.
Boulegue, J., *Le Grand Jolof, XIIIe-XVIe siècle (Les Anciens Royaumes Wolof)*, Paris: Diffusion Karthala, 1987.
Bouveignes, O., *De Les Anciens Rois du Congo*, Namur: Grands Lacs, 1948.
Boxer, Charles R., 'Background to Angola, Cadornega's Chronicle', *History Today*, 11, 1961, pp. 665–672.
  Portuguese Seaborne Empire, London: Hutchinson, 1969.

Salvador de Sá and the Struggle for Brazil and Angola,1602–1686, London: Athlone Press, University of London, 1952.

The Church Militant and Iberian Expansion 1440–1770, Baltimore, ML, and London: The John Hopkins University Press, 1978.

The Dutch in Brazil, 1624–1654, Oxford: Clarendon Press, 1973.

Boxer, Charles R. (ed.), *South China in the Sixteenth Century: Being the Narratives of Galeote Pereira, Fr. Gaspar da Cruz, O.P. [and] Fr. Martín de Rada, O.E.S.A. (1550–1575)*, London: Routledge, 2010.

Brásio, Padre António, 'As Misericórdias de Angola'. *Studia*, 4, 1959, pp. 106–149.

Monumenta Missionária Africana, África Ocidental (1490–1508), volumes I–XIII, Lisbon: Agência-Geral do Ultramar, 1952.

Os Pretos em Portugal, Lisbon: Agência Geral das Colônia, 1944.

Brinton, Selwyn, *The Gonzaga, Lords of Mantua*, London: Methuen, 1927.

Brooks, Thom, *'Just War' Theory*, Leiden; Boston: Brill, 2013.

Brough, Michael W. et al. (eds.), *Rethinking the 'Just War' Tradition*, Albany, NY: SUNY Press, 2007.

Brown, Leslie, *The Indian Christians of St. Thomas, An Account of the Ancient Syrian Church of Malabar*, Cambridge: Cambridge University Press 1956.

Brusher, Joseph, *Popes Through the Ages*, Whitefish, MT: Van Nostrand, 1959.

Buxton, Thomas F. *The African Slave Trade and Its Remedy*, London: J. Murray, 1839.

Cabral, Amilcar, *Return to the Source: Selected Speeches of Amilcar Cabral*, New York: Monthly Review Press, 1973.

Unity and Struggle: Speeches and Writings of Amilcar Cabral, New York: Monthly Review Press, 1979.

Cadamosto, Luís L. de, *Navegações de Luís de Cadamosto, Texto Italiano, e Traducao Portuguesa*, Lisbon: Instituto para a Alta Cultura (1507), 1944.

Cadas, Iozé Antonio 'Notícia Geral de Toda Esta Capitania da Bahia Desde o Seu Descobrimento Até O Prez.te Anno de 1759, Salvador, Bahia.

Cadornega, Antonio de Oliveira, *História Geral das Guerras Angolanas 1680*, vol. I, II and III Lisbon: Agência Geral das Colónias, 1972.

Caetano, Marcello, *O Conselho Ultramarino, Esboço da Sua História*, Lisbon: Agência- Geral do Ultramarino, 1943.

Caldeira, Arlindo Manuel, 'Formação de uma cidade afro-atlântica: Luanda no século XVII,' *Revista Tempo, Espaço, Linguagem*, 5(3), 2014, pp. 12–39.

Candido, Mariana P., *An African Slaving Port and the Atlantic World: Benguela and Its Hinterland*, New York: Cambridge University Press, 2013.

'Conquest, Occupation, Colonialism and Exclusion: Land Disputes in Angola', in José Vicente Serrão, Bárbara Direito, Eugénia Rodrigues and Susan Münch Miranda (eds.), *Property Rights, Land and Territory in the European Overseas Empires*, Lisbon: CEHC-IUL, 2014, pp. 223–233, http://hdl.handle.net/10071/2718.

'Dimensão Sociopolítica do Município de Luanda Durante o Século XVII', *Cadernos de Estudos Africanos*, 30, 2015.

'Jagas e Sobas no "Reino de Benguela": Vassalagem e Criação de novas categorias políticas e sociais no contexto da Expansão Portuguesa na África durante os Séculos Xvi E Xvii', in Alexandre Vieira Ribeiro, Alexsander Lemos de Almeida Gebara and Marina Berther (eds.), *África: Históricas Conectadas*, Niterói: ppghistória-UFF, 2014, pp. 39–76.

'O Limite Tênue entre a Liberdade e Escravidão em Benguela durante a Era do Comércio Transatlântico', *Afro-Ásia*, 47 (2013), pp. 239–268.

'The Transatlantic Slave Trade and the Vulnerability of Free Blacks in Benguela, Angola, 1780–1830', in Mark Meuwese and Jeffrey A. Fortin (eds.), *Atlantic Biographies: Individuals and Peoples in the Atlantic World*, Leiden: Brill, 2013, pp. 193–210.

Carneiro, Edison, *O Quilombo dos Palmares* [1947], 2nd ed., São Paulo: Brasiliense, 1958.

'Panteão da Liberdade e da Democracia', in *Coleção das Leis da República Federativa do Brasil*, Brasília: Imprensa Nacional, 1996.

Carreira, A., 'O Céu, Deus e a Terra', *Boletim Cultural da Guine Portuguesa*, 2(6), 1947, pp.461–463.

Carreira, António, *As Companhias Pombalinas de Navegação Comércio e Tráfico de Escravos entre Africana e o Nordeste Brasileiro*, Bissau: Centro de Estudos da Guiné Portuguesa, 1969.

Carretta, Vincent, *Equiano, the African: Biography of a Self-made Man*, New York; London: Penguin Books, 2006.

Carvalho, Aline Vieira de, 'Archaeological Perspectives of Palmares: A Maroon Settlement in 17th-Century Brazil', *African Diaspora Archaeology Newsletter*, 10(1), 2007, pp. 1–18.

Carvalho, António Pedro de, *Das Origens da Escravidão Moderna em Portugal*, Lisbon: Tipografia Universal, 1877.

Carvalho, Ariane, 'Guerras nos sertões de Angola: Sobas, Guerra Preta e Escravização (1749–1797)', unpublished Ph.D. thesis, Federal University of Rio de Janeiro, 2020.

Carvalho, Carlos and Moraes Sato, 'Geoprocessando as Relações Sociais na Cidade da Bahia – Século XVI', in Carlos Valencia Villa and Tiago Gil, *O Retorno dos Mapas: Sistemas de Informação Geográfica em História*, Porto Alegre: Ladeira Livros, 2016.

Carvalho, Flávia Maria de, 'O Reino do Ndongo no Contexto da Restauração: Mbundus, Portugueses e Holandeses na África Centro Ocidental', *Sankofa. Revista de História da África e de Estudos da Diáspora Africana*, 4(7), 2011, pp. 7–30.

Sobas e Homens do Rei. Relações de Poder e Escravidão em Angola (séculos XVII e XVIII), Maceió, Alagoas: Edufal, 2015.

Castro Borges de et al., *Collecção dos Tratados, Convenções, Contratos e Actos Publicos: Celebrados Entre a Coroa de Portugal e as Mais Potencias Desde 1640 ate ao Presente*, Lisbon: Imprensa Nacional, 1856.

Chalhoub, Sidney, 'Interpreting Machado De Assis: Paternalism, Slavery, and the Free Womb Law,' in Sueann Caulfield, Sarah C. Chambers and Lara Putnam (eds.), *Honor, Status, and Law in Modern Latin America*, Durham, NC: Duke University Press, 2005, pp. 87–108.

Cavagnaro, Nahuel, 'Los Hombres de Negocios: las Redes Genovesas en la Edad Moderna,' in Bernard Vincent et al. (eds.), *Estudios en Historia Moderna*

desde una visión Atlántica Libro Homenaje a la Trayectoria de la Profesora María Inés Carzolio, La Plata: Universidad Nacional de La Plata, 2017.
Cavalcanti, Nireu Oliveira, 'O Comércio de Escravos Novos no Rio Setecentista', in Manolo Florentino (ed.), *Tráfico Cativeiro e Liberdade (Rio de Janeiro, Séculos XVII – XIX)*, Rio de Janeiro: Civilização Brasileira, 2005, pp. 15–77.
Cerejeira, M. Gonçalves, *O Renascimento em Portugal*, Coimbra: Imprensa da Universidade, 1918.
Chamberlain, Robert Stoner, 'Pre-Conquest Labor Practices' in John Francis Bannon (ed.), *Indian Labor in the Spanish Indies: Was there Another Solution?* Boston: D. C. Heath and Co., 1966.
Cheney, Glenn Alan, *Quilombo dos Palmares: Brazil's Lost Nation of Fugitive Slaves*, Hanover, CT: New London Librarium, 2014.
Clarkson, Thomas, *An Essay on the Slavery and Commerce of the Human Species: Particularly the African, Translated from a Latin Dissertation, Which Was Honoured with the First Prize in the University of Cambridge, for the Year 1785*, London: Longman, Hurst, Rees, and Orme, 1808.
'A Summary View of the Slave Trade and of the Probable Consequences of its Abolition', London: J. Philips, 1787.
The History of the Rise, Progress and Accomplishment of the Abolition of the African Slave Trade by the British Parliament (1808), vol. I, New York: John S. Taylor, 1836.
Cohen, Robin, *Global Diasporas: An Introduction*, London: Routledge, 2008.
Cooper, Barbara, 'Oral Sources and the Challenge of African History', in John Philips (ed.), *Writing African History*, Rochester, NY: University of Rochester Press, 2005, pp. 191–215.
Conrad, Robert Edgar, *Children of God's Fire: A Documentary History of Black Slaves in Brazil*, 3rd ed., University Park, PA: Pennsylvania State University Press, 1997.
Cont, Alessandro, 'Sotto Tutela: Il Sovrano Bambino in Italia (1659–1714), '*Rivista Storica Italiana*, 124(2), 2012, pp. 537–581.
Cookey, Sylvanus John Sodienye, *King Jaja of the Niger Delta: His Life and Times, 1821–1891*, New York: Nok Publishers, 1974.
Cortesão, Armando and Avelino Teixeira da Mota (eds.), *Portugalliae Monumenta Cartographica* (6 vols.), Lisbon: Imprensa Nacional-Casa da Moeda, 1960–1962.
Costa, Carlos Alberto Santos, Fabiana Comerlato and Cinthia de Silva Cunha, 'Arqueologia do Baixo Sul da Bahia: Engenho Rio de Contas, Itacaré, Bahia, Brasil', *Revista de Arqueologia*, 31(2), 2018, pp. 256–281.
Costa, E. V. D., 'The Portuguese-African Slave Trade: A Lesson in Colonialism.', *Latin American Perspectives*, 12(1), 1985, pp. 41–61.
Costa, F. A. Fereira da, *Anais Pernambucanos* 4, Recife: Arquivo Público Estadual, 1951–1958.
Cruz, Gaspar da (O.P.), *Tractado em que se Co[m]tam Muito por Este[n]so as Cousas da China, co[n] suas Particularidades, [e] assi do Reyno Dormuz*, Madrid: Em Casa de Andre de Burgos, 1569.
Cugoano, Ottobah, *Thoughts and Sentiments on the Evil of Slavery (1791)*, New York: Penguin, 1999.

Curtin, Philip D. *Economic Change in Precolonial Africa: Senegambia in the Era of the Slave Trade*, vol. I., Madison, WI: University of Wisconsin Press, 1975.
'Sugar Planting: From Cyprus to the Atlantic Islands', in Philip D. Curtin (ed.) *The Rise and Fall of the Plantation Complex: Essays in Atlantic History*, Cambridge: Cambridge University Press, 1990, pp. 17–28.
'The Mediterranean Origins', in Philip D. Curtin (ed.), *The Rise and Fall of the Plantation Complex: Essays in Atlantic History*, Cambridge: Cambridge University Press, 1990, pp. 1–16.
Curtin, Philip D. (ed.), *The Rise and Fall of the Plantation Complex: Essays in Atlantic History*, Cambridge: Cambridge University Press, 1990.
Curtin, Philip D. and Steven Feierman, Leonard Thompson, and Jan Vansina, *African History: From Earliest Times to Independence*, Edinburgh: Longman Pearson Education, 1995.
Curto, José C., *Enslaving Spirits: The Portuguese-Brazilian Alcohol Trade in Luanda and Its Hinterland c. 1550–1830*, Leiden: Brill Academic, 2004.
'Experiences of Enslavement in West Central Africa.' *Social History*, 41(82), 2008, pp. 381–415.
'The Legal Portuguese Slave Trade from Benguela, Angola, 1730–1828: A Quantative Re-appraisal', *África*, 17(1), 1993/1994, pp. 101–116.
'The Story of Nbena, 1817–20: Unlawful Enslavement and the Concept of 'Original Freedom' in Angola, in Paul E. Lovejoy and David Trotman (eds.), *Trans-Atlantic Dimensions of Ethnicity in the African Diaspora*, New York: Continuum, 2003, pp. 43–64.
'Un Butin Illégitime: Razzias d'esclaves et relations luso-africaines dans la région des fleuves Kwanza et Kwango en 1805,' in ed. Isabel de Castro Henriques and Louis Sala-Molins (eds.), *Déraison, Esclavage et Droit : Les fondements idéologiques et juridiques de la traite négrière et de l'esclavage*, Paris: Unesco, 2002, pp. 315–327.
Curto, José C. And Renée Soulodre-lafrance (eds.), *Africa and the Americas: Interconnections During the Slave Trade*, Trenton, NJ: Africa World Press, 2005.
'Álcoól e Escravos: O Comércio Luso-brasileiro do Álcool em Mpinda, Luanda e Benguela Durante o Tráfico Atlântico de Escravos (c. 1480–1830) e o Seu Impacto nas Sociedades da África Central Ocidental', *Tempos e Espaços Africanos*, 2002, pp 273–276.
Cuvelier, J., *L'Ancien Royaume de Congo*, Bruxelles: Desclée, 1946.
Cuvelier, J. & L. Jadin, *L'Ancien Congo d'Après les Archives Romaines (1518–1540)*, Bruxelles: IRCB., 1954.
Dampier, Captain William, *A Voyage to New Holland Etc in the Year 1699, Wherein are described, The Canary Islands, the Isles of Mayo and St. Jago. The Bay of All-Saints, with the forts and town of Bahia in Brazil. Cape Salvador. The winds on the Brazilian coast. Abrolho Shoals. A table of all the variations observed in this voyage. Occurrence near the Cape of Good Hope. The course to New Holland. Shark's Bay. The isles and coast, etc. Of New Holland. Their inhabitants, manners, customs, trade, etc. Their harbours, soil, beasts, birds, fish, etc. Trees, plants, fruits, etc. Illustrated*

with several maps and draughts: also divers birds, fishes and plants not found in this part of the world, curiously engraven on copper plates, 3rd ed., London: Printed for James and John Knapton at the Crown in St. Paul's Churchyard, 1729.

Darby, Graham, 'Pope Innocent XI: The Saviour of Christendom?' *History Today*, 61(5), 2011, pp.

Davidson, Basil, *Black Mother, Africa: The Years of Trial*, London: Victor Gollancz Ltd, 1961.

Davis, David Brion, *Inhuman Bondage: The Rise and Fall of Slavery in the New World*, Oxford: Oxford University Press, 2006.

Deakin, Simon, Angus Johnston and Basil Markesinis, *Tort Law*, Oxford: Oxford University Press, 2003.

Debret, Jean-Baptiste, *Viagem Pitoresca e Histórica ao Brasil, 1834–1839*, Belo Horizonte: Itatiaia, 1978. The original was published as *Voyage Pittoresque et Historique au Brésil*, vol. II, Paris: Firmin Didot Frères, 1835.

Decker, J. M., *Les Clans Ambuund (Bambundu) d'Après Leur Littérature Orale*, Bruxelas: Institut Royal Colonial Belge, 1950.

De Koch, Christophe G. and Frédéric Schoell, *Histoire Abrégée des Traités de Paix entre les Puissances de l'Europe Depuis la Paix de Westphalie*, vol. XI, Paris: Nabu Press, 1817–1818.

Delgado, José Matias, 'Notes', in António de Oliveira Cadornega, *História Geral das Guerras Angolanas 1680*, vols. I, II and III, Lisbon: Agência Geral das Colónias, 1972.

Descartes, René, *Discourse on Method and Meditations on First Philosophy*, Oxford: Basil Blackwell, 1986.

Specimina philosophiae, Amsterdam: Elzevier, 1644.

Dias, Gastão Sousa, 'A Defesa de Angola: a Estratégia Militar Portuguesa no Período da Grande Guerra, do Gapitão Gastão Sousa Dias', *Revista Militar*, 1932, pp. 598–620.

Dias, Mariza de Araújo, 'Os Jesuítas e a Escravidão Africana no Brasil Colonial: Um Estudo Sobre os Escritos de Antonio Vieira, André João Antonil e Jorge Benci (sécs. XVII e XVIII)', unpublished Master's thesis, State University of São Paolo, 2012: https://repositorio.unesp.br/bitstream/handle/11449/93370/dias_ma_me_assis.pdf?sequence=1.

Dias, Pedro, *A Arte da Língua de Angola, Oferecida à Virgem Senhora N. Do Rosário, Mãe e Senhora dos Mesmos Pretos*, Lisbon: Na officina de Miguel Deslandes, impressor de Sua Magestade, 1697.

Diop, Cheikh Anta, *The African Origin of Civilization, Myth of Reality*, ed. and trans. Mercer Cook, Chicago, IL: Lawrence Hill Books, 1974.

Disney, Anthony R., *A History of Portugal and the Portuguese Empire*, vol. II, New York: Cambridge University Press, 2009.

Documentos Históricos do Arquivo Municipal de Salvador, 1640–1680, vol. V, 1928.

Documentos Históricos do Arquivo Municipal de Salvador, Atas da câmara, vol. IV, 1949.

Documentos Históricos dos Arquivos Municipal, Cartas do Senado 1673– 1684, vol. II, Prefeitura do Municipio do Salvador, Bahia, 1952.

Documentos Históricos, Cartas Régias, 1667–1681, vol. LXVII, Ministério da Educação e Saúde, Biblioteca Nacional, Rio de Janeiro: Batista de Sousa, 1945, pp. 213–214.

Documentos para a Hitória do Açúcar – Legislação, Rio de Janeiro: Instituto do Açúcar e do Álcool, 1954.

Donelhas, A., 'Outra Relação em 14 Capítolos que fez Andre Donellas, ao Governador e Capitão Geral Fr. De Vaz Concellos da Cunha; Sobre a Serra Leoa, Reys e Senhores que a Habitão, e Secunvezinhos,Ritos, Costumes e Todas Variedades de Rios, Portos, Arvores, Animais Aves Pexes com os Proveitos que Dela se Tirão', Ms. 51-IX-25, in Palácio de Ajuda, Lisbon, 1625

Downs, Wilbur G., 'History of Epidemiological Aspects of Yellow Fever', *The Yale Journal of Biology and Medicine*, 55, 1982, pp. 179–185.

Dubik, James M., *'Just War' Reconsidered: Strategy, Ethics, and Theory*, Lexington, KY: University Press of Kentucky, 2016.

Durán, Francisco Xavier de Garma y, *Theatro Universal de España: Descripcion Eclesiastica y Secular de Todos sus Reynos y Provincias, tomo IV*, Barcelona: En la Imprenta de Mauro Martí, 1753.

Earle, Tom F. and Kate J. P. Lowe (eds.), *Black Africans in Renaissance Europe*, Cambridge: Cambridge University Press, 2005.

Ehret, Christopher, *The Civilizations of Africa, A History to 1800*, Oxford: James Currey, 2002.

Eisenberg, José, 'António Vieira and the Justification of Indian Slavery', *Luso-Brazilian Review*, 40(1), 2003, pp. 89–95.

Elbl, Ivana, 'The Horse in Fifteenth-Century Senegambia', *The International Journal of African Historical Studies*, 1991, 24(1), pp. 85–110.

Elkin, Judith Laikin, 'Colonial Origins of Contemporary Anti-Semitism in Latin America', in David Sheinin and Lois Baer Barr (eds.), *The Jewish Diaspora in Latin America: New Studies on History and Literature*, New York: Garland Publishing, 1996, pp. 127–141.

Engerman, Stanley L., 'Slavery at Different Times and Places', *The American Historical Review*, 105(2), 2000, pp. 480–484.

Ennes, Ernesto, *As Guerras dos Palmares (Subsídios Para a Sua Sistória), Domingos Jorge Velho e a 'Tróia Negra'*, vol. I, 1687–1700, Rio de Janeiro: Companhia Editora Nacional, 1938.

Equiano, Olaudah, *The Interesting Narrative of the Life of Olaudah Equiano, or Gustavus Vassa, the African, Written by Himself*, vol. I, London: Printed and folded for the Author, by T. Wilkine, 1789, online: https://www.bl.uk/collection-items/the-%20life-of-olaudah-equinao.

Fage, J. D., 'Slavery and the Slave Trade in the Context of West African History', *The Journal of African History*, 10(3), 1969, pp. 393–404.

Faria, Manuel Seuerim de, 'Discyrso Sexto, Sobre a Propagaçam do Evangelho nas Provincias de Guiné, Das Condições, com que os Summos Pontifices derão Reys de Portugal Senhorio de Guiné,' in *Noticias de Portvgal*, Lisbon: Na Officina Craesbeeckiana, 1655.

'Sobre a Fundação de Seminários para a Guiné', Academia Real de la Historia, Madrid, [ARHM], Salazar y Castro, ms. B-4, fls. 95–105 v; MMA, vol. VII, January 1622, pp. 697–698.

Faulkner, Raymond O., Ogden Goelet, Eva Von Dassow and James Wasserman, *The Egyptian Book of the Dead: The Book of Going Forth by Day: Being the Papyrus of Ani (royal scribe of the divine offerings), Written and Illustrated circa 1250 B.C.E., by Scribes and Artists Unknown, Including the Balance of chapters of the Books of the Dead Known as the Ban Recension, Compiled from Ancient Texts, Dating Back to the Roots of Egyptian Civilization*, San Francisco, CA: Chronicle Books, 2008.

Felner, Alfredo de Albuquerque, *Angola: Apontamentos Sobre a Ocupação e Início do Estabelecimento dos Portugueses no Congo, Angola e Benguela Extraídos de Documentos Históricos*, Coimbra: Imp. Da Universidade, 1933.

Ferlini, Vera Lúcia Amaral, 'A subordinação dos Lavradaores de Cana aos Senhores de Emgenho: Tensão e Conflito no Mundo dos Brancos', *Revista Brazileira de História*, 6(12), 1986, pp. 151–168.

Fernandes, V., *Description de la Côte Occidentale d'Afriqe (Sénégal au Cap de Monte, Archipels) par Valentim Fernandes (1506–1510)*, Bissau: Centro de Estudo da Guiné Portuguesa, 1951.

Fernão de Sousa a El-Rei Angola-are [A Letter of Governor Fernão de Sousa to the King and Angolans], BAL – Ms. 51-VIII-30, fls. 242-242 v, 27 March 1627; also, in MMA, pp. 506–507.

Ferreira, Eugénio, *Feiras e Presídios: Esboço de Interpretação Materialista da Colonização de Angola*, Lisbon: Edições 70, 1979.

Ferreira, Roquinaldo Amaral, *Cross-Cultural Exchange in the Atlantic World: Angola and Brazil During the Era of the Slave Trade*, Cambridge: Cambridge University Press, 2014.

  'Slaving and Resistance to Slaving in West Central Africa', in David Eltis and Stanley L. Engerman (eds.), *The Cambridge World History of Slavery*, vol. III, Cambridge: Cambridge University Press, 2011, pp. 111–131.

  The Costs of Freedom: Central Africa in the Age of Abolition, 1820 ca.–1880 ca. Princeton, NJ: Princeton University Press: (forthcoming).

Ferreiro, Elvira Pérez, *El Tratado de Uceda contra los Estatutos de Limpieza de Sangre: Una Reaccíon ante el Establecimiento del Estatuto de Limpieza en la Orden Franciscana*, Madrid: Aben Ezra Ediciones, 2000.

Ferronha, António Luis, *As Cartas do 'Rei' do Congo, D. Afonso*, Lisbon: Grupo de Trabalho do M. Da Educação para as Comemorações dos Descobrimentos Portugueses, 1992.

Ferronha, António Luís (ed.), 'Introdução', in Andre. A. De Almada, *Tratado Breve dos Rios de Guiné do Cabo-Verde, Feito peleo Capitão André Álvares d'Almada, Ano de 1594, Leitura, Introdução, Modernização do Texto e Notas*, Lisbon: Grupo de Trabalho do Ministério da Educação para as Comemorações dos Descobrimentos Portugueses, 1994.

Filho, Ivan Alves, *Memorial dos Palmares*, Rio de Janeiro: Xenon, 1988.

Filho, Luís Viana, *O Negro na Bahia*, Rio de Janeiro: Martins Editora, 1976.

Fu-Kiau, Kimbwandende K. B., *African Cosmology of the Bantu-Kongo – Principles of Live and Living*, [Place of publication not identified]: African Tree Press, 2001.

Finlay, John, 'The Petition in the Court of Session in Early Modern Scotland', *Parliaments, Estates & Representation*, 38(3), 2018, pp. 337–349.

Finnis, John, *Natural Law and Natural Rights*, Oxford: Oxford University Press, 1980.
Fitz, Francisco García, 'La Reconquista: un Estado de la Cuestión', *Clio & Crímen*, 6, 2009, pp. 142–215.
Fonseca, George J., *Religião e Liberdade: os Negros nas Irmandades e Confrarias Portuguesas (séculos XV a XIX)*, Lisbon: Papelmunde, V. N. Famalicão, 2016.
'A Historiografia Sobre os Escravos em Portugal', *Cultura*, 33, 2014, pp. 1–22.
Foucault, Michel, *Discipline and Punish: The Birth of the Prison*, New York: Random House, 1977.
The Archaeology of Knowledge, New York: Pantheon, 1972.
The Birth of the Clinic, London: Tavistock, 1973.
The Order of Things: An Archaeology of the Human Sciences, London, New York: Routledge, 2002.
Frade, Florbela Veiga and Sandra Neves Silva, 'Medicina e Política em dois Físicos Judeus Portugueses de Hamburgo, Rodrigo de Castro e o Medicus Politicus (1614), eManuel Bocarro Rosales e o Status Astrologicus (1644)', *Sefarad*, 71 (1), 2011, pp. 51–94.
Freitas, Décio, *Palmares: A Guerra dos Escravos* [1973], 5th ed., Porto Alegre: Mercado Aberto, 1984.
Freitas, Mario Martins de, *Reino Negro de Palmares* [1954], 2nd ed., Rio de Janeiro: Biblioteca do Exército, 1988.
Freudenthal, Aida and Selma Pantoja, *Livro dos Baculamentos que os Sobas Deste Reino de Angola Pagam a Sua Majestade 1630*, Luanda: Arquivo Nacional de Angola, D.L., 2013.
Freyre, Gilberto, *Casa Grande & Senzala, Formação da Família Brasileira Sob o Regime de Economia Patriarcal*, 4th ed., Rio de Janeiro: Livraria José Olympio, 1943.
Fromont, Cécile, *The Art of Conversion: Christian Visual Culture in the Kingdom of Kongo*, Chapel Hill, NC: University of North Carolina Press, 2014.
Fuller, F. Lon, *The Morality of Law*, New Haven, CT, London: Yale University Press, 1964.
Funari, Pedro Paulo A., 'Conflict and the Interpretation of Palmares, a Brazilian Runaway Polity', *Historical Archaeology*, 37(3), 2003, pp. 81–92.
Furtado, Francisco Xavier de Mendoça and Marcos Carneiro de Mendonça (eds.), *A Amazôniana era Pombalina*, 2nd ed., vol. I (vol. 49a), *Correspondência do Governador e Capitão-General do Estado do Grão-Pará e Maranhão, Francisco Xavier de Mendonça Furtado, 1751-1759, Edições do Senado Federal*, Brasília: Senado Federal.
Gail, Marzieh, *The Three Popes: An Account of the Great Schism*, New York: Simon and Schuster, 1969.
Garstein, Oskar, *Rome and the Counter-Reformation in Scandinavia: Until the Establishment of the S. Congregatio de Propaganda Fide in 1622, Based on Source Material in the Kolsrud Collection*, vol. I, Oslo: Universitetsforlaget, 1963.
Gaspar, David Barry and Darlene Clark Hine (eds.), *Beyond Bondage: Free Women of Color in the Americas*, Urbana, IL.: University of Illinois Press, 2004.

Genovese, Eugene D., *From Rebellion to Revolution: Afro-American Slave Revolts in the Making of the Modern World*, Louisiana: Louisiana State University Press, 1981.
Gilroy, Paul, *The Black Atlantic*, London: Verso, 1993.
Gitlitz, David M., *Secrecy and Deceit: The Religion of the Crypto-Jews*, Philadelphia, PA: Jewish Publication Society, 1996.
Golding, Martin P., *Philosophy of Law*, Englewood Cliffs, NJ: Prentice-Hall, 1975.
Gomes, Flávio dos Santos, *Histórias de Quilombolas: Mocambos e Comunidades de Senzalas no Rio de Janeiro, Século XIX*, Rio de Janeiro: Arquivo Nacional, 1995.
Palmares: Escravidão e Liberdade no Atlântico Sul, São Paulo: Contexto, 2005.
Gomez, Michael A. *African Dominion: A New History of Empire in Early and Medieval West Africa*, Princeton, NJ: Princeton University Press, 2018.
'African Identity and Slavery in the Americas', *Radical History Review*, 75, 1999, pp. 111–120.
Gordon, Jacob U., 'Yoruba Cosmology and Culture in Brazil, A Study of African Survivals in the New World', *Journal of Black Studies*, 10(2), 1979, pp. 231–244.
Gorr, Michael and Sterling Harwood (eds.), *Controversies in Criminal Law*, Boulder, CO: Westview Press, 1992.
Gray, Richard, *Black Christians and White Missionaries*, London and New Haven, CT: Yale University Press, 1990.
'The Papacy and the Atlantic Slave Trade: Lourenço da Silva, the Capuchins and the Decisions of the Holy Office', *Past and Present*, 115, 1987, pp. 52–68.
Green, Toby, *A Fistful of Shells, West Africa from the Rise of the Slave Trade to the Age of Revolution*, Milton Keynes: Penguin Random House UK, 2019.
'Baculamento or Encomienda?: Legal Pluralisms and the Contestation of Power in Pan-Atlantic World of the Sixteenth and Seventeenth Centuries', *Journal of Global Slavery*, 2, 2017, pp. 310–336.
'Beyond an Imperial Atlantic: Trajectories of Africans from Upper Guinea and West-Central Africa in the Early Atlantic World', *Past and Present*, 230(1), 2016, pp. 91–122.
'Masters of Difference: Creolization and the Jewish Presence in Cabo Verde, 1497–1672', unpublished Ph.D. thesis, University of Birmingham, 2006.
The Rise of the Trans-Atlantic Slave Trade in Western Africa, 1300–1500, Cambridge: Cambridge University Press, 2012.
Gross, Hyman, *A Theory of Criminal Justice*, Oxford: Oxford University Press, 2005.
Gunn, Jeffrey, 'Creating a Paradox: Quobna Ottobah Cugoano and the Slave Trade's Violation of the Principles of Christianity, Reason, and Property Ownership', *Journal of World History*, 21(4), 2010, pp. 629–656.
Haag, Ernest van den, *Punishing Criminals: Concerning a Very Old and Painful Question*, Chicago, IL: University of Chicago Press, 1978.
Hall, Stuart, 'The Spectacle of the Others', in Stuart Hall (ed.), *Representation*, London: Sage, 1997.
Representation, London: Sage, 2013.

Hall, Trevor P., *Before Middle Passage: Translated Portuguese Manuscripts of Atlantic Slave Trading from West Africa to Iberian Territories, 1513–26*, Farnham: Ashgate, 2015.
Hart, H. L. A., *Punishment and Responsibility*, Oxford: Oxford University Press, 1968.
The Concept of Law, Oxford: Clarendon Press, 1961.
Hanke, Lewis, *The Spanish Struggle for Justice in the Conquest of America*, Boston, MA: Little, Brown, 1965.
Hansen, João Adolfo, 'Representações da Cidade de Salvador no Século XVII', *Sibila Sibila, Revista de poesia e crítica literária*, 2010: http://sibila.com.br/mapa-da-lingua/representacoes-da-cidade-de-salvador-no-seculo-xvii/3343.
Haveaux, G. L., *La Tradition Historique des Bapende Orientaux*, Brussels, 1954, pp. 35–37 and 46–47.
Havik, Philip J., *Silences and Soundbites: The Gendered Dynamics of Trade and Brokerage in the Pre-Colonial Guinea Bissau Region*, Münster: Lit Verlag, 2004.
Hawthorne, Walter, *From Africa to Brazil, Culture, Identity, and Atlantic Slave Trade 1600–1830*, Cambridge: Cambridge University Press, 2010.
Hegel, F., *The Philosophy of History*, trans. J. Sibree, New York: Dover Publications, 1956, p.18.
Heidegger, Martin, *What is Metaphysics?*, trans. Siavash Jamadi, Salisbury: Phoenix Publishing, 2014.
Heintze, Beatrix and Katja Rieck, 'The Extraordinary Journey of the Jaga Through the Centuries: Critical Approaches to Precolonial Angolan Historical Sources', *History in Africa*, 34, 2007, pp. 67–101.
Heintze, Beatrix, 'Angola nas Garras do Tráfico de Escravos: As Guerras Angolanas do Ndongo (1611–1630), *Revista Internacional de Estudos Africanos*, 1, 1984, pp. 11–59.
Angola nos Séculos XVI e XVII. Estudo Sobre Fontes, Métodos e História, Luanda: Kilombelombe, 2007.
'Luso-African Feudalism in Angola? The Vassal Treaties of the Sixteenth to the Eighteenth Century', *Revista Portuguesa de História*, 18, 1980, pp. 111–131.
'Ngonga a Mwiza: um Sobado Angolano sob Domino Português no Século XVII', *Revista Internacional de Estudos Africanos*, 8–9, 1988, pp. 221–234'.
'Propaganda Concerning "Man Eaters" in West Central Africa in the Second Half of the Nineteenth Century', *Paideuma*, 49, 2003, pp. 125–135.
'The Angolan Vassal Tributes of the 17th Century', *Revista de Historia Economica e Social*, 6, 1980, pp. 57–78.
'Written Sources and African History: A Plea for the Primary Source. The Angola Manuscript Collection of Fernão de Sousa', *History in Africa*, 9, 1982, pp. 77–103.
Helms, Mary W., 'The Cultural Ecology of a Colonial Tribe', *Ethnology*, 8(1), 1969, pp. 76–84.
Henderson, Lawrence W., *Angola: Five Centuries of Conflict*, Ithaca, NY: Cornell University Press, 1979.
Henriques, Isabel Castro, *Os Africanos em Portugal História e Memória Séculos XV-XXI, Inauguração da Exposição*, Lisbon: Torre de Belém, 2011.

Heywood, Linda M., *Njinga of Angola: Africa's Warrior Queen*, Boston, MA: Harvard University Press, 2017.
'Slavery and Its Transformation in the Kingdom of Kongo: 1491–1800', *The Journal of African History*, 50(1), 2009, pp. 1–22.
Heywood, Linda M. and John K. Thornton, *Central Africans and Cultural Transformations in the American Diaspora*, Cambridge: Cambridge University Press, 2002.
Heywood, Linda M. and John K. Thornton, *Central Africans, Atlantic Creoles, and the Foundation of the Americas, 1585–1660*, Cambridge: Cambridge University Press, 2007.
Hilton, Anne, 'The Jaga Reconsidered', *The Journal of African History*, 22(2), 1981, pp. 191–202.
Hoare, Prince, *Memoirs of Granville Sharp*, London: Henry Colbourn, 1828.
Hoogbergen, W., *Palmares: A Critical View on its Sources*, 2001, pp. 23–55: https://publications.iai.spk-berlin.de/servlets/mcrfilenodeservlet/Document_derivat e_00001778/BIA_070_023_055.pdf;jsessionid=888A9913152645 68BF28EA3 C1CEB1192.
Holl, Augustin, BBC interview: 'Slavery and Suffering: The History of Africa with Zeinab Badawi', episode 16: https://www.youtube.com/watch?v=ajI8lkYdmAk.
Howes, R. 'The British Press and Opposition to Lord Salisbury's Ultimatum of January 1890', *Portuguese Studies*, 23(2), 2007, pp. 153–166.
Hume, David, *Essays, Moral, Political, and Literary, Part I, Essay XXI, 'Of National Characters (LF ed.) [1777]*, Indianapolis, IN: Liberty Fund 1987.
Hussey, Ronald D., 'Text of the Laws of Burgos (1512–1513) Concerning the Treatment of the Indians', *The Hispanic American Historical Review*, 12(3), 1932, pp. 301–326.
Ilídio, Amaral do, *O Reino do Congo, Os Mbundu (ou Ambundos), O Reino dos 'Ngola' (ou de Angola) e a Presença Portuguesa, de Finais do Século XV a Meados do Século XVI*, Lisbon: Ministério da Ciência e da Tecnologia, Instituto de Investigação Tropical, 1996.
Inikori, Joseph E., 'Africa and the Globalization Process: Western Africa, 1450–1850', *Journal of Global History*, 2(1), 2007, pp. 63–86.
Jaca, Francisco José de and Epifanio de Moirans, Order of Friars Minor Capuchin (Ordo Fratrum Minorum Capuccinorum) – O.F.M. Cap., *Servi Liberi Seu Naturalis Mancipiorum Libertatis Iusta Defensio (Freed Slaves or the Just Defence of the Natural Freedom of the Emancipated)*, Archivo General de Indias, Sevilla, Audiencia de Santo Domingo, Legajo 527, 1682, in José Tomas López García, *Dos Defensores de los Esclavos Negros en el Siglo XVII*, Maracaibo, Caracas: Biblioteca Corpozulia, 1982.
Jackson, Guida M., *Women Who Ruled: A Biographical Encyclopedia*, Santa Barbara, CA: ABC-CLIO, 1990.
Jackson, John G., *Introduction to African Civilizations*, New York: Citadel Press, 1970.
Jeal, Tim, *Livingstone*, London: Heinemann. 1973.
Jerade, Miriam, 'Mors Certa, Hora Incerta: Derrida on Finitude and the Death Penalty', *The New Centennial Review*, 17(3), 2017, pp. 103–121.

Joner, Henrique, 'Impressions of Luis de Molina about the Trade of African Slaves', *Patristica et Mediaevalia*, 36, 2015, pp. 39–50: https://core.ac.uk/do wnload/pdf/322579935.pdf.

Jouve-Martín, José R., 'Death, Gender, and Writing: Testaments of Women of African Origin in Seventeenth-Century Lima, 1651–1666', in Kathryn Joy McKnight and Leo J. Carofalo (eds.), *Afro-Latino Voices: Narratives from the Early Modern Ibero-Atlantic World, 1550–1812*, Indianapolis, IN, Cambridge: Hackett Publishing Company, Inc., 2009, pp. 105–125.

Kallestrup, Louise Nyholm, *Agents of Witchcraft in Early Modern Italy and Denmark*, Basingstoke and New York: Palgrave, 2015.

Karttunen, Liisi, *Les Nonciatures Apostoliques Permanentes de 1650 a 1800*, Geneva: E. Chaulmontet, 1912.

Kellogg, Susan and Matthew Restall (eds.), *Dead Giveaways: Indigenous Testaments of Colonial Mesoamerica and the Andes*, Salt Lake City, UT: University of Utah Press, 1998.

Kent, R., 'Palmares: An African State in Brazil', *The Journal of African History*, 2, 1965, pp.161–175.

Kiple, Kenneth F. and Virginia Himmelsteib King, *Another Dimension to the Black Diaspora: Diet, Disease and Racism*, Cambridge: Cambridge University Press, 2003.

Lahon, Didier, 'Da Redução da Alteridade à Consagração da Diferença: as Irmandades Negras em Portugal (Séculos XVI–XVIII)', *Projecto História*, 44, 2012, pp. 53–83.

Langan, J., 'The Elements of St. Augustine's "Just War" Theory',*The Journal of Religious Ethics*, 12(1),1984, 19–38.

Lara, Silvia Hunold, 'Depois da Batalha de Pungo Andongo (1671): O Destino Atlântico dos Príncipes do Ndongo', *Revista de História*, 2016, pp. 205–225.

'Palmares & Cucaú: O Aprendizado da Dominação, Tese Apresentada Para o Concurso de Professor Titular, Área de História do Brasil, Disciplina HH384 – História do Brasil I', unpublished thesis, State University of Campinas, São Paulo, 2008.

'Palmares and Cucaú: Political Dimensions of a Maroon Community in Late Seventeenth-Century Brazil', Conference paper, 29–30 October, Yale University, New Haven, CT, 2010.

Las Casas, Bartolomé de, *Brevisima Relacion de la Destruccion de Africa (1556)* (estudo Preliminar, edição e notas de Isacio Perez Fernandez), Salamanca: Viceconsejería de Cultura y Deportes del Gobierno de Canarias, 1989.

Lawal, Babatunde, *The Gèlèdé Spectacle: Art, Gender, and Social Harmony in an African Culture*, Seattle, WA: University of Washington Press, 1996.

Leite, S. J. Serafim, *História da Companhia de Jesus no Brasil*, vol. VIII, Rio de Janeiro: Imprensa Nacional, 1949, pp. 278–279.

'Jesuítas do Brasil, Naturais de Angola', *Brotéria: Revista Contemporânea de Cultura*, 3(3/4), 1940, pp. 254–261.

Lenhart, J. M., 'Capuchin Champions of Negro Emancipation in Cuba, 1681–1685', *Franciscan Studies*, VI, 1946, pp. 195–217.

Léry, Jean and Janet Whatley, *History of a Voyage to the Land of Brazil, Otherwise Called America*, Berkeley, CA: University of California Press, 1990.
Lesko, Barbara S., *The Great Goddesses of Egypt*, Norman, OK: University of Oklahoma Press, 1999.
Lewin, Boleslao (ed.), *Confidencias de dos Criptojudíos en la Cárcel de la Inquisición*, Buenos Aires: Tall. Gráf. J. Kaufman, 1975. 1975.
Lima, José Ignacio de Abreu, *Synopsis ou Deducção Chronologica dos Factos Mais Notaveis da História do Brazil*, Pernambucco: Na typographia de M. F. De Faria, 1845.
Lindsay, Lisa A., *Atlantic Bonds: A Nineteenth-Century Odyssey from America to Africa*, Chapel Hill, NC: University of North Carolina Press, 2017.
Lingna Nafafé, José , 'African Orality in Iberian Space: Critique of Barros and Myth of Racial Discourse', *Portuguese Studies Journal*, 28(2), 2012, pp. 126–142.
Colonial Encounters: Issues of Culture, Hybridity and Creolisation, Portuguese Mercantile Settlers in West Africa, Frankfurt am Main: Peter Lang, 2007.
'Europe in Africa and Africa in Europe: Rethinking Postcolonial Space, Cultural Encounters and Hybridity', *European Journal of Social Theory*, 16(1), 2013, pp. 51–68.
'Mission and Political Power: Subversive Power Relations in Luso-West Africa (Guinea-Bissau) 1886–1914', in A. Seldtkeller (ed.), *Series, Missionsgeschichtliches Archiv. Studien der Berliner Gesellschaft für Missionsgeschichte*, vol, X, Franz Steiner Verlag: Berlin, 2005, pp. 229–241.
Lipiner, Elias, *Izaque de Castro: o Mancebo que veio Preso do Brasil*, Recife: Fundação Joaquim Nabuco/Editora Massangana, 1992.
Lisska, Anthony J., *Aquinas's Theory of Natural Law: An Analytic Reconstruction*, Oxford: Clarendon Press, 1996.
Livermore, Harold, 'Padre Oliveira's Outburst', *Portuguese Studies*, 17, 2001, pp. 22–41.
'The Anglo-Portuguese Crisis of 1890: Another Look at the Ultimatum', *Studia*, 56–57, 2000, pp. 23–59.
Livingstone, David and James I. Macnair (ed.), *Livingstone's Travels*, London: J. M. Dent, 1954.
Logerfo, James, 'Sir William Dolben and "The Cause of Humanity": The Passage of the Slave Trade Regulation Act of 1788', *Eighteenth-Century Studies*, 6(4), 1973, pp. 431–451.
Lovejoy, Paul E., *Transformations in Slavery: A History of Slavery in Africa*, Cambridge: Cambridge University Press, 2011.
Lovejoy, Paul E. and Nicholas Rogers, *Unfree Labour in the Development of the Atlantic World*, London: Frank Cass Publishers, 1995.
Luchte, James, *Kant's Critique of Pure Reason: A Reader's Guide*, London, New York: Continuum, 2007.
MacGaffey, Wyatt, 'African History, Anthropology and the Rationality of the Natives', *History in Africa*, 5, 1978, pp. 101–120.
M'bokolo, Elikia, *África Negra: História e Civilizações, vol. I (até o século XVIII)*, Slavador: EDUFBA; São Paulo, Casas das África, 2008, pp. 185–205.

Magalhães, Pablo Antonio Iglesias, 'A Relação do Engenho de Sergipe do Conde em 1625', *Afro-Ásia*, 41, 2010.
Malekandathil, Pius, 'Cross, Sword and Conflicts: A Study of the Political Meanings of the Struggle Between the Padroado Real and the Propaganda Fide', *Studies in History*, 27(2), 2011, pp. 251–267.
Mamiami, Luiz Vicencio, *Arte de Gramatica da Lingua Brazilica da Nação Kiriri*, Rio de Janeiro: TYP, Central de Brown & Evaristo, 1877.
Manning, Patrick, *Slavery and African Life*, Cambridge: Cambridge University Press, 1990.
Manso, Visconde Paiva, *Historia do Congo*, Lisbon: Typ. Da Academia, 1877.
Marcussi, Alexandre Almeida, 'Cativeiro e Cura: Experiências Religiosas da Escravidão Atlântica nos Calundus de Luzia Pinta, Séculos XVII-XVIII', unpublished Ph.D. thesis, Federal University of São Paulo (USP), 2015: https://bv.fapesp.br/pt/bolsas/134878/cativeiro-e-cura-experiencias-religiosas-da-escravidao-atlantica-nos-calundus-de-luzia-pinta-secul/.
  'O Dever Catequético A Evangelização dos Escravos em Luanda nos séculos XVII e XVIII': http://www.historia.uff.br/7mares/wp-content/uploads/2014/04/v01n02a06.pdf.
Maritain, Jacques, *Man and the State*, Chicago, IL: University of Chicago Press, 1951.
Mark, Peter, *'Portuguese' Style and Luso-African Identity: Precolonial Senegambia, Sixteenth-Nineteenth Centuries*, Bloomington, IN: Indiana University Press, 2003.
Marques, Guida, 'Do Índio Gentio ao Gentio Bárbaro: Usos e Deslizes da Guerra Justa na Bahia Setecentista', *Revista Histórica*, 171, 2014, pp. 15–48: https://www.revistas.usp.br/revhistoria/article/view/89006.
Marques, José, *A Arquidiocese de Braga no Século XV*, Lisbon: Imprensa Nacional-Casa da Moeda, 1998.
Martin, Richard, 'Zumbi dos Palmares: Um Novo Tiradentes?', *Clio – Revista de Pesquisa Histórica*, 20(1), 2002, pp. 233–247.
Martin, Phyllis, 'Sources and Source–Criticism', *Journal of African History*, 29(3), 1988, pp. 537–540.
Martins, Jorge, *O Senhor Roubado a Inquisição e a Questão Judaica*, Lisbon: Heuris – Europress, 2002.
Marx, Karl, *Capital: A Critique of Political Economy*, vol. I, London: Lawrence & Wisehart, 1954.
Mattos, Hebe, '"Pretos" and "Pardos" Between the Cross and the Sword: Racial Categories in Seventeenth Century Brazil', *European Review of Latin American and Caribbean Studies*, 80, 2006, pp. 43–55.
Maxwell, John Francis, *Slavery and the Catholic Church: Teaching Concerning the Moral Legitimacy of the Institution of Slavery*, London: Rose [for] the Anti-Slavery Society for the Protection of Human Rights, 1975.
Mbiti, John S., *African Religions & Philosophy*, London: Heinemann, 1969.
Mcknight, Kathryn Joy and Leo J. Carofalo (eds.), *Afro-Latino Voices: Narratives from the Early Modern Ibero-Atlantic World, 1550–1812*, Indianapolis, IN, Cambridge: Hackett Publishing Company, Inc., 2009.

Mcmurdo, Edward, *History of Portugal*, vol. III, London: S. Low, Marston, Searle, & Rivington, 1889.
Melo e Souza, Marina de, 'Congo in the Americas and Brazil', Oxford Encyclopedia, 2020: https://oxfordre.com/africanhistory/view/10.1093/acre fore/9780190277734.001.0001/acrefore-9780190277734-e-430.
Mendes.Albano, Ramon Sarró and Ana Temudo, *O Museu Ethnográfico Nacional da Guiné-Bissau: Imagens Para uma História – El Museu Ethnográfico Nacional de Guiné-Bissau: Imágenes Para una Historia*, Lisbon: Instituto Camões, 2018.
Miers, Suzanne and Igor Kopytoff, 'African "Slavery" as an Institution of Marginality', in Suzanne Miers and Igor Kopytoff (eds.), *Slavery in Africa: Historical and Anthropological Perspectives*, Madison, WI: University of Wisconsin Press, 1979, pp.1–26.
Miller, Joseph C., 'Capitalism and Slaving: The Financial and Commercial Organization of the Angolan Slave Trade, according to the Accounts of Antonio Coelho Guerreiro (1684–1692)', *'The International Journal of African Historical Studies*, 17(1), 1984, pp. 1–56.
 Kings and Kinsmen: Early Mbundu States in Angola, Oxford: Clarendon Press, 1976.
 'Mortality in the Atlantic Slave Trade: Statistical Evidence on Causality,' *Journal of Interdisciplinary History*, 13(2), 1981, pp. 317–329.
 'Requiem for the Jaga', *Cahiers d'Études Africaines*, 11(3), 1981, pp. 385–423.
 Way of Death: Merchant Capitalism and the Angolan Slave Trade, 1730–1830, Madison, WI: University of Wisconsin Press, 1997.
Molina, Luis de, *De Iustitia et Iure: Opera Omnia, Tractatibus Quinque, Tomisque Totidem Comprehensa*, Coloniae Allborogum: Sumptibus Fratrum de Tournes, 1759.
Montecúccolo, Giovanni Antonio Cavazzi, *Descrição Histórica dos Três Reinos do Congo, Matamba e Angola*, vols. I–II., trans. Graciano Maria de Leguzzano, Lisbon: Junta de Investigações do Ultramar, 1965.
 Istorica Descrizione de Tre Regni Congo Matamba ed Angola, book 5, Bologna: Giacomo Monti, 1687.
 'Missione Evangelica al Regno de Congo', MSS Araldi, Modena, vols. A, B, C, trans. John Thornton, 2008.
Morenz, Siegfried, *Egyptian Religion*, Ithaca., NY: Cornell University Press, 1973.
Mota, Lucia Silva da, 'A Familia Mesquita em Portugal e em Terras de Piratiningas', unpublished Master's dissertation, University of São Paulo, 2008.
Mott, Luiz, *Egipcíaca, Rosa (1719–1771)*, Oxford African American Studies Center, 2016 and online version 2017: https://oxfordaasc.com/view/10.1093/acref/9780195301731.001.0001/acref-9780195301731-e-73870.
 Rosa Egipcíaca: Uma Santa Africana no Brasil, Rio de Janeiro: Bertrand Editors, 1993.
Moura, Clóvis, *Rebeliões da Senzala*, São Paulo: Lech Livraria Editora Ciências Humanas Ltd, 1959.
 Sociologia do Negro Brasileiro, São Paulo: Ática, 1988.

Mudimbe, Valentin-Yves, *The Invention of Africa: Gnosis, Philosophy and the Order of Knowledge*, Bloomington and Indianapolis, IN: Indiana Press University, 1988.
Mundadan, A. Mathias, *History of Christianity in India*, vol. I, Bangalore: Church History Association of India, 1984.
Münzer, Jérome, 'Itinerarium, De Inventione Africae Maritimae et Occidentalis Videclicet Genee Per Infantem Heinrichum Portugallie', fls. 280-88, 1494 and in P. A. Brásio, *Monumenta Missionaria Africana 1342–1499*, Segunda Série, vol. IV, Lisbon: Academia Portuguesa da História, 1958.
Myrup, Erik Lars, 'To Rule from Afar: The Overseas Council and the Making of the Brazilian West, 1642–1807', unpublished Ph.D. thesis, Yale University, 2006.
Nabuco, Carolina, *The Life of Joaquim Nabuco*, Stanford, CA.: Stanford University Press, 1950.
Nascimento, A., *O Quilombismo – Documentos de uma Militância Pan-africanista*, Petrópolis: Editora Vozes, 1980.
Naro, Priscilla, Roger Sansi-Roca and David Treece (eds.), *Culture of the Lusophone Black Atlantic*, London: Palgrave Macmillan, 2007.
Natividade, Manuel Vieira de, *O Mosteiro de Alcobaça*, Coimbra: Imprensa Progresso, 1885.
Needell, Jeffrey D., 'Identity, Race, Gender, and Modernity in the Origins of Gilberto Freyre's Oeuvre', *The American Historical Review*, 100(1), 1995, pp. 51–77.
Newton, John, *An Authentic Narrative*, Edinburgh: Chapman & Co, 1880.
Niehaus, Isak, *Witchcraft and a Life in the New South Africa*, Cambridge: Cambridge University Press, 2012.
Novinsky, Anita, 'Padre Antônio Vieira, a Inquisição e os Judeus', *Jewish History*, 6(1-2), 1992, pp. 152-162.
Nowell, Charles E., *The Rose-Colored Map: Portugal's Attempt to Build an African Empire from the Atlantic to the Indian Ocean*, Lisbon: Junta de Investigates Científicas do Ultramar, 1982.
O'Malley, John W., *Trent: What Happened at the Council*, Cambridge, MA: The Belknap Press of Harvard University, 2013.
Oliveira, Fernando, *A Arte da Guerra e do Mar*, Lisbon: Biblioteca National, 1937.
Oliveira, Freire de, *Elementos para a História do Município de Lisboa*, Lisbon, 1885.
Oliveira, Ingrid Silva de, 'As "Histórias" de Angola e Seus Autores nos Séculos XVII e XVIII: um Estudo de Caso dos Militares Antonio de Cadornega e Elias Alexandre Correa', *Anais do XV Encontro Regional da História da ANPUH-RIO*, 2012, pp.1–11: http://www.encontro2012.rj.anpuh.org/resources/ana is/15/1338340715_ARQUIVO_Textocompletoanpuh2012.pdf.
Oliveira, Vanessa, 'A África no Brasil: as Irmandades Religiosas como Símbolos de Resistência,' *Caderno do Estudante*, 1, 2008, pp. 75–81.
  'Devoção e Distinção Étnica na Irmandade do Homens Pretos do Rosário da Cidade de São Cristóvão-Sergipe,' *Portuguese Studies Review*, 22(2), 2014, pp. 79–112.

'Donas, Escravas e Pretas Livres em Luanda (séc. XIX), *Estudos Ibero-Americanos*, 44(3), 2018, pp. 447–456.
Orser Jr., C. E., *A Historical Archaeology of the Modern World*, New York: Plenum Press, 1996.
Pagden, Anthony, *The Fall of Natural Man: The American Indian and the Origins of Comparative Ethnology*, Cambridge: Cambridge University Press, 1982.
Painter, Nell Irvin, *The History of White People*, New York: W. W. Norton & Company, 2011.
Papy, Louis, 'La Valée du Sénégal: Agriculture Traditionnelle et Riziculture Mécanisée', Les Cahiers d'Outre-Mer, 4(16), 1951, pp. 277–324.
Parfitt, Tudor *Black Jews in Africa and the Americas*, Cambridge, MA, London: Harvard University Press, 2013.
  Hybrid Hate: Conflations of Antisemitism and Anti-Black Racism from the Renaissance to the Third Reich, Oxford: Oxford University Press, 2020.
  The Lost Tribes of Israel: The History of a Myth, London: Weidenfeld and Nicolson, 2002.
Parfitt, Tudor and Yulia Egorova, *Genetics, Mass Media and Identity: A Case Study of the Genetic Research on the Lemba and Bene Israel*, London: Routledge, 2006.
Parés, Luis Nicolau, 'A Formação do Candomblé: História e Ritual da Nação Jeje na Bahia', *Revista de História*, 158, 2008, pp. 309–314.
Parry, J. H., *The Spanish Theory of Empire in the Sixteenth Century*, Cambridge: Cambridge University Press, 1940.
Peel, John D. Y., *Religious Encounter and the Making of the Yoruba*, Bloomington, IN: Indiana University Press, 2003.
Pereira, Júlio César Medeiros da Silva, *À Flor da Terra: O Cemitério dos Pretos Novos no Rio de Janeiro*, Rio de Janeiro: Garamond, 2007.
Pereira, Pacheco, *Durate Pacheco Pereira, Esmeraldo de Situ Orbis*, series II, vol. LXXXI, London: Hakluyt Society, 1892.
Petter, Margarida, 'Línguas Africanas no Brasil: Vitalidade e Invisbilidade', in Ivana Lima Stolze and Laura Carmo (eds.), *História Social da Língua Nacional: Diápora Africana*, Rio de Janeiro: FAPERU, 2014, pp. 19–39.
Pimentel, Maria do Rosário, 'Aspectos do Quotidiano no Transporte de Escravos do Século XVII: do Sertão africano à Costa Americana', *Estudos Ibero-americanos*, 25(2), 1999, pp. 233–244.
Pimentel, Maria do Rosário and Maria do Rosário Monteiro (eds.), *Senhores e Escravos nas Sociedades Ibero-Atlânticas*, Lisbon: CHAM, 2019.
Pitta, Sebastião da Rocha, *Provincia da Bahia, História da America Portugueza, Collecção de Obras Relativas á História da Capitania Depois a Sua Geographia Mandadas Reimprimir ou Publicar pelo Barão Homem de Mello, Do Conselho de Sua Magestade o Imperador, Presidente da Mesma Provincia*, Bahia: Imprensa Econômica, 1878.
Plato, *Gorgias*, trans. W. Hamilton, Harmondsworth, Middlesex: Penguin Books Inc., 1960.
Podipara, Placid J., *The Thomas Christians*, London: Darton, Longman and Tidd, 1970.

Pope Alexander VII's Brief to the Queen Ana de Sousa Njinga, 'Carissimae in Christo filiae Nostrae Annae Reginae Singae Alexander Papa VII', AV, Epistolas ad Principes (EaP), vol. 64, fls. 70 v–71, doc. 115, 19 June 1660.

Prestage, Edgar, *As Relações Diplomáticas de Portugal com a França, Inglaterra e Holanda de 1640 a 1668*, Coimbra: Imprensa da Universidade, 1928.

Price, R., 'Palmares Como Poderia Ter Sido', in João José Reis and Flávio dos Santos Gomes (eds.), *Liberdade Por Um Fio: História Dos Quilombos no Brasil*, São Paulo: Companhia das Letras, 1995, pp. 52–59.

Pullan, Brian, *The Jews of Europe and the Inquisition of Venice, 1550–1670*, Oxford: Basil Blackwell, 1983.

Querino, Manuel, *O Negro Na Bahia*,: São Paulo: Livraria José Olympio Editor a Rua do Ouvidor, 1946.

Ramos, Arthur, 'O Espírito Associativo do Negro Brasileiro', *Revista do Arquivo Municipal*, 47(4), 1939, pp. 105–126.

Ramos, Rui, 'Rebelião e Sociedade Colonial: "Alvoroços" em São Tomé (1545–1555)', *Revista Internacional de Estudos Africanos*, 4&5, 1986, pp. 101–136: https://www.africabib.org/rec.php?RID=119523795.

Reddie, Richard, *Abolition! The Struggle to Abolish Slavery in the British Colonies*, Oxford: Lion Books, 2007.

Redford, Donald B., *Ancient Gods Speak: A Guide to Egyptian Religion*, Oxford, New York: Oxford University Press, 2002.

Reginaldo, Lucilene, '"África em Portugal": Devoções, Irmandades e Escravidão no Reino de Portugal, século XVIII', *Studia Historica, Historia Moderna*, 38 (1), 2016, pp. 123–151: https://www.scielo.br/j/his/a/qvqDbVM7RsyLp7jrFNWySwG/?lang=pt.

'André do Couto Godinho: Homem preto, formado em Coimbra, missionário no Congo em fins do século XVIII,' *Revista História*, 173, 2015, pp. 141–174.

'"Não tem Informação": Mulatos, Pardos e Pretos na Universidade de Coimbra (1700–1771)', *Estudos Ibero-Americanos*, 44(3), 2018, pp. 421–434.

Os Rosários dos Angolas – Irmandades de Africanos e Crioulos na Bahia Setecentista, São Paulo: Alameda, 2011.

'Rosários dos Pretos, "São Benedito de Quissama": Irmandades e Devoções Negras no Mundo Atlântico (Portugal e Angola, Século XVIII)', *Studia Historica, Historia Moderna*, 38(1), 2016, pp. 123–151.

Reis, João José, *Domingos Sodré, um Sacerdote Africano: Escravidão, Liberdade e Candomblé na Bahia do século XIX*, São Paulo: Companhia das Letras, 2008.

Slave Rebellion in Brazil: The Muslim Uprising of 1835 in Bahia, London: Taylor & Francis, 1995.

Reis, João José, Flávio dos Santos Gomes and Marcus J. M. de Carvalho, *O Alufá Rufino: Tráfico, Escravidão e Liberdade no Atlântico Negro (1822–1853)*, São Paulo: Companhia das Letras, 2010.

Relaçam/ Do FELICE SVCCESSO, QUE / configuiraõ as armas do Sereniffimo Princepe D. Pedro N. S. gouernadas por Francifco de Tauora, Gouernador, & Capitam General do Reyno de Angola contra a Rebeliaõ de Dom Ioaõ Rey

das Pedras, & Dongo, no mez de Dezembro de 1671', Biblioteca Nacional de Lisboa, Reservado, 903, pp. 1–11.
Richardson, David, 'Shipboard Revolts, African Authority, and the Atlantic Slave Trade', *The William and Mary Quarterly*, 58(1), 2001, pp. 69–92.
Rodney, Walter, 'African Slavery and Other Forms of Social Oppression on the Upper Guinea Coast in the Context of the Atlantic Slave Trade', *Journal of African History*, 7, 1966, pp. 431–443.
Rodney, Walter, *History of the Upper Guinea Coast: 1545–1800*, Oxford: Clarendon Press, 1970.
How Europe Underdeveloped Africa, London; Brooklyn, NY: Verso, 2018.
Rodrigues, Jose Honorio, 'The Influence of Africa on Brazil and of Brazil on Africa', *The Journal of African History*, 3(1), 1962, pp. 49–67.
Rodrigues, Nina, 'As Sublevações de Negros no Brasil Anteriores ao Século XIX. Palmares', *Os Africanos no Brasil* [1905], 5th ed., São Paulo, Companhia Editora Nacional, 2010, pp. 130–195.
Rorty, Richard, 'Feminism and Pragmatism', in Russell S. Goodman (ed.), *Pragmatism: Critical Concepts in Philosophy*, New York: Routledge, 1995, pp. 1–35.
Rugendas, Johann Moritz, *Viagem Pitoresca Através do Brasil*, São Paulo: Martins, 1972. This book was translated from German into Portuguese and was first published with the German title *Malerische Reise in Brasilien*, Paris: Engelmann, 1835.
Russell-Wood, A. J. R., 'Black and Mulatto Brotherhoods in Colonial Brazil: A Study in Collective Behavior', *Hispanic American Historical Review*, 54 (4), 1974, pp. 567–602.
Fidalgos and Philanthropists: The Santa Casa da Misericordia of Bahia, 1550–1755, London: Macmillan, 1968.
The Black Man in Slavery and Freedom in Colonial Brazil, Oxford: Macmillan Press, in association with St Antony's College, 1993.
Russell, F., *The 'Just War' in the Middle Ages*, Cambridge: Cambridge University Press, 1975.
Said, Edward, *Orientalism*, London: Penguin, 1995.
Saldanha, M. J. Gabriel, *História De Goa (Politica E Arqueologica)*, New Delhi: Asian Educational Services, 1990.
Salles, Wesley Dartagnan, 'Lei das Arqueações de 1684: Por uma Nova Interpretação', *Oficina do Historiador*, 4(2), 2011, pp. 75–95.
Salvador, José G., *Os Cristãos Novos e o Comércio no Atlântico Meridional*, São Paulo: Pioneira, 1978.
'snas Capitanias do Sul. (Séculos XVI e XVII). Os Cristãos-Novos do Sul e Suas Relações com a Igreja', *Revista de História*, 25(51), 1962, pp. 49–86.
Sanceau, Elaine, *The Perfect Prince: A Biography of the King Dom Joao II*, Porto: Livraria Civilização-Editora, 1959.
Sandoval, Fray Prudencio de, *Historia de la Vida y Hechos del Emperador Carlos V, Biblioteca de Autores Españoles*, vol. 82, Madrid: Ediciones Atlas, 1955.
Santos, Catarina Madeira, 'Um Governo "Polido" para Angola: Reconfigurar Dispositivos de Domínio (1750–1800)', Unpublished Ph.D. thesis, New University of Lisbon, 2005.

Santos, Milton, *A Rede Urbana do Recôncavo*, Salvador: Imprensa Oficial do Estado, 1958.
Santos, Vaniclèia Silva, 'As Bolsas de Mandingas no Espaço Atlântico: Século XVIII', unpuplished Ph.D. thesis, State University of São Paulo, 2008.
Sargiacomo, M., 'Michel Foucault, Discipline and Punish: The Birth of the Prison', *Journal of Management and Governance*, 13(3), 2009, pp. 269–280.
Sarmento, Genisete de Lucena, *A Ocupação das Terras do Quilombo dos Palmares e a Criação de Vilas, Introdução à Hitória de União dos Palmares*, Maceió: CBA Editora, 2019.
Saunders, A. C. de C. M., *A Social History of Black Slaves and Freedmen in Portugal 1441–1555*, Cambridge: Cambridge University Press, 1982.
Schorsch, Jonathan, 'Blacks, Jews and the Racial Imagination in the Writings of Sephardim in the Long Seventeenth Century', *Jewish History*, 19, 2005, pp. 109–135.
Jews and Blacks in the Early Modern World, New York: Cambridge University Press, 2003.
Schultz, Kara, 'Interwoven: Slaving in the Southern Atlantic under the Union of the Iberian Crowns, 1580-1640', *Journal of Global Slavery*, 2, 2017, pp. 248–272.
Schwan, Anne and Stephen Shapiro, *How to Read Foucault's Discipline and Punish*, London: Pluto Press, 2011.
Schwartz, Stuart B. *Blacks and Indians: Common Cause and Confrontation in Colonial Brazil*, no date, Yale University: https://glc.yale.edu/sites/default/fil es/files/maroon/schwartz.pdf.
'Mocambos, Quilombos e Palmares: A Resistência Negra no Brasil Colonial', *Estudos Econômicos*, 17, 1987, pp. 61–88.
'Rethinking Palmares: Slave Resistance in Colonial Brazil,' in Stuart B. Schwartz, *Slaves, Peasants and Rebels: Reconsidering Brazilian Slavery*, Urbana, IL: University of Illinois Press, 1992, pp. 1294–1325.
Segredos Internos: Engenhos e Escravos na Sociedade Colonial, São Paulo: Companhia das Letras, 1988.
Slaves, Peasants, and Rebels: Reconsidering Brazilian Slavery, Urbana, IL: University of Illinois Press, 1996.
Sovereignty and Society in Colonial Brazil: The High Court of Bahia and its Judges, 1609–1751, Berkeley, CA.: University of California Press, 1973.
Sugar Plantations in the Formation of Brazilian Society: Bahia, 1550–1835, Cambridge: Cambridge University Press, 2010.
Schwartz, Stuart B. (ed.), *A Governor and His Image in Baroque Brazil: The Funeral Eulogy of Afonso Furtado de Castro do Rio de Mendonça by Juan Lopes Sierra*, trans. Ruth E. Jones, Minneapolis. MN: University of Minnesota Press, 1979.
Schwartz, Stuart B. andFrank Salomon, 'New Peoples and New Kinds of Peoples: Adaptation, Readjustment, and Ethnogenesis in South American Indigenous Societies (Colonial Era)', in Stuart B. Schwartz and Frank Saloman (eds.), *Cambridge History of Native Peoples of the Americas*, vol. III, Cambridge: Cambridge University Press, 1999, pp. 467–471.

Socorro Maria do, F. Barbosa et al. *Fontes Repatriadas: Anotações de História Colonial Referenciais para Pesquisa*, Recife: University Publisher of the Federal University of Pernambuco, 2006.

Seaver, George, *David Livingstone: His Life and Letters*, New York: Lutterworth Press, 1957.

Seibert, Gerhard, 'São Tomé and Príncipe: The First Plantation Economy in the Tropics', in Robin Law, Suzanne Schwarz and Silke Strickrodt (eds.), *Commercial Agriculture, the Slave Trade and Slavery in Atlantic Africa*, Oxford: James Currey, 2013, pp. 54–78.

'São Tomé's Great Slave Revolt of 1595: Background, Consequences and Misperceptions of One of the Largest Slave Uprisings in Atlantic History,' *Portuguese Studies Review*, 18(2), 2010, pp. 29–50.

Shaw, L. M. E., *Trade, Inquisition and the English Nation in Portugal, 1650–90*, Manchester: Carcanet Press, 1990.

Sharp, Granville, *The Law of Retribution: Or, a Serious Warning to Great Britain and Her Colonies, Founded On Unquestionable Examples of God's Temporal Vengeance Against Tyrants, Slave-holders and Oppressors*, London, 1776.

A Short Sketch of Temporary Regulations, (until Better Shall Be Proposed) for the Intended Settlement on the Grain Coast of Africa, Near Sierra Leona, London: H. Baldwin Publication, 1786.

Signorotto, Gianvittorio and Maria Antonietta Visceglia (eds.), *Court and Politics in Papal Rome, 1492–1700*, Cambridge: Cambridge University Press, 2002.

Silva, Daniel B. Domingues da, *The Atlantic Slave Trade from West Central Africa, 1780–1867*, New York: Cambridge University Press, 2017.

'The Atlantic Slave Trade to Maranhão, 1680–1846: Volume, Routes and Organisation', *Slavery & Abolition*, 29(4), 2008, pp. 477–501.

'The Kimbundu Diaspora to Brazil: Records from the Slave Ship Brilhante, 1838', *African Diaspora*, 8(2), 2015, pp. 200–219.

Silva, Sandra Neves, 'A "Obra ao Rubro" na Cultura Portuguesa de Seiscentos: o Cristão-Novo Manuel Bocarro Francês e seus Versos Alquímicos de 1624', *Cadernos de Estudos Sefarditas*, 8, 2008, pp. 217–244.

Silveira, L. (ed.), *Peregrinação de André de Faro à Terra dos Gentios*, Lisbon: Na Officina Tipographia Portugal – Brasil, 1945.

Simpson, Lesley Byrd, *The Encomienda in New Spain*, Berkeley, CA: University of California Press, 1950.

Skidmore, Thomas E., 'O Negro no Brasil e Nos Estados Unidos', *Argumento*, 1 (1), 1993, pp. 25–45.

Smith, John Holland, *The Great Schism: 1378*, New York: Weybright and Talley, 1970.

Soares, Mariza de Carvalho, 'Engenho Sim, de Açúcar Não o Engenho de Farinha de Frans Post', *Varia História*, 25(41), 2009, pp. 61–83.

Sokol, B. J., *Shakespeare and Tolerance*, Cambridge: Cambridge University Press, 2008.

Souza, Laura de Mello e, *Diabo e a Terra de Santa Cruz: Feitiçaria e Religiosidade Popular no Brasil Colonial*, São Paulo: Companhia das Letras, 1987.

Sparks, Randy J., 'The Two Princes of Calabar: An Atlantic Odyssey from Slavery to Freedom', *The William and Mary Quarterly*, 59(3), 2002, pp. 555–584.

Spicksley, Judith, 'Contested Enslavement: The Portuguese in Angola and the Problem of Debt, c. 1600–1800', *Itinerario*, 39(2), 2015, pp. 247–275.

Spivak, Gayatri Chakravorty : 'Can the Subaltern Speak?', in: Cary Nelson and Lawrence Grossberg (eds.), *Marxism and the Interpretation of Culture*, Urbana, IL: University of Illinois Press, 1988, pp. 271–313.

Staller, Jared, *Converging on Cannibals: Terrors of Slaving in Atlantic Africa, 1509–1670*, Athens, OH: Ohio University Press, 2019.

Stein, Peter, *Roman Law in European History*, Cambridge: Cambridge University Press, 1999.

Stolze, Ivana Lima and Laura Carmo (eds.), *História Social da Língua Nacional, Diápora Africana*, Rio de Janeiro: FAPERU, 2014.

Sweet, James H., *Domingos Álvares, African Healing, and the Intellectual History of the Atlantic World*, Chapel Hill, NC: University of North Carolina Pres, 2011.

'Mistaken Identities? Olaudah Equiano, Domingos Álvares, and the Methodological Challenges of Studying the African Diaspora', *The American Historical Review*, 114(2), 2009, pp. 279–306.

Recreating Africa: Culture, Kinship and Religion in the African-Portuguese World, 1441–1770, Chapel Hill, NC: The University of North Carolina Press, 2003.

Swinburne, Richard, *The Coherence of Theism*, Oxford: Clarendon Press, 1989.

Taber, Robert '"To Strengthen the Colonies": French Labor Policy, Indentured Servants, and African Slaves in the Seventeenth Century Caribbean', *Library Research Grants*, 10, 2007. pp. 1–35.

Tardo-Dino, Frantz, *Le Collier de Servitude: La Condition Sanitaire des Esclaves aux Antilles françaises du XVIIe au XIXe siècle*, Paris: Éditions Caribéennes; Agence de Coopération culturelle et technique, 1985.

Temudo, Marina, 'Men Wielding the Plough: Changing Patterns of Production and Reproduction Among the Balanta of Guinea-Bissau', *Journal of Agrarian Change*, 18, 2018, pp. 267–280.

Terra, Paulo Cruz, 'Free and Unfree Labour and Ethnic Conflicts in the Brazilian Transport Industry: Rio de Janeiro in the 19th Century', *Internationaal Instituut voor Sociale Geschiedenis* (IRSHo), 59, Special Issue, 2014, pp. 113–132.

Thiong'o, Ngũgĩ wa, *Decolonising the Mind: The Politics of Language in African Literature*, Nairobi: Heinemann, 1994.

Thornton, John K., *A Cultural History of the Atlantic World, 1250–1820*, Cambridge: Cambridge University Press, 2012.

Africa and Africans in the Making of the Atlantic World, 1400–1800, Cambridge: Cambridge University Press, 1998.

'Legitimacy and Political Power: Queen Njinga, 1624–1663', *The Journal of African History*, 32(1), 1991, pp. 25–40.

'New Light on Cavazzi's 17th-Century Description of Kongo', *History in Africa*, 6, 1979, pp. 253–264.

'The Art of War in Angola, 1575–1680', *Comparative Studies in Society and History*, 30(2), 1988, pp. 360–378.

'The Kingdom of Kongo, ca. 1390–1678: The Development of an African Social Formation', *Cahiers d'Études Africaines*, 87–88, 1982, pp. 325–342.

The Kingdom of Kongo: Civil War and Transition, 1641–1718, Madison, WI: University of Wisconsin Press, 1983.

The Kongolese Saint Anthony: Dona Beatriz Kimpa Vita and the Antonian Movement, 1684–1706, Cambridge: Cambridge University Press, 1998.

'The Origins and Early History of the Kingdom of Kongo, c. 1350–1550', *The International Journal of African Historical Studies*, 34(1), 2001, pp. 89–120.

Thornton, John K. and Andrea Mosterman, 'A Re-Interpretation of the Kongo-Portuguese War of 1622 According to New Documentary Evidence', *The Journal of African History*, 51(2), 2010, pp. 235–248.

Tognetti, Sergio, 'Trade in Black African Slaves in Fifteenth-Century Florence', in Tom F. Earle and Kate J. P. Lowe (eds.), *Black Africans in Renaissance Europe*, Cambridge: Cambridge University Press, 2005, pp. 213–224.

Tollenare, Louis-François de, *Notas Dominicaes Tomadas Durante uma Residencia em Portugal e no Brasil nos Annos de 1816, 1817 e 1818, Parte Relativa a Pernambuco*, Recife: Empreza do Jornal do Recife, 1905.

Tracy, Alexandre Prouville de, 'Réglement de M. de Tracy, Lieutenant Général de l'Amérique, touchant les Blasphémateurs et la Police des Isles, 19 June 1664,' in Moreau de Saint-Méry, *Loix et Constitutions des colonies françoises de l'Amérique sous le vent*, vol. I., Paris, 1786, pp. 119–120.

Turpin, William, 'Imperial Subscriptions and the Administration of Justice', *Journal of Roman Studies*, 81, 1991, pp. 101–118

Ullman, Walter, *The Origins of the Great Schism: A Study in Fourteenth-Century Ecclesiastical History*, Hamden, CT: Archon Books, 1967.

Vainfas, Ronaldo, *A Heresia dos Índios: Catolicismo e Rebeldia no Brasil Colonial*, São Paulo: Companhia das Letras, 2010.

Valencia, Robert Himmerich y, *The Encomenderos of New Spain*, Austin, TX: University of Texas Press, 1991.

Vansina, J., 'Ambaca Society and the Slave Trade c. 1760–1845,' *Journal of African History*, 46(1), 2005, pp. 1–27.

How Societies Are Born: Governance in West Central Africa before 1600, Charlottesville, VA: University of Virginia Press, 2004.

Kingdoms of the Savanna, Madison, WI: University of Wisconsin Press, 1968.

'Long-Distance Trade-Routes in Central Africa', *The Journal of African History*, 3(3), 1962, pp. 375–390.

Paths in the Rainforests: Toward a History of Political Tradition in Equatorial Africa, Madison, WI: University of Wisconsin Press, 1990.

Vicente, António Pedro, *Espanha e Portugal: Um Olhar Sobre as Relações Peninsulares no Século XX*, Lisbon: Tribuna de Historia, 2010.

Vieira, Alberto, 'Sugar Islands: The Sugar Economy of Madeira and Canaries, 1450–1650', in Stuart B. Schwartz (ed.), *Tropical Babylons: Sugar and the Making of the Atlantic World, 1450–1680*, Chapel Hill, NC: University of North Carolina Press, 2004, pp. 42–84.

Vieira, Mildred Evelyn and Frank Ephraim Talmage (eds. and trans.), *The Mirror of the New Christians (Espelho de Christãos Novos) of Francisco Machado*, Toronto: Pontifical Institute of Mediaeval Studies, 1977.

Vieira, Padre António, 'Padre António Vieira – "O Problema de Escravatura"', in J. A. da Graça Barretto, *Monstruosidades do Tempo e da Fortuna, Diário de Factos que Sucederam no Reino de 1625 a 1780, até hoje Atribuído Infundamente ao Benedictino Fr. Alexandre da Paixão*, ms. P. 202, fl. 189 v. [1673], Lisbon: Tipografia da Viúva Sousa Neves – Editora, 1888.

Escritos Sobre os Índios, Lisbon: Temas & Debates, 2015.

Obras Escolhidas, Lisbon: Sá da Costa, 1951–1954.

Sermões (15 vols., Lisbon, 1679–1748), 2nd ed., Lisbon: Editorial Comunicação, 1982.

Sermões, Porto: Lello, 1959.

Vilhena, Luis dos Santos, *Recopilaçã de Noticias Soterpolitanas e Brasilicas Contidas em XX Cartas que da Cidade de Salvador, Bahia de Todos os Santos, Escreve hum a Outro Amigo em Lisboa*, Salvador: Imprensa Official do Estado, 1921–1922, II.

Vincent, Bernard, C. Lagunas, E. Reitano, I. Sanmartín Barros, G. Tarragó, J. Polo Sánchez and O. Pereyra, *Estudios en Historia Moderna desde una visión Atlántica Libro Homenaje a la Trayectoria de la Profesora María Inés Carzolio*, La Plata: Universidad Nacional de La Plata, 2017.

Vicent, Vicente de Cadenas y, *Revista Hidalguia, La Revista de Genealogia*, Nobleza y Armas, (6) 1954, pp. 417–436.

Vinhas, Joaquim Alves, *A Igreja e o Convento de Vilar de Frades, das Origens da Congregação dos Cónegos Secular de São João Evamgelista (Lóios), À Extinção do Covento 1425–1834*, Barcelos: Junta de Freguesia de Areias de Vilar, 1998.

Viotti, Ana Carolina de Carvalho, 'As Proposições de Antonio de Saldanha da Gama para a Melhoria do Tráfico de Escravos, "Por Questões Humanitárias e Econômicas"', História, Ciências, Saúde, 23(4), 2016, pp. 1169–1189.

Wadström, Carl Bernhard, *An Essay on Colonization, Particularly Applied to the Western Coast of Africa*, London: Darton and Harvey, 1794.

Observations on the Slave Trade: And a Description Of Some Part of the Coast of Guinea, during a Voyage, Made in 1787, and 1788, in Company with Doctor A. Sparrman and Captain Arrehenius, by C. B. Wadstrom, Chief Director of the Royal Assay and Refining Office; Member of the Royal Chamber of Commerce, and of the Royal Patriotic Society, for Improving Agriculture, Manufactures, and Commerce in Sweden, London: Printed and sold by James Phillips, George-Yard, Lombard-Street, 1789.

Walvin, James, *Black Ivory: A History of British Slavery*, London: Harper Collins, 1992.

White, J. L., *The Form and Structure of the Official Petition: A Study in Greek Epistolography*, Missoula, MT: Society for Biblical Literature, 1972.

Whitehorne, J. E. G., 'Petitions to the Centurion: A Question of Locality?', Bulletin of the American Society of Papyrologists, 41, 2004, pp. 155–170.

Whitman, James Q., *The Legacy of Roman Law in the German Romantic Era: Historical Vision and Legal Change*, Princeton, NJ: Princeton University Press, 1990.

Wilkinson, Richard H. *The Complete Gods and Goddesses of Ancient Egypt*, New York: Thames & Hudson, 2003.
Williams, Caroline A., '"If You Want Slaves Go to Guinea": Civilisation and Savagery in the "Spanish" Mosquitia, 1787–1800', *Slavery and Abolition*, 35 (1), 2014, pp. 121–141.
Williams, E. E., *Capitalism & Slavery*, Chapel Hill, NC: University of North Carolina Press, 1994.
Woolf, Greg, *Becoming Roman: The Origins of Provincial Civilization in Gaul*, Cambridge: Cambridge University Press, 1998.
'Monumental Writing and the Expansion of Roman Society in the Early Empire', *Journal of Roman Studies*, 86, 1996, pp. 22–39.
Zavala, Silvio, *Las Instituciones Jurídicas en la Conquista de América*, 3rd. ed., Mexico City: Porrúa, 1935.
Zimmermann, Reinhard, *The Law of Obligations: Roman Foundations of the Civilian Tradition*, Oxford: Oxford University Press, 1996.
Zurara, Gomes Eanes de, *Crónica de Guiné, Introdução, Novas Anotações e Glossário de José de Bragança*, Lisbon: Livraria Civilização, 1972.

ARCHIVES AND MUSEUMS

Angola

Arquivo de Antropologia de Angola, Luanda
Museu de História Militar, Luanda

Portugal

Arquivo de Torre do Tombo
Arquivo Histórico Ultramarino de Belém
Arquivo Público de Braga & Biblioteca de Braga
Biblioteca Nacional de Lisboa, Lisbon
Mosteiro de Alcobaça, Alcobaça;
Mosteiro de Tibães, Braga.
Mosteiro de Vilar de Frades
Museu de Peniche, Peniche
Museu de Vila Viçosa, Portugal
Palácio Nacional da Ajuda

Brazil

Arquivo da Cúria do Rio de Janeiro, Rio de Janeiro
Arquivo da Cúria Metropolitana de Salvador, Universidade Católica do Salvador
Arquivo da Santa Casa de Misericórdia
Arquivo Geral da Cidade do Rio de Janeiro
Arquivo Histórico da Bahia
Arquivos Municipal e Público de Salvador

Arquivo Nacional do Rio de Janeiro; Biblioteca Nacional do Rio de Janeiro
Arquivo Público do Estado do Rio de Janeiro
Arquivo Público de Pernambuco, Recife
Engenho da Vitória, Cachoeira, Bahia
Instituto Geográfico e Histórico da Bahia, Salvador
Instituto Geográfico do Rio de Janeiro
Instituto Histórico e Geográfico de Alagoas, Maceió
Museu Carlos Costa Pinto, Salvador
Museu de Arte da Bahia
Museu Nacional do Rio de Janeiro
Quilombo dos Palmares [Parque Memorial], Maceió

Spain

Archivo Diocesano de Toledo
Archivo General de Madrid
Archivo General del Palacio de Madrid
Archivo General de Simancas, Valladolid
Museu del Prado, Madrid

Italy

Archivio Storico de Propaganda Fide, Congregazione per l'Evangelizzazione dei Popoli o "de Propaganda Fide", Città del Vaticano, Rome, Italy
Archivio Apostolico Vaticano, Città del Vaticano, Rome, Italy and Biblioteca Apostolica Vaticana, Città del Vaticano, Rome, Italy
Basilica di Santa Maria Maggiore

USA

Brown University Library, Rhode Island

Index

abolition. *see* Black Atlantic Abolition Movement:concept of
abuse of enslaved Africans, 35, 198, 275, 323, 327, 355
   attempts to stop, 346, 347, 352, 366, 385
acquiring enslaved people
   direct warfare, 30, 60, 168, 336
   trade with chiefs, 168
   tribute, through, 109, 168
actus reus of slavery, 348, 369, 415
Afonso I, king of Kongo, 60–63, 330
   Portuguese Crown, relationship with, 63–66, 336–338
African agency, 28, 141, 240, 420
   suppression of, 208
African involvement in the Atlantic slave trade, 43, 55, 329, 382–383, 386, 422, 429–430
   African practices of slavery, 335, 346–348
   mutual relationship, 73
   sobas, 9
   unequal footing, 73
Alexander VI (pope), 297, 372
Alexander VII (pope), 377
Álvares, Domingos, 195
Álvares, Gaspar, 118–122, 137
   arrest, 102, 114
   Correia de Sousa's relationship with, 75, 80, 118–123
   inheritance dispute, 118–128
Álvaro II, king of Kongo, 154, 310
   networks/alliances against Portuguese occupation, 142–144

amnesties
   customary right for escapees, 146, 161, 162, 244
   kijiko, 146
   safe haven principle, 245
Angola
   Dutch occupation, 71
   See also Ndongo.
Antonil, Antonio Andreoni, 198, 218, 245, 404
   engenhos in Bahia, 222–223, 224–230
Apostolic Notary of Luanda, 77
Araujo, Captain Major Payo d', 122–124
asylum principle, 245
Azzolino, Cardinal Decio, 352

baculamento, 12, 55, 68, 157, 167–168
   Hari I, 169, 174–175
   Hari II's refusal to pay, 188
   introduction of, 9–10, 35, 52
   Portuguese exploitation of, 170–176, 206, 390, 412
   Sousa, Fernão de, 9, 35, 68, 146, 169–176, 419
   traditional Mbundu understanding, 169–170
Bango Bango, João, 207, 210, 417
Barreira, Baltasar, 156–158
Barreto, Dionizio de Faria, 83, 97, 123
Benton, Lauren, 35–36
bias of historical sources, 37–40

Index

Birmingham, David, 105, 138–140, 168–169, 171, 176, 177, 205, 212, 389, 423, 429
Black Atlantic Abolition Movement
concept of, 4, 36–37, 49, 55
Black Brotherhoods, confraternities of, 25, 27–29, 40, 53, 81, 220, 358, 378, 421
Vatican court case, 41, 328, 348, 419, 423
See also confraternities of Our Lady of Rosary of the Black Men
Boxer, Charles R., 66, 211–212, 392
Brásio, António, 27–28, 51, 71, 145, 294, 309, 339
Bumbi
invasion by Correia de Sousa, 81, 100, 102, 116, 132, 135, 137
economic rationale, 101
runaway slaves rationale, 101, 135
return of Bumbi people, 129
Buxton, Thomas, 2, 326, 328

Cabangua, Dom Diogo, 200–206, 209, 280, 282–284, 287–288
See also João (John) Hari II.
Cadamosto, Luís de, 332, 333
Cadornega, Antonio de Oliveira de, 27, 118, 124, 148, 159–161, 165, 418
kijikos, 155
Mbundu culture, 165, 166
Ndongo's political structure, 174, 177, 183, 184, 186, 187, 206
Calixtus III, 372
Candido, Mariana, 30, 31, 68, 141, 179, 389
raiding and taxation, 60
cannibalism justification for enslavement, 333–334, 406, 410
Cardoso, Bento Banha, 99, 104, 114, 115, 123, 171, 174, 175
Cardoso, Mateus
enslavement of the Kazanze, 91, 92, 93, 94
Carlos II, king of Spain, 392
confraternities of Rosary of Our Lady of Star for the Black Men, 317
Carvalho, Pedro de, 29–30, 255
Casas, Bartolomé De las, 25, 357
Christianisation of Africa, 375–378
Western narrative, 269–270, 405–406, 410

Christianisation rationale for conquest/invasion, 231, 324, 342–345, 377, 411
just war principle, 89, 94–95, 97
slavery as a crime against *jus canonico*, 360
Church and slavery, intersection between, 76, 80, 116–118, 137
See also Álvares, Gaspar; Christianisation rationale for conquest/invasion
civil law, 364
slavery as contravention of, 27, 42, 49, 153, 371, 379, 414
Clarkson, Thomas, 2
Clement X (pope), 312
Coelho de Sousa, Pero, 90, 101, 116, 123, 132, 133
coercion into slave trade by Portuguese, 7, 11, 16, 34, 58, 74, 149, 334, 335, 383, 412, 415, 419
Mendonça's family, 391
Western misinterpretation of, 66–68, 175
colonos of Palmares, 256–258
complicity of African rulers in slave trade, 60
See also African involvement in the Atlantic slave trade; coercion into slave trade by Portuguese
confraternities of Our Lady of Rosary of the Black Men, 304
constitutional rights of members, 300–302
São Tomé, 305–309
liberation of members from slavery, 300
Mendonça as attorney of, 53, 309–312, 317, 322
See also Black Brotherhoods, confraternities of
conquered Indigenous people, 262–269
Contreiras, Cristovão de Burgos de, 53, 198, 238, 256–260, 273
Correia de Sousa, João
Álvares, relationship with, 75, 118
See also Álvares, Gaspar
arrest, 116
corruption, 114–116
invasion of Bumbi, 100–104
invasion of Kazanze, 84–86
personal account of, 91–93
Kazanze people, enslavement of, 81–93
illegal exile to Brazil, 93–100

Index

Spanish Crown, relationship with, 86–89
war captives, 102–104
crime against humanity concept, 43–44
Crown intervention, 104
See also Fajardo, Antonio Bezerra:
criminal investigations of governors.
Cugoano, Ottobah, 4, 324–325, 328
Curto, José, 31
complicity of African rulers in slave trade, 60, 66, 141

Dávila y Osori, Antonio Pedro Sancho (Marquise of Astorga and Great Spain), 353–355, 423
death toll during Atlantic crossing, 41, 130, 360, 395, 398, 399
diseases, 400
debt and judicial proceedings as enslavement methods, 9, 31–32, 62–65, 70–71, 145
Del Real, Dom Lorenzo, 318–319
Delgado, José Matias, 140, 163, 177
demand for labour as a rationale for slavery, 81–82, 136, 225, 234
Dias, Henrique, 24, 140
Dias, Paschoal, 40
divine law
slavery as contravention of, 27, 42, 49, 153, 371, 379, 414
Dom João de Sousa. *see* João (John) Hari II
Dongo *see* Ndongo
Doria, Vincenzo Gonzaga (Prince of Gonzaga), 353–355, 423

economic rationale for enslavement, 113, 157, 206, 356, 366, 400, 405, 407, 418, 428–429
Bumbi, 101
Cayru, 233
Kazanze, 85–90, 93
Overseas Council, 403–404
economic rationale for war *see* just war principle
education of Mendonça, 11, 20, 53, 142
education of Ndongo royals
political resistance, as a tool to suppress, 281–296
See also education of Mendonça
encombros, 9, 72, 109, 173
enslaved Africans in Portugal, 302–304
See also exile of Ndongo's royals: Portugal

enslaved Africans in the Americas
solidarity with New Christians and Indigenous people, 36, 236–239, 321
See also exile of Ndongo's royals: Brazil
enslavement of Africans as fundamental part of conquest, 7–10
enslavement of the Kazanze, 88–93
Equiano, Olaudah, 4, 69, 325, 326–327, 328
exile of Ndongo's royals, 52
Brazil, 9, 20, 52, 209–212, 275
status as prisoners of war, 213
Portugal, 9, 20, 280–282, 320–322
Dom Diogo Cabangua, 287–288
Dom Philipe (Ngolamano), 281–288
prisoners of war, 282
silence by separation, 294–296
exploitation of customary gifts
encombros, 72
ocombas and *ynfucas*, 71, 72–73

Fajardo, Antonio Bezerra
City Council of Luanda Constitution, 107–111
criminal investigations of governors, 104–114
ill-treatment of *sobas*, 107, 112
relationship with local authorities, 106
enslavement of the Kazanze, 91
Falcão, Antonio de Souza, 196–197
Ferrás, Bento, 115
Ferreira, Roquinaldo, 31, 60, 141
festivals
Christian festivals, 269
enslaved Africans in Brazil, 220, 229, 230
Figueiredo, Marçal de, 115, 116
financial importance of raiding and taxation, 30–31, 32, 60, 68, 110
See also taxation as an enslavement method
forced gifts, 71, 72, 327
See also ocombas and *ynfucas*

Garcia II, king of Kongo, 329, 330, 356, 403, 429
ally of Dutch, 339
networks/alliances against Portuguese occupation, 142–144
General Congregation (6 March 1684), 19, 42, 57, 306, 328, 346, 351, 352, 353, 414
See also Vatican criminal case

Godinho, André do Couto, 194
Gouvêa, André de
  engenhos in Bahia, 223–224
Gray, Richard, 22, 23–24, 34, 140, 302, 402, 414
Green, Toby, 33, 143, 173, 239
guerra preta (Angola), 12, 85, 92, 101, 177, 179, 186, 188, 193, 198, 204, 207, 273, 294, 417

Hebrew Nation. *see* New Christians
Heintze, Beatrix, 30, 140
  raiding and taxation, 60, 68
Heywood, Linda, 104, 428
  baculamento, 170
  complicity of African rulers in slave trade, 60, 340–344
  Queen Njinga, 141, 160
Holl, Augustin, 67–68
homogenisation of culturally diverse groups, 275–278
human dignity argument against slavery, 106, 155, 342, 369, 371
human law
  slavery as contravention of, 27, 42, 49, 153, 369–370, 379, 414
humanity argument against slavery, 7, 16, 42, 135, 137, 196, 269, 275, 279, 322, 349, 364, 371, 377, 382, 407, 411, 420

identity of Mendonça, 23
  surname and confusion surrounding, 19–20, 21
Indigenous people, 6, 235
  Pan-Atlantic solidarity, 11, 328, 420, 426
  Quilombo dos Palmares, alliance with, 239–256
  See also Quilombo dos Palmares alliance with Indigenous people
  solidarity with enslaved Africans in Americas, 36, 53, 236–239, 321, 420, 426
  Vatican court case, 328
Innocent XI (pope), 112, 260, 297, 312–313, 322, 348, 352, 372, 373, 379, 381, 419
Inquisition of the New Christians
  end of, 316
investigations
  illegal enslavement in Brazil, 129–130

invasion of Kazanze and enslavement of its people, 91–93
Jesuit High Court of Appeal, 93–100
land return to *sobas*, 105
slave trade of São Tomé and Angola, 158
See also Fajardo, Antonio Bezerra: criminal investigations of governors.

Jaca, Francisco José de, 25–27, 47, 330, 332
  evidence, impact of, 361–366
João (John) Hari II, 52
  blockade of slave trade, 189
  death, 8, 139, 190–192
  education, 205
  independence from Portugal, 193–194, 198, 205
  refusal to pay *baculamento*, 188
  networks/alliances against Portuguese occupation, 189
  Overseas Council, relationship with, 55, 385, 390–392
  succession, 176–177
João II, King of Portugal, 335
John VI, King of Portugal, 385
just war principle, 111–114, 327
  invasion of Bumbi, 100–104
  See also Bumbi
  invasion of Kazanze, 93, 95–96
  Christianity rationale, 89, 94–95, 97
  See also Kazanze
  manipulation of, 424

Kazanze
  deception by Correia de Sousa, 88–91
  enslavement by Correia de Sousa, 91
  exile to Brazil, 91, 98
  return policy, 129–135
  invasion by Correia de Sousa, 85–86, 137
  economic rationale, 85–90, 93
  land distribution, 86
  runaway slaves rationale, 99–100, 135
  violence, 86, 94
  See also Correia de Sousa, João
  return of Kazanze people, 129
kidnapping, 26, 31, 32, 49, 81, 104, 110, 137, 321, 329, 336, 337, 408, 412, 418
kijikos, 93, 113–114, 146, 151, 155–156, 162

Kongo
  background, 416–419
  See also Bumbi; Kazanze

Lahon, Didier, 28, 310
land distribution, 12, 87, 233
Lara, Silvia, 140, 160, 294
liberation and return of captives, 24, 142, 197, 221, 274, 296, 301, 315, 365, 379
  carta de alforria, 307
  Crown intervention, 129–135
  See also universal liberty concept
liberation as a question of power, 53, 198, 238
Lindsay, Lisa, 195
Livingstone, David, 2, 326, 328

macamba, 241, 271
  mocambo distinguished, 242, 271
Manuel, king of Portugal, 74
  Afonso I (Kongo), relationship with, 63–66
Mascarenhas, Simão de, 130, 131–133, 175
Mattos, Hebe, 22, 24–25, 140
Mbandi, king of Ndongo
  death, 15
  legal policies around slavery, 161–163
  Portuguese governors, relationship with, 80, 83–85, 161–162
Mendonça family tree, 14–16, 417
Mendonça, Afonso Furtado do Rio de Castro de, 19
  Cayru, invasion of, 232–234
Mendonça's racial heritage, 22–23
Mendonça's exile, 416
  Brazil, 141–142, 192, 200–201
  Portugal, 293, 296–300, 320
    Confraternity of Our Lady of Rosary of Black Men, 300–312
Mendonça's experience of people being taken into slavery, 57–59, 141–144, 213–214, 219–222, 273, 372, 412
Mendonça's relationship with Overseas Council, 402
mens rea of slavery, 348
Mesquita, Gaspar da Costa, 11, 54, 313–314
  Mendonça, relationship with, 315–316
Miller, Joseph, 31, 140, 399

misinterpretation of custom by Western world, 66–68, 175
  kitanda/feiras, 68–70
  mobuka, 33–34
  terreyro, 66–67
mobuka
  Western misinterpretation of custom of, 33–34
mocambos, 75, 229, 239, 242, 246
  macamba distinguished, 242, 271
  Quilombo dos Palmares, 271–272
mocanos
  incorporation in outposts, 71–72
Moirans, Epifanio de, 25–27, 47, 330, 332
  evidence, impact of, 361–366
Molina, Luis de, 326–327, 337–338, 349, 356, 364, 372
Montecuccolo, Giovanni Antonio Cavazzi da, 60–64, 377
Municipal Council of Luanda
  Apostolic Notary, 77
  budget and financing, 12–14
  Crown, relationship with, 78–80
  dismissal of council members, 102
  involvement in slave trade, 8, 11–14, 51–52, 59–60
  policy, 59
  structure, 76–77

natural law argument against slavery, 26, 27, 42, 49, 95, 135, 153, 186, 370, 379, 411, 414
Ndongo
  background, 138, 147, 416–419
  Christianity, 148
  exile of royal family, 139
  geography, 147
  Hari I, election of, 163–169
  language, 147
  rule and succession, 148, 163–167
  slavery, concept of, 153–154
    servitude versus slavery, 154–155
    war captives, 154–156
  system of governance
    political hierarchy, 148–151
    social divisions, 151–153
  See also Angola.
Ndongo people
  Correia de Sousa, relationship with, 83–85

networks/alliances against Portuguese occupation, 142–144, 192, 378, 414, 426
    Hari II, 189
    Quilombo dos Palmares alliance with Indigenous people, 239–256
New Christians, 6, 275, 321
    network with elite classes in Central West Africa, 20–22, 53, 316–317
    Pan-Atlantic solidarity, 11, 328, 420, 426
    solidarity with enslaved Africans in Americas, 36, 53, 321, 420, 426
    Vatican court case, 328
Ngola Aiidi, *see* João (John) Hari II
Ngolamano, Dom Philipe, 194, 209, 280, 282–288
Nicholas V (pope), 344–345, 372, 427
Novais, Paulo Dias de, 11, 78, 156–157, 158, 207

ocombas and *ynfucas*, 71–72
Oliveira, Fernando, 331
Overseas Council of Portugal, 386–388, 409–410
    African culture justification for slavery, 403, 410, 411
    economic justification for slavery, 403–404, 421
    Hari I, relationship with, 55, 385, 388–390
    Hari II, relationship with, 55, 385, 390–392
    'nature' justification for slavery, 404
    political struggles with, 55, 385, 402–408
    social disorder justification for slavery, 403

papal bulls
    conquest of Africa in the name of the Christian God, 372–373, 427–428
    Mendonça's challenge, 374, 415
Peçanha, Diogo Nabo, 116
    Álvares inheritance dispute, 125
Pedro II, king of Kongo, 129, 417
    liberation and return of captives, 131
Pedro II, king of Portugal, 355, 391, 392
    Quilombo dos Palmares, 261, 263, 272
    slave trade shipment reforms, 393–402
Pereira, Manuel Cerveira, 81
    Correia de Sousa, relationship with, 82–83

Philipe Hari I, 417
    baculamento, 169, 174–175
    election to throne, 52, 145
    Portuguese influence, 163, 166
    succession disputes, 163–167
    family background, 159–161
    Overseas Council, relationship with, 55, 385, 388–390
Philipe III, king of Spain, 334
Philipe IV, king of Spain, 417
Portuguese Crown, 74
    Afonso I (Kongo), relationship with, 63–66
    Crown intervention liberation and return of captives, 104, 131, 133
    Municipal Council in Luanda, relationship with, 78–80
    See also João II, king of Portugal; John VI, king of Portugal; Manuel, king of Portugal; Pedro II, king of Portugal; Sebastião, king of Portugal.
Portuguese Inquisition
    Gaspar, 313
    Mesquita, 314
    punishment of slavery, 351
    witchcraft, 229
Praça, Simão da Rocha, 207
presidio (outposts), 9
    legal system, 70
    mocano, incorporation of, 71–72
    slave markets, 70
    sobas, relationship with, 105–106
Preto, Gaspar, 116
proposals to end slavery, 359–360
Pungo-Andongo
    destruction of, 8, 20, 52, 139, 188, 201–205, 391
    loyalty to Portugal, 207–209
punishment of enslaved Africans, 225–229, 356–358
    punishment as a form of education, 227

Queen Njinga, 52, 377
    Correia de Sousa, relationship with, 83–84
    networks/alliances against Portuguese occupation, 142–144
    succession dispute with Hari I, 163–167

Quilombo dos Palmares (Maroon community in Brazil), 10, 53, 239–242
  alliance with the Native Americans. *see* Quilombo dos Palmares alliance with Indigenous people
  asylum principle, 245–246
  colonos, 256–258
  exiled royals of Ndongo, 258–260, 270
  safe haven principle, 245–246
  Vieira, 260–261
  Christianisation of Palmares, 263–270
  creation of 'tamed hamlets', 262–270
Quilombo dos Palmares alliance with Indigenous people, 239, 242–243, 245–256

Reginaldo, Lucilene, 28–29, 141, 194, 196
Reis, João José, 195
religious freedom
  denial of, 6, 322, 420
return/mucuâ principle, 244
Rodney, Walter, 67, 154, 336
Rufino, Alufá, 195
runaway slaves, 229
  amnesties, 162
  rationale for invasion, 10, 53, 424
  See also Quilombo dos Palmares (Maroon community in Brazil)

Sá, Salvador Correia de
  Pungo-Andongo, destruction of, 201–205, 208–209
safe haven principle, 245–246
Salvador and the slave trade, 214–219
Sebastião, king of Portugal, 156
servitude/endenture, history of, 60–65, 154, 335, 424
  French law, 360
Sharp, Granville, 2
slave markets, 60, 66–67, 68–70, 156–158, 327
slave resistance, 331
slavery debate
  African-led legal debates, 6, 18–20
  former enslaved Africans, 3
  Western narrative, 2–3, 6, 32, 38, 56, 67–68, 194–195, 327, 328, 338–341, 424–426, 430
sobas (Angolan local rulers)
  involvement in slave trade, 9
  taxation of, 175, 179–180
solidarity between oppressed and enslaved, 36–37, 52–53, 236–239, 276–278, 321, 419–421, 426
  Black Atlantic Abolition Movement, 37
  See also networks/alliances against Portuguese occupation; Quilombo dos Palmares alliance with Indigenous people
Sousa, Fernão de
  Álvares inheritance dispute, 126, 128
  appointment as governor of Luanda, 167
  baculamento, 9, 35, 68, 146, 169–176, 419
  forced gifts, 72
  Hari I, election of, 168
  Kazanza succession dispute, role in, 90
  runaway slaves, 161
Sweet, James, 195

Távora, Francisco de, 20, 52, 178
  appointment as governor of Luanda, 178–179
  exploitation of political division, 179
  supply of enslaved to the Americas, 180
  trade and military strategy, 180–181
  taxation as an enslavement method, 30, 67, 68
  See also baculamento; financial importance of raiding and taxation
theological rationale for slavery, 97
  See also Christianisation of Africa; Christianisation rational for conquest/invasion
Thornton, John, 73, 104, 141
  complicity of African rulers in slave trade, 60, 62
  concept of slavery, 155–156
  kijikos, 113, 155
  war against Kazanze, 86
Tristão da Cunha incident, 202

universal liberty concept, 7, 16, 40, 41, 53–54, 379
  See also Black Atlantic Abolition Movement: concept of

Vasconcelos, Luís Mendes de, 83, 85, 104, 174
vassalage and tribute payments, 109, 110, 168
xicacos, 30
  See also baculamento; forced gifts

Vatican criminal case, 1, 16–20, 40, 42–44, 54–55, 382–383
   categories of documents, 45–46, 349–351
   closing statement, 367–371, 379–381
   confraternities of Black Brotherhoods, 40–42
   Council of Trent, influence of, 47–48
   evidence, 349–351
   eye-witnesses, 46–47, 330
   first legal challenge, 5, 57
   impact, 408
      slave trade shipment reforms, 392
   Mendonça's argumentation, 371–379
      closing statement, 379–381
   Mendonça's presentation, 345–353
      response to, 353–367, 384
   second complaint, 5
   universal liberty, 36
   See also General Congregation (6 March 1684)
Vatican's implication in slavery, 323
Vaughan, James Churchill, 195–196
Velho, Domingos Jorge, 256–260, 273
Vidal de Negreiros, André, 81

Vieira, António
   New Christians, 315
   Quilombo dos Palmares, 260–261
      Christianisation of Palmares, 263–270, 273
      creation of 'tamed hamlets', 262–270
voices of protest against the enslavement of Africans
   Africans, 332
      Cadamosto, 332
   Brotherhoods of enslaved Africans, 348
   Correia de Sousa's actions, 93–100
   Hari II, 182
   Jaca and Moirans, 25, 356
   See also networks/alliances against Portuguese occupation; Quilombo dos Palmares alliance with Indigenous people; solidarity between oppressed and enslaved

Wadstrom, Carl, 81, 326
war as an enslavement method, 30
Wilberforce, William, 2, 328
witchcraft, 229–231

www.ingramcontent.com/pod-product-compliance
Ingram Content Group UK Ltd.
Pitfield, Milton Keynes, MK11 3LW, UK
UKHW020240170225
455193UK00013B/204